MW01630213

# THE PRINTED PICTURE

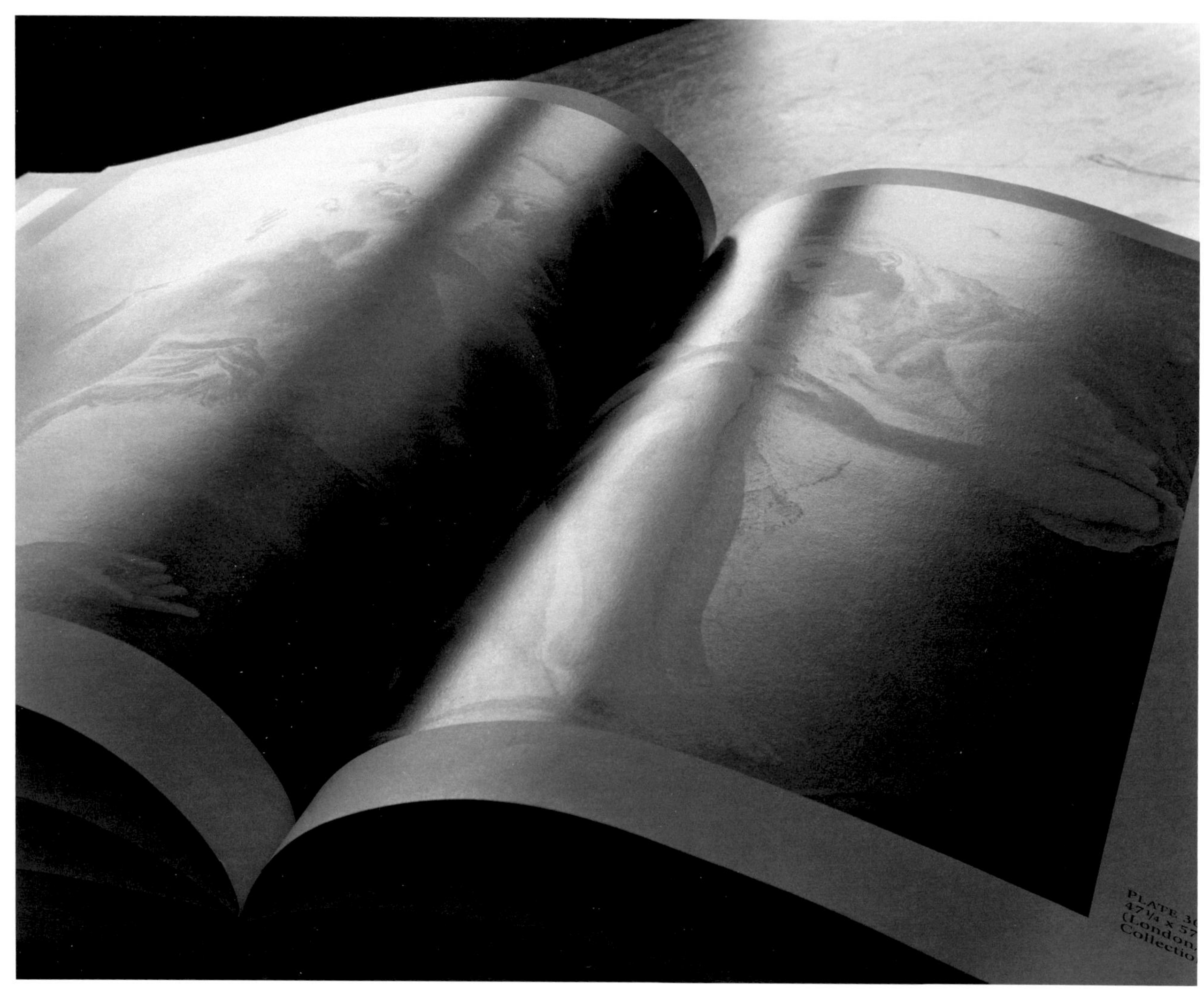

**Gelatin silver print.** Abelardo Morell. *Pietà by El Greco.* 1993. 18 x 22½ in. (45.7 x 57.2 cm)

# THE PRINTED PICTURE

Richard Benson

THE MUSEUM OF MODERN ART · NEW YORK

To accompany the publication of this book, an exhibition, also titled *The Printed Picture*, is presented in The Edward Steichen Photography Galleries of The Museum of Modern Art, October 2008 through spring 2009.

The book is made possible by the John Szarkowski Publications Fund.

Produced by the Department of Publications,
The Museum of Modern Art, New York

Edited by David Frankel
Design and separations by Richard Benson
Cover design by Beverly Joel, pulp, ink.
Production by Marc Sapir
Printed and bound by GHP, West Haven, Conn.

This book is typeset in Adobe Garamond Pro.
The paper is 100-lb. Value Silk

Published by The Museum of Modern Art,
11 W. 53 Street, New York, New York 10019



Distributed in the United States and Canada by
D.A.P./Distributed Art Publishers, Inc., New York
Distributed outside the United States and Canada by
Thames & Hudson Ltd, London

Library of Congress Control Number: 2008932757
ISBN: 978-0-87070-721-6

Front cover (left to right, top to bottom): see sections 4.9, 9.8, 5.3, 10.2, 11.7, 5.6, 3.3, 9.5, 5.10, 3.6, 2.1, 12.5, 3.7.
Back cover (left to right): see sections 13.5, 1.2

Dedication page: Richard Benson. *Apples*. 2007. Inkjet print, ⅝ x 17 ⅜ in. (24.6 x 44.2 cm)

Printed in the United States

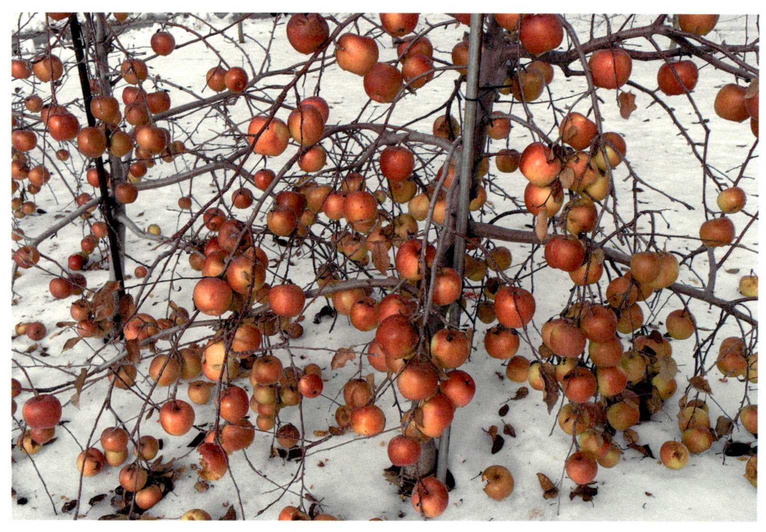

For John

## FOREWORD

It is impossible to conceive of modern visual culture apart from the very particular contributions of highly creative individual artists, and the preservation, display, and study of their work constitute the principal mission of The Museum of Modern Art. It is equally impossible to ignore the vast and ultimately anonymous transformations wrought by technological change. MoMA has grappled steadily with that very complex domain as well, without ever attempting a comprehensive program.

Richard Benson's book *The Printed Picture* is a major contribution to the latter tradition. Its marvelous illustrations include more than a handful of outstanding works of art, but the great bulk of the pictures are utterly commonplace. For Benson, these humble things are more important than their exquisite, rare, and sometimes very valuable cousins because their social function has been enormously more influential. That influence rests upon the capacity to multiply the image, and the book's essential subject is just how that physical capacity is created: the way pictures are made shapes the way they look and behave, and hence what they can mean.

Richard Benson is uniquely qualified to guide us through this sprawling territory, which today, with the advent of digital technologies, is once again expanding rapidly. A dedicated artist and teacher, he is also an inspired tinkerer, who four decades ago led a revolution in printing that would radically improve the quality of photographs in reproduction. He has himself made nearly all of the many kinds of pictures he discusses here, and that hands-on experience makes itself felt on every page.

The Museum is proud to present this landmark contribution to our understanding of the life of pictures in the modern world. We thank the excellent staff of the Department of Publications, led by Christopher Hudson, and we salute in particular David Frankel, who edited the book, and Marc Sapir, who collaborated with the author in producing it. Finally we are grateful to Robert B. Menschel and his fellow members of the Committee on Photography, who nearly twenty years ago generously established the John Szarkowski Publications Fund, whose support has been indispensable. Never was a name more rightly linked to a project, for John Szarkowski initiated and shared some of Richard Benson's most ambitious and fruitful experiments in offset lithography, notably the four-volume *The Work of Atget* (1981–85).

Glenn D. Lowry, Director
Peter Galassi, Chief Curator of Photography
The Museum of Modern Art

# Introduction

This book is about pictures and the ways in which they are printed. Many of the pictures in the book are "representational," by which I mean that they attempt to show the form of some object, rather than acting as symbols in the manner of letters and numbers. When letters and numbers, whether drawn or printed, are used to communicate, they are understood through a set of meanings embedded in the language that the writer and reader share. All a letter or number has to do pictorially is to be recognized as itself and not some other character. A representational picture is different: the details of its visual structure dominate the meaning, to the point where any small change in form results in a change of meaning. Any given representational picture might have a broadly recognizable subject, and even an obvious meaning, but the specifics of its form shape that meaning.

It follows that when a representational picture becomes complex, different people may attach widely different meanings to it. To make matters worse, at any given moment in history cultural influences strongly direct our interpretation of pictures — yet since even pictures on fragile paper may outlast their makers, much of that cultural influence may have disappeared before the picture does. All this implies that it is hard to know just what any picture might "mean." We can be sure, though, that the form of the picture is the dominant influence on how we understand it, and that is where my interest lies: not so much in meaning as in form. This book examines how pictures look — by reproducing a lot of them — but carries out that examination by describing the manner in which they were made. To my mind the making dictates the form, and whatever meaning there might be flows from those steps and from the cultural context in which the picture is viewed.

When a picture is a skillfully made drawing or painting its meaning surely derives to a huge degree from the intention of its maker. But when a picture is a reproduction of a drawing or painting, the case is very different, because the form and therefore the meaning of this second-generation picture are then heavily influenced by the technology used to produce the reproduction. This issue has been examined beautifully by William Ivins, whose books on prints and their appearances are still the benchmarks for anyone studying the interaction of form and meaning in printed material. When the picture-making system is photography, though, everything becomes muddled, because even in original work — photographs taken out in the world — the mind of the maker has to share the driver's seat with the form of the picture as it is shaped by the technology of photography. And when a photograph is reproduced, things get still more difficult, because such reproductions can only be made by rephotographing the photograph. It then becomes very hard to tell whether the person doing the reproduction or the technology itself might be in charge. The intention of this book is to explore this many-layered subject through an examination of the different ways in which printed pictures are made. An underlying premise of the book is the fact that printing, photography, and digital technology, as applied to pictures, are all aspects of a single ancient process: that of creating fixed visual forms in multiple copies. I believe that pictures are as important as language, and that together they form the glue that holds society together.

Because printing and photography have become so commonplace I have chosen to concentrate on everyday pictures rather than just those exotic birds that reside in museums. Some of the pictures found here are rare and valuable but most of them are scraps gathered through my forty years of work as a photographer, printer, and junk collector. In every case the picture facing the text is related to the process described, but in many cases the text does not refer to the particular picture that is illustrated. The picture is there as an example of the process but not always as an object to be discussed. As far as possible the essays follow a chronological thread, but because the various processes have originated and disappeared at different times, and because the essays and pictures are grouped by process, there is necessarily some jumping back and forth in time. The various processes and inks shown in this book are all reproduced by conventional process-color printing in photo offset lithography.

We live in a time of tremendous technological change. One of the most far-reaching innovations has been the creation of moving pictures. The earliest examples of these, locked onto chemical film and projected in strips, became the ubiquitous movies. Today we find radically new versions in television, video, computer imaging, and the World Wide Web. This book is not about those new forms of pictures; what follows is a survey of "still" images, those fixed on paper and other substrates. I leave it to some other, far younger author to give an overview of the moving picture.

This book grows out of a series of lectures given at Yale University over the last thirty years. Each time I gave one it was different, varying according to the prints I hung on the wall that day. The following pages still retain the tone of a lecture being delivered in the first person.

# Introduction

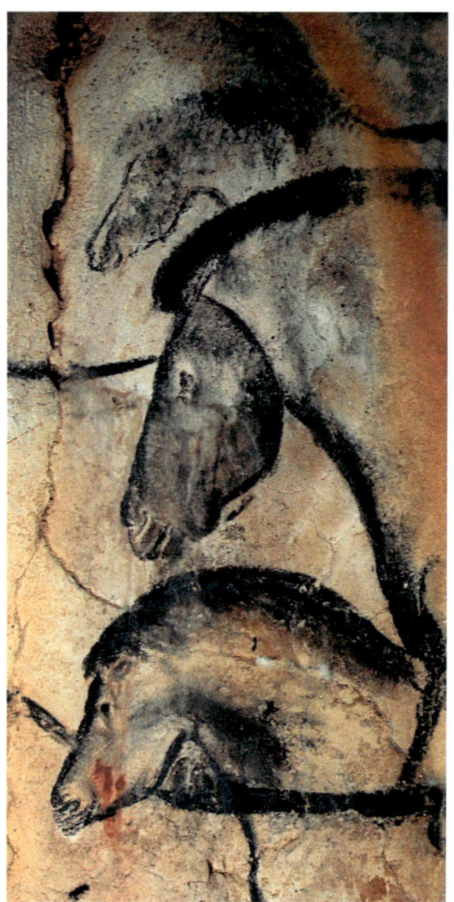

Horses from the walls of the Chauvet cave, Ardèche, France. c. 30,000 B.C.

The oldest pictures we know appear on cave walls in Europe. They were drawn with carbon black, derived from burned wood or bone, and with red ocher, a naturally occurring iron compound. The oldest of these pictures, dating back as far as 30,000 years, display fully evolved representational art. Linear description is handled magnificently, shading is used to render rounded forms, and picture structure is so well handled that these paintings rival anything made since. If we look at representational painting in the West for the thousand years preceding the Renaissance, we can only shake our heads in wonder at how much had been forgotten since the artists worked in the caves.

Mixed in with the hand-drawn pictures in the caves are clear examples of printing. The most common of these printed pictures are of the human hand. Sometimes the image is dark, obviously made by impressing a pigment-covered hand onto the wall, while in other cases the hand appears as a negative, clear but surrounded by colored material. As we go along in this book we shall be defining the basic types of printing, and the hands we find in prehistoric caves represent two of the fundamental forms. The positive images (those made by the hand itself carrying the pigment) are examples of relief printing, the system that underlies printing with moveable type or with wood or linoleum blocks. The negative images (those blank hands surrounded by colored pigment) are examples of stencil printing, in which image-bearing pigment is passed through or around some form that holds the picture information.

We can make an argument that printing has existed as long as people have been making pictures. While this book concentrates on pictures on paper, we should always remember that the practice of printing—of using an object to control the form of a repeated picture—has had a role in human culture from its earliest days. We should note as well that while most of the examples in this book are European or American, printing was in use in East Asia and in the Islamic world centuries before it became common in the West.

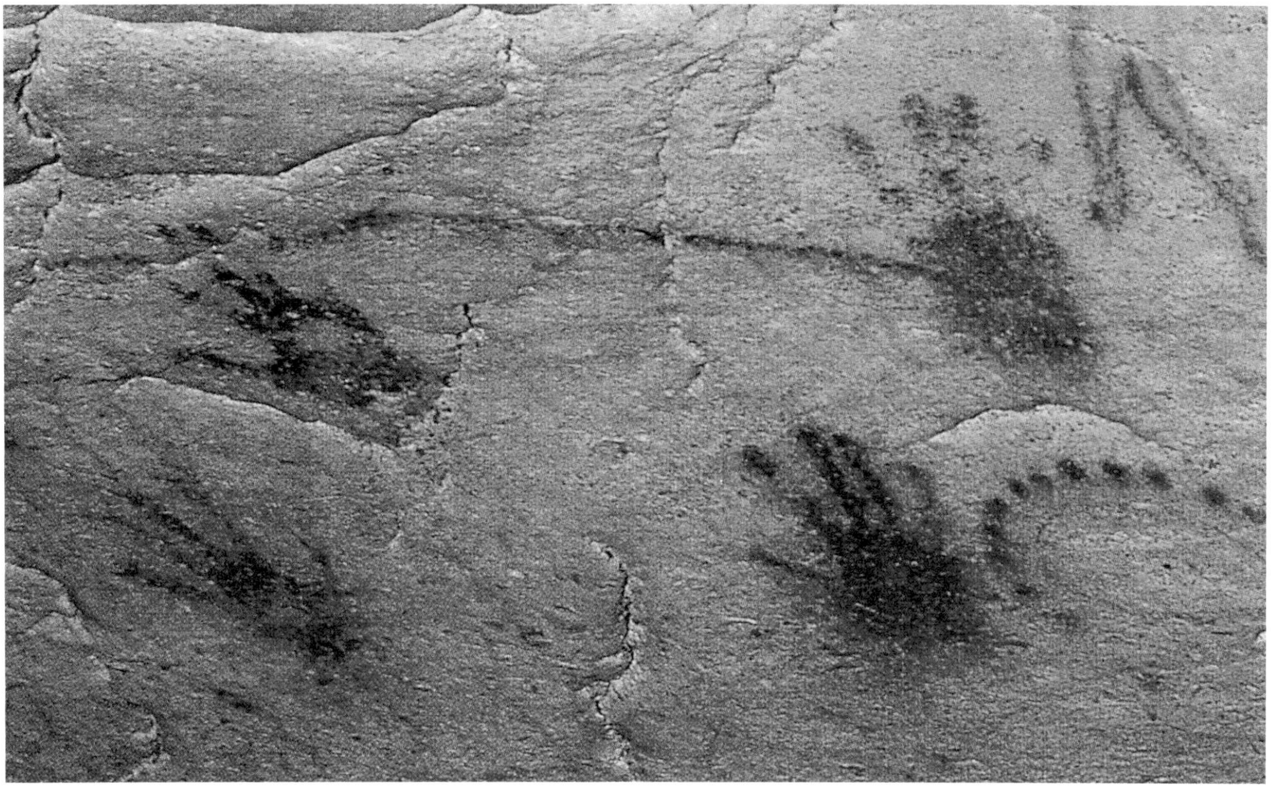

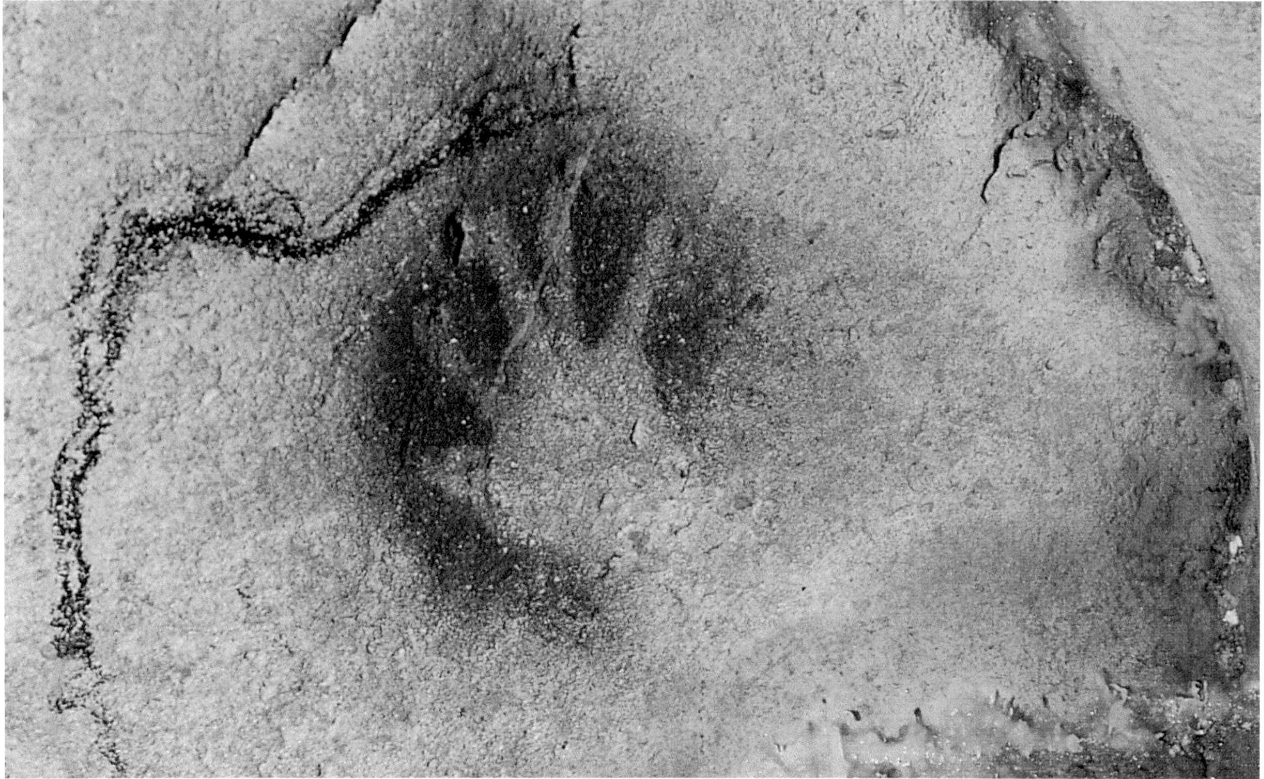

**Pigment prints.** Hands from the walls of the Chauvet cave, Ardèche, France. c. 30,000 B.C.

# Part 1

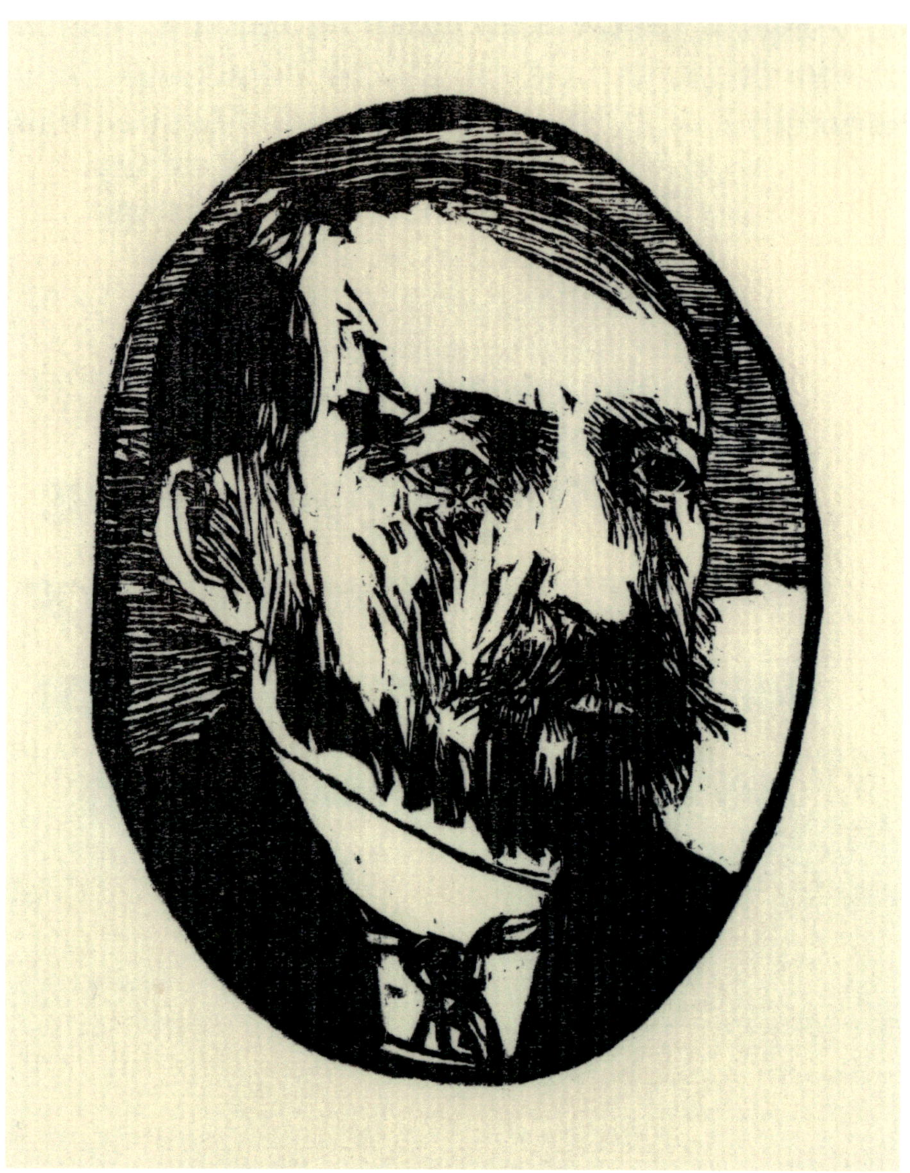

The oldest and simplest of all printing processes involves printing from the high parts of some surface. In the picture we see here, printed by woodblock, parts of the block's surface have been cut away, and leave no mark, appearing in the image as white. The high parts of the block have not been cut away, and they print black. We call this class of printing "relief" printing, and this first section describes some of those historic processes.

**Woodcut.** Leonard Baskin. *Joseph Conrad.* c. 1970. 5¼ x 4 in. (13.3 x 10.1 cm)

# Relief printing

1.1 Woodcut
*The most basic form of relief printing.*

1.2 Woodcut printing
*Cross-hatching as a form of tonal emulation.*

1.3 A hand-lettered manuscript page
*Handmade books before the invention of moveable type.*

1.4 Letterpress
*A plain eighteenth-century Bible page.*

1.5 Woodcut letters
*The use of woodblock to print letters.*

1.6 Woodcut printing
*Single-color printing from multiple blocks.*

1.7 Woodcut and metal type
*Words and pictures printed in a single form.*

1.8 Wood engraving
*Engraved images cut in end-grain woodblocks.*

1.9 Wood engraving
*Wood engraving as a reproductive medium.*

# Relief printing

## 1.1 WOODCUT

This print was made in Europe in the late fifteenth century. The image is in ink—in this case black pigment that was held in oil—and is printed onto a paper support. That little scrap of paper is revolutionary in its technology: paper is cheap, light, flexible, and above all portable. Where the drawings on the stone walls of the caves are firmly stuck in their original location, this paper print could be made and passed on to users somewhere else. As soon as pictures were able to move, they assumed a new power, since in serving multiple users they could permeate society. Like language itself, the paper image spread throughout human culture. Pictures on stone, whether painted on cave walls or carved as monumental inscriptions, existed as single copies that were stuck in one location. Paper, in its capacity to move freely, completely overwhelmed these massive older forms of communication.

The picture has been made with a woodblock. The image is not a unique drawing but the visual record of a carving in a flat wooden plank. Those areas that were not intended to print were carved away, and the remaining surface of the wood, after being inked, transferred the image to a sheet of paper. There were probably multiple copies, and they may, at some earlier time, have been bound into a book. This particular copy now resides in Newport, Rhode Island, among the thousands of bits of paper that I have collected through the years. Fragile and small, this little object has managed, over the course of 500 years, to travel across the Atlantic, survive hundreds of wet and freezing winters and hot and humid summers, and still be absolutely clear and legible. Because a few hundred or so might have been made, the odds have favored some remaining to this day. This safety in numbers is the same method used by some biological species that produce many offspring in the hope that some will survive.

The design of the picture is fundamentally linear. The use of lines as descriptive tools, found as far back as the cave paintings, is perhaps the most remarkable innovation in the entire history of picture-making. While lines appear in nature in many forms—from blades of grass to winding rivers—in pictorial terms they are completely artificial. In life the leg and foot of the person we see here are soft and rounded; the lines that describe them in the picture are artificial, yet their meaning is absolutely clear. There must be some remarkable circuitry in our brains that we can so effortlessly see the lines and imagine the object.

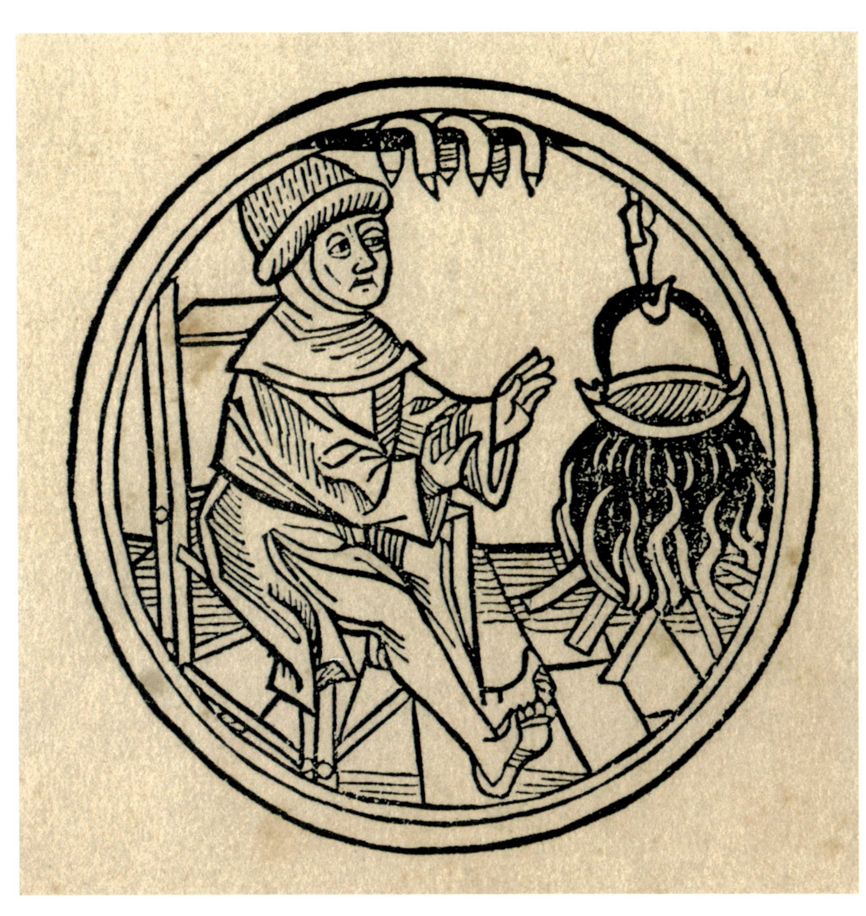

**Woodcut.** Artist unknown. *February.* c. 1484. 3⅝ x 3½ in. (9.2 x 8.9 cm) From *Calendar Deutsch.*

## 1.2 WOODCUT PRINTING

Relief printing is so named because the image-bearing part of the printing matrix—in this case a wooden block—stands higher than those areas that do not print. The woodblock is made by carving, with a chisel or gouge, into the side of a hard plank. Once carved, the block is inked, either with a roller covered in an even layer of ink or with an ink-covered rag applied with care to deposit ink on the high surfaces only. Since the sunken, cut-away areas receive no ink and are in any case kept away from the paper by the higher parts of the surface, they appear white in the print. Conversely, the lines and solids we see in the print were printed by the parts that were not carved; each has had material removed along its sides and remains as the high part of the block, still possessing its original surface. It is ironic that what we see as a black line is actually the part of the block that the carver never touched.

We often assume that the printing takes place in a press, but far more woodblock prints have been made by simply placing the paper on the inked block and rubbing the back. The carved plank holding the image tends to warp and lose its flatness, and it doesn't do too well under the pressure needed in a press.

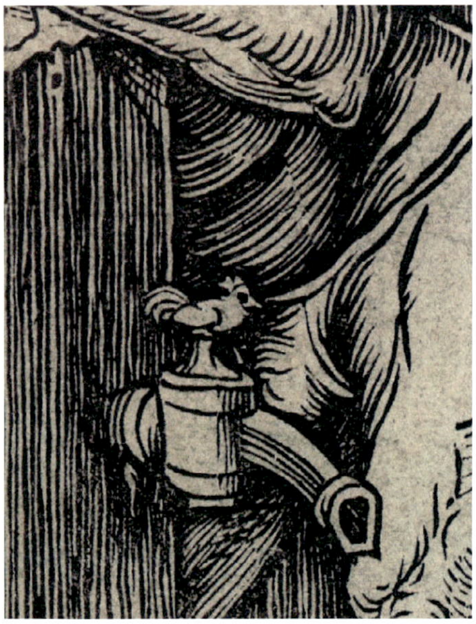

Relief printing has no mechanism for making black ink print gray. We could print with gray ink, of course, but then we would have no black in the picture. As print technology evolved, methods of printing were developed that used multiple blocks, inked with different-colored inks, to generate complicated tones; the height of that technique is the Japanese woodblock print, which we will see later in the book. For a single impression, however, we need some means to describe gray values with black ink if we wish the printed picture to portray tonal variation. Much of the technological development of printing has focused on this problem: how do you describe gray when your ink is black? Groups of closely arranged lines are the most common solution: if the lines, though black, are narrow enough, and the print is viewed from far enough away, they create the illusion of gray. In our Dürer print the quality of the carving is remarkable. The dense array of carved channels and raised lines in the block represent a high point in the wood-carver's trade. When the print is seen from only a short distance away the eye blends the lines and spaces to read variable tone, and so the challenge of achieving the illusion of tone, and with it of volume and perspective, is elegantly solved.

A detail enlarged about 1.2 times from the original print.

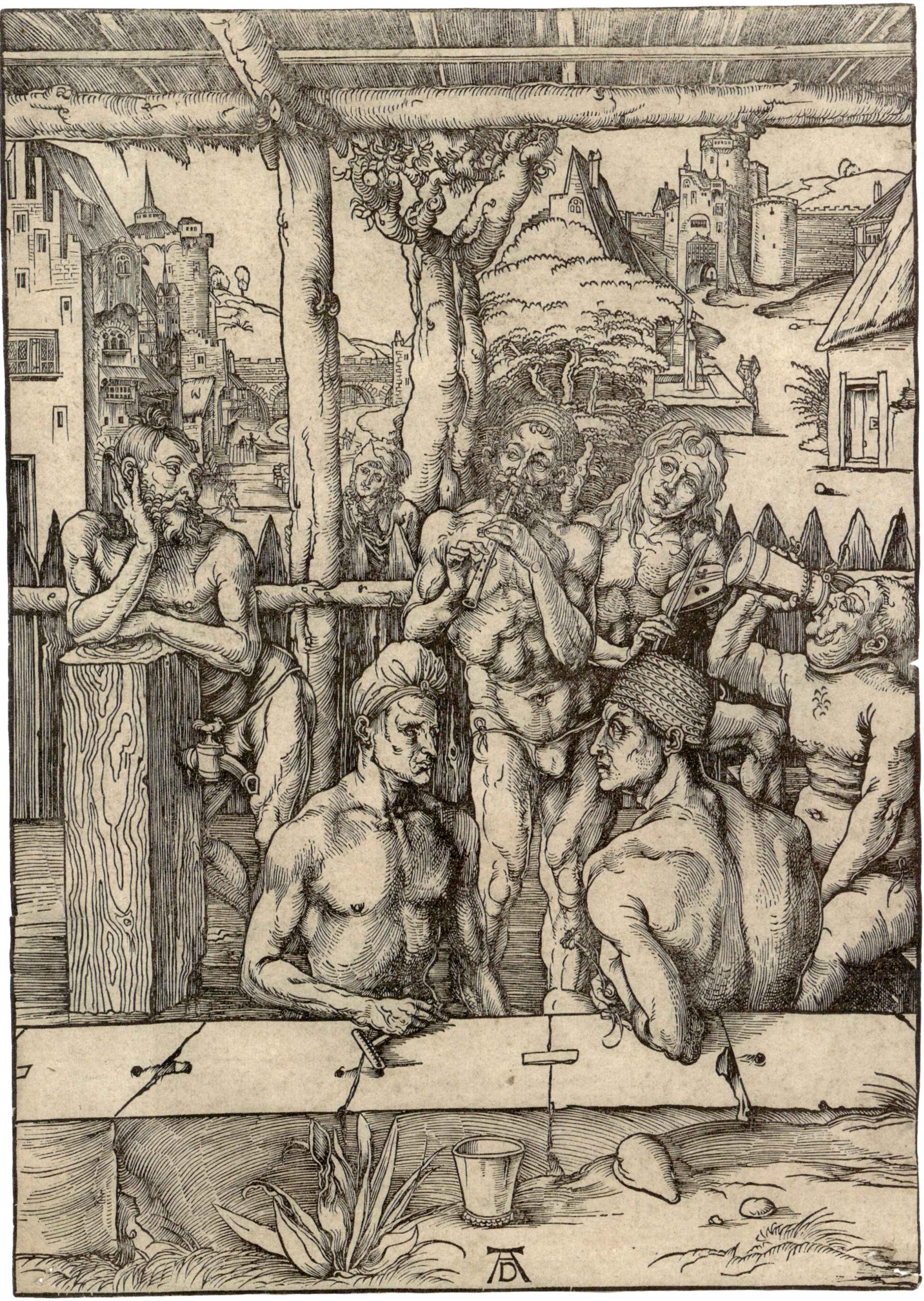

**Woodcut.** Albrecht Dürer. *The Men's Bath.* c. 1496. 15¼ x 11¼ in. (38.7 x 28.6 cm)

## 1.3 A HAND-LETTERED MANUSCRIPT PAGE

This small and simple manuscript page dates from the fourteenth century. The letters are run-of-the-mill, written rapidly by a scribe on a sheet of calfskin. This is not part of a large and splendid Bible, worth thousands of dollars; rather it is a remnant of a Catholic missal that I bought in a junk shop for $20 some years ago. Before the invention of lead type such pages existed by the hundreds of thousands. Bound up in books, they were the primary carriers of language in a fixed form, as opposed to the fluid and changeable information buried in the spoken word.

Centuries before this page was written, human culture had learned the remarkable lesson that language could be laid out, in all its tremendous variety, through the use of a limited set of letters and words. This is simply astonishing. Not only could the mind direct alterations of the physical world, the building of cities and the plowing of fields, but its workings could also be codified by such a simple set of tools as the letters of the alphabet and their astonishingly versatile arrangement into words and sentences. Once these words were written down they acquired the extraordinary ability to outlast their makers: this page, like our little woodcut in plate 1.1, has managed to last dozens of times longer than the life of the person who made it, even outliving anyone who might have used it for its original purpose. This persistence has shown that accumulated knowledge, set down in ink on paper, has the ability to last through generations. In the animal kingdom some artifacts do last — pathways and burrows can be used over decades — but by and large the knowledge each individual accumulates through experience dies once the biological shell fails. The written word gave humanity a tool far beyond that of any other animal; it is the perfect Darwinian step to ensure the survival and dominance of the species.

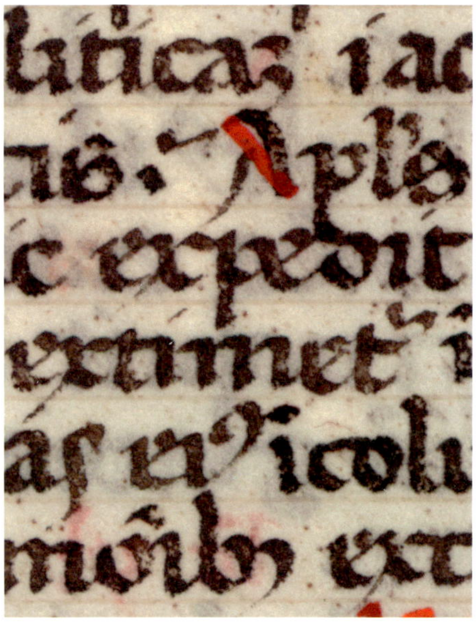

Handwritten letters can vary according to their neighbors, and individual letters often run together. This practice gives a strong identity to the words, and reinforces the fact that letters by themselves mean nothing; content only exists when words and sentences are formed.

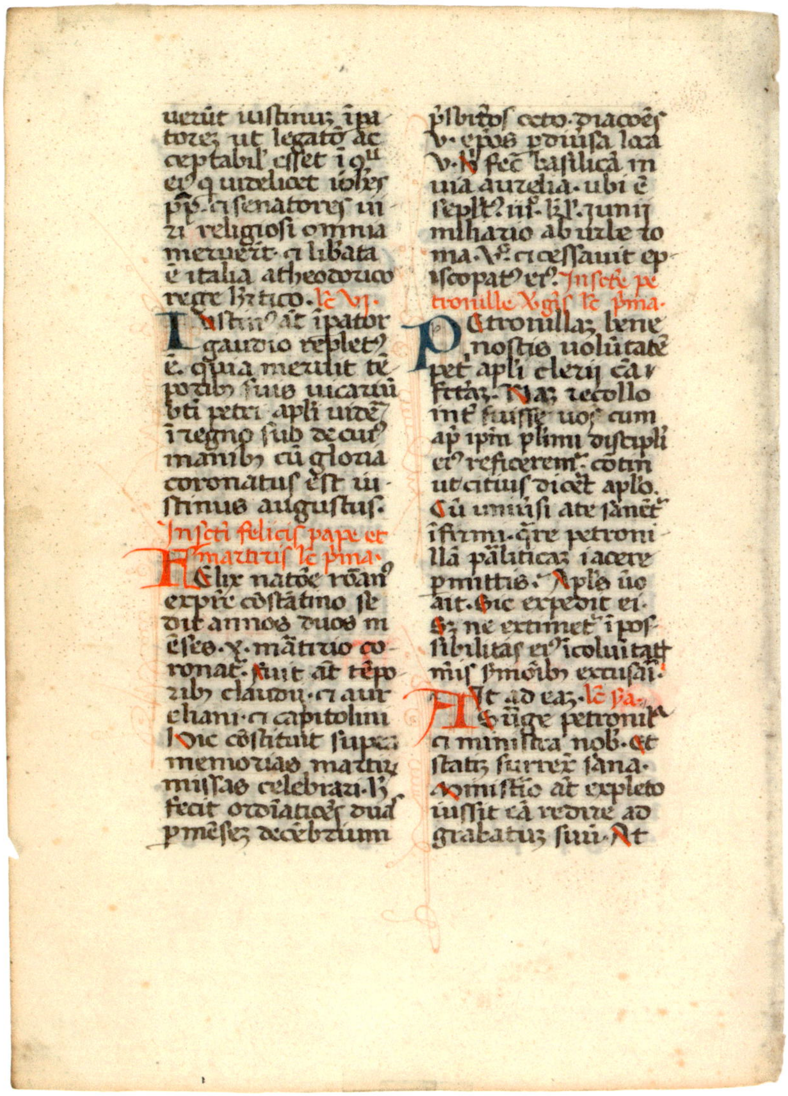

**Hand lettering.** Artist unknown. Page from a missal. c. 1350. 5¾ x 4⅛ in. (14.6 x 10.5 cm). A small manuscript page written in a southern Gothic book hand.

## 1.4 LETTERPRESS

Handwritten manuscripts were costly to make, and could exist only in limited numbers, available to the well-to-do and the powerful. In the mid-fifteenth century, in their efforts to produce less expensive versions of written language, printers began to use metal type, unleashing the great revolution of language-based information available to the masses. Prince and pauper alike got the same information from the printed page, and I have always thought that democracy as we know it would have been impossible without this innovation. The use of metal type spread rapidly, and over the 400 years from 1500 to 1900 the technology of printing words by making them up out of little metal letters in relief remained basically unchanged. Technological innovation tends to derive from need, and the development of printing from moveable type was such an innovation that its initial technology did not require much further development for this astonishingly long period.

This is a leaf from a Bible, printed at the end of the eighteenth century. It is a pale thing compared to the little manuscript page that precedes it, but in this blandness resides the tremendous power of printing from moveable type. The page once resided in a bound book, long since destroyed. Not only do books hold huge amounts of information, they also act as tough protective devices; one can spill a whole glass of water on a book (as I have done on a number of occasions) and come away with only some stains along the edge.

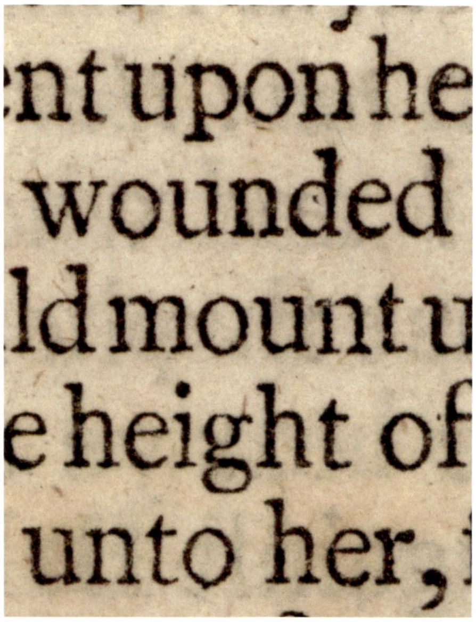

The sheet is elegantly laid out—good design, after all, doesn't really cost more than bad, so the relative simplicity of this Bible didn't mean that it had to be poorly designed. The letters run across two columns, to avoid a wide block of type that would be hard for the eye to follow from line to line. A fine rule separates the columns, allowing them to be closely spaced and so fitting more on the page. The margins leave room for printed commentary and perhaps notes written in by the reader. The page also has a beautiful evenness; its "gray"—the modulation of the white paper by the black type—is smooth and lightly rippled by the verse endings and number indents. The type itself is formed with great regularity. We assume this is because the letters were well drawn by their maker but their shape actually derives from a complex set of punches. Laboriously filed by hand in the actual size of the type being made, these punches struck the type mold to make the negative spaces into which the molten metal flowed when the type was cast. Multiple punches were needed for most letters, but the stems and curves for different letters were often made with the same punch. This process of making led to comfortable family relationships between letters, so that they could visually coexist together on the page.

Words printed with moveable type look completely different from those made by hand: no letter can touch another, and when they are packed onto the page the distances between the letters and between the words they form can be very similar. It is little wonder that those accustomed to handmade books considered early printing from metal type mediocre.

Before CHRIST 595.

and I will ſtretch out mine hand upon thee, and roll
thee down from the rocks, and will make thee a
burnt mountain.
26 And they ſhall not take of thee a ſtone for a
corner, nor a ſtone for foundations ; but thou ſhalt
be † deſolate for ever, ſaith the LORD.
27 Set ye up a ſtandard in the land, blow the trum-
pet among the nations, prepare the nations againſt
her, call together againſt her the kingdoms of Ararat,
Minni, and Aſhchenaz; appoint a captain againſt her;
cauſe the horſes to come up as the rough caterpillers.
28 Prepare againſt her the nations, with the kings
of the Medes, the captains thereof, and all the rulers
thereof, and all the land of his dominion.
29 And the land ſhall tremble and ſorrow: for
every purpoſe of the LORD ſhall be performed againſt
Babylon, to make the land of Babylon a deſolation
without an inhabitant.
30 The mighty men of Babylon have forborne to
fight, they have remained in *their* holds; their might
hath failed, they became as women: they have burnt
her dwelling-places; her bars are broken.
31 One poſt ſhall run to meet another, and one
meſſenger to meet another, to ſhew the king of Babylon that his city is taken at *one* end ;
32 And that the paſſages are ſtopped, and the reeds
they have burnt with fire, and the men of war are
affrighted.
33 For thus ſaith the LORD of hoſts, the God of
Iſrael, The daughter of Babylon *is* like a threſhing-
floor, ‖ *it is* time to threſh her: yet a little while, and
the time of her harveſt ſhall come.
34 Nebuchadrezzar the king of Babylon hath devour-
ed me, he hath cruſhed me, he hath made me an empty
veſſel, he hath ſwallowed me up like a dragon, he hath
filled his belly with my delicates, he hath caſt me out.
35 † The violence done to me and to my ‖ fleſh *be*
upon Babylon, ſhall the † inhabitant of Zion ſay;
and, My blood upon the inhabitants of Chaldea,
ſhall Jeruſalem ſay.
36 Therefore thus ſaith the LORD, Behold, I will
plead thy cauſe, and take vengeance for thee; and
I will dry up her ſea, and make her ſprings dry.
37 And Babylon ſhall become heaps, a dwelling-
place for dragons, an aſtoniſhment and an hiſſing
without an inhabitant.
38 They ſhall roar together like lions; they ſhall
‖ yell as lions' whelps.
39 In their heat I will make their feaſts, and I will
make them drunken, that they may rejoice, and ſleep
a perpetual ſleep, and not wake, ſaith the LORD.
40 I will bring them down like lambs to the
ſlaughter, like rams with he-goats.
41 How is Sheſhach taken! and how is the praiſe
of the whole earth ſurpriſed! how is Babylon become
an aſtoniſhment among the nations!
42 The ſea is come up upon Babylon; ſhe is covered with the multitude of the waves thereof:
43 Her cities are a deſolation, a dry land and a
wilderneſs, a land wherein no man dwelleth, neither
doth *any* ſon of man paſs thereby.
44 And I will puniſh Bel in Babylon; and I will
bring forth out of his mouth that which he hath ſwal-

*† Heb. everlaſting deſolations.*
*‖ Or, in the time that he threſheth her.*
*† Heb. My violence.*
*‖ Or, remainder.*
*† Heb. inhabitreſs.*
*‖ Or, ſhake themſelves.*

lowed up: and the nations ſhall not flow together any
more unto him; yea, the wall of Babylon ſhall fall.
45 My people, go ye out of the midſt of her, and
deliver ye every man his ſoul from the fierce anger
of the LORD.
46 And leſt your heart faint, and ye fear for the
rumour that ſhall be heard in the land, a rumour
ſhall both come *one* year, and after that in *another*
year *ſhall come* a rumour, and violence in the land,
ruler againſt ruler.
47 Therefore, behold, the days come, that I will
† do judgment upon the graven images of Babylon;
and her whole land ſhall be confounded, and all her
ſlain ſhall fall in the midſt of her.
48 Then the heaven, and the earth, and all that *is*
therein, ſhall ſing for Babylon: for the ſpoilers ſhall
come unto her from the north, ſaith the LORD.
49 ‖ As Babylon *hath cauſed* the ſlain of Iſrael to fall,
ſo at Babylon ſhall fall the ſlain of all ‖ the earth.
50 Ye that have eſcaped the ſword go away, ſtand
not ſtill. remember the LORD afar off, and let Jeruſalem come into your mind.
51 We are confounded, becauſe we have heard re-
proach; ſhame hath covered our faces: for ſtrangers
are come into the ſanctuaries of the LORD's houſe.
52 Wherefore, behold, the days come, ſaith the
LORD, that I will do judgment upon her graven images,
and through all her land the wounded ſhall groan.
53 Though Babylon ſhould mount up to heaven, and
though ſhe ſhould fortify the height of her ſtrength, *yet*
from me ſhall ſpoilers come unto her, ſaith the LORD.
54 A ſound of a cry *cometh* from Babylon, and
great deſtruction from the land of the Chaldeans:
55 Becauſe the LORD hath ſpoiled Babylon, and de-
ſtroyed out of her the great voice; when her waves do
roar like great waters, a noiſe of their voice is uttered;
56 Becauſe the ſpoiler is come upon her, *even* upon
Babylon, and her mighty men are taken: every one
of their bows is broken; for the LORD God of re-
compences ſhall ſurely requite.
57 And I will make drunk her princes, and her wiſe
*men*, her captains, and her rulers, and her mighty men:
and they ſhall ſleep a perpetual ſleep, and not wake,
ſaith the King, whoſe name *is* The LORD of hoſts.
58 Thus ſaith the LORD of hoſts, ‖ The broad
walls of Babylon ſhall be utterly ‖ broken, and her
high gates ſhall be burnt with fire; and the people
ſhall labour in vain, and the folk in the fire, and they
ſhall be weary.
59 ¶ The word which Jeremiah the prophet commanded Seraiah the ſon of Neriah, the ſon of Maa-
ſeiah, when he went ‖ with Zedekiah the king of Ju-
dah into Babylon, in the fourth year of his reign:
and *this* Seraiah *was* a ‖ quiet prince.
60 So Jeremiah wrote in a book all the evil that
ſhould come upon Babylon, *even* all theſe words *that*
*are* written againſt Babylon.
61 And Jeremiah ſaid to Seraiah, When thou comeſt
to Babylon, and ſhalt ſee, and ſhalt read all theſe words,
62 Then ſhalt thou ſay, O LORD, thou haſt ſpoken
againſt this place to cut it off, that none ſhall remain
in it, neither man nor beaſt, but that it ſhall be † deſolate for ever.

Before CHRIST 595.
*† Heb. viſit upon.*
*‖ Or, Both Babylon is to fall, O ye ſlain of Iſrael, and with Babylon, &c.*
*‖ Or, the country.*
*‖ Or, The walls of broad Babylon.*
*‖ Or, made naked.*
*‖ Or, on the behalf of.*
*‖ Or, prince of Menucha, or, chief chamberlain.*
*† Heb. deſolations.*

63 And

**Letterpress from metal type.** Mark and Charles Kerr, Edinburgh, printers. Holy Bible. 1795. page from Jeremiah 51: *God's judgment against Babylon: her utter destruction.* 9¾ x 8 in. (24.6 x 20.3 cm)

## 1.5 WOODCUT LETTERS

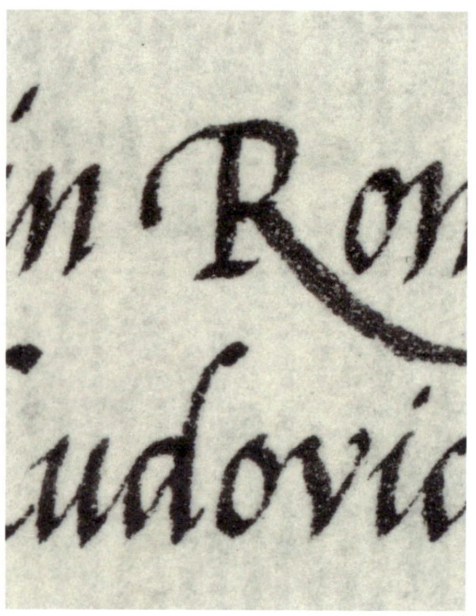


A piece of pen lettering handwritten in the style of Arrighi.

Moveable type shifted the printing of words away from the older technology of the woodblock, but chisel and wooden plank continued to be used for the printing of pictures and of words that couldn't easily be cast in metal. This page is from a book published in Rome in 1522 to teach the craft of fine handwriting. The text is printed in the same script that is being taught, which a calligrapher would have done with a broad-edged pen, held so that the nib made strokes ranging from wide to thin depending upon the angle of any given line. A pen such as this gives letter forms an elegant complexity, creating curves of varying thickness. Such active lines persist to this day in most printed type, including the Adobe Garamond face in which this book is printed.

It was a tremendous challenge to convert the handwritten letter into a printable woodblock. The basic fact of printing is that the data in the printed picture must come from somewhere and be moved onto a printing matrix that can hold this data and pass it on to the printed sheet. The data source for this page was a piece of pen lettering; the matrix was the woodblock that would receive the ink and move it onto the paper. To transfer the lettering to the block, someone carved the wooden surface into a replica of the letters in which the pen lines became the only parts of the original wood surface that remained after the cutting was completed. The carving was not done by the scribe; from its earliest stages, printing with ink onto paper involved technical skills almost never commanded by those who supplied the information. We can be sure that one person wrote this text, another cut the block, and others carried out the printing. One of the nice things about printing is that it demands cooperation between diverse groups; information is disseminated by the printed page, and this powerful act comes from the cooperative efforts of many people.

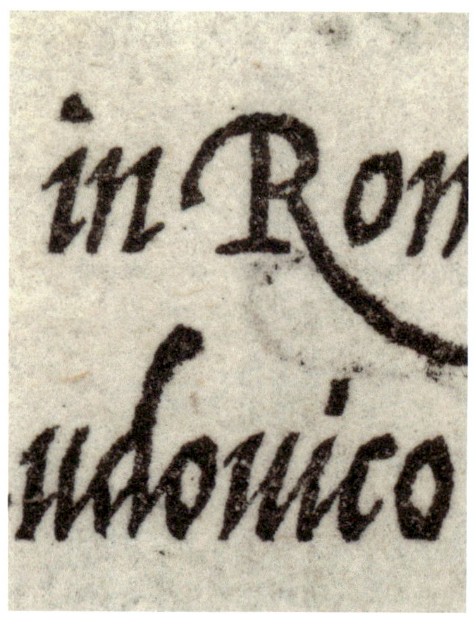


An enlargement of the same detail from the woodcut-printed book. The carving is remarkable, especially considering that the plate on the right shows the page in its original size, but the calligrapher's extreme variations of thick and thin have been lost in the printed version.

In the relationship between artist and printer there has always been a question of who owns what. In the case of this book from Rome the writer owned the original pen work and the carver believed that he owned the woodblocks. The two parties had a disagreement about this and at one point Ugo da Carpi, who made the blocks, printed an edition without permission from the writer, Ludovico Vicentino Arrighi. In the first editions of the book da Carpi gets a credit on this page; in this later edition his name has been replaced by a decorative woodblock claiming "CUM GRATIA PRIVILEGIO," "with favor and privilege," a designation that the author had copyrighted the book. To this day there are misunderstandings on this subject: unless a publisher negotiates with the printer ahead of time, the printer, not the publisher, may own the digital files that produce the book.

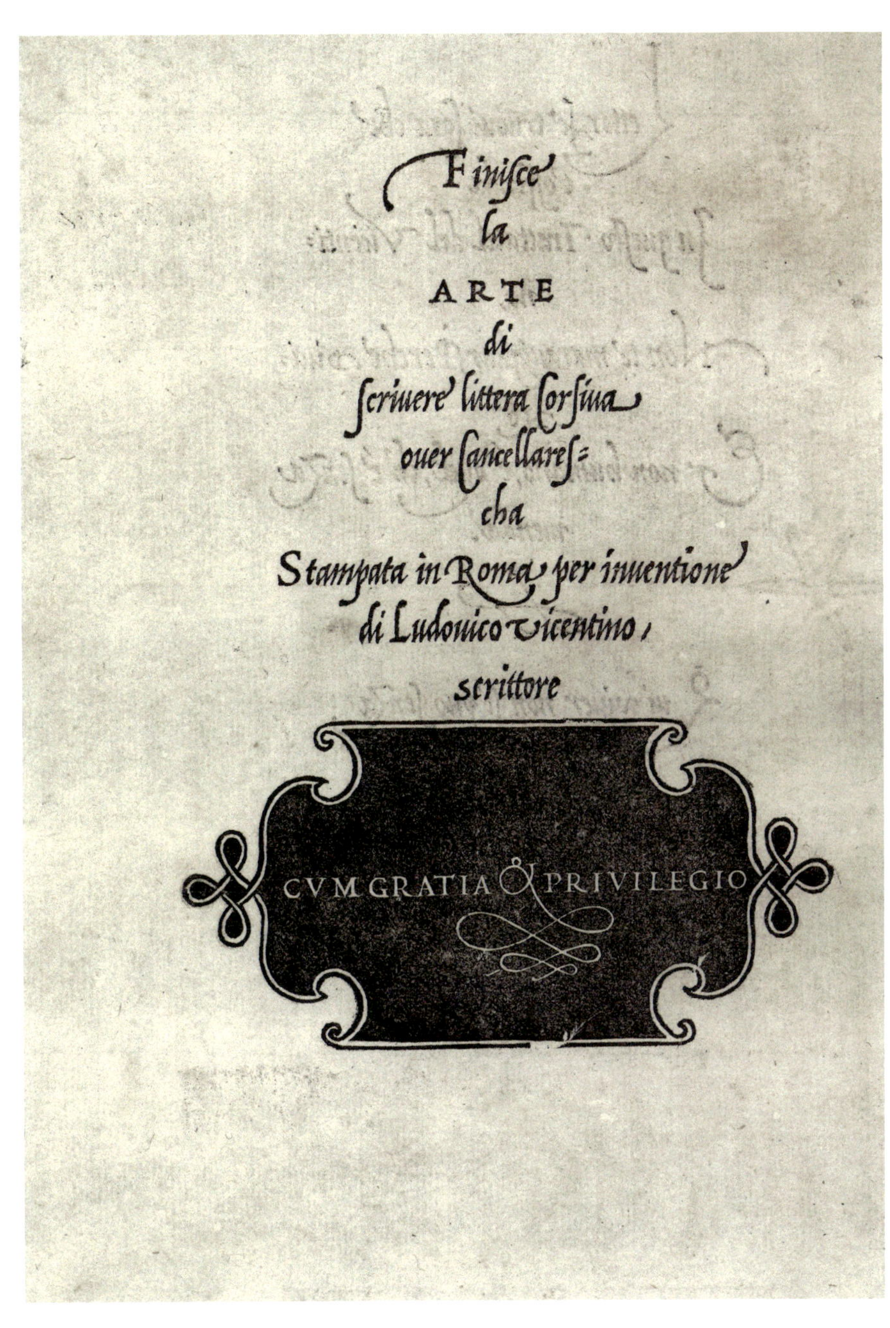

Finiſce
la
ARTE
di
ſcriuere littera Corſiua
ouer Cancellareſ=
cha
Stampata in Roma per inuentione
di Ludouico Vicentino,
ſcrittore

CVM GRATIA & PRIVILEGIO

**Woodcut.** Ludovico Vicentino Arrighi. Leaf from *La Operina.* 1522. Print: Ugo da Carpi. 6⅝ x 4⅝ in. (16.8 x 11.8 cm)

## 1.6 WOODCUT PRINTING

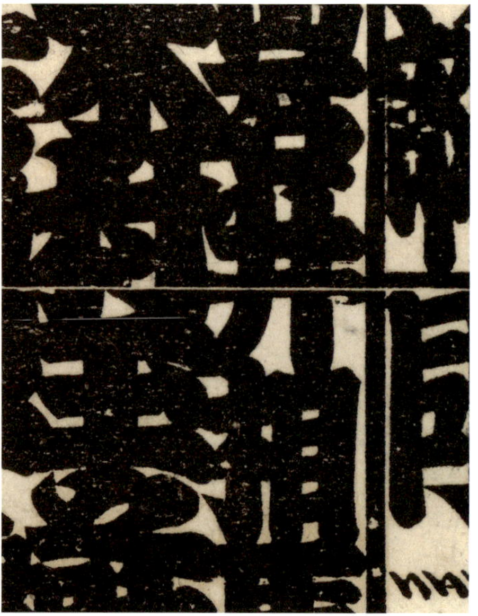

A detail from the upper center of the print, showing the joint between two of the primary blocks.

This magnificent sheet was printed in Japan sometime in the 1930s to announce the results of a wrestling match. It was made by woodblock, exactly the same technology as the previous plate, but these two samples of the printer's art look remarkably different: the letters on the older, Roman-alphabet sheet are delicate and thin, completely dominated by the white space of the unprinted paper, while the Japanese print is as densely packed with characters as a can is with sardines. The Japanese characters are perfectly suited to the carver's chisel; instead of thin, sweeping curves, forms with fairly straight edges that can be far more rapidly cut. We almost feel that the characters on this sheet have been designed to be squeezed together, to make an overall pattern with great graphic effect.

The lesson here is the astonishing versatility of this old printing process. Using the same sort of wood and carving tools, both cut by hand on the side grain, and printed with similar ink and paper, these two prints fully respond to the character of the culture and language out of which each came. The woodblock relief-printing process really has little character of its own; instead it is poised to take on the qualities of the data that the print must display. I started out as a printer trying to learn to reproduce photographs in ink, and this was the first big lesson I absorbed: the printer and the process must be in total subservience to the work being reproduced.

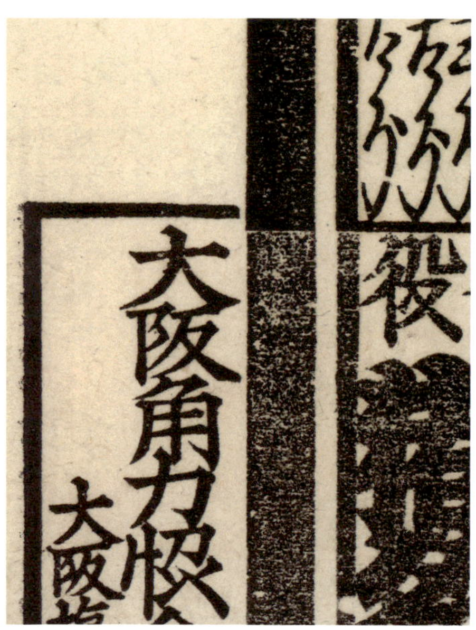

A detail from the lower left of the print, showing the different impression from two blocks that varied somewhat in their surface. The characters to the left are from yet another woodblock.

The Italian sheet is small, about seven inches high, while this one is nearly two feet tall. Even more remarkable than the paper's size is the fact that its information is time sensitive—it is a broadside, printed to get the word out about an athletic event. The match took place on one day and this announcement came out on the following one. A close examination of the original shows that the print was actually made from six separate blocks. A single brush-drawn tissue was painted with the text, cut into pieces, pasted onto the different blocks, and handed to different people to do the carving. Then the blocks were held together while the impression was made. Once again the division of labor inherent in printing shows up, but this time it was done to speed the process so that the news could get out fast.

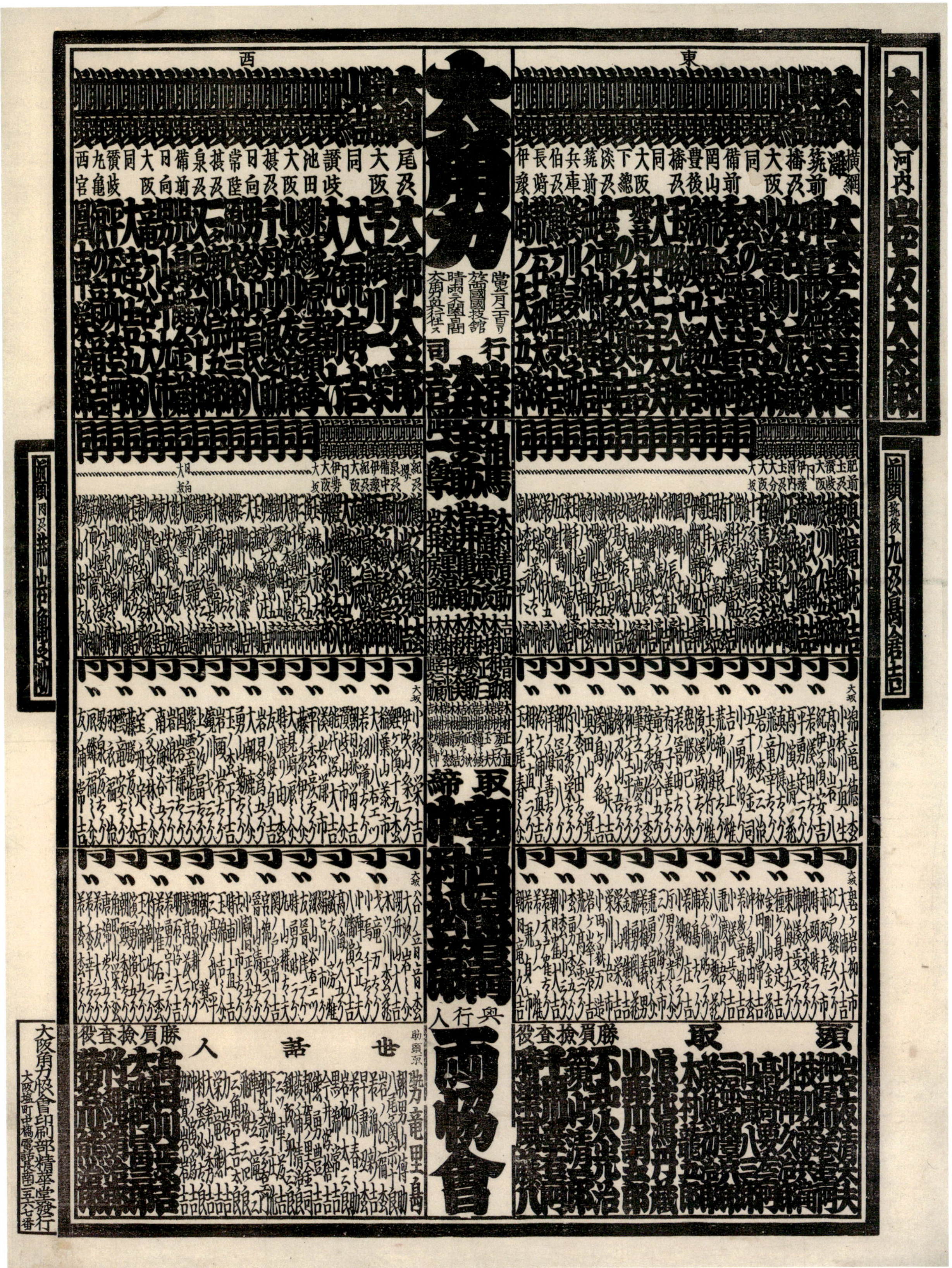


**Woodcut.** Japanese broadside. c. 1935. 22½ x 17½ in. (57.2 x 44.5 cm)

## 1.7 WOODCUT AND METAL TYPE

Since the very beginning of printing on paper, printers have struggled to accommodate words and pictures on a single page. Both types of images are pictures—the former symbolic and the latter representational—but the methods used to print them have been very different.

While woodblocks carrying representational pictures were often printed by hand, letters cast in metal type were always printed in a press. They were locked up in a metal frame, called a "chase," that was fitted into the press, and ink was transferred from their surfaces to paper by the application of mechanical pressure. The chase had to hold the tiny letters so firmly that it could be lifted without a piece falling out. To secure them in place, they were packed along with spacers (called "furniture") that were less tall than the letters—"less than type high" was the phrase—and the whole aggregate was further held in the frame by wedges driven between the type and furniture and the inside wall of the chase. The body of the lead type was usually cast so accurately in the mold that a full page of it would lock immovably in the chase. If even a single piece was pulled out, tugged by the sticky bond between ink and paper, it would be crushed with any adjacent type during the following impression.

This page, an early effort to combine words and pictures, was made by locking a woodcut into the chase along with the letters and furniture. This was a dubious practice: the woodblock could be made type high, so that the printing surfaces of both picture and words came to the same level in the press, but the block was flexible while the type was not. As the wedges used in the "form" (the printer's name for the assembled contents of the chase) pressed the assembly together, the woodblock, at right angles to the direction in which it had grown in the tree, would compress. The metal type, on the other hand, would hold its shape under pressure, so picture and letters were held with different degrees of firmness and the whole package was unstable. Such instability could be tolerated in a slow, manually driven hand press as long as the printer kept a close eye on the chase and its contents, but the system could never work once the presses ran at any sort of speed. This particular page was made in 1493, well before the arrival of the steam-driven printing press, so it could be slowly printed by this union of side-grain wood and metal type. Three hundred and fifty years later, when presses were mechanically driven at high speeds, a different method for uniting words and pictures would be needed.

Eneas pius bin ich genāt
Mein lob vnd preis ist hohbekāt

Eneas pius der babst　　Friderich der dritt ein romischer kaiser

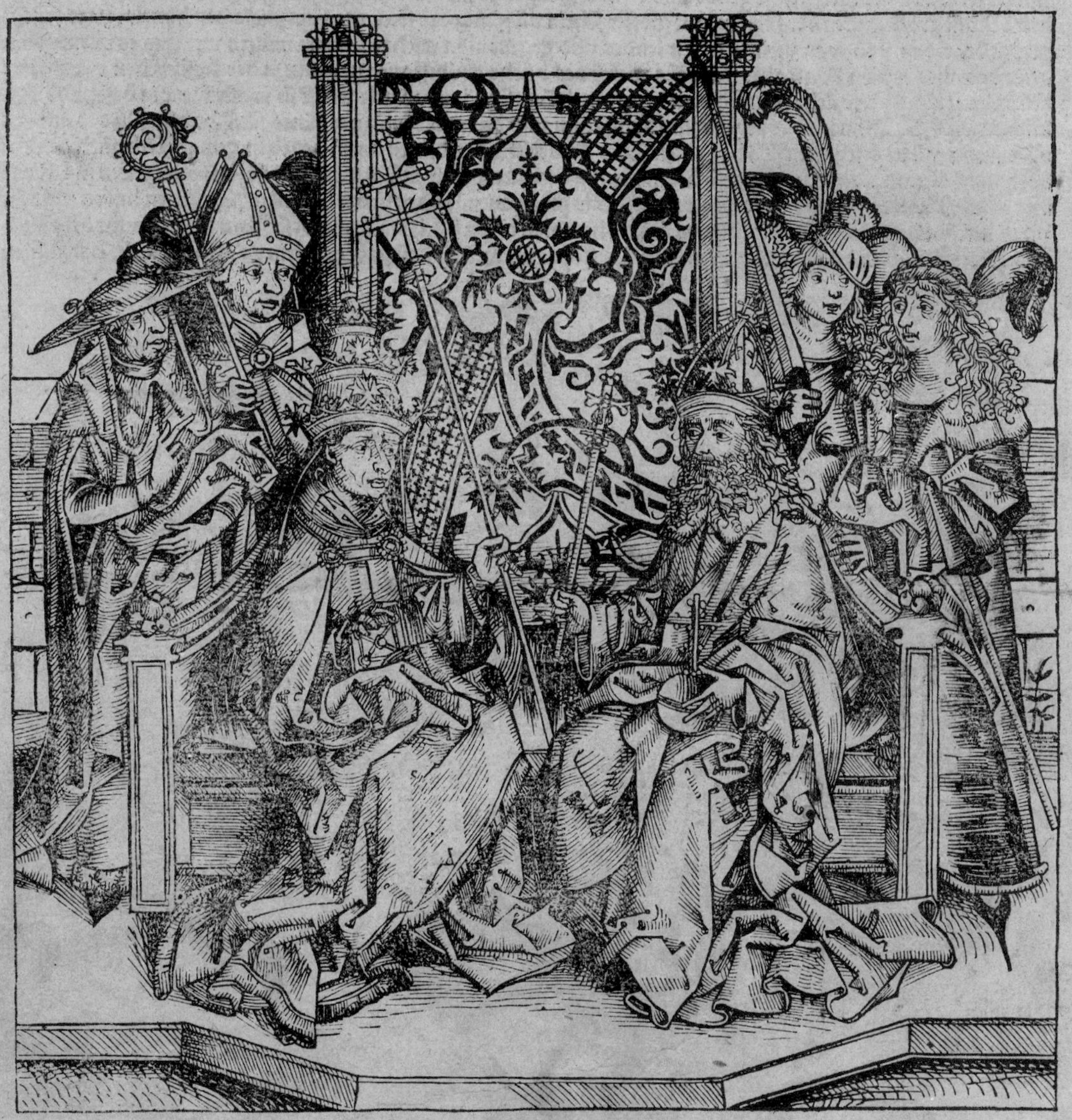

Der zornig leob verschonen thut
Dess: der gein im zaiget demūt
Also soll auch ein herrscher thon
Dem gelyhen ist des gewalts kron

**Letterpress from woodcut and metal type.** Anton Koberger and the workshop of Michael Wohlgemut. *King Friderich and the Roman Pope.* 1493. 13½ x 10 in. (34.3 x 25.4 cm). A page from the German version of the Nuremberg Chronicle.

## 1.8 WOOD ENGRAVING

The solution to the problem of combining words and pictures on press came in England in the late eighteenth century, with Thomas Bewick's refinement of wood engraving. Bewick worked as an artist, making precise, beautiful, tiny wood engravings, but the process quickly became established as a commercial system for printing illustrations because the wood engravings could be used in conjunction with metal type. Like woodcut, wood engraving was a relief printing process, but the method differed in the orientation of the wooden printing block and in the cutting tools applied in carving it. Woodcut had used a plank, cut from the tree in the direction of its growth, so that the grain ran along the printing surface. Wood engraving used a block taken horizontally out of the tree, so that the engraving was cut into the end grain of the wood.

The blocks for wood engraving had to be very hard; the favored material was boxwood, which is a small tree, so the printing blocks often had to be glued up out of small pieces. But boxwood is dense enough to lock up decently with type in a printing chase. Still more important, the height of the block is extremely stable, since wood undergoes little dimensional change along the direction of its grain when temperature or humidity varies. The wood could be carefully dried, accurately finished to type height, and cut to the size needed for illustrations. The early, semirotary steam-driven presses could dependably print forms properly locked up with metal type and end-grain picture blocks. When presses became fully rotary, around the time that this print was made, the printing was often done from a "stereotype," a precise casting made from the type and picture blocks. Stereos were thin and could fit the curved shape of the printing cylinder. Far higher printing speeds were possible on these new presses, in which flat reciprocating surfaces were eliminated.

The great print scholar William Ivins once said that all civilization grew out of written language pointing to a picture. The combination of the wood engraving with metal type made this practice widespread, through the creation of inexpensive volumes of illustrated text. Some of these reproduced art, but many technical publications were also made in which the explanatory words could finally refer to a picture on the same page.

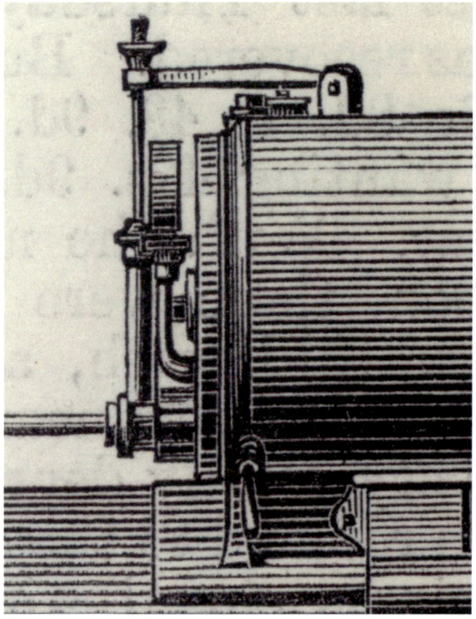

The horizontal lines describing the roundness of the engine's cylinder move flawlessly from thin black lines on a white ground to equally thin white lines on a black ground. The scheme in no way mirrors the actual appearance of such a cylinder; instead it is a printer's invention, reflecting a theoretical conception of how such a form might be described. This picture comes not from an interpreted observation of the world but from the mind of its maker.

## COMPOUND SEMI-FIXED ENGINE.

CONSTRUCTED BY MESSRS. WALLIS AND STEEVENS, ENGINEERS, BASINGSTOKE.

(*For Description, see next Page*).

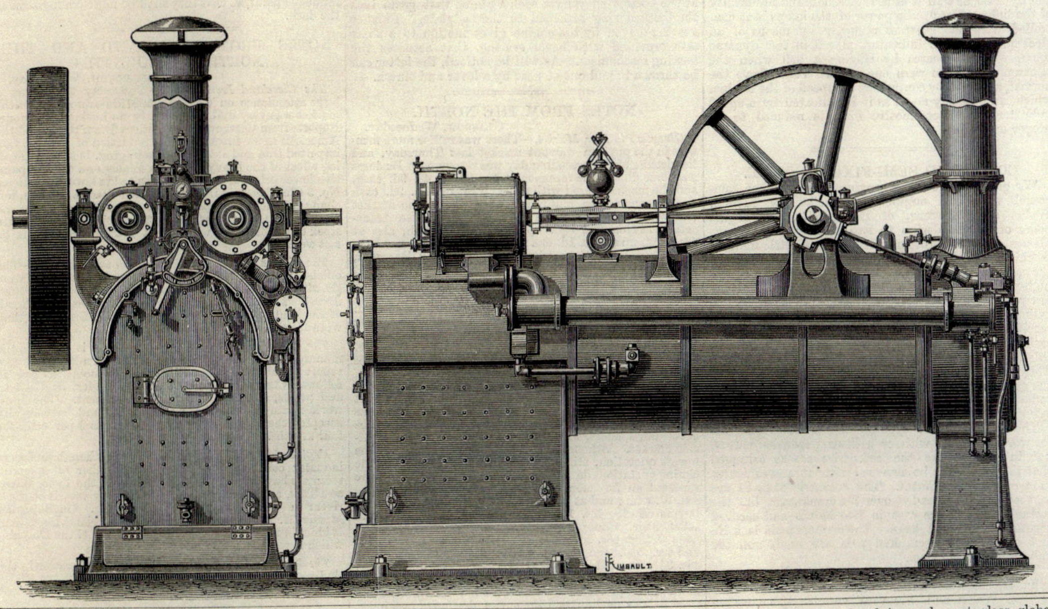

### THE ELECTRIC LIGHT ON THE S.S. "TARAWERA."

THE Edison Electric Light Company, Limited, received a contract recently for lighting two ships belonging to the Union Steamship Company of New Zealand, the Tarawera and the Waihora. The Tarawera was built by Messrs. Denny Brothers, at their yards at Dumbarton, and on the 21st of November the staff of the Edison Company commenced wiring the vessel. The dynamo and engine were placed in a small room, 12 ft. by 11 ft. and 7 ft. high, opening into the engine room, the floor being on a level with the gallery running round the top of the cylinders of the main engines. The wiring of the vessel is done in the most careful manner, nothing but the most highly insulated wire, protected by an india-rubber covering, and over that a waterproof covering of waxed thread, being used. The wires were all laid under the woodwork of the vessel in wood beading, made for the purpose, and at proper places safety catches with fusible lead wires were placed to obviate any danger of over-heating. The fixtures to carry the lamps are nickel-plated and of an elaborate character; in the saloon, arrangements have been made by which the incandescence lamps are suspended inside the shade of the ordinary oil lamps, but can be removed at pleasure at a moment's notice; the state rooms are lit by a single lamp, controlled by a switch placed within hand reach of the occupant of the berth; the lamps, which are enclosed in opalescent glass shades, are all the ordinary Edison 16-candle type, requiring an electromotive force of 96 volts to make each yield its normal light. In the gangways and the ladies' drawing-room the lamps are suspended from the ceiling enclosed in opalescent glass globes. The lamp in each state room is controlled by its own tap on the socket; the lamps in the saloon are all controlled by a single switch placed in the engine-room, so that the light can be shut out at eleven o'clock, leaving the lamps burning in the state rooms.

The generator is one of the Edison 150-light dynamos, which has been slightly modified in order to reduce the normal speed; it is capable of being driven practically and conveniently without belting. The following data supply the necessary information as to the dynamo.

Resistance of armature, 0.1 ohm; resistance of each leg of field magnets, 20 ohms; speed, 475 revolutions per minute, electromotive force, 96 volts; current, 120 ampères; length of armature, 5 ft. 5½in.; diameter of armature, 10 in.; 150 lamps of 16 measured candle power are maintained, each lamp having a resistance of 125 ohms hot, and taking 0.8 ampères of current.

The dynamo was driven by one of Mr. Peter Brotherhood's well known three-cylinder engines, 7 in. diameter of cylinders, 4½ in. stroke, working up to 20 horse power. Both generator and engine are fixed on the same base-plate, which is bolted down to a teak bedding 3 in. thick, through the deck beams, the dynamo being further stayed by cross-stays holding it in position. The extreme size of the bed-plate is 9 ft. by 3 ft., the height of the machine over all being 6 ft. 6 in. The illustration which we annex shows the arrangement clearly. The engine takes steam from the main boilers.

The preliminary trials having been made of the machinery, to show that everything was in perfect working order, on the 2nd of December a numerous company were invited by the Union Steamship Company of New Zealand to witness the trial runs on board the vessel which was lying in the Albert Harbour, Greenock. At two o'clock the engine was started, and the lights all over the vessel illuminated simultaneously. The engine ran with extreme smoothness, and there was an entire absence of any flickering or unsteadiness in the light. Saloons were illuminated with a uniform and steady light, and in the state rooms the single Edison lamps gave about eight or ten times the light ordinarily afforded to the occupants. A special feature of this generator is its high economy in the conversion of mechanical power into electrical energy, and the very moderate speed at which it runs. This speed of about 475 revolutions a minute, is one at which the Brotherhood engines have run with the greatest ease for long periods of time without adjustment or repairs. The gentlemen present on Saturday, comprising as they did, in addition to representatives of

**Letterpress from wood engraving and metal type.** J. H. Rimbault. *Compound Semi-fixed Engine.* 1882. 12 x 8¾ in. (30.5 x 22.2 cm). From the journal *Engineering,* December 8, 1882.

## 1.9 WOOD ENGRAVING

The woodblock had always been cut with a chisel or gouge, woodworking tools with an ancient lineage. The newer wood engraving, cut in end-grain wood, got its name because it was made with a burin, a completely different cutting tool. The burin is small, fits tightly into the hand, and is used horizontally, moving along the wood surface rather than being hammered down into it. At the cutting end there is a lozenge-shaped face, set at an angle, and the lower point of this end is pushed into the surface to make a groove. The burin was probably first developed to do decorative metalwork but is adapted to the cutting of engravings in wood as well. The term "engraving" is connected to the use of this tool; copper engravings, for example, are made with intaglio plates worked with a burin to make grooves in the metal that hold ink. The word "engraving" causes a lot of confusion and we need to remember that it applies to very different sorts of printing.

One of the great capacities of wood engraving was as a reproductive medium, a role in which it reached a high point in the 1880s, when it was used to make reproductions before the development of purely photomechanical methods. In plate 1.8 we saw wood engraving used in a technical journal from 1882. Those pictures are schematic in nature rather than deriving from human vision or a photograph. The wood engraving opposite, made three years later, is different: it is a carefully executed reproduction of a pen-and-ink drawing by a first-rate visual artist. The original drawing, by the nineteenth-century New York political caricaturist Thomas Nast, was animated and lifelike. Slavishly following Nast's lines, the engraved block has produced a printed ink replica of a drawing originally made by hand.

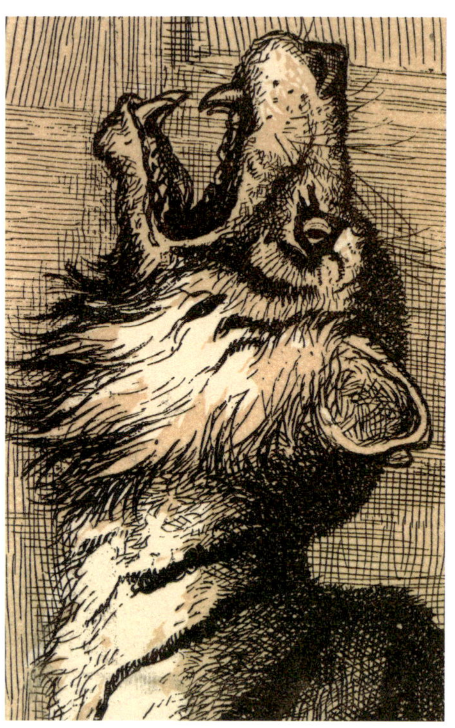

The second impression gives the appearance of printing white in parts of the tiger, an effect it actually creates by laying down a surrounding pale-yellow color.

The Tammany Tiger has been printed in two impressions. The dominant one, in black ink, is from an intricate block portraying the original drawing. The second impression, made in careful register with the first, is from a simple block that prints a solid pale-yellow color everywhere except in the ruff of the tiger's throat and chest. This is an example of two-impression printing. Further on in the book, when we examine color printing, we will find that this practice of printing in multiple layers would be developed into the most common method for generating color prints.

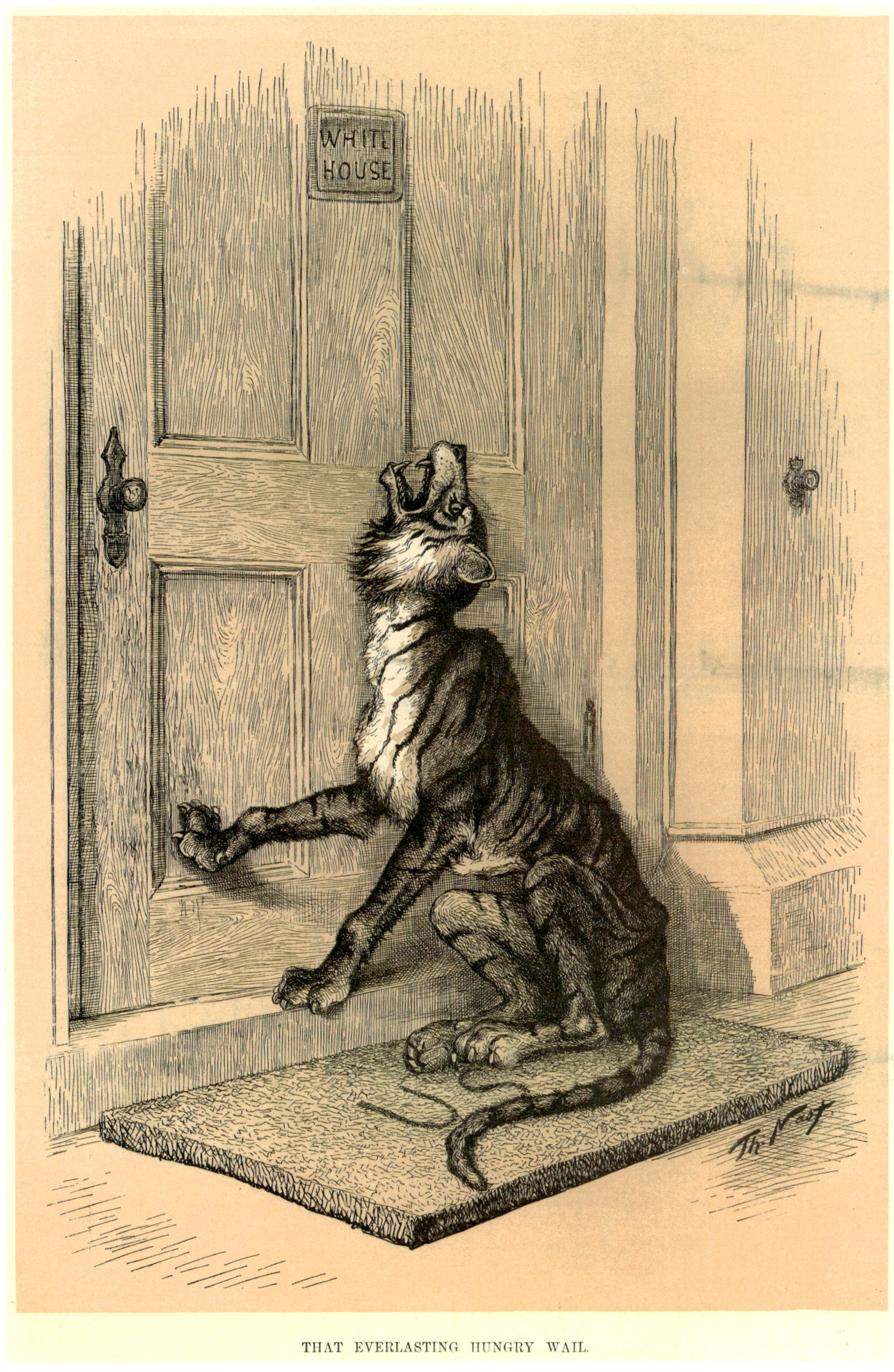


THAT EVERLASTING HUNGRY WAIL.

**Letterpress from wood engraving.** Thomas Nast. *That Everlasting Hungry Wail.* 1885. Print: 14¼ x 9¼ in. (36.2 x 24.1 cm). A two-color wood engraving by an anonymous engraver from a drawing by Nast. From *Harper's Weekly*, October 1885.

# Part 2

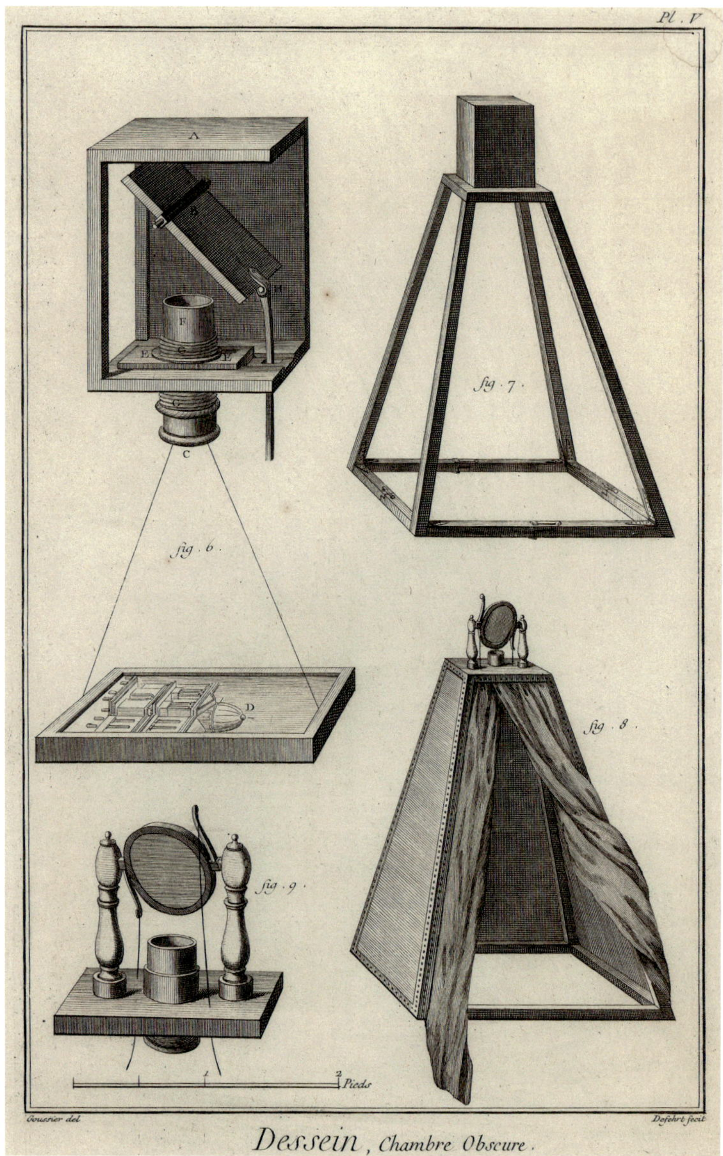


This section examines two of the great printing processes: intaglio, which means printing from the low part of a printing plate (as opposed to the high parts used in relief printing), and planographic printing, which prints from a material with a smooth surface. The most common intaglio processes are engraving and etching; the best-known of the planographic processes is stone lithography.

**Copper engraving.** Jacques-Louis Goussier. *Dessein, Chambre Obscure.* c. 1772. Print: Desehrt. 13¼ x 8¼ in. (33.6 x 21 cm). From *L'Encyclopédie de Diderot.* c. 1772

# Intaglio and planographic printing

2.1 Copper engraving
*Printing from lines cut with a burin into a copper plate.*

2.2 Etching
*Deriving the linear structure of a plate by chemical etching.*

2.3 Etching and engraving
*A simple overview of intaglio printing.*

2.4 Steel engraving
*Steel replacing copper to achieve longer editions.*

2.5 Aquatint
*Tonal printing through the use of etching and a randomly applied resist.*

2.6 Mezzotint
*Printed pictures generated from a burnished copper plate.*

2.7 Stipple in etching and engraving
*The height of handmade intaglio pictures.*

2.8 Monotypes
*Prints made from the inked surface of a flat plate.*

2.9 Stone lithography
*A method of printing from a chemically defined surface.*

2.10 Stone lithography
*Lithography as a system for printing smooth tones.*

# Intaglio printing

## 2.1 COPPER ENGRAVING

With this rather stiff picture of Monsieur Helyot we enter a completely different world from that of wood-based relief prints. The print is a copper engraving that has been printed by the intaglio process. "Intaglio" comes from the Italian *intagliere*, to "cut in" or carve, and describes the class of printing that uses grooves in metal to hold the printing ink. Relief printing, such as the woodcut and the wood engraving, is done by applying ink to the high parts of a printing matrix; intaglio uses the low parts instead. Using a burin, the engraver cuts lines into a polished plate. These lines hold the ink, which the pressure of the printing press transfers to the paper.

Engravings were a hugely important pictorial system for centuries, starting to be common in the 1500s and dominating fancy printing until the industrial revolution. Most intaglio printing of this period was done with copper plates. Copper is a tough material to cut with the burin—it is stringy and resists the tool—but when properly handled it can produce precise and delicate plates that last for many impressions. The burin is a small, lightweight thing, and pushing it in a controlled way across the copper surface is very hard. Much engraving was done instead by holding the tool tightly and moving the plate against it; that way the engraver was using both hands together to guide the line. One easy way of doing this was to rest the plate on a leather pad and rotate it. As a result, many old engravings include a lot of smoothly curved lines, making them the perfect medium for describing the fashionable wigs that swell people wore at one time. We see a perfect example of this in Monsieur Helyot's absurd hair.

In the hands of a master, copper engraving could make great pictures, but many are awkward. They were often used to make reproductions of paintings, and in the example here, the lettering and the geometric and floral borders are fine, but the articulated cloth shows signs of a struggle on the engraver's part; the difficulties of cutting the plate have overcome the descriptive requirements of the picture. The face, on the other hand, is beautifully done. Many of the engravings that have survived in museum and private collections are terrific but a vast number are simply terrible, because of the difficulties of engraving the copper.

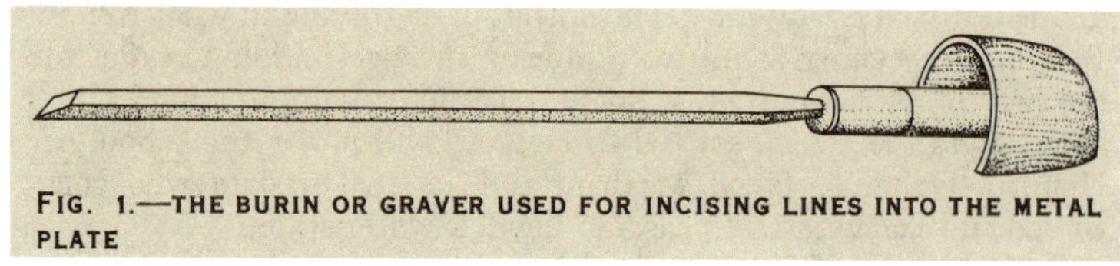
FIG. 1.—THE BURIN OR GRAVER USED FOR INCISING LINES INTO THE METAL PLATE

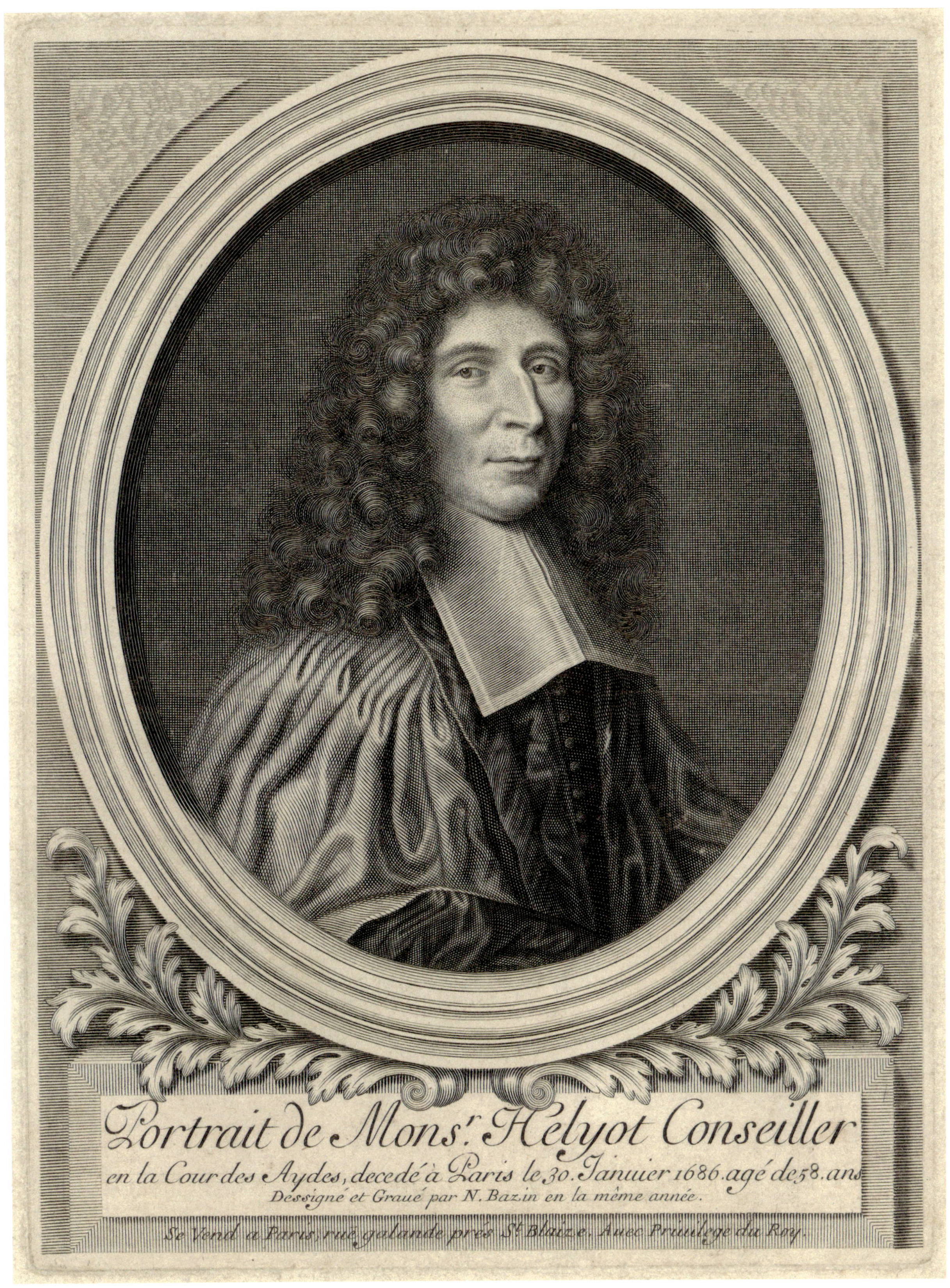


**Copper engraving.** Nicolas Bazin. *Portrait de Monsieur Helyot Conseiller.* 1686. 10¼ x 7¾ in. (26 x 19.7 cm)

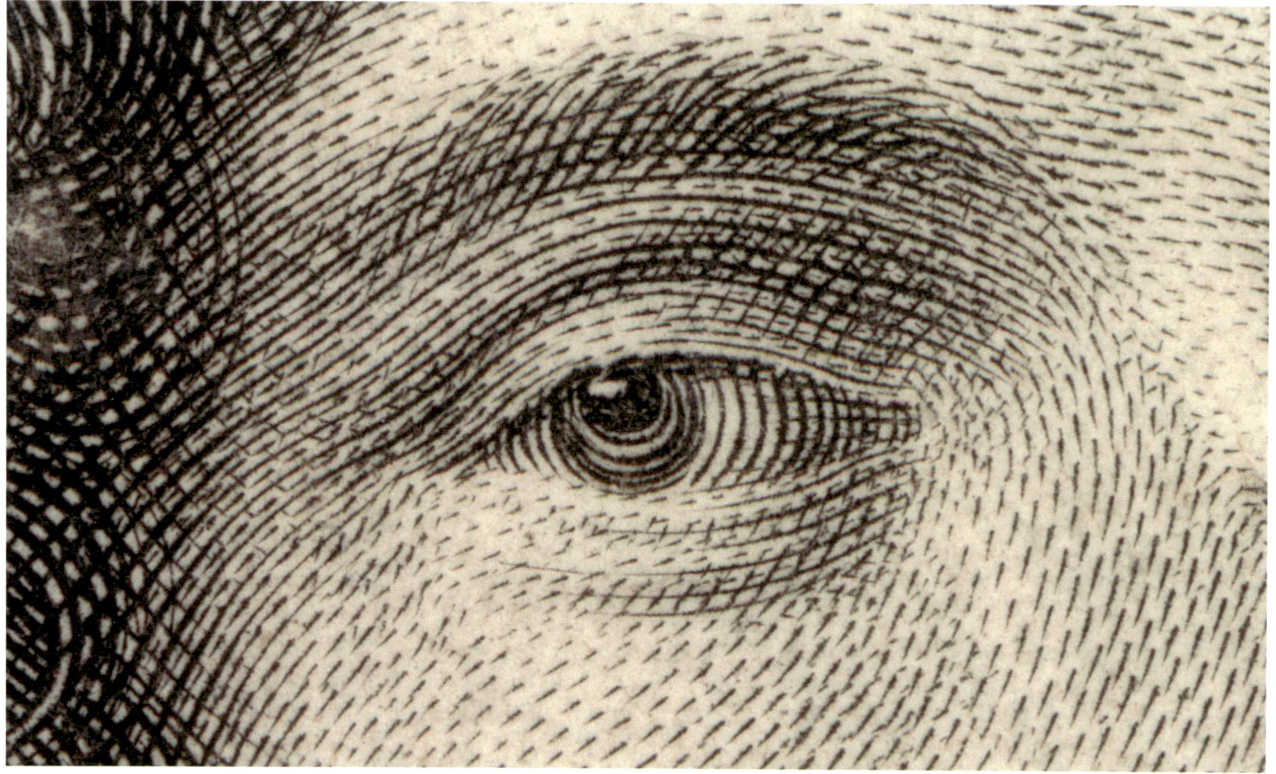

All of these details are enlarged to eight times actual size. The short strokes begin thin and then broaden as the burin enters the copper. In areas where they portray the desired tone inadequately, the engraver has added small marks between them.

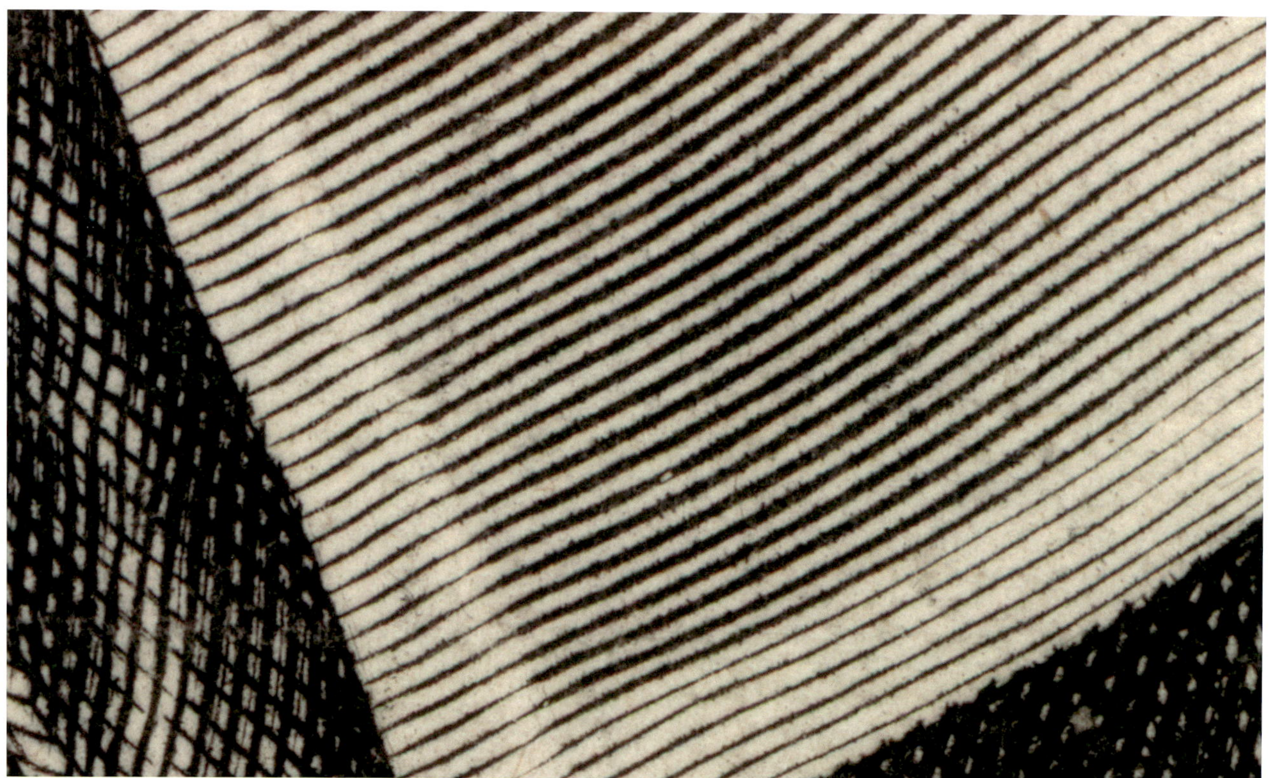

Tone is described by engraved black lines, some cross-hatched to form a fluctuating grid, as at the left side of this detail, some parallel but varying in depth and hence width. The curves and varying thicknesses of the lines in this part of the collar beautifully suggest the shape of the piece of cloth.

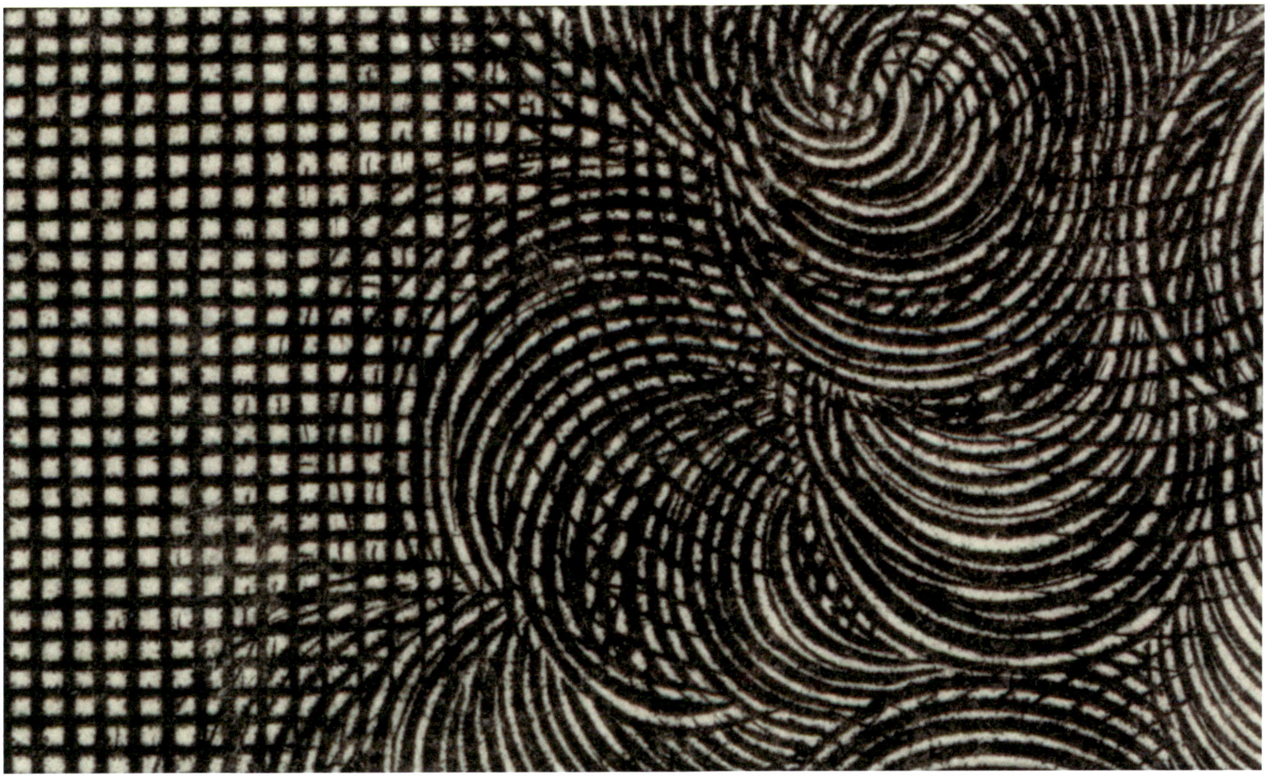

The curls of Monsieur Helyot's wig were made by rotating the plate. The square-mesh background was engraved using some sort of straightedge as a guide for the burin.

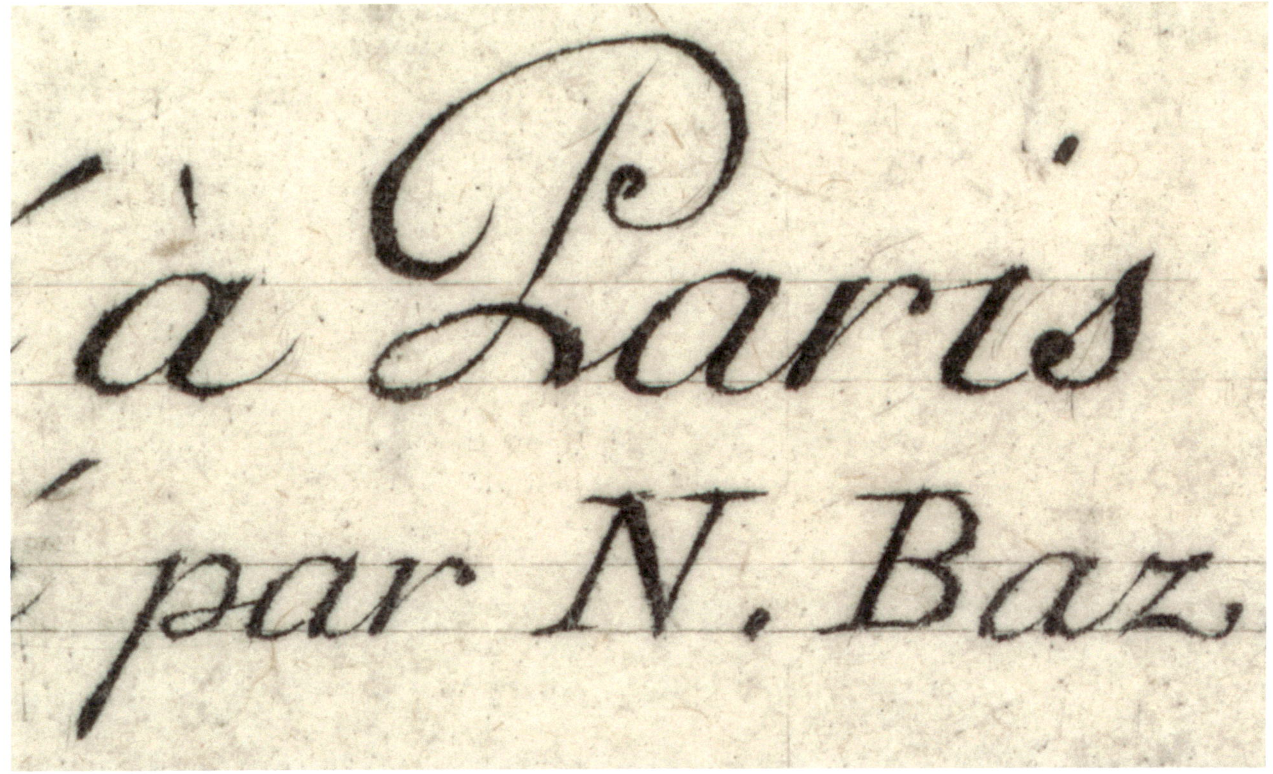


Many copper engravings contain lettering as well as pictures. The letters in this one are simple, fluid, and beautifully cut. Before carving them the engraver scored the copper plate with narrow guidelines, which retained enough ink to print faintly, despite their delicacy.

## 2.2 ETCHING

Etching was a remarkable technical breakthrough in intaglio printing. It had been known for many years that some acids could dissolve metal, and that some waxy materials could be applied to the metal surface to resist the acid and so produce etched designs. This technique had long been used in metalwork having no connection whatever to printing. At some point, probably in the 1500s, the idea of etching through a resist was applied to intaglio printing.

The technique itself is simple. If a copper plate (of the same kind used for engraving) is coated with a thin layer of soft wax, an artist can draw through the wax with a sharp needle. If the plate is then placed in an acid bath, the lines bared by the needle will be etched into it while those areas protected by the wax will remain intact. The etched lines will be rougher than the smooth grooves cut by the burin, but they will hold ink and be printable.

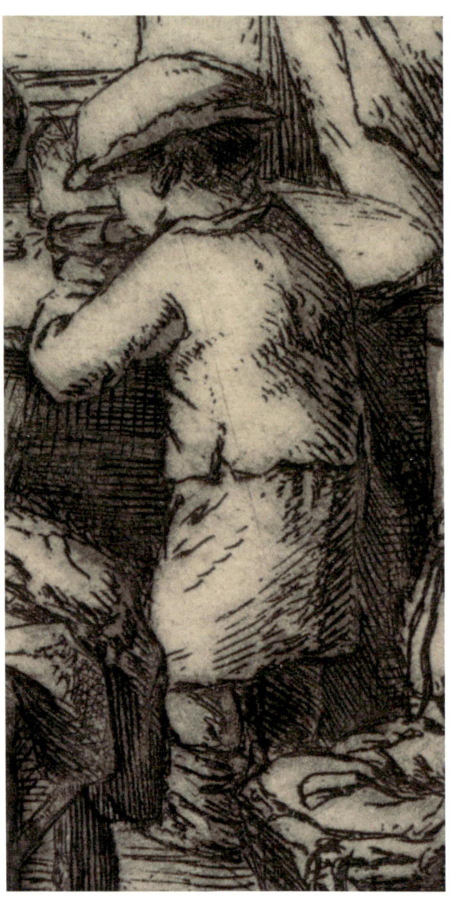

Etching's characteristically loose lines contrast strongly with the precise linear description in the copper-engraved plate of Monsieur Helyot (plate 2.1).

Etching transformed intaglio printing. The older method of hand engraving had been a predominantly reproductive medium. It was so hard to do, and required so much skill, that a class of engravers evolved who were not artists but craftsmen concerned only with reproducing the work of painters. Etching allowed artists to apply linear designs to a copper plate themselves, with the same ease with which they might draw on paper. Little pressure was needed to make the needle move freely through the resist. Once a plate was etched and the resist removed, further work could be done on the plate by using the needle to draw with more pressure, raising burrs capable of holding ink. This technique, called "drypoint," did not require etching, and allowed the artist to do rapid work that could be seen on a proof print without the delay necessitated by an additional etching stage.

Etching and drypoint produced prints with a different character from the older, more restrained forms of reproductive copper engraving. Almost as soon as etching was developed, engravers began to use it to help them make their hand-cut plates; many prints combine both methods. In the etching we see here the lines have the nervous quality of the hand rather than the stiff appearance of the burin meeting intransigent copper. When engravings were printed, the inked plates were wiped so thoroughly that the background was absolutely clean. When etching came along things became more casual, and sometimes the printer would leave ink on the plate surface, to add to the tonality of the print. This "plate tone" often showed up in the corners of a print, as it does here at the lower right.

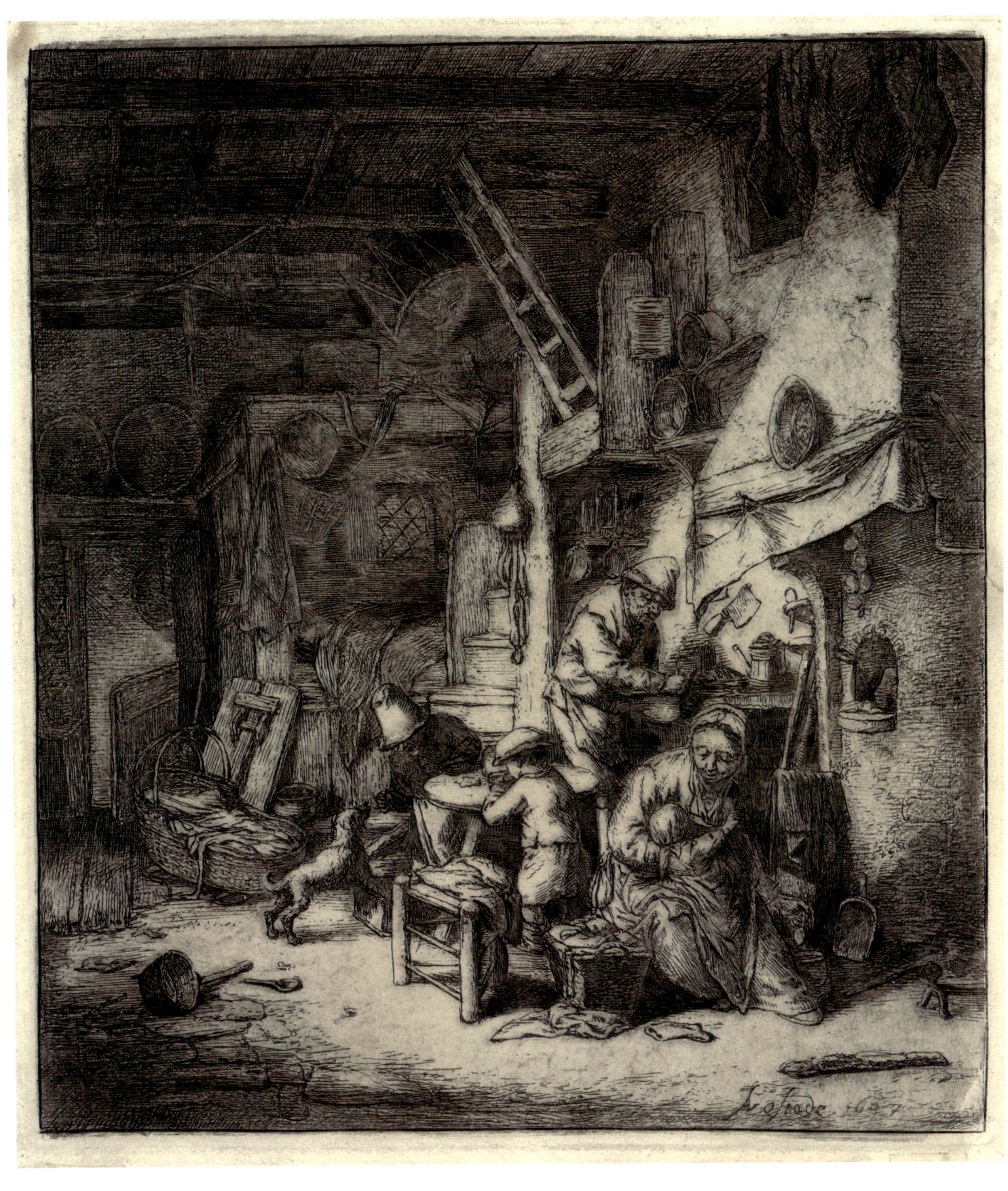

**Etching with aquatint.** Adriaen Van Ostade. *The Family.* 1647. 7⅛ x 6¼ in. (18.1 x 15.9 cm). This impression is a late one, made after the artist's death. The copper plate from which it was printed was worn, and some aquatint (described in section 2.5) was added to strengthen the image.

# Intaglio printing

## 2.3 ETCHING AND ENGRAVING

Engravings and etchings, although differently produced, were printed in exactly the same way. I want to describe this in some detail because the same printing technique was used for later intaglio techniques: the aquatint, the mezzotint, and even the glorious photogravure, which didn't come along until the mid-nineteenth century. We will look at photogravures later on; those prints were the perfect union of ancient ink-printing and modern photographic description (plate 10.9 introduces them). A decent intaglio printer of the seventeenth century would have had no problem printing a photogravure plate made in 1900.

All copper intaglio printing plates had a smooth polished surface into which the engraved or etched lines were incised. The printer would cover the plate completely with a fairly stiff ink, consisting of pigment in oil, and then wipe off the excess ink using a series of heavily starched cloths scrunched into balls. The wiping gradually removed ink from the plate surface, but the ink in the engraved grooves or lines would remain. After wiping with progressively cleaner cloths, the printer would give the plate a final wiping with the palm of his hand, often after lightly dusting the skin with chalk, to remove every trace of ink from the plate surface. Finally the plate was placed face up on the flat bed of a press that had two rigid rollers between which the bed could move. A sheet of damp rag-based paper was set on top of the inked plate; two or more layers of thick felt went on top of that; and the bed was passed between the rollers. The press—properly called a mangle—could exert tremendous pressure on the sandwich of plate, paper, and felt. The pressure was so high that the edges of the plate had to have smooth bevels, to avoid cutting the paper and felts.

Once through the press, the paper could be pulled off the plate, and the ink held in the grooves would have been transferred to it. If the relationship between ink, paper, and pressure had been right, the printed lines would have a physical height that no other printing process could produce. No mark in printing can compare with a fine intaglio line.

Etching allowed the artist to draw freely on the plate, but it also did something else: the labor of cutting the copper with a burin was replaced by an acid eating away the copper. It didn't take long for engravers to figure out that they could begin a plate by etching, then complete it by cleaning up the lines with a burin, and that in doing so they could avoid much of the labor of pure engraving. By the early 1700s many prints called "engravings" were actually made by using both etching and engraving on the same plate.

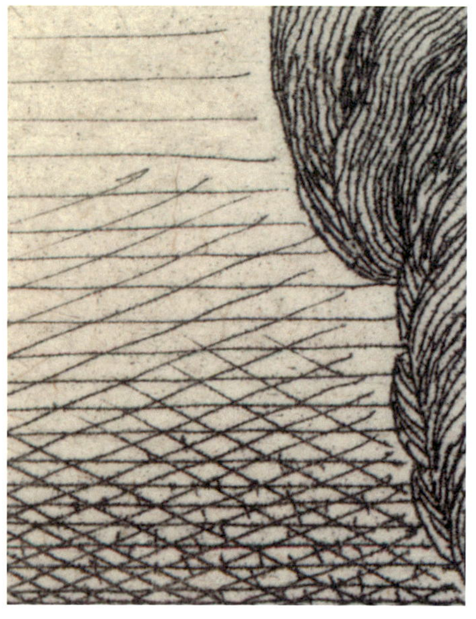

It is almost impossible to tell exactly which parts of some prints are engraved and which are etched. This beautiful little print has the cleanness of an engraving yet most of it is etched. The parallel lines we see in this detail are very similar to those made with a burin and straightedge, yet the topmost diagonal line changes direction at its end, and this mark could only have been made by an etching needle.

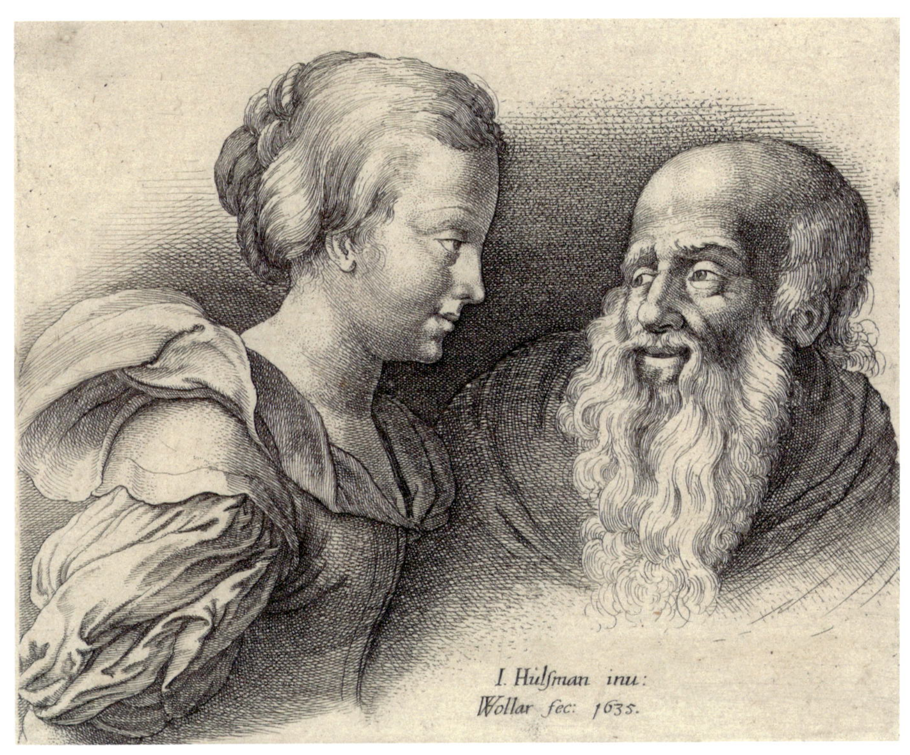

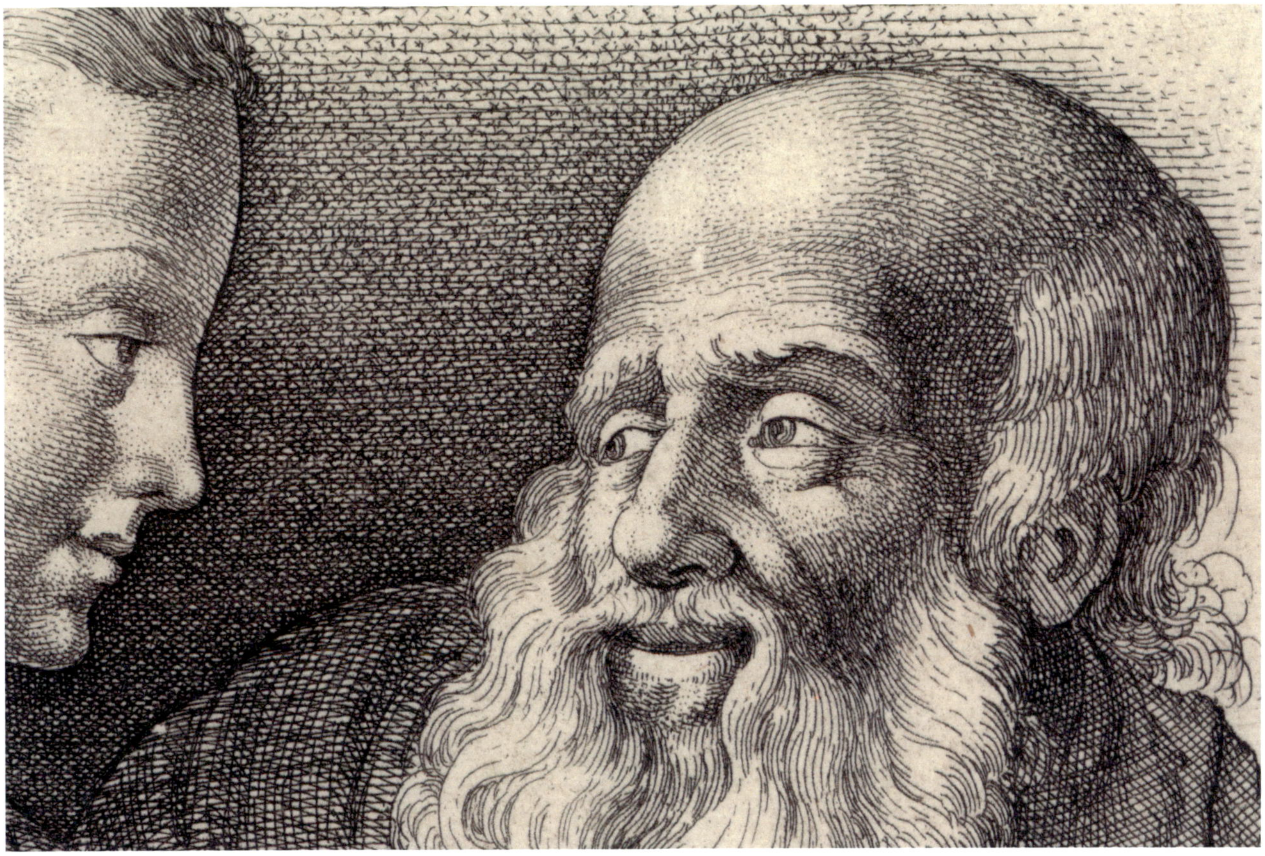

**Etching.** Johann Hulsman. *The Elder and the Maiden.* c. 1634. Print: Wenceslaus Hollar. 1635. 4 x 4¾ in. (10.2 x 12.1 cm). An etching with some afterwork done by engraving.

## 2.4 STEEL ENGRAVING

Copper printing plates wear out with use. The abrasion of wiping and the pressure of printing can affect the plate quite rapidly: the edges of the incised grooves become rounded and the wiped plate holds less ink, so the print gradually becomes lighter through the successive impressions of an edition.

One way to print intaglio in longer editions was to engrave the plates in steel instead of copper. Steel was difficult to work; instead of simply holding the burin by hand, the engraver often had to strike it with a hammer. The problem was compounded by the fact that a steel tool was being used to cut steel, but one characteristic of that material is that it can be prepared soft or hard—the steel burin could be tempered until it could cut the softer plate. Steel plates produced a new class of prints that look very different from those made with copper. They were called "steel engravings," but a great deal of etching was almost invariably present as well. Cuts made with a burin tend to curve in one direction only; a line drawn with an etching needle can freely change direction in a single stroke. These different lines can often indicate whether a print was made by engraving or etching. Almost every piece of steel engraving that I have seen includes a substantial amount of etching, so the process name is somewhat of a misnomer.

Steel engravings were very popular in the 1870s and '80s and often turned up in art books. The usual practice in these volumes was mostly to use run-of-the-mill illustrations printed from wood engravings locked up with the metal type used for the text. Scattered throughout the book, though, would be lush steel engravings, printed on beautiful thick paper bound into the more humble letterpress signatures. This particular plate is from *Picturesque America*, a two-volume publication by D. Appleton & Co. Beautiful books like this one are sought out by print dealers who cut out the pages to sell as single prints in antique shops. It is a tragedy that this happens, but I am as bad as they are: the plate we see here is one of a half dozen or so that I cut out of my copy of the book, to use in teaching my graduate students about the pictorial history of ink on paper.

In almost all steel engravings that depict a delicate pale sky, the appearance of tone is generated by the use of a burin guided by a straightedge. The two sets of lines we see in this detail, both made in that way, are angled at approximately thirty degrees to each other. This angle was chosen because overlapping linear designs often create disturbing "moiré" patterns, and printers learned that a thirty-degree difference minimized them.

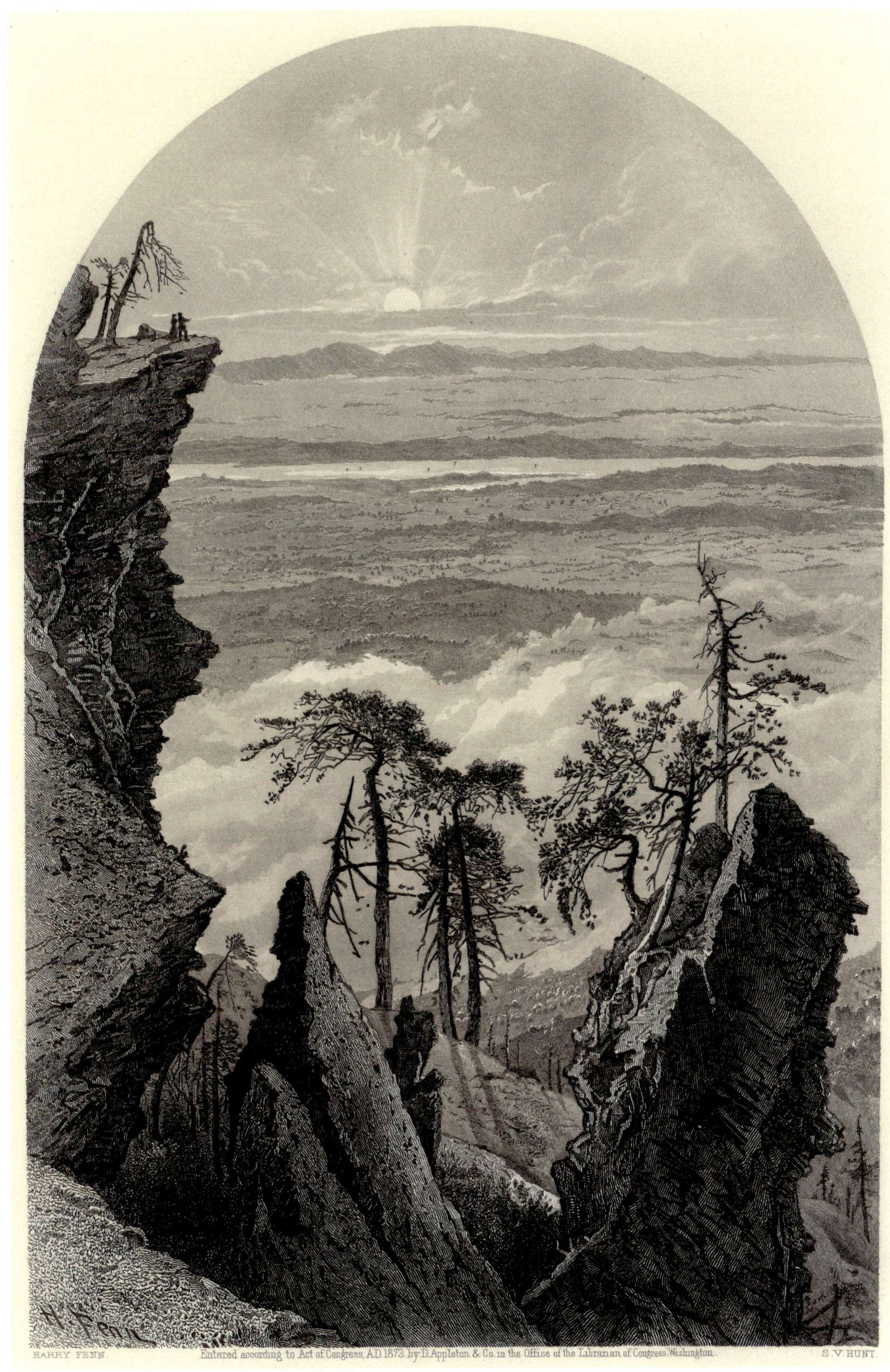


**Steel engraving.** Harry Fenn. *The Catskills.* c. 1870. Print: S. V. Hunt. 1874. 9 x 6 in. (22.6 x 15.1 cm). From *Picturesque America*, volume II (New York: D. Appleton & Co., 1874).

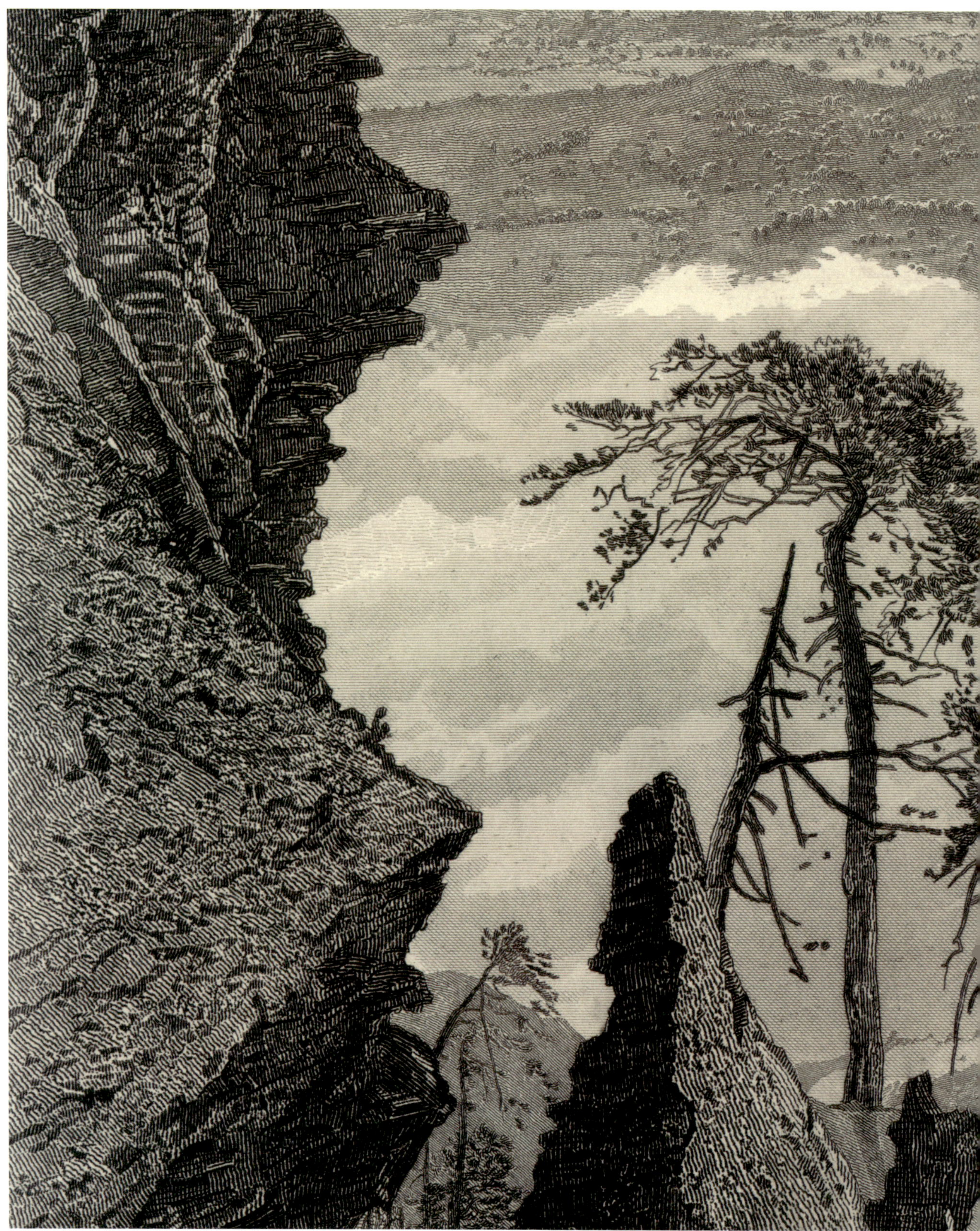

This detail, enlarged 1.7 times, shows the marvelous variations in apparent tone typical of steel engravings. Most of the dark lines were etched; the lighter ones tend to have been engraved. Etching relieved the great labor of engraving deeply into the steel plates.

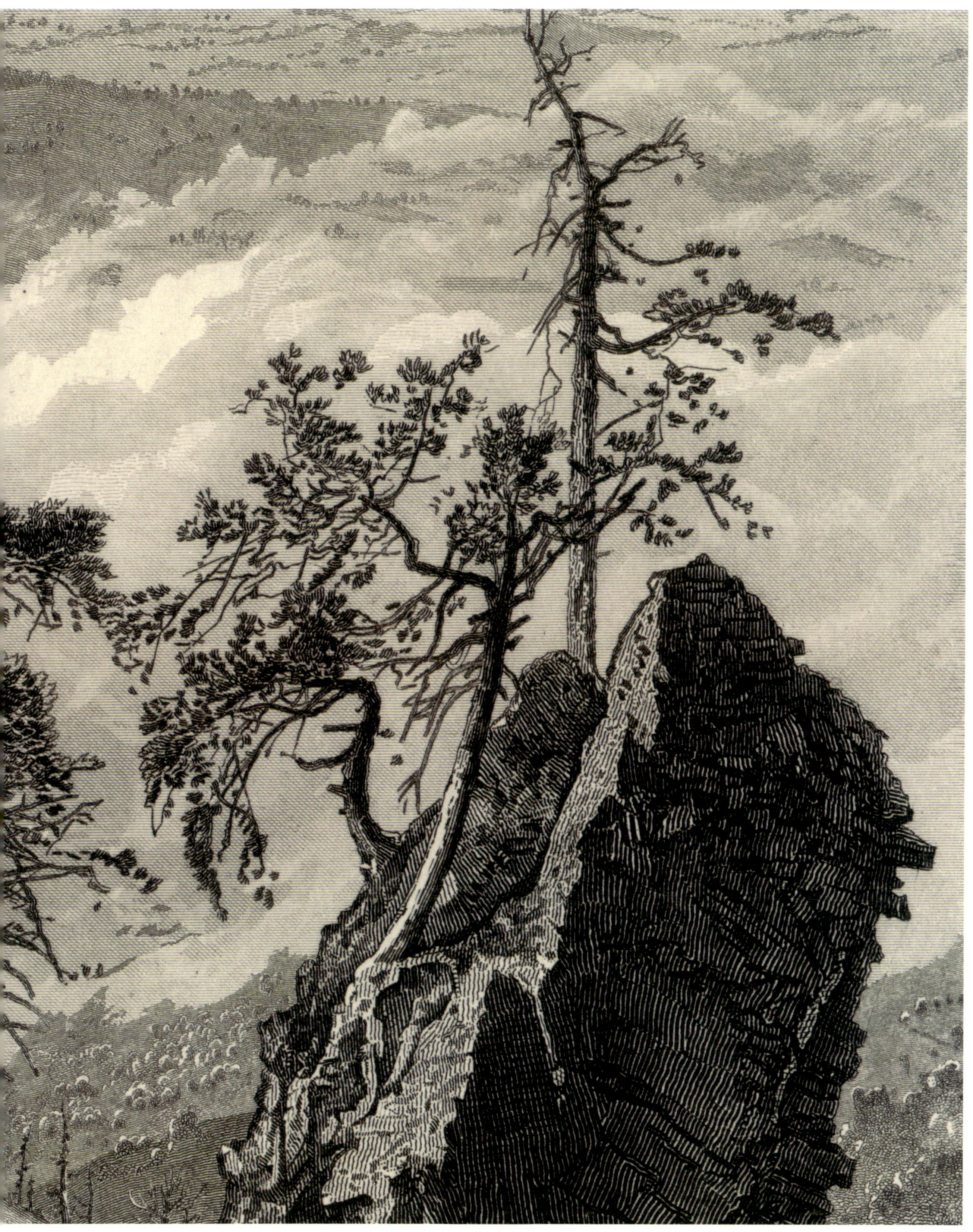

## 2.5 AQUATINT

Aquatint is a form of etching. Developed in the eighteenth century, it was the first truly tonal system of ink printing. The cross-hatching used in relief printing and engraving had involved small marks that allowed black ink to appear to the eye as various shades of gray, but that did so by tricking the eye. Aquatint managed this by generating a printing plate with a fine array of cells etched to variable depths, so that the ink was actually put down in different thicknesses. The ink was manufactured so that a thin film looked pale, a thicker one darker, and, when finally thick enough, the deposit appeared black. Aquatint could portray tone in beautiful gradations. It was used for hand-drawn prints in the eighteenth and nineteenth centuries and then was adapted to photogravure in the 1850s.

The basis of an aquatint was a fine deposit of acid-resistant grains—usually asphaltum or rosin—applied in a random pattern to a copper plate. The printer could spread these particles evenly with a device called a "dusting box" or could scatter them onto the plate more irregularly by sifting them through a piece of cloth, traditionally a sock, which could be squeezed or shaken over the plate to put down an aquatint grain in any desired area. Once applied, and set with heat, the particles would resist the etching chemical, protecting the original plate surface during the etch. If they covered more than 50 percent of the plate surface they tended to form a connected network, and the etching took place in the gaps in the net; if the aquatint was light, it was the etched areas that would form a network while the nonetched areas became separate points. In either case the result was a delicate pattern of pockets in the plate—tiny etched areas that could hold ink.

After etching, the printer would remove the asphaltum or rosin grains with a solvent. He would ink the plate, then wipe it, and his wiping cloth or hand would run across the higher, nonetched areas without removing the ink from the pockets. If the etching was deep the tone produced would be dark; if the etching was light—only a few seconds or so—the tone would be pale and smooth. Complex pictures such as the one we see here were made by etching a single aquatint in many discrete steps, each deeper than the one before. To fully understand this we need to examine a magnified section of the plate.

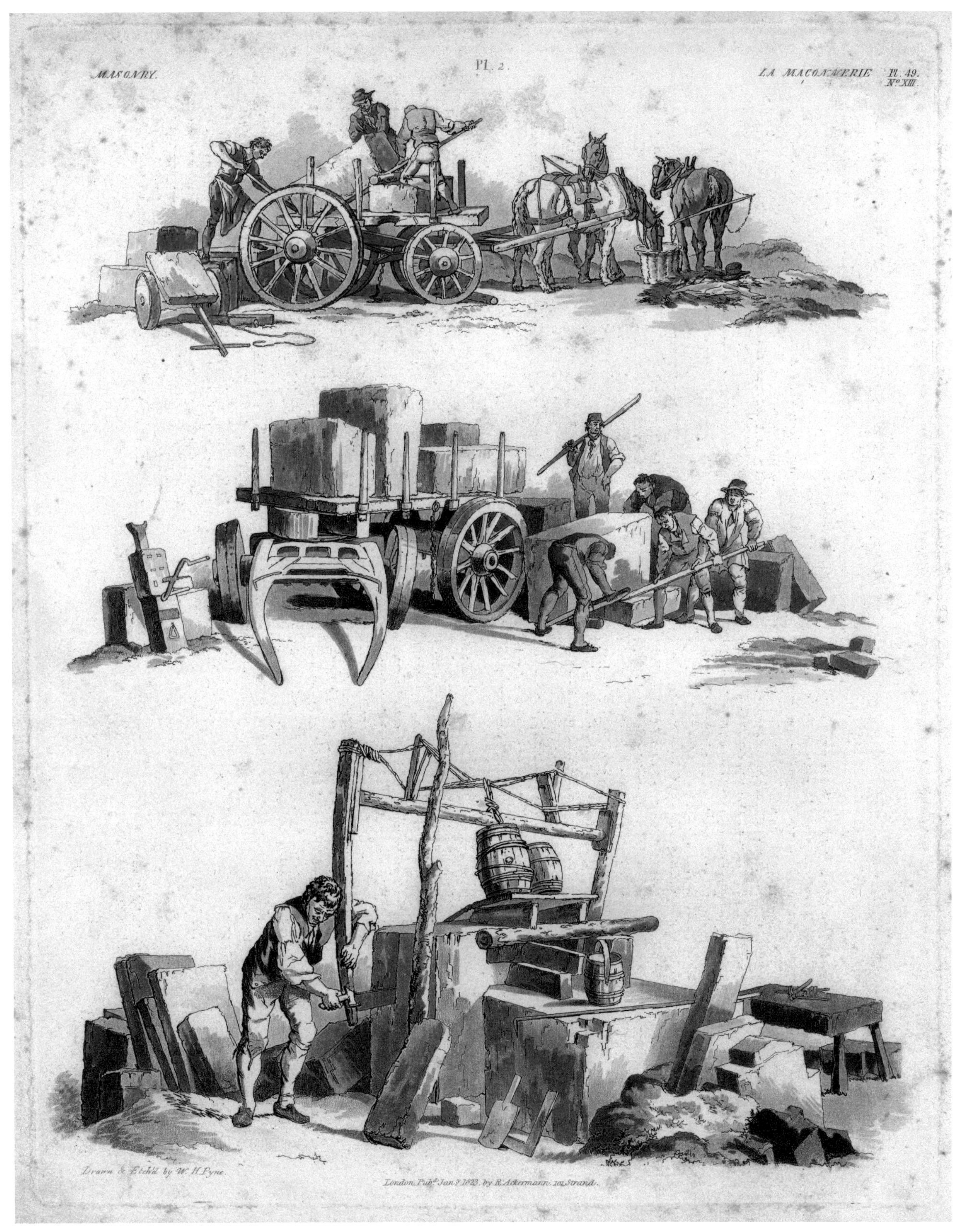


**Aquatint.** W. H. Pyne. *Masonry.* c. 1823. 11½ x 9¼ in. (29.2 x 23.2 cm). From *Picturesque Groups for the Embellishment of Landscape* (London: M.A. Nattali, 1845). This particular plate was published some years earlier, in January 1823, by R. Ackerman. Pyne is given credit for the drawing and etching and J. Hill for the aquatint.

## 2.5 AQUATINT

This four-times enlargement of Pyne and Hill's print shows the delicate random pattern of the aquatint-generated cells. It also shows that the picture has a simple line-drawn skeleton, an initial drawing into which the tones generated by the aquatint have been fitted. The tones themselves do not gradate smoothly from one value to another but change in discrete steps. I have set small squares of the six visible tonal levels in the print, along with the plain paper base as the lightest step, below the detail. In fact there are eight tones in the picture: the paper, six levels of aquatint, and the dark value of the etched linear drawing.

The print was begun as a plain etching—a line drawing made with a needle in a plate. Once it was etched and a trial print or "proof" was made to check the drawing, the plate was cleaned and a superb aquatint was applied over the entire surface. Before any further etching was done, the areas of the picture that were to remain plain, unprinted paper were "staged out" by being painted over with a resist (probably asphaltum dissolved in turpentine). The plate was then given a short acid-bath etch, just enough to lightly etch between the aquatint grains the shallow cells that would produce the lightest printed tone we see—the tone in block 1, one step darker than the bare paper. The plate-maker then shielded the areas that were to retain that tone by painting them with the resist, and the plate was etched again. That bite went to a sufficient depth to produce the tone we see in block 2. And so the procedure continued until the plate had received six etchings, each with different degrees of staging of the plate surface and each to a different depth. Only once these were completed was all of the resist (aquatint particles and staging paint) removed and the plate proofed to see the results. Further corrections were still possible, using etching, drypoint, or even a fresh aquatint, but the bulk of the image was done through the initial linear etching, the single aquatint, and its successive etchings.

Aquatint could produce smooth tonal areas with a grain so fine that it was completely invisible to the unaided eye. The process was fairly widely used, most often as a supplement to a conventionally etched picture. The tonal capacity of the aquatint was far greater than a hand-generated print could ever achieve. Photogravure, invented in the 1850s, was the process that harnessed the untapped wonders of the aquatint's full tonal range.

Every aquatint is a puzzle when we try to determine exactly how any given one was made. This detail—an eight-times enlargement of the wheel on the facing page—shows evidence of two aquatints: a fine one, which produced the gray tone in the center of this blowup, and a coarser one, slightly vertical, that managed the rest of the tones. The darkest part, at the bottom of the picture, shows evidence of needle work done through the aquatint to make an even darker tone.

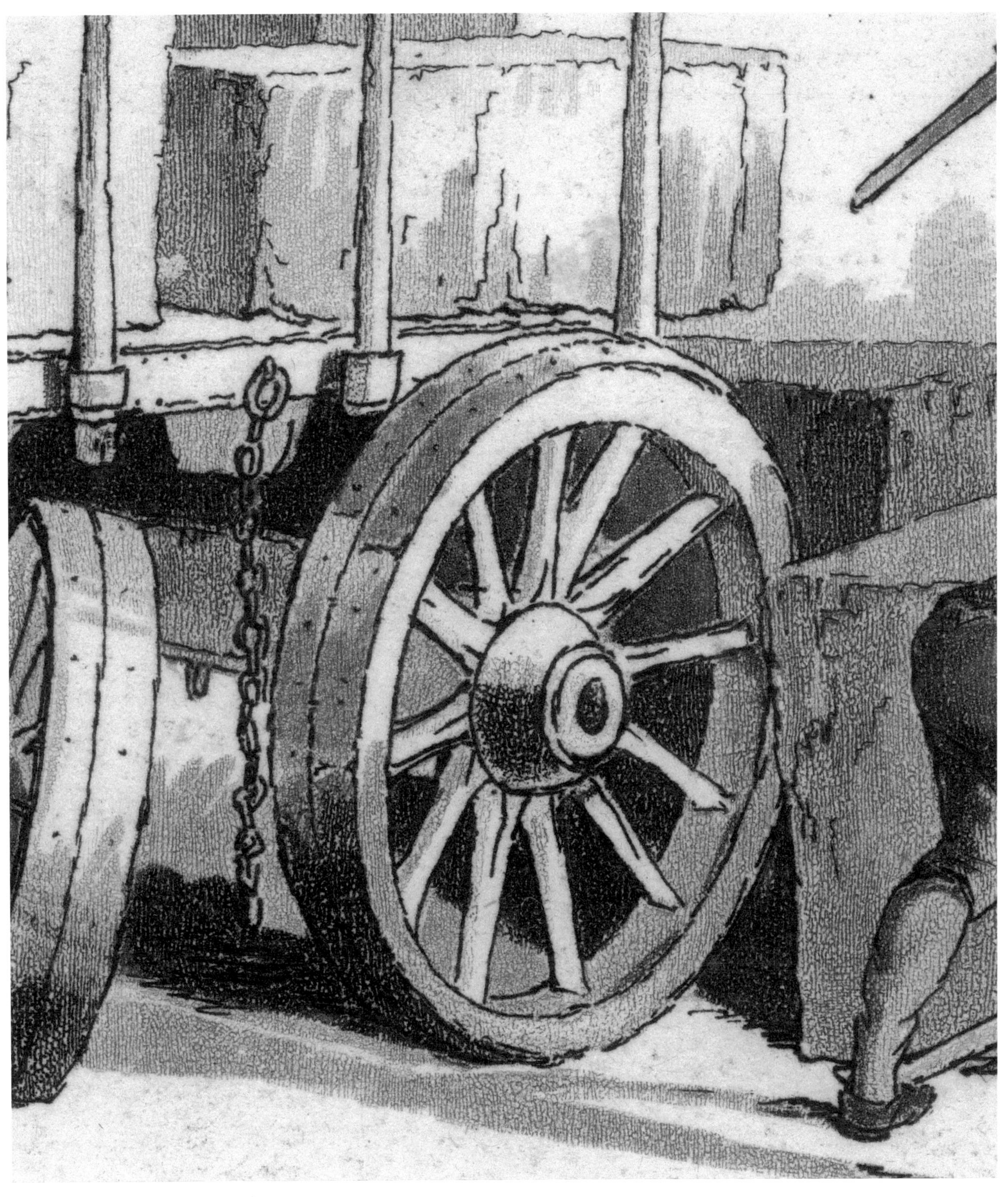

paper 1 2 3 4 5 6

## 2.6 MEZZOTINT

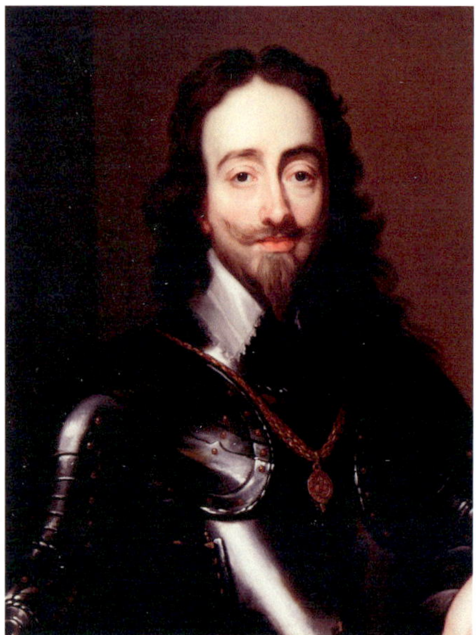

This detail from a copy of Van Dyck's painting shows the image that Beckett copied when he made the mezzotint. All direct printing processes, in which the plate transfers ink to the paper in one step, reverse the image. The image on the plate of the mezzotint had the same orientation as the painting; once printed, it was flopped horizontally.

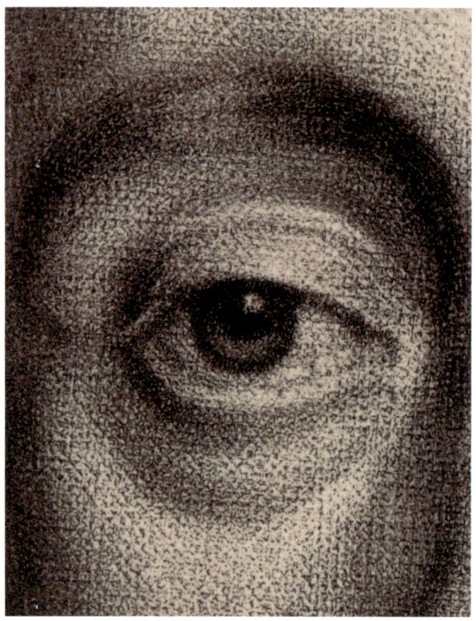

This four-times enlargement shows the somewhat mechanical marks of the rocker. The burnishing that makes the picture does not create new marks but simply lightens those already on the surface. Much effort went into rocking the plate in such a way that the marks left as little pattern as possible.

The mezzotint is a strange intaglio process that was developed in the early 1600s. The basis of the process was to cover a plate with ink-holding surface indentations such that it would print a deep, even, black tone, then to polish out some of those serrations to make them print lighter. This variation of light and dark produced the picture. The nickname for mezzotint was "*manière noire,*" reflecting the fact that the picture was extracted from blackness.

The initial plate preparation was done by someone in the printshop—certainly not the artist—and was carried out by roughening the plate surface with a tool called a "rocker," a chisellike instrument with a curved cutting edge and with grooves running along the length of the blade. When this tool was rocked firmly back and forth on the plate, and gradually moved across it, the plate took on a mixture of indentations and raised burrs across its entire surface. If inked, a plate thus prepared would have printed a smooth black tone. First, though, the artist worked on it with a burnisher, a small handheld tool with a rounded, highly smooth tip. The polished areas of the surface held less ink than the rougher ones and produced the lighter tones of the picture. The process is considered intaglio—printing from the low—but as well as sinking grooves, the rocker raised burrs that probably held just as much ink, making the technique in many ways related to drypoint. However we classify it, mezzotint produced beautiful values and a fundamentally different look from any other kind of print, but the plate was extremely delicate and had to be printed with great care. Mezzotint editions were far smaller than those of engravings or etchings because of this fragility of the plate.

It is very hard to make a good picture with an eraser, which is what the artist was doing in burnishing the plate. In many mezzotints, then, the technique dominates the image and the pictures suffer accordingly. This beautiful and eccentric picture of King Charles of England shows the tonality that mezzotint made possible, but also its potential weaknesses: uneven areas of large tone when no detail is present, and a somewhat odd appearance in the lighter values, which comes from the difficulty of knowing just how the burnished plate will carry ink. When mezzotints were just right, though, their beauty was breathtaking and their degree of technical refinement astonishing.

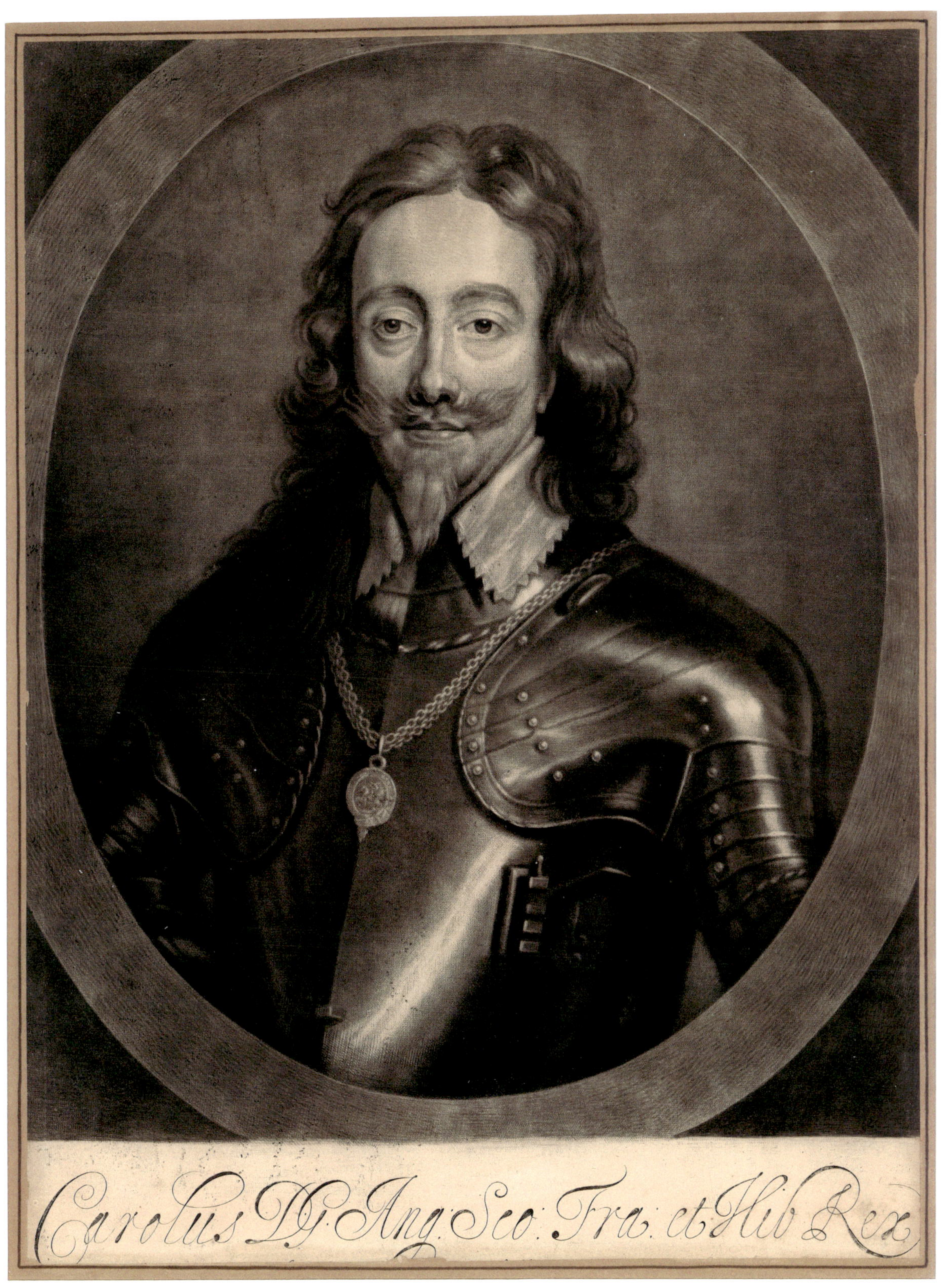


**Mezzotint.** After Sir Anthony Van Dyck. *King Charles I.* c. 1635. Print: Isaac Beckett. c. 1685. 13⅛ x 9⅞ in. (33.3 x 25 cm). Beckett's title, beautifully engraved on the mezzotint plate, is "Charles, by the grace of God King of England, Scotland, France, and Ireland."

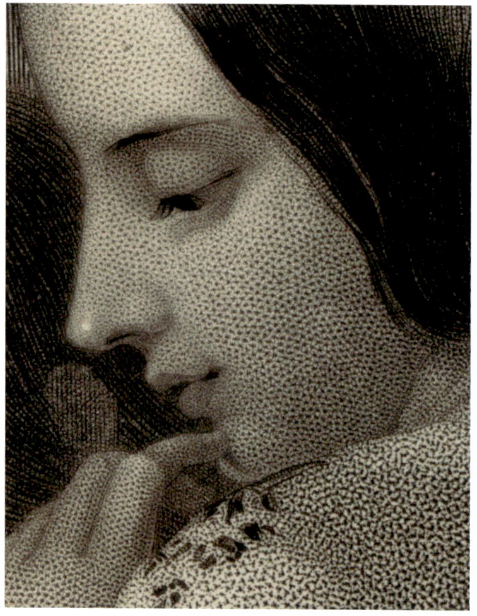

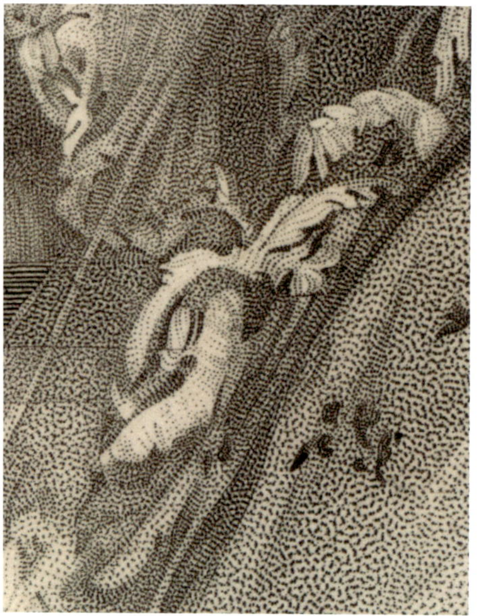

These details, enlarged three times, show the extraordinary precision of the printing plate. Ink, paper, and press have no trouble handling this complex visual data.

## 2.7 STIPPLE IN ETCHING AND ENGRAVING

We leave intaglio printing with a look at an extraordinary work, a stipple etching and engraving made in the 1840s and published in *The Art Union, Monthly Journal of the Fine Arts* in 1846. This publication, produced in London in sections during the year, showed prints that represented the height of the printing craft in various technologies. I found leather-bound annuals of this publication in a bookstore in 2003, bought them each for about $100, and thereby got myself examples of the most astonishing craft applied to the most insipid pictures imaginable. Everything in the *Journal* is heavily dated in visual terms, representing the current art trends in England at the time. I think that, in a way, it is rather like one of the fashion magazines we find on newsstands today, packed full of the latest and greatest that will be forgotten tomorrow.

It is a bit sad, because the plates in this old publication demonstrate the absolute height of handmade printed pictures. Most of them are engraved, etched, or lithographed reproductions of paintings, and each plate gives credit to both the painter of the original and the craftsman who made the printing plate. *Young Kitty* was painted by J. Wright and engraved by E. Finden. The printer who wiped and printed the plate remains anonymous, but that is all right because the printing is the most literal and clear impression of the plate, with virtually no visual content added to the engraving by techniques of wiping and printing.

The image is composed of etched and engraved lines and also thousands of tiny individual black dots, called "stipples," that describe subtle passages of tone. This is a reproductive etching; visually it doesn't have much to do with the modern notion of art, but as pure craft it demonstrates a high point in the practice of transcribing information onto a printing plate. We will see a further step, comparable to this, when we examine wood-engraved photographs in section 10.2. Prints such as these show that the technology of the printing processes in the mid-nineteenth century was so advanced that the hand and eye were becoming inadequate to develop the information that they could display. The presses, thirsty for visual data, were ready for the information-gathering net of photography, which was invented just about the time this print was made.

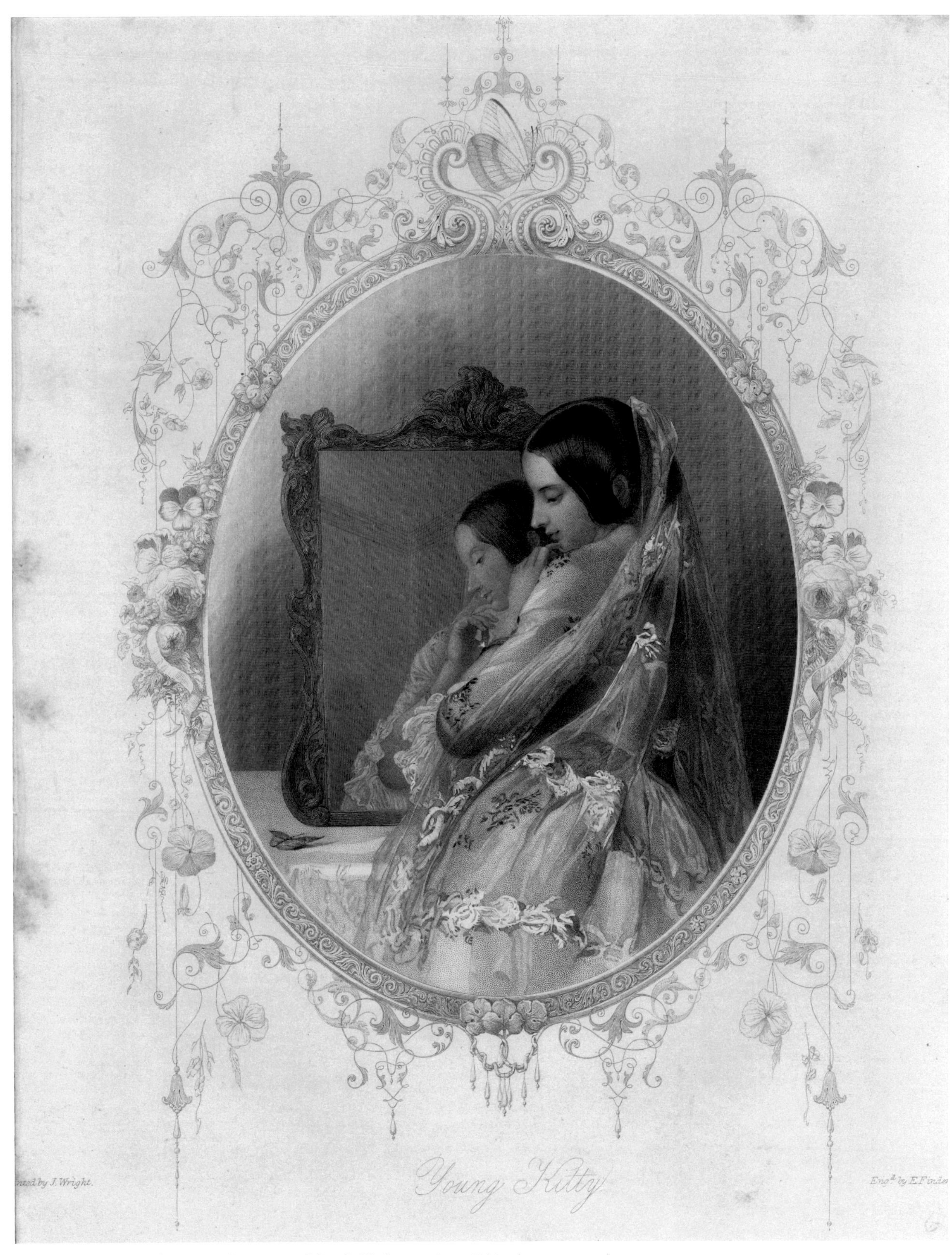


**Stipple etching.** J. Wright. *Young Kitty.* c. 1842. Print: E. Finden. 1846. 11 x 8¾ in. (29.9 x 22.2 cm).
A plate from *The Art Union, Monthly Journal of the Fine Arts*, 1846.

## 2.8 MONOTYPES

Planographic printing can be done from an evenly smooth-surfaced printing plate with neither raised areas, such as we find in relief printing, nor low ones, as in intaglio printing. The most basic form of planographic printing is the monotype, which can most easily be described as printing from a finger painting done on a copper plate. The press is the same press used for intaglio printing and the plate is the same copper plate used in engraving and etching, because that is the kind of plate we find in printshops that have those presses. No work is done to the plate, though, except to make sure it is polished and to bevel the edges to avoid cutting the paper and felts during printing.

If we smear ink on such a plate and run it through the press with dampened paper on top, the ink will transfer onto the paper. It is surprising to find, though, that not all of the ink transfers; quite a lot is left on the plate. With no additional work to it, the plate can be printed again and a much lighter version of the print will appear. Despite the name of the process, then, we do find monotype editions, which the artist can make by repainting the plate after each impression, using the residue left on the plate as a guide for the new work. Every print in a monotype edition is unique, but all are related through the visual foundation maintained by the succession of pale residual ink images that act as guides to the artist doing the printing.

This business of ink left on a plate is extremely important, affecting processes as simple as monotype and as complex as modern offset printing. In all print processes the signal conveyed from plate to paper is generated not only by ink applied for the present impression but by residues of ink left from earlier impressions. The plate prints a union of these inks, so it is obvious that the first impression of any plate cannot represent what the plate will do when printed in an edition. This sounds like a minor point, but it is central to the practice of printing in multiple copies. The simple monotype brings to light some of the complexities of printing plates and the manner in which they transfer ink to paper.

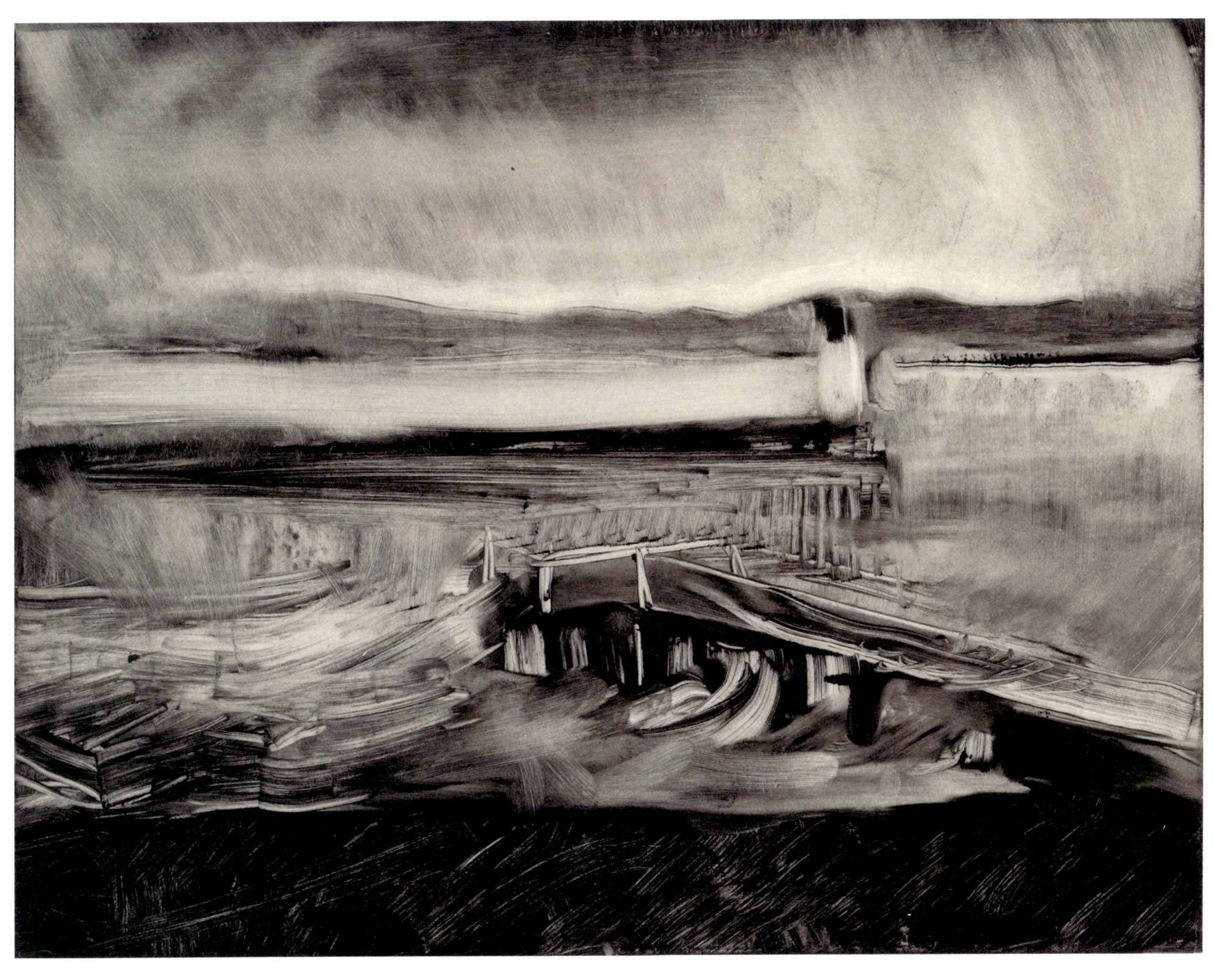

**Monotype.** Christopher Benson. *View of Narragansett Bay.* 1987. 9 x 11¾ in. (22.9 x 29.9 cm)

# Planographic printing

## 2.9 STONE LITHOGRAPHY

Relief and intaglio printing are both old processes, gradually developed hundreds of years ago, with no identifiable moment of invention. Not so with lithography, which was invented in 1799, by Alois Senefelder, who developed it as a cheaper alternative to other printing methods. The industrial revolution was rooted in the eighteenth century, built on a foundation of scientific and technical work that created the fields of modern engineering, physics, and chemistry. We think of the nineteenth century as a time of iron beams and steam engines, but all that heavy gear grew out of the fledgling understanding of chemistry in the century before. Lithography could only have happened in this context, since it used chemistry, rather than the older chisels and burins, to define printing surfaces.

Lithographic printing is done from the smooth surface of a piece of limestone. The artist draws directly on the stone, using a crayon composed mainly of beeswax and dark pigment (to give visibility). After the drawing is done the stone is treated with a weak acid called "etch"—like "engraving," a very confusing word. In intaglio printing the etch removes material from the surface; in lithography it doesn't alter the height of the surface but rather induces a chemical change, leaving the surface—wherever it isn't covered by the crayon—in a state that will hold a continuous film of water when wetted. The crayon is then removed with a solvent, but the limestone under the drawing retains the crayon's ability to repel water. (This is all too familiar to someone—like me—who has spent a lifetime washing dishes: the presence of a grease film prevents the formation of a water film.) Once etched and cleaned, the stone is carefully worked up with ink and water to stabilize the printing image. Repelled in its turn by the damp areas of the stone, the ink adheres only to the area of the drawing. Repeated applications of ink and water allow the stone surface to print many copies.

This three-times enlargement shows the grain of stone lithography's black crayon, which allows it to create the illusion of tone.

If a lithographic crayon has been properly made—often with additional materials added to the wax and pigment—the lines it draws take on a fine grain that can range from light to dark. The ink particles are still black, but their size varies, and so lithographs have the wonderful ability to give the appearance of tonal variation. Like etching, lithography responds beautifully to the hand of the artist, and much original work was done in this medium when it was used to print cartoons and satires in newspapers during the nineteenth century.

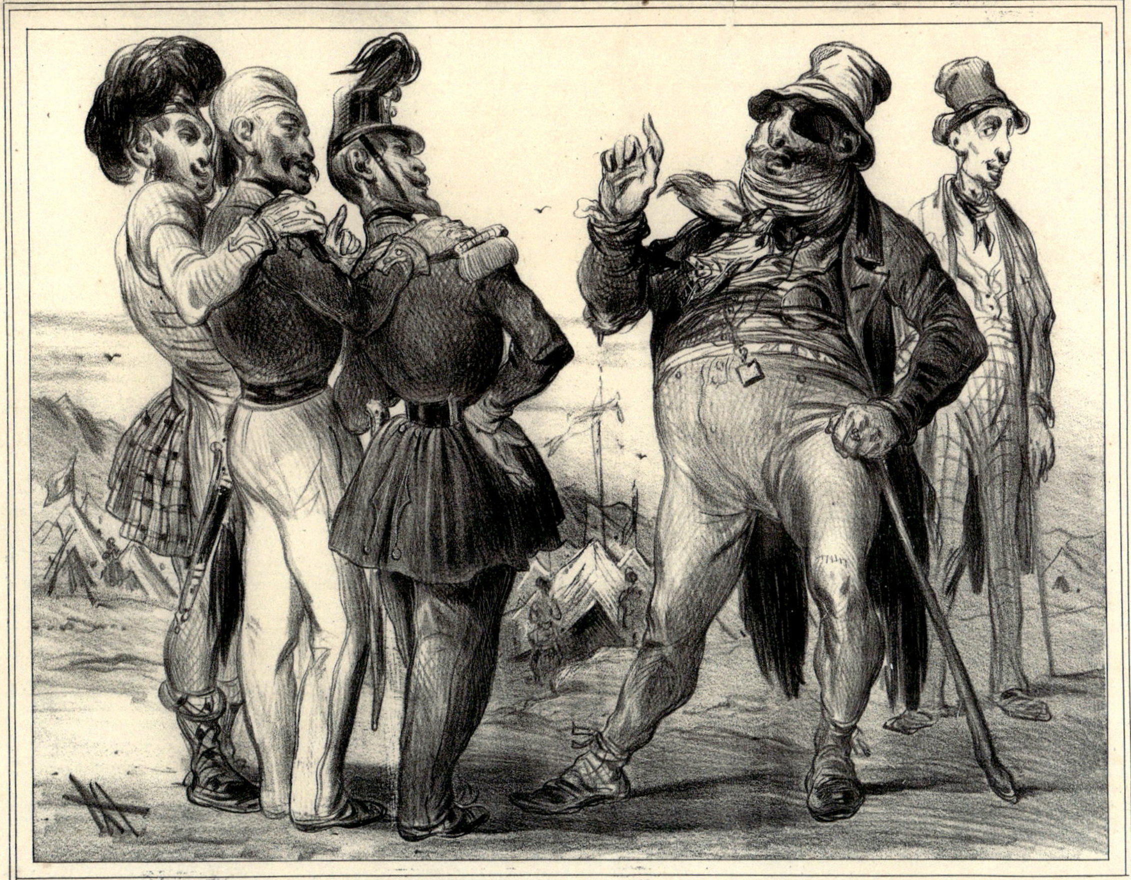


**Stone lithograph.** Artist unknown. *Propositions de la Russie.* c. 1850s. 9⅜ x 10½ in. (23.7 x 26.5 cm)

## 2.10 STONE LITHOGRAPHY

The lithographic crayon can render delicate lines of varying shades, but the process also does something else that was new when it was invented: it produces perfectly smooth areas of even tone. Intaglio printing could not do this; there the ink was always held in small pockets, which inevitably gave some texture to the prints. Earlier relief printing had also done a poor job over large areas because the flat platens of the presses could never apply enough pressure to a large printing area. (Relief improved in this respect later on, with the invention of cylinder presses.) But lithographic presses use a scraper—a stiff leather or synthetic blade—to press the paper against the inked stone. This blade is drawn across the paper, so that, at any one point in the printing, all of its pressure is applied to a thin line beneath its working edge, allowing an even transfer of ink from stone to paper. The tonalities generated by printing this way, along with the ability to register multiple impressions, led to the beautiful lithographic posters of the nineteenth century. And the ability of lithography to print even tonal fields lay beneath its eventual adaptation to photo offset lithography in the twentieth century.

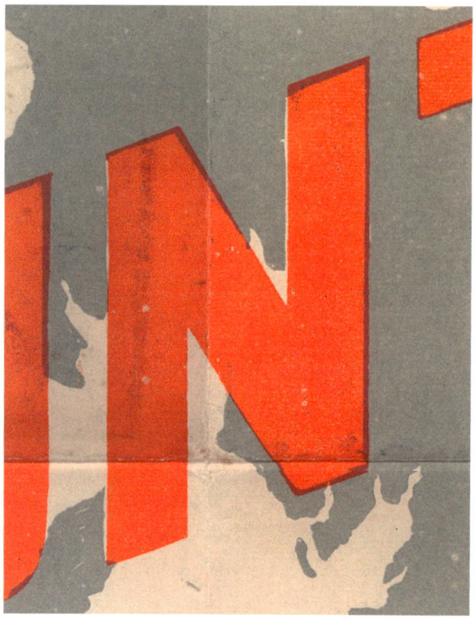

I should probably place this poster later in the book, in the section on color printing, but I leave it here as an introduction to color and to emphasize the radically new nature of lithography in relation to the other ancient processes. Lithographs were fundamentally different from relief and intaglio prints, and they opened the door to the modern era of intricate multiple-impression printing in color. This poster, made entirely by hand around the time of World War I, gives us a crucial lesson about the challenges of registration when printing in more than one impression. When the gray was printed, the shapes of the letters were left blank; their red ink was applied in the second impression, filling the spaces left open for them. Unfortunately the two impressions didn't perfectly align—the registration was not accurate (and it never was)—so a white, uninked line runs down one side of the N and a dark, double-inked line down the other. The solution, called "trapping" in the printing trades, was to make the letter larger than the space it was to fit into, or to make the space it fitted into smaller. The reproduction of the entire poster shows that most of the red letters have a dark line at their edges where they butt up against the gray impression. This dark trap line is less offensive than occasional white lines would be had the image not been adjusted to create an overlap. The lesson here is that if a picture is cut up into pieces and printed in more than one impression, getting all those parts to assemble correctly on press is a technical problem. Only by adjusting the size of the picture elements can we make a print that seems to fit together properly.

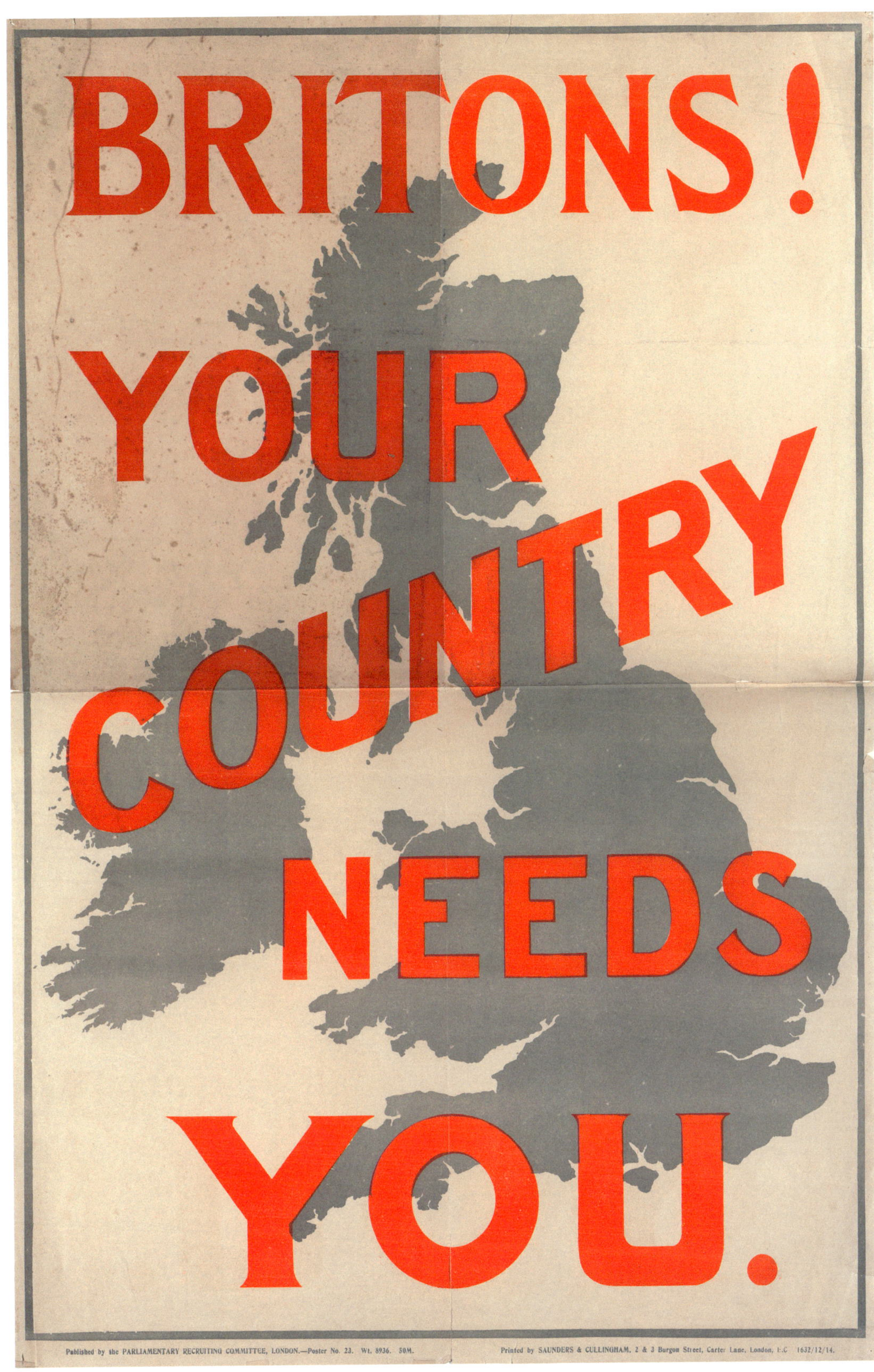


**Stone lithograph.** Artist unknown. *Britons! Your Country Needs You.* c. 1914. 28⅜ x 18⅝ in. (72 x 47 cm)

# Part 3

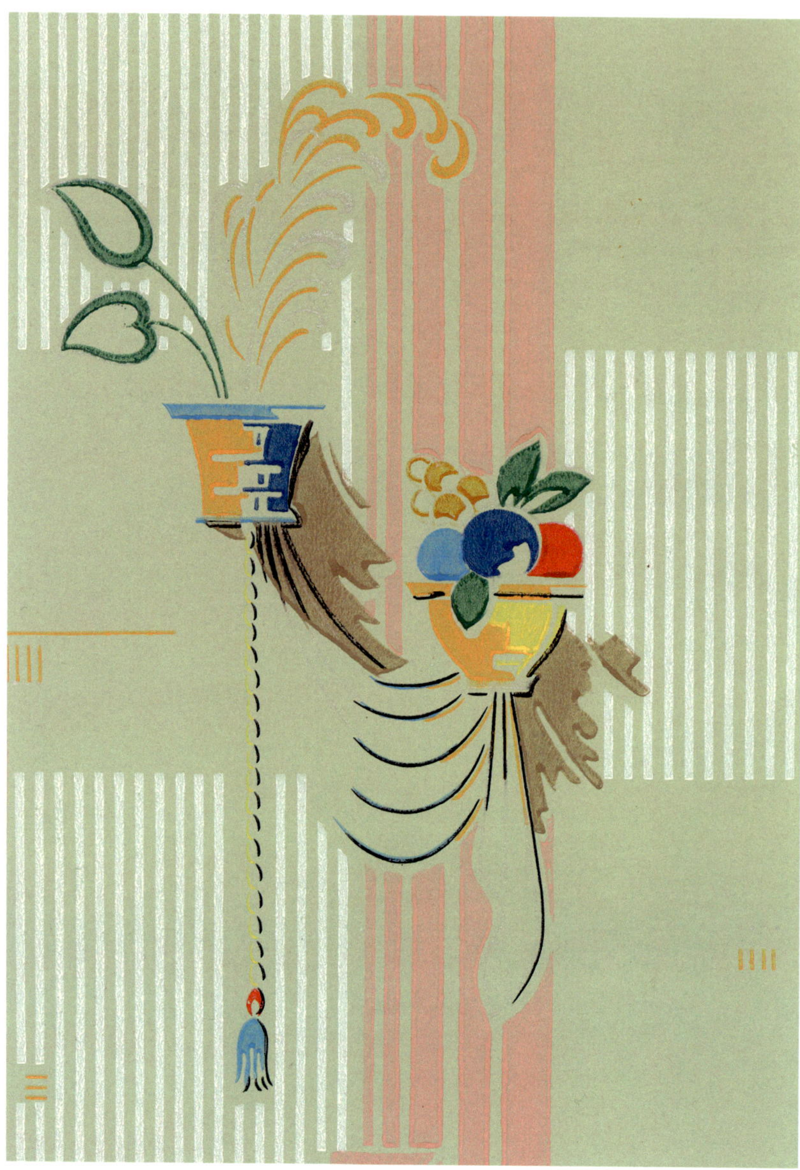

Color printing began with the simple expedient of using inks of different colors—if a particular color was needed then an ink was mixed to match it. In the twentieth century, color printing turned into a different system based upon the mixing of primary colors. The earlier method continues to this day, and we briefly trace its history in this section. Primary colors and their use in color printing are dealt with in Part 8.

**Relief-printed wallpaper.** American. c. 1920. 11 x 7½ in. (28 x 19 cm)

# Color printing

3.1 Hand coloring and stencil
*Color applied to a black-and-white engraving.*

3.2 Two-color letterpress
*A page of type printed from two separate forms.*

3.3 Multipass intaglio
*Currency printed dry from two separately inked steel plates.*

3.4 Chromolithography
*Stippling and transparent ink in color lithography.*

3.5 Chromolithography
*Complex color reproductions generated from multiple stones.*

3.6 Stencil
*Color prints generated from multiple hand-cut stencils.*

3.7 Japanese woodblock printing
*Complex color structure derived from multiple woodblocks.*

3.8 Woodblock progressives
*The successive stages of a Japanese woodblock print.*

# Color printing

## 3.1 HAND COLORING AND STENCIL

This map is an engraving, printed in black ink from a single copper plate. Once the sheet was dry it was colored by hand, using watercolors. It is hard to tell whether the colors were applied by painting or put on with stencils, to give some repeatability to the washes throughout the edition. In either case this picture is really both a print and a painting, part of its information deriving from a printing plate and part coming from the hand.

If the map was painted, the colors were applied with a brush, but if it was stenciled the artist probably used a cloth ball called a "dauber," patting it first on an ink source and then gently on the print surface. Stencilers also used specialized round brushes, which could be held vertically to apply controlled amounts of color. When properly used these tools could create the blended edges of the colors that we see along the river borders in this print. Often the stencils, cut in stiff paper, could give a hard, sharp edge that looks just as if it has been painted with a conventional brushstroke; then the dauber, carefully applied, could produce a blend on the other side. We can see such an application in the upper left, where a yellow area meets a red, without a black engraved line obscuring the join.

The technical term for a black-and-white print colored through the use of stencils is "pochoir," a French term for "stencil." Pochoir is still practiced today, and we will find an example in plate 11.4, in which modern photographic printing is used to create the black-and-white skeleton for a color picture.

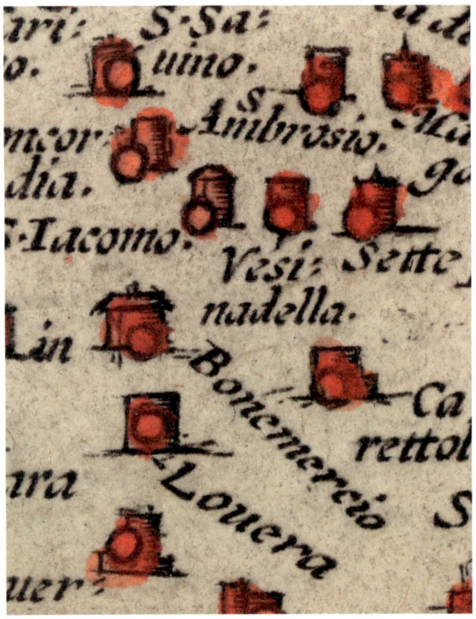

The small red spots applied to the individual towns have been rapidly painted by a dab with a brush, for which no stencil was necessary.

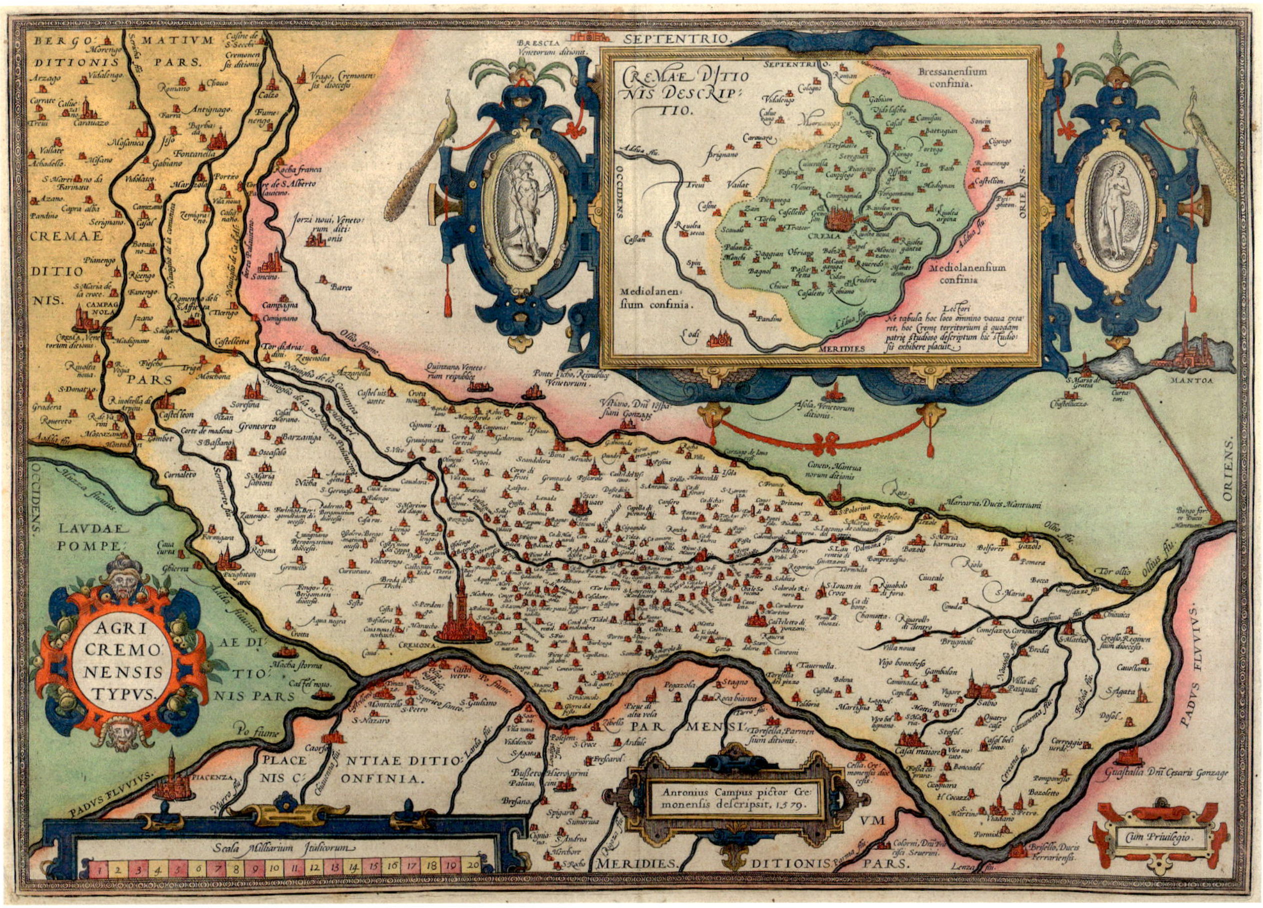

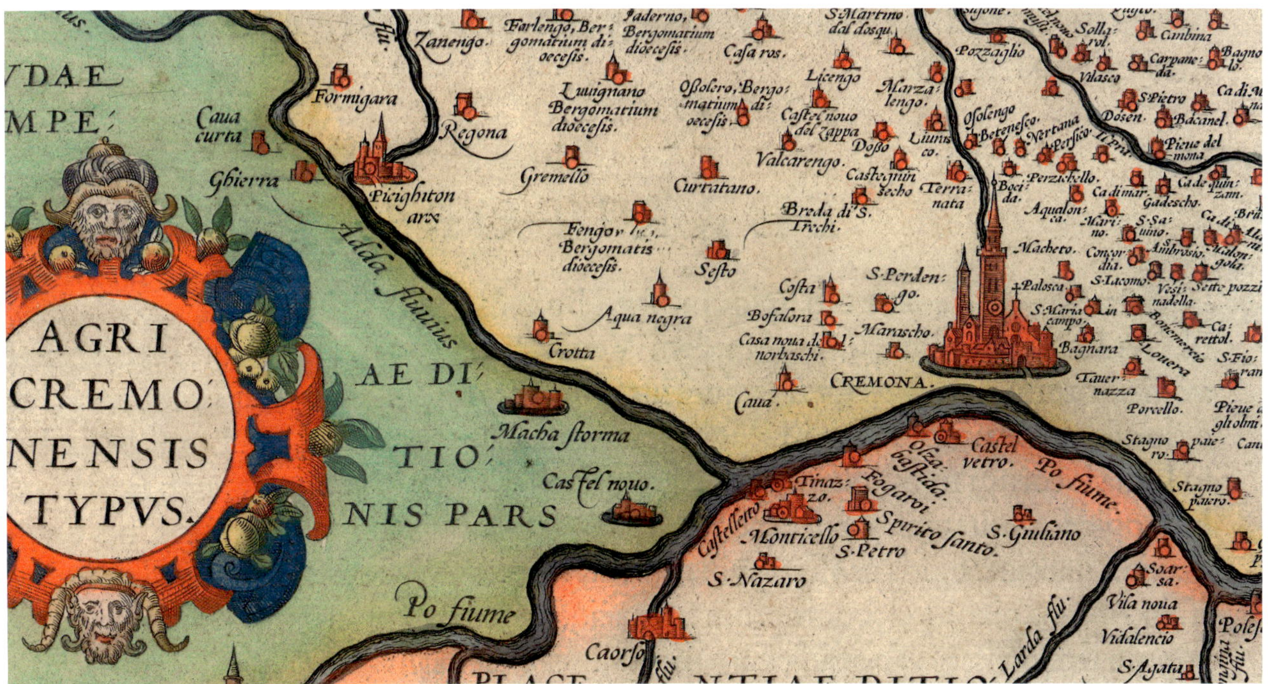


**Hand-colored copper engraving.** Antonius Campus. *Map of the Fields of Cremona.* 1579. 13½ x 19½ in. (34.3 x 49.5 cm)

### 3.2 TWO-COLOR LETTERPRESS

Where the map in section 3.1 combined single-impression printing with hand coloring, this sheet was printed in two colors using a press for both. Two different forms of type were set, the one to be printed in black leaving blank spaces where the red words would go, the one to print red being mostly empty to accommodate the black impression. The sheet was put through the press twice—the black surely printed first—and the hand press was carefully manipulated to impress the red words as accurately as possible in their intended location. Registration on these early presses was crude at best. Our example was laid out so that no part of the print required absolutely accurate registration; the two impressions needed to be fitted to each other within only about a sixteenth-of-an-inch tolerance to be acceptable.

There are two ways to print a picture in more than one color. The simplest method is to ink different parts of the form with different colors. This was sometimes done when there was a large capital letter at the start of a page or section; it was relatively easy to ink that one letter with a bright color, such as red or blue, and then ink the rest of the form with black. When printed the two colors would be in perfect register, since the type was never moved and the sheet was printed only once. Other decorative initials were simply colored in by hand, so they are similar to the hand-colored map in the previous plate.

The other way to print in multiple colors is with the method used for this sheet. The practice of putting a piece of paper through the press more than one time has become the basis of all complex color printing. The biggest problem faced in the development of this multiple-impression technique was to achieve accurate registration of the two images. Our example, made by letterpress, was printed on tough rag paper that was dampened before printing. Because the paper was printed wet, it varied slightly in size from one pass to the next, which meant that multiple impressions could never be registered accurately enough to print pictures. Once the nineteenth century came along, machinery could be made more accurately; sheets could then be printed dry, at high speed, with a delicate impression, and it became possible to maintain superb registration. Even at its best, however, letterpress never achieved the accuracy of photo offset lithography, which is used to create most of our books today.

nks for the 2 vol.

Christopher THE GREAT Marshall

# HISTORICAL,

## Geographical, Genealogical and Poetical

# DICTIONARY;

BEING

## A Curious Miſcellany

OF

*SACRED and PROPHANE HISTORY.*

Containing, in ſhort,

The LIVES and moſt REMARKABLE ACTIONS

Of the Patriarchs, Judges, and Kings of the Jews; Of the Apoſtles, Fathers, and Doctors of the Church; Of Popes, Cardinals, Biſhops, *&c.* Of Hereſiarchs and Schiſmaticks, with an Account of their Principal Doctrines; Of Emperors, Kings, Illuſtrious Princes, and Great Generals; Of Ancient and Modern Authors; Of Philoſophers, Inventors of Arts, and all thoſe who have recommended themſelves to the World, by their Valour, Virtue, Learning, or ſome Notable Circumſtances of their Lives. Together with the Eſtabliſhment and Progreſs both of Religious and Military Orders, and the Lives of their Founders. As alſo, The Fabulous Hiſtory of the Heathen GODS and HEROES.

THE DESCRIPTION

Of Empires, Kingdoms, Common-Wealths, Provinces, Cities, Towns, Iſlands, Mountains, Rivers, and other conſiderable Places, both of Ancient and Modern Geography; wherein is obſerved the Situation, Extent and Quality of the Country; the Religion, Government, Morals and Cuſtoms of the Inhabitants; the Sects of Chriſtians, Jews, Heathens and Mahometans. The principal Terms of Arts and Sciences; the Publick and Solemn Actions, as Feſtivals, Plays, *&c.* The Statutes and Laws; and withal, the Hiſtory of General and Particular Councils, under the Names of the Places where they have been Celebrated.

The Whole being full of Remarks and Curious Enquiries, for the Illuſtration of ſeveral Difficulties in Theology, Hiſtory, Chronology and Geography.

COLLECTED

From the beſt Hiſtorians, Chronolcgers, and Lexicographers; as *Calviſius, Helvicus, Iſaacſon, Marſham, Baudrand, Hoffman, Lloyd, Chevreau,* and others: But more eſpecially out of *LEWIS MORERY,* D. D. his Eighth Edition Corrected and Enlarged by Monſieur *LE CLERC*; In Two Volumes in Folio.

To which are added, by way of Supplement, intermix'd throughout the Alphabet,

The Lives, moſt Remarkable Actions, and Writings of ſeveral Illuſtrious Families of our *Engliſh, Scotch* and *Iriſh* Nobility, and Gentry, and moſt Famous Men of all Profeſſions, Arts and Sciences: As alſo, an Exact Deſcription of theſe Kingdoms; with the moſt Conſiderable Occurrences that have happened to this preſent Time.

The SECOND VOLUME.

*The Second Edition Reviſ'd, Corrected and Enlarg'd to the Year* 1688;
*By* JER. COLLIER, *A. M.*

*LONDON,*

Printed for *Henry Rhodes,* near *Bride-Lane* in *Fleetſtreet*; *Thomas Newborough,* at the *Golden-Ball* in St. *Paul's Church-Yard*; the Aſſigns of *L. Meredith,* at the *Star* in St. *Paul's Church-Yard*; and *Elizabeth Harris,* at the *Harrow* in *Little-Britain*; MDCCI.

**Two-color letterpress.** Jeremy Collier. *The Great Historical, Geographical, Genealogical and Poetical Dictionary.* 1701. Title page. 14¾ x 9 in. (37.5 x 22.9 cm)

## 3.3 MULTIPASS INTAGLIO

Sometimes one comes across a piece of printed paper that is pure pleasure to look at. It is lucky that this sheet of currency, one of the most beautiful things I own, fits nicely into our examination of multiple-impression printing, so I have an excuse to put it in the book. It is an uncut sheet, intaglio printed, that retains its original borders and registration marks. The bills were probably printed sometime between 1839 and 1842, because the names of two banknote-engraving companies appear on each bill, and we have records that one of the companies was created in 1839 and that they combined into a single organization, with a different name, in 1842. In the early years of the nineteenth century banks issued a huge variety of currencies, which were printed by many engravers. In 1863 the U.S. government put a stop to this and became the country's sole issuer of paper money. At about the same time, virtually all the small printers of currency merged to become the American Bank Note Company, which remained active until electronic banking reduced the need for paper bills in the late 1990s.

Unlike the older etchings and engravings, this sheet was not printed by hand: although intaglio printing remains a hand process for "art" prints even today, mechanical methods emerged early on to meet the need for huge editions of currency, postage stamps, and fancy certificates. The paper is very thin, about .002 inches thick (.05 mm), and the quality of the registration speaks of a sheet printed dry, instead of dampened, as hand printing required. The two colors on this sheet—black as the key impression, orange as the second—were both printed from steel plates that had been etched and then engraved. The four register marks—the crosses in the margins—demonstrate the oldest method of aligning multiple impressions. On modern presses, in almost all of the processes, the impression is light and the paper undergoes little distortion. Before the invention of rotogravure in the late nineteenth century, though, intaglio always distorted the sheet severely, and a second impression could never be aligned exactly with the first. The compromise solution to this problem was to use four register marks on the borders, arranged like those on this sheet, which could be aligned as well as possible. This gave the center of the sheet the best "fit"; registration errors increased toward the edges.

Mechanical methods capable of decorative details such as these had appeared by the mid-nineteenth century. The filigreed orange circle around the fives was engraved or etched by a pantograph working from a larger image.

In the early years of the United States, currency was printed by plain old letterpress, but it always had a shaky reputation and coin was regarded as the genuine specie. It is no wonder that intaglio printing became the standard for money because its rich appearance gives some sense of solidity to the bills. Today there are hordes of currency collectors and I have always thought part of the attraction they feel toward old money is based on its visual beauty.

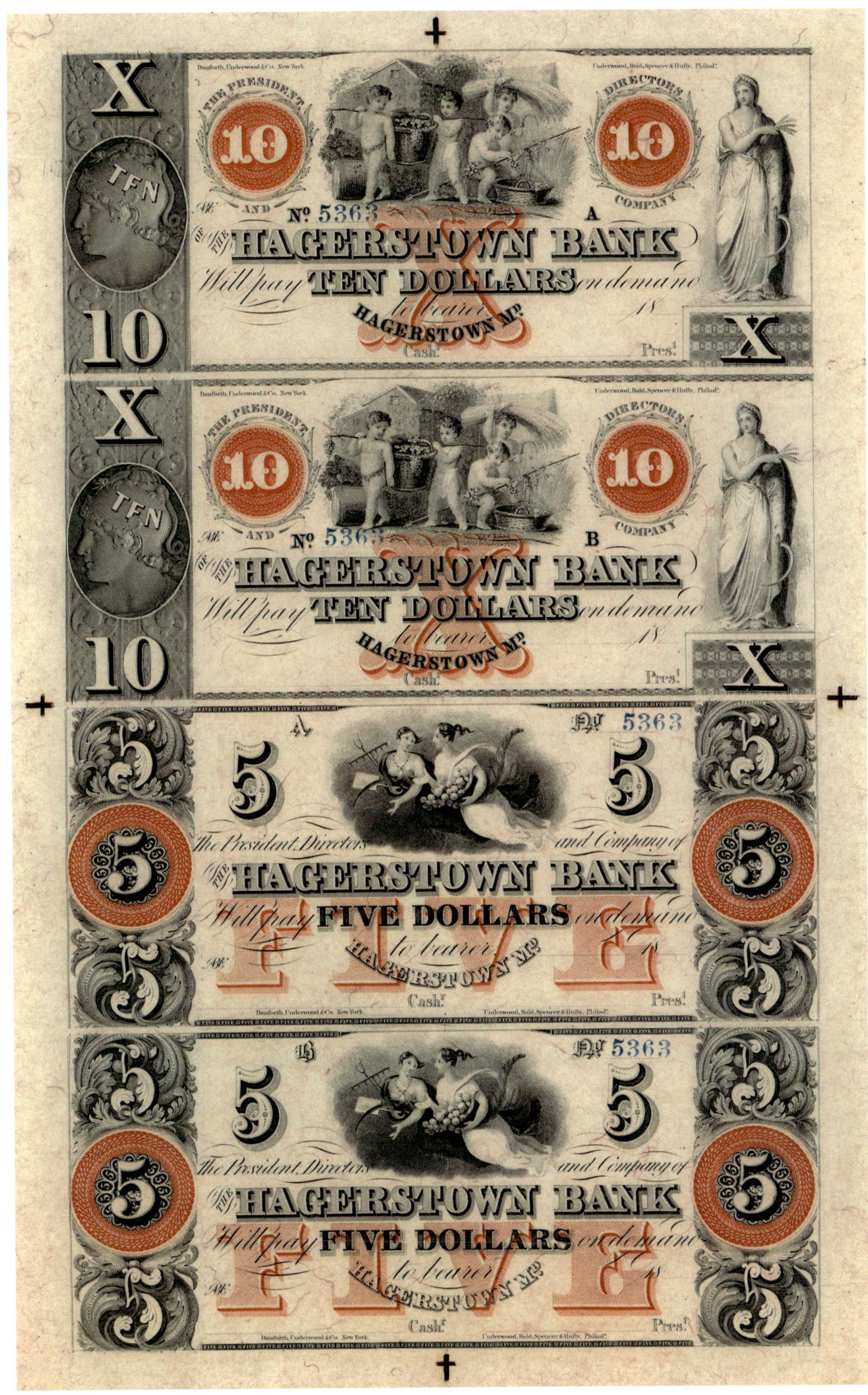


**Two-color steel engraving.** Danforth, Underwood & Company. Banknote proof sheet. c. 1839. 12¼ x 7¾ in. (31.1 x 19.7 cm)

### 3.4 CHROMOLITHOGRAPHY

Three of the four major systems of printing—relief, intaglio, and planographic—struggled with the difficulties of registration. Until the introduction of mechanized presses, the first two methods used dampened paper, which expanded and shrank as it absorbed water and dried, so that accurate registration over the several impressions needed for complex color images was impossible. Planographic printing, in the form of stone lithography, used a dry sheet, and the presses applied pressure with a stiff scraper, which, when handled properly, could leave a printed sheet close to its original size. Paper will take up water when possible, and expand accordingly, and lithography had the drawback of bringing the paper in contact with the dampened stone; still, with careful manipulation, accurate registration of multiple impressions was possible. Chromolithography grew out of this technical window, and it served to produce the best and earliest full-color printed pictures.

The principle of chromolithography was to print in multiple colors from multiple stones. Each stone held a printable image, drawn or transferred from paper, in black ink. This image, once etched, could be inked up with the right color and printed in register with a "key" plate, which tended to be a black skeleton of the picture. The idea that each color impression originated as a black-and-white image is important: this is the technical trick that has allowed simple monochromatic printing to be used to generate complex color images. To this day all color printing is based upon groups of single-color plates, each carrying its own portion of the color structure of the picture.

The black key plate in this early chromolithograph, made in about 1846, was printed by letterpress. The linear form is characteristic of woodcut or wood engraving, and either way of printing could have been done on a dry sheet, creating little distortion in that first impression.

Each of the color plates was drawn so that there are areas of solid color but also areas of stippling, with quite large dots in certain areas. The detail shows both solid colors and areas in which dot patterns diffuse the strength of the colors. Two printed colors, when transparent, can overlay to make a third. The small pink flower shape to the right side of the detail is printed in the same color used for the figure's head; this pink also underlies the blue area on the right of the detail, but not the man's cowl, which, however, is printed in the same blue. Thus two colors—pink and blue—produce three separate colors in the print: pink, blue, and the fused pink-and-blue. When the overlay is also modulated by stippling, the variation in color can become extensive even though only a few actual ink colors are used, with correspondingly few plates.

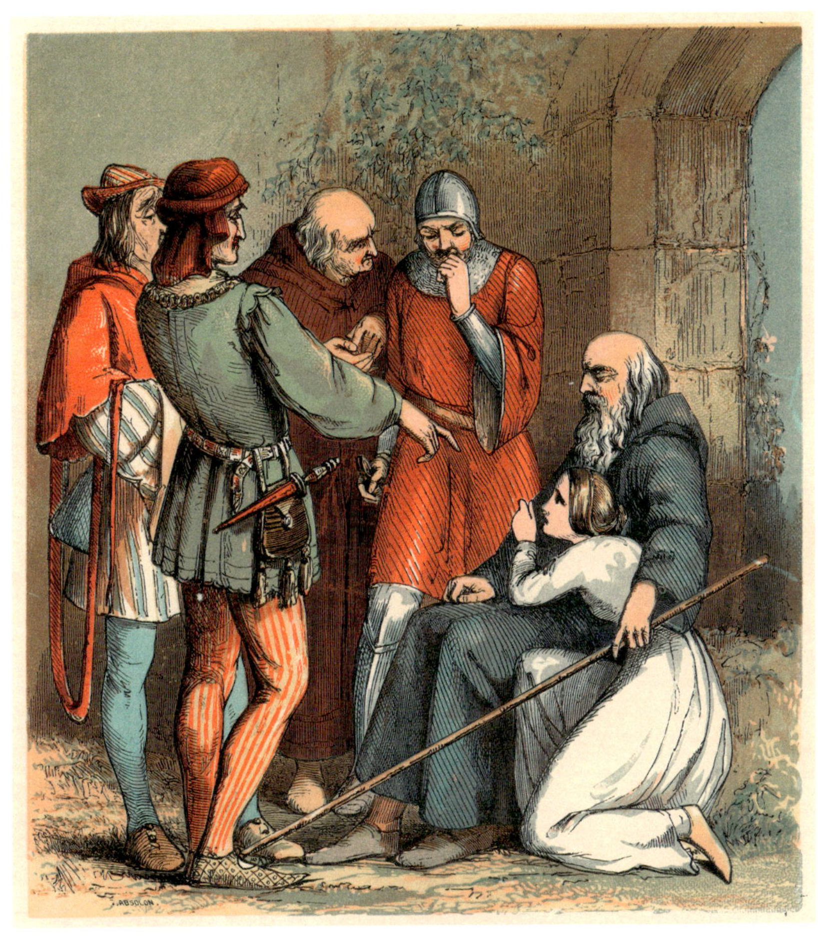

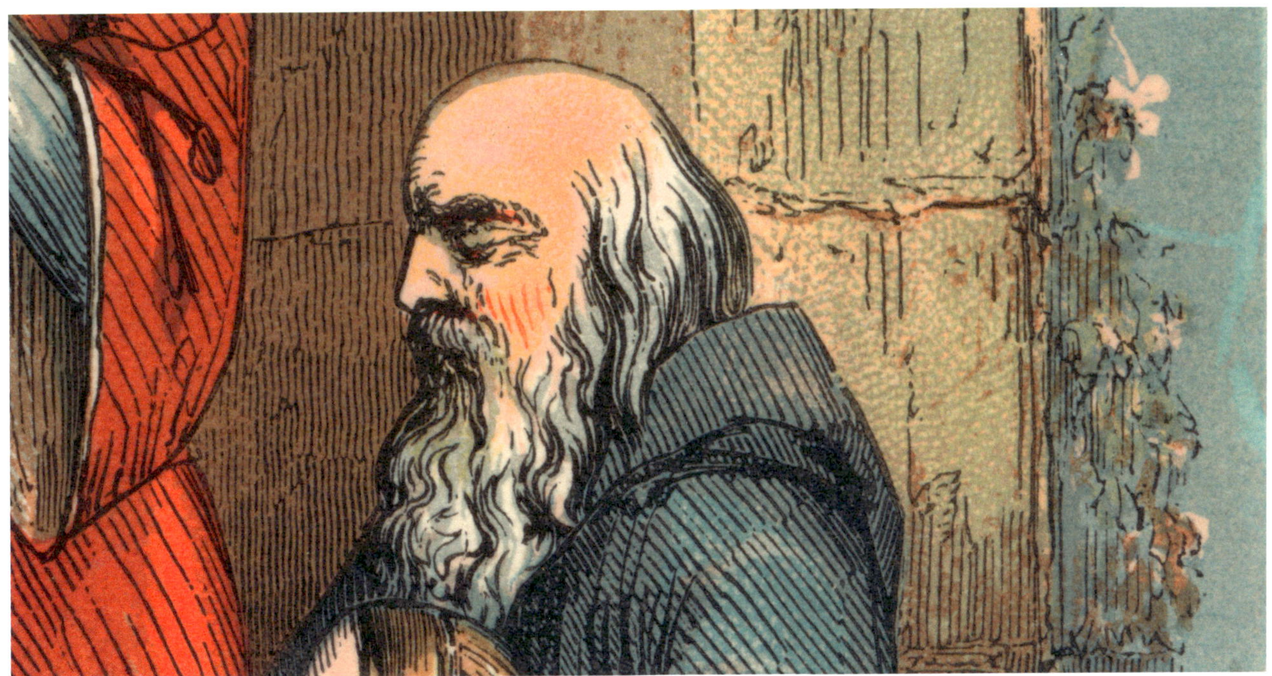

**Chromolithograph.** Artist unknown. Sample print from the *The Art Union, Monthly Journal of the Fine Arts.* c. 1846. 4¾ x 4¼ in. (12.1 x 10.7 cm). This print has a skeleton of black lines printed by letterpress.

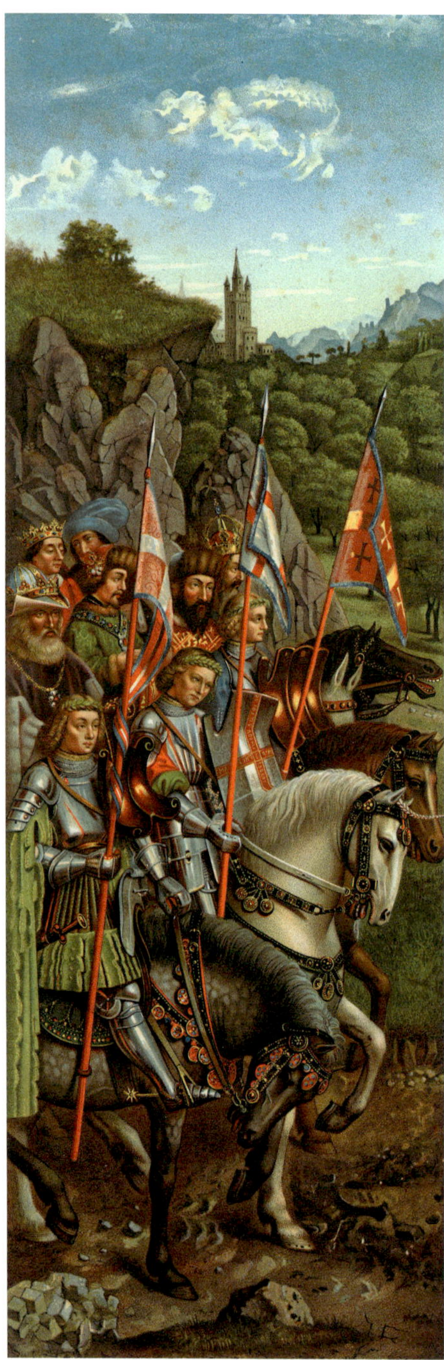

**Chromolithograph.** Hubert and Jan Van Eyck. Panel from The Ghent Altarpiece. c. 1432. Print: Storch & Kramer. 1877. 15½ x 5⅛ in. (39 x 13 cm)

## 3.5 CHROMOLITHOGRAPHY

Chromolithography reached an extraordinary level of complexity. This picture reproduces one of the four lower side-panels from Hubert and Jan van Eyck's Ghent Altarpiece of 1432. The full panel, shown on the left, is 15½ inches (39 cm) high in the reproduction, from which the detail on the right is shown enlarged three times. In the detail we can see the delicate stippling that has been used to generate the appearance of many colors and tonal variations. The stippling is far finer in the heads of the crusaders than in the rest of the picture, as though the human being deserved more care in the reproduction than did the flora and fauna. It is important to remember that the stippling we see in this detail is three times larger than it was in the handmade drawings used to make the reproduction. There was no photomechanical method allowing the printer to draw large and then print smaller.

I have long since given up trying to figure out how many colors were printed in this reproduction. At least eight stones were used and perhaps many more. The color separations have nothing to do with the scientifically based separations used today for "process" color printing, shown in plate 8.3. Instead the separator has chosen the key colors in the picture, drawn separations for those, and used stippling to make blends for intermediate colors and tones.

Like the Japanese woodblock print in plate 3.7, this picture shows an astonishing degree of technical skill. In both cases the printers were making a copy—their job was strictly to reproduce a piece of original art, without embellishing or altering it at all. In the case of the chromolithograph the printer must have used the original painting itself, or some hand-painted copy of it, as a guide. For the Japanese woodblock, the artist's painting, and perhaps even the artist himself, were nearby to direct the work. In both cases there was no room for expression on the part of the printer, beyond the goal of being completely invisible for the sake of the job at hand.

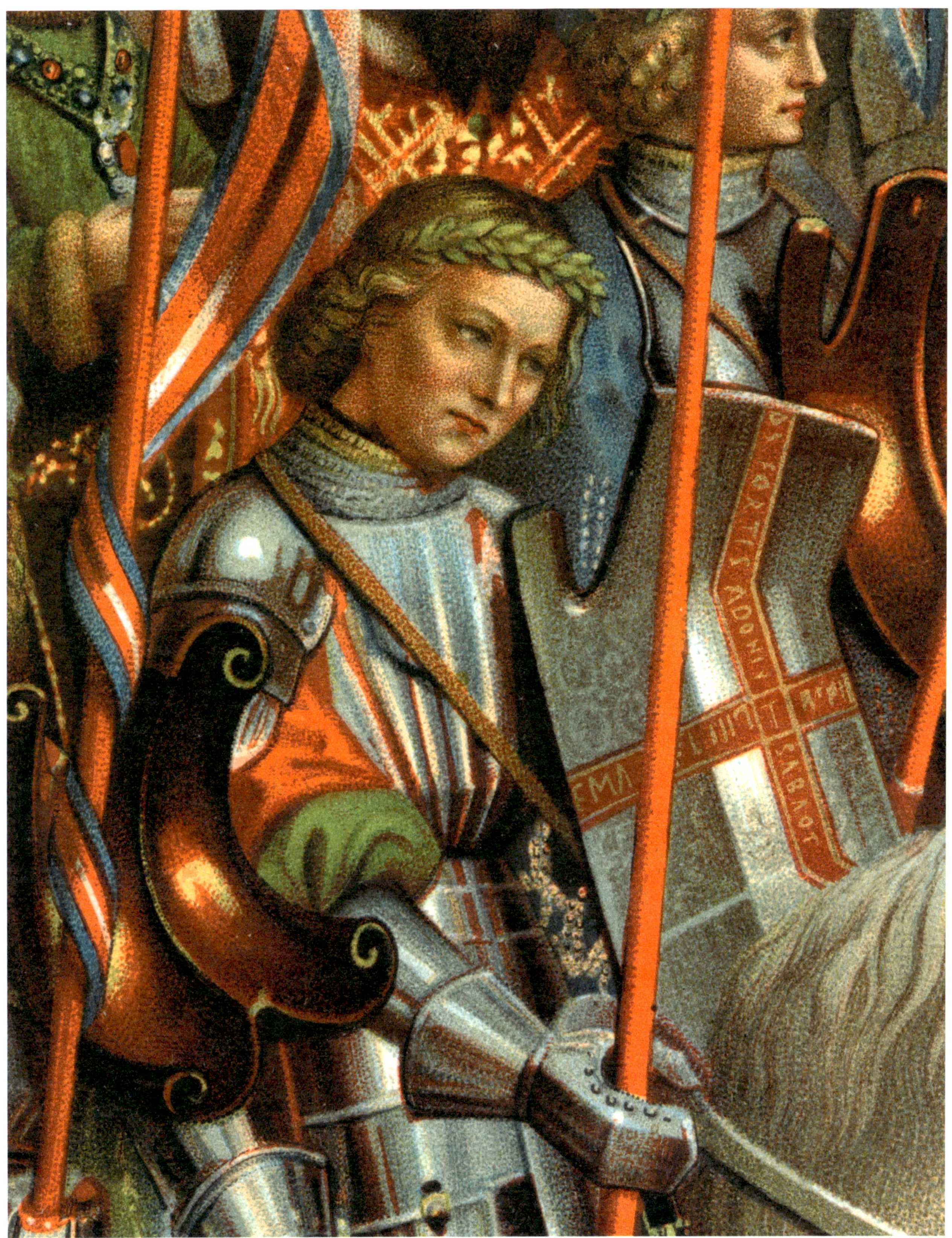

A detail from the chromolithograph, enlarged three times.

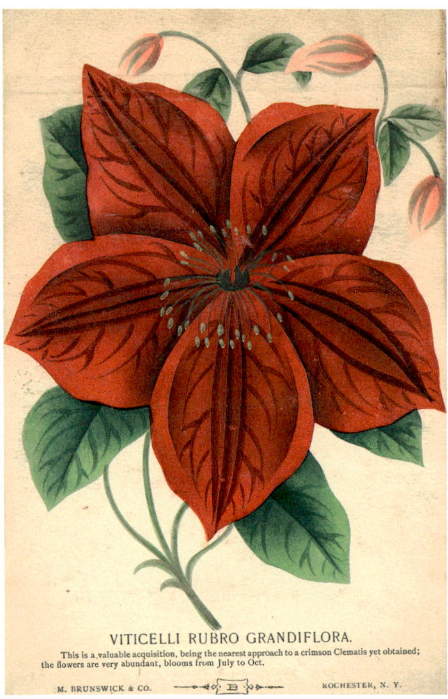


Another plate from the seed catalog.

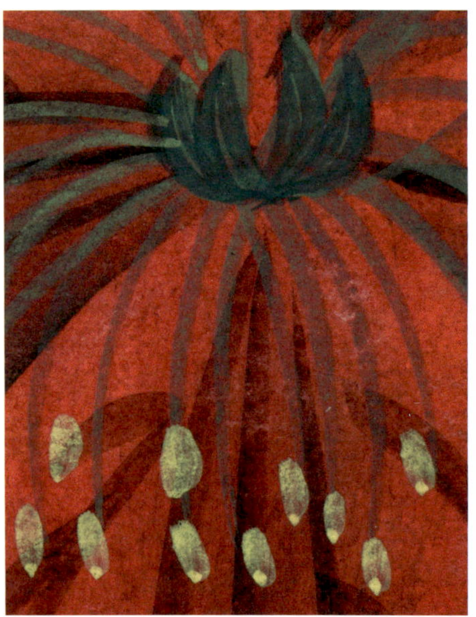

This detail is enlarged three times from the original shown above. While the overall picture is dominated by the stiff forms of the stencils, most of the small details have been freely put in with a brush. What we see here is virtually all hand painting.

## 3.6 STENCIL

There was a class of stencil printing in color that resembled pochoir except that the black key plate, or skeleton plate, was eliminated. This sort of printing was used for small editions and most often for the botanical plates used in seed and plant catalogs. I have come across two such books, as well as numerous plates that have been cut out of them and matted for sale individually in junk shops. The stencil process allows smooth and beautiful areas of color, and when the inks are transparent, complex pictures can be built up with a relatively small number of stencils.

The stencils for this image were certainly made of paper, and the ink was applied through them using a dauber of some sort—probably a rounded bundle of cloth—that could gently press the ink onto the sheet. The printer used a number of inks and stencils to make the picture and applied the ink carefully so that many of the edges are soft. This is most visible in the modeling of the red values in the flower. Probably the stems and leaves of the clematis were stenciled, and then the veins and small tendrils were quickly painted in with short strokes of a paintbrush, without the benefit of any stencil as a guide. The mixture of these two technologies—stencil and painting—makes every page in this book an original work of art, because the hand never repeats itself in the manner of a true repetitive printing process.

It has always seemed odd to me that the sort of stencil work we see in this book of flowers was not more widely used, since it is a great pleasure to do, lends itself to terrific color values, and can be done with almost no expensive equipment. Silk screen printing—the most common form of pictorial stenciling done today—evolved into a fairly complex process primarily used for reproductive work, with opaque inks. Pictures like the one we see here, made in pure stencil using washes of transparent color, are almost nonexistent today.

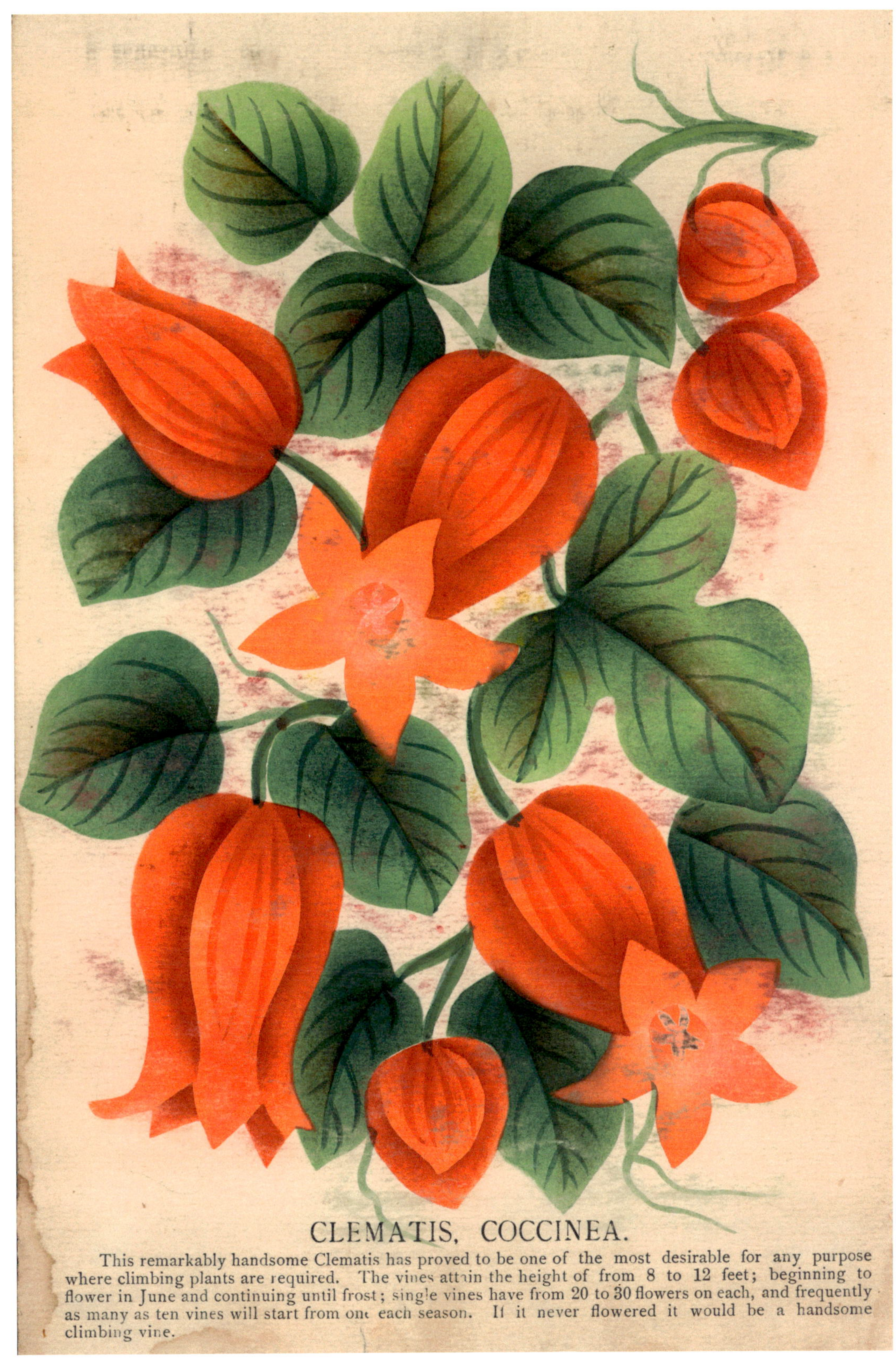


**Color stencil.** M. Brunswick & Co. *Clematis, Coccinea.* c. 1900. 8 x 5¼ in. (20.3 x 13.3 cm). A plate from S.T. Cannon's seed catalog.

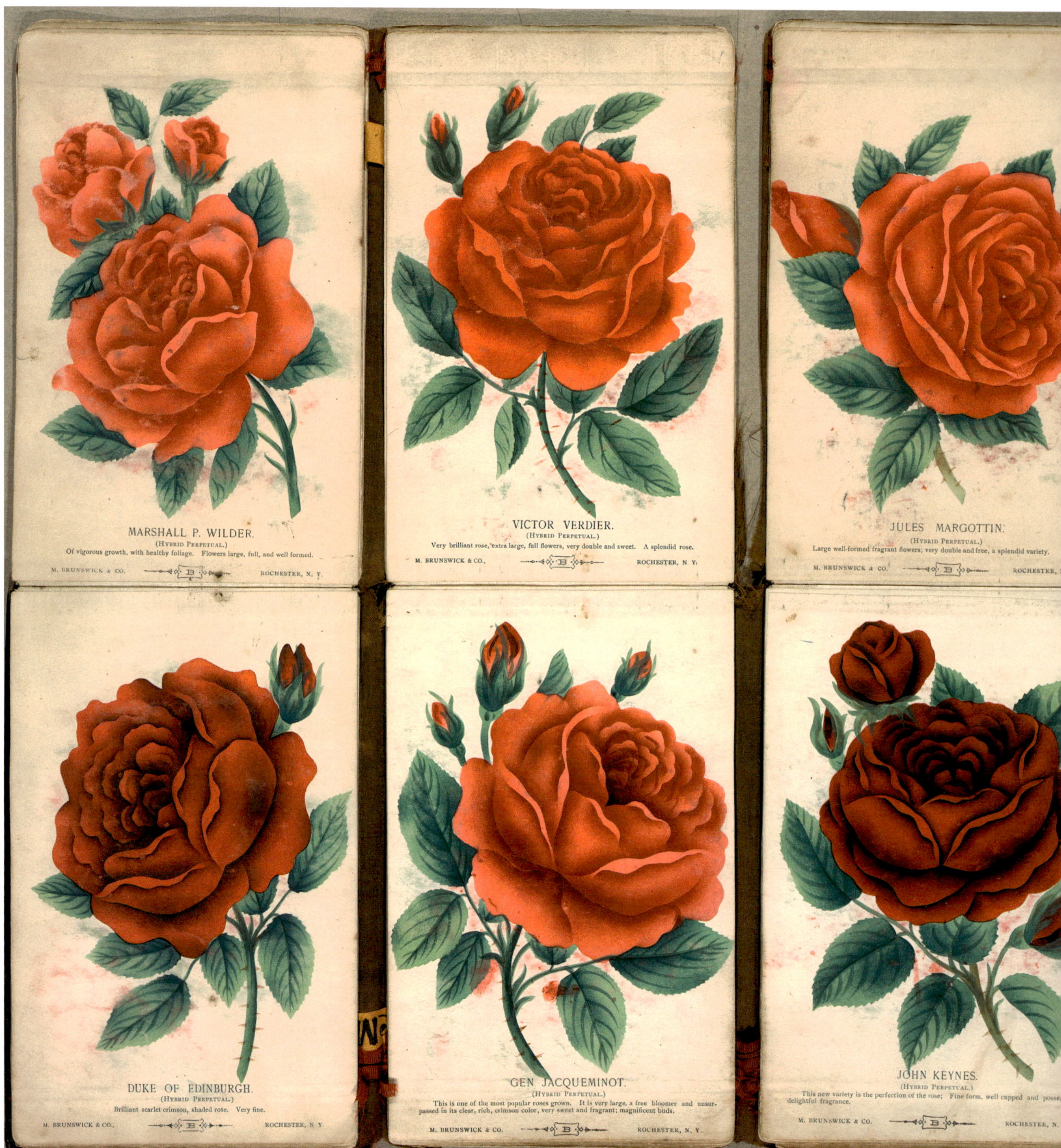


Each spread of the book holds twelve remarkable pictures. I show a group of roses here, but all sorts of flowers are hidden away among the 120 plates in the book. Bits of yellow and red ribbon can be seen between a few pages; these strips of cloth connected groups of six pages, and all the pages were bound together by a foldable joint running across the twelve at the center. This arrangement allowed a single motion of the hand to switch all twelve images by folding a group of six over. It must have been dazzling to see such a sweep of color revealed in a single pass, and it would have taken a strong-willed store manager or housewife to resist the riches shown in the book.

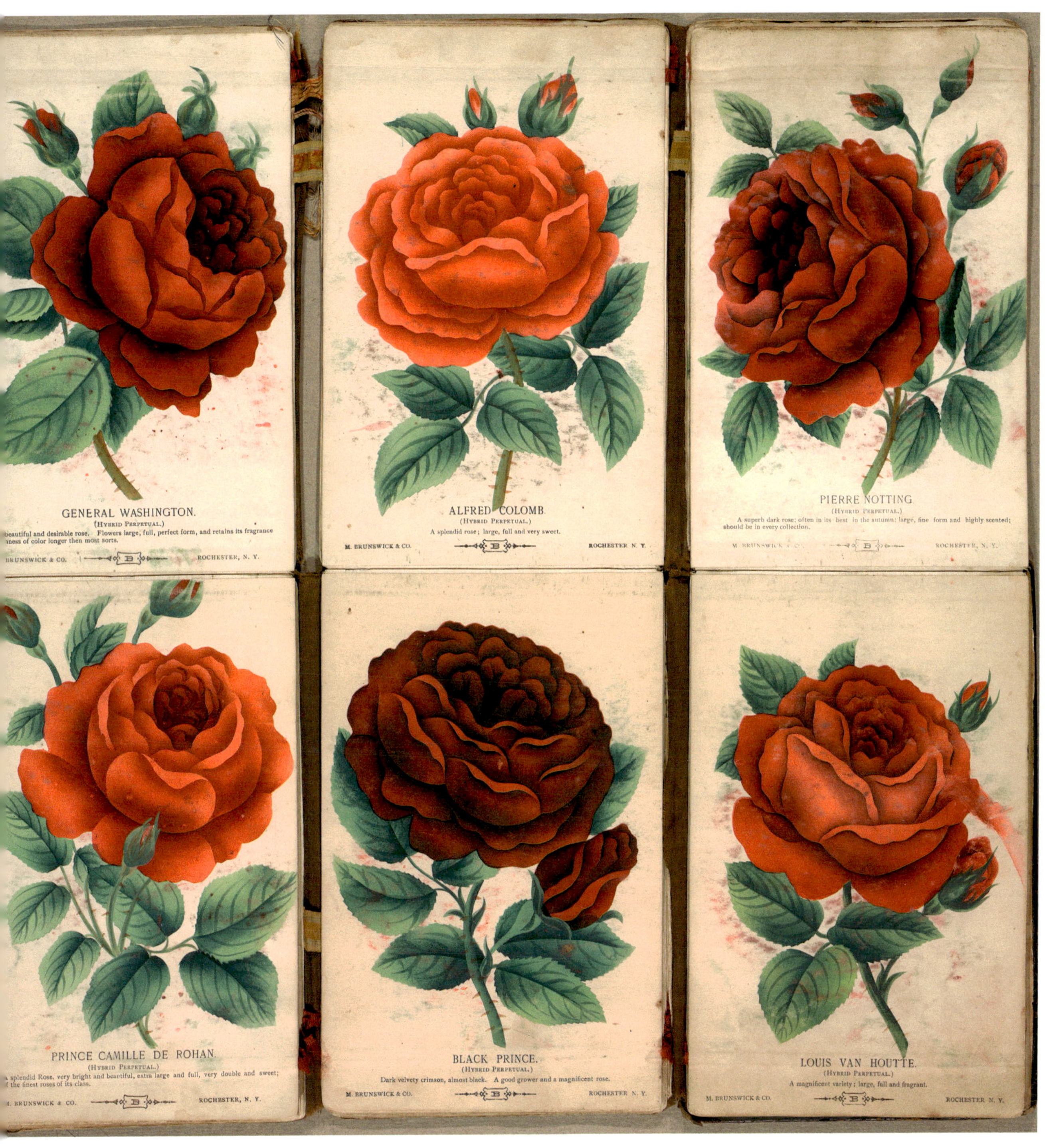


**Color stencil.** M. Brunswick & Co. Spread from S.T. Cannon's seed catalog. c. 1900. 17¼ x 35 in. (43.8 x 88.9 cm)

## 3.7 JAPANESE WOODBLOCK PRINTING

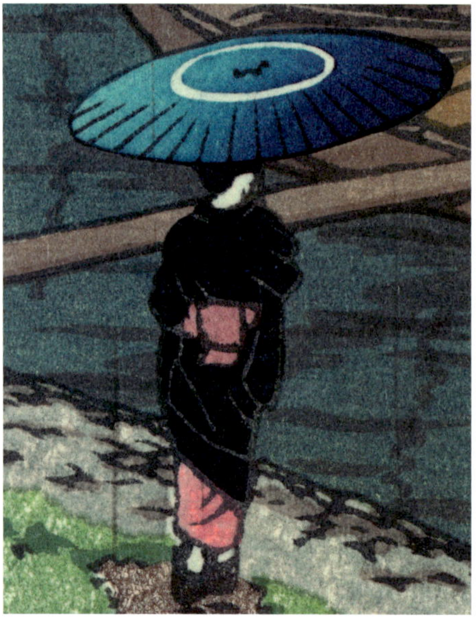

This small detail, enlarged 1.7 times from the original, shows two different, distinctive blues in the umbrella and a pink in the kimono. These color accents, standing out from the field of muted green and blue that constitutes most of the picture, push the figure out of the picture plane toward the viewer.

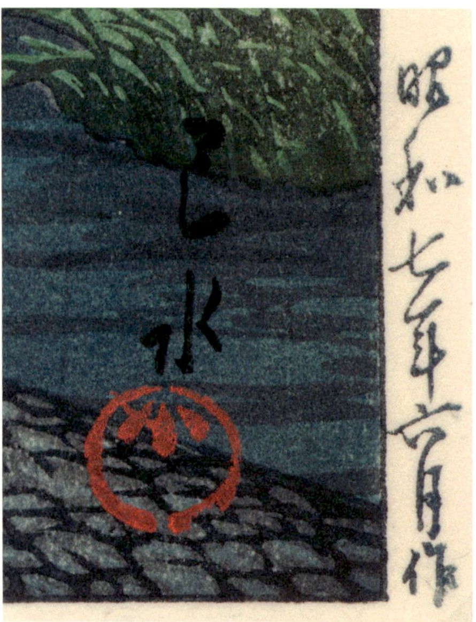

The writing in the right margin of the print resembles original brushwork but it, too, is printed from a woodblock. The red mark in the lower right corner of the image—a signature stamp that Hasui used late in his career—is also a relief print, in this case printed from an engraved stone stamp.

Handmade color separations, printed without the benefit of photography, reached their most highly refined states in chromolithography and Japanese woodblock printing. An example of the former technique appears in plate 3.5, and here we see the latter in a color print by the artist Kawase Hasui.

An artist of the first half of the twentieth century, Hasui traveled widely, making sketches and watercolors of scenes that embodied old Japan. Master carvers translated his delicate pictures into multiple blocks that could be inked and printed to generate astonishingly complex color pictures. Most Western woodblock color printing assumes that each block will be inked evenly, in a somewhat mechanical way, to make all the prints in an edition identical. In Japan the printers didn't hesitate to ink their blocks with tonal gradations, making far more complex color structures than were achieved in the West. The only hand-generated Western color printing that approaches this degree of refinement is chromolithography, which is based upon the completely different principle of stippling: tiny dots, all inked the same way, create the appearance of tonal change.

Japanese woodblock prints illuminate a crucial principle of color pictures. This is that the color decisions of an artist (and in this case a printer as well) working with pigments or dyes can create a set of relationships within a picture that form the foundation of its meaning. This particular print is about two different greens, two different blues, and their interaction to produce transitional shades. The brown used in the boats, small accents of other colors, and the black key plate support these picture-defining colors, but the artist has stated the theme of the picture through the blue-green structure. This is what painters have always done with color, and this level of refinement has always showed up in the best original printmaking. Photography, the new and dominating picture medium of our time, had no method for handling color in this way until the recent introduction of digital tools. When traditional color photographs were printed, all of the colors were "connected," being derived from three dye layers, each of which had to be manipulated globally. If a color in a photograph wasn't quite right, the printer could alter the filtration and shift that color to the right place, but all of the others were dragged along with it and the whole picture changed. Traditional artists have always been suspicious of photography, labeling it a minor art because of its machine-generated origins. This is a stupid idea, but if photography's handling of color was really understood, then the old skeptics might realize they actually had a point.

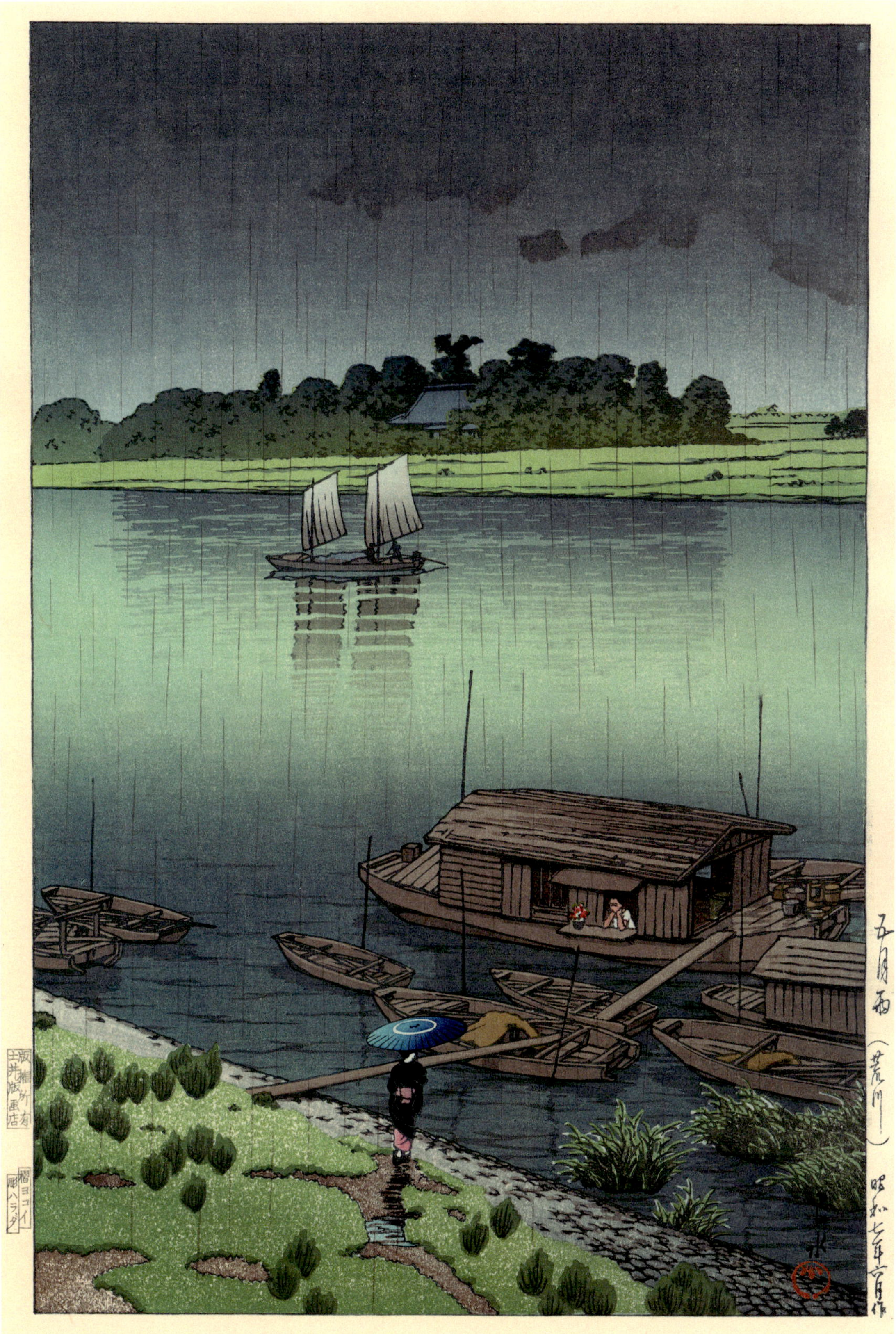


**Japanese woodblock printing.** Kawase Hasui. *Early Summer Rain.* c. 1940. 14¾ x 10⅛ in. (37.5 x 25.7 cm). This is a late impression of a set of blocks cut in 1932.

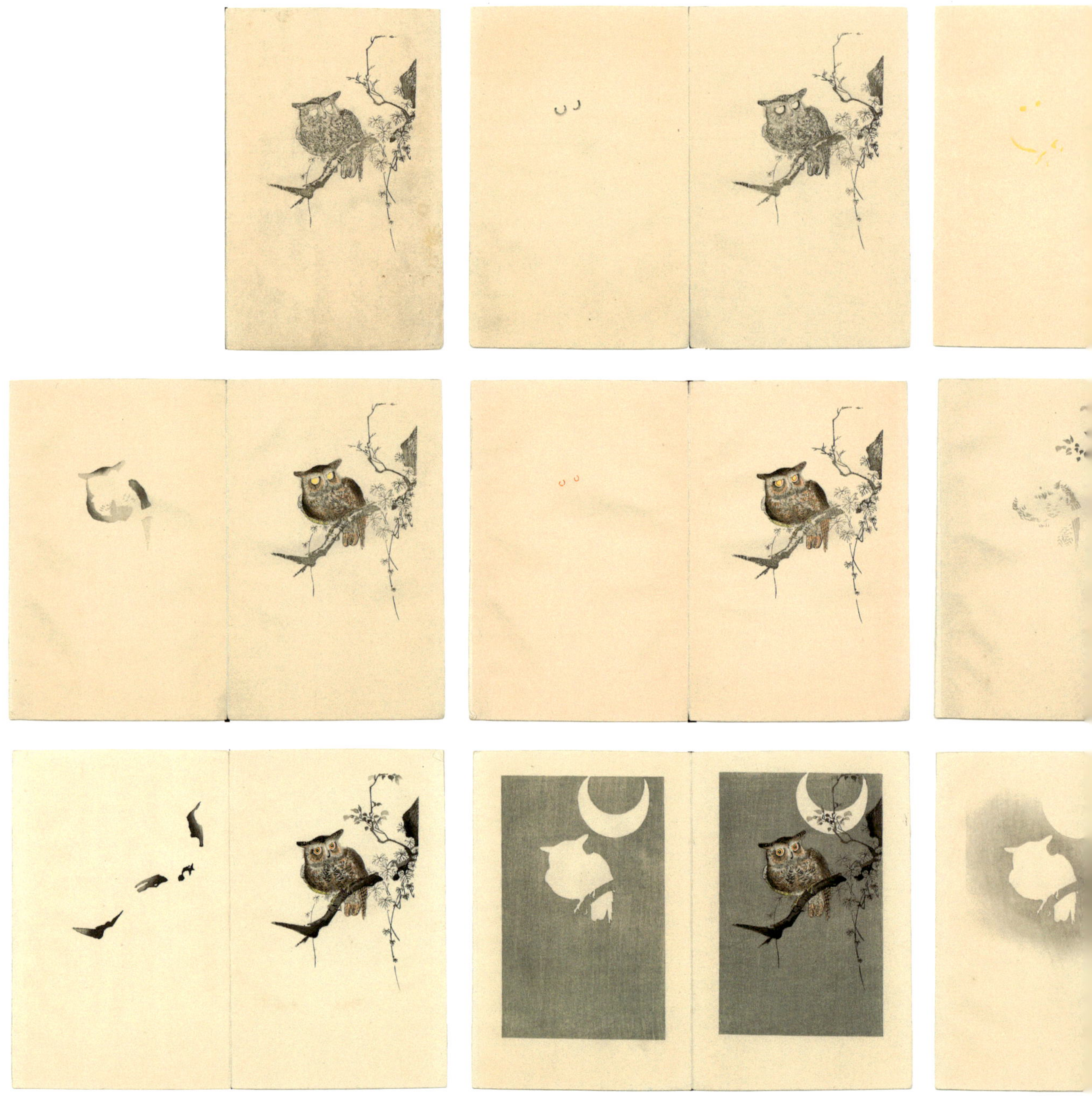

Japanese woodblock printers would occasionally make small booklets showing the progressive stages of a single print. We see here the fifteen stages of a small print of an owl in a tree. In modern color printing, such as four-color process, each printing plate holds information for the entire picture. In handmade color such as this woodblock print, the artist has the option of making color decisions about separate parts of the picture. We see this clearly here, since individual parts of the owl and the tree each have their own blocks and colors. In this print the color structure of the picture tends to be about discrete steps of tone and color rather than smooth transitions between broad areas.

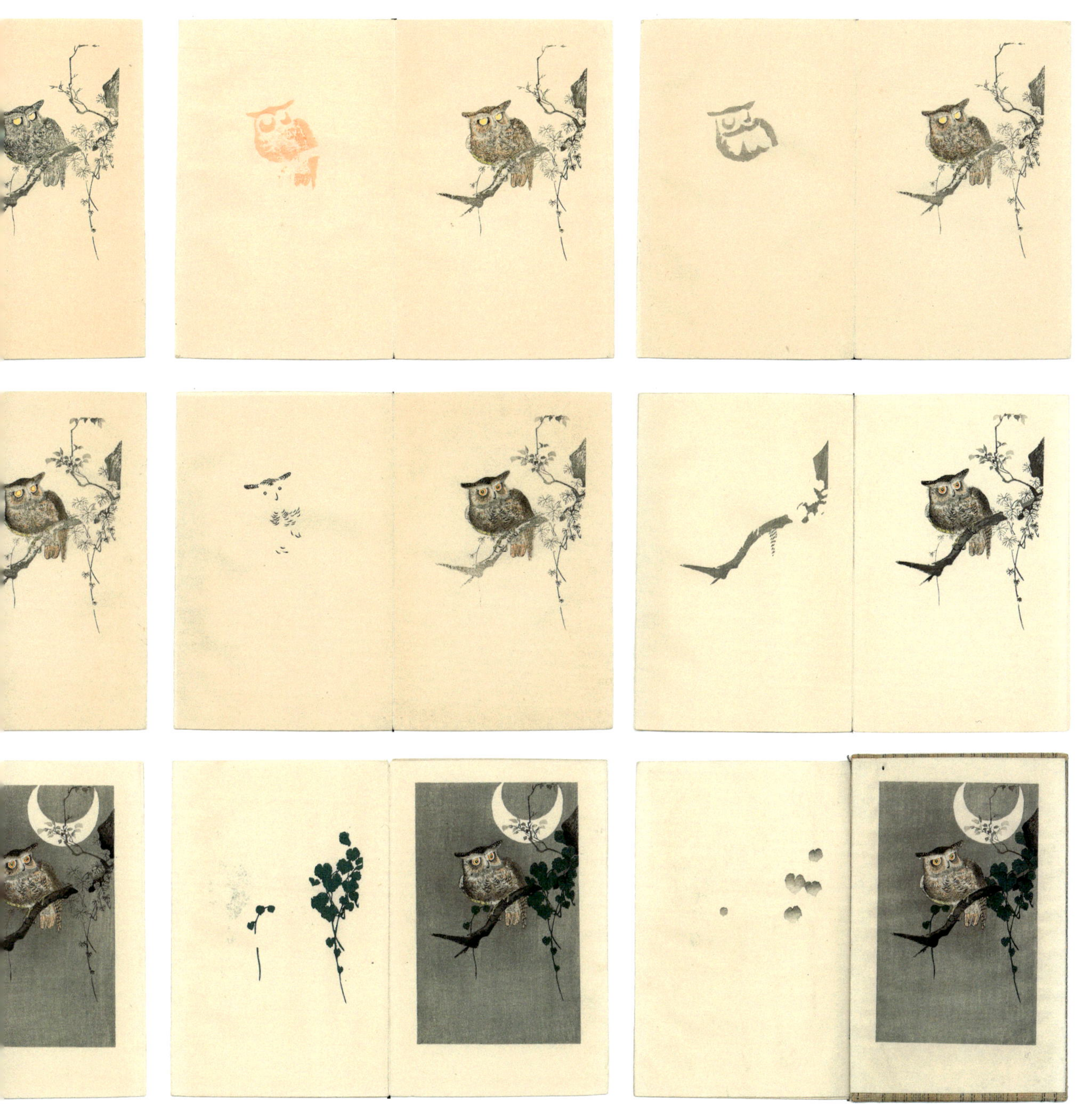

**Woodblock progressives.** Artist unknown. Publisher's process book. c. 1930. Each spread: 7⅛ x 9⅜ in. (18.1 x 23.8 cm)

# Part 4

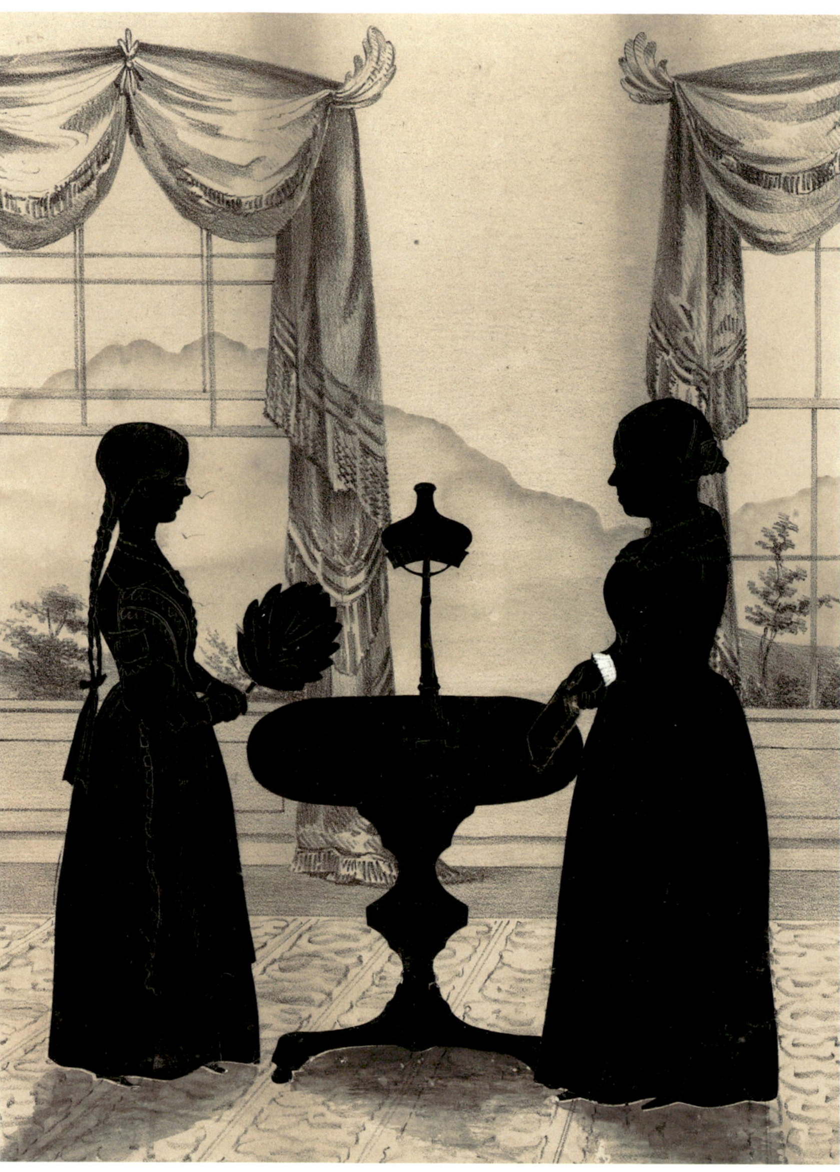

This section deals with a group of techniques that I have chosen to isolate from the main thread of our story. Stencil, lithography, and etching are here, but in their surviving, vestigial forms as art processes. I have also stuck the typewriter in here. The second half of this section is devoted to mechanical systems of picture-making that preceded photography. They introduce Part 5, which will begin our examination of the photographic processes.

**Silhouettes pasted onto a lithograph.** Samuel Metford. *The Sherman Family* (detail). c. 1830. 11 x 7⅞ in. (28 x 20 cm)

# Bits and pieces

4.1 Stencil letters
*Modern uses of simple stencil printing.*

4.2 Silk screen printing
*Stencil's pictorial method.*

4.3 Modern stone lithography
*Artists preserving out-of-date techniques.*

4.4 Modern etching
*Printmaking as a personal or distributed practice.*

4.5 The typewriter
*Relief printing for personal use.*

4.6 Weaving
*A diversion to consider a remarkable woven photograph.*

4.7 Rubbings
*Pictures made by the mechanical transcription of information.*

4.8 The squeeze
*An obscure method of copying inscriptions.*

4.9 Pantograph etchings
*Etched prints derived from pantographic tracings of relief surfaces.*

4.10 Silhouettes
*Pictures made by tracing.*

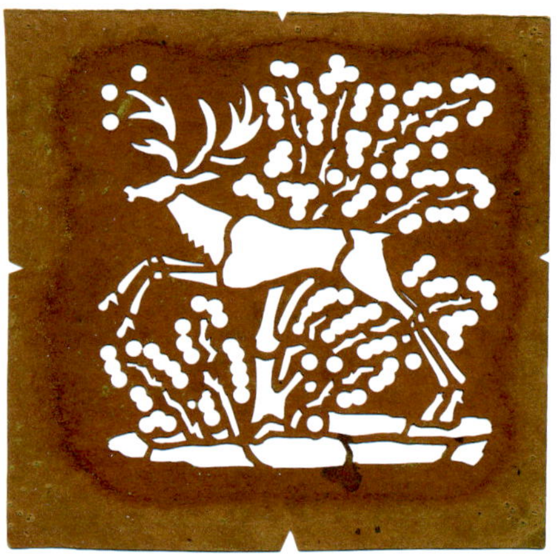

A small decorative stencil by the painter Durr Freedley, cut in cardboard. c. 1935. 5 x 5 in. (12.7 x 12.7 cm). The stencil shows four V-cuts, one on each side, used to register the print. These registration marks would only have been necessary if the stencil was to be used to make multiple impressions in more than one color.

## 4.1 STENCIL LETTERS

Stencil depends upon a printing matrix with holes in it, through which the ink passes on its way to the support. An ancient system of print technology, stencil had a long life as a method for applying color to black-and-white prints, as in the engraved map in plate 3.1, but it has had very little use in bookmaking. (Our stenciled seed catalog, shown in plate 3.6, is a rare exception.) The other processes—relief, intaglio, and planographic—all managed to adapt themselves to mechanized production; the plates they use to carry information were refined to fit printing machinery, so that the inking and printing could be done at high speed. But the physical action that stencil entails is too hard to handle and too slow to be easily adapted to the printing press. The closest we have come is silk screen printing, in which the holes have become tiny and are spread across a sheet of fabric—a rigidly rectangular weave of threads and the apertures between them, which the printer either leaves open to pass ink or closes with a stencil to block the flow.

Stencil has enjoyed a wide application in simple lettering, for packing cases, pedestrian crosswalks, and hundreds of other marking chores. The stencils, often cut out of stiff paper, are held against the support; paint or ink wiped or sprayed across them passes through the areas that have been cut away, leaving the writing behind. The letters we see here are from a set of brass stencils made for the U.S. military during World War II. This alphabet shows the primary design requirement for a stencil: that all interior voids in the letters be connected to the surrounding background. This is necessary because letter parts such as the center of an "O" would fall away in the stencil if not held by small strips to the outside of the letter. The need to hold all the parts together gives stenciled lettering its characteristic look: the letters are simple and read well, but, once printed, have gaps in them to accommodate this structural requirement.

In this particular set, the brass sheets holding every letter have edges designed so that each letter can slip into the one next to it, making a paint-tight connection. A string of letters is put together, like the word "stencil" in our example, and can then be handled as a single object to print repeatedly. When these letters were put away a few of them were left uncleaned, so we see the residual paint from an earlier use. One of the great sins of stenciling is to fail to clean a freshly used stencil—that is as bad an error as failing to clean letterpress type before it is distributed back to its case after printing.

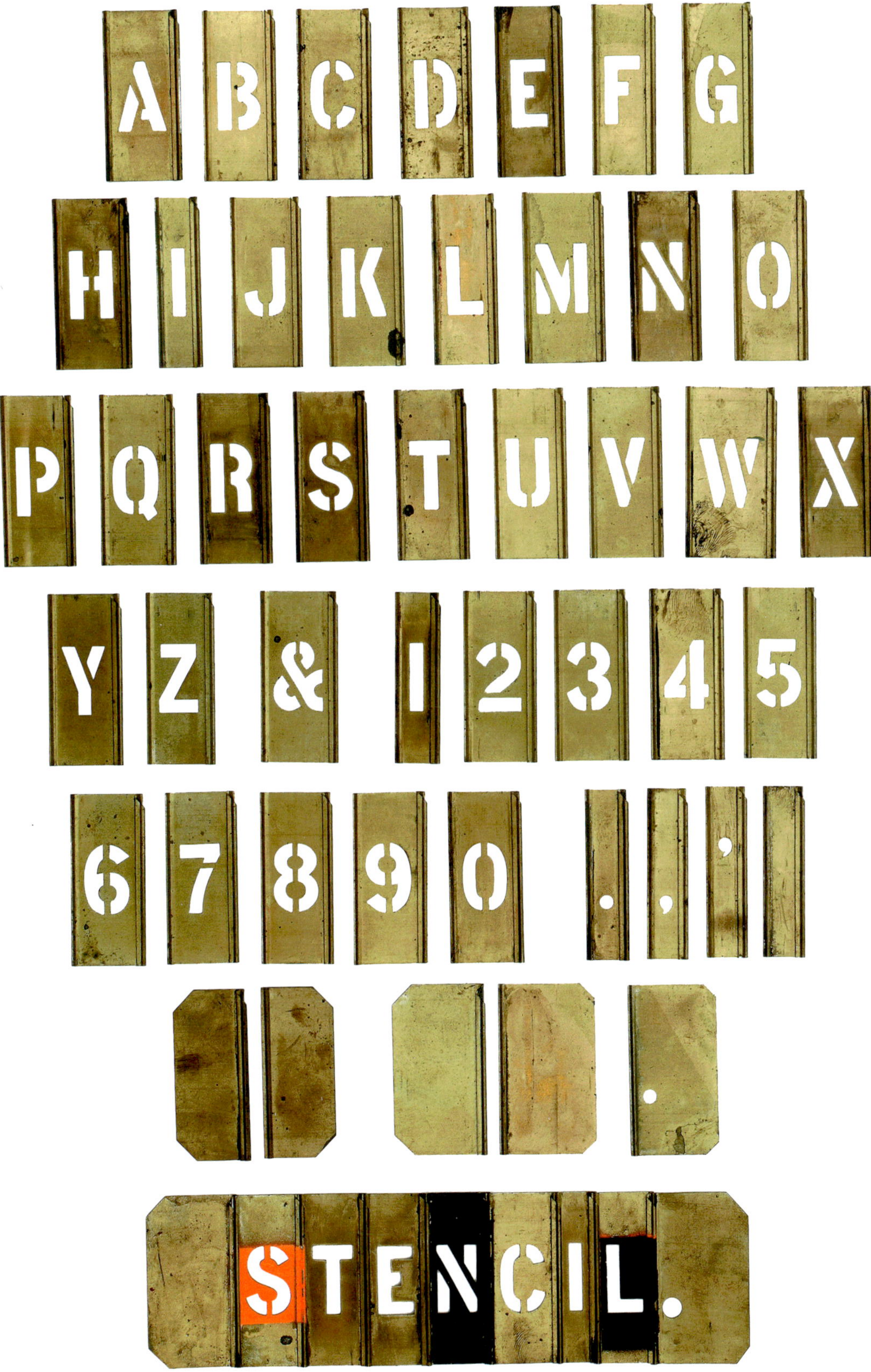


**Stencil letters.** C. H. Hanson Company. *Stencil Set, Marking, Lockedge, Adjustable, Brass, 1 inch size. FSN 7520-298-7043.* c. 1945. 2½ in. (6.4 cm) high, width variable. A set of marking stencils made for the U.S. military during World War II.

## 4.2 SILK SCREEN PRINTING

Even if stencil never had a large role in the book world it is a great process, and reached spectacular form in silk screen printing. The fancy gallery folks call prints made this way "serigraphs," one of those names, like those used for car models in the automobile industry, that sound swell and don't mean much. The underlying principle of the silk screen is to hold the stencil parts on a panel of cloth, one woven openly so that there are spaces within the grid formed by warp and weft. The threads hold the stencil, eliminating the structural requirements we saw in the stenciled letters of the previous plate, and the apertures in the cloth are so fine that the ink that passes through them goes down onto the sheet as an unbroken film.

The stencils can be cut paper—like those used for the print we see here—or they can be made photographically, with a store-bought, light-sensitive jelly that is coated on the screen and exposed. A washing removes the unexposed areas; where the stencil of jelly has been exposed, it remains, and blocks the passage of ink. Silk screen has the nice characteristic of not requiring a press: the screen is stretched on a simple wooden frame hinged to a table top and is printed by placing the paper beneath, pouring the ink into one end of the frame, and then passing a squeegee across the screen to apply the ink through the fabric. Multiple impressions, made with a separate screen for each color, are possible because the printing does not distort the sheet. The printing frames are simple and the registration is never exact, but this isn't much of a problem because all silk screen printing is low resolution. The fabric might have a very fine thread count—over 200 threads per linear inch—but the apertures formed in the screen are printed in a binary way; they either pass ink or don't. They behave like a halftone dot (which we will examine in Part 10) that has only one size, so lacks any decent method for describing tonal change.

Silk screen printing's lack of tonal flexibility is compensated for by its beautiful layers of flat color. The inks used are usually opaque, with great covering power, and when complex color pictures are silk-screened, with as many as twenty or more colors, amazingly beautiful prints can be made. Because the process has great presence, silk-screening turns up in fabrics, T-shirts, high-end signs, and a wide range of art reproductions. Sometimes a coarse halftone is used with the photographic resists in an effort to introduce tonal modulation, but the primary characteristic of a silk screen print tends to be sharply defined chunks of opaque colors, printed in complex layers to produce physically enticing prints.

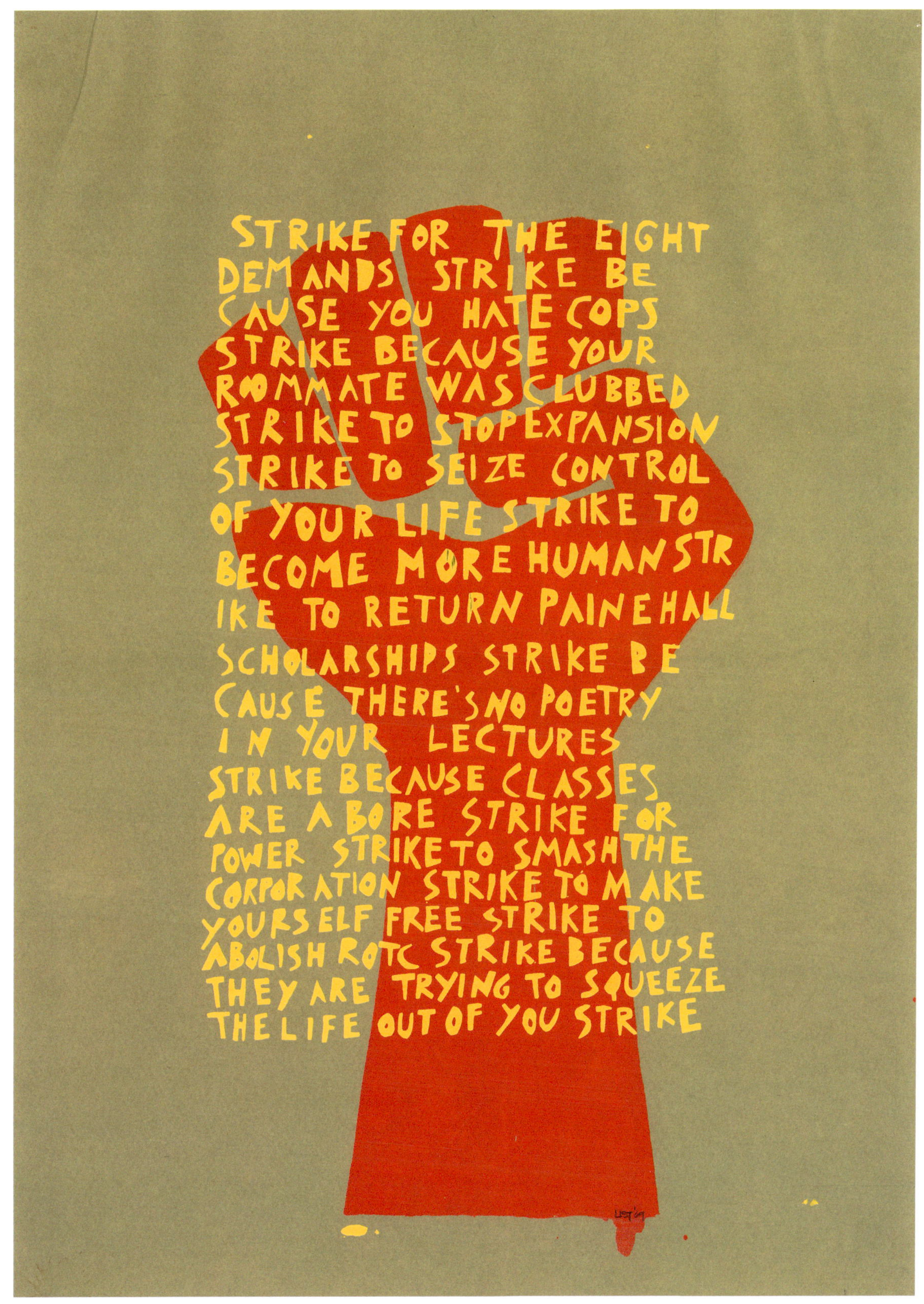


**Silk screen print.** Strike Poster Workshop, Graduate School of Design, Harvard University. *Strike for the Eight Demands.* 1969. 21½ x 15¾ in. (54.6 x 40 cm)

## 4.3 MODERN STONE LITHOGRAPHY

Invented at the end of the eighteenth century, stone lithography rapidly reached a state of technical development that has remained stable ever since. Shortly after the medium's invention it became a printing system for illustrated newspaper work, and later on was used to make art prints. In the twentieth century those jobs were taken over by high-speed processes, first letterpress and then photo offset (which applies the lithographic principle to flexible metal plates). Surprisingly, lithography in its older, stone-based form has survived: it is still around because it has become a primary tool for artists' printmaking.

Like the etching plate, the stone surface used in lithography can accept direct drawing by the artist. "Transfer" papers are made that allow a drawing on paper to be transferred to the stone, but all through the twentieth century and still today, artists have worked right on the stones to make terrific prints. The presses are expensive, the stones heavy, and the chemistry moderately dangerous, so artists rarely set up their own shops; instead they work in specialized ateliers, where all the equipment is available, along with technical help. Lithography also crops up in educational printshops in art schools and college art departments, where students can use the tools under the direction of a teacher. Even as digital methods are making their inroads into art education we still find students drawing directly on the stone surfaces to make prints.

The interesting thing that we see here is the artist's way of hanging onto old technologies after their glory years are over. Woodblock printing, engraving, etching, lithography, and even the more basic picture-making practices of drawing and painting—all of these technologies were tremendously influential in their day, but each has moved away from the broad cultural forefront and shifted over into the narrower realm of art. This is happening now with photography: the new digital methods convey a great deal of photographic description, but they don't look quite like chemical photography, and will look less and less like the chemical forms as digital photography evolves. There will always be artists using the earlier technology in vital and effective ways, to make pictures that simply can't be produced with the new methods. Art is like some sort of backward country where old cars are sent to be kept running indefinitely, while modern times and new models race on ahead elsewhere.

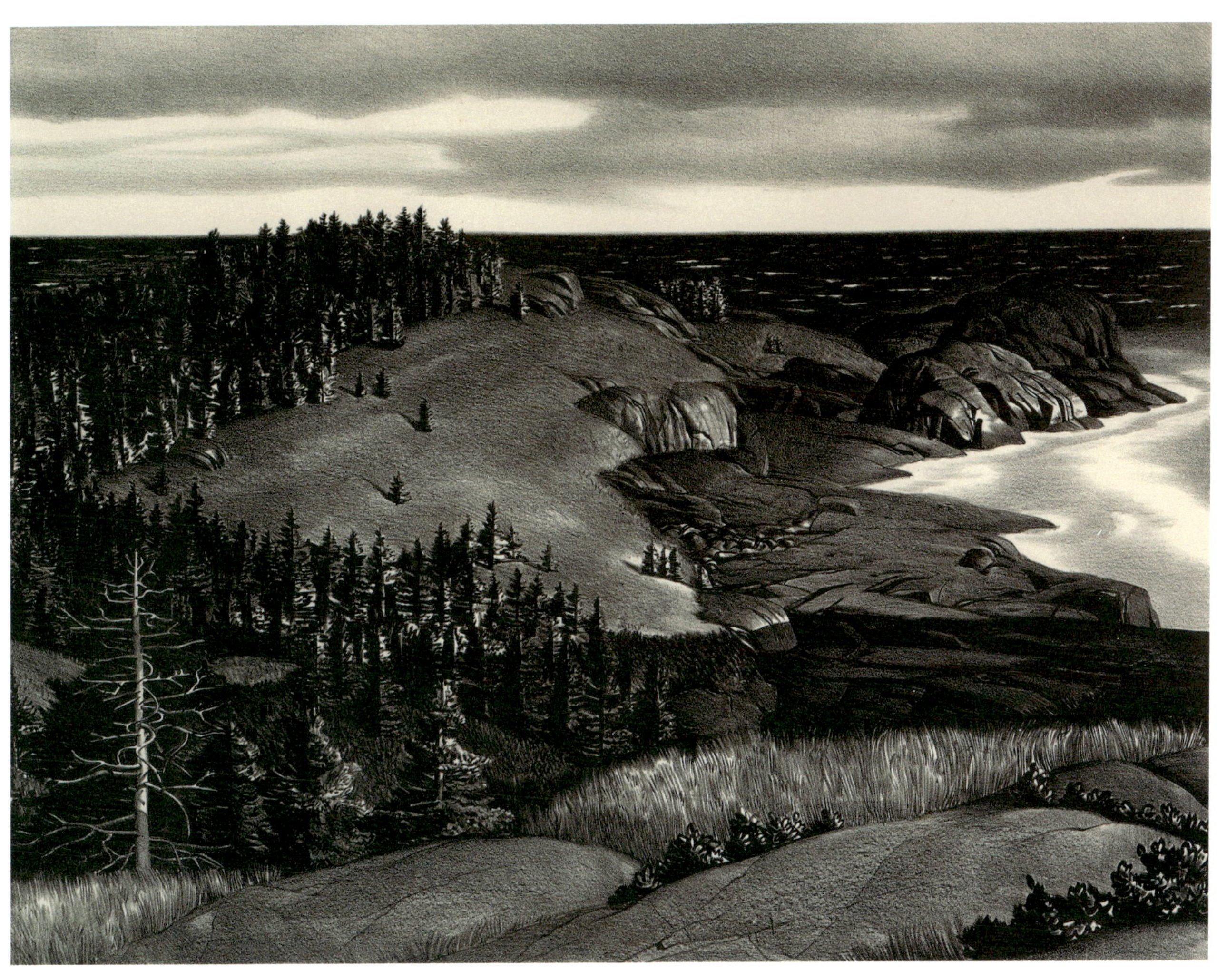

**Stone lithograph.** Stow Wengenroth. *Monhegan, Maine.* 1938. 11½ x 15 in. (29.2 x 38.1 cm)

## 4.4 MODERN ETCHING

This is an etching made by my friend Sam Messer, who teaches at the Yale University School of Art. The print uses linear etching, drawn in the resist with a needle and then chemically etched, but also has large areas of aquatint, creating the darkness in the background and between the typewriter keys. Sam teaches painting and printmaking and after hours goes into the printshop at the School, where students are doing projects, and works alongside them making pictures for himself. Art education is a tough thing to do well and many of us in that trade think this is the best (and perhaps only) really good way to teach: to make your own art along with the students, so they come to understand the process as a whole, and can see the complex physical and intellectual activity needed in such work. I don't raise this subject here to praise Sam, but instead to point out that there are two very different ways in which artists practice printmaking today.

The old technologies have survived in schools and privately run workshops, but their technical demands are so intimidating (and dirty) that many artists have chosen to leave that side of the activity to hired professionals. The artist goes to the shop, draws on the plate or stone, and then watches while the skilled technician does the chemical and physical work of producing the print. By engaging in printmaking this way the work can have a physical perfection and slickness not available to most artists who might do the work themselves. But working this way also tends—I believe—to sterilize the work, eliminating all those delights that occur when the holder of the artistic vision skates close to the edge of physical disaster while driving a recalcitrant medium in unexpected directions.

Artistic printmaking is a big business; successful artists working with professional ateliers can generate large incomes for themselves and their marketers. The work will be technically perfect—appropriate for a grand living room wall—and will spread the artist's work far and wide, making multiple copies available at a modest cost compared to that of an original painting. Whatever we think of this practice, it is one of the primary engines that preserves the old technologies long after they have outlived their original uses. Even so, those atelier-produced prints are the antithesis of the one we see here, derived entirely from the hand of the artist himself.

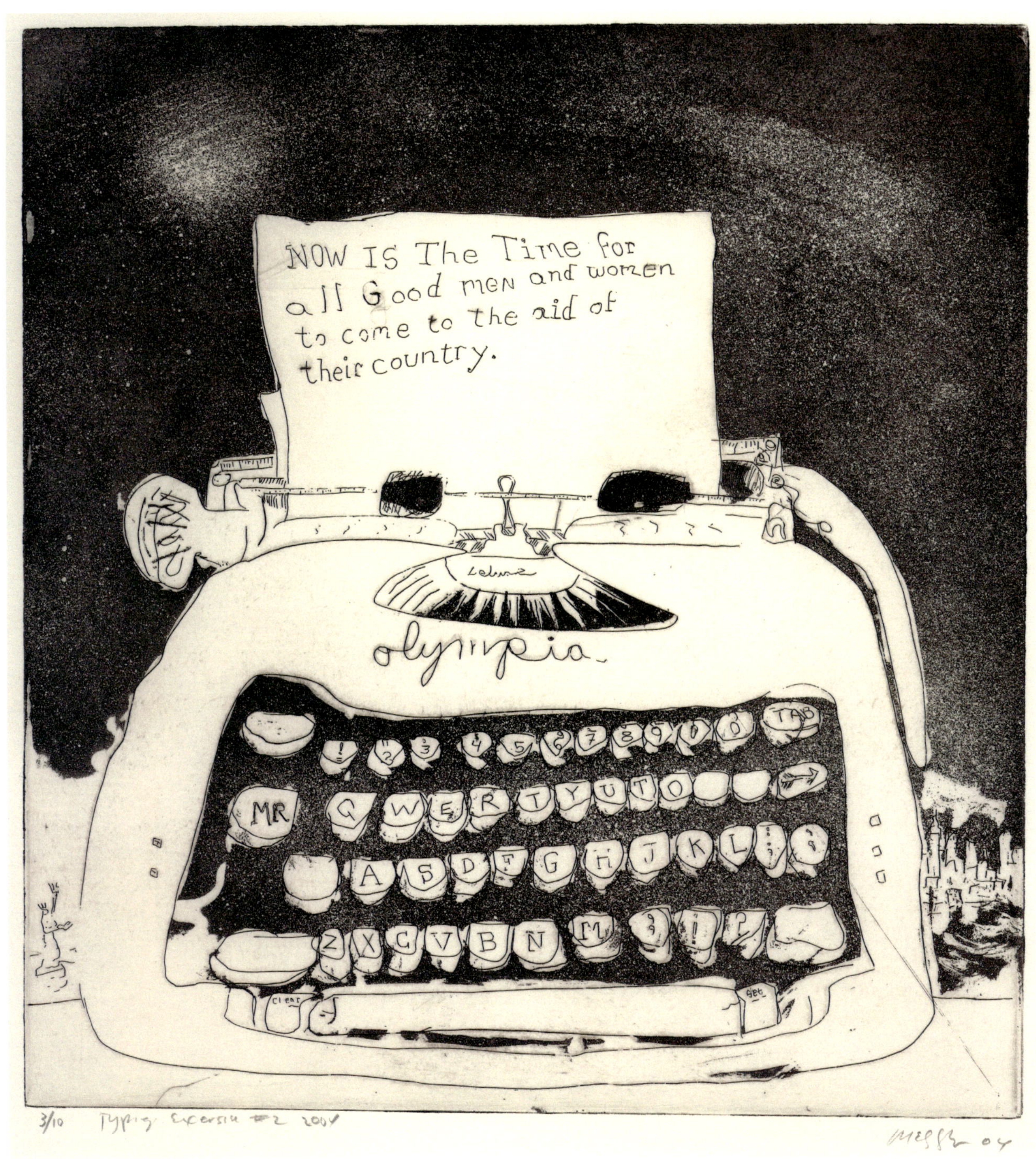


**Etching with aquatint.** Sam Messer. *Typing Exercise #2.* 2004. 11 x 10⅛ in. (27.9 x 25.7 cm)

## 4.5 THE TYPEWRITER

In the nineteenth century the metal type used in letterpress printing was stored in specialized cases that allowed the typesetter to pick out letters without having to look at each one as it was chosen. The process of setting type this way was rapid but still extremely time-consuming, and for many years attempts were made to invent a machine with a keyboard that could reduce the labor of typesetting by hand. Two such machines finally appeared. The first one, called the Linotype, was invented in about 1890, and it cast lines of metal type by using a keyboard to access individual letter molds, which were assembled, clamped, and used to cast a line of letters. The second machine, invented slightly later, was called the Monotype, and it too cast type, but did so by rapidly creating molds for individual letters that could be cast and locked up in a form. The Monotype used a keyboard to punch paper tape, which in turn passed the letter-sequence information to the type-caster. The paper ribbon of the Monotype machine was closely related to the data cards that ran the Jacquard looms of the time, which could be "programmed" to weave a pattern; both of these punched objects were binary data systems. Neither the Linotype nor the Monotype actually took letters out of a type case and then set them — in both cases it proved easier to arrange molds and cast fresh type. One beauty of these new methods was that the type, once used, could simply be melted down into slugs of metal that could later be recast into new letters. This procedure avoided the labor of replacing used type back into its case.

Keyboard-driven relief letters also turned up in the typewriter. This versatile machine was invented in the nineteenth century, when it started out looking very much like a piano. It has always seemed to me to be a vital and useful branch of printing's evolutionary tree that sprouted, flourished for a century or so, and then died without any real descendants. The keyboard has hung around as a useful data interface between the human mind and the computer, and even performs similar functions to the typewriter when used for word processing, but the old typewriter, with a set of keys each holding a metal letter, has disappeared. When coupled with carbon paper these machines, which ultimately were compact and inexpensive, could make multiple copies that were perfectly suited for the bureaucratic tasks to which they were applied. Typewriter letters struck the paper through an inked ribbon, which meant the letters themselves never became clogged with ink. Toward the end, typewriters were electric, and the later models even had digital memories, which allowed them to produce editions printed in crisp carbon-black letters, each showing the imprint of the keys, to convince the readers that the missive was unique and typed out for their use alone. Even these fancy models were swept away in the computer revolution.

-2-

October 30, 1974
Rt. #3, Box 610
Madison Hts, Va.
24572

Dear Mr. Feltham:

I have decided to part with some more of my whistle collection and thought I would write you first, since you have bought from me before. I plan to have 1000 listings printed soon and these will be circulated throughout the country, to mostly NRHS members, but also well known whistle collectors and museums and the like. Some of these whistles have already been sold, but the collection must be reduced in size as I need the added space. So I am personally writing 25 of the fellows prior to mailing of the lists. Here is what I have to offer.

NATHAN 6" diam. 3-chime, all brass, heavily built, nicely cleaned, no valve, from NYO&W loco. Can probably get valve. Nice acorn on flat top. $325.00

AMERICAN 6" diam. 3-chime, all brass, nicely polished, flat top with fancy acorn, no valve. From NYC RR K class 4-6-2, very nice steamboat tone. $325.00.

SOUTHERN RY 6" diam. 3-chime, super tall, 30 1/4" high, 78 LB weight, all brass except the highly desired top lever mount feature, best of the valve types, is from SRY engine #1402, only 10 such engines built and these whistles were built by SRY, wall thickness on bell is 5/16", bell alone is 48 LB bronze, very, very beautiful tantalizing tone that will start out with a whisper and go up to a beautiful crescendo and leave ones emotions to the wildest imagination. A very rare and highly sought after whistle. Only 10 built and 5 are known to have been melted down at the old Spencer, N.C. shops in the early 1950's. Mine was a personal gift to a friend of mine, presented by former Pres. of SRY, Harry de Butts who is still living. Engine was of the beautiful green and gold PS-4 class 4-6-2 that pulled the Crescent Limited, Tennessean, Pelican and other named trains. Due to the origin and circumstances of this rare and perfect item, I will be interested in offers. One man has a standing offer of $750 on it, but I paid more than that for it in 1969 and would pay gladly that much to get another if I wanted and could find another. I feel that many of the museums around, would be greatful to add this to their collection, but if we can keep it out of museum hands, then it will not be gone forever. This is probably the largest loco whistle ever put in service, at least it is the tallest I have seen and the arches are nicely shaped.

Caliope whistle: 3-tubes, each different length, each tube 1 1/8" diam, hand made by old engineer from West Va. Tube lengths are: 11 1/4", 9 5/8" and 7 3/4", each capped with dome top, all fastened to a very unuqie shaped cast bowl especially made for these 3 tubes, 3/4" inlet and separate but included 3/4" whistle valve. Overall height with valve is approx; 18" high, very, very beautiful tone. Each tube is made from small boiler flue tubes, sprayed 5 coats of heavy duty Dupont gold that is very pretty, not gaudy as many gold paints are. An ususnal whistle that really sings a song, price including valve is only $80. A real bargain and will go quickly.

Another unusual whistle, 2 1/2" diameter, bell is 12 5/8" high, separate but included valve, with overall height of about 18", is a brass 4-chime, of most beautiful tone that sounds more like a 4" diameter whistle, nice valve and has been cleaned up, still needs minor buffing, but very nice, with valve $90.00.

Still another rare type unusual whistle. This is a "tee" shaped one with 2 bells of 2 1/2" diameter, each bell is diff. length, for two chime, all brass and the bells lay horizonal and feed from central bowl that has spreader plate on each side, with valve and is beautifully polished like a mirrior, two acorns, all is brass and blows a very beautiful tone. Can be adjusted to blow from 2 LB to 150 LB PSI, a very versatile and old whistle. Overall length is 17", overall height is 7". Price with valve included is $125.00. At these prices, all should go

(OVER)----

**Typewriter.** L. G. Simpson. Letter to David Feltham. 1974. 11 x 8½ in. (28 x 21.6 cm). Every letter in the typewriter responds to the impulse of a struck key. When the area covered by a letter is small, as in a period or comma, the impact is great and so the impression strong; when large, such as in the letter "m," the impact is diffused and the impression is lighter.

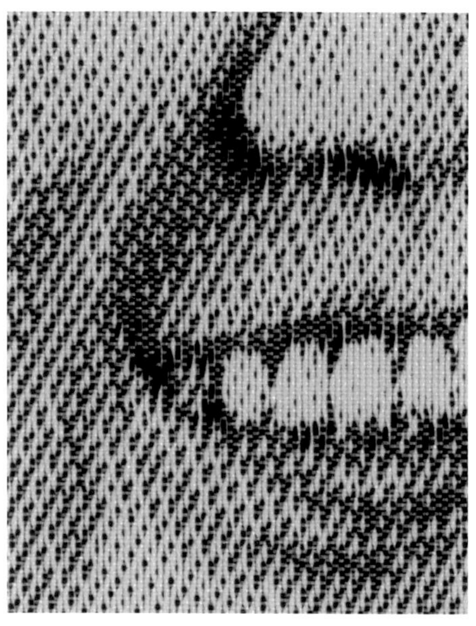

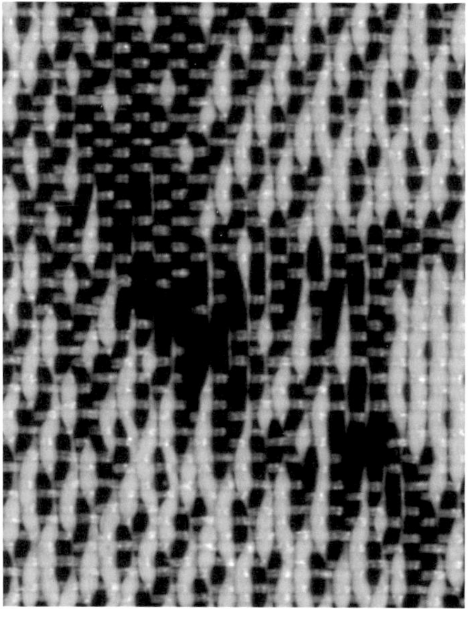

The delicate threads of the warp run horizontally, while the thicker (and thus visually dominating) threads of the weft run vertically.

## 4.6 WEAVING

This piece of cloth, shown from both front and back, is a picture of Chairman Mao. Probably woven in the 1980s, it is full of lessons about printing and photography, and even though it is modern its lessons are of such importance that I am showing it here, early on in the book, out of any reasonable chronological sequence.

First of all, it is a piece of weaving that holds a representational picture. Pictures of all kinds—representational, decorative, symbolic—have long appeared in weaving, but this one was made with a Jacquard-type loom, a loom driven by punch cards that translated the tones of the image into patterns of stitches displaying values from dark to light. Invented at the start of the nineteenth century, these looms are the first known practical instance of binary numerical data being applied to a visual end. The one that wove this was already obsolete when it did its weaving.

Chairman Mao might be made of threads woven into cloth, but he unquestionably started out as a photograph. This is the second lesson from this weaving. We have not yet examined photography in this book, but from the start we should understand that the description of the world made by lens and camera is radically unlike that of traditional artists. When a portrait painter made a picture of a famous figure, the form and content of the picture inevitably revealed what was thought about the subject—what the artist, the sitter, or both wished to have projected to the viewing audience. Photography, on the other hand, makes its pictures out of reality, and brings to the viewer objects and structures whose description is far from the traditional ideals. Mao's pudgy hands, the tabletop on which they rest, and the inactive pencil were the photographer's props, but their appearance comes from the world itself, without the embellishments of traditional art. We must not confuse a photograph with the world from which it is made, but there is little question that photography's connection to that world gives it a radically new visual character when compared to the old handmade pictures.

The third lesson comes from the back of the cloth. The weaving was done with two sets of threads in the weft: one black, the other white. Tones were made by grouping stitches in a grid and controlling the amount of white and black shown in any given grid area. The interesting thing is that as white threads were shown on the front, the black threads had to move to the back, and vice versa. So the positive image on the front generated a negative one on the back. This is a beautiful way to see the relationship between positive and negative: if you have an even tonal field and remove a positive picture from it, a reversed negative image remains. Almost all color photography would end up using this principle to generate positive images in one step.

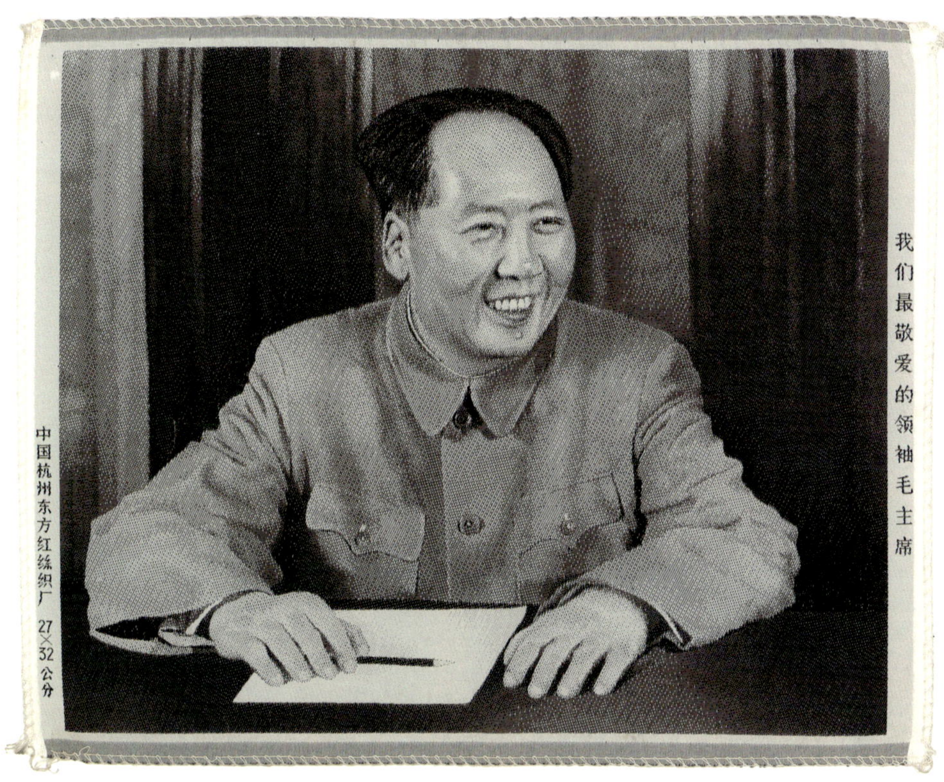


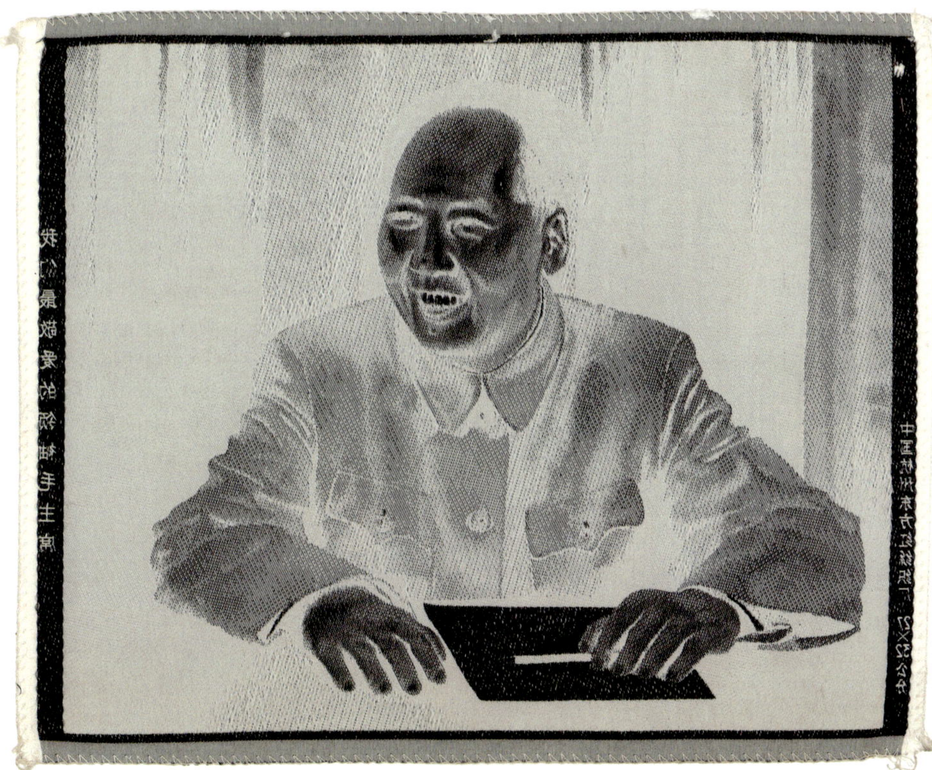

**Weaving.** Photographer unknown. *Chairman Mao.* c. 1950. 11¼ x 14⅛ in. (28.5 x 35.8 cm). Print: this textile was probably made in the 1980s by the Chinese company Silk Line. I purchased it on Canal Street in New York City.

## 4.7 RUBBINGS

The mechanically derived picture was an age-old pursuit. The ultimate solution was photography, in which light itself formed the image, but long before that medium's invention there were attempts to somehow make pictures without having to learn to draw. The problem here was to find a physical analog—some structure that mimics the modulations of another—for the object being copied. (For the baby boomers among us the most common analogs used to be the old vinyl records; the wiggles and ups-and-downs of the groove on each side of the record imitated the frequency and intensity levels of the recorded music.) Three-dimensional analogs could be made from the earliest years of civilization, by casting objects: a mold could perfectly imitate the form of the original, and multiple copies could be made easily. The most common of these was and is the building block, cast from a fabricated mold to imitate the carved stone blocks of earlier times. Copying two-dimensional pictures proved to be far more complex. There were many efforts to find pictorial analogs, and this small section of the book describes a few of them.

The most basic pictorial analog is the rubbing. Since I come from a stone-carving family I can't resist illustrating one made from an early American tombstone. The letters and floral border are beautifully described, and the picture has that marvelous characteristic of only showing part of the original, like some Greek sculptural fragment where the arms and head tantalize us with their absence. This sheet also has a great patina of brown spots running across the surface and there is even a large water stain on the bottom edge. All in all it makes a great picture, and does so by transmitting information from the original carved stone into a new context: the meaningless degradation of the paper support. The artists among us should always be cautious about letting such beautiful haphazard patterns coexist with intended meaning.

Rubbings are extremely easy to make. This one was done by holding a soft sheet of paper against the vertical stone and then rubbing the paper surface with a block of black cobbler's wax called "heel ball." Multiple rubbings aren't too good for the object underneath, but if the work is done with soft ink-bearing pads, virtually no harm is done to the original. A few artists use rubbing as their medium, laying down different colors with different pressures to make rich renditions that owe as much of their content to manual skill as to the mechanical transmission of information from one form to another.

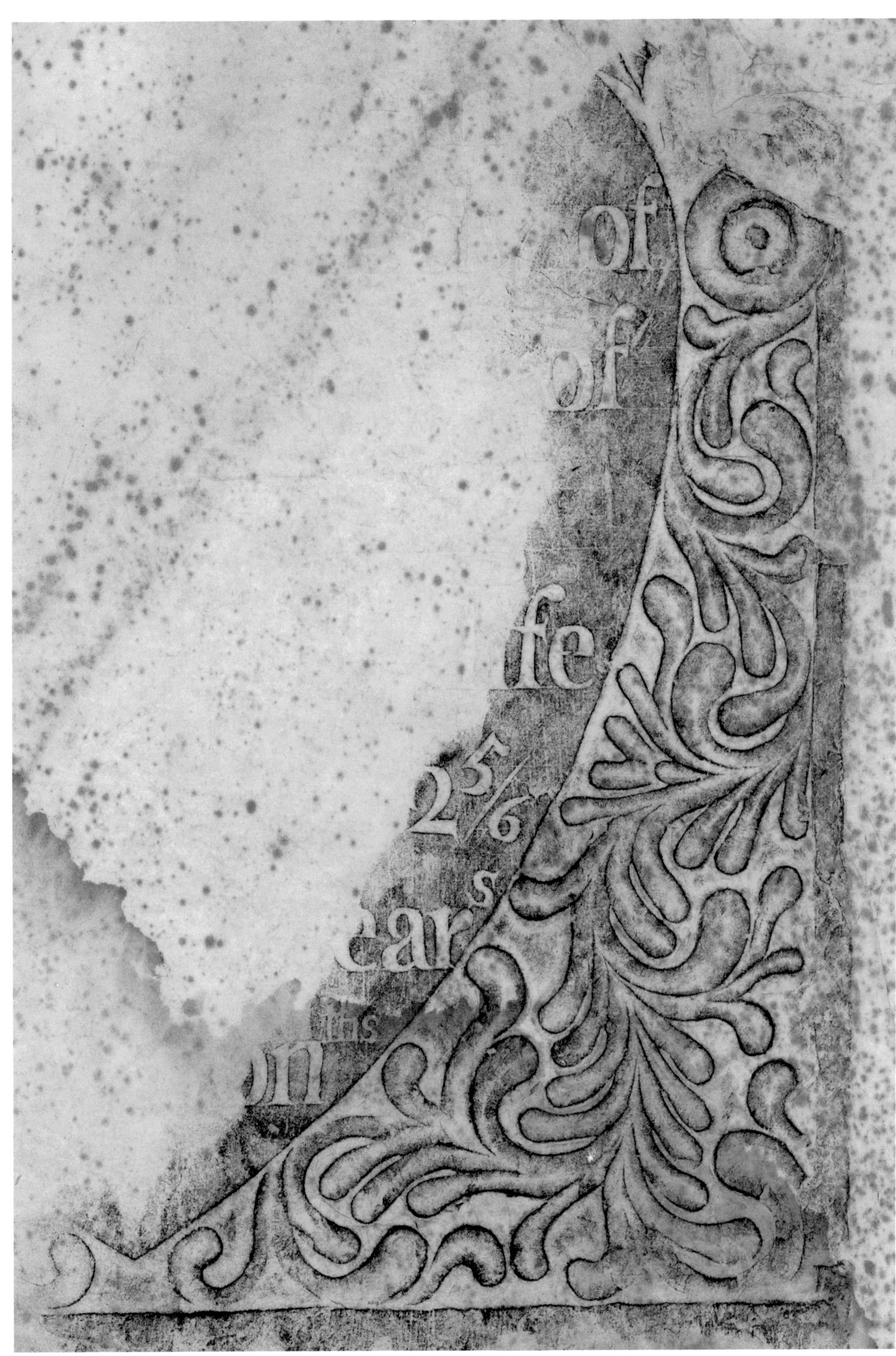

**Rubbing.** John Stevens. Decorative tombstone border carved in slate. c. 1715. Print: John Howard Benson. c. 1940. 17½ x 11¼ in. (44.5 x 28.6 cm)

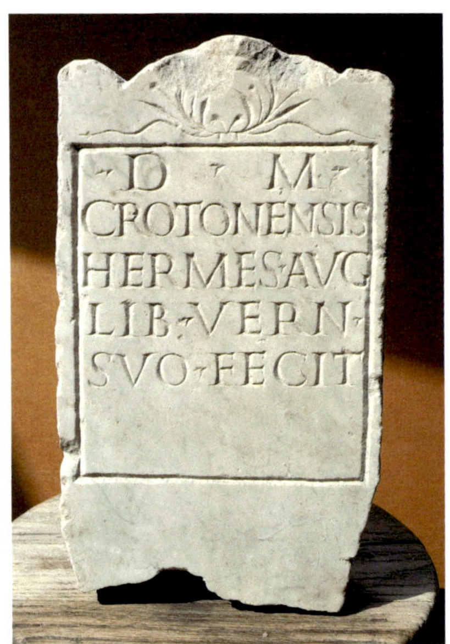


A modern photograph of the stone.

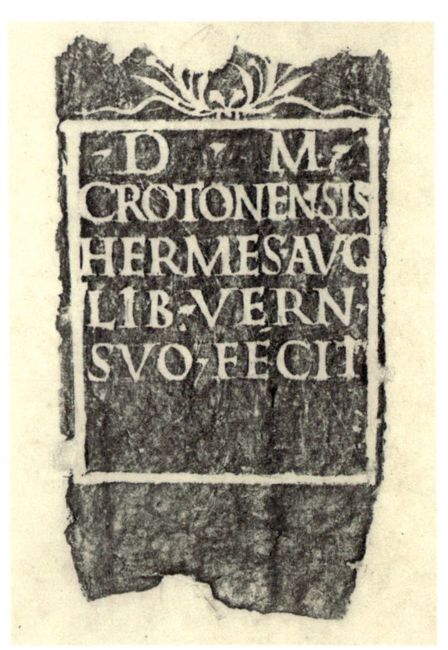


A rubbing of the stone.

## 4.8 THE SQUEEZE

The greatest inscribed letters were made in Rome during the days of empire. Later carvers were anxious to have models of those letters, and made rubbings and even in some cases plaster casts of formal inscriptions. One technique that developed for copying inscriptions was the squeeze. I only include this truly obscure process because I am aware of it from my stone-cutting background, but it is interesting and yet another method for making a mechanical picture.

I need to admit right away that the squeeze is actually a form of casting, but one that leaves no mess, works vertically, and doesn't damage the original. Squeezes are made by soaking a sheet of thin tissue (usually Japanese, with a good tacky sizing), laying the damp paper over the original, and beating it into the letters with a brush. The brush looks like a wide, flat dust brush, with horsehair bristles set to stick out at right angles to the handle. Once the tissue is beaten down onto the stone, another is laid on top of it, beaten, and so on until a dozen or so have been applied. Then the thick stack of tissues is pulled off, turned face up, and laid on a blotter to dry. The sizing on the paper glues the sheets together, and the thin pieces of tissue, deformed by the beating of the brush, retain the full depth of the letters. The squeeze is really a form of papier-mâché.

Squeezes have the nice characteristic of bringing the low parts of the letters up to the top—the sharp interiors of the V-shaped cuts stand up. The one we see here is from a Roman stone 1,800 years old. The piece of marble is heavily worn, but the bottoms of the V's are as sharp as the day they were made. They stand up out of the surface of the squeeze and give new life to this old piece of work.

In the early days of photography, Roman inscriptions were often photographed as a way of making a record of the carving. In one famous case, the only capital M in the inscription was in a corner, where the primitive camera lens distorted the image, curving the letter's stems. Modern carvers copied this flawed photograph slavishly, producing a whole generation of curved M's. A decent squeeze would have avoided this misinterpretation.

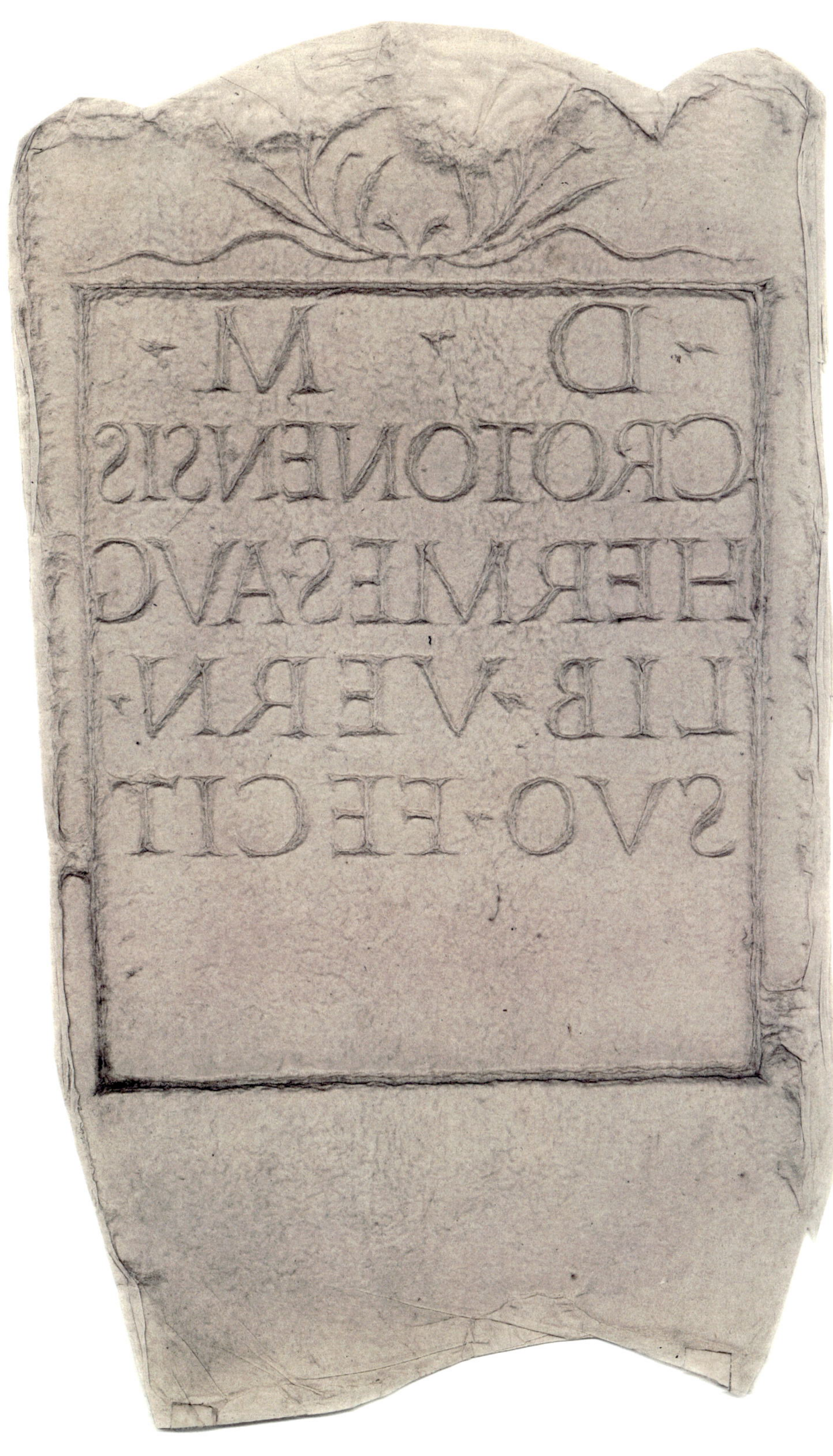


**Squeeze.** Memorial inscription. c. 200 A.D. Print: John Everett Benson. c. 1985. 14¾ x 8¾ in. (37.5 x 22.2 cm). A relief impression in Japanese tissue.

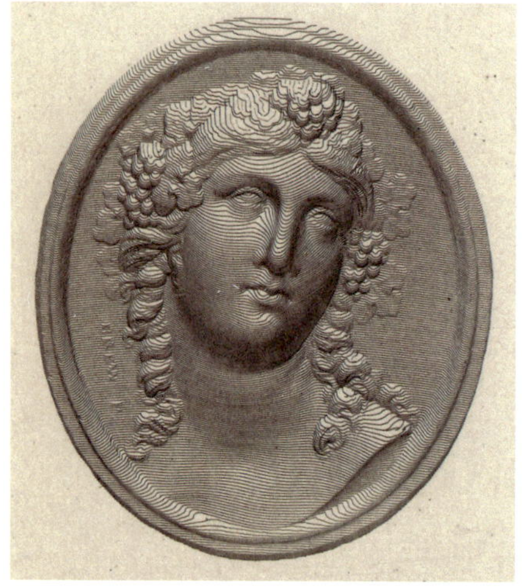

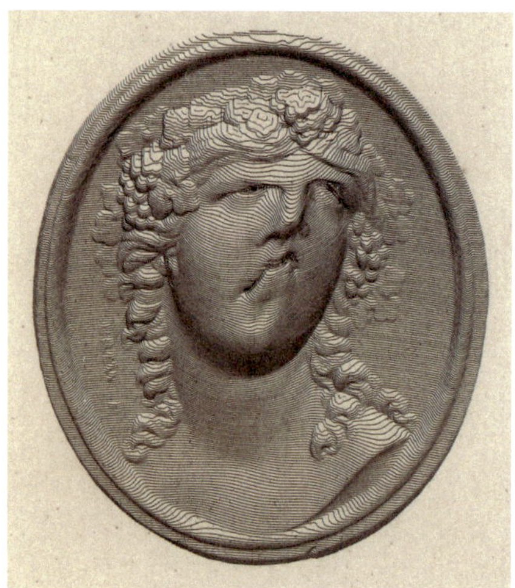

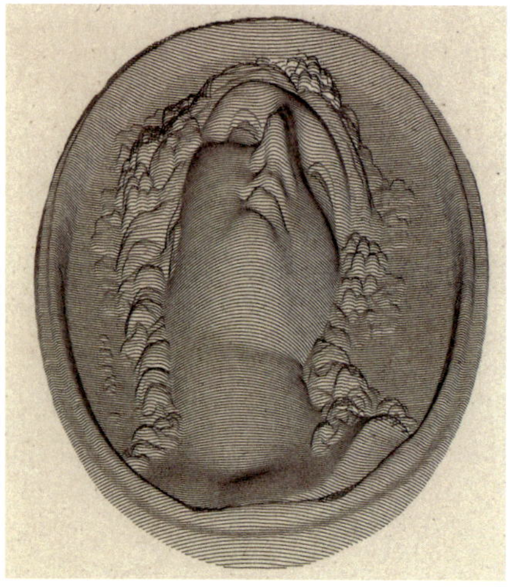

The lower two of these details show etchings made from the medal at the top, with the pantograph settings altered to emulate changes of perspective, as though the viewer were looking at the original medal from different points of view.

## 4.9 PANTOGRAPH ETCHINGS

The nineteenth century was the age of commemorative relief medals. They were made to honor notable occasions and famous people, and were cast in multiple copies of great precision and beauty. I came across a book of extraordinary etchings made from these medals, and include one here because the etched printing plates were generated mechanically from the medal's relief modulations.

The work was done with a pantograph, a mechanical device that uses a series of bars on pivots to trace forms and produce analogs of them in different sizes. Pantographs were used in silhouette-making, and to reduce or enlarge drawings and sculptural work. In this particular case the pantograph was asked to translate the vertical modulations of the medal's surface into variously spaced lines scored in an etching ground. One end of the pantograph ran over the medal and was constrained to run in a straight line only. In the background of the print, showing the flat part of the medal, vertical, close, evenly spaced parallel lines produced the effect of an even tone. When the operator raised the tracing stylus by moving it over the relief section of the medal, the line being drawn in the etching ground by the other end of the pantograph was shifted slightly to the right (actually to the left, because the print is reversed). By running the stylus repeatedly across the medal's surface, and shifting each line minutely forward from the one before, the printer drew a topographical map of the medal on the prepared plate surface. Once etched, this plate could be inked, wiped, and printed to produce the picture we see here.

It is a remarkable process, and only understandable by looking at highly magnified sections. The changing spacing between the lines causes a lightening in areas that rise up on the left of the print; as the form begins to fall off on the right side, the line spacing is reduced and the tone darkens. The increasing and diminishing of the line spaces is perfect, so that the flat surround retains its even gray tone even while the lightening of the head on one side is perfectly compensated for by a darkening on the other. The viewer's impression is that the medal has been lit from the left side—an apparently perfect lighting, coming not from one point but from parallel rays skating at a low angle across the surface of the medal.

This technique turns up occasionally in art prints and currency, but it is rare, and it is always a delight to find it in unexpected places. Plate 3.3 shows an example of it on the left-hand side of the ten-dollar bill.

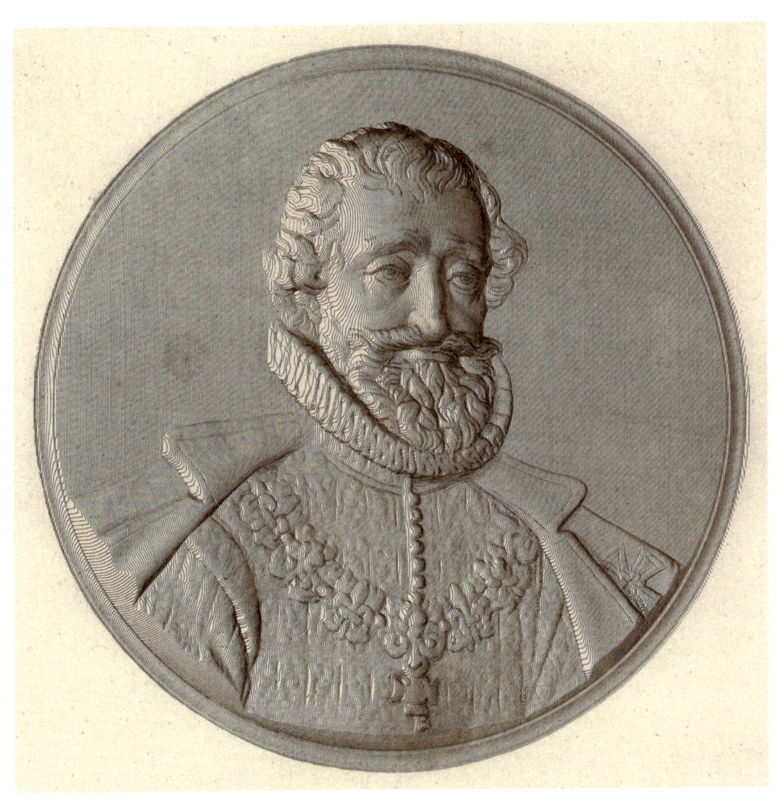

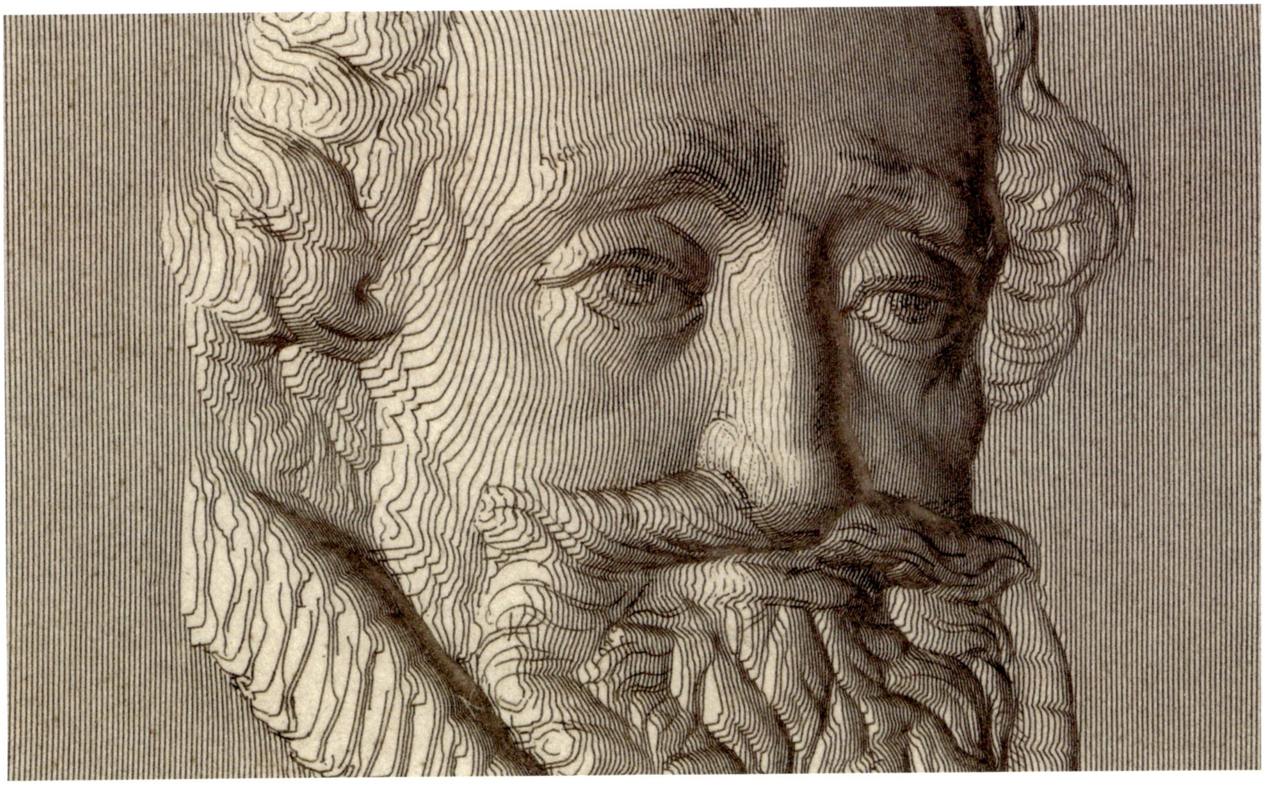

**Etching.** Artist unknown. *The Head of Henry IV.* n.d. Relief medallion. Print: Achille Colas. Pantographically derived etching. 1837. 3¾ x 3¾ in. (9.5 x 9.5 cm). From "Answer to Mr. Bate's Challenge," *Literary Gazette* no. 1047 (London), February 11, 1837.

## 4.10 SILHOUETTES

The life-sized silhouette of Phebe Hough opposite and above was made in 1856 in Philadelphia, Pennsylvania, by Anna Wharton, who signed it with her initials. For much of the previous century, the cutting of silhouettes had been a pastime at parties and family gatherings. They were made through the use of light, by tracing the shadow of a person's profile. The traditional way to do it was to have the subject sit with a book, or some like-shaped object, pressed between their head and the wall, and with a piece of paper between their head and the book. The book both supported the piece of paper and served the useful role of keeping the subject from moving. A candle across the room cast a shadow; this outline was traced, the paper was removed, and the silhouette was cut out from it with scissors. Multiple copies were often made so that everyone could take the pictures home with them as mementos. In viewing a silhouette, we are most often looking at negative space—not the positive figure but the white paper from which it has been cut, and which is set against a sheet of black paper.

Although this picture-making practice goes back into the eighteenth century, well before the invention of photography, the pictures it produced have always seemed to me as photographic as anything else: they record the actual form of the subject, and it is very easy to identify silhouettes of those one knows. In the eighteenth and nineteenth centuries, silhouettes of full-length figures were made, not based on the tracing of light but cut by eye. Similar silhouette-making is done today at carnivals and tourist destinations, with the maker usually just looking at the person to be depicted and then cutting a reduced-size silhouette directly. This method is closer to caricature than to photography, since the outline comes from an image in the maker's mind, rather than being generated by some mechanical means from the subject itself.

Silhouettes were also made with a pantograph, which could trace the person's actual profile in a reduced size. The pair shown here come from an album put together in the early nineteenth century in Philadelphia. Most of the album's silhouettes were cut at the Peale Museum in that city, and bear a small blind stamp identifying that source. The subject's profile was traced by a metal stylus in a pantograph machine, which drew a reduced-size silhouette on a piece of paper. This small outline was then cut by hand, at which point such small embellishments as Mr. Morton's lock of hair were added. Friends exchanged these beautiful little silhouettes, and put them in albums, in exactly the same way that we put away family snapshots today.

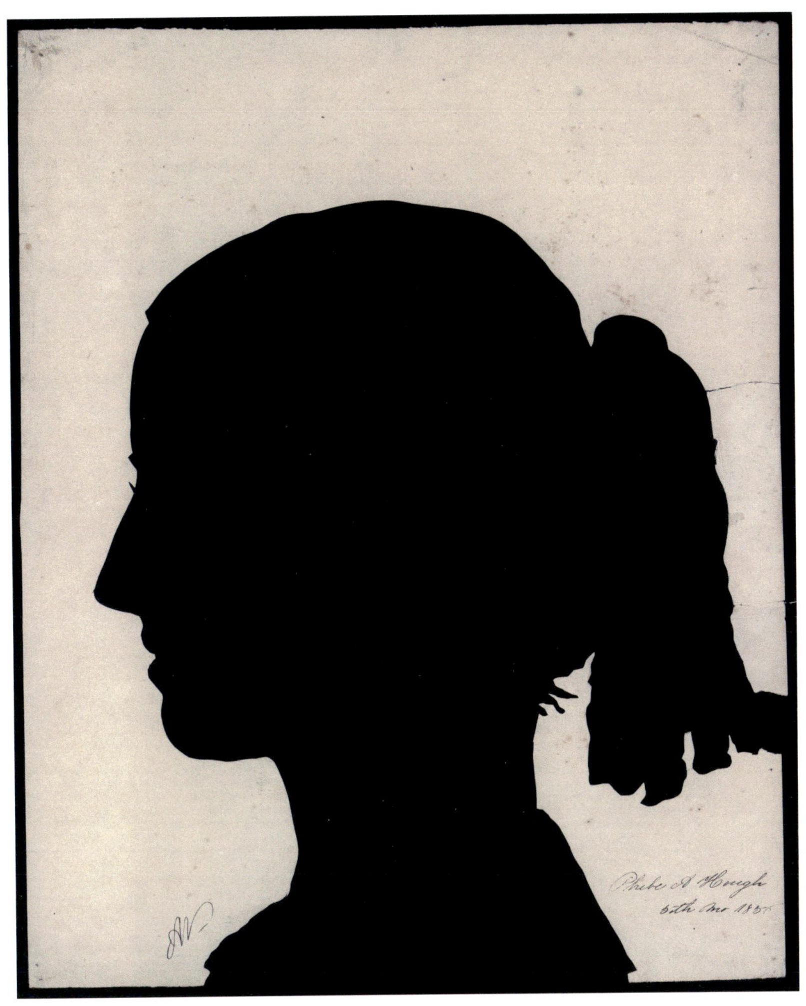


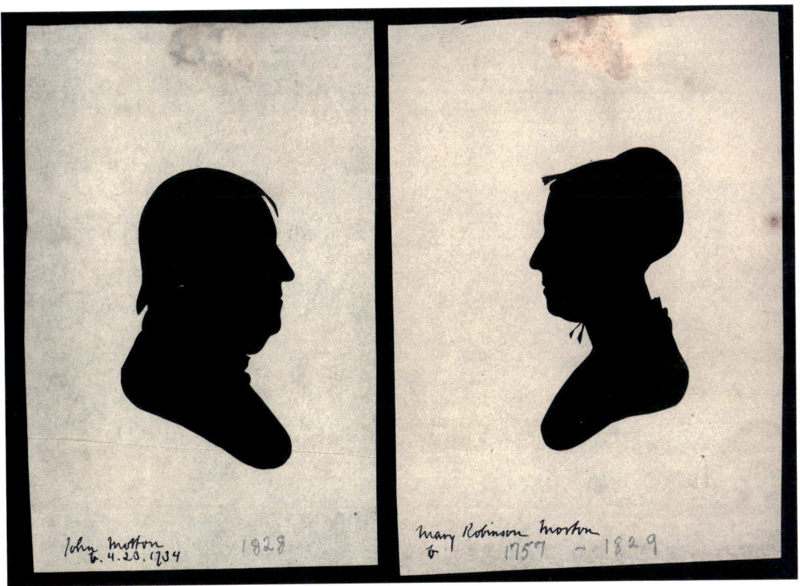


**Silhouettes.** Top: Anna Wharton. *Phebe A. Hough.* 1856. 15½ x 12¾ in. (39.4 x 32.4 cm). Bottom: Peale Museum. *John Morton and Mary Robinson Morton.* c. 1795. Black paper support: 5½ x 7¼ in. (14 x 18.4 cm). The two small silhouettes, from Anna Wood's album of profiles, are approximately one-sixth life size.

# Part 5

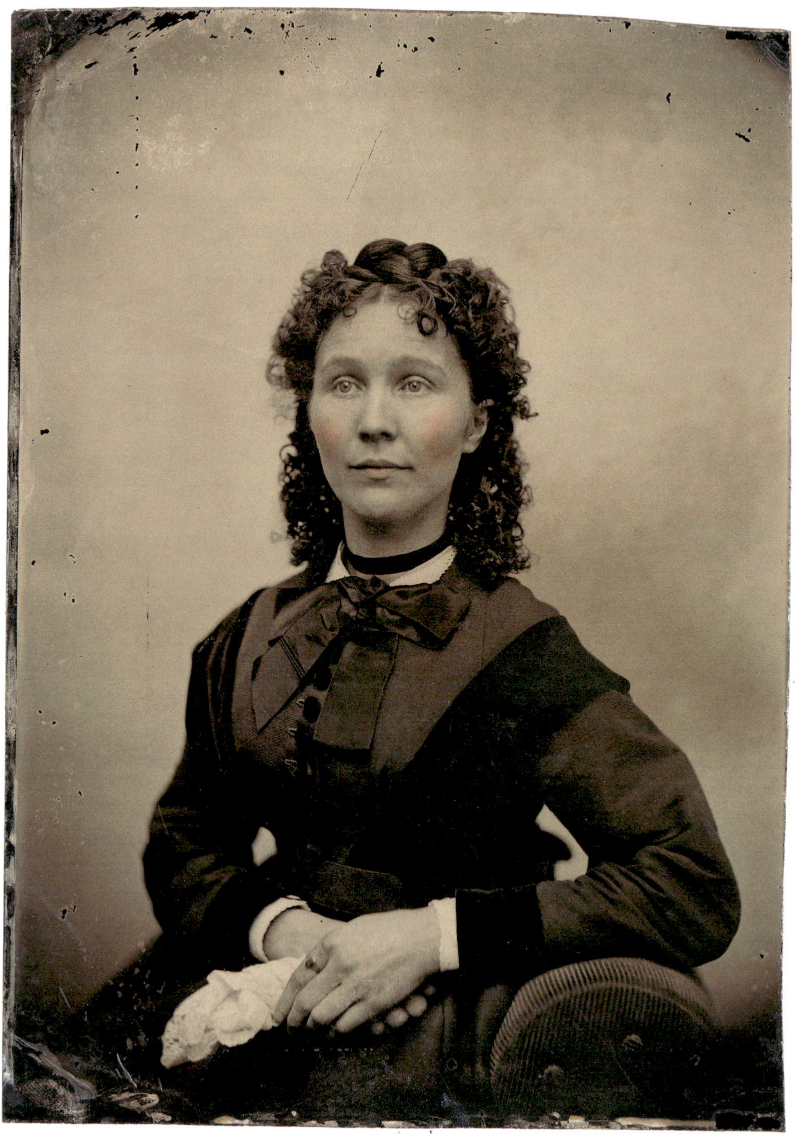

This section concerns itself with silver-based photography in the nineteenth century. Silver was the capture medium, used to gather information in the camera, and it was also used in various printing processes of the time. Other chemical systems used for printing in the early years of photography are dealt with in Part 6.

**Tintype.** Photographer unknown. Portrait of a woman. c. 1895. 9¼ x 6½ in. (23.6 x 16.5 cm)

# Early photography in silver

# Early photography in silver

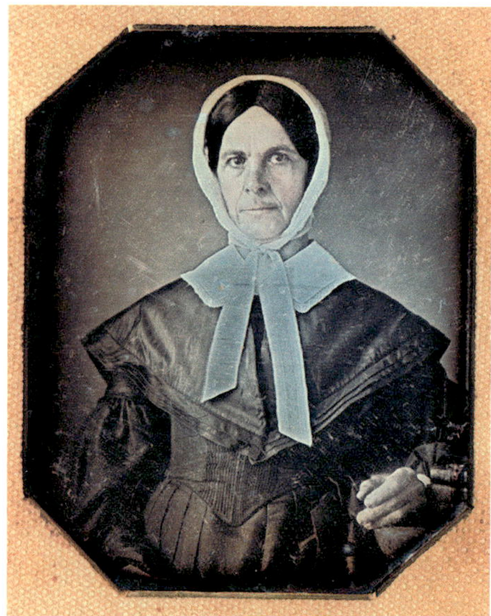

The overwhelming majority of daguerreotypes are anonymous portraits like this one, only three or four inches in height. Recording not only faces but clothing, they give us direct evidence of how people looked and what they wore a hundred and fifty years ago.

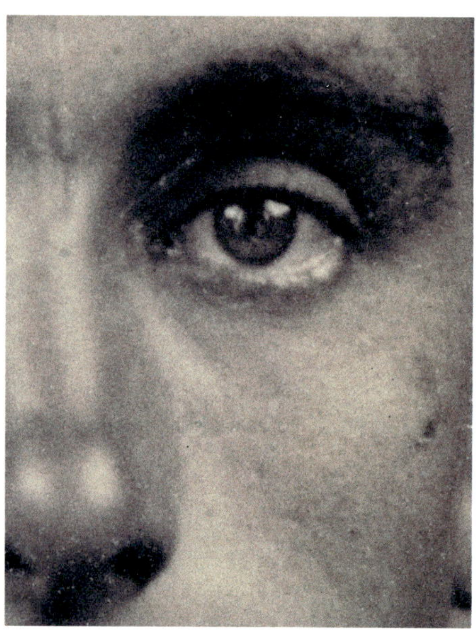

A seven-times enlargement from the original on the right, showing the seamlessness of the daguerreotype's description.

## 5.1 THE DAGUERREOTYPE

The invention of photography was formally announced in 1839. During the previous decades, though, many people had worked on the task of capturing an image by the agency of light alone, and as early as 1826, a Frenchman, Joseph Nicéphore Niépce, had made a lens-generated image in hardened asphaltum. What happened in 1839 was that two completely different processes reached a practical state of development that would quickly allow photography to spread throughout society. One method—invented by another Frenchman, Louis Jacques Mandé Daguerre—allowed precise and sharp lens images to be captured on silver-plated sheets of copper. The other method, invented by the Englishman William Henry Fox Talbot, produced rougher images on paper. The history of these inventions has been told many times, and we need not repeat it here, but some extremely interesting technical points should be noted.

All photographic capture methods from 1840 until the development of digital technology depended upon the sensitivity of silver compounds to light. By photographic "capture" I mean the generation of specifically lens-based images. Through the balance of the nineteenth century, many processes evolved for photographic printing, a number of them using not silver but other compounds responsive to the high levels of illumination that could be used to print photographic negatives by contact. But only silver salts were sensitive enough to record the relatively weak light that could pass through an image-forming lens. And even if Niépce's invention came first, it turned out to be a complete dead end for photography per se; his method of hardening a substance by exposure to light was too insensitive for use in a camera. The principle of a light-hardened material would ultimately be the basis of most photographically produced printing plates.

Silver dominated photography for a century and a half, and from the start it exhibited two completely different ways of making images. The first method—in which a silver compound darkens directly as it is exposed—is referred to as "printing out" and was essential to the earliest paper processes. The second—using the ability of some silver compounds to hold a latent image, invisible yet developable—was the basis of the daguerreotype and of all of the glass and film processes that followed. It is of the utmost importance to recognize this miracle of some silver compounds—that they not only respond to light in a manner that can be made permanent, but do so in two radically different ways.

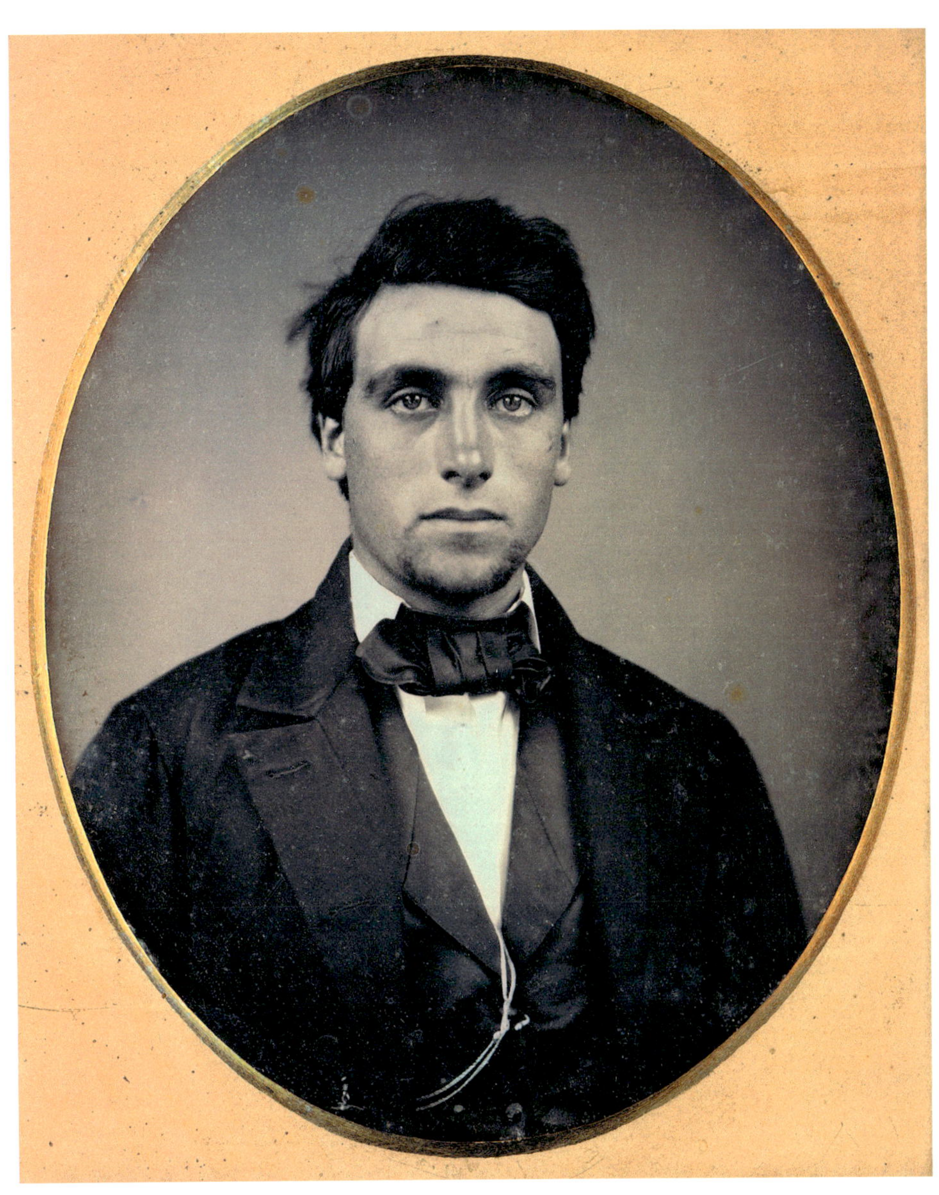

**Daguerreotype.** Photographer unknown. Portrait of a young man. c. 1865. 3 x 2½ in. (7.6 x 6.4 cm)

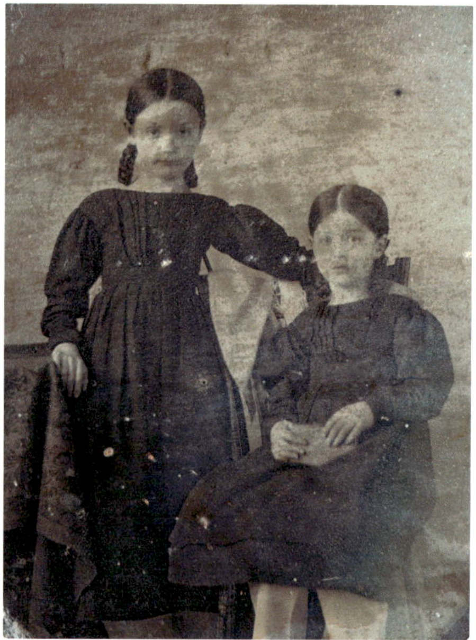

The earliest daguerreotypes were not toned with gold and were pale, cool in color, and fragile. This one, by an anonymous photographer, was made in Philadelphia in June 1843, an extremely early date for an American daguerreotype. On the left it shows Anna Wharton, who twenty-three years later would make the large silhouette shown in plate 4.10.

## 5.2 THE DAGUERREOTYPE

The first practical photographic processes—the daguerreotype and the paper-based method—were at war in early photography. Sharp, clear, and permanent, the daguerreotype was perfection itself, while the paper image was rough, tonally poor, and subject to terrible fading. But paper would win the war, simply because it was cheap, easy to use photographically, and—above all—because it could generate multiple copies by printing a negative more than once. Since the daguerreotype produced a direct, camera-made positive, no negative was available for later printing.

The daguerreotype thrived until the 1860s, then died a slow death, but it has left us with extraordinary images, in many cases as perfect today as when they were made. Daguerreotypes were made by silver-plating a sheet of copper, then treating it with an iodine compound to produce a coating of light-sensitive silver iodide. After exposure the plate was subjected to mercury vapor, which condensed onto the latent image, most thickly where the light had been brightest. When the silver areas in a daguerreotype reflect a dark ground, the mercury appears as diffuse white, producing a positive image. After the formation of the mercury image, the plate was "fixed" with sodium thiosulfate, which photographers nicknamed "hypo." As a final step the pictures were toned with gold, which stabilized them and made the image more robust. Since the metal support did not absorb these destructive fixatives, the daguerreotype avoided the fading that has always plagued paper photography, but all daguerreotypes had to be sealed to prevent tarnishing of the silver coating upon which the mercury image rests. The small frames, glass covers, and cases in which daguerreotypes live add a whole layer of physical protection. Daguerreotypes can easily be mistaken for tintypes, which, whether by accident or intent, are often placed in daguerreotype cases and misidentified in the stores. But daguerreotypes have a brilliant mirror finish and become nearly blank mirrors under bright light—they only show an image when placed so that they reflect from a dark surface. Tintypes and ambrotypes (plates 5.10 and 5.11) look the same regardless of the angle at which they are viewed.

Every daguerreotype is a unique object that once sat in the camera facing the subject of the picture. Pieces of the True Cross of photography, these technological relics bring us as close to the past as any other mnemonic devices that exist. The little girl on the left in the image opposite, Abby Sophia Greene, was born in 1844 and was my maternal great-grandmother. On those rare occasions when I look in a mirror I see this young woman staring back out at me, transformed into an aging hippie with a lucky understanding of his origins that only photography could have brought.

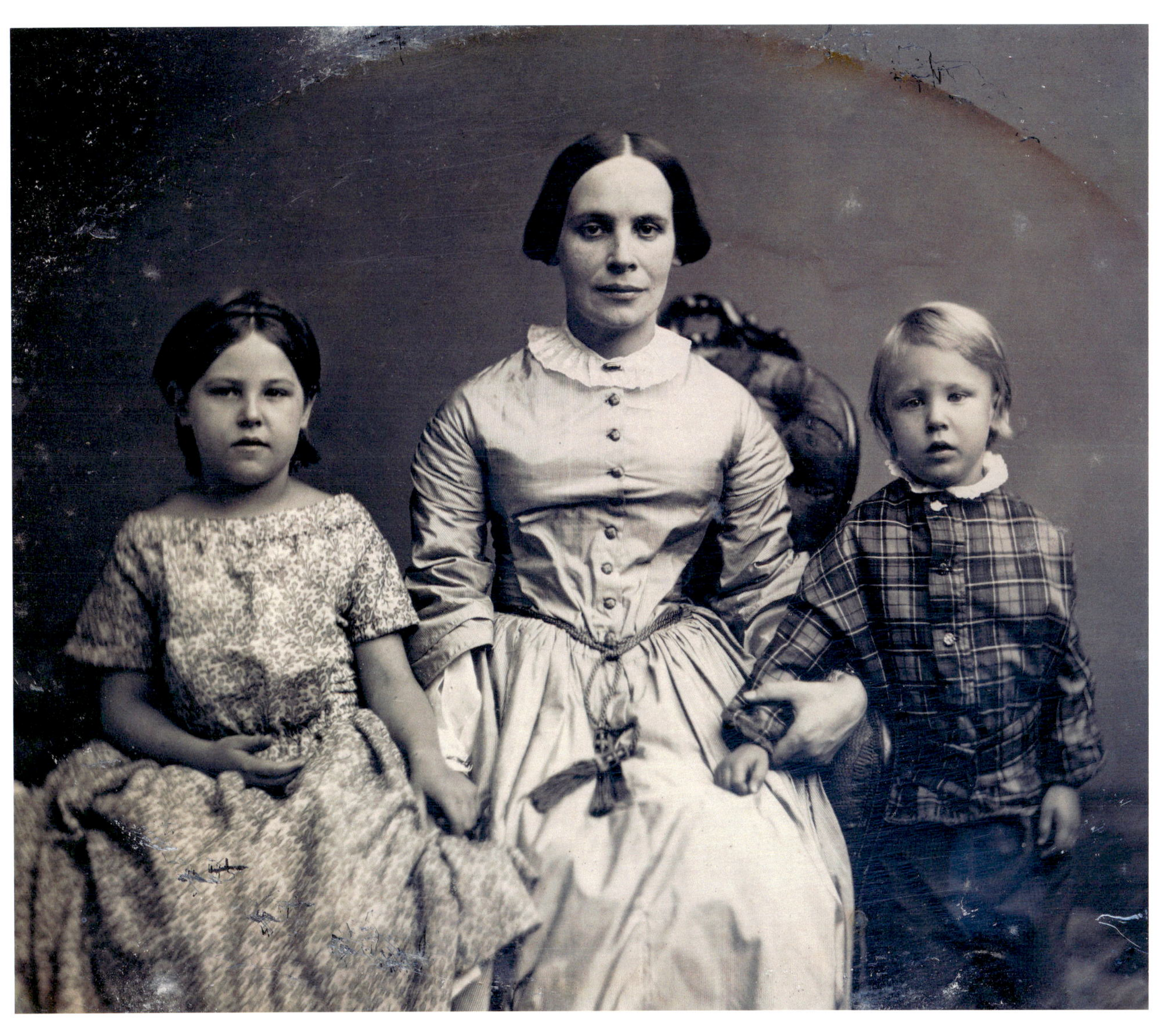

**Daguerreotype.** Photographer unknown. *Sarah Anna Chace Greene and Her Children.* c. 1850. 3⅝ x 4¼ in. (9.2 x 10.8 cm)

## 5.3 SALTED-PAPER PRINTS

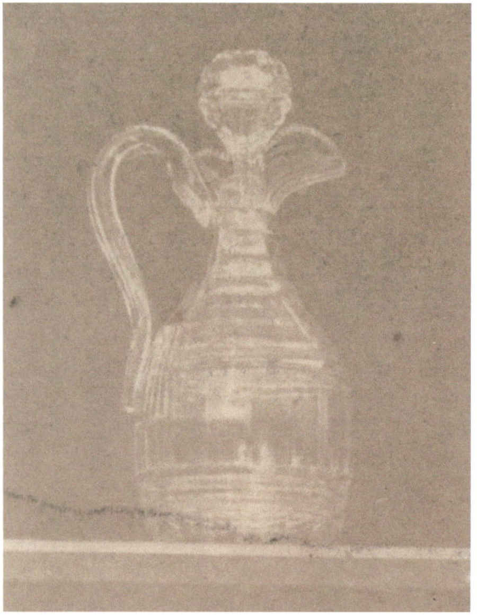

A small detail—about 1¾ by 1½ inches—of a Talbot print showing the severe fading that afflicted most early paper photography. This print faded through improper processing. Even though it spent 150 years in darkness inside a book, it still changed as residual chemistry attacked the silver image.

The first paper photographs were contact prints of objects. The small Talbot print of lace that we see to the right, made in 1845, is a negative image, made by pressing the lace against a sensitized sheet of paper. Where the lace blocked the light, no silver deposit was formed; in other areas, where light struck the paper, it darkened. By a happy coincidence, the lace, white but opaque, looks like a positive in this reversed print.

The early paper photographic processes utilized both types of silver response—they started out as printing-out processes but quickly adapted to the use of the latent image. Talbot's first camera-made pictures were on silver chloride–coated paper that darkened directly as it was exposed. It was apparent from the start, though, that this would only work with long exposures, and that even then the camera would have to be tiny because no large lenses with relatively large apertures existed that could provide adequate exposure for a big picture. Within a few years Talbot and other workers had figured out how to use latent images, exposing the paper lightly and then developing a strong image afterwards through chemical treatment. This way pictures could be made with exposures of a minute or less, making paper photography practical. At the same time, however, all the early users of paper-based photography made their prints using the other method—allowing the agency of light to darken the paper with no later development of the image.

Whether images print out or are developed, they are dark where light strikes the sensitive material. Because of this, camera images are negative. To reverse them, so that the white of the paper support mimics the light of the world that formed the original image, they must be printed.

The silver compound most commonly used in early photography was silver chloride, which involves an interesting technical problem in that it is completely insoluble in water. You cannot make a solution of silver chloride and coat it on a sheet of paper, no matter how hard you try. The way around this problem was to coat the paper with a salt solution—perhaps even using plain old table salt—that had a small amount of gelatin mixed in as a binder. Once that coating was dry, a second coating, of a solution containing silver nitrate, was put on the sheet. The moment the silver nitrate and the salt came into contact they produced silver chloride, and because the salt was evenly coated, the silver chloride was as well. This is the origin of the term "salted paper." It was possible to apply the salt coating and then dry and store the sheets; the silver nitrate had to be applied shortly before the material was used, since the sensitive paper degraded in a day or so. Virtually all salted-paper prints were toned with gold prior to fixing, which gave them their characteristic reddish-purple color.

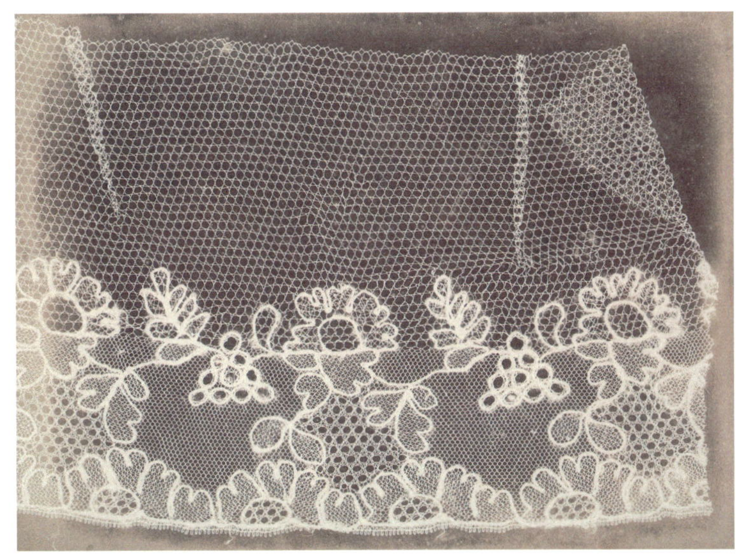

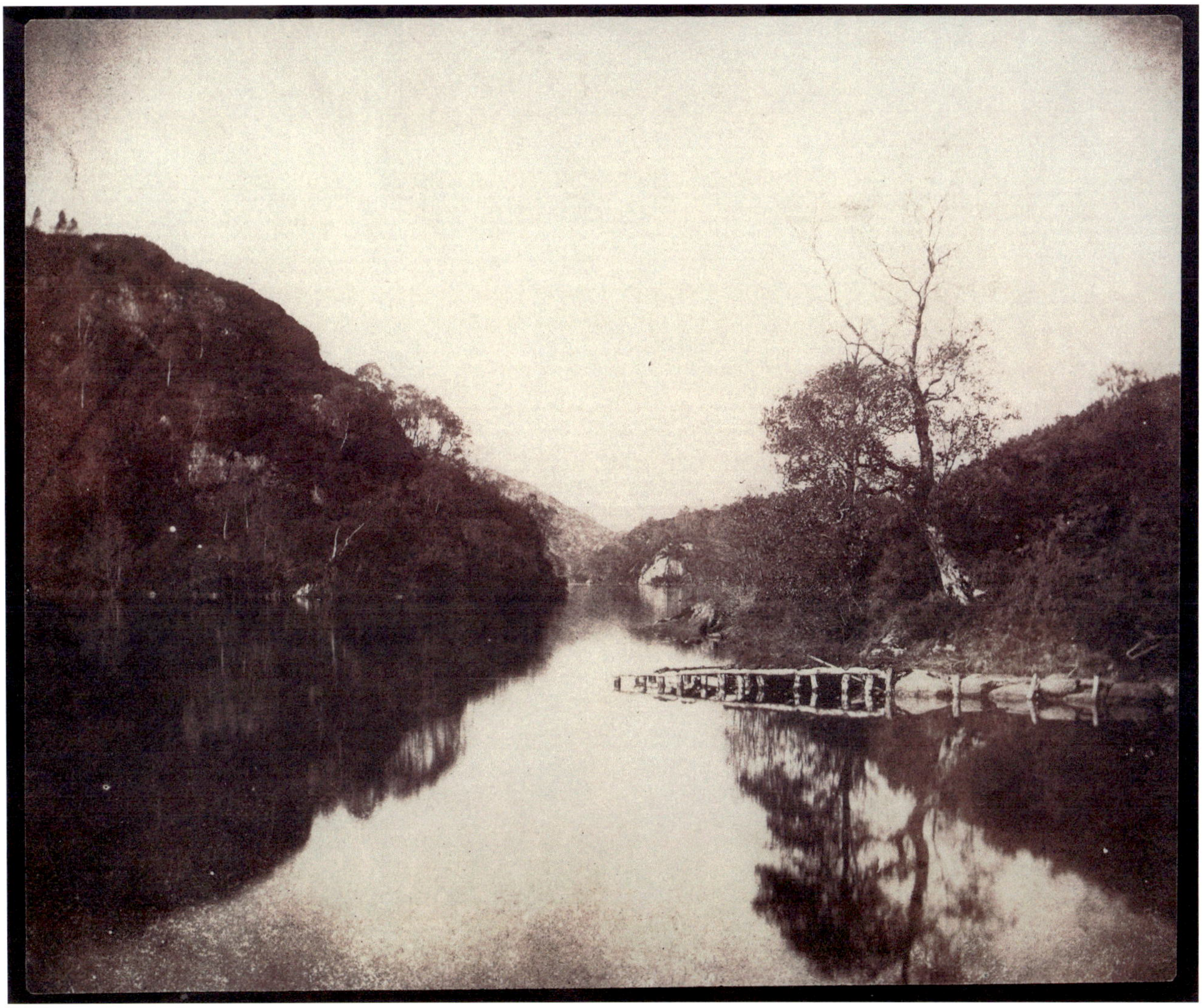

**Salted paper.** Top: William Henry Fox Talbot. *Lace.* 1845. 6½ x 8¾ in. (16.5 x 22.3 cm). Silver chloride contact print. Bottom: William Henry Fox Talbot. *Loch Katrine.* 1844. Salted-paper print from a calotype negative, 6⅞ x 8¼ in. (17.4 x 21.1 cm)

## 5.4 PAPER NEGATIVES

This is a platinum print, made by me some years ago from a paper negative of about 1850. This modern print shows just how strong an image could come out of paper photography after a decade or so of development.

The picture has dark corners because the lens did not fully cover the paper negative. All lenses give circular images, and camera formats are designed to crop rectangles out of these circles of description. Even in the best of circumstances, lens-derived images grow progressively darker as we move away from their centers. This happens with certain camera designs because the mounting barrel of the lens blocks some off-axis light, but it always happens to some degree because the lens's aperture, circular when viewed straight on, becomes elliptical when seen from the side, and an ellipse admits less light than the perfect circle on axis does. Great effort has been exerted in lens design to minimize this vignetting, and modern lenses perform far better than did the older one used for this picture.

Decked out in black cape and white clothes, the subject of the picture is great looking—just the sort of person we might hope would have been active in the revolution of early photography. Despite his youth, he has to lean against the wall, and to clasp his hands together, to make sure that he does not move during the minute or so of exposure. The direct look he gives us brings home what a time machine photography is: as he stares out at us from the past, his unknown identity and fate become irrelevant under the force of his presence transported through the years.

The picture also offers another lesson in the power of photography: the delicate precision of the daguerreotype is not required for a strong picture. Soft, grainy paper does the job perfectly well, allowing a picture full of details that no painter would have understood before the invention of photography. The perspective-defining lattices of the shutter, occupying nearly a quarter of the picture space; the ornate doorstop at the far right; even the folds in the trousers are defined with as much clarity as the man himself, revealing the dispassionate tendency of photography to treat all things in the most democratic manner possible. Every element in the picture has received the full benefits of the medium, and the task of the artist/photographer is to make every part of this richly described world be essential to the picture.

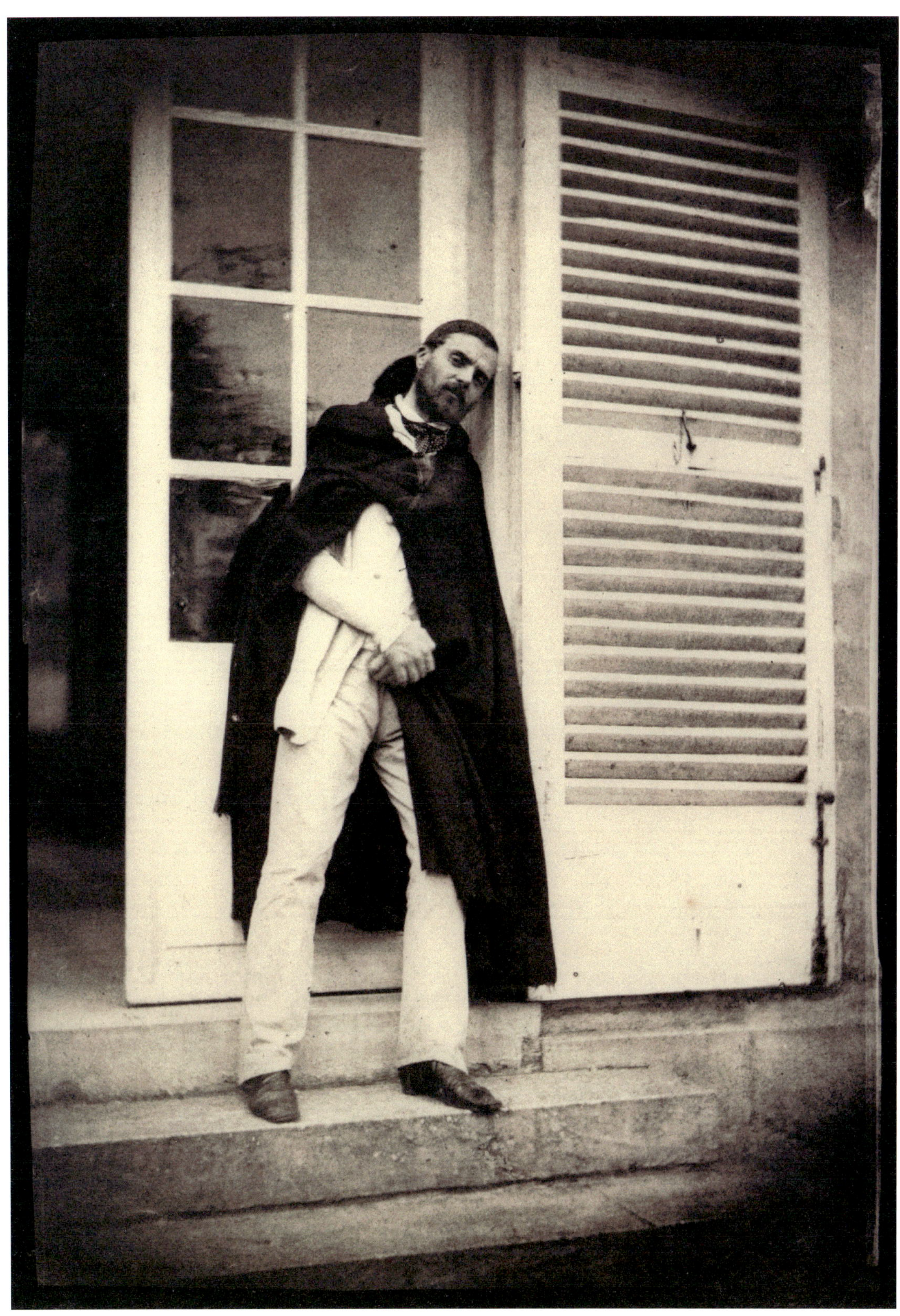

**Salted-paper negative.** Photographer unknown. Portrait of a man. c. 1850. 9 x 6¼ in. (22.7 x 16 cm). The negative from which this print was made was produced with salted paper. The print, made in the 1970s, is a platinum print (see plate 6.7).

## 5.5 WET-PLATE PHOTOGRAPHY

Early photographs on paper were poor in their rendition of tone and detail because the negative image was embedded in the rough paper of the support. The negatives were usually waxed, to make them translucent and to reduce the effect of the paper's fibers, but even so the images they produced could not compete with the daguerreotype for precision and exactness. A tremendous improvement came in the 1850s with the invention and refinement of the wet-plate process, which used a glass support for the negative and captured sharp, intricately detailed images that could be printed with a long and smooth range of tones. We can say with some confidence that with the wet-plate process the image quality of black and white photography reached a level that matches anything done since.

It was a difficult process to master; like most crafts, wet-plate photography is easy to do badly but very hard to do well. The collodion — the chemical solution that held the light-sensitive silver salts onto the glass — tended to catch dust, curl off the edges of the plate, and generally misbehave. Most prints from wet-plate negatives have been trimmed and mounted, but the one we see here shows the entire negative, and the photographer's struggle with the collodion at the plate edges is quite apparent. The process only worked when the coated glass plate was exposed while still damp, which meant that the photographer working outside the studio needed a portable darkroom. Like the older paper negative and even the daguerreotype, wet-plate negatives were only sensitive to blue light. That meant that delicate skies were usually overexposed; if the rest of the image was adequately exposed the sky would disappear into blank white in the finished print. Conversely, since the plates were completely insensitive to red light, the skin of portrait subjects tended to be underexposed — dark and ruddy. Despite all this, magnificent work came out of the wet-plate era. Hardworking photographers lugged their plates and cameras all over the world, and since no good enlargement process existed — printing was only done by direct contact between negative and paper — those plates and cameras were generally as large as possible. Nineteenth-century photography during the era of the wet-plate has a purity and clarity that largely disappeared in the twentieth century.

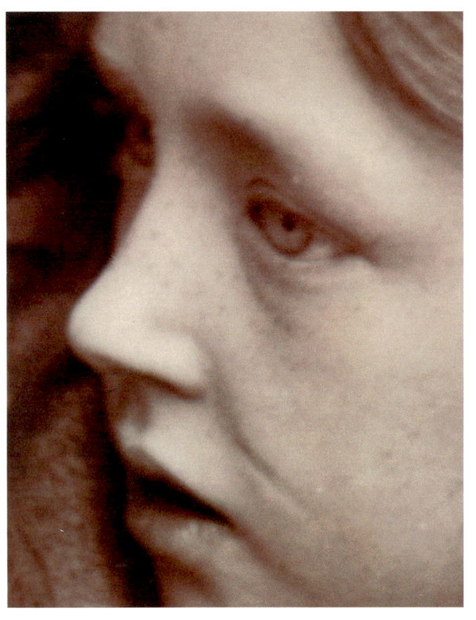

Like the daguerreotype, a print from a glass-plate negative has superb tonal description, as we can see in this six-times enlargement from the print.

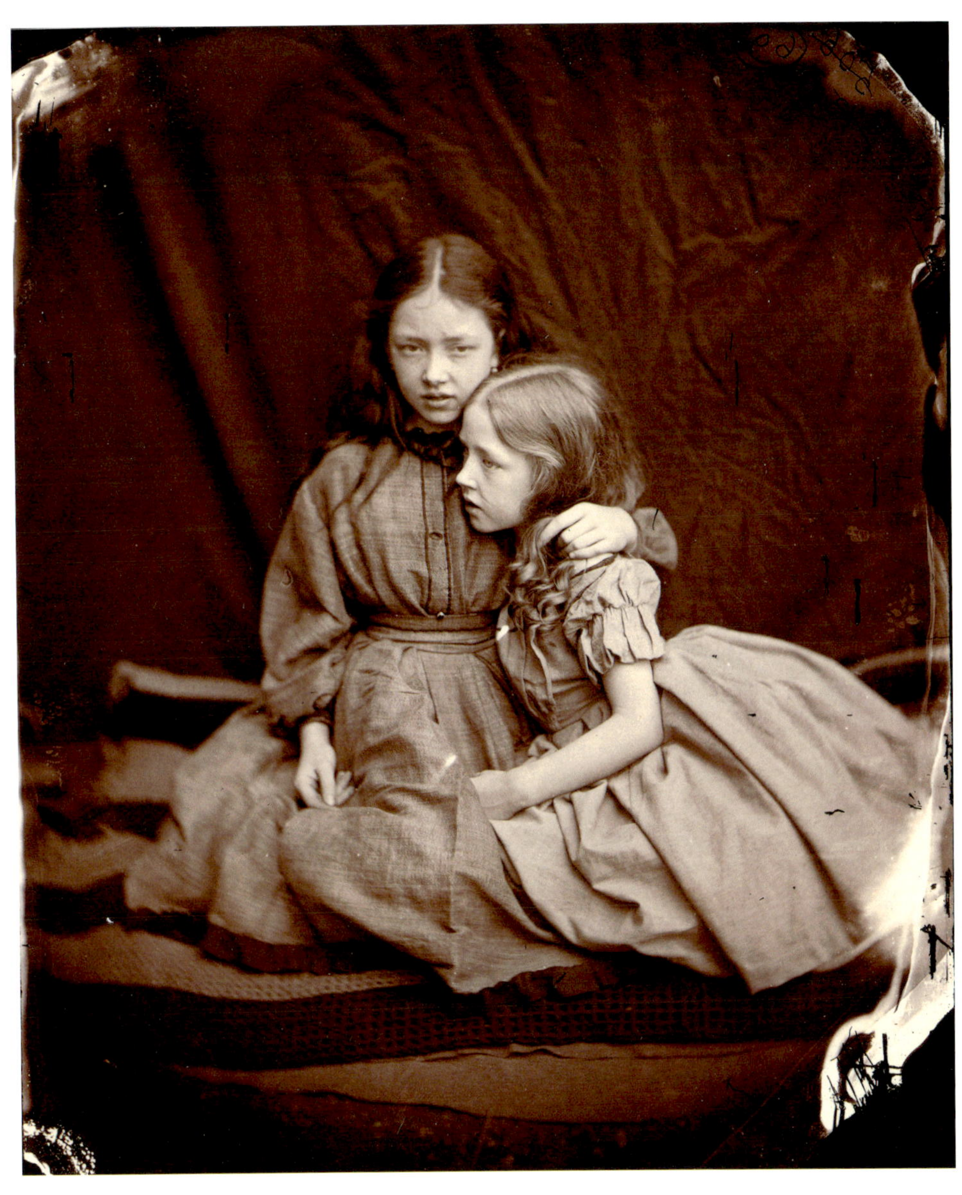

**Wet plate.** Lewis Carroll. *The Terry Sisters.* 1875. 6 x 5 in. (15.2 x 12.7 cm). This modern print was made in 1980 by the author, from the original wet-plate negative.

## 5.6 ALBUMEN PRINTS

The wet-plate era demanded a new printing process that could do justice to the wide range of tone held in the glass negatives. The older method of printing on paper—the salted-paper method—produced images that sat directly on the paper fibers, which made them somewhat rough. They were also completely matte, which meant that they could never have strong black values; matte surfaces diffuse the light reflecting off them, preventing the high degree of light absorption that is necessary to portray a strong black value. Because of their superb scale the wet-plate negatives opened the door to a new range of tonal description in the darker values that had not been possible with the salted-paper process.

The solution was albumen printing. The name comes from the fact that the image-bearing material was held onto the paper support by a relatively thick layer of albumen, the soluble protein found in egg white. This binder allowed prints to be made that carried the image not on the paper fibers but above them, in the smooth egg-white coating. Albumen also produced a beautiful semigloss surface, which could describe a very dark value if enough silver was present—and in fact the new method increased the amount of silver available in the print. The albumen coating could hold far more sensitive salt than salted paper did and hence could produce a much heavier metallic deposit.

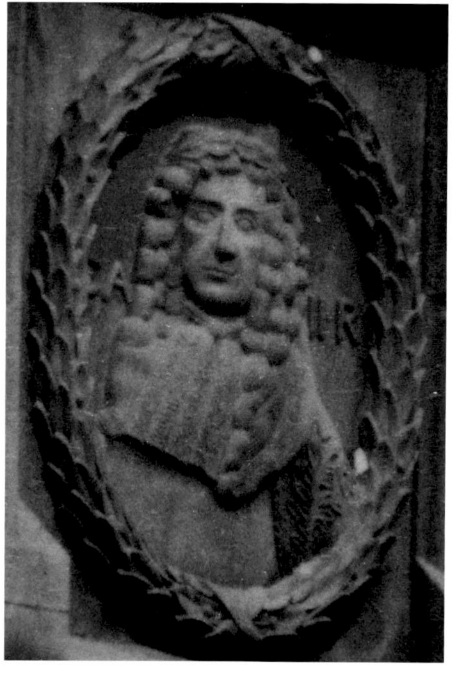

A six-times enlargement from the lower photograph opposite.

The combination of the wet-plate negative and the albumen print transformed positive/negative photography; once this pair of techniques spread, the daguerreotype was effectively dead. It is important to review just what changes these new processes represented. In the older salted-paper-based photography the negative was exposed dry, had a low sensitivity, and produced a rough and tonally limited image. The newer glass negative was far more sensitive, held superb detail and tone, but had to be coated and exposed just moments before being used. In printing, both the old and the new method used a sheet of paper that was exposed dry, by contact, fixed with sodium thiosulfate, and then toned with gold. A thorough wash in plain water removed any residual chemicals. In both cases the image "printed out," so no developing was needed. The chief difference between the salted-paper and the albumen print was simply the binder used to hold the sensitive salts (and subsequently the image) onto the paper support. The use of albumen gave the prints a new surface, deeper tonality, and far more detail. In many ways albumen printing was just an improved version of the older salted paper. The wet-plate negative, on the other hand, had been a radical innovation.

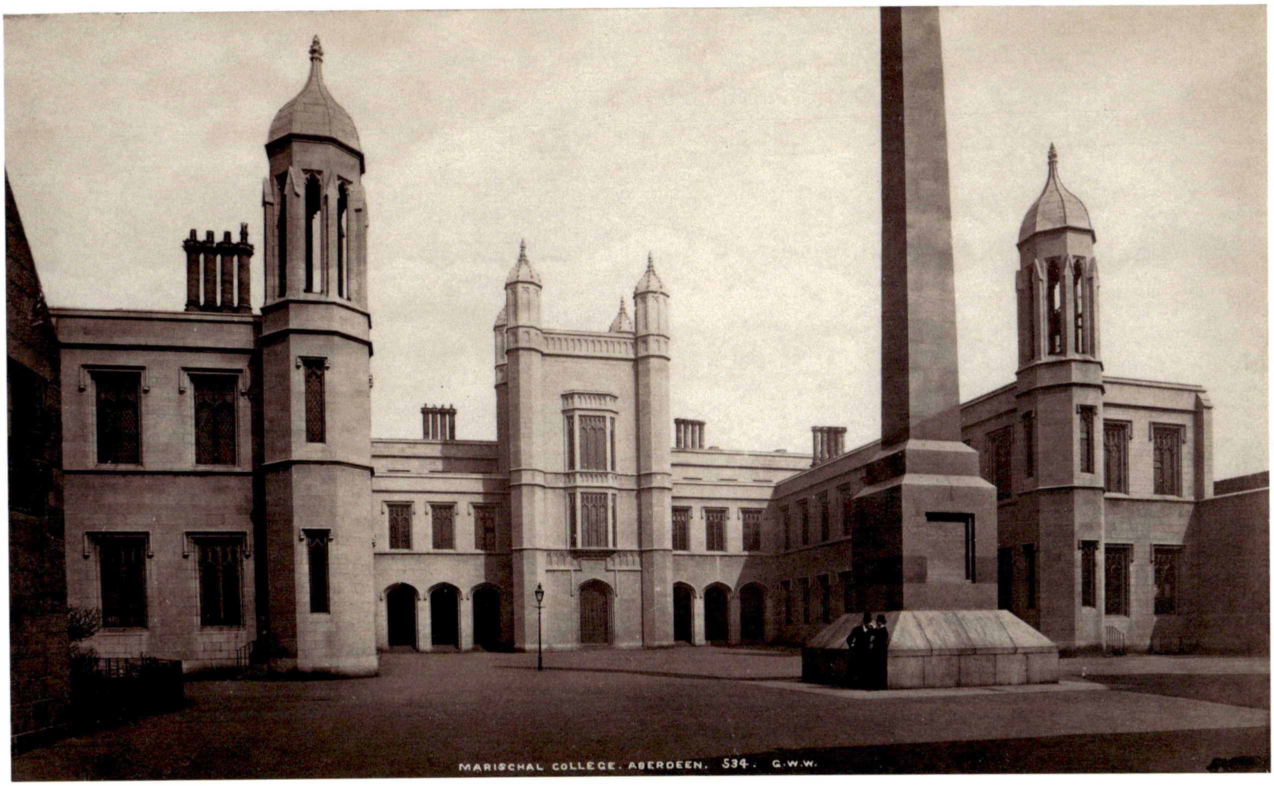

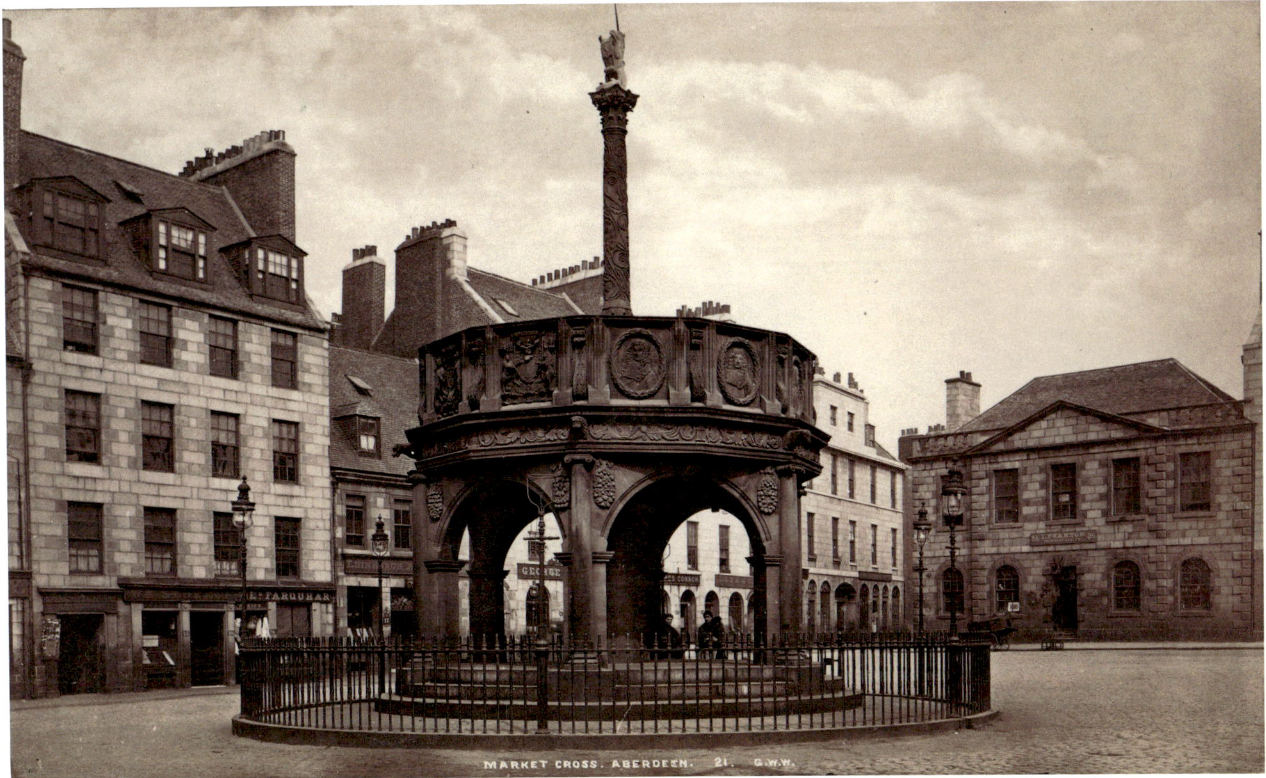


**Albumen print.** Top: George Washington Wilson. *Marischal College, Aberdeen.* c. 1875. 4½ x 7½ in. (11.4 x 19 cm).
Bottom: George Washington Wilson. *Market Cross, Aberdeen.* c. 1875. 4½ x 7½ in. (11.4 x 19 cm)

## 5.7 ALBUMEN PRINTS

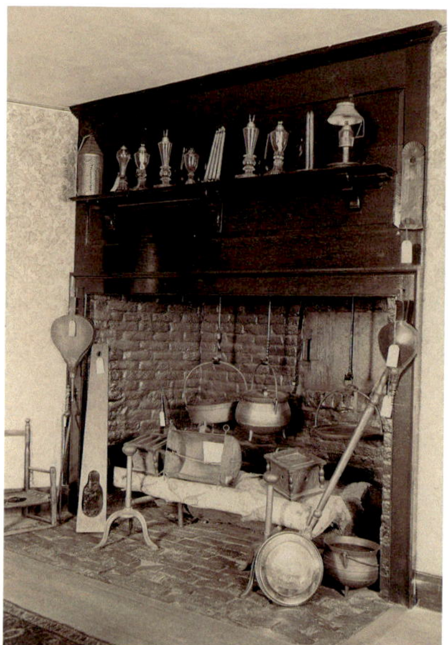

An albumen print with a moderate degree of gold toning—neither too red nor too purple.

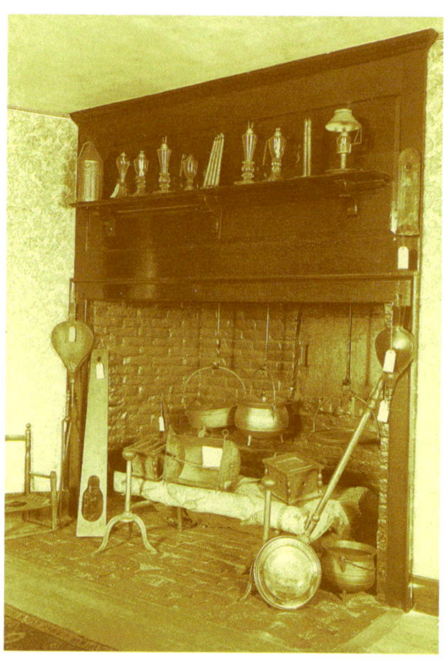

The same picture showing how the print might have looked had gold toning not been used.

Albumen prints dominated nineteenth-century photography. As I go on to describe other printing techniques it will be important to understand that the albumen process produced far more prints than all of the other chemical printing methods of photography's early years combined. Toward the century's end, the inked photographic image became more common, and eventually the numbers produced that way would far surpass all chemical prints. The printing press was destined to rule the roost of photographic printing, but this didn't really take place until the twentieth century.

The albumen print required no developing—it was made by direct exposure to the sun, with the image forming as the print was exposed. In the trade, a paper of this kind is called a "printing-out paper," or "POP." As the print darkened in the printing frame the darker portions of the picture, which were being heavily exposed, masked themselves and therefore were exposed at a slower rate than the lighter values. This altered the scale of tones in the negative, resulting in prints that described middle and light values beautifully while still holding detail in the shadows. In many ways the tonal description of an albumen print surpasses that of modern developing papers.

The silver deposit of an albumen print is extremely fine grained, and when fixed with hypo it weakens and changes to a distressingly yellow color. To prevent this color change, albumen prints were toned with a gold solution, which gave them a purplish color cast. It was discovered early on that if a print was immersed in a bath containing gold chloride before being fixed, its color would alter and the image would become far more permanent. Most daguerreotypes and virtually all salted-paper and albumen prints had gold applied to them. Silver is a reasonably stable metal but it does change over time when exposed to the air—witness the tarnishing of silverware. Gold, the noblest of metals, is virtually indestructible.

The amount of toning affected the color: more gold made for a deeper purple, less tended toward a reddish brown. All through the nineteenth century the dominant color of photography was purplish red, a direct result of the use of gold toners. Since gold was expensive, many early prints were trimmed down right to the edge of the image, to avoid wasting gold toner on the dark borders of the print. I have always suspected that a great deal of the motive for devising alternative printing processes was to avoid the high cost of the gold and to get away from the insistent purple color that came to characterize most photographs.

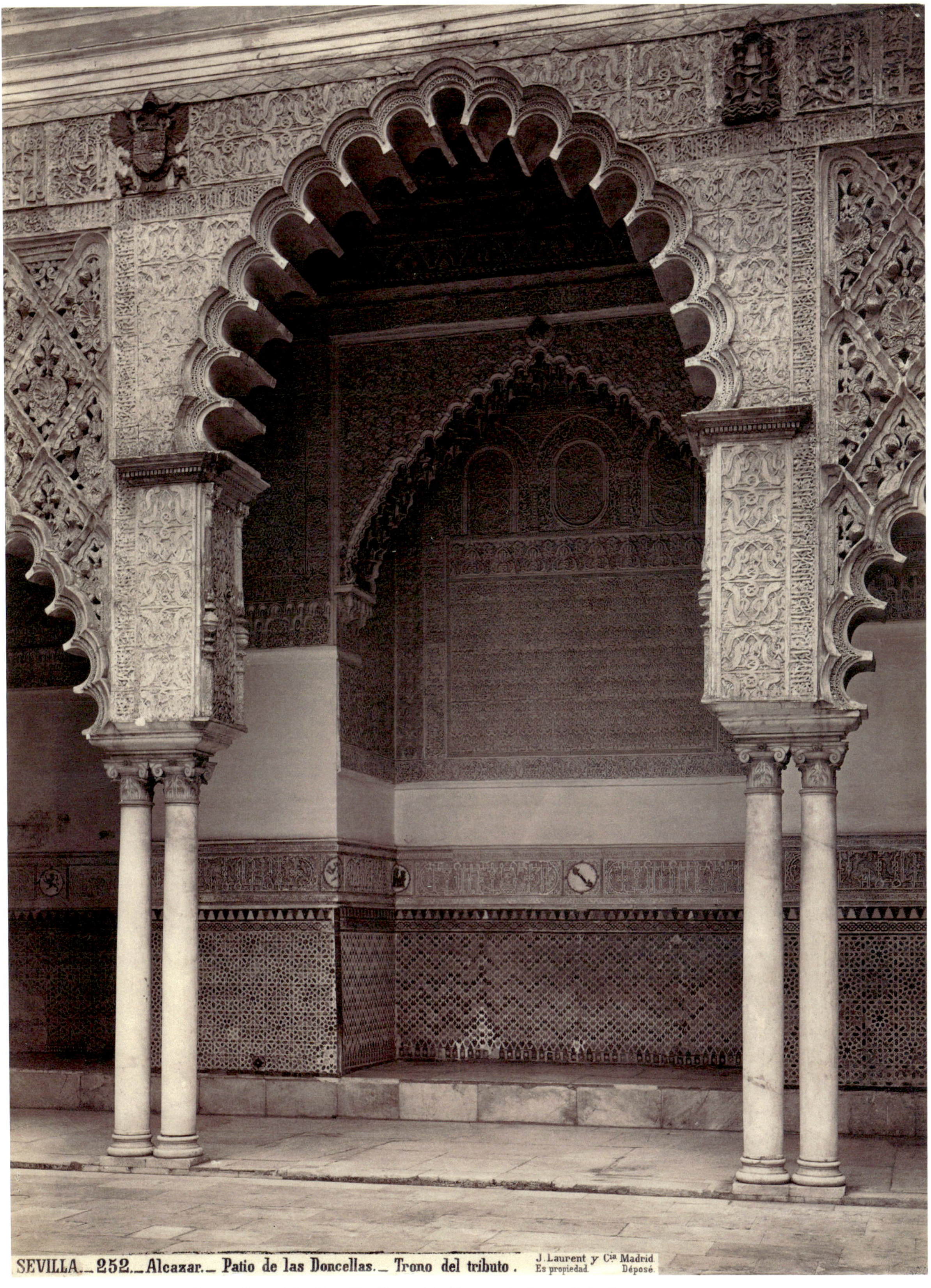


**Albumen print.** J. Laurent. *Alcazar–Patio de las Doncellas–Trono del tributo.* c. 1896. 13 x 9¾ in. (33 x 24.8 cm)

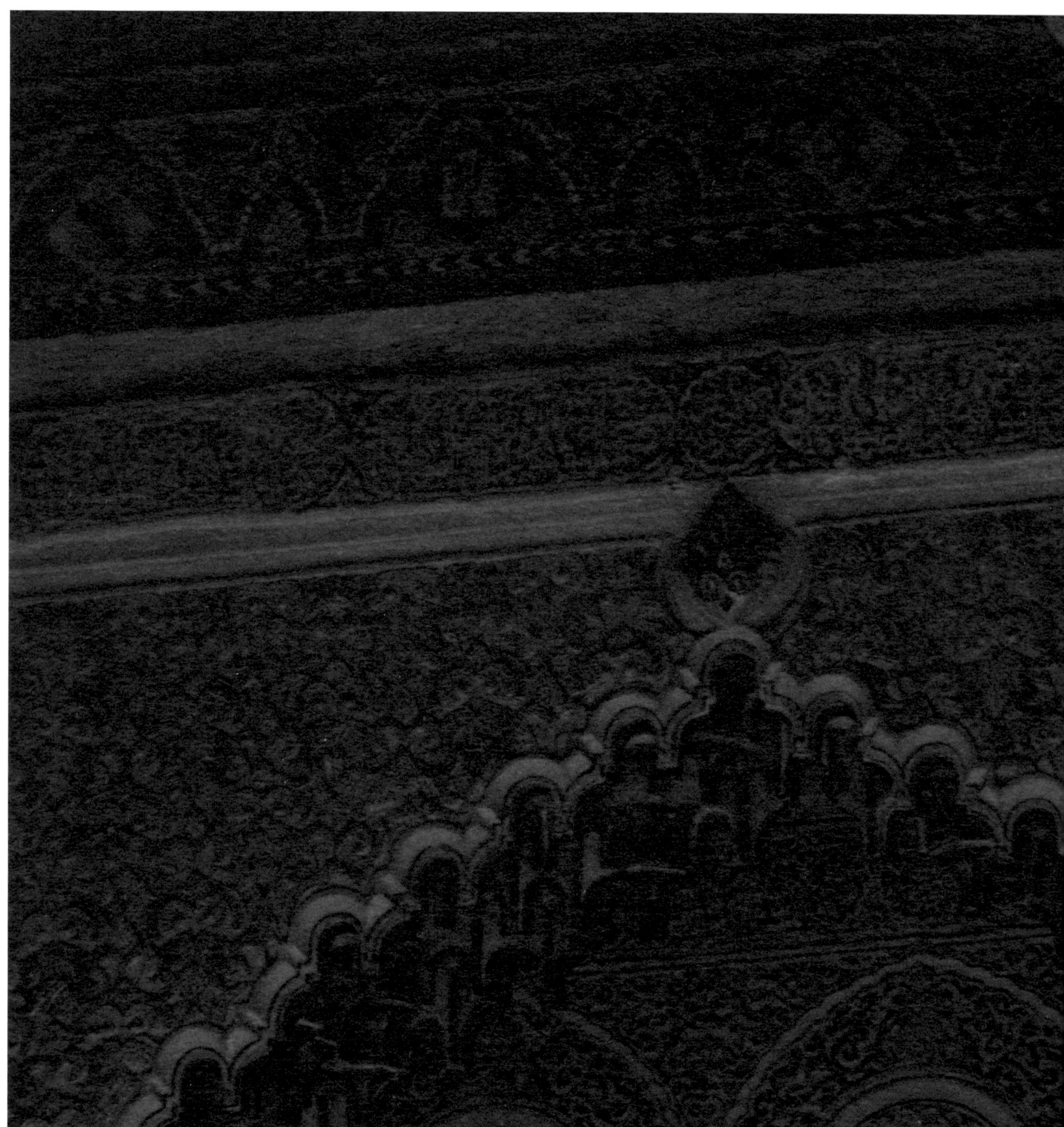

This plate shows a three-times enlargement of a detail of the previous one. As photography matured during the latter half of the nineteenth century it reached a remarkably advanced stage of development. Glass negatives, whether wet-plate or the later dry plate, recorded a long range of tones, and semigloss, gold-toned albumen prints rendered this long tonal scale flawlessly. Because the pictures were printed by contact, meaning that the negative and the printing paper were exposed while held together, the negatives had to be the same size as

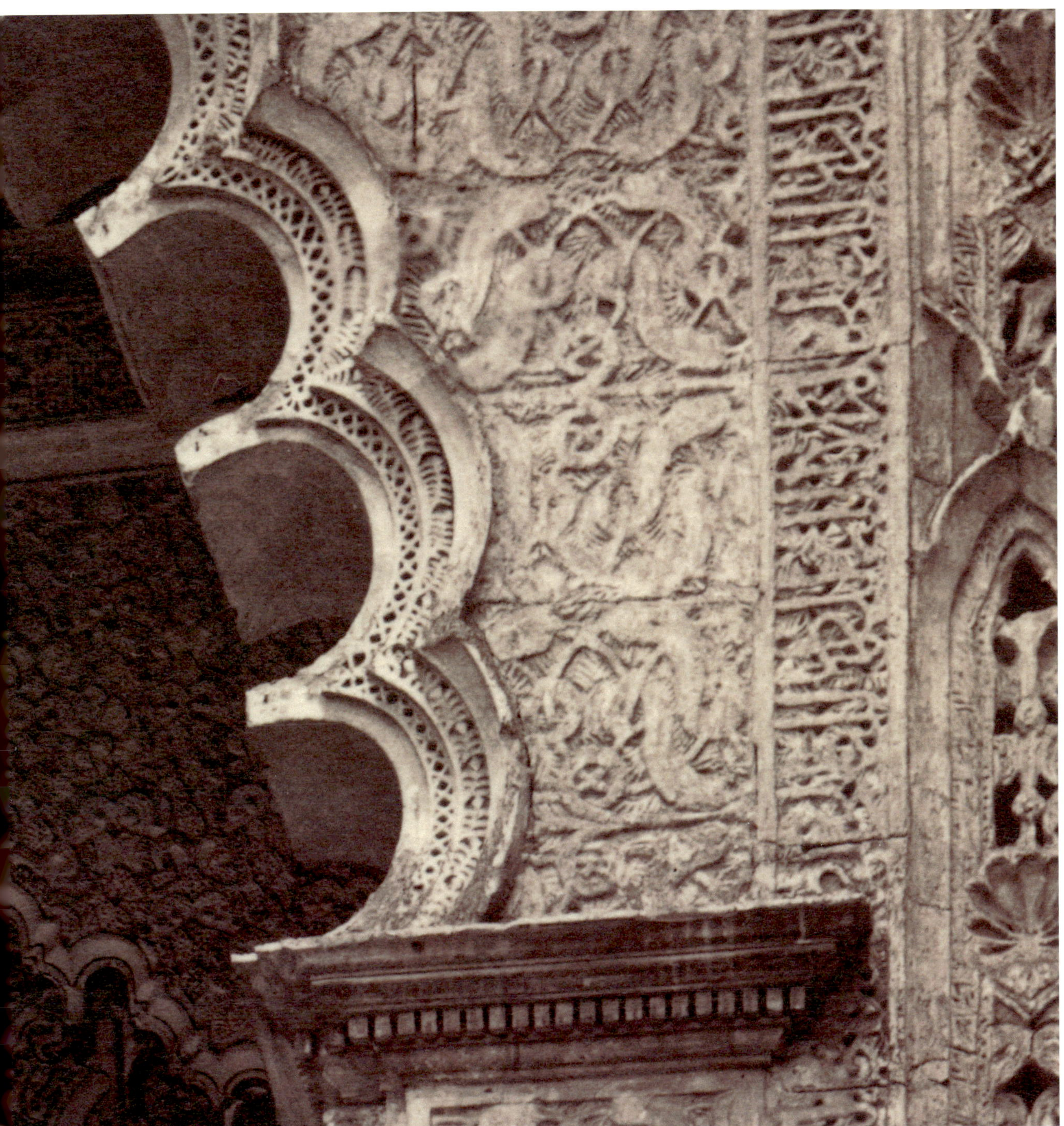

the desired print, so photographers used large glass plates that often recorded a wealth of detail seldom found in today's photographs made by enlargement. The pictures were still black and white, and did not do a very good job of translating color into black and white tones because the plates were only sensitive to blue light, but a fine nineteenth-century albumen contact print can have as strong an impact as any other example of the photographic medium.

## 5.8 ALBUMEN PRINTS: STEREO CARDS

The first cameras, like most cameras today, used a single lens, and the photographs they took were consequently made from a single location. But human vision is stereoscopic, being produced with two eyes that view the world from slightly different locations. The left eye sees the relative positions of things slightly differently from the right eye, and the brain interprets the two images to give us information about depth. It wasn't very long before photographers figured out that if they too made a pair of images from slightly different positions, and set them up so that the right eye saw the right image and the left eye the left, the brain would carry out its usual magic and interpret the pictures in three dimensions.

Stereo cards became extremely popular. To fit human eyes, they had to be a standard size, and they could easily be seen with a handheld viewer that forced each eye to see only the image associated with it. It is actually possible to look at a stereo card without the viewer by crossing our eyes until the images fuse, then shifting focus until the combined image is sharp. (When we cross our eyes we automatically shift focus to a closer distance, where the views of the crossed eyes meet—the focus needed for stereo viewing is somewhat farther away.) Many people can do this instinctively and others can quite easily learn.

The first makers of stereo cards were mainly locals in vacation destinations who photographed the sights for tourists. Before long, larger companies took over this task, producing stereo sets of virtually everything a tourist might visit. The photographers faced an interesting problem: a stereo could be boring if it did not contain dramatic differences of depth in its subject. This simple need, not hard to understand, led the photographers to make radically different images from any that had existed before. It is ironic that a large number of the more innovative single images in early photography were originally one half of a stereo. Seeing just one half, without the illusion of three dimensions, we can be enthralled by the strange new sort of flat picture that can be made when the depth of the scene is an important part of the picture structure. Also, stereo halves are nearly square, and this format, rare in early photography, made its own contribution to producing more surprisingly structured pictures.

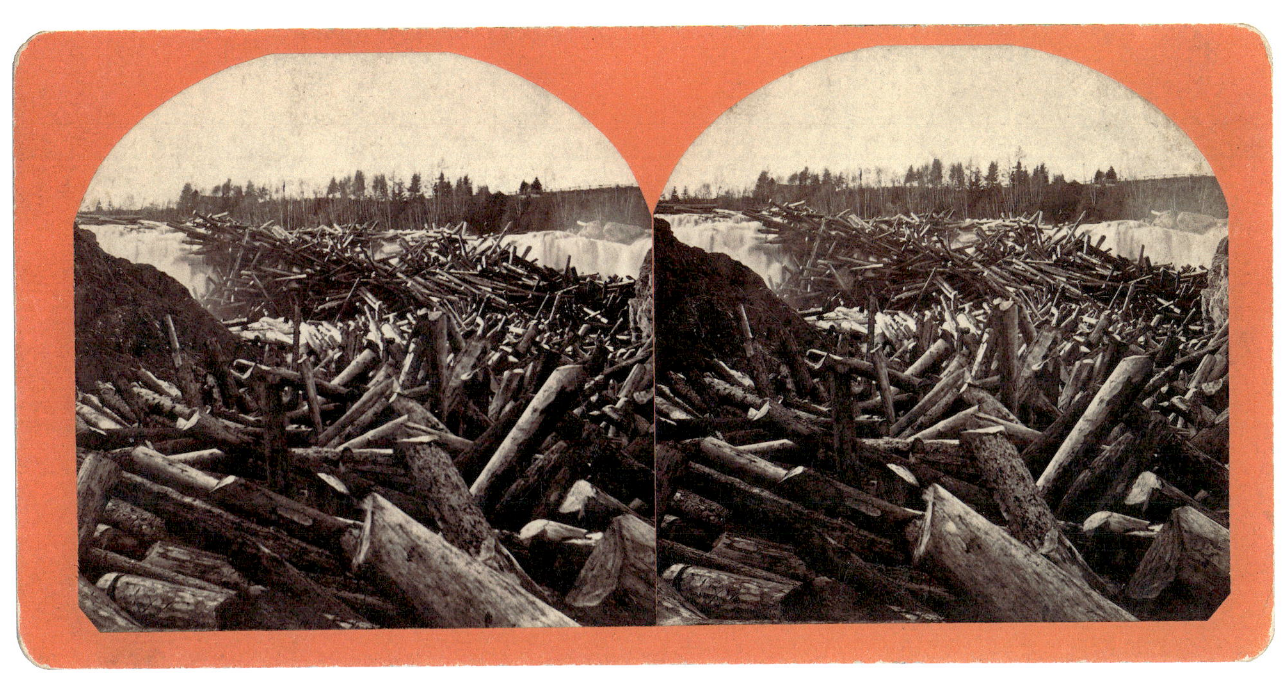

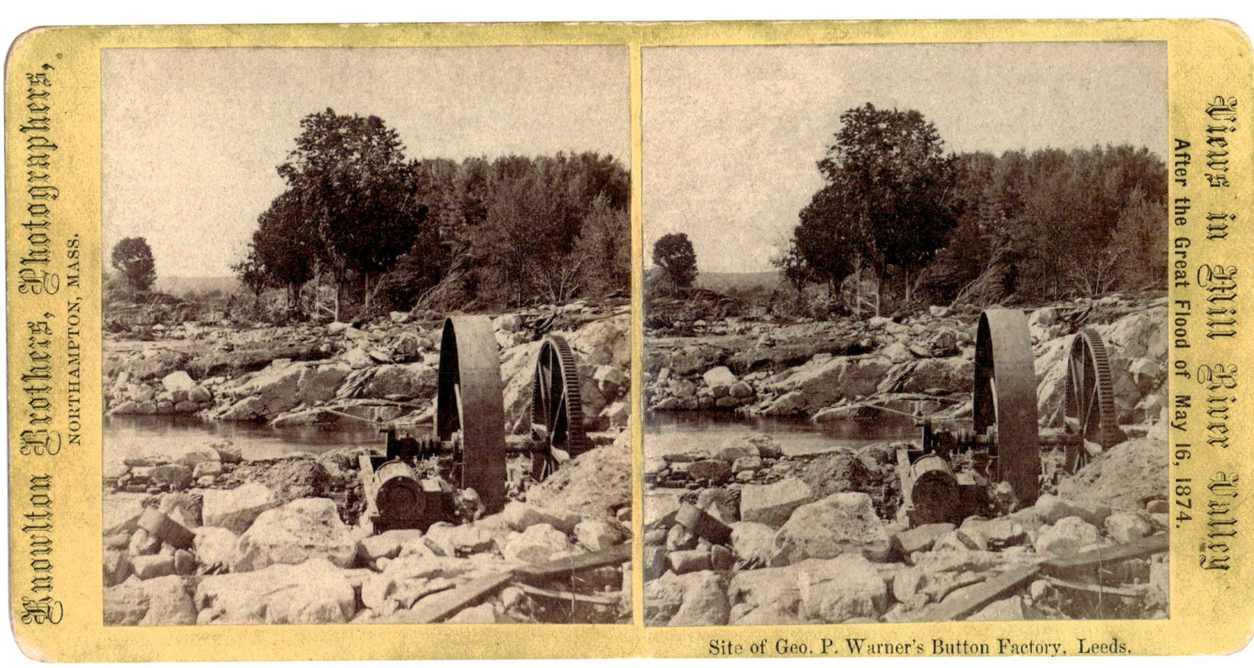


**Albumen print.** Top: George Taylor. *Logjam.* c. 1880. Bottom: Knowlton Brothers. *Site of Geo. P. Warner's Button Factory, Leeds.* 1874. Each: 3½ x 7 in. (8.9 x 17.8 cm)

## 5.9 ALBUMEN PRINTS: THE CARTE DE VISITE

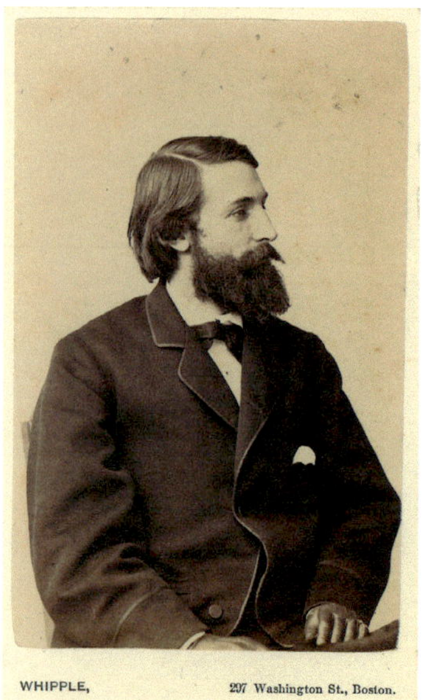


Many cartes de visite have the name of the subject handwritten on the back; the inscription on this one tells us that the picture shows Norwood Penrose Hallowell.

Photographs are fragile. The older daguerreotypes were protected by their glass covers and tough cases, but the mass of paper prints from the albumen era had no such safety. So, when tourists traveled abroad, they often pasted any prints they made into large albums to take back home. There, they also kept smaller family albums of photographs and notes on the pictures' subjects. Mercifully most of these albums held the prints in sleeves, so glue and rubber cement had no chance to ruin the prints. Today it is quite common to find such books intact, their leather covers firmly closed with brass clasps, and the pictures in perfect shape inside. Nothing preserves a photograph as well as being in a dry book that is stored closed, since light is the great destroyer of the photographic image.

The family album was an outgrowth of the practice of making cartes de visite, small cards holding photographs of their bearers which were produced in multiple copies to be passed among friends and family. These little pictures were usually about 4 by 2½ inches, in a vertical format. This odd size came about because the overwhelming majority of the pictures are portraits, and they were sized to match the standard visiting cards. Most small photographs from the nineteenth century were fractional divisions of the old whole plate size—6½ by 8½ inches—but the carte de visite broke this pattern.

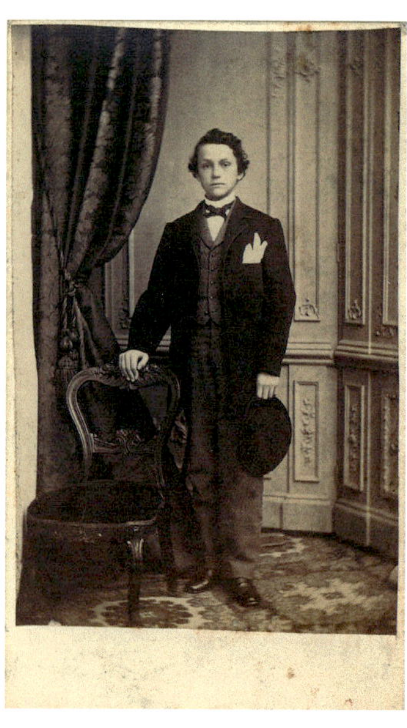

Photographer and subject unknown. c. 1875

In some cases these small pictures were made by using a multiple-lens camera to copy a large print. These cameras had baffles inside them, and their array of lenses—sometimes six or more—would produce that number of separate images on a single large plate. Each print from this negative could then be cut down into many copies to be pasted on cards. A multiple-lens camera was occasionally used to photograph the actual portrait subject; there are pictures of Abraham Lincoln made this way, and collectors obsess over the tiny differences in each small image that comes from the stereo effect of each lens being in a slightly different location. If we assemble any adjacent pair of these in copy prints that are close in tone and the same in size, we can cross our eyes and see the great man in three dimensions.

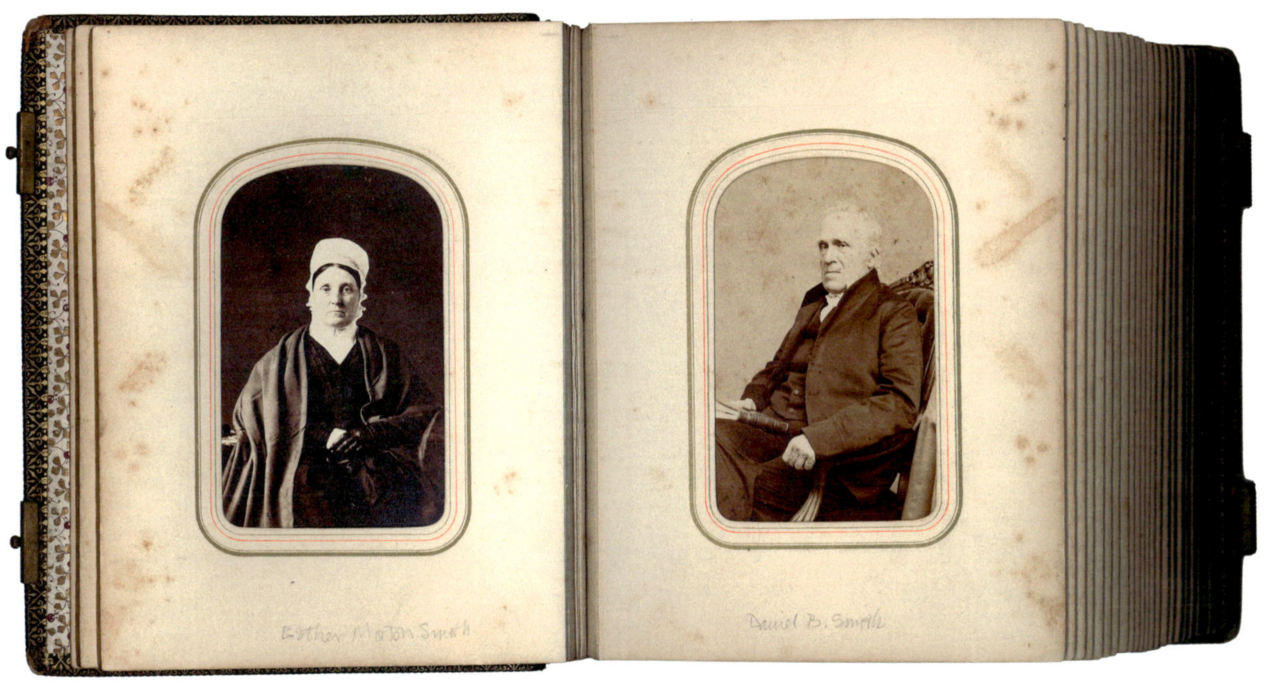


**Albumen print.** F. Gutekunst. *Esther Morton Smith* and *Daniel B. Smith.* c. 1875. Each carte de visite is 4 x 2¼ in. (10.2 x 6 cm). The album, by an unknown maker, has pages that are 6 x 4¾ in. (15.2 x 12 cm).

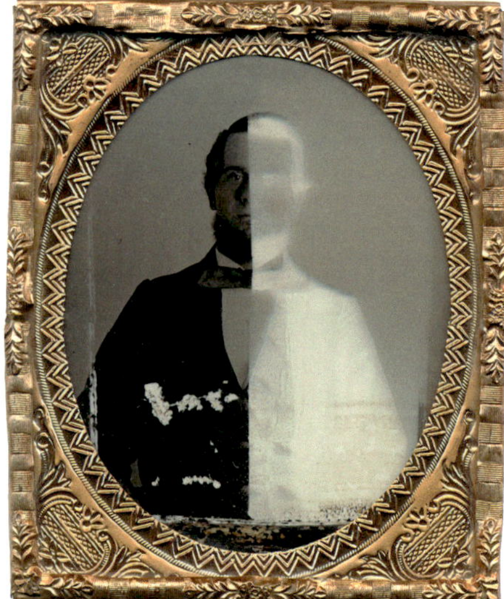

A small ambrotype from which half of the black backing has been removed. The right-hand side shows the image as a negative, while the left, still backed with black paint, appears as a positive.

## 5.10 AMBROTYPES AND TINTYPES

Most photographers who have worked in the darkroom are aware that negatives can sometimes appear as positives. Often we will lift an underexposed negative out of the fixer, disappointed that it is of insufficient density, and find that it suddenly appears as a positive. This occurs when the silver deposit is illuminated by the overhead light but we see it against a dark background, perhaps the old darkroom trays made of black rubber. The silver, which appears light gray, shows as a positive instead of a negative, since it is much lighter than the background against which we see it.

This phenomenon was noticed early on, and some wet-plate photographers turned it to use by intentionally underexposing their plates, then coating the back of the glass with black paint. The resulting pictures—unique, direct-positive images—were called ambrotypes. Usually small, they were put in cases and entered the same market as the dying daguerreotype. The tintype was a variant of this process, made by applying the wet-plate coating not to glass but to a sheet of black-lacquered metal. These little pictures were cheaper, and seldom got into the fancy cases; instead they were usually sold in simple paper holders with lithographed borders.

The ambrotype was never very popular compared to the vast number of negatives generated for albumen printing. Part of the problem with both the ambrotype and the tintype was that they were unique—each exposure produced just one picture. Like the daguerreotype, every one still around once sat in the camera facing its subject; it is a relic of the origins of photography. Another drawback was that the highlights were always gray—the beautiful white of paper, capable of holding a long range of tones, did not exist for either process. Even so, the tintype, the cheaper of the two methods, became very popular, and millions of small examples are still to be found in family albums and the antique malls cropping up in small fading towns across the country.

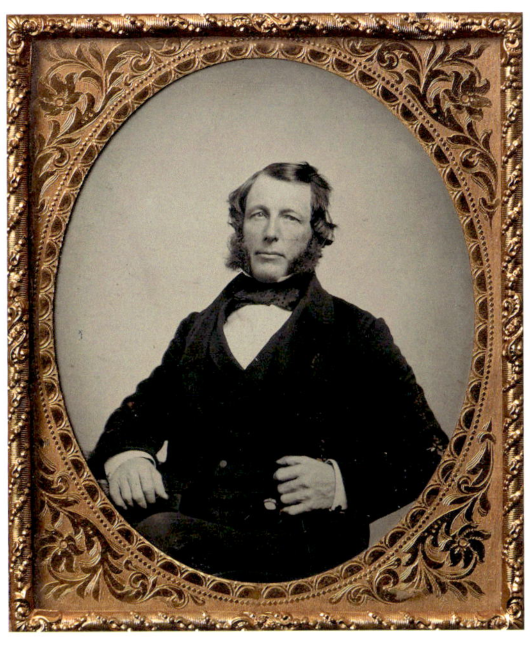

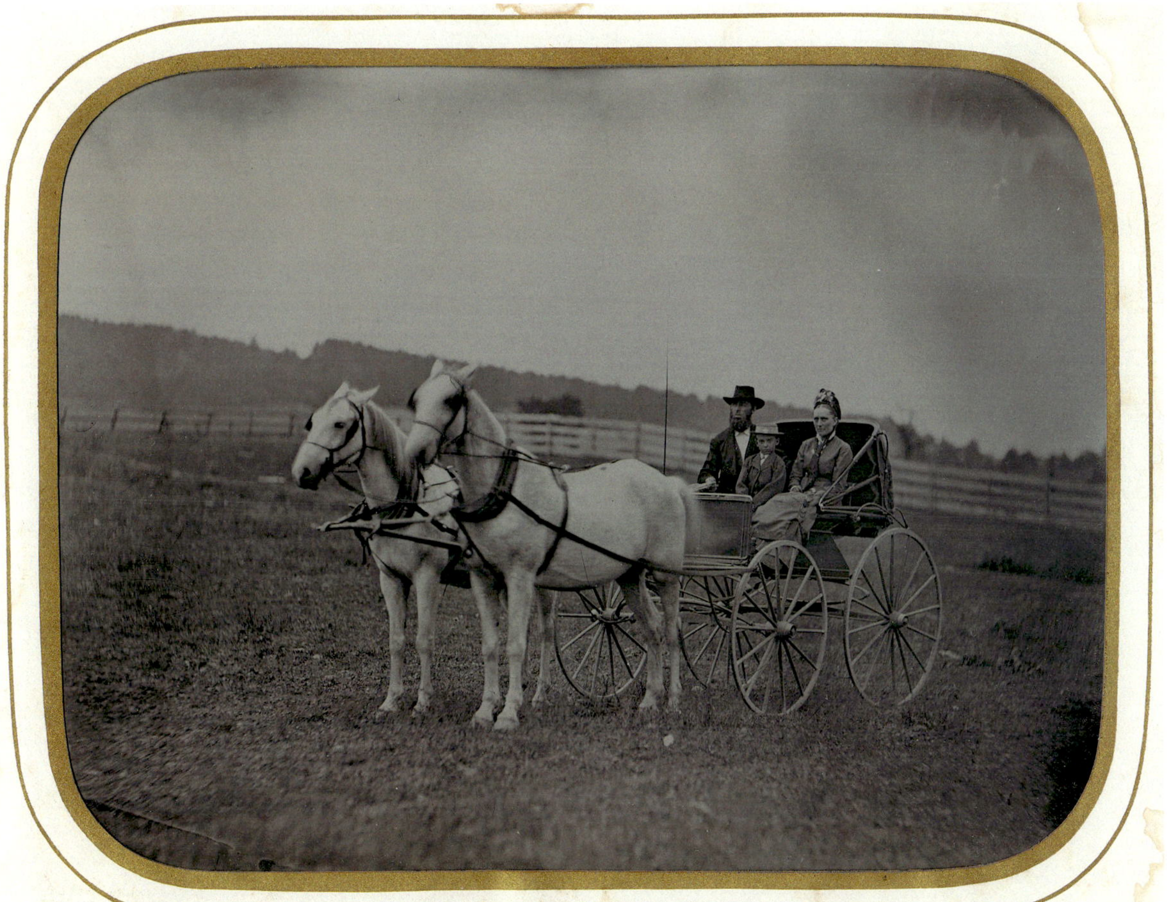

Top: **Ambrotype.** Photographer unknown. Portrait of a man. c. 1880. 3¼ x 2¾ in. (8.4 x 7 cm)
Bottom: **Tintype.** Photographer unknown. Family in a carriage. c. 1880. 6⅞ x 8⅞ in. (17.5 x 22.5 cm)

## 5.11 TINTYPES

Most of the tintypes that we find today have long since lost their simple paper holders and instead are loose, scratched, and bent. Many of them have been roughly cut out of larger sheets of metal with shears, so they don't have neat edges like the more formal one we see on the right. The tintype survived for years. It was cheap, easy to do in a small size, and because the metal base didn't absorb water it could be exposed, developed, dried, and then immediately given to a tourist or other traveling customer to carry away. Tintypes were also made in the studio, as was this beautiful one of a young man posed in a corner of mirrors, so that we see five of him in one shot. I only know who he is because he was my mother's late cousin and she wrote his name on a piece of tape stuck on the back. The overwhelming majority of these pictures are anonymous.

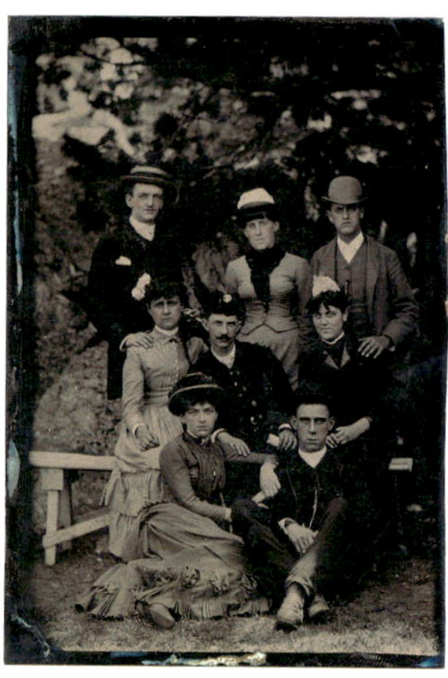

A tintype group portrait and its lithographed paper holder. The pink ground has remained as fresh as the day it was printed because the usually fugitive color was protected by the tintype. The tintype is approximately 5 x 3 inches.

Tintypes were made in whole-plate size, half-plate size, and down through the divisions until they became tiny. They appeared on campaign buttons and in minute albums of pictures no more than half an inch high. Most are uninteresting from a physical point of view—dull in tone and often quite beaten up—but even the most pedestrian of them provides a direct view through the time machine of photography back to the moment of its origin. Paper photography, which has long since won the game, inevitably gives a secondhand view of the past through the fact of being printed from the negative, which was what faced the subject in the camera. As printing technologies have changed and famous old pictures have been copied, retouched, and reprinted, the paper-based photograph has lost some of its always questionable connection to the truth. The little tintypes, and their more elegant cousins the ambrotypes and daguerreotypes, provide the oldest direct connection to the visual past that we can depend upon. All photography is fictional, by which I mean that any photograph is a picture, not the world from which it was generated. But these little bits of early photography pull that fiction closer to the world than any other pictures known. Many other photographic techniques make pictures that "look" more like the world, but the early direct-positive photographs on glass and metal bear the actual stain of light from the past.

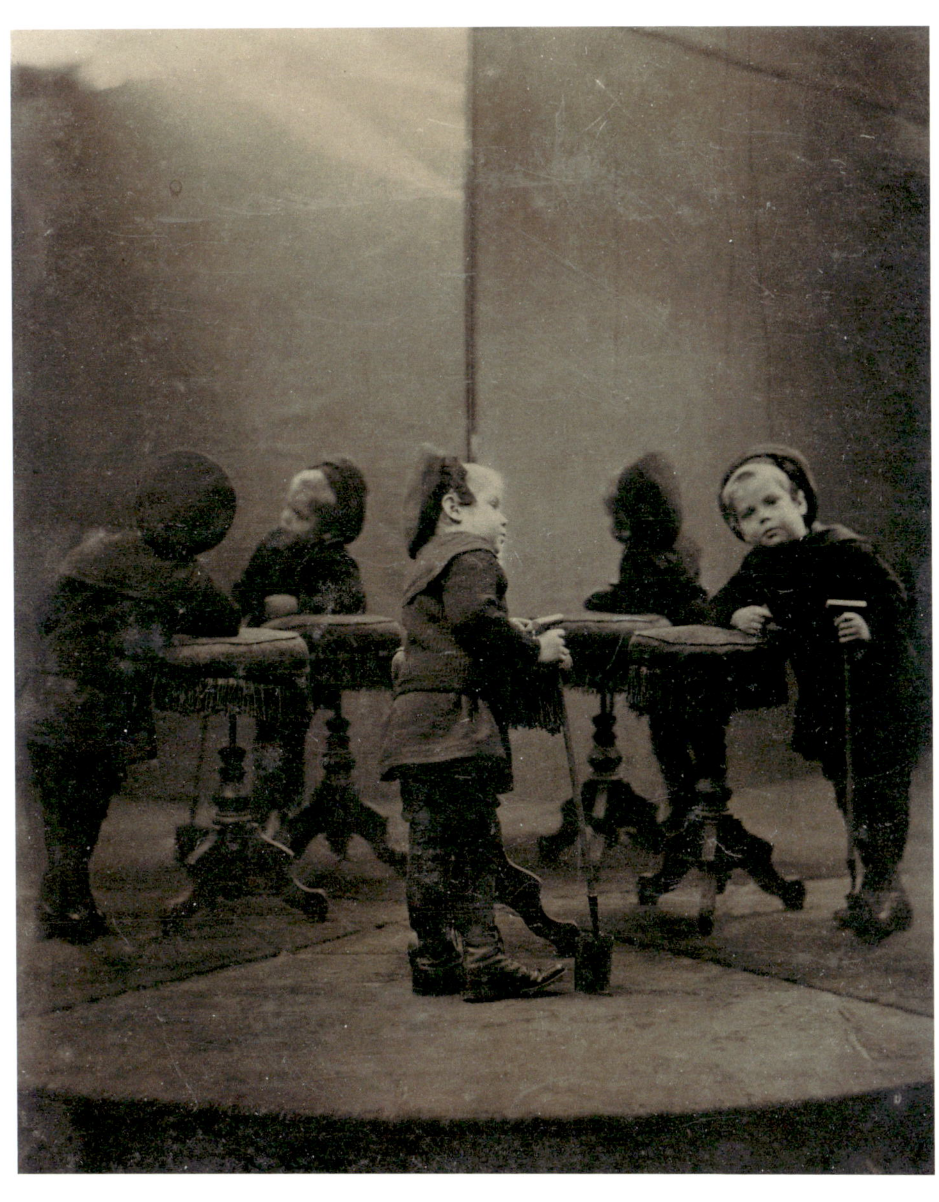

**Tintype.** Photographer unknown. *Arthur Cleveland.* c. 1895. 4 x 3¼ in. (10.2 x 8.4 cm). Arthur Cleveland grew up and lived most of his life in Chadds Ford, Pennsylvania. When he was a middle-aged man, Andrew Wyeth painted his portrait.

## 5.12 GELATIN-BASED PRINTING-OUT PAPER

As the nineteenth century drew to an end, photography began its deep transition to the dry plate. That process, introduced in Part 7, changed the medium from one in which the materials could be homemade to a different sort in which almost every consumable was bought in a store. Albumen, the giant of all the nineteenth-century photographic printing mediums, was doomed by the spread of the dry plate, but it underwent a few changes on its way out. Gelatin printing-out paper (POP) was the most widespread of these.

Gelatin is a tremendously versatile material, and it was mass produced. (It was a byproduct of animal husbandry—sending the old horse to the glue factory meant it was to become a source not just of glue but of gelatin and animal feed.) Once purified, this organic polymer behaved predictably and lent itself to manufacturing processes with a dependability and ease that albumen did not. A gelatin POP differed from an albumen sheet only in the substitution of gelatin for egg white as the binder that held the silver salts. This new paper was still exposed to the sun, it printed out with no developing necessary, and it was gold toned for permanence before fixing. The surface of these new prints, though, was hard and glossy. Albumen's beautiful, articulated, semigloss surface gave way to the high shine that later modern papers would also have, since they too would be factory coated with gelatin emulsions. While albumen paper had completely disappeared by the 1920s, gelatin printing-out paper continued to be made throughout the twentieth century. Because it produced a superb image that needed no developing, portrait photographers could easily make prints on this paper as proofs for their customers. Being neither gold toned nor fixed, the pictures would gradually darken as they were viewed, so the client would have to come back to the photographer to buy a permanent, final print.

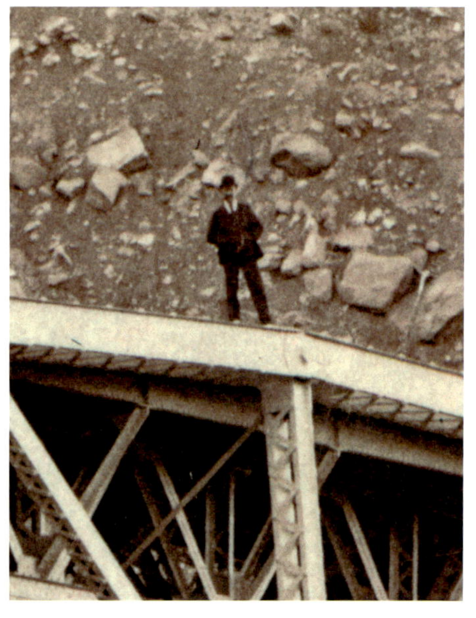

An eight-times enlargement from the original print.

The picture we see here celebrates the building of the Canadian Pacific Railway's Stoney Creek Bridge, British Columbia, in about 1893. It includes a perfect example of the old photographic practice of putting a human being in a picture to demonstrate the scale of the scene. In drawings and prints made for the tourist trade before the invention of photography, the viewer might expect a bit of exaggeration when sights such as ancient Egyptian monuments are shown with a tiny camel or guide in the picture. Early photographs continued this practice but provided irrefutable evidence of the immensity of such subjects.

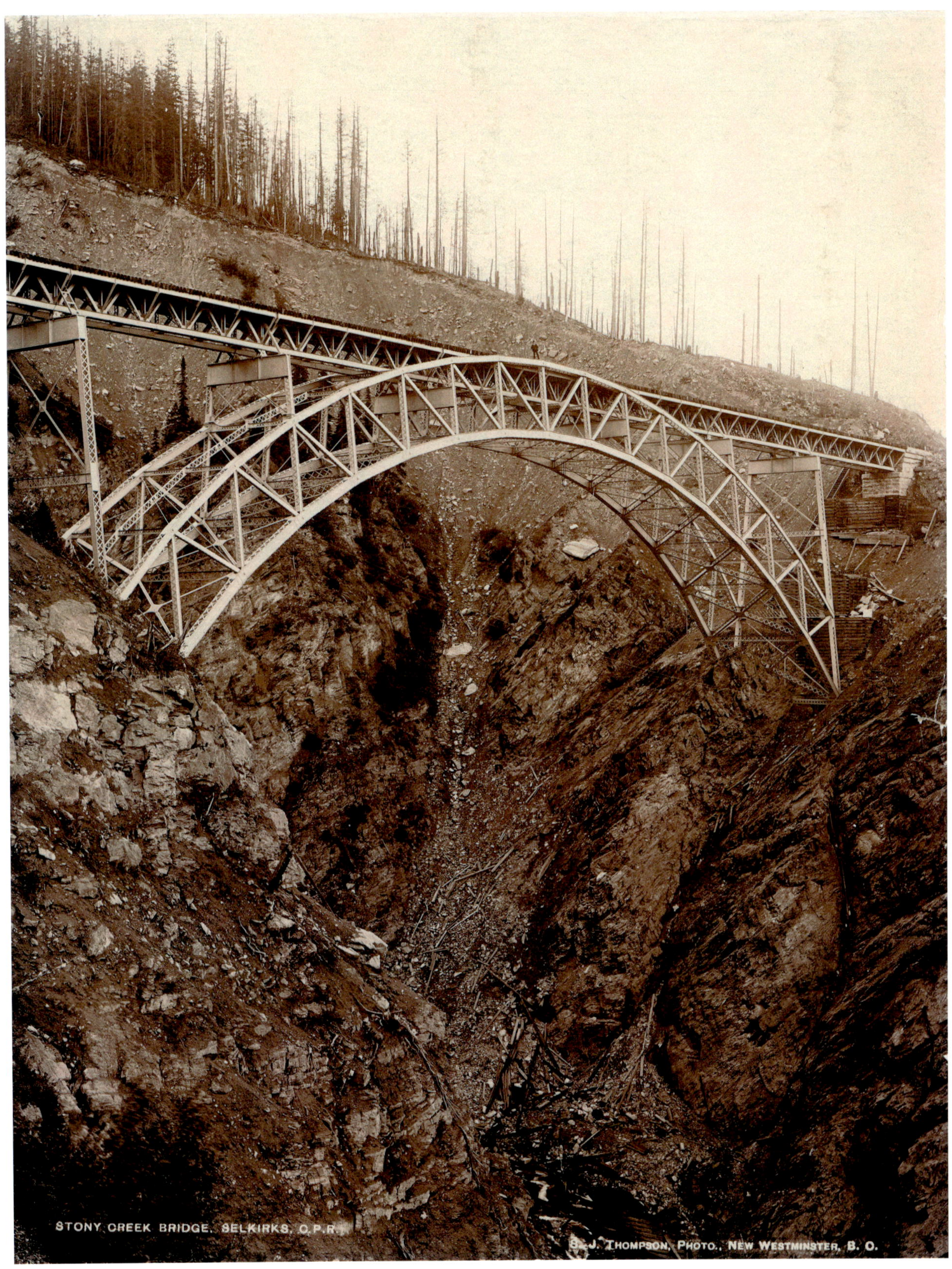


**Gelatin-based printing-out paper.** S. J. Thompson. *Stoney Creek Bridge. Selkirks. C.P.R.* c. 1893. 9⅛ x 7⅛ in. (23.2 x 18.1 cm)

# Part 6

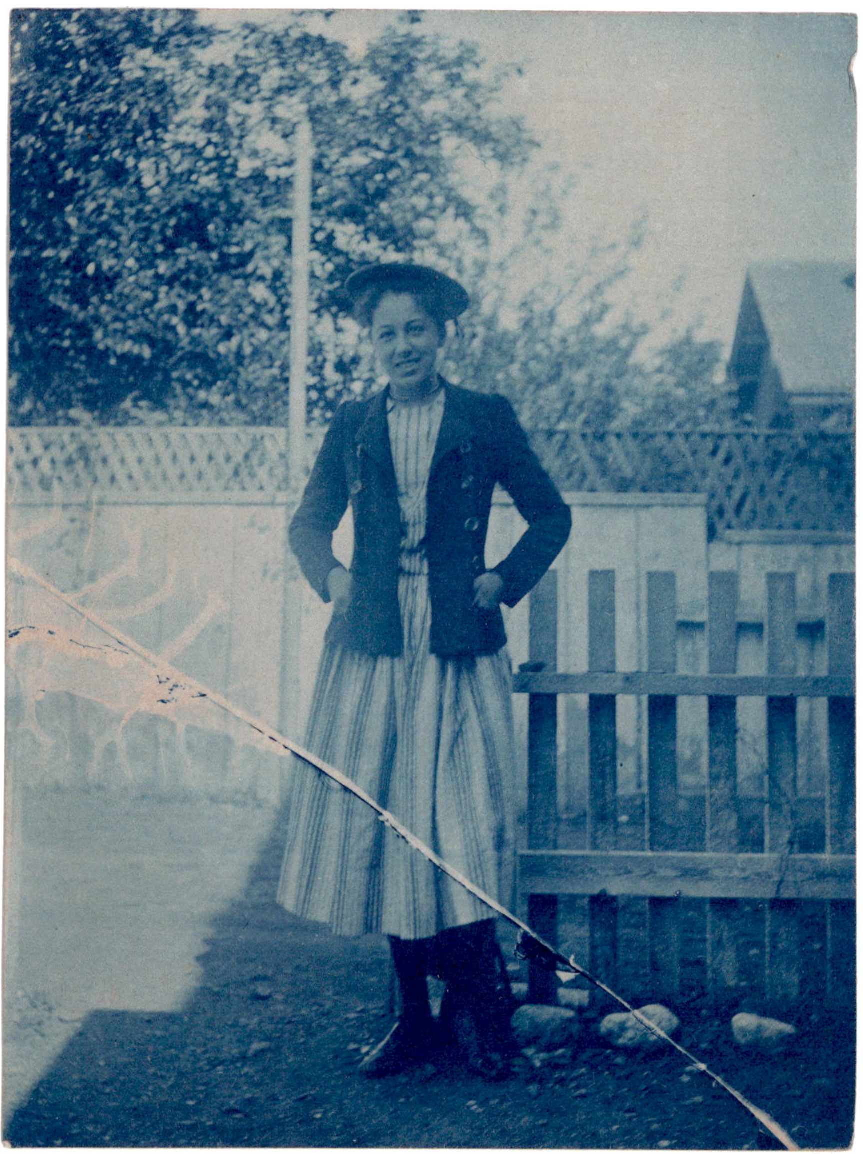

In the nineteenth century a great many odd and obscure printing processes were developed that did not involve silver, the most significant of them using either colloids (such as gelatin) that could be hardened or iron compounds that would change upon exposure to intense light. This section makes no attempt to list all of the alternative processes but concentrates on those that were most widely used.

**Blueprint.** Photographer unknown. *Elizabeth Perry Howard.* c. 1890. Printed from a cracked glass dry-plate.

# Non-silver processes

# Non-silver processes

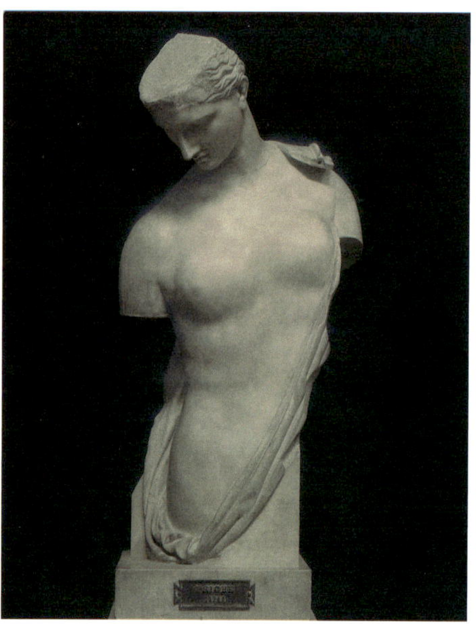

A print from the same negative, but one made with a greenish pigment.

## 6.1 CARBON PRINTING

There is a large difference in the light energy needed to make a negative and to make a print. The negative is usually made in a camera, whose lens focuses the light that goes through it so that any point on the negative only receives light from a single point on the subject. The lens might be "fast," which means that it has a large aperture in relation to its focal length, but even so the illumination landing on the negative is minute compared to the light running in all directions out in the world. Only silver compounds are sensitive enough to record the faint levels of light that come through the lens. When we make a print by contact—that is, by holding the negative directly in contact with the material to be printed—the light we use has no need to carry information. It can be as bright as we wish, and can come from a large source, so that many points on the surface of the light send their energy to every point on the print. The result is that compounds with low sensitivity can be used in contact printing, and there are many materials sensitive enough for this use.

Silver salts are of course one such material, and were used as printing-out media as well as for making the latent image in the camera. Iron too exists in a whole range of light-sensitive compounds that, when coated and handled properly, can leave a deposit of their own or reduce other compounds to a visible metallic state. A third group of materials is the colloids, a rather loosely defined family of glues and proteins that can be sensitized to light in such a way that they will harden upon exposure and lose their natural solubility in water. The most commonly used colloid for photographic printing purposes is gelatin, the same material found in photographic films and plates.

The great printing process based on hardened gelatin is the carbon print. The process gets its name from the early use of carbon black as a coloring, but almost any pigment will work. The underlying principle of the carbon print is that a thick layer of gelatin, holding some form of pigment, can be sensitized to light and exposed by contact to a photographic negative. The thin parts of the negative will expose the gelatin layer heavily, the dense areas only slightly. After the exposure, the unexposed gelatin—which remains soluble—can be washed away and a positive print, made of pigmented gelatin, will result. If only it was really that easy.

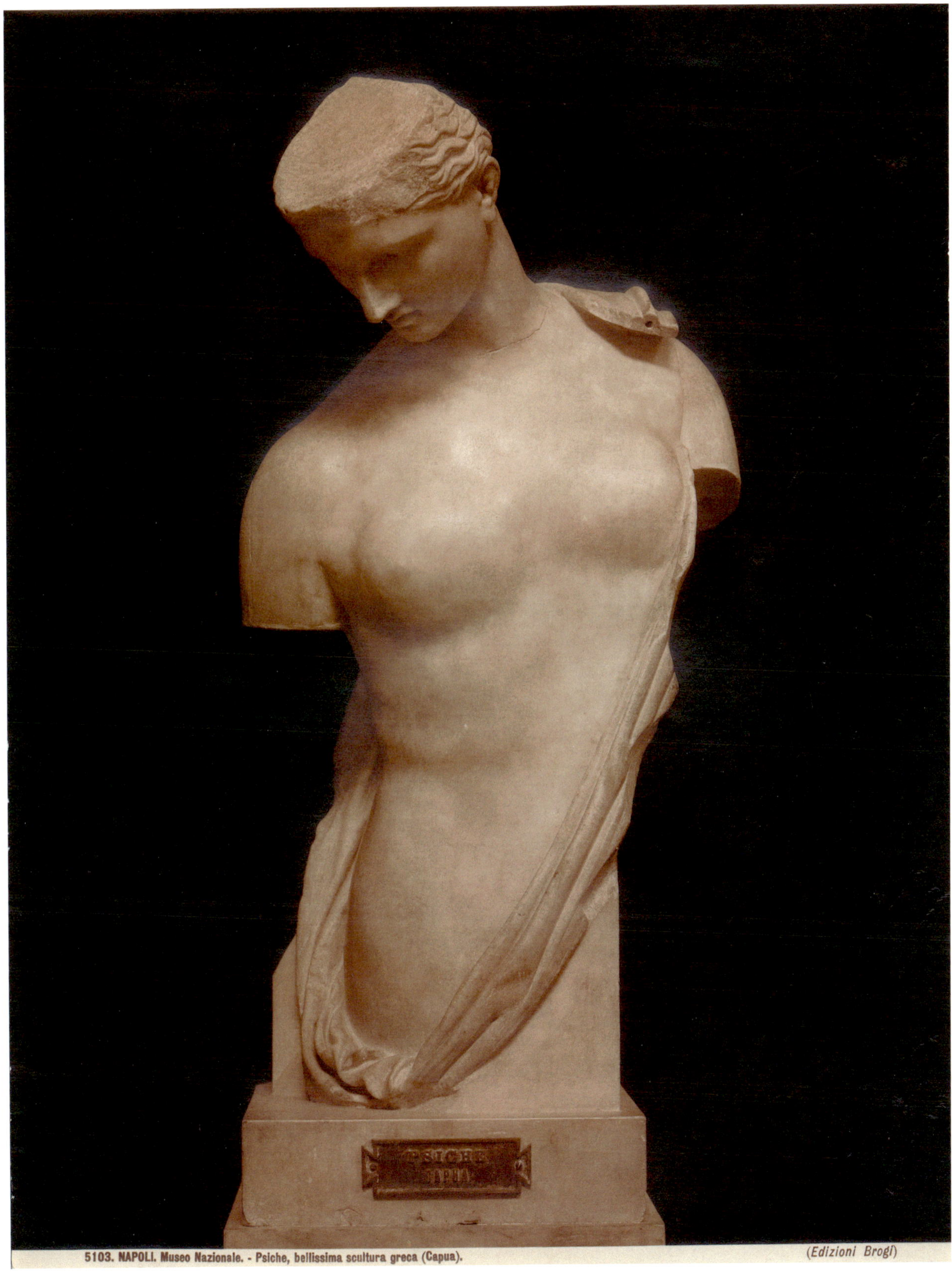


**Carbon print.** Edizioni Brogi. *Psiche, bellissima scultura greca (Capua).* c. 1910. 14½ x 11 in. (36.8 x 27.9 cm)

## 6.2 CARBON PRINTING

Here is a simplified description of carbon printing.

It starts with a sheet of gelatin-coated paper, which would have been purchased ready made. This paper is insensitive to light, but holds a relatively thick coating of gelatin that has had a great deal of pigment worked into it. The paper, called "carbon tissue," curls severely because the gelatin is only coated on one side. A sheet of it is cut to the desired print size and immersed in a weak solution of potassium bichromate, then withdrawn and squeegeed onto a polished sheet of chrome-plated steel called a "ferrotype tin." After being dried, usually with a fan, the sheet comes off the ferrotype with a highly polished surface. This carbon tissue—which the potassium bichromate has sensitized to blue light—is exposed by contact to a negative, usually with sunlight or an electric arc lamp. After exposure, the paper is immersed in a tray of cold water for a few minutes and then, while submerged, brought into contact with a sheet of "receiver" paper, which has a prepared surface that will stick to the gelatin. This sandwich of two sheets—hopefully with no bubbles between them—is then taken out of the tray and placed under a weight for about a half hour. Next, the pair is immersed in a tray of hot water at about 100 degrees Fahrenheit. After a few minutes in the hot water, gelatin and pigment can be seen oozing out of the sandwich, indicating that the gelatin has softened. The carbon tissue can then be gently peeled off the receiver sheet. Once this is done, the print appears on the receiver, and a few more minutes of gentle rocking washes away the remaining soluble gelatin and its pigment. The process is completed by shifting to cold water and then air-drying the print (which will tenaciously try to ruin itself by curling).

If this sounds complex, it is. Unfortunately the print thus made is backward—reversed from left to right. This is corrected by once more wetting the print and transferring the gelatin from the old receiver to a new one. Then the final print can be dried and mounted to permanently counteract its tendency to curl.

The print opposite is a magnificent large carbon made with greenish-black pigment. It has suffered somewhat over time by mishandling, and the paper base has turned unevenly yellow. That is too bad, because carbon prints are the most stable of all photographic prints as long as they are protected from extremes of humidity. I mention the size because it is difficult to make one of these prints well, and the challenges become all the more extreme as the size increases.

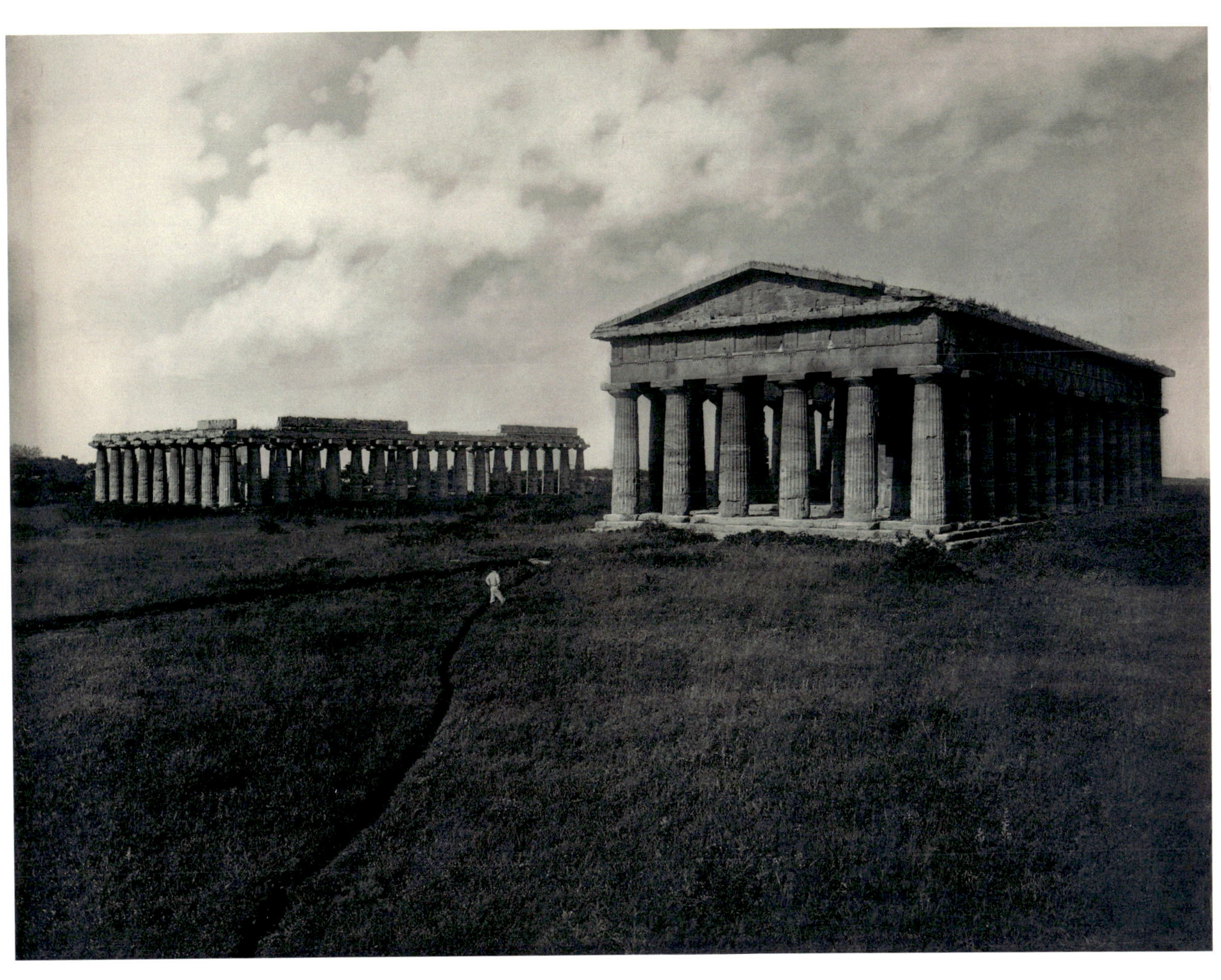

**Carbon print.** Edizioni Brogi. Temple of Neptune, Paestum. c. 1910. 15½ x 20½ in. (39.4 x 52.1 cm). This large carbon was undoubtedly made from an enlarged negative, itself most likely generated from an 18-x-24-cm original glass negative.

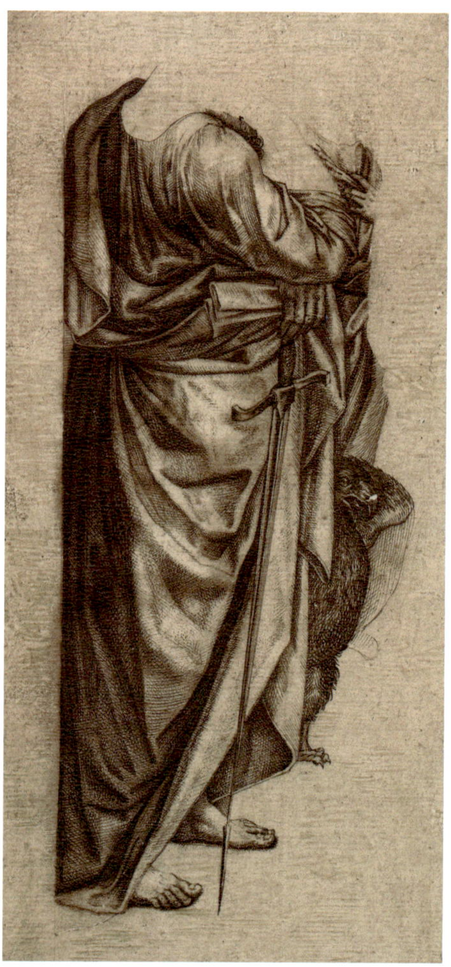

Another carbon print by Braun of a drawing by Raphael. The original carbon print is 12 x 4¾ inches (30.5 x 12.1 cm), but is shown here cropped a bit at top and bottom.

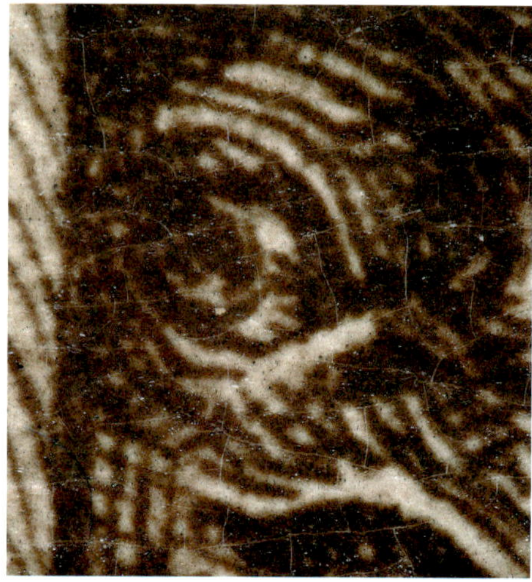

A small detail of the print above, enlarged twenty-five times from the original, showing the sort of cracks that often occur in old carbon prints.

## 6.3 CARBON PRINTS OF DRAWINGS

Carbon printing is the only practical photographic process that can make monochromatic prints in any color. The tissue is prepared with pigmented gelatin, and the pigment used can be virtually any that is available to painters. Since most of those colorants are inert, which is to say that they can be mixed in water or oil without reacting or changing color, carbon tissue could be manufactured and sold in a wide range of colors.

The print we see here uses an iron oxide pigment that closely imitates the color of the original Raphael drawing. In fact the red pigment in the print is the same we saw in the handprints on the cave walls at the start of the book, and is virtually identical to that in the red chalk with which Raphael made the drawing in the first place. This most ancient of pictorial materials works beautifully in photographic pigment printing.

There has always been a market for reproductions of art, and the carbon print was superbly suited to this task because the print color could be tailored to the original. Far more carbons were made of art than of pictures taken with cameras out in the world. The reproductions are often large, to look well on a parlor wall, and they show no grain whatsoever under a magnifying glass, so it is easy to mistake them for originals until they are taken out of their frames. Their surfaces are almost always a beautiful near-matte, and they are usually mounted on thick cardboard supports to keep them flat.

If a carbon print has been stored under poor conditions—changing back and forth from damp to dry and hot to cold—it can sometimes crack in a distressing pattern resembling a dried-out riverbed. If a print has never been mounted, it will usually show puckering of the surface where the gelatin layer is thick and the print dark. Other than these problems the only thing that can kill a carbon (short of pouring boiling water on it) is to mount it on bad board or frame it on top of an acidic wood backing. If well taken care of, these prints remain in perfect condition long after all other chemical prints would have self-destructed. Carbon tissue is still used in the revival of hand gravure, which is described later in the book, but carbon has completely died out as a printmaking technique.

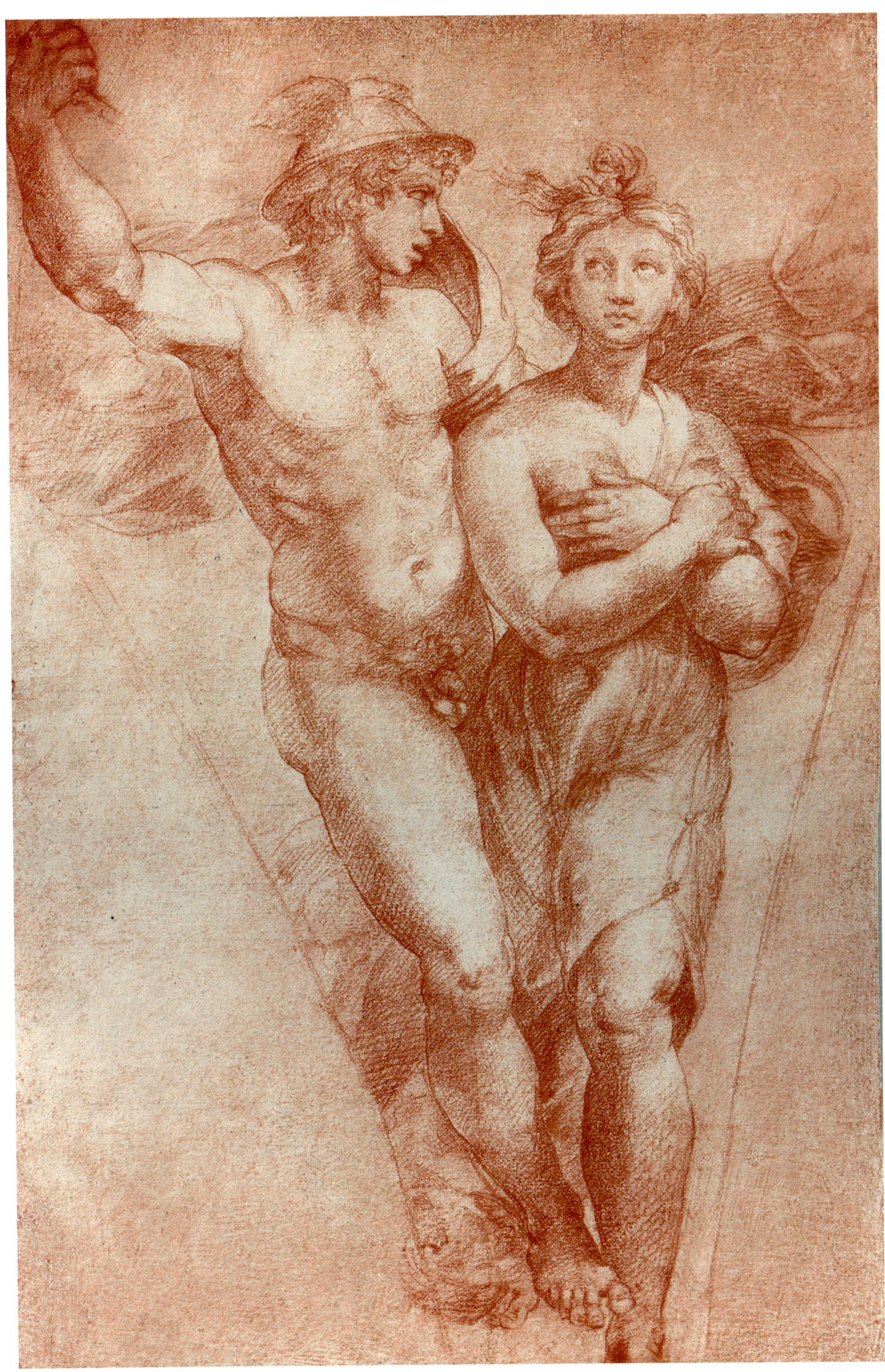

**Carbon print.** Raphael Sanzio. *Cupid and Psyche.* c. 1510. Drawing in red chalk. Photograph: Adolphe Braun. c. 1880. 13½ x 9 in. (34.3 x 22.9 cm)

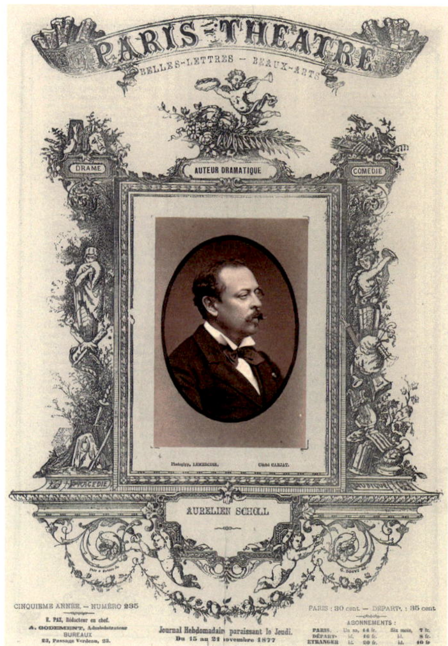


A typical woodburytype used as a theater advertisement, from 1877. The full sheet is about 14 inches (36 cm) high, but the print is only 5 x 3½ in. (12.7 x 8.9 cm).

## 6.4 THE WOODBURYTYPE

Chemically based photographic processes derive their color from characteristics of the chemicals used. Gold-toned albumen prints are purplish because that is the color produced by that particular chemistry. The carbon print avoids this restriction because it can be made with any pigment as its colorant. The woodburytype too has this freedom, since it is actually a cast replica of a carbon print, made out of the very same gelatin and pigment as the carbon original. I have little doubt that the woodburytype is the craziest process of them all.

The carbon print varied in thickness according to the amount of hardened gelatin left on the print. Where a tone was dark, the pigmented gelatin was thick; where light, the layer was thin. A woodburytype began with a carbon print, developed not onto a sheet of paper but onto a piece of glass. Once dry, the thin layer of gelatin—carrying all the modulations of height that derived from exposure—was pressed under extreme pressure into a sheet of lead, which took on the form of the gelatin (but as a negative, of course—thin where the gelatin was thick). This lead sheet was then used as a mold: hot, pigment-bearing gelatin was poured into it; a piece of paper, carefully manufactured to be of a consistent thickness, was placed on top of the hot gelatin; and the sandwich thus made—lead/gelatin/paper—was put in a press and squeezed. The excess gelatin ran out the sides, and after it cooled, a perfect print could be pulled off the mold. The gelatin, bearing its pigment, then varied in thickness in exactly the same way that it had in the original carbon.

The woodburytype plate was hard to make, but once done it could generate a lot of inexpensive prints. They curled terribly and the borders were always a mess, from the excess gelatin squeezing out, so they were always mounted. The woodburytype used no silver, which saved money, and it could produce monochromatic prints in any color, according to the pigment used. The prints were also never wet, so all the complex handling of wet paper was avoided. Most of them were colored to imitate albumen prints, so the viewers believed they were seeing a "real" photograph. The technology didn't allow prints much bigger than eight by ten inches, but these beautiful little prints never had to go into a hypo bath so they are remarkably permanent. Woodburytypes were most often used for theater bills and popular magazines; this one is from *Galerie Contemporaine*, a Parisian publication that was more or less the *People* magazine of its time. Both woodburytypes and their parent, the carbon print, sometimes show relief in the images when viewed along their surface in a hard light.

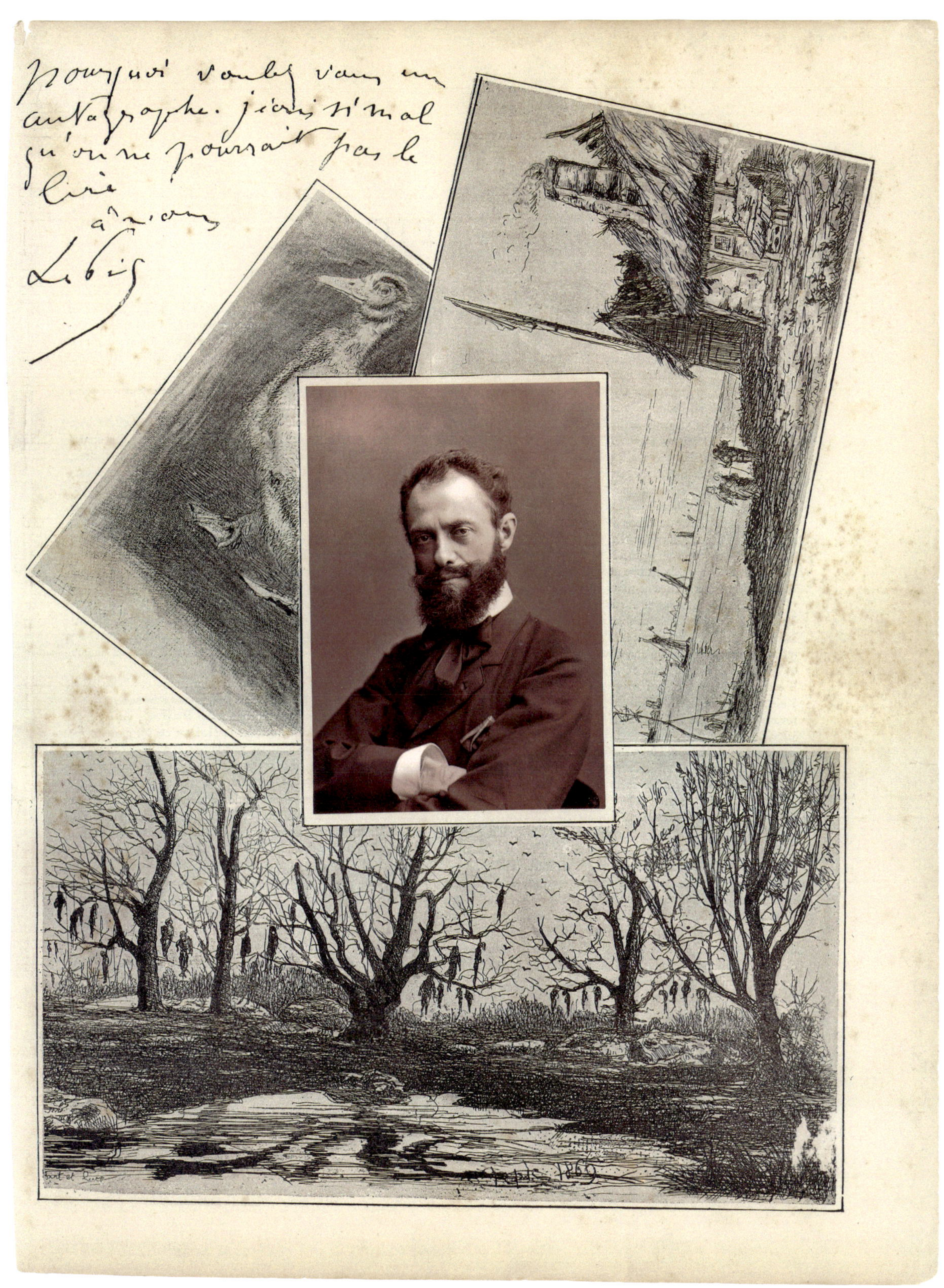

**Woodburytype.** Photographer unknown. Page from *Galerie Contemporaine.* c. 1896. 13¼ x 10 in. (44.7 x 25.4 cm). The small woodburytype has been pasted onto a sheet that has letterpress reproductions of drawings printed on it.

## 6.5 GUM BICHROMATE

Most photographic processes were capable of rendering an accurate series of tones, running smoothly from dark to light. When the images were made with pigment, as in the carbon process, a technical problem arose because between the exposed, hardened surface of the gelatin and the paper was soft, unexposed gelatin. If such a print was processed in hot water the soft gelatin would melt and the hardened image would simply float off the paper. This difficulty was met by attaching the exposed surface to a different support from the one that had originally held it—in other words, transferring the image to a new sheet.

A lot of work went into finding a way to make pigment prints that did not require such a transfer, and one method that survived and enjoyed some popularity was the gum bichromate process. In this case the colloid used was gum arabic instead of gelatin, and it was heavily pigmented and coated on a sheet by brushing it on while warm. A "toothy" sheet of rag paper was used, and the coating was designed so that, after exposure, it could be wetted and rubbed manually to loosen the soft gum while leaving the hardened gum and its pigment stuck to the paper fibers. Unlike all the other processes we have examined, gum bichromate did not produce a fine scale of tones. The retention of gum and pigment was haphazard, and since the toothy paper itself was the matrix that defined the tonal particles, the images were grainy. The rubbing that developed the image was done by hand and could strongly affect the way the picture looked. In some cases gum was printed on top of a platinum print (section 6.7), which allowed the smooth rendition of the latter process to support the heavy blacks that gum could produce while simultaneously covering up the graininess inherent in gum bichromate prints.

Gum bichromate did allow the artist who developed the print a great deal of tonal control, and the process became a favorite of the photographers working in the Pictorial style just after the turn of the twentieth century, when ideas about painting and photography became muddled together. It is a poor process, which we see here at its best in this landscape made in a French town in about 1910. Despite its occasional successes, gum bichromate is a poor process, unable to render the clear and beautiful tonalities that lie at the core of the photographic medium.

This detail, enlarged seven times, shows the random graininess typical of a gum print.

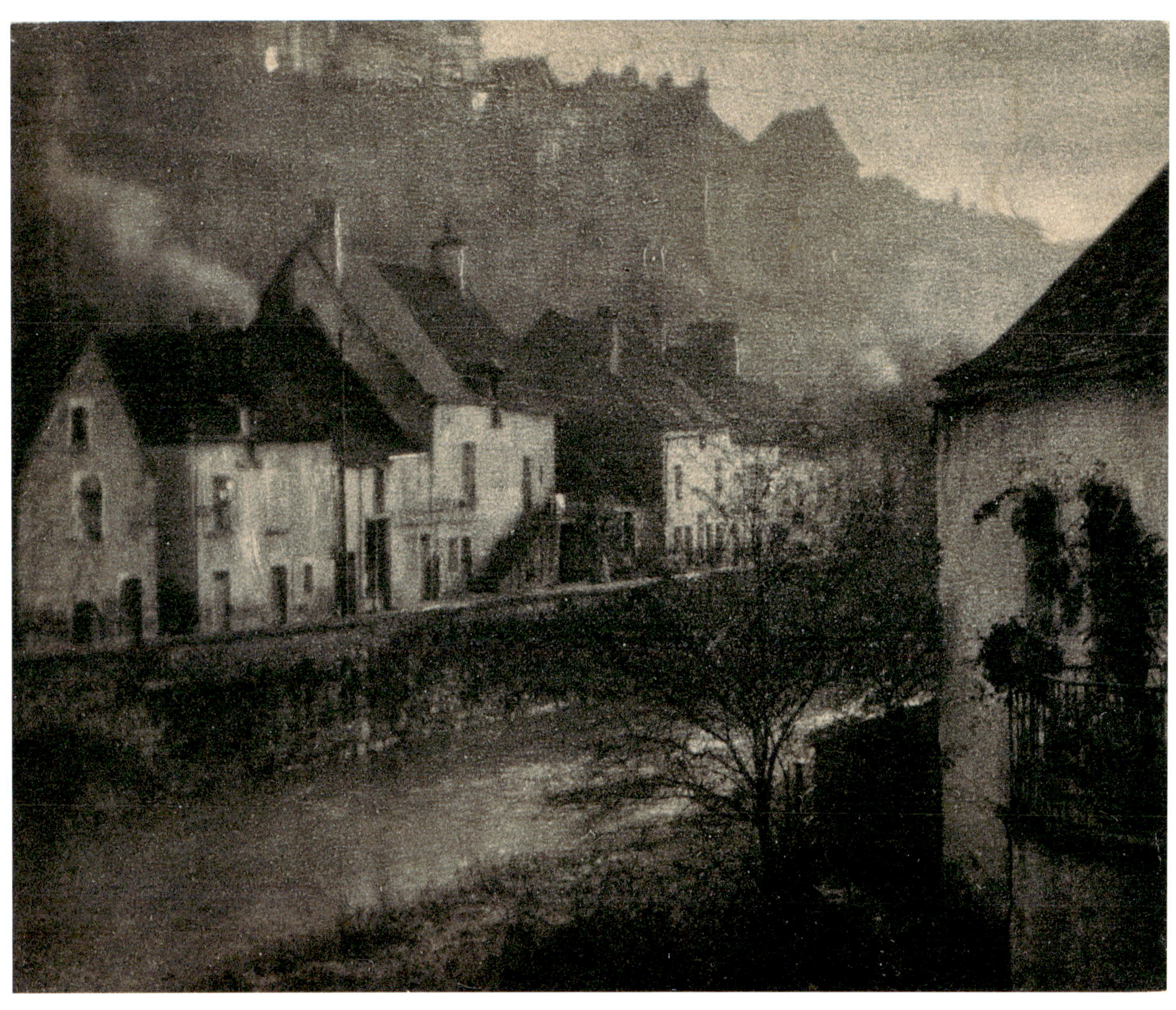

**Gum bichromate.** C. H. Roblot. Untitled. c. 1910. 6¼ x 7¾ in. (16 x 19.7 cm)

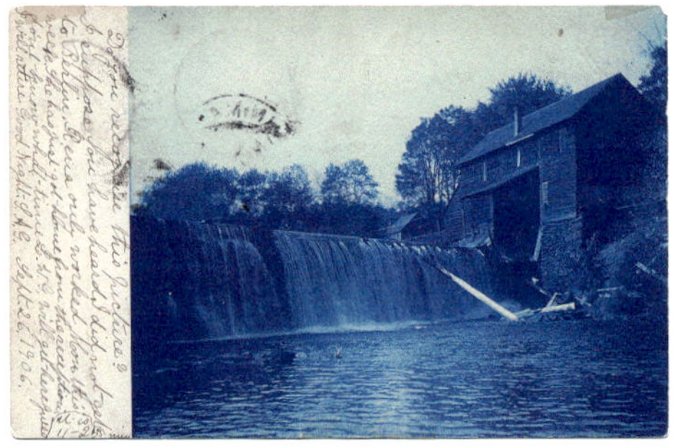

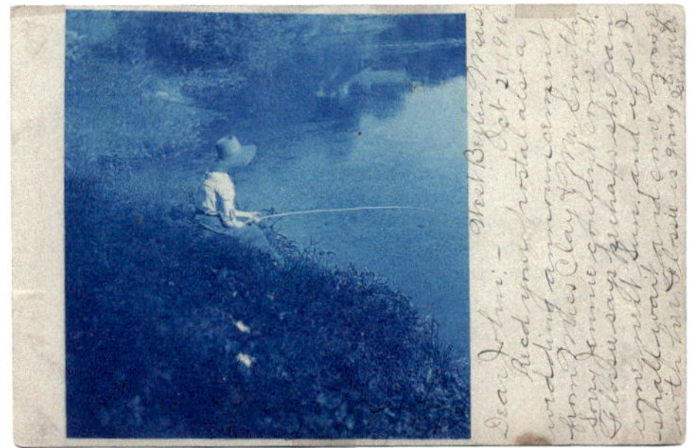

Blueprinting lent itself to the homemade postcard. These two date from 1906, when there was still some confusion about whether writing could appear on the address side of the card.

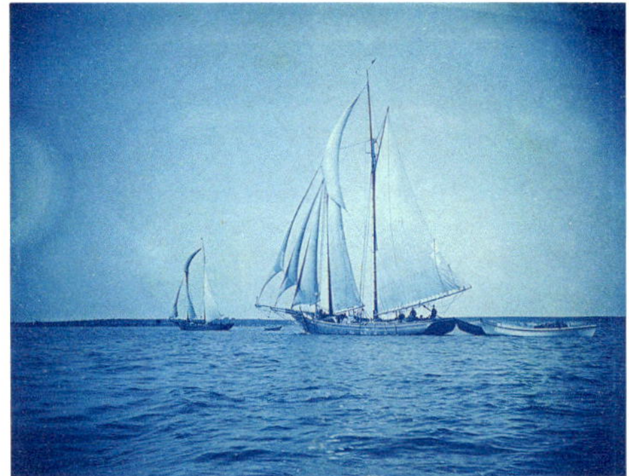

Many thousands of amateur photographs were made with small glass-plate cameras and printed by contact as blueprints. This picture comes from an album of New England coaster schooners photographed by Edward Wanton Smith in the early years of the twentieth century.

## 6.6 BLUEPRINTS

A number of "ferric" iron compounds undergo a chemical change when exposed to high levels of light, becoming "ferrous" instead and behaving very differently from the way they did in their former state. Of the several printing processes that use this mechanism the most common is the blueprint, which in fancy circles is known as the "cyanotype." The image is formed from an insoluble iron compound known as Prussian blue. This material has a long history as a dye, and was also used in machine shops to reveal inaccuracies in bearing surfaces that were being finished by hand.

Blueprints are contact prints made from original pen-and-ink drawings. They are really negatives: the blue background is composed of the iron compound. If an expensive material like silver were used, the prints would cost many times as much; instead they are extremely cheap, and the processing is simplicity itself—just washing the exposed print in water. For decades this was the process used to make all the blueprints that codified and dispensed engineering information, which had to be shared if people were to work together to make battleships, skyscrapers, and other complex constructions. In the 1950s the blueprint began to be replaced by the diazo print, a dye process that lends itself to mechanization and the use of automatic exposure and developing equipment. This new process avoided the messiness of developing the large blueprints needed for industry.

The blueprint has a beautiful photographic tonal scale, never seen in the engineering drawings that the process reproduced; those are chiefly composed of solid lines without intermediate tones. Many photographers working out in the field, or with severe financial restraints, used the blueprint as their primary process because it was simple, cheap, and permanent. These prints had just one serious drawback: they were brutally blue. We can accept the world turned into neutral gray, and even into the range of purples and reds that characterized early silver printing, but the blue does become tiresome after a while. Only a few serious artists used this medium, and then only sparingly. When we look outside the sphere of the well-known early photographers, though, we find a wide range of marvelous pictures printed this way. Almost all of them show a straightforward, workaday approach to the medium that can be a great relief if we have spent too much time wandering the halls of proper, refined photographic art.

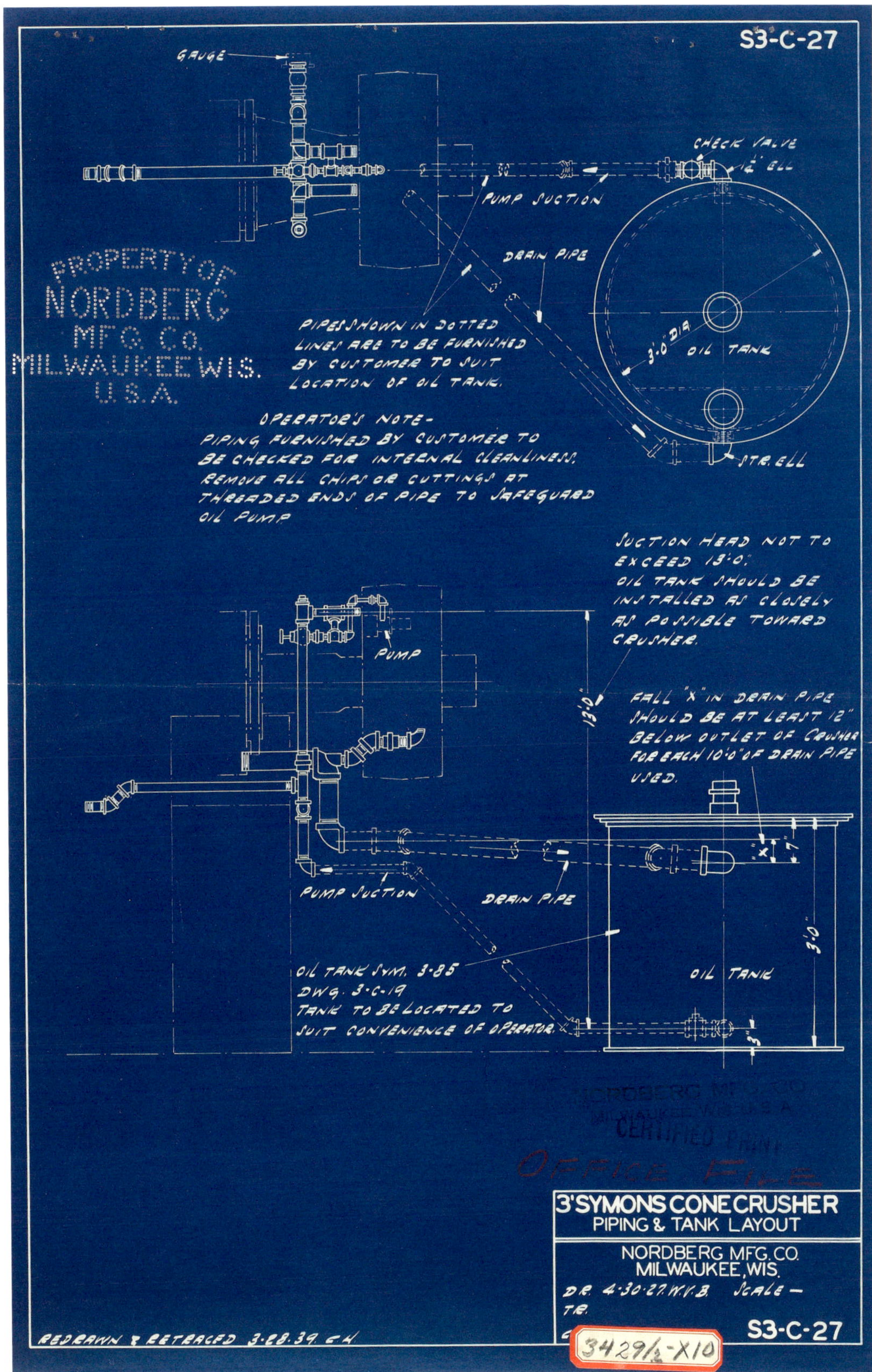


**Blueprint.** *3' Symons Cone Crusher: Piping & Tank Layout.* 1939. 17¼ x 11¼ in. (43.8 x 28.6 cm). Produced by the Nordberg Manufacturing Company, Milwaukee, Wisconsin. Nordberg's in-house identification stamp has been applied to this print at the upper left through a series of punched holes giving the company name.

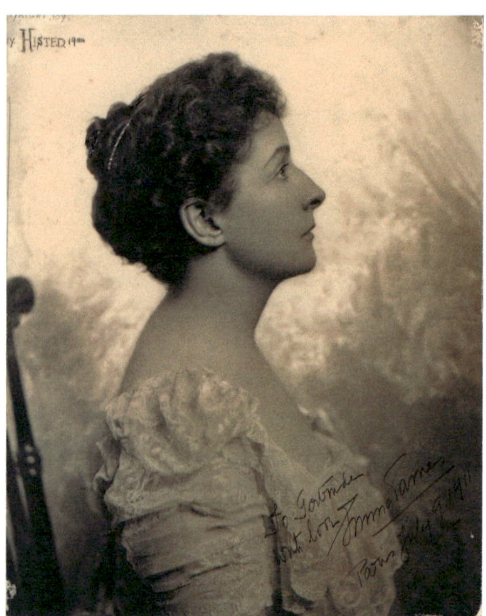

**Platinum print.** Ernest W. Histed. *Emma James.* 1900. 9½ x 7⅝ in. (24.2 x 19.5 cm). A professional studio portrait, printed in platinum and probably toned with mercury to alter the neutral platinum color.

## 6.7 PLATINUM

The blueprint might have made more pictures but the visual king of the iron processes was the platinum print. This method, invented in 1877 by William Willis, used the iron compound ferric oxalate as a sensitive material that, after exposure, could reduce a platinum salt to a visible metallic deposit. The paper was very sensitive to moisture but after manufacture could be sealed in metal containers and sold, so that photographers could make these prints without having to do complex chemical shenanigans. The irony is that the process is very easy to do from scratch without buying anything except the raw chemicals and the paper onto which they will be coated. It is worth explaining, because the practice of hand-coating a sheet for photographic printing purposes is simple and greatly enjoyable as a craft.

A coating made this way is not an emulsion—not a suspension of some material in another, like the silver salts dispersed in the gelatin coatings of film. To make a platinum print the raw chemicals are just dissolved in water, stored in bulk in separate bottles, and then mixed in careful proportions just before coating. The measuring is done with eyedroppers—so many drops of sensitizer (the iron compound), so many of metal (the platinum salt), and so many of other chemicals that control contrast. The drops are swirled together (perhaps in a ramekin stolen from the kitchen) and then poured right onto the center of the paper. The liquid is evenly spread with a broad, high-quality watercolor brush, then dried with a hair dryer (perhaps stolen from the family bathroom). In the print shown here we can see the marks of the watercolor brush extending past the image area. Unfortunately some photographers mistake these brushmarks for pictorial content and we occasionally see them in mounted or matted prints.

After the sheet is dry it is exposed to the negative, by contact, using either sunlight or some short-wavelength lamp. Once exposed (for five minutes or so in good sunlight), the print is placed face up in a tray and a developer is poured on top of it. The image appears instantly. Modern gelatin-silver papers develop slowly, as the gelatin emulsion controls the action of the developing chemicals. The platinum print uses no emulsion so the chemical reaction of development is nearly instantaneous. After a minute or so the print is cleared in a weak acid (which removes the iron compounds and unused platinum), rinsed for a while in running water, then dried on a screen. The wet print is always more beautiful than when it dries. It takes a strong mind to put the memory of the wet print away and to accept the one that has dried by a few hours later. Some photographers in the past varnished or waxed their prints to try to retain this enticing wet look, but these treatments almost always yellowed over time and caused more damage than good.

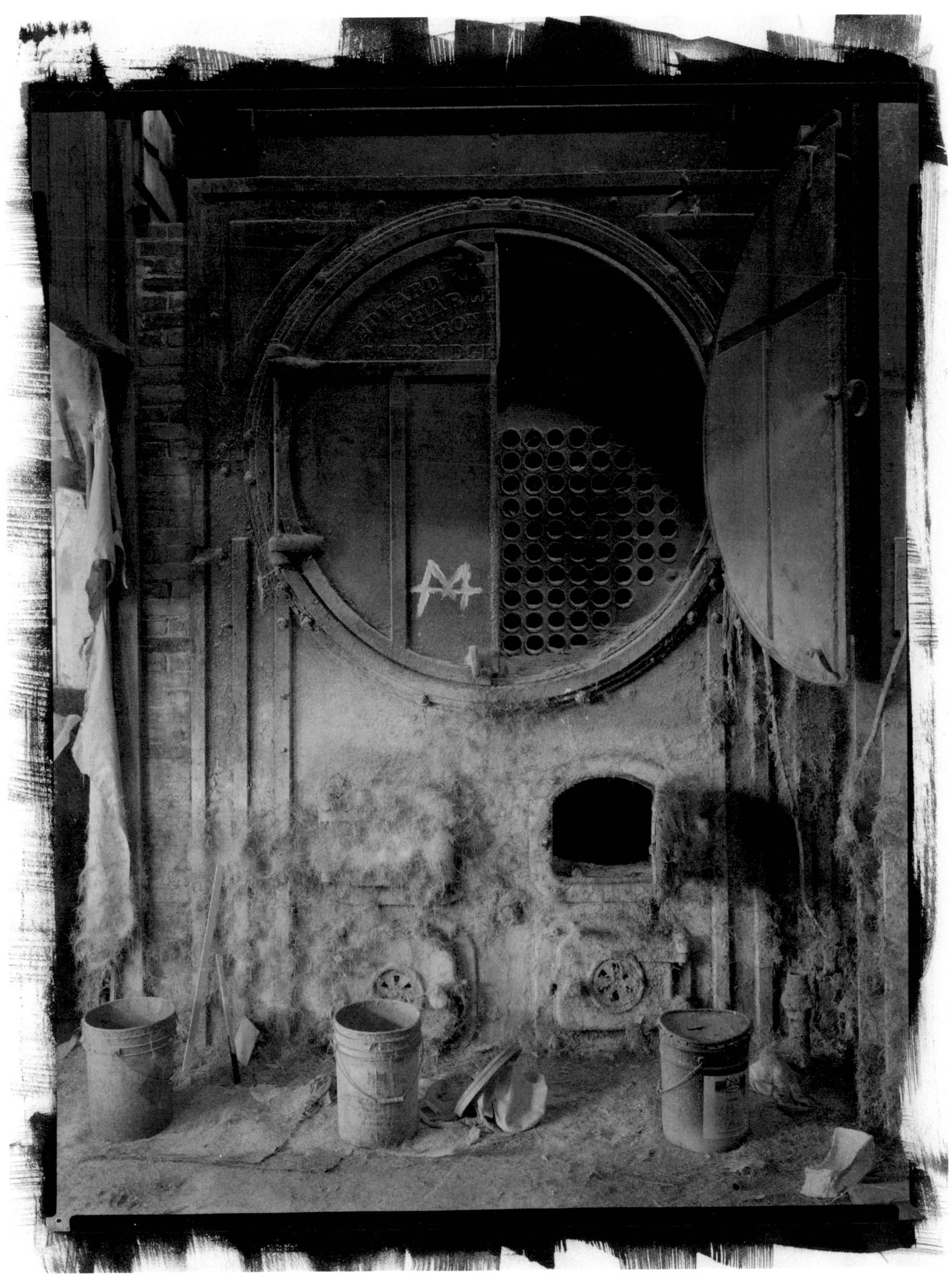

**Platinum print.** Richard Benson. *Fall River Boiler.* 1978. 11 x 8½ in. (28 x 21.6 cm). This print is untrimmed, showing the brushmarks made when the sensitive iron/platinum coating was applied to the sheet of Crane's stationery that was the basis for the print.

## 6.8 PALLADIUM

The iron compound ferric oxalate turns upon exposure into ferrous oxalate, which can react to a number of salts and reduce them to their metal components. The three metals most often used in old papers involving this iron process were platinum, palladium, and silver. Platinum produced a beautiful neutral-to-slightly-bluish tone, depending on the sizing used on the paper. Palladium was much warmer, and the overall print color was brown, but this metal could also produce a far blacker deposit in the shadows than could platinum. Silver reduced by iron made a greener deposit. A paper called "Satista," made with this less expensive metal, was used a bit in the first part of the twentieth century, most notably by Paul Strand, but it was quite unstable and never very popular. Both platinum and palladium papers were extraordinarily stable, and prints made with these metals are the most long-lasting of all chemical photographs. The prints must be properly cleared and washed, but no hypo is involved in their production. A properly made platinum might degrade after many years through changes in the paper support; the metal deposit itself is absolutely permanent.

The Platinotype company manufactured papers that were pure in either platinum or palladium. They also made some alternate versions that used a mixture of the metals, with names like "Black Palladio." Homemade platinum prints almost always incorporate both metals. One reason for this is expense: palladium is much cheaper than platinum. The other reason is to get the deep black of palladium coexisting with the neutral tones of platinum. When I printed this way I always kept an eye on the Russian wheat harvest; when it was bad, Russian reserves of palladium and platinum flooded the market, to generate income for the purchase of grain from the United States. The prices of these precious metals fell and I filled my bottles to the brim.

Platinum and palladium prints were touted as having the finest tonal scale, but this is simply not true. The papers had matte surfaces, which cannot hold as long a range of tones as glossy ones. Platinum and palladium have the additional problem of being deposited right in the paper fibers, so that not only are the blacks weak (compared to a gloss black) but the detail in the shadows tends to be obscured by the paper. Nevertheless, a great platinum or palladium print is a wonder, and can convey photographic description in a manner unlike any other process. The secret here is not to judge these prints by comparison to other processes but to view them by themselves. Comparison drags things being judged down to their common denominators, and clouds our eyes to the special qualities of each one.

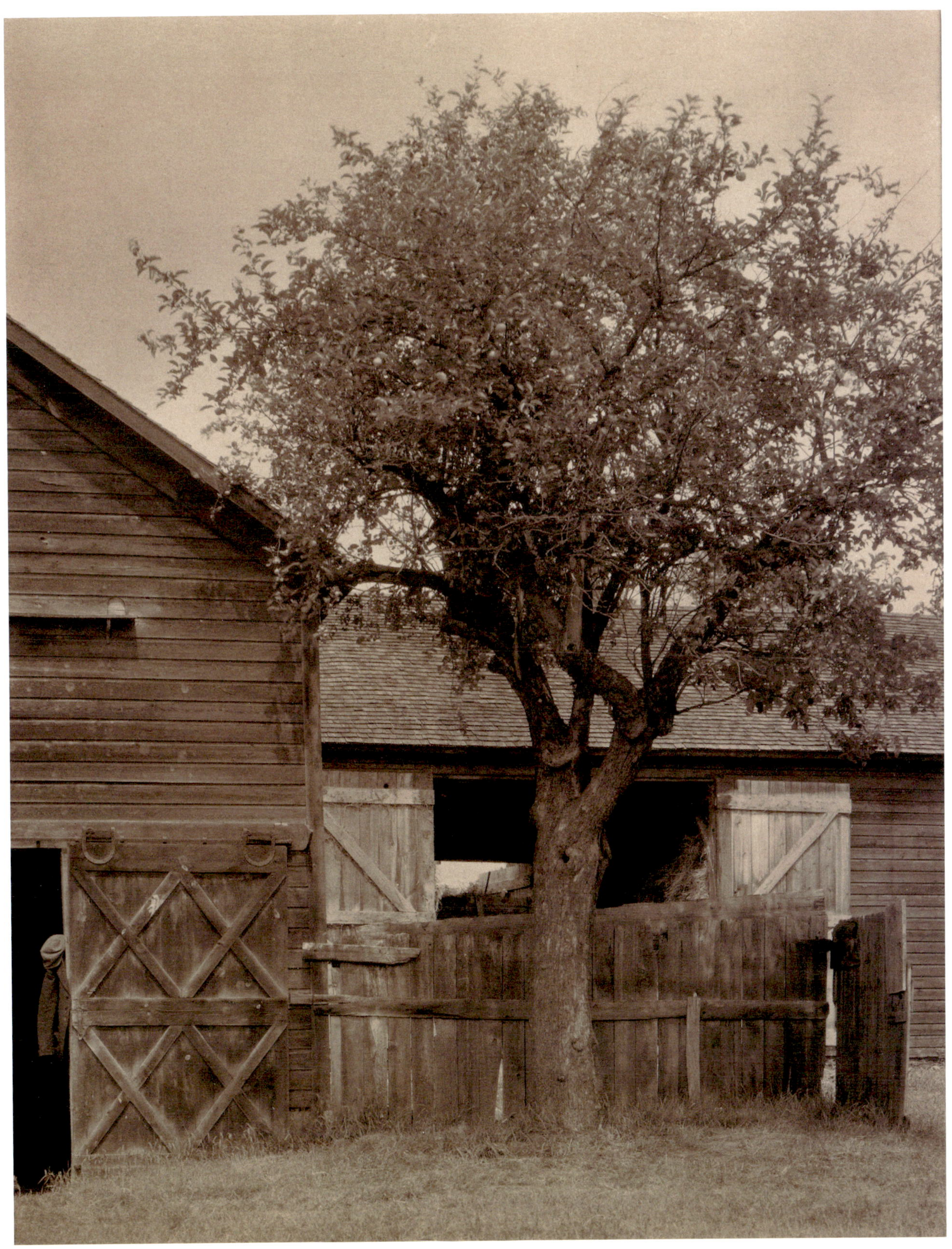

**Palladium print.** Alfred Stieglitz. *The Barn.* 1922. 9⅛ x 7⅛ in. (23.2 x 18.1 cm)

## 6.9 MODERN PLATINUM PRINTING

Platinum paper enjoyed a vogue during the late Pictorial years but its commercial manufacture ended in the 1930s. Many early processes stumbled along in the first part of the twentieth century and then gradually died. From about 1940 until 1980 the overwhelming majority of the chemical photographs made were modern, black and white, gelatin silver prints, and that process, along with the rapidly increasing use of color photography, dominated the field. In the 1970s a few people began to revive some of the old technologies. Platinum was at the forefront of this revival because it was suited to homemade coatings. In the area of ink printing, hand photogravure underwent a similar revival, since it, too, could be easily done on a small scale with available tools. A subset of photography grew up called "alternative processes," and art galleries and museums began to show work made in the twentieth century using technologies developed in the nineteenth.

The picture we see here is a perfect example of this fertile new patch of old photography. Both the photograph and its print were made by the great photographer Irving Penn. He shot the picture with an obsolete old camera that had a twelve-by-twenty-inch negative size, having been designed for photographing large groups—another return to earlier technologies. The print was made on a sheet of rag paper, using a tremendously rich coating, full of expensive platinum and palladium. Penn was working free of the financial constraints of mass manufacture. He chose these two metals to take advantage of the qualities of each material: the platinum produces relatively neutral tones while the palladium produces a blacker deposit. The coating, exposure, and processing are absolutely perfect, and the print, with deep blacks, brilliant whites, and smooth intermediate tones, is a high point in photographic printing regardless of the medium used. In his other work in platinum Penn even went so far as to make multiple negatives, each dealing with a particular part of the photographic scale, to be printed onto a single sheet of paper through more than one exposure. To allow accurate registration, he made some of these prints on a sheet of paper mounted on aluminum. The technique of multiple exposures comes out of the printing trades, which use multiple impressions to build picture structure not available in a single pass. Penn, on the cutting edge of modern photographic technology in his conventional work, turned the other way, grabbed hunks of the nineteenth century and the ink printing crafts, and created exciting new pictures using long-dead methods. The lesson is that traditional chemical photography is an extraordinarily flexible field, which, even as it disappears, has hardly been touched.

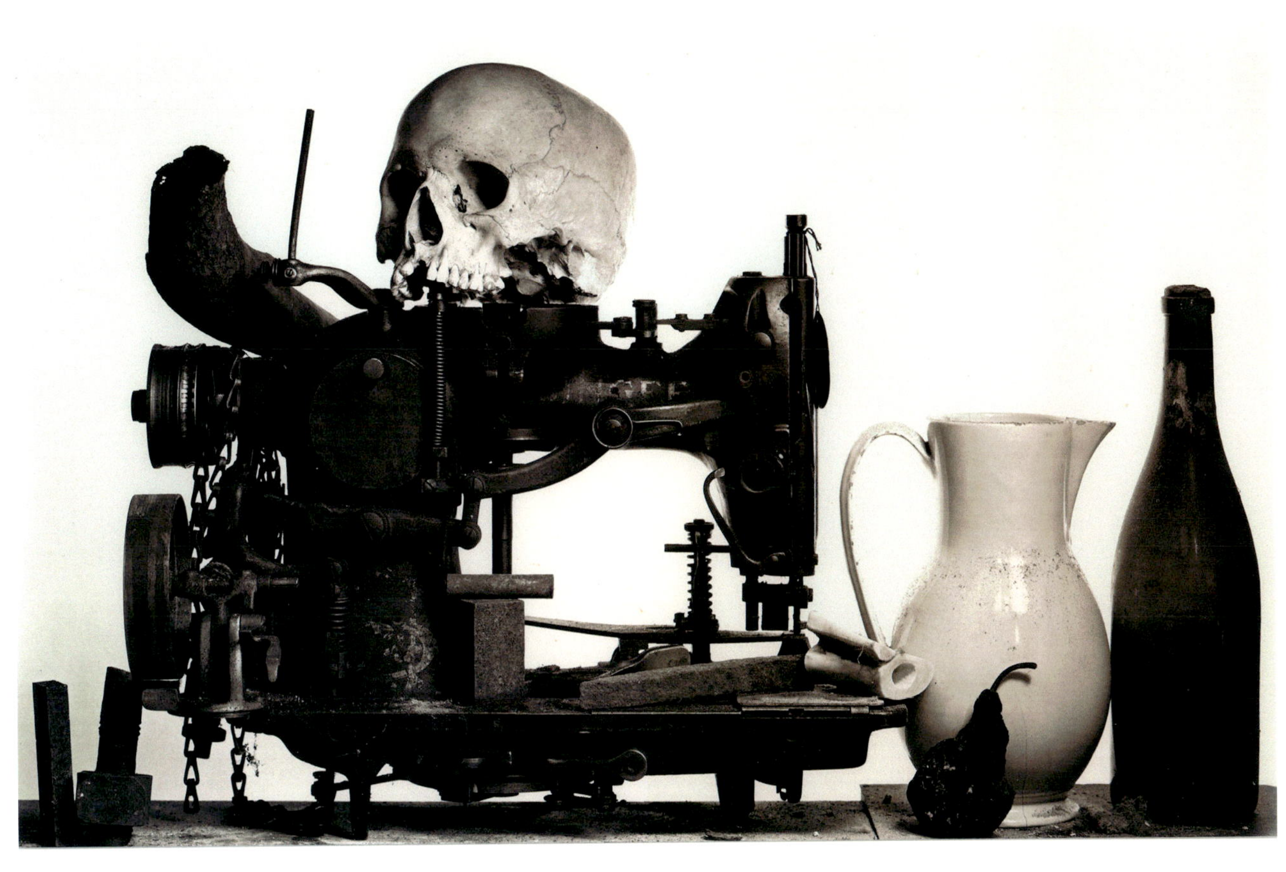

**Platinum and palladium print.** Irving Penn. *Composition with Skull and Pear, New York.* 1979. 11⅞ x 19 in. (30.2 x 48.3 cm)

# Part 7

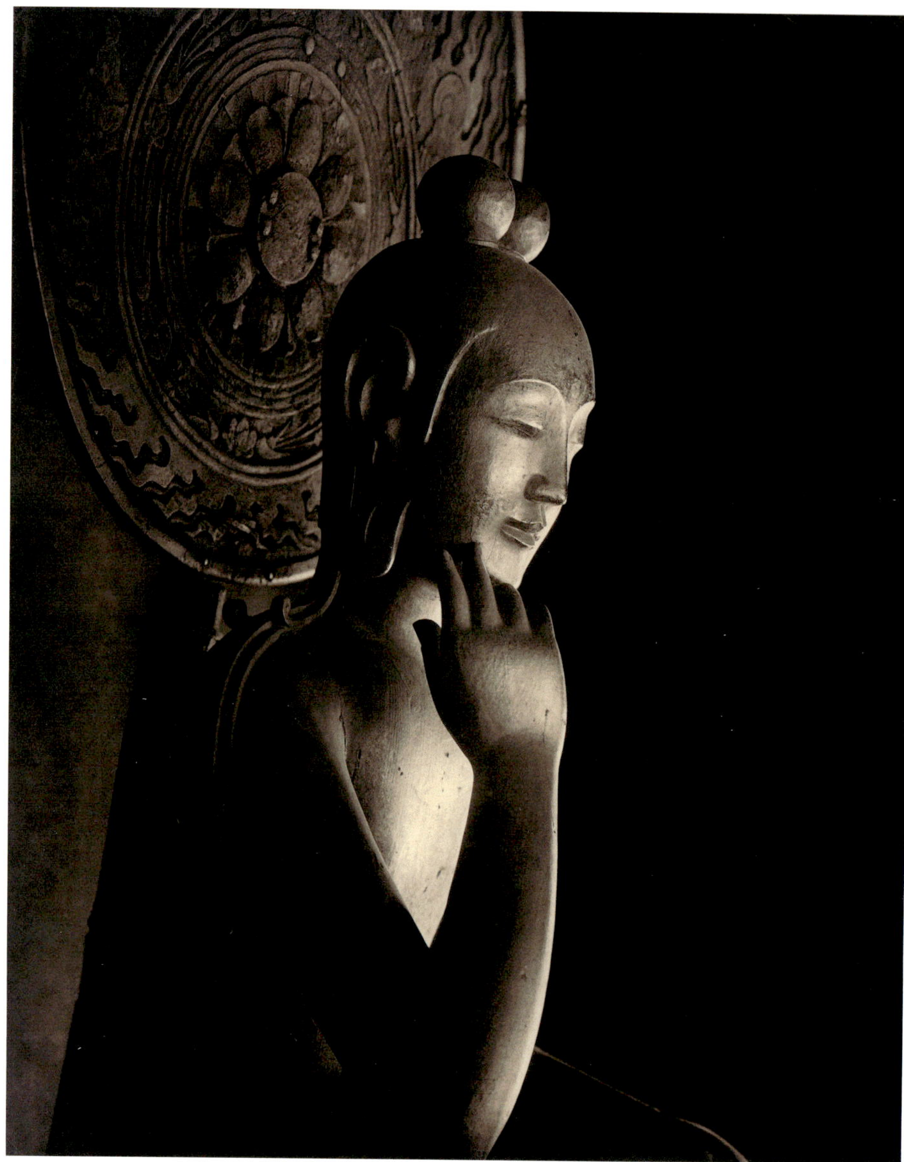

The era of modern photography began with the great innovation of the dry plate. Now that camera-ready materials could be purchased off the shelf, the medium underwent far more than a technical change: the physical manipulations of photography shifted to the background and concerns with picture content came to the front. According to the photographer Tod Papageorge, this invention opened the door for photography to become more like poetry than carpentry.

**Gelatin silver print.** Photographer unknown. *Nyoirin Kwannon.* c. 1933. 10¾ x 8¾ in. (27.2 x 22.2 cm)

# Modern photography

7.1 The dry plate
*The dry plate and its application to paper prints.*

7.2 Developing-out gelatin silver paper
*Neutral print tone in black and white photography.*

7.3 The Kodak Number 1
*Photography for the masses using roll film and factory processing.*

7.4 The hypo problem
*The destructive properties of fixative.*

7.5 Sepia toning
*Color toning for black and white prints.*

7.6 Professional photography
*Weddings and such immortalized by photography.*

7.7 Family albums
*Vast numbers of photographs made by amateurs as family records.*

7.8 The negative
*The negative record, unseen but essential.*

7.9 Lantern slides
*Still photographs projected in the theater setting.*

7.10 Contact printing
*Low-sensitivity photographic papers.*

7.11 35mm photography
*The miniature camera evolves into the ubiquitous amateur and professional camera.*

7.12 Enlargements
*Highly sensitive papers used to enlarge small negatives.*

7.13 Black and white Polaroid
*Instant chemical pictures as a new art medium.*

7.14 Resin-coated paper
*Quick and dirty processing using papers that don't get wet.*

# Modern photography

## 7.1 THE DRY PLATE

The transforming technical innovation that created modern photography was the dry plate. Invented in the late nineteenth century, this new negative material completely supplanted the wet-plate process. All the old photographic technologies, whether for capturing images in cameras or printing them on paper, were chemical systems that the photographer assembled from raw materials. Photography had been much like cooking, with recipes to guide the practitioner, and secret formulas jealously guarded. The dry plate was a completely different thing. As the name implies, it was a light-sensitive plate that could be used dry without the need for immediate assembly that the wet-plate required. The chemistry of the new materials was far more complex than any photographic material that had come before, and the new plates could only be produced in a carefully controlled laboratory. Because they were used dry, these plates could be manufactured and sold later on; because they were hard to make, their manufacture was taken out of the hands of photographers and instead was done in large manufacturing plants. These two changes marked the turning point between old and new photography.

The dry plate held a light-sensitive silver salt in a gelatin emulsion on glass. The plates were far more sensitive to light than the older wet-plate; we say they had more "speed." The coatings were also perfect, something that had never happened before, and to top it all off, any given box of plates tended to be absolutely consistent in quality. All of these characteristics gave photography a great boost in ease of use, as they took the task of making materials out of the hands of the artist. A similar thing had happened in painting when paints and canvas became available in manufactured form, but painting is difficult whether we make our own paints or not. Photography, on the other hand, turned out to be remarkably easy if the materials came in a store-bought box and had only to be exposed and developed. Whether the pictures so made were good or not is another question altogether. It is impossible to know if the dry-plate era made photography better or worse.

The technology of dry-plate coatings quickly moved over to flexible film and then to paper for printing purposes. These new chemical coatings, whether on glass, film, or paper, completely supplanted all the older photographic processes. Wet-plate, albumen, platinum, and carbon all went into the junk heap under the assault of inexpensive, easy-to-use materials bought off the shelf of the local supplier. Now that the technical success of the picture was taken for granted, photography as a medium had to scramble to get its content back.

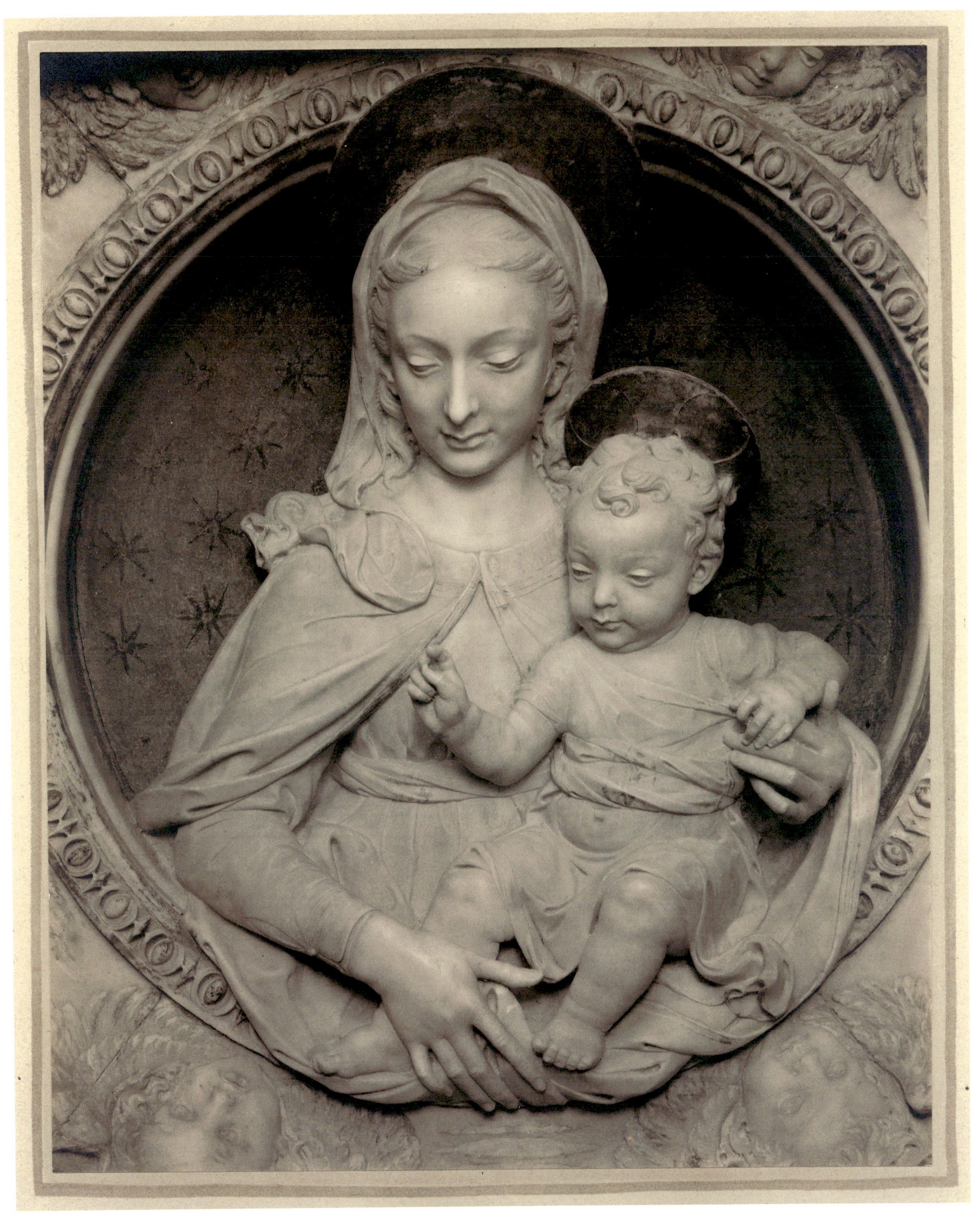

**Gelatin silver print.** Clarence Kennedy. *Madonna and Child (Tondo Relief of the Madonna and Child).* 1933. 11½ x 9 in. (29.2 x 23.8 cm)

## 7.2 DEVELOPING-OUT GELATIN SILVER PAPER

The story of the dry plate hovers in the background of photographic history because at first it was only used to make negatives, photographic artifacts that are never seen by the viewing public or bought by the traveling tourist. Negatives slide back into envelopes, to be printed later for new orders or to be simply lost in the closets of amateurs. When the dry-plate chemistry moved over to the printing side of photography things really began to look different. The gelatin coating of the dry plate, put onto a paper support, produced our modern "gelatin silver paper" (as the museums call it). This material uses the latent image—no more printing out—and produces an image color that is far closer to neutral than most earlier photographic printing processes do. The papers were exposed and then had to be developed, so we can call them "developing-out papers," or "DOP" (as opposed to the older POP, or printing-out papers). It really wasn't until the spread of gelatin silver papers and dry-plate negatives that the darkroom came into its own. Most nineteenth-century printing materials could be handled in room light and even the wet-plate could be manipulated under a red safelight. The new papers were in some cases as sensitive as the film was, and light-tight darkrooms became standard in photographic practice. Early in the twentieth century, dry-plate materials began to be made with full color sensitivity, and these required absolute darkness for handling films and plates.

The neutral tone of the new papers caused a stir. Except for relatively rare processes such as carbon, platinum, and blueprint, photographic printing had mostly been reddish purple, and in some way the new prints didn't seem to be "real" photographs in the way the older albumens had. The woodburytype printers had had a similar problem, and had often used purplish pigments to make the viewer think the prints were albumen. It didn't take too long for the public assessment to shift, and for photographers and their clients to accept neutrality as the norm in photography, but we find prints from the transition period that were made the new way but toned to look like the old. This pair is a perfect example. Both pictures were made for the tourist trade, and, because I found them together and they are of the same subject, I have always assumed they were made at about the same time. Both are on modern developing-out gelatin silver paper, but the lower one has been toned—quite beautifully—to imitate an albumen print. Toning hung around for a while, but later on it tended to be done to make the prints somehow more "artistic."

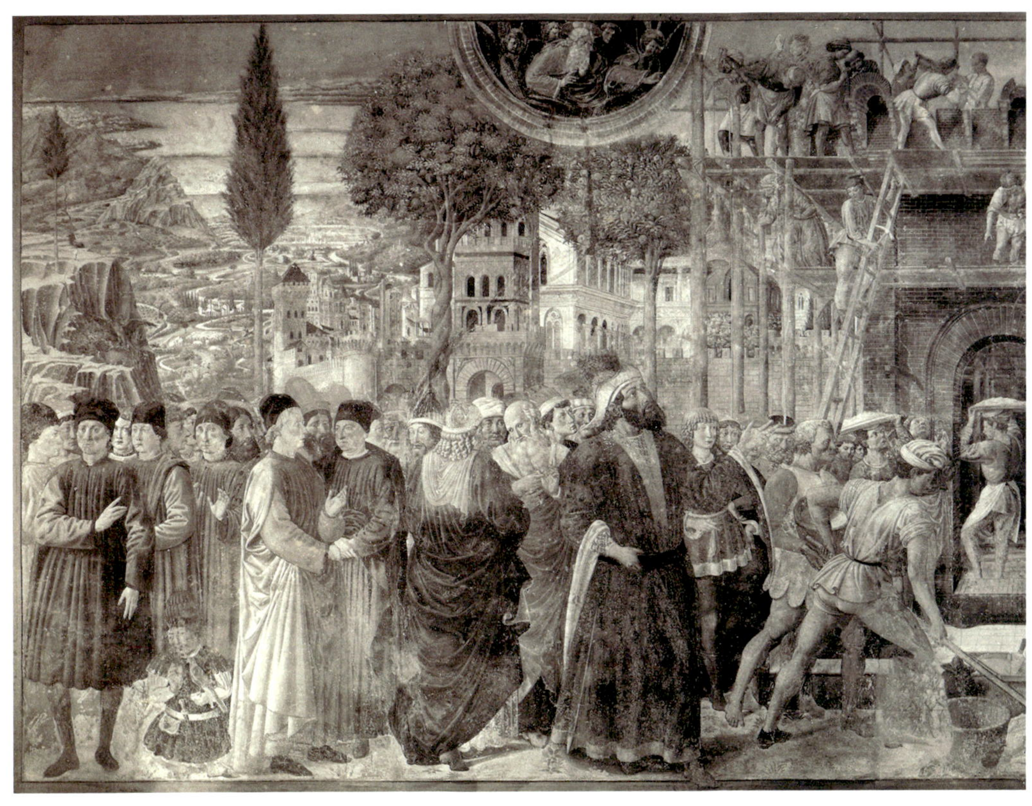

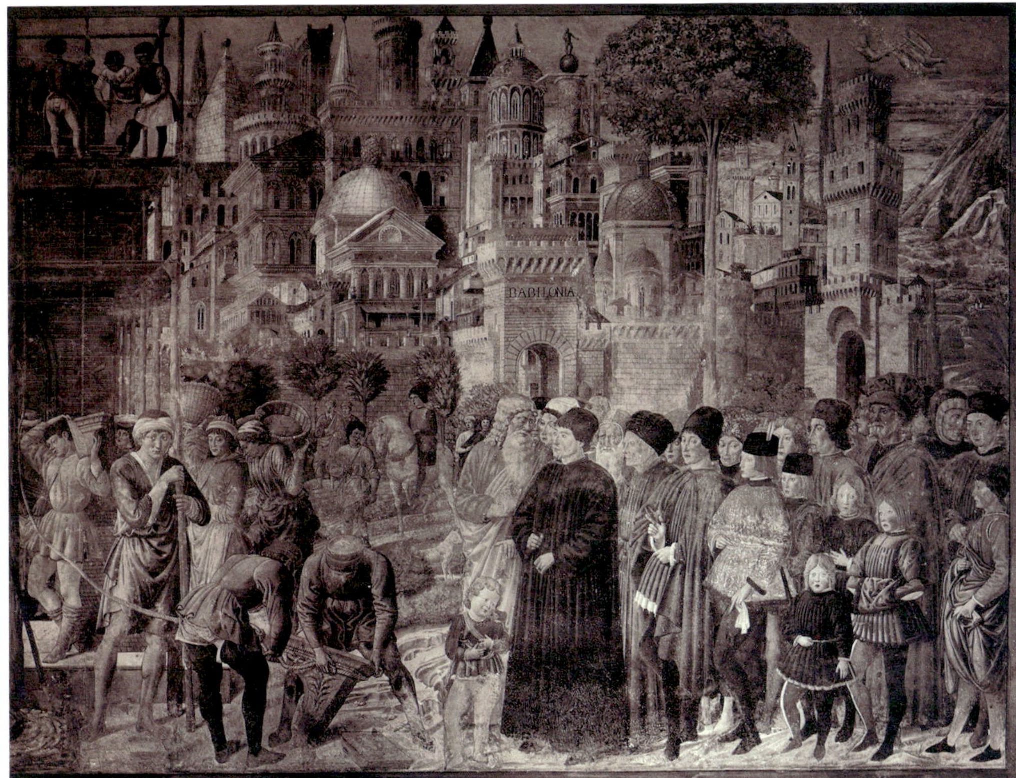


**Gelatin silver print.** Benozzo Gozzoli. Two frescoes of *The Tower of Babel*, Campo Santo, Pisa. c. 1470. Prints: photographer unknown. c. 1910. Each: 7 x 9¼ in. (17.8 x 23.5 cm)

## 7.3 THE KODAK NUMBER 1

If we think of the development of photography as some sort of evolutionary process taking the form of a branching tree, then we could say that the tree split, and grew a second trunk, with the development of George Eastman's amateur cameras. Eastman cobbled up a system combining his own ideas with those of others and produced cameras that were sold preloaded with a roll of flexible film. The user exposed the roll, then shipped the whole camera, its film inside it, to the factory for processing. The film was processed, the camera was reloaded with a new roll, and camera and prints were mailed back to their owner. All the user had to do was aim the camera, click the shutter, and use the mail—all of the technical chores were taken over by Eastman's company.

These extremely basic cameras used a single-element lens and a single-speed shutter. Because the lens was crude it did not cover the corners adequately so a round mask was placed in front of the film to crop them out, making the earliest Kodak pictures round in format. It was also a very wide-angle lens, which meant that as often as not the subject managed to be in the picture, despite the inaccuracy of the camera's viewing system. The wide angle of view from such a short-focal-length lens produced a description of the world very different from the previous photographic norm. For centuries, painters had been structuring their pictures so that figures, buildings, and landscapes appeared "normal," which is to say undistorted by a close point of view. We can even go so far as to say that the vision of the traditional painter was that of a photographer using a long lens. The Kodak camera, with its short-focal-length lens, distorted the perspective of a scene when compared to traditional pictures. We can see this distortion in the two photographs opposite: feet in the foreground turn down and enlarge as they approach the picture edge. Trees in the right-hand picture go from very tall to very short as they run from left to right. The young woman in that photograph, who appears abnormally small compared to the two men in front of her, is not in fact so small; her odd size is a result of the picture structure. While her head is lower than the men's, her feet also have risen up in the picture plane. Both these shifts of scale derive from the lens.

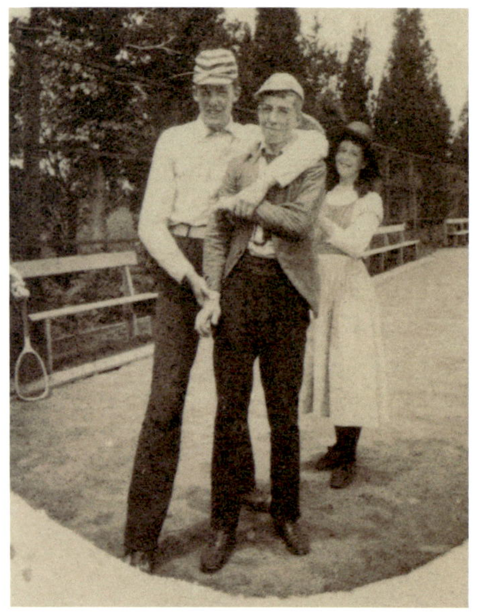

In some ways we can say that the history of photography has been one of steadily shortening focal lengths. From the classical, distanced view of the painter, photographic description shifted to encompass wider and wider angles of view. Both Eugène Atget, the great French photographer who so often worked in cramped spaces, and George Eastman, the American entrepreneur, moved photography a huge step in this direction through their adoption of radically descriptive wide-angle lenses.

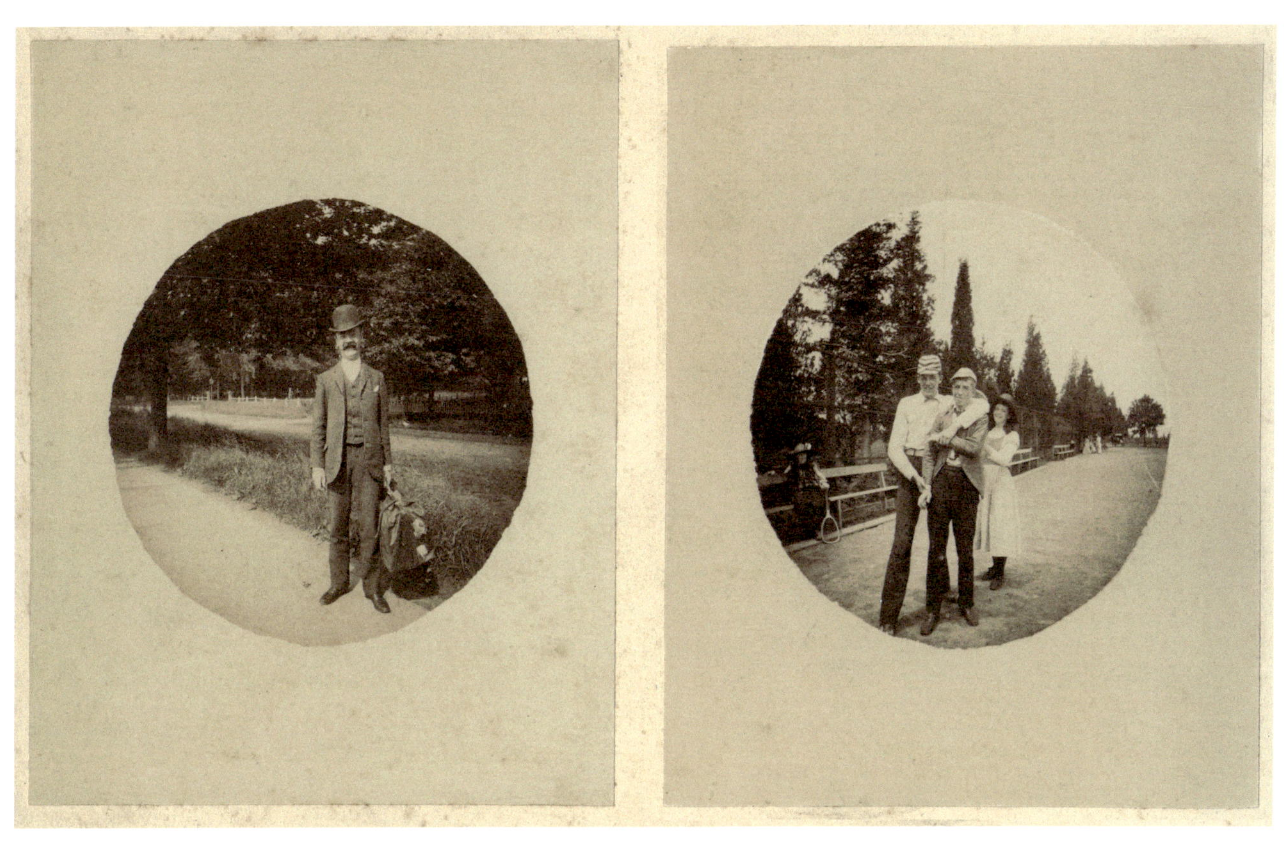

**Albumen silver print.** Photographer unknown. Two snapshots. c. 1890. Each circular image: 2½ in. (6.3 cm) in diameter

## 7.4 THE HYPO PROBLEM

I always like to say that photography had five inventors. We all know three: Niépce, Daguerre, and Talbot. A fourth, my favorite because of his pictures, is the Frenchman Hippolyte Bayard, who invented an autopositive paper process in the early 1840s. The fifth would be Sir John Herschel, a member of that small group of the wealthy English upper class who all seemed to know each other in the mid-nineteenth century. Herschel solved the great problem of how to make photographs permanent, suggesting to Talbot that he "fix" his pictures with the chemical sodium thiosulfate. This compound, and its cousin ammonium thiosulfate, have remained the primary fixing chemicals for nearly all silver-based photographic processes, from the very earliest until those modern chemical processes that are presently disappearing under the digital onslaught.

If you tried to think of the worst possible chemical with which to treat a piece of paper, "hypo," as the fixer came to be called, would be near the top of the list. Baths using thiosulfates do a superb job of clearing out undeveloped silver salts, which are unstable, but no matter how well a print is washed, it retains some residue from the fixer, and this chemical trace slowly eats away at the photograph and can turn the silver in the image into silver sulfide. If a black and white print is thoroughly washed and stored in a dry, cool, dark place, its life span is very long, but the hypo probably waits in there and could ultimately cause trouble.

As photographic prints degrade they can change color in two ways. First, when hypo converts the silver image to silver sulfide, the neutral gray metallic deposit becomes brown. Second, residual hypo (or other leftover chemicals from the print processing) can cause the paper itself to yellow. We see both these flaws in this eighty-year-old print. The first problem—of the silver turning—can actually be fixed, by wetting the print, bleaching the image, and then redeveloping it to its original silver state. If the print is old, there is a chance of losing it when it is rewetted, but if it survives that process the image can be dramatically restored. The second problem, of the paper turning yellow, has no solution that I know of, aside from trying a mild bleach that may or may not affect the silver image. The short version of all this is that photographic prints are delicate and doomed. They have the maddening habit of lasting well as long as no light falls on them and allows them to be seen, just as the proverbial tree falling in the forest may make no sound if no one hears its crash. Does the picture really exist locked away in a dark box? I think not. Better to look at it, enjoy it, and let it wear out like everything else in the world.

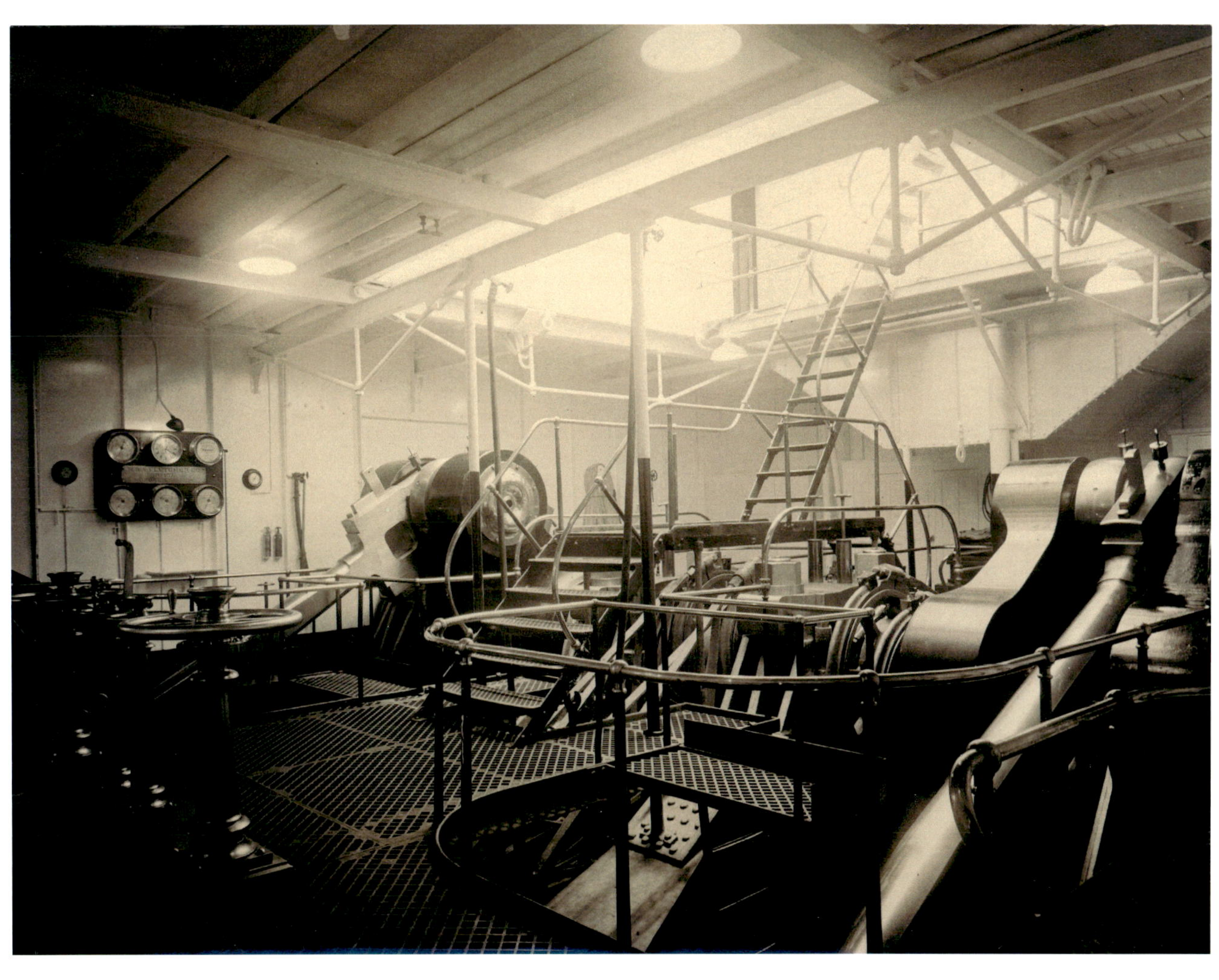

**Gelatin silver print.** Photographer unknown. Engine room of a Fall River Line steamer. c. 1925. 7⅜ x 9½ in. (18.7 x 24.1 cm)

### 7.5 SEPIA TONING

We simply have to mention sepia toning. It is probably the worst thing that has ever happened to photographs but, like neckties and hair dye, it's out there and has long been around to make things look silly. Somehow the idea grew in the first half of the century that a photograph would be better if it was brown. I have always assumed that this was a nostalgic link to the nineteenth century, when black and white photography was so colorful, but those early processes derived their color from the unavoidable nature of their chemical processes. Intentional toning of photographs is more like putting a veneer on a piece of wood: it provides a false appearance, as often as not covering up something that isn't too good in the first place.

I am being a bit unfair here, particularly with this photograph made by a Western photographer named Frank Jacobs who had a small studio in Montana in the 1920s. He has the glacier, mountains, tall fir trees, and even the children, in there for scale in this pleasant and dramatic view. Unfortunately the whole damn thing is brown—not a nice, albumeny purple-brown but a heavy yellow-brown that can only make us think of molasses or maple syrup. It is ironic that sepia-toned prints tend to be more permanent than those of silver alone, since the silver sulfide that produces the brown tone is a more stable compound than metallic silver.

Toning has persisted, and it found a truly useful niche when selenium was used for a light toning, giving a stronger black and an ever-so-slightly purple cast to gelatin silver prints. Many photographers used selenium toning because it was thought to make the image more stable. On a slow, fine-grained photographic paper, selenium can cause remarkable color shifts in selected tones of the picture, which came to be called "split toning." Some photographers use this color alteration intentionally as a way to enhance the impact of their prints.

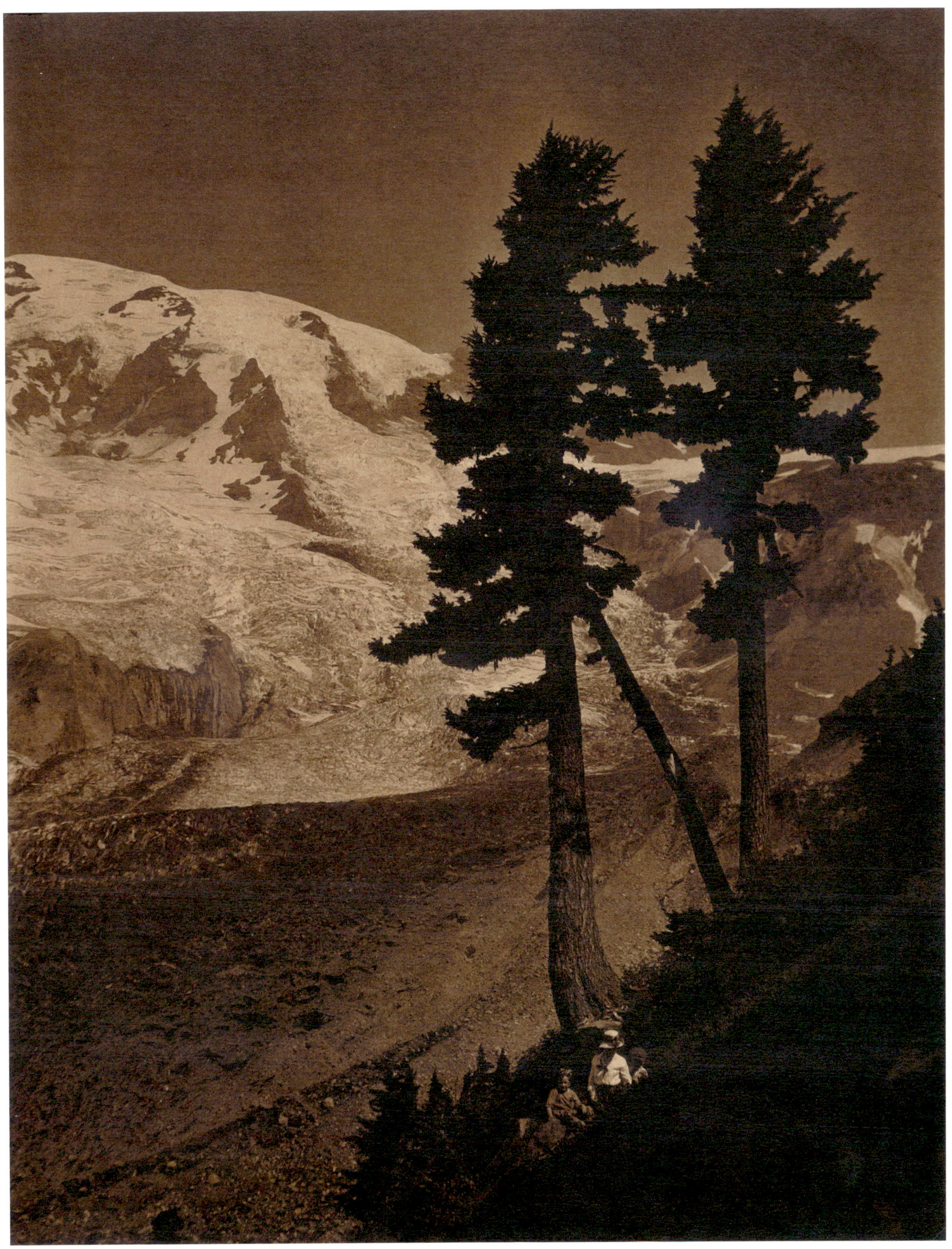

**Gelatin silver print.** Frank Jacobs. *View in the Rocky Mountains.* c. 1930. 13⅝ x 10½ in. (34.6 x 26.7 cm)

## 7.6 PROFESSIONAL PHOTOGRAPHY

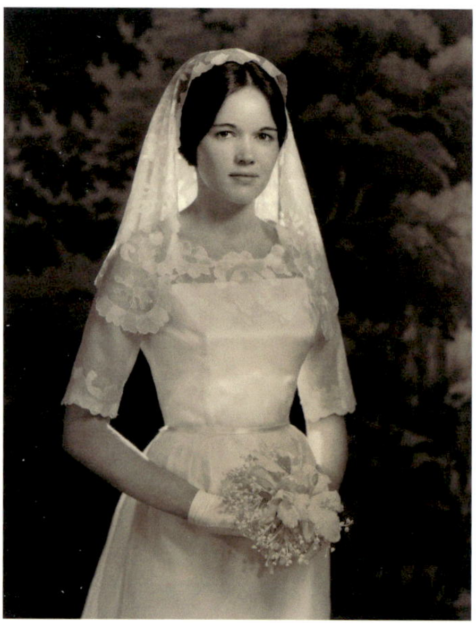

**Gelatin silver print.** Bradford Bachrach. *Barbara Murray on the Occasion of Her Wedding.* 1966. 13½ x 10½ in. (34.3 x 25.4 cm). As she saw herself.

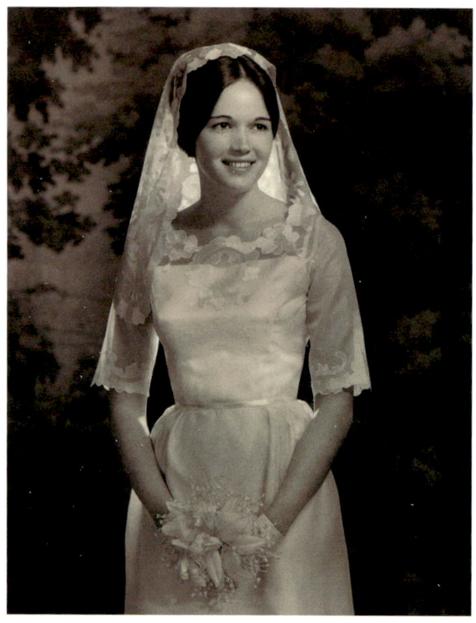

**Gelatin silver print.** Bradford Bachrach. *Barbara Murray on the Occasion of Her Wedding.* 1966. 13½ x 10½ in. (34.3 x 25.4 cm). As her mother wished her to be.

Photography is practiced by the amateur and the professional. The pros, called either "professional" or "commercial," work in studios, where lighting and sets can be controlled, or out in the field, with cameras, lights, and sometimes even assistants along to handle the gear. These photographers serve a wide range of clients and specialize in a particular version of the truth: reality depicted to approach an ideal that can replace our memory of the actual subject or give us a version of events not personally witnessed. The subject might be a wedding, as in this picture; a bowl of cereal carefully arranged for an advertisement; or a piece of reportage from the other side of the world. In all cases reality and picture often have a strained relationship. Artists are a different group; some know more than the most seasoned pro but most know embarrassingly less. The artists and the pros all pursue their own version of photographic "truth."

This picture was taken on the occasion of my wife's parents' wedding. It really is very good. The photographer knows just how to arrange that long dress, how to move the description to darkness in the corners (a painter's old trick to make a picture look good), and how to hold the attention of each participant in the scene. The photograph was made with a large-format camera and printed on a warm-toned, pebbled-surface portrait paper, perfectly exposed and so well processed that even today, over sixty-five years after the event, the photograph is nearly perfect. Teaching in an art school, I often find myself wishing that my students could handle a picture as well as this photographer did.

The problem, of course, is that Bachrach—first the founder, then the son, and later just the name of the firm—made this picture again and again. The same pose and technique were used endlessly, to crank out a series of pictures that the photographer never intended to hang on the wall together, so their sameness would never be revealed. Believe it or not, the child of this couple, born a few years after the wedding, had her wedding picture taken in the very same studio. Her husband (me) refused to pose for such a picture but her mother, whom we see opposite, demanded that at least the bride be photographed. She was, and we still have the picture, in two poses. In one she smiles the false smile put on to please her mother; in the other (her favorite) she has the same stern look her mother-to-be has in this photograph. We need to be careful about criticizing pictures such as these, since once the years have eliminated most of them, the few remaining won't be such clichés. The subjects will then stare back out at us freed from the cultural net that directed their interpretation at the time when they were made.

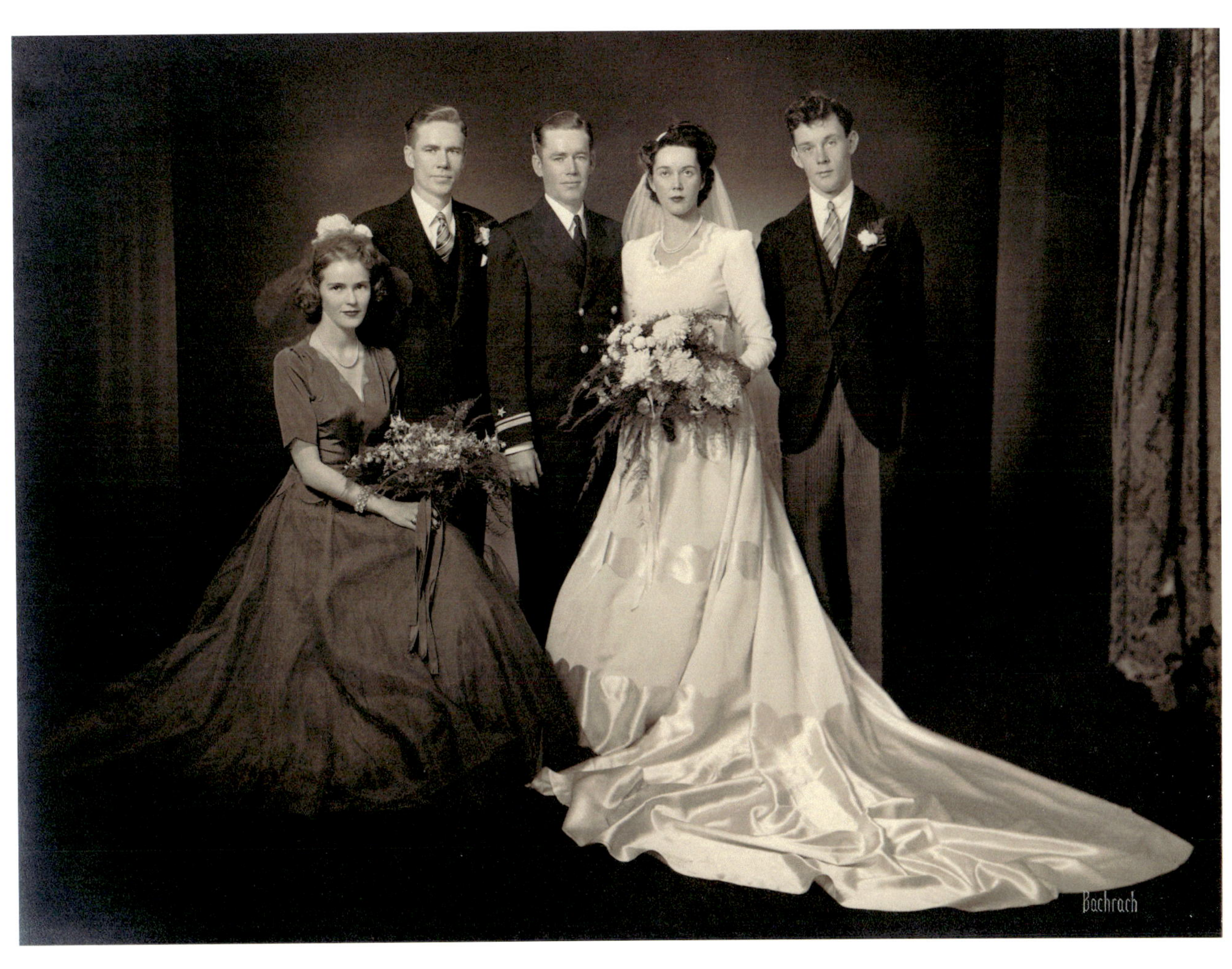


**Gelatin silver print.** Louis Fabian Bachrach. *The Wedding Party for Daniel Murray and Rita Callan.* 1941. 8⅜ x 11⅜ in. (21.3 x 28.9 cm)

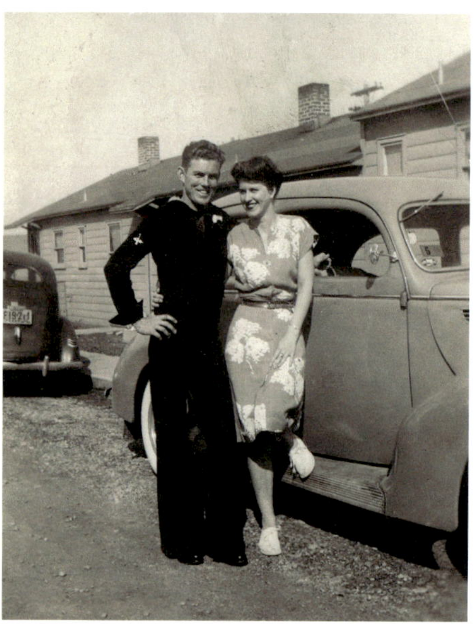

**Gelatin silver print.** Photographer unknown. *Tommie Freeman Daly and Loretta Franklin Daly.* c. 1944. 2½ x 2 in. (6.4 x 5.1 cm). After babies, events relating to the military are the most common subjects in many of these old albums.

## 7.7 FAMILY ALBUMS

Every junk shop in America has a family album or two for sale. They are usually rotting away, full of small yellowing snapshots, processed by the local drugstore or some mail-order lab and then lovingly stuck on black paper with rubber cement or fancy black photo corners. Most of the pictures are uninteresting. The person tends to be in the middle, too small, and as often as not barely recognizable. That is certainly not the case here. The photograph on the right is terrific, the figures posed beautifully on some half-collapsed wooden structure, the cigarette smoker framed by two brothers, each holding a rifle, and all the parts arranged to support the astonishing view of the eagle, dead and stretched out to show the eight-foot wingspan of America's national bird. The diagonal cable would never have sprung from the mind of a painter—only photography could have drawn it—and the backdrop of pine trees perfectly sets the stage for the wilderness where the eagle has lived and that the human beings have invaded.

Pictures like these were almost always made with roll-film cameras, direct descendants of the Kodak Number 1. The lenses tended to be pretty poor but since the prints were almost always contact prints—they were rarely enlarged—the image quality was passable. Because the cameras had poor systems for setting focus (if they had any at all), the main subject was usually out of focus, but this fault too was seldom noticeable unless the pictures were enlarged. Despite their drawbacks, old family albums remain treasure troves of photography. They bring home the fact that the medium draws much of its power from the richness of the world it records. These records only grow in power as they move away from the point of their origin, whether through physical distance or time. The eagle was a fact of life out in the woods where this picture was made; it became dramatic when viewed in the parlor back east, and even more so when looked at by the middle-aged son of the man on the right, who first showed me his father's album fifty years after it had been made.

Walker Evans said that there wasn't much that could go wrong if the sun was out and you made sure it was shining behind you as you made the photograph. He also knew that nothing could replace a remarkable subject. Evans's brilliance was often in seeing the extraordinary in the commonplace, then recording it with a directness that was unflinching. Even without his intelligence, the two guidelines of good light and a great subject can often lead to remarkable pictures. Millions of these are thrown out as the old albums fall apart and are discarded. The ease with which interesting photographs can be made is matched by the likelihood that most will ultimately be discarded.

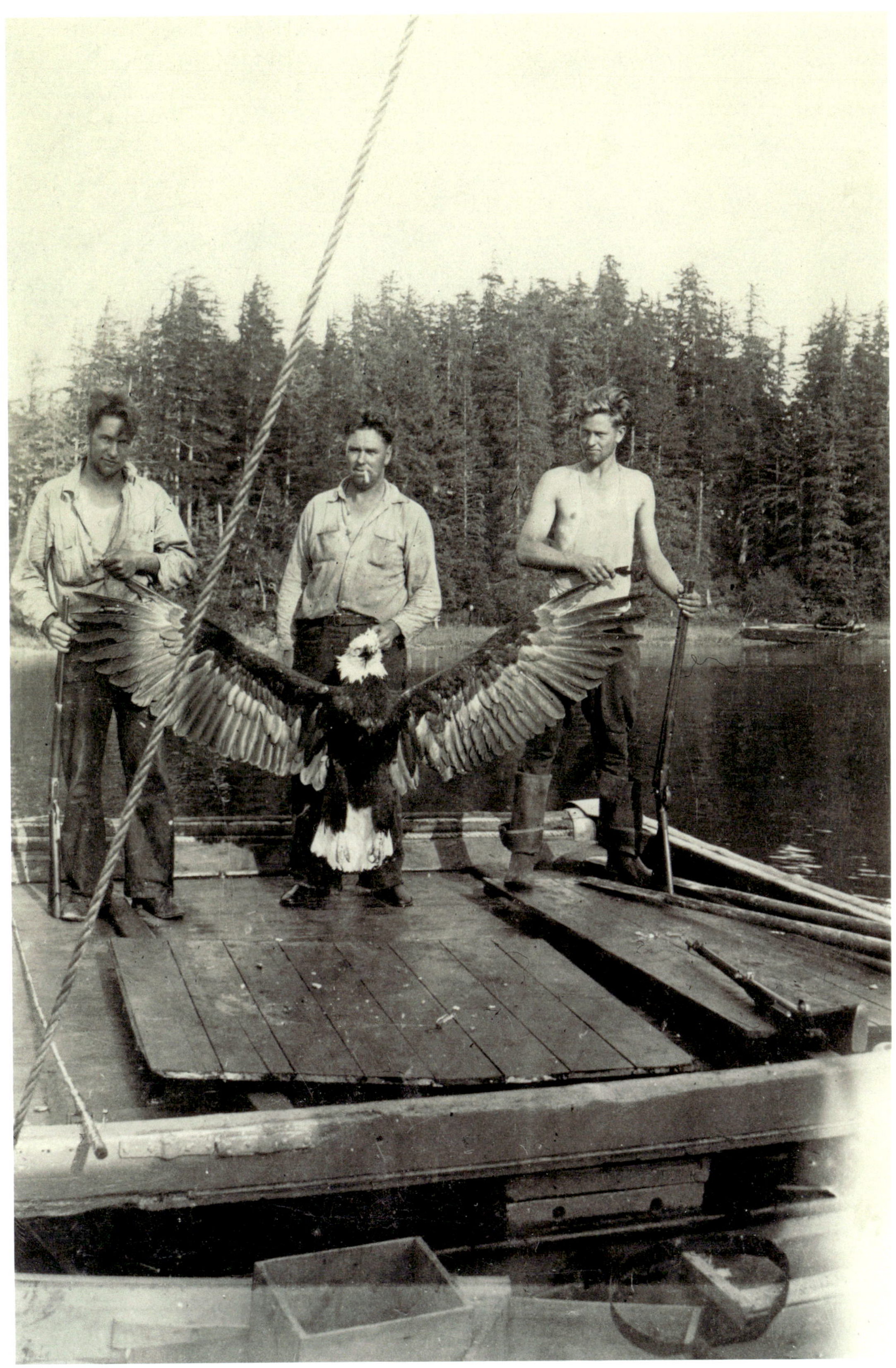

**Gelatin silver print.** Photographer unknown. Reece Franklin (on the right) and friends in Washington State. c. 1938. 5¼ x 3½ in. (13.3 x 8.9 cm)

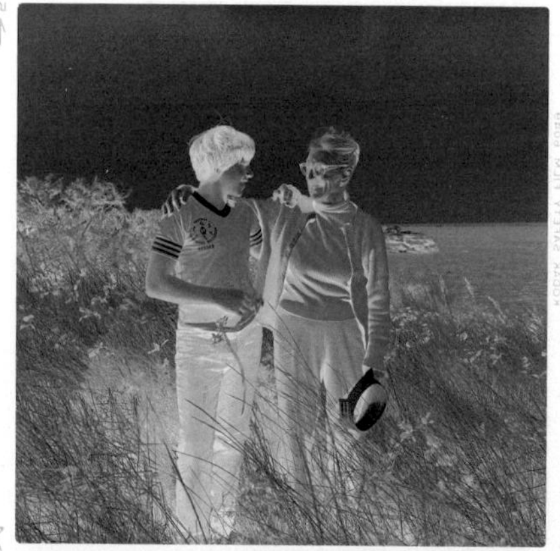
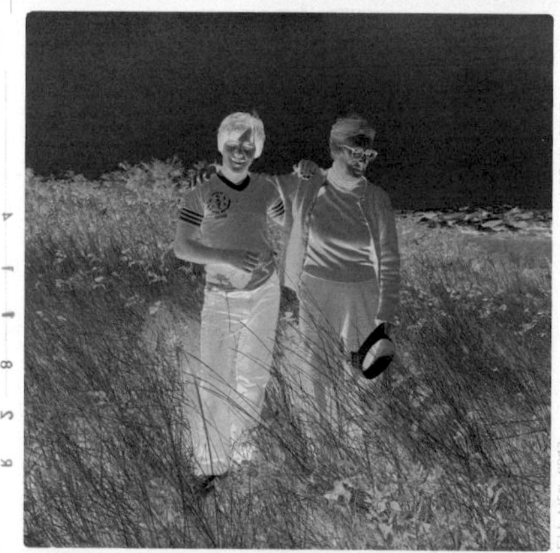
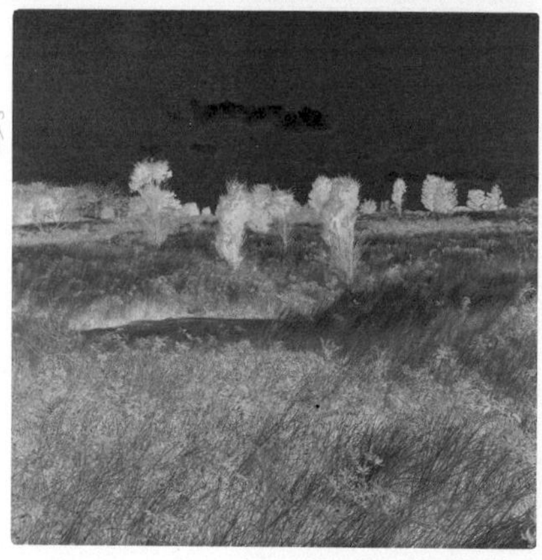

A three-frame section of a 2¼ in. (5.7 cm)-wide roll-film negative, exposed in a square-format camera.

## 7.8 THE NEGATIVE

Behind almost every black and white photograph (and many color ones too) there is a glass or film negative, the actual record of the light that came out of the world into the camera. A properly exposed and developed negative is a smooth and uninterrupted analog of the intensity and distribution of that light. Ansel Adams used to compare the negative to a musician's score: a tonal record, it waits in the darkroom for the photographer to play out an interpretation of it in a print. Adams had a good point, because the negative—when correctly made—holds neither black nor white but instead a long scale of grays. It is made this way because those extremes of tone are actually informational voids; rather than have the negative irrevocably determine what parts of the picture will be black and white, the photographer prefers to make that decision in the darkroom.

The negative does two extraordinary things that are often overlooked. One is that it can provide a record of the passage of light over time. The one illustrated here was exposed for about a half hour, in the dark recesses of an old fort. The heaviest silver deposit is in a window through which brilliant sunlight shone, but in the negative that area is still deep gray rather than black, because I restrained the development of the film. The upper parts of the picture, showing the brickwork around a ventilation passage, hold clear information, which, however, was barely visible to the naked eye—it only became clear after I had avoided the bright window for a minute or so and allowed my eyes to adjust to the darkness. A negative, properly handled, can make a record of an extreme range of illumination.

A second miracle of the negative is that it can record things that are simply invisible to the naked eye. The clearest example of this is its ability to record faint light, in work such as astronomy, where exposures are routinely many hours long. But silver salts are also sensitive to electromagnetic radiation far outside the small window of frequency that our eyes use, so that a negative can gather X-rays and infrared light and turn them into usable silver deposits. The extraordinary thing that happens then is not so much that something invisible is translated for our use, but rather that the technology of photography can go somewhere that the human being cannot. As we expand our understanding of the physical world we increasingly find that our machines interact and interpret it with far more capacity than we can ourselves.

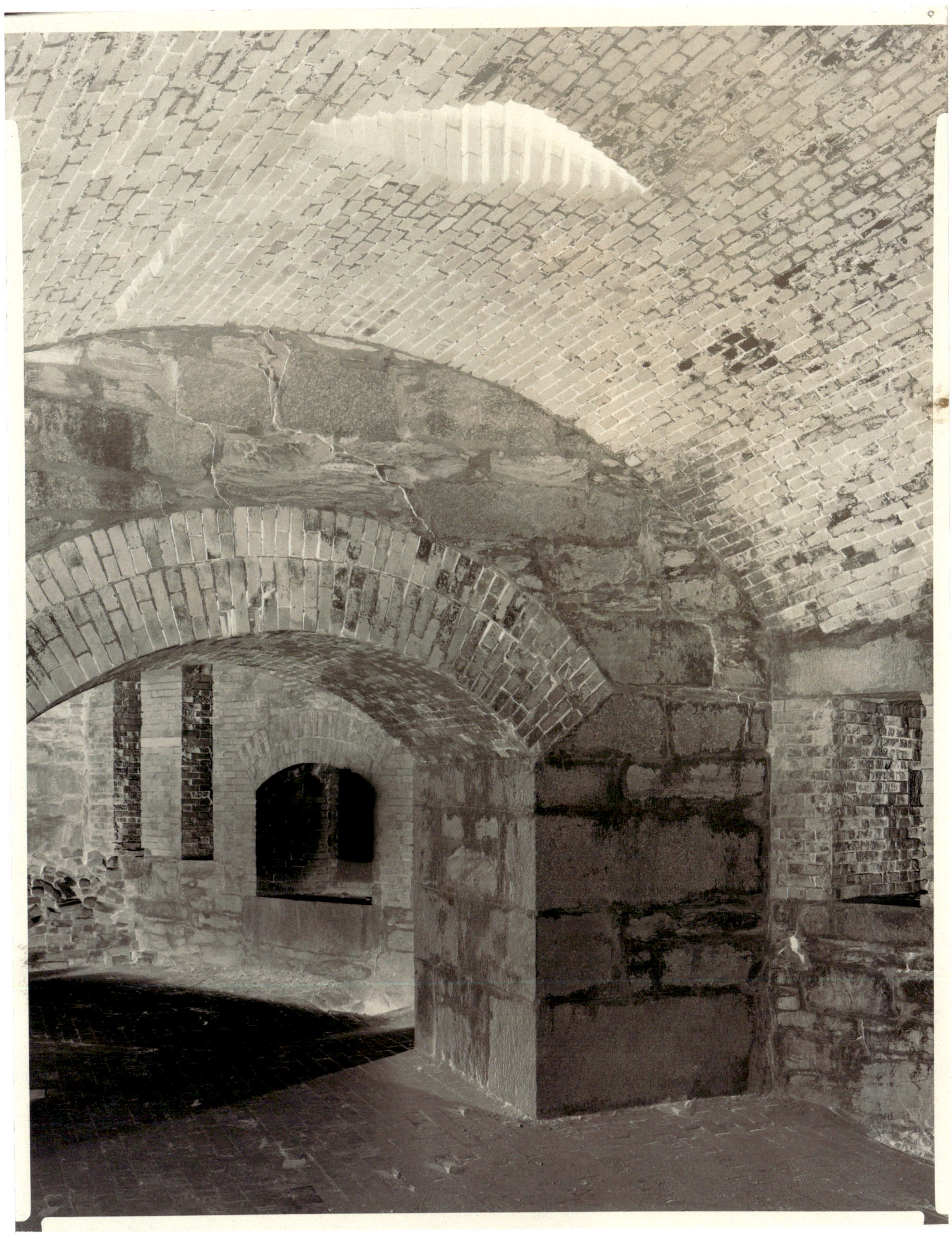

**Black and white film negative.** Richard Benson. *Fort Adams.* 1975. 10 x 8 in. (25.4 x 20.3 cm)

## 7.9 LANTERN SLIDES

In the early years of photography its audiences accessed it through books, albums, and pictures hanging on walls. The medium eventually migrated to museums and galleries, but even before then movies were invented, and photographic images, linked into time-based sequences, began to appear in theaters that had so far been inhabited only by living actors and musicians. This book is not about moving pictures, which lie outside the field of printing, but a powerful dynamic occurs when groups of people sit close to each other in the dark and look at some brilliantly illuminated scene. The power of this effect was adapted to education through the invention of the lantern slide, and ultimately led to the widespread use of color slides by amateur photographers.

The lantern slide was largely replaced by the 35mm slide, but in old universities we still occasionally find the larger glass slides being used, cherished by the older faculty for their tendency to stay in better focus than the newer, flexible film transparencies (which themselves are now being replaced by digital projections). They were always made on thin 3¼-by-4-inch glass plates, which were usually exposed from copy negatives made from photographic prints or drawings. To prevent the image from being scratched as it was moved in and out of the projector, a cover glass was attached with black tape, and stuck on this border there was almost always an information label and a red dot to show which way up the slide was to be placed in the projector. Lantern slides have nearly disappeared, but they still turn up in junk shops, often in perfect condition packed away in boxes.

The quality of these positive images tends to be surprisingly low. In the first place they are almost always two generations away from the original photograph: a negative was made in a camera out in the world, then printed; a copy negative was made of that print; and the copy negative was printed onto the glass slide. Every time a photograph is copied by chemical means, the information it contains is eroded. Another difficulty with the lantern slide is that the tonal range was usually made very light, to make the image adequately bright when projected. This results in washed-out images that have lost much of the beauty we have come to expect of photographic prints.

A few artists, notably Alfred Stieglitz, used lantern slides to present their photographs publicly, but almost every other application they were used for had to do with education. They were instrumental in establishing the copyright status of "fair use," which says that an image can be used for educational purposes without the owner receiving compensation. That practice is being challenged for today's digital imagery.

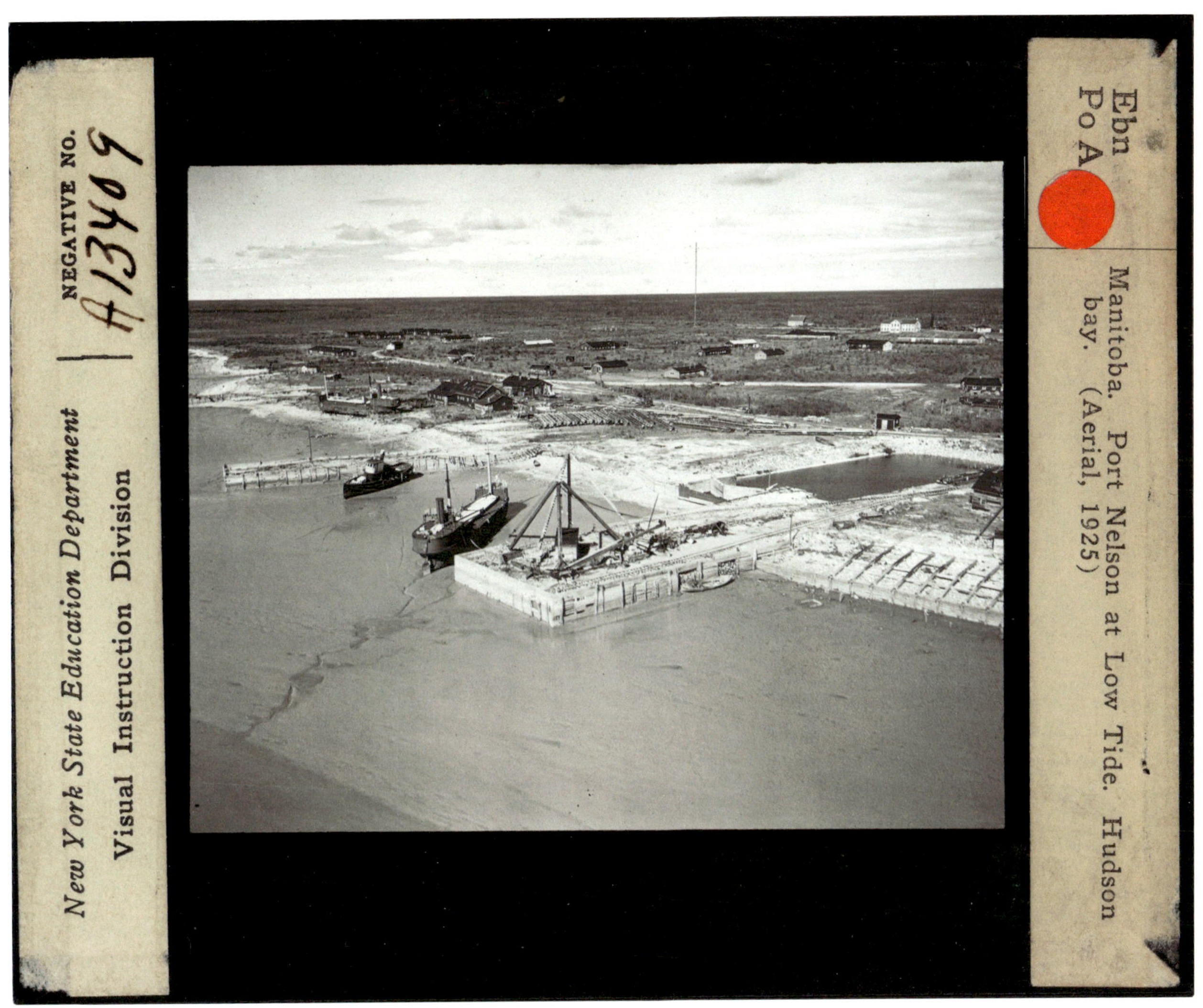


**Lantern slide.** Photographer unknown. *Manitoba. Port Nelson at Low Tide. Hudson Bay.* 1925. 3¼ x 4 in. (8.3 x 10.2 cm)

## 7.10 CONTACT PRINTING

By the 1920s modern photographic papers had evolved into two classes. One group had a low sensitivity to light, and were referred to as "contact" papers. The other group were highly sensitive—some even approaching film in their speed—and were made for use in the enlarger, to make big prints from little negatives. Both of these modern papers were far more sensitive than the older POPs, which had required light of the sun's intensity for exposure.

The first type of these new papers was used by placing negative and paper into a spring-loaded frame, so that the emulsions of each were held closely together. Then an exposure was made with a normal lightbulb from a few feet away. The second type of paper was exposed in an enlarger, which is really just a camera turned inside out: the small negative is held in a frame and brightly illuminated from behind, and the light passes through it to a lens, which projects the picture onto the paper at a larger scale. I call the enlarger a camera because the subject being photographed is the negative and the print paper takes the role of the film. Unlike a normal camera, the enlarger contains both light and subject within a light-tight bellows, while the paper recording the image is out in a large dark room. This inversion of light and dark allows the printer to manipulate the light on its way to the paper, altering the overall tonalities by shading with hands or specialized tools.

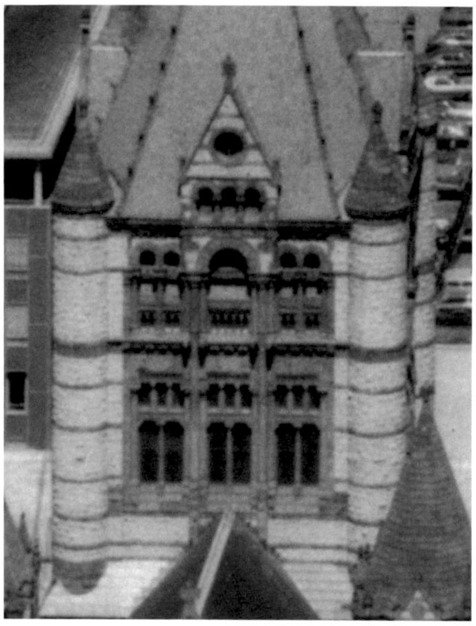

This twelve-times enlargement shows the remarkable detail and tonal smoothness of a modern eight-by-ten-inch contact print.

The two classes of paper were based on two different silver salts. The slower paper was usually made with silver chloride, which produced a warm tone. The faster, enlarging papers were usually made with silver bromide, which produced colder colors. Many intermediate papers were produced with mixtures of these salts, and the manufacturers kept the formulas for them secret. By the 1930s a wide variety of papers was available, in many surfaces, speeds, and subtle colors (although all of them were basically neutral). The emulsions of many of these papers contained a great deal of silver. The papers were coated slowly, and had a relatively soft gelatin surface that was delicate but very beautiful; these papers could produce tonally rich prints. As the technology of manufacture advanced over the years, the silver content went down and the coating speeds went up, giving less appealing surfaces. At one point the manufacturers added a top coating to the papers, called a supercoating, made of harder gelatin, which made them easier to handle. As time went by, emulsion design was greatly improved, and even with less silver and harder surfaces, today's materials are as good as—if not better than—anything made in the past.

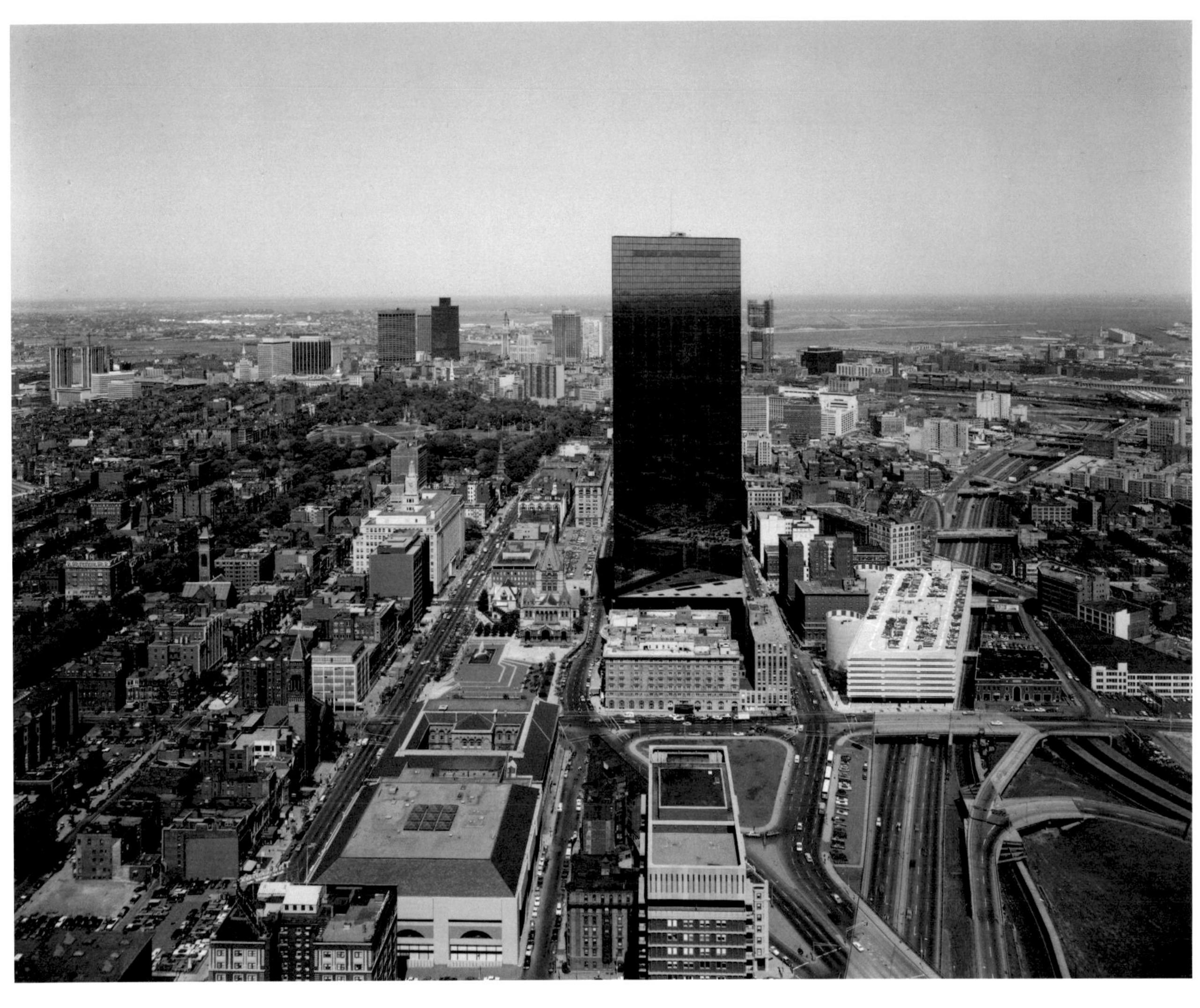

**Gelatin silver print.** Nicholas Nixon. *View of the New John Hancock Building.* 1975. 7⅝ x 9⅝ in. (19.4 x 24.4 cm). This print was made by contact on Kodak Azo paper, a silver chloride–based, contact-speed, gelatin developing-out paper that remained available long after other such papers disappeared from the market.

## 7.11 35MM PHOTOGRAPHY

The cameras of the nineteenth century were almost all stuck on a tripod. They needed it because the negative materials required long exposures and the cameras used large, heavy glass negatives, suitable for contact printing. As film migrated onto flexible supports and the sensitivity of the emulsions was increased, the door was open for small cameras with fast shutter speeds, which could stop action in the thin slice of time that they recorded. The technology for this change was driven by the invention of movies, which depended upon a rapid sequence of small-format pictures made with very brief exposures. The first popular still camera to grow out of the film trades was the Leica, which came on the market in the 1920s. It used the same 35mm-width film as the movies did, and used the sprocket holes along both sides to control the position of the film as it was advanced through the camera. This is no surprise, since the Leica itself originated as a device for testing samples of film that were to be exposed in the long reels necessary for moviemaking. The difference was that where this film ran through the movie camera vertically, it ran through the Leica horizontally. The picture format chosen was quite long—the width being half as long again as the height—and this extended rectangle proved to be a great container for the broad and simple forms that the grainy enlargements from miniature film produced. These little cameras directed the photographer's attention to form rather than detail, and a whole new type of picture structure grew out of their use.

The Leica had a simple viewing system built alongside the lens. Later models used a rangefinder to set the focus. As small-camera technology developed, a viewing system that had been used in larger-format Graflex cameras was adapted to miniature size and a new type emerged: called "single lens reflex" cameras, these machines let the photographer view the subject to be photographed through the actual lens that would make the picture, by using a mirror interposed in the light path. As the exposure was made, this mirror was rapidly raised and the light that had been directed to the viewing window went instead to the film. These new cameras shared the market, in many models, with the older class of rangefinder cameras.

The miniature camera, which gradually came to be called simply the 35mm camera, changed photography dramatically. Along with slightly larger models that used unsprocketed film, these machines allowed pictures to be made anywhere, under almost any conditions. In this picture we see the bed upon which Josef Koudelka slept for many years while he was traveling and photographing. All the old baggage of the traveling photographer had gone by this time, and a Leica camera—all the technical resources Koudelka needed—could easily fit into his jacket pocket.

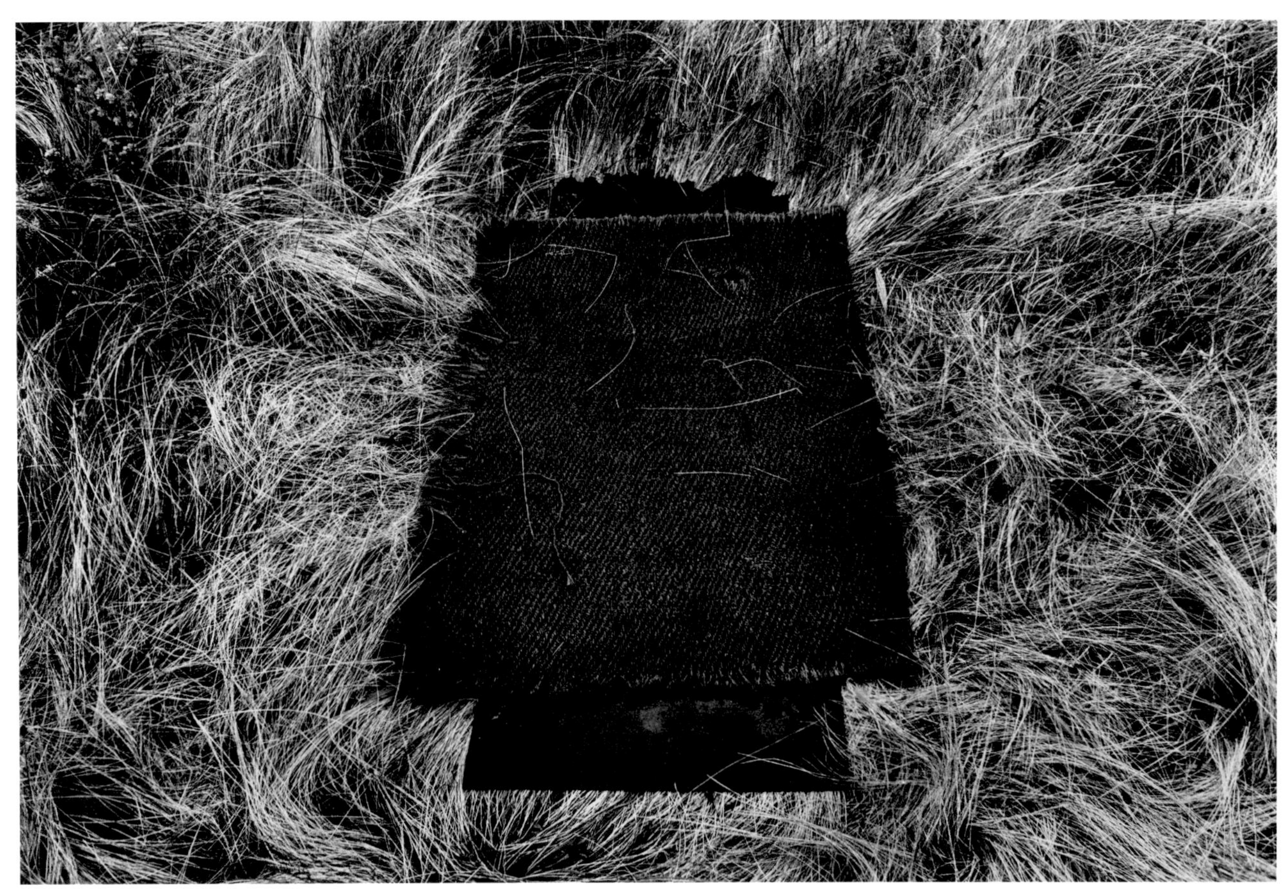

**Gelatin silver print.** Josef Koudelka. *Wales.* 1977. 8 x 11¾ in. (20.3 x 29.9 cm)

## 7.12 ENLARGEMENTS

As the years went by, films, lenses, and papers became better and better, and enlargement from small negatives became the most common photographic practice. Photographers continually complained that everything was getting worse, but I believe that photographic materials steadily improved through the twentieth century.

Cameras made for the casual amateur tended to use larger formats than 35mm, so that inexpensive contact prints made with them, while small, were still usable in albums. The film was always on rolls, so that multiple photographs could be taken with a single loading of the camera. By the 1970s, most of the odd old film sizes had disappeared and we were left with only two: 35mm, still with its sprockets, and 2¼-inch-wide roll film. Both came in various lengths. Not all of the cameras made pictures using the same rectangle; most 35mm cameras retained the two-by-three proportion of the original Leica, but the roll-film camera formats ranged from square—which we see here—to rectangles as long as the 35mm shape. Black and white photography was king, and hundreds of thousands of amateurs and professionals printed in their own darkrooms.

When we expose and develop film we capture a range of tones to be interpreted when the picture is printed. At that point the photographer must make tough decisions about what is black and what is white in the picture. The earliest of the modern papers had so much silver in them that they could be developed to different degrees—the photographer could adjust the light and dark end of the print to suit the negative. As time went on, and papers gradually lost their earlier richness in silver, this became impossible. As a result, papers came to be sold in different-contrast "grades," ranging from 0 (very low contrast) to 5 (very high). The average darkroom held at least three or four boxes of each paper, each box a different grade, to cope with the varying tonal scale of negatives made under different lighting conditions.

A great change took place in the 1960s when a new class of enlarging paper became available that had two different silver compounds coated on it. One was of low and one of high contrast. The two types were sensitive to different colors of light, so the printer could adjust the color of the enlarger's light with filters to produce any needed contrast on a single sheet of paper. By the 1980s the old graded papers were far less common than these new "variable contrast" materials, and today perhaps 95 percent of all black and white darkroom printing is done out of a single box in the darkroom. Today, as digital techniques replace chemical printing, the market for all photographic papers is shrinking and old favorites of even this new class of paper are disappearing.

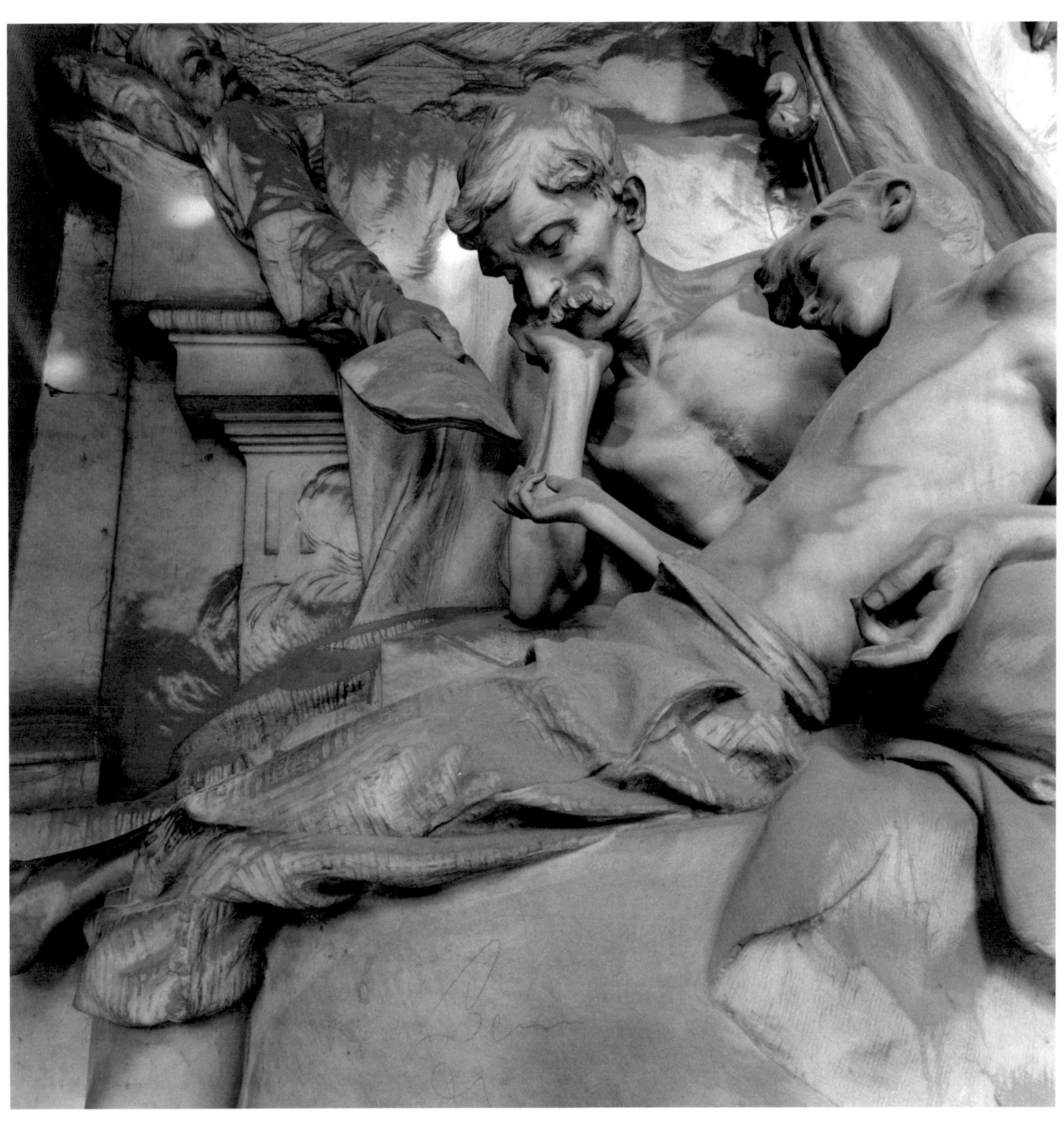

**Gelatin silver print.** Lee Friedlander. *Staglieno Cemetery, Genoa, Italy.* 1993. 14¾ x 14⅝ in. (37.7 x 37.2 cm)

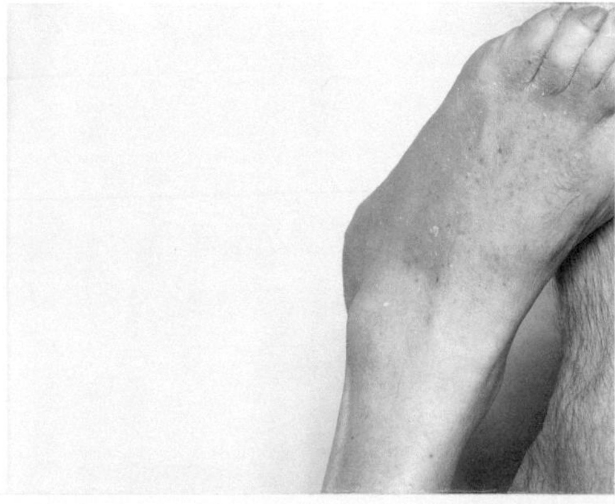

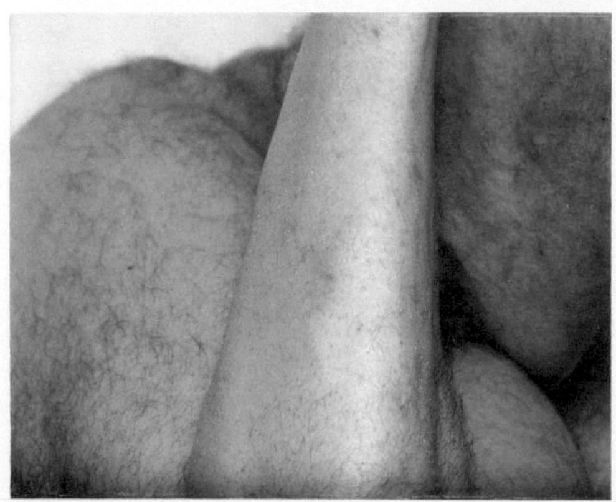

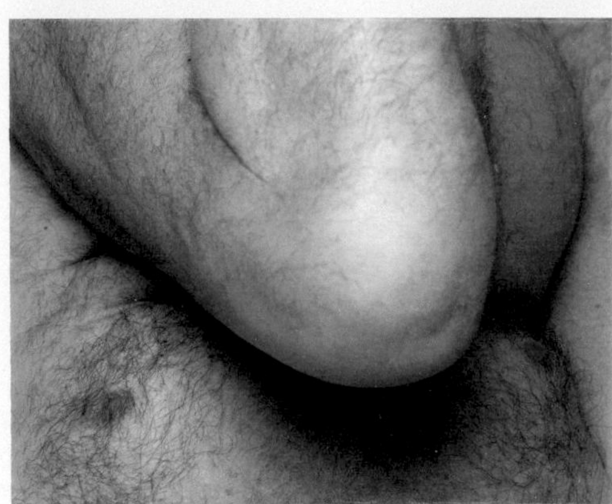

## 7.13 BLACK AND WHITE POLAROID

When we study the history of technology we face a great temptation to liken its development to that of the biological kingdom. In the evolution of life we have that nice, solid underlying premise of genetic connection, which lets us be absolutely certain that every living thing is related to every other. Not so with the stuff we make. Odd things come out of the blue in technology, rise up, fill a gap we didn't even know existed, and then disappear. I put the fax machine, the typewriter, and the Polaroid process all in that category.

Polaroid materials came out of the mind of Edwin Land, who spent years developing a type of photography that did not require a darkroom. Land believed there would be a great market for the instant picture that the photographer could expose and see immediately. He devoted years of brilliant research to this project, and out of it came an entire branch of photography that was completely different from anything that had gone before. The underlying chemistry still involved the exposure, development, and fixing of silver-based images, but Land made films and cameras that did all this on the spot, right after the picture was taken.

The first Polaroid pictures, in black and white, were made in the 1950s. The company flourished, produced specialized cameras for its films, developed color materials in various sizes, made tons of money, and went bankrupt around the year 2000. The idea of the instant picture was buried (along with the giant of conventional silver photography) by the digital revolution, which lets a photographer snap a picture, then view it instantaneously on a screen on the camera back; no chemicals, no silver, and no cost (after the cost of buying the camera). Even before the digital assault, though, Polaroid was in trouble, because the materials were always quite expensive and the process depended upon specialized cameras.

**Polaroid instant prints.** John Coplans. *Untitled Study for Self Portrait. (Upside Down no. 9).* 1992.
Three black and white Polaroid prints, each: 3½ x 4½ in. (8.9 x 11.4 cm)

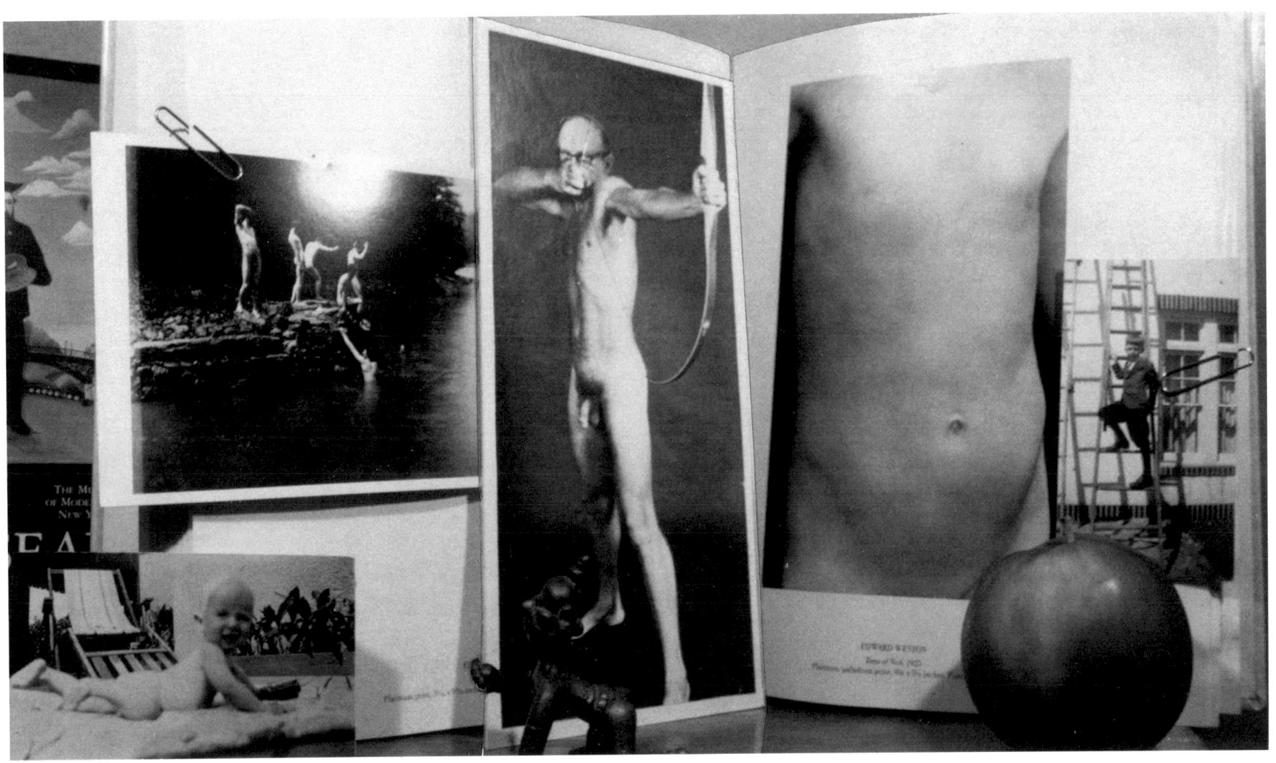

All of us who used view cameras bought Polaroid backs and made four-by-five-inch black and white Polaroid pictures. They were absolutely great. Like the daguerreotype, each one was unique, and had a connection to the light of the world that was immediate and enthralling. Ansel Adams made terrific ones, and became a spokesman for the company. Once color materials, with an enticing palette, were available in the 1970s, other photographers took up the system. In the commercial world the Polaroid became the great test material: the photographer could shoot a complex studio setup with a Polaroid back as a check before exposing the conventional transparency, which would have to be sent out for processing. Land's dream process burst into maturity, had its day, then disappeared. It left a lot of interesting photographic artifacts in its wake. Artists loved Polaroids, whether in black and white or color; the prints could be altered, ganged up, and used in collages, all without having to engage the darkroom and its high-tech demands.

**Polaroid instant prints.** John O'Reilly. *Mythic Still Life.* 1985. Collage of black and white Polaroid prints. 3¾ x 6⅝ in. (9.5 x 16.8 cm)

## 7.14 RESIN-COATED PAPER

Both the dry plate and the developing-out papers that dominated black and white photography in the twentieth century used gelatin, which has the characteristic of absorbing water, to allow gradual chemical reactions to take place, while retaining its structure as a coating. When gelatin was coated on the nonabsorbent glass support of the dry plate, it could be processed and rapidly dried. Films, made of synthetic polymers but still coated with a gelatin emulsion, tended to take up water, so the drying time was longer. When the dry-plate emulsion moved over to paper, for use in printing, there was the additional difficulty of the paper becoming wet and also requiring a long time to dry. This was not a new problem; all the old paper-based processes had suffered in the same way. Paper gets wet, changes size, takes up any bad chemicals that are around, and then tends to stain when it dries and gets old.

In the 1980s a new class of paper emerged called "resin-coated" or "RC" paper. This material was still paper, and still carried a gelatin emulsion, but the paper substrate was completely sealed in plastic so the paper itself never got wet. Since RC papers could be developed, rinsed, and dried in only a few minutes, they became a popular proofing material. Many photographers—the author included—used these papers for their terrific convenience. The old hypo problem—of the print retaining destructive fixing chemicals—had more to do with the paper holding the chemistry than with the emulsion, and with RC papers the paper itself never got wet, so most of the hypo was removed with a short rinse.

This sounds like a great development, and it did make things easier in the darkroom. By and large, though, these new papers were dreadful. The early ones used a sealing material that broke down in a few years, far less time than the old enemy hypo would have needed to do its destructive work. Worse, the papers tended to be made in only three surfaces—all bad. One was highly polished, with a brilliant shine that the manufacturers somehow thought would be better for reproduction purposes. In reality these papers scratched easily, which made them terrible to rephotograph. There was also a dead matte surface, so flat that no black appeared anywhere in the print, no matter how heavy the silver deposit. The final insult was the "pearl" surfaces, which had a texture applied to them. These surfaces were widespread in color papers (most of which were resin coated, to ease handling in the processing machines) and invariably produced terrible-looking prints. RC papers became common, and we now find traditional photographic papers being called "fiber based," to distinguish them from this newer, inferior type that is so easy to use.

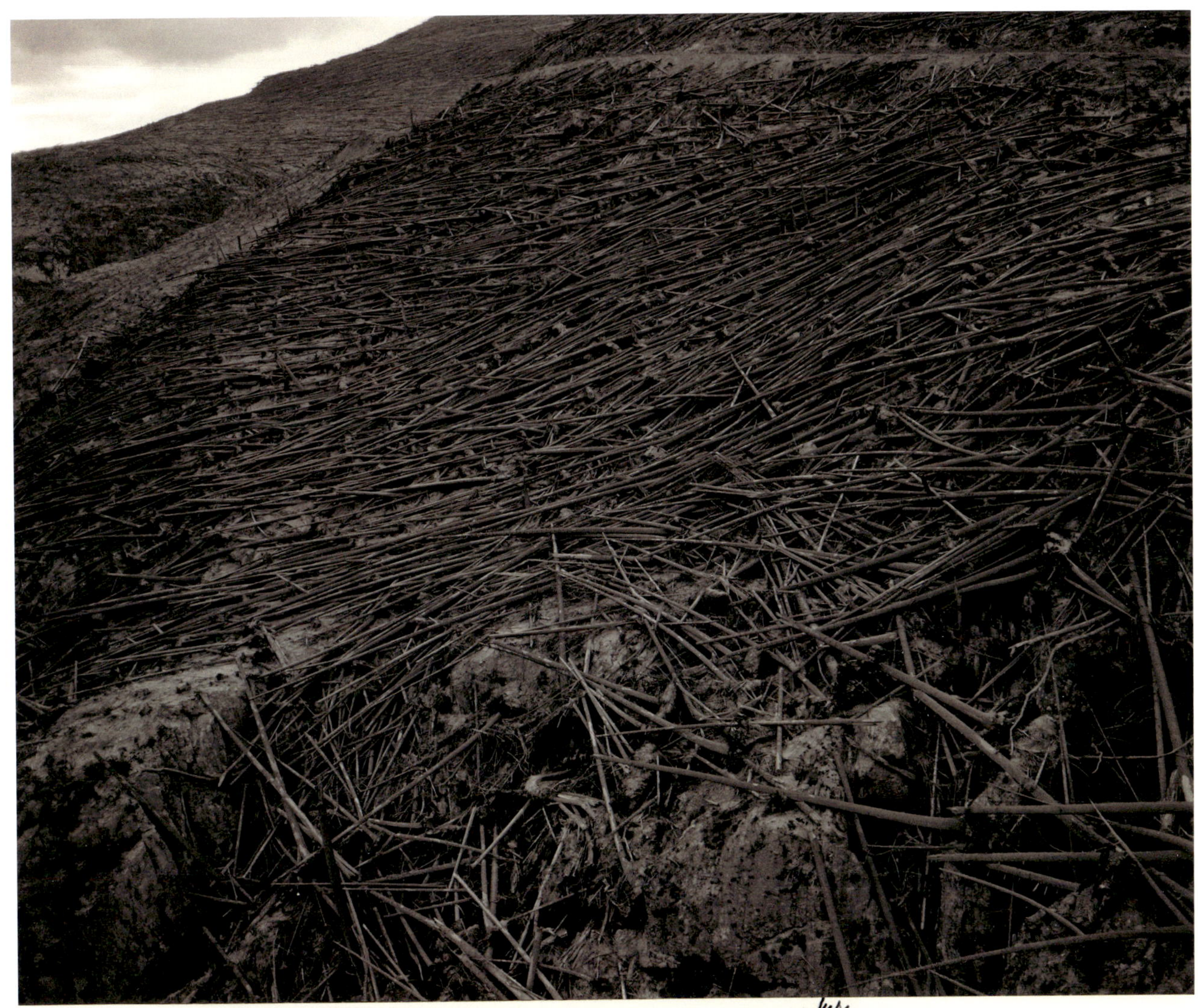


**Resin-coated proof print.** Frank Gohlke. *Aerial view–Downed forest 8 miles from crater–Mt. St. Helens, July 1981.* 7½ x 9⅛ in. (19 x 23.2 cm)

# Part 8

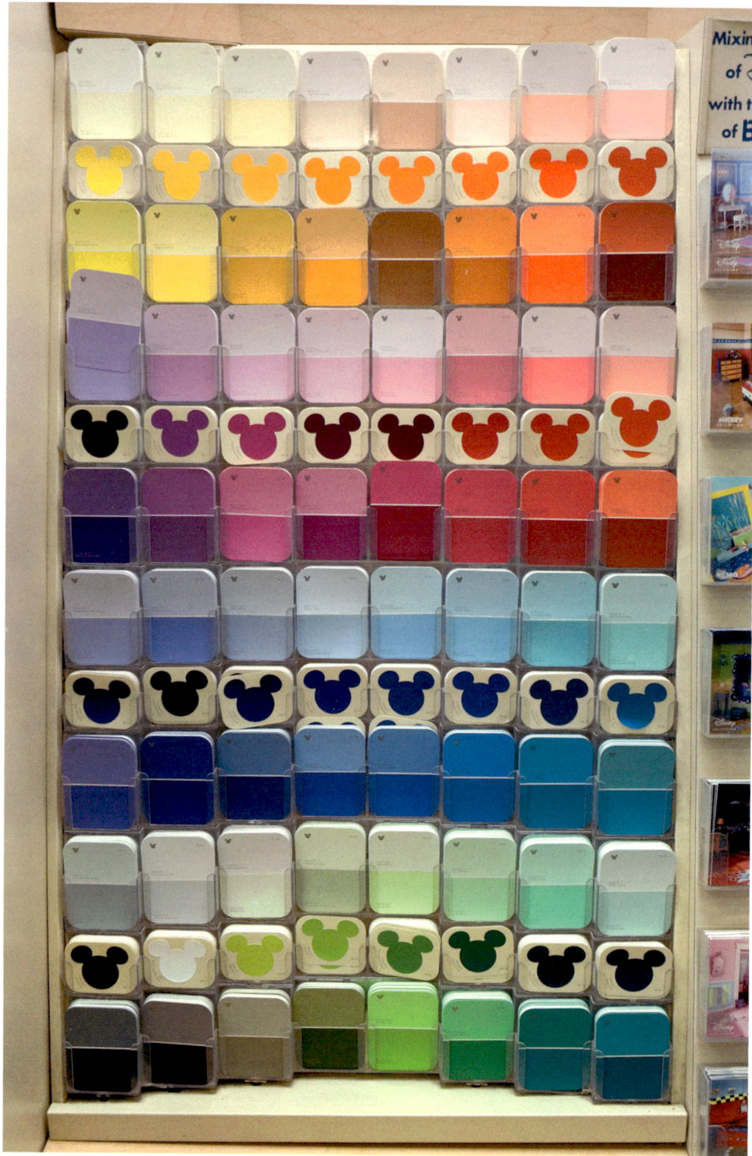

Color is the most subjective of all qualities; I really don't know whether or not the red I see is the same as the red someone else does. For centuries the only practical way to define color was to show samples of it. Color photography and computer imaging require a more scientific understanding of color, and this brief section touches upon this immensely complex subject.

Behr Paints and the Walt Disney Company. Paint sample display. 2007

# Color notes

8.1 Primary colors
*What are the primaries after all?*

8.2 James Clerk Maxwell and color
*Sorting out the primary colors.*

8.3 Color separations
*Photography and printing with color separations.*

8.4 The question of neutrality
*Using gray to understand color.*

# Color notes

## 8.1 PRIMARY COLORS

There has always been some idea that certain colors are more important than others, and these special ones came to be called "primary" colors. If you ask any reasonable painter to name them you will almost always get the same answer: red, yellow, and blue. But this answer is incorrect today because those colors are the old set, chosen through hundreds of years of work with paint on canvas. They are not picked to fit the scientific description of primary colors. Red, yellow, and blue are a perfectly appropriate set of colors for the painter to think of as primary in work in that medium, but as we engage the modern technologies of color photography and digital display, we must dig deeper and try to understand just what the term "primary color" might mean.

For the painter the term "primary" refers to a color that stands by itself as a visual entity, instead of being generated by mixing other colors. We know today that a pure magenta can be mixed with yellow to produce red, but in the past, painters used earth-based pigments that were never so pure as to produce good color when mixed. Meanwhile beautiful reds, yellows, and blues existed in natural pigments that could be used by themselves. Those pigments could also be mixed, the blues and yellows, for example, combining to produce greens; but greens produced by mixing yellow and blue tended to be quite "dirty," which meant that they had fairly strong gray components in their colors, making them less pure. The green seen out the window in this Matisse painting is a perfect example of a "dirty" green. Yet green is the color to which our eyes are most sensitive, and it is ironic that this color was not widely regarded as a primary simply because it had to be derived by mixing other pigments.

When we paint we are dealing with a form of color called "subtractive" color. Most painting entails the assumption that the support is light in value (often the white of gesso, applied to the canvas as a primer, or of bright paper) and that the paints "subtract" particular colors from this whiteness by absorbing light as it passes through them. This is true when the paint is transparent, such as watercolor, and even to some extent when the paint is relatively opaque, like oil, which can be applied with some degree of transparency. As printing technologies developed and attempts were made to print in color, it became obvious that the subtractive principle could be used, and that transparent inks in a limited number of colors, applied overlying each other, could produce many additional colors not present in the actual ink set. This interesting fact lies at the foundation of all modern color printing, whether in ink on presses or in the traditional materials of color photography in the darkroom.

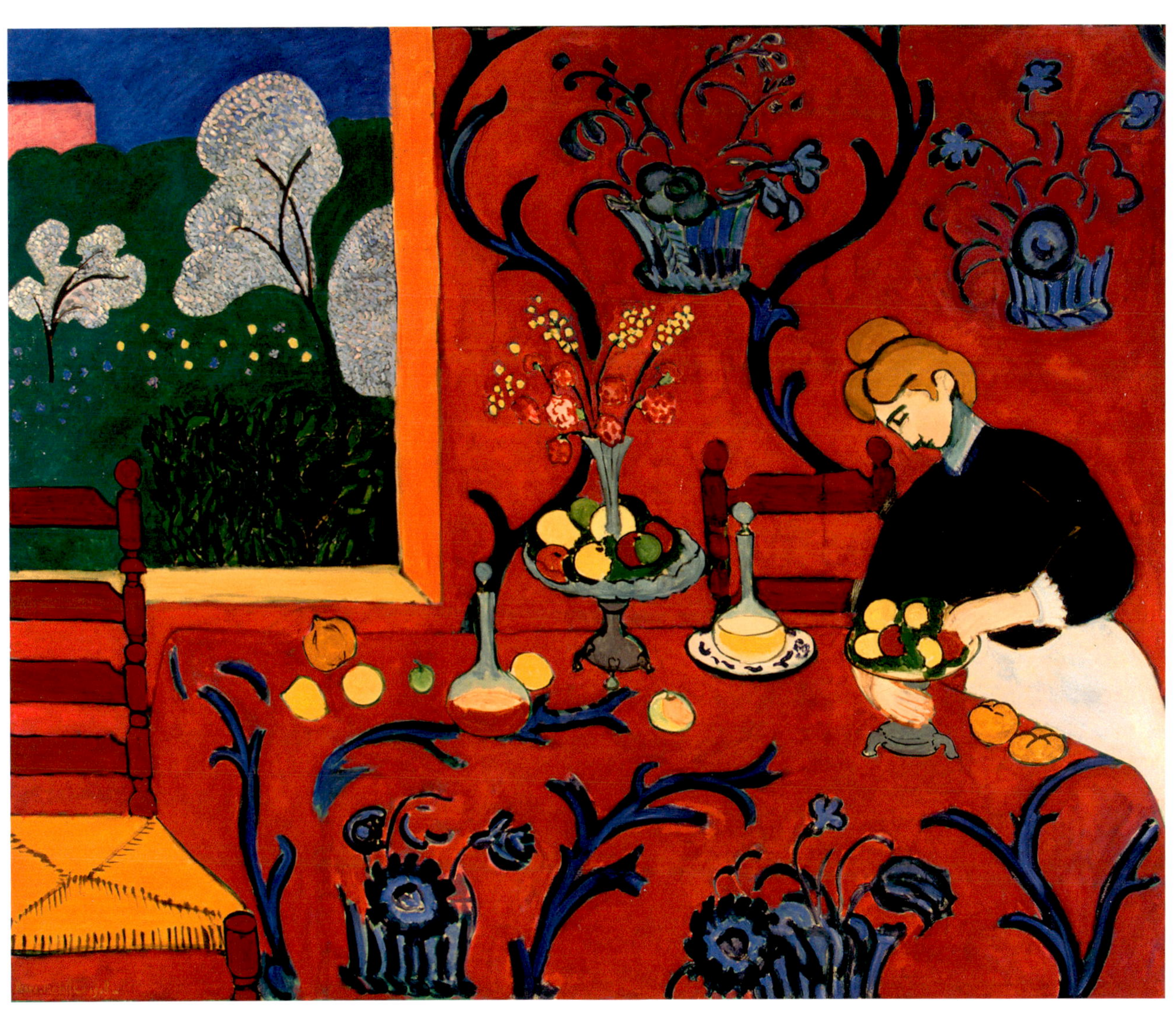

**Oil on canvas.** Henri Matisse. *Red Room (Harmony in Red).* 1908. 70⅞ in. x 7 ft. 2⅝ in. (180 x 221 cm)

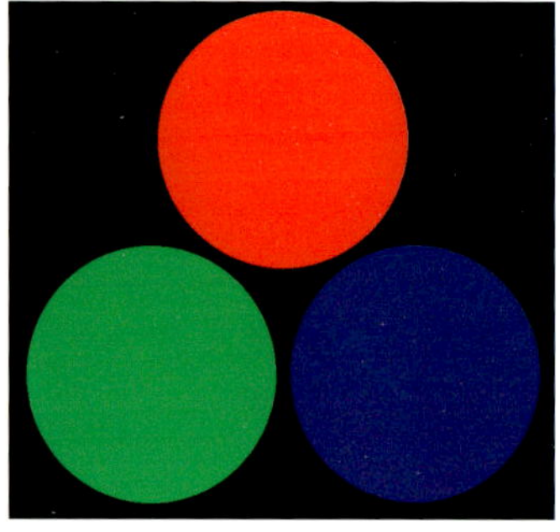

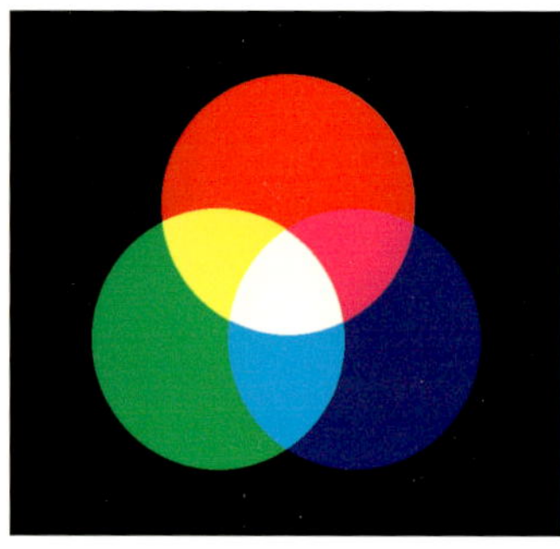

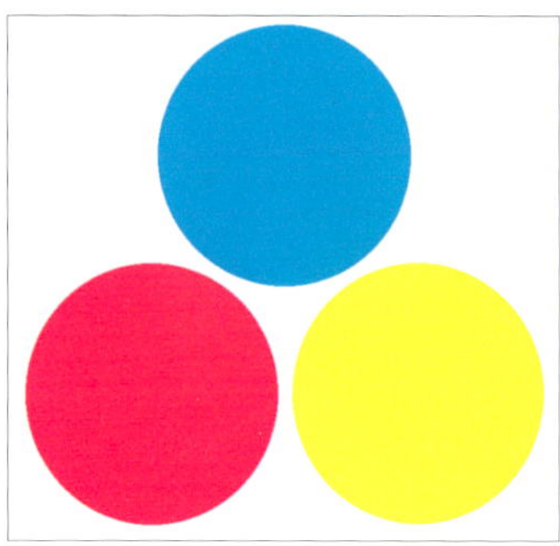

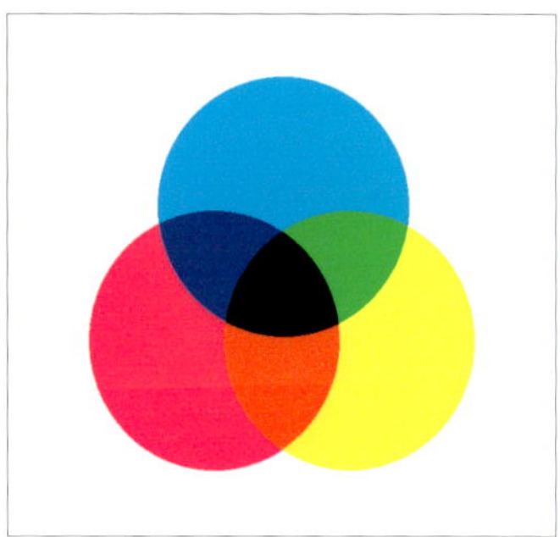

## 8.2 JAMES CLERK MAXWELL AND COLOR

The first person I am aware of to grasp the scientific basis of subtractive printing was the Scottish physicist James Clerk Maxwell. In the mid-nineteenth century he stated that three widely spaced points in the spectrum could be chosen, and that the colors at these points could be combined in varying levels of brightness to produce virtually every color we can see. In arguing this Maxwell also made the point that there are actually two different sets of three primary colors. One set, used in painting, eventually in printing, and later still in photography, is called the subtractive primaries: cyan, magenta, and yellow. Please note that although cyan and magenta are close relatives of blue and red, they are not the classic primaries of the painters. The second set, used when mixing projected (rather than reflected) light, is called the "additive primaries," and these are red, green, and blue.

Before we grapple with these colors and their intriguing relationships we would do well to understand more about the extraordinary implications of Maxwell's statement. If his system works, it could explain how our eye-and-mind combination deals with color. Implicit in his proposal is the possibility that we only actually perceive three colors. Subsequent advances in understanding vision have confirmed that our eyes have peak sensitivity to red, green, and blue—that it is information about these parts of the spectrum that are sent to the brain, where they are interpreted to produce the sensation of other colors. This is shocking—the idea that we make our rich world of perceived color out of three primaries almost defies belief, but the truth of it is borne out by the success of modern color printing and the effectiveness of electronic displays such as the television screen and computer monitor.

The three additive primaries with which we see—red, green, and blue—are intimately connected to the three subtractive primaries—cyan, magenta, and yellow—with which we print. The relationship between these two color sets must be understood by anyone working with photography, printing, and digital images. As we spend our days reading books and magazines and then looking at the computer and the television set, we move effortlessly between the worlds of print and projection (the first subtractive, the second additive). If we have any hope of photographing with digital tools, then both systems must be seen as parts of a single whole, with additive and subtractive color working together seamlessly in a system based upon six primary colors.

Circles of color like those to the left appear in almost any publication that attempts to describe color and how it works. The red, green, and blue, seen against a black background, represent what we might see if three slide projectors each had a color filter over the lens and each projected one color circle. The second image, showing these same three circles moved closer together so that they overlap, accurately describes how projected, or additive, primary colors add up: red and blue light make magenta, blue and green make cyan, and green and red make yellow. The first two combinations follow our instinctive sense of how the primaries would mix: magenta and cyan seem to be logical productions of the overlap. The third—green and red making yellow—is not intuitive at all, and remains one of the most surprising aspects of additive color. Where all three colors overlap we see white light. This is a clear demonstration of the flip side of Isaac Newton's great observation that white light contains all the colors, which he demonstrated using a prism. Here we see those same colors mixing together to produce white (which Newton also demonstrated).

The three circles of color on a white ground represent spots of printer's ink printed on white paper. These are the subtractive primaries—cyan, magenta, and yellow—which, when overlapped as in the fourth illustration, produce blue, red, and green. Where all three inks combine, the image is black.

We can immediately see that the subtractive primaries combine to produce the additive ones and the additive primaries combine to produce the subtractive ones. This is the key to understanding modern color structure. The circles of color also show us the relationships between complementary colors. The yellow we see in both illustrations is the absence of blue; in the same way, the magenta area depicts the absence of green. Our diagrams give us a further bit of information: yellow is the "complement" of blue, magenta of green, and cyan of red. This is true in either additive or subtractive color, and is another bridge between the two color types.

The importance of understanding the relationships between the two sets of primary colors cannot be emphasized enough. As I work with photography students, I usually find that they are handicapped by lacking a clear foundational understanding of how color works. I do need to emphasize that I have discussed here only a small part of what we can learn about color; I haven't dealt with any of the visual effects studied by the great colorists—such as Johannes Itten and Josef Albers—nor have I dealt with saturation or value. I have also presented the six primaries in ideal terms; the realities of color in actual use are much more complicated. The most blatant of these complications is the need to add a fourth color—black—into the palette used for subtractive printing.

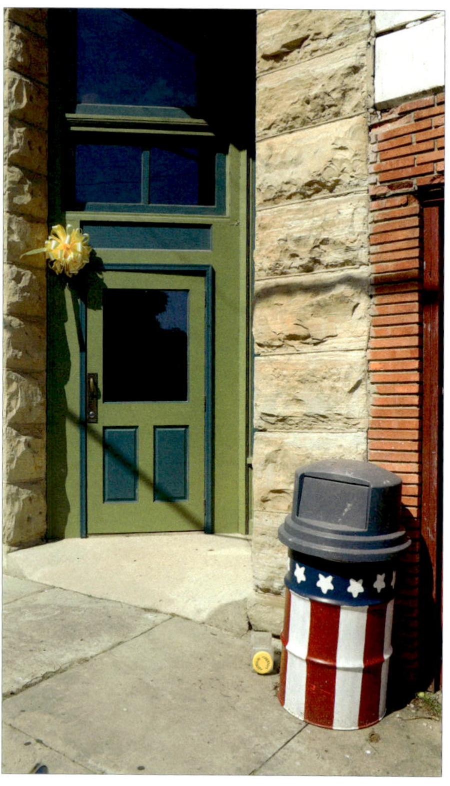

A digital photograph made by the author.

## 8.3 COLOR SEPARATIONS

The way in which Maxwell's work has been used, in both printing and photography, is through color "separations." His principle of selecting three points in the spectrum and recording the color values at those points to define a wide range of colors found a practical application through photographic records of colored objects made with filtration in the primary colors. These color separations were routinely made with red, green, and blue filters to record the values that were subsequently printed with cyan, magenta, and yellow. Color photography, which we come to in the next section, uses complex coatings with three light-sensitive layers that each respond to a particular primary, all applied to a single substrate. In the printing trades the separations are separate, and generate printing plates for the press; in modern color photography they are stacked up together on a single sheet, and we don't need to know that such complexity exists in these photographic materials we use. The interesting early transitional stages of color photography wrestled with separations in various ways, before the technology evolved to allow them to be used together on a single support.

The example shown here is a hypothetical set of color separations made to be printed in the subtractive primaries of cyan, magenta, and yellow. On the printing press these separations need to be accompanied by a fourth printer that uses black ink, denoted by the letter "K" (the letter "B" was not used to avoid confusion with blue), leading to the abbreviation CMYK for this system of printing. In an ideal world the three primaries, when printed together at full strength, would produce a black value, but things don't work out that way: the dyes or pigments in the inks are not strong enough, and it is very difficult to print three heavy layers of wet ink on top of each other. These problems are solved by using a fourth printer, in black ink, which only affects the darker values in the picture. Photographic papers need no black layer, since the dyes are stronger, and there is none of the handling difficulty that exists with heavy layers of ink.

This book is about printed images on paper, but it is important to point out that modern electronic devices such as the computer monitor use additive rather than subtractive primaries to produce colors. A quick look at a computer screen with a magnifying glass shows an array of red, green, and blue rectangles, each glowing to a varying degree. For pure reds, greens, and blues, those points alone are illuminated. In a yellow area the red and green points are bright and the blues are dark; in the pink (or magenta) areas the blues and reds are illuminated while the greens are dark. Through these combinations, the additive primaries are used to generate the subtractives, in the same way that combinations of the subtractive primaries are used to produce the additive set in color printing. The computer monitor needs no black printer, since black can be achieved simply by turning all the points off.

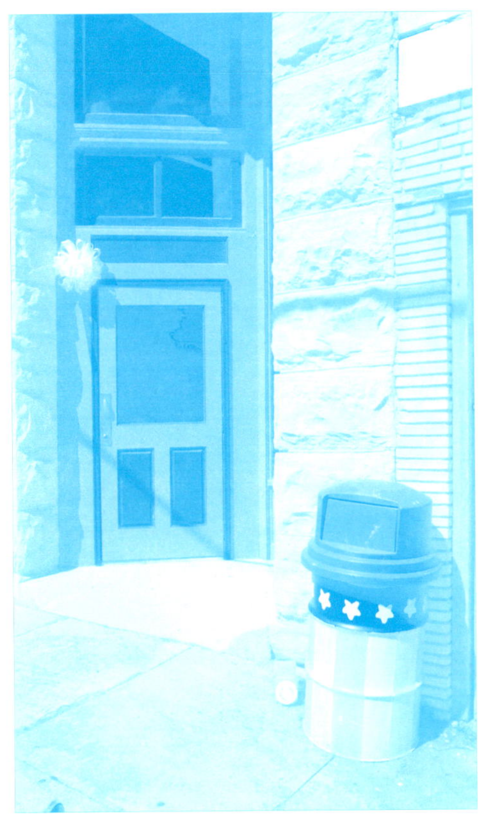

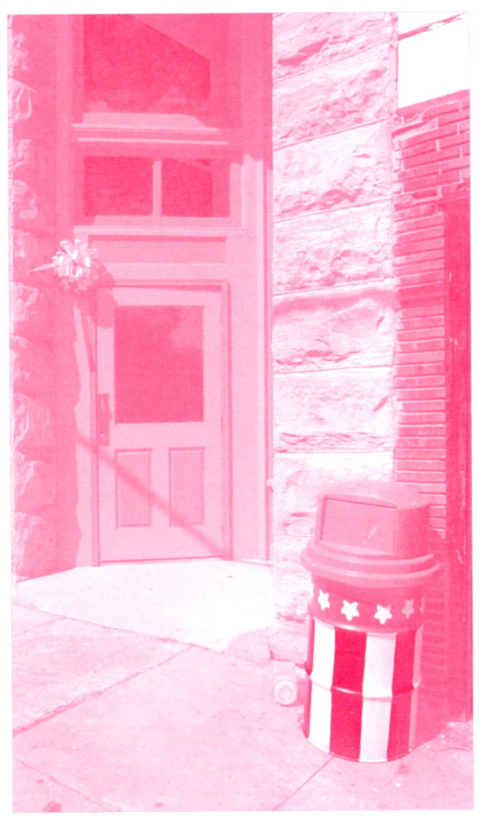

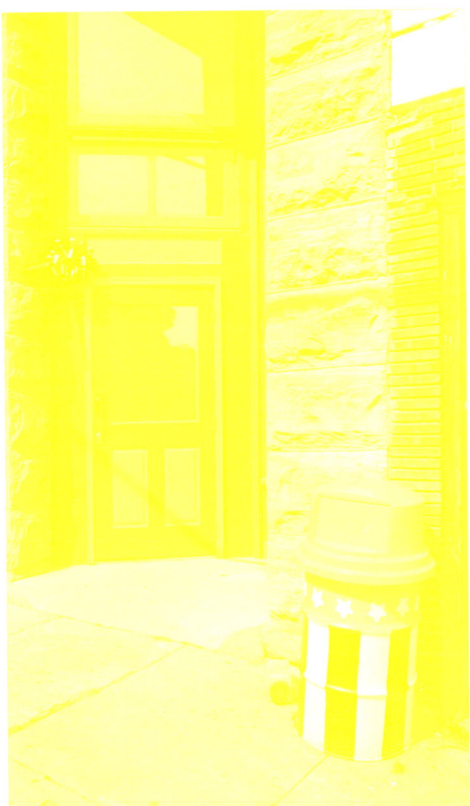

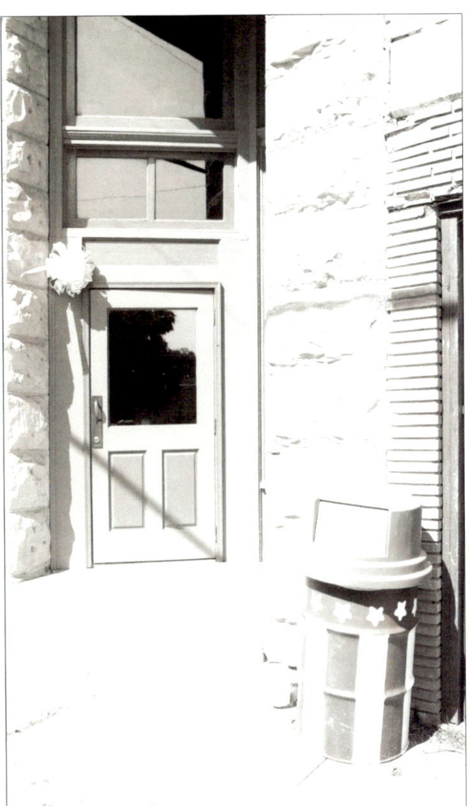

A sample set of color separations: top left, cyan; top right, magenta; bottom left, yellow; and bottom right, black. These are single impressions of the actual separations used to make the full-color reproduction on the left.

## 8.4 THE QUESTION OF NEUTRALITY

The last point we need to examine before moving on to color photography is the question of "neutrality." Black and white photographs are assumed to be "neutral" in color, which is to say that the tones are gray, carrying no color information. In reality most of the early photographic printing processes produced images with some color, but it was unrelated to the color in the scene that had been photographed. Blueprints were blue, but they did not imply that the world was blue. Modern photographic printing, using dry-plate emulsions on photographic paper, came far closer to true neutrality. A definition of a neutral color would be that no color appears; the value shows no tendency toward any primary, so it is "neutral" in relation to the primaries. It is unfortunate that in all the dictionary definitions of the word "neutral" we almost never find it used in relation to color.

The reason we must obsess about neutrality is that the areas in color photographs and on computer screens that appear neutral are actually made up of the primary colors used in that particular system. In a color photograph, or a reproduction of one made on the printing press, a light and perfectly neutral gray value is produced by making the amounts of the three subtractive primaries equal in that area of the picture. On a computer screen the neutrals exist where equal amounts of the additive primaries are present. Equality of primaries generates neutrality of color—that is the key point we must understand.

Each printing system handles this rule in a slightly different way. When we print color photographs in the darkroom we don't really need to know how much of each primary is present in the neutrals; instead we simply make a gray part of the world appear gray in the photograph by filtering the enlarger light until it looks right in the print. On the printing press, where the inks use inferior dyes, visual neutrality is produced by slightly unequal amounts of the primaries, since none of the inks is completely pure. In the darkest values much of the neutral color may also be held by the black ink used in CMYK printing. On the computer screen the system is completely pure: any neutral point has exactly equal levels of intensity in the three additive primaries of red, green, and blue.

Many of our struggles in printing color images come from this practice of the neutrals being made up of the primaries, instead of being printed with pigments that are actually neutral themselves. In modern black and white chemical photography, the silver deposit in the print is neutral in color, so the print is as well. In the old days, when we printed images like the currency shown in plate 3.3, we simply mixed inks that had the correct colors for those parts of the picture that needed it. The small numbers on those bills were done with a blue ink, the orange details with an orange, and the overall design with a black ink. Pictures in "full" color can't use such simple methods; instead, all parts of the image must be made up of primary colors, with some addition of black where necessary.

In an engaging reversal of what we might expect, this issue of neutrality ends up being the best method we have for controlling color. If a color photograph is printed in ink, and if this picture has any neutral grays in it, the color separations and the presswork must be precise if the neutrals are to remain so. For example, if the magenta ink is run too heavily on a job we might not be able to tell that by looking at a red color, which would simply appear a bit redder. If we looked at a neutral value, though, we would immediately see that it had taken on a pink color cast. The same is true of a television or computer screen. Our eyes and mind have some wonderful built-in mechanism for perceiving neutrality, and when we calibrate these additive devices the primary tool we use is the technique of tuning the neutrals.

By correcting the neutral values in a picture, we don't necessarily ensure that the colors are all correct, since dyes and pigments have varying degrees of purity. But we come a long step closer to setting things right. In nearly all crafts the practitioner faces the difficulty of deciding what must be accurate and what is less important; it is the old issue of the forest or the trees, and much of the work we see suggests an obsession with detail at the expense of the entire object being made. Neutrality of color is a perfect example of this: textbooks and guidelines, densitometers and printing profiles, all obsess on the minutiae of color calibration. If we only used our eyes, and made the neutrals correct, we could throw all that junk out the window and get far-better-looking color prints. This extreme statement doesn't necessarily apply to high-end work in laboratories and professional shops, but I offer it as a mantra for the working artist. Eye and mind give us the perfect method for handling color. Make the neutral framework correct and the wide and enticing range of hues in our colorful world of pictures will have the best background against which they can be seen.

# Part 9

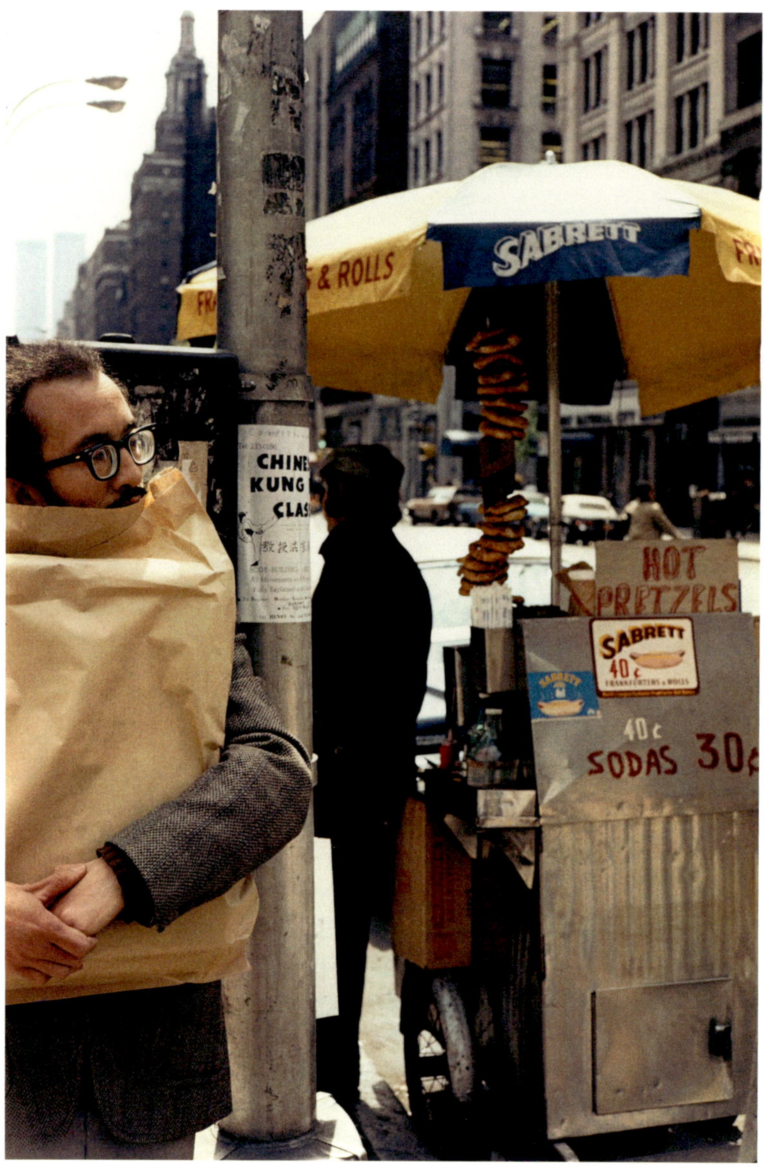


Silver—the sensitive agent for all in-camera photography until the digital came along—is inherently sensitive only to blue light. In the early twentieth century scientists figured out how to sensitize emulsions to the entire spectrum, and shortly thereafter practical color photography was born. During the first three quarters of the last century color was secondary to black and white photography, but it steadily grew, and now, with digital tools, color is on top and black and white is all but disappearing.

**Dye transfer print.** Helen Levitt. *New York.* 1976. 14 x 9¼ in. (35.6 x 23.7 cm)

# Color photography

9.1 Hand-colored photographs
*Coloring applied to black and white photographs.*

9.2 The Lumière Autochrome
*An early method for producing full-color photographs.*

9.3 Color carbon printing
*Subtractive color printing using multilayer carbon prints.*

9.4 Carbro
*An adaptation of color carbon printing to the advertising trades.*

9.5 Dye transfer
*The final multilayer color process.*

9.6 Kodacolor and Kodachrome
*Color photographic materials assembled on a single support for consumer use.*

9.7 Large-format transparencies
*Color transparencies for use as printing intermediates.*

9.8 Chromogenic or type-C printing
*Modern negative and print processes using color coupling methods.*

9.9 35mm slides
*Small color transparencies for the amateur.*

9.10 Cibachrome
*An autopositive method for printing from color slides.*

9.11 Polaroid color
*The twenty-by-twenty-four-inch color Polaroid camera.*

9.12 The SX-70
*Polaroid's elegant amateur color camera.*

# Color photography

## 9.1 HAND-COLORED PHOTOGRAPHS

Throughout the nineteenth century photography was entirely black and white. The prints might have had different colors according to the processes used to make them, but the data captured in cameras was monochromatic. This was because the silver halides — the family of salts that are light sensitive enough for the camera — only respond to light at the blue end of the visual spectrum, so recording colors in other parts of it was difficult. There had been a long history of hand-coloring etchings and engravings, though, and this practice easily moved over to the photograph.

The daguerreotype in its earliest form had a dull gray look, which was often relieved by applying pale red to the subject's cheeks or spots of gold to the buttons on a jacket. In Japan, albumen prints made for the tourist trade were often given wild applications of color — cherry blossoms became pink, hanging wisteria blue. These modifications were made with dilute oil paints prepared for the purpose. Long after the invention of color photography these oil colors were still sold in kits, so that the favorite family portrait could be customized and made more lifelike.

There is an interesting technical difficulty in hand coloring. A black and white photograph translates the colors of the world into gray tones. In early photography, when the materials of the negative were sensitive to blue and insensitive to red, or "orthochromatic," they translated blues into light shades of gray and reds into dark ones. The print of a picture made this way was dark where a color image would have been red, so any hand application of color in those areas was obscured by the heavy tone already present. The solution — and a half-baked one at that — was to make a light print and hope that it had enough tonal "space" to allow applied colors to show. This is interesting because it relates to the fact that there are two completely different ways to make a color picture. One way — the one we find in hand-colored photographs — is to create a monochromatic skeleton and fill in the colors on top of it, as if we were hanging colors on a neutral framework. The other method — the basis of true color photography — is to build up an image out of primary colors, which themselves create the neutral values in areas where all three of them are present. The black and white skeleton is absent and color alone makes the framework. This is the practice that leads to the riches of color, and also to substantial technical problems when the balance of the primaries distorts the neutrality of the gray tones in the picture.

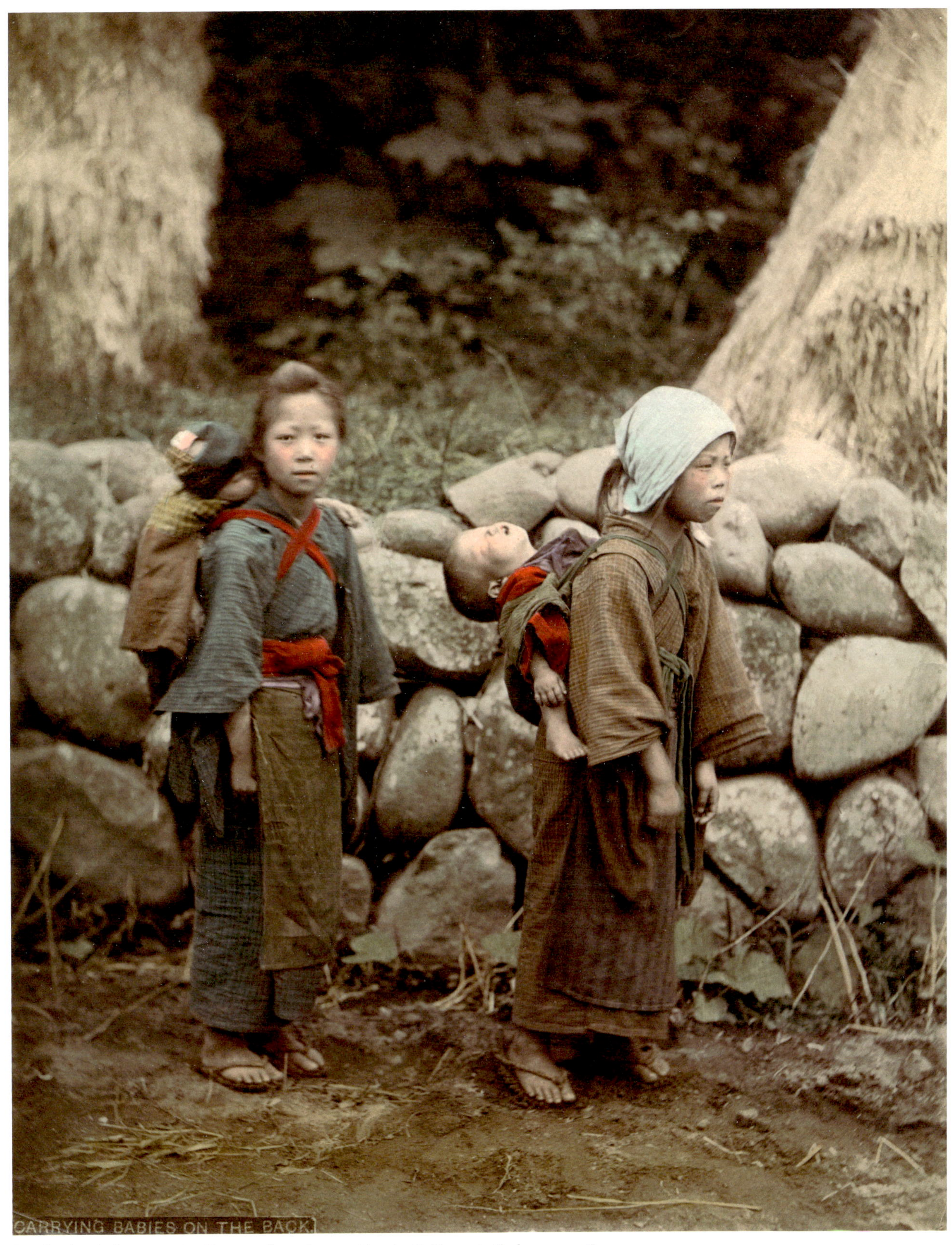


**Hand-colored albumen print.** Photographer unknown. *Carrying Babies on the Back.* c. 1900. 9¼ x 7¼ in. (23.5 x 18.4 cm)

## 9.2 THE LUMIÈRE AUTOCHROME

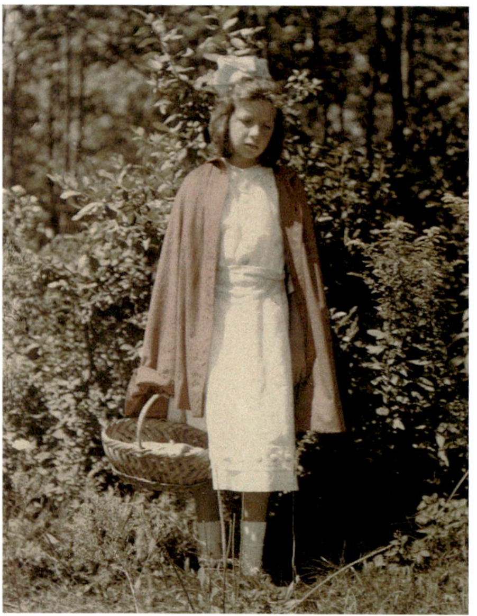

A faded Autochrome, by an unknown photographer, depicting Little Red Riding Hood dressed up for her adventure with the wolf. c. 1910. 5 x 3½ in. (12.7 x 8.9 cm)

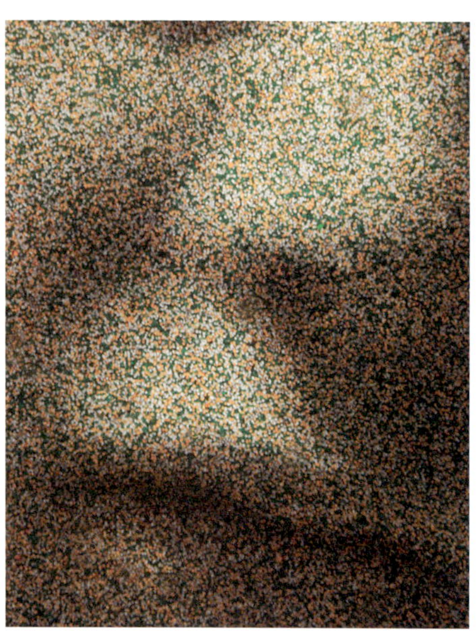

A detail of the Autochrome above enlarged twenty-five times, showing the grainy structure that produced the additive primaries. The blue grains have faded severely and the red and green are also weak. The Autochromes that have survived in good condition were almost always stored in the dark.

The first practical color process was the Lumière Autochrome, invented and marketed by the same Lumière brothers, Auguste and Louis, who made the first movies. These color pictures were on glass plates and were viewed as transparencies. They consisted of a color screen superimposed upon a black and white positive, which modulated the light going through the color screen. The wild thing about the Autochrome is that it used additive color; when the more modern color processes were developed—even those used to make transparencies—they used subtractive color exclusively. The structure of the Autochrome is so crazy that I can't resist describing it.

A glass plate was coated with tiny transparent grains of potato starch that had been dyed in the additive primaries—red, green, and blue. These colors were mixed in even proportions over the plate, which therefore appeared gray when viewed through transmitted white light. The areas between the grains were dyed black. On top of this was coated a black and white photographic emulsion, which the photographer exposed in the camera with the color-screen side facing the lens. Instead of being processed as a normal black and white negative the plate was subjected to reversal processing: the negative was developed, the developed silver was bleached out before the image was fixed, and finally the remaining silver salts were developed, producing a positive image. Once the plate had been processed and dried, it could be viewed as a transparency and appeared as a full-color photograph.

The Autochrome worked because the positive image—even though monochromatic—acted to modulate the amount of light that went through each grain of dyed starch. In a red area of the picture, for example, a lot of light would have passed through the red grains onto the coating of black and white emulsion when the picture was taken. The positive was correspondingly light in that area, so a lot of light went through the red grains when the sandwich was viewed. The green grains in that same area would have blocked the red light when the exposure was made; little light went to the plate there, the positive was correspondingly dark, so the green grains, when viewed later, were "turned off" by the heavy deposit of silver behind them. In controlling the intensity of the three additive primaries, the Autochrome worked exactly the same way as the modern television or computer screen.

The brightness range of the Autochrome was limited for two reasons: the black matrix in which the grains were dispersed reduced the overall transmission of light, and saturated colors were created by diminishing the brightness of unwanted colors. To make a strong blue, the red and green grains were darkened, so saturated areas were less bright, giving the Autochrome a tonal scale unlike any other process.

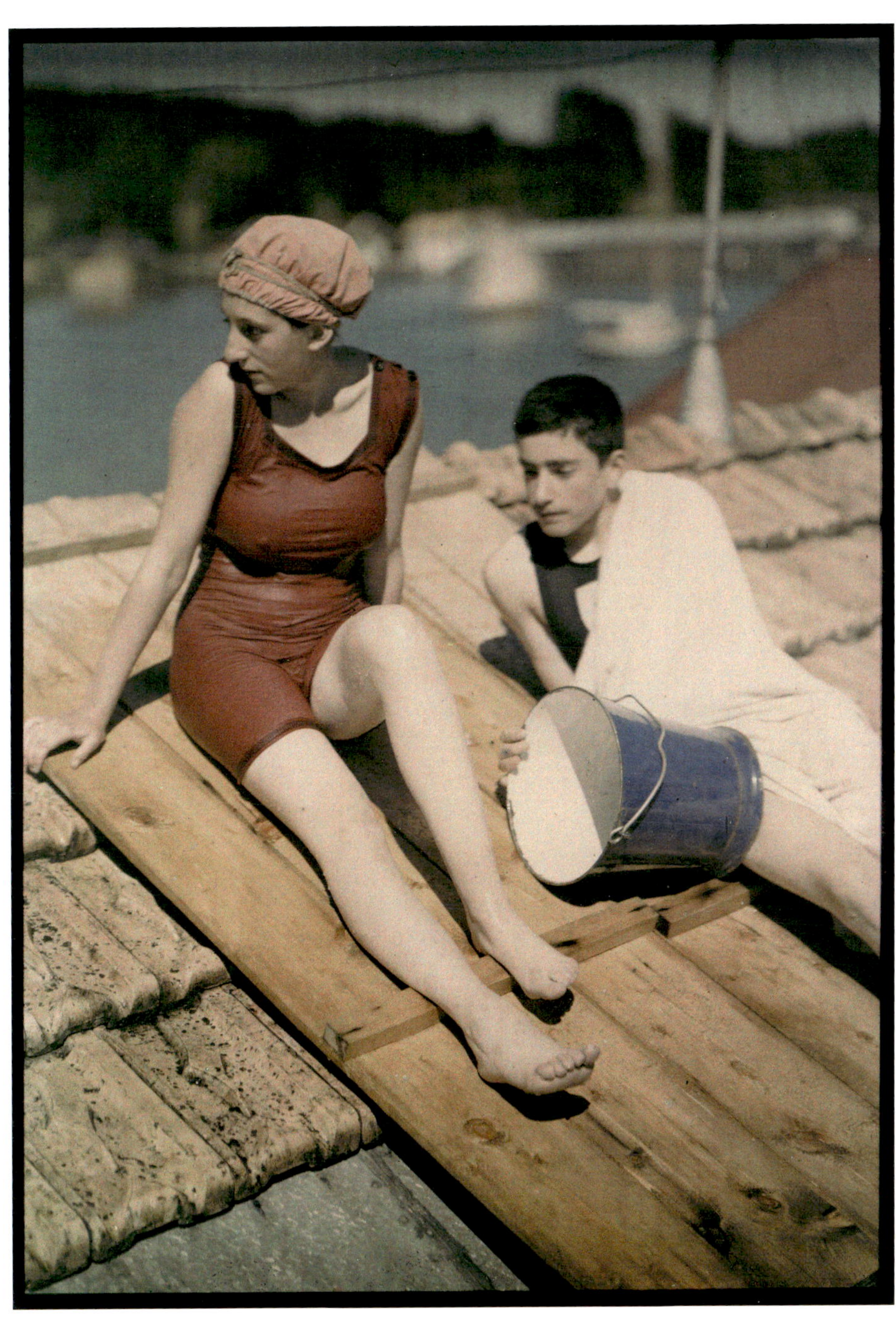

**Lumière Autochrome.** Photographer unknown. *Bathers at Lake George.* c. 1918. 7 x 5 in. (17.8 x 12.7 cm)

## 9.3 COLOR CARBON PRINTING

The Autochrome was followed by a flurry of additive-color processes that used screens, but none was widespread and all were eventually buried by the development of subtractive-color photography. The principle behind the subtractive method is that three black and white negatives can be made of a color subject, each exposed through a filter in one of the additive primary colors, and these three negatives will then hold all the information needed to make a full-color picture. This is of course Maxwell's principle applied again (as it was in the Autochrome): we capture a signal in three discrete parts of the spectrum, knowing that from that information we can generate the illusion of full color.

The separation negatives were printed in the complementary colors to the filters used to make them, so that the red-filter negative was used to print cyan; the green, magenta; and the blue, yellow. Conventional chemical photographic processes could not be used to print these separations because none handled color with any versatility: silver deposits were gray in color, gold toning was purple, and iron deposits were blue. Carbon printing, however, used pigments of any color, allowing the color of the print to be controlled by the selection of the pigment used to make the carbon tissue. If relatively pure cyan, magenta, and yellow colorants were used to make three tissues, the separations could be printed in register, one on top of the other, to make a full-color picture.

My earlier description of the carbon print gives some idea of how difficult these prints were to make, and if you multiply these difficulties by three you get some notion of just how hard it was to make a carbon print in color. And yet such prints were made, producing the first terrific color photographs on paper. There was much to-do about the permanence of these pictures, but the one we see here, made in the 1930s, spent part of its life under an overmat, which protected the outer edges from exposure to light, and it is easy to see how badly the rest of the picture has faded. There is a lesson in here: that pigments, touted as permanent, can fade just as badly as dyes if they are inherently unstable. All color is fugitive to some degree or another, and great care must be used in selecting the dyes or pigments used in color processes if we wish the pictures to be permanent. Most of our modern printing in books would fade badly if exposed to light, and the same is true of color photographs. The only safe thing to do is to keep them in the dark. Light erodes color in almost any medium we choose to use.

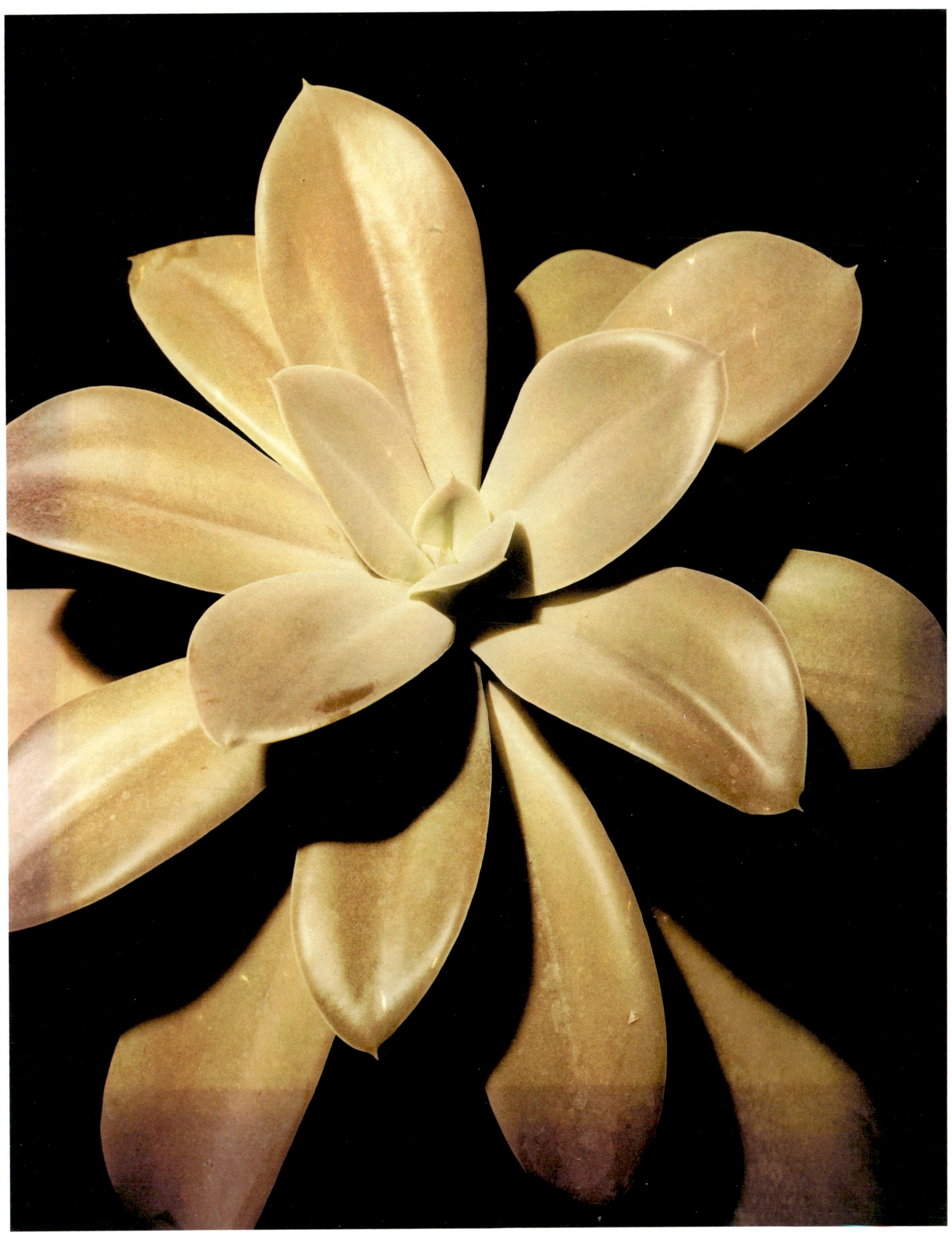

**Color carbon print.** Hi Williams. *Echeveria.* c. 1935. 16¾ x 13¼ in. (42.6 x 33.7 cm)

## 9.4 CARBRO

The making of color separations was the foundation of all color photography until the invention of single-sheet color materials, such as Kodachrome and Agfacolor, shortly before World War II. Those materials would use separations too, but they would be invisible, embedded in the multiple coatings of a new generation of color films and papers. In the meantime photo labs used separation negatives to make color carbons, color "carbros" (of which this picture is an example), and dye transfer prints.

The carbro print was an odd duck. It was really a variation on the color carbon process, but it gained popularity in photo labs making color masters for the advertising trade. Color was moving onto the printing presses during World War II and separations would also be the basis for printing color in ink. There was a need for superb originals to be reproduced by the presses. Since the ink separations then used would badly degrade the quality of the color, these originals had to be as good as possible. The carbro answered this need. It was controllable under lab conditions, used separations that could be manipulated and retouched, and became the color standard until the invention of modern color materials.

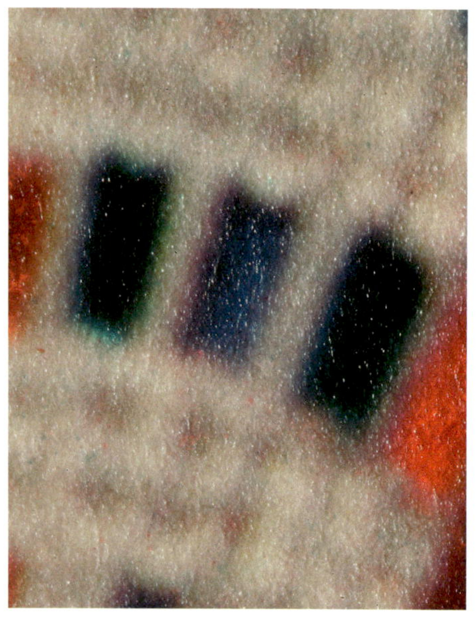

This detail, enlarged ten times from the original, shows the smooth, grainless quality of the carbro but also a slight misregistration, seen in the color fringes on the edges of the small blocks of color.

The difference between the carbon and the carbro was in the separations and in the way the pigmented gelatin layers were hardened. Color carbon used full-sized separation negatives while the carbro used an intermediate set that were exposed to photographic paper to create a set of positives. These paper positives were bleached and placed in contact with pigment-bearing carbon tissue; the bleach migrated across to the gelatin and hardened it. After hardening, the tissue was transferred to the final support in exactly the same manner as in carbon printing.

The terrible truth about carbros is that they often failed technically and aesthetically. They were extremely hard to do well, but even worse, they were almost always made for the advertising trade, so the images tend to have that feeling of decadence that the combination of fashion and commerce so often produces. Every once in a while we find a good one, but even the worst of them have a visual nostalgia that comes from their reflection of the tastes of the time in which they were made.

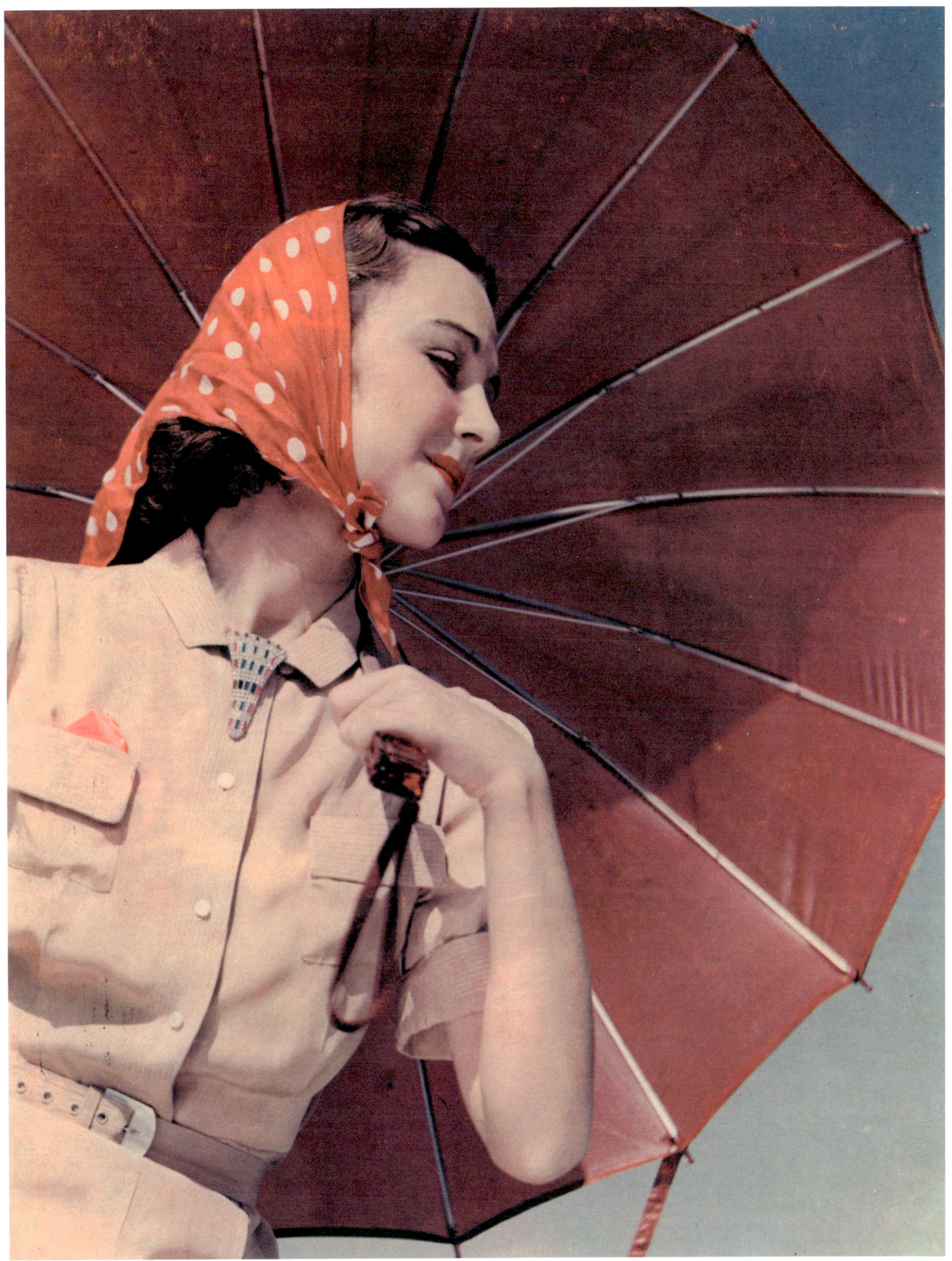

**Carbro print.** William Rittase. *Model with Umbrella.* c. 1935. 13½ x 10⅜ in. (34.3 x 26.4 cm)

## 9.5 DYE TRANSFER

The final chemical method using individual separations to make color photographic prints was called "dye transfer." The process was designed to make superb color prints from transparencies rather than from negatives. The color original was placed in an enlarger and a set of three filtered separations was made from it. These new negatives were then exposed by contact onto a new sort of film called "matrix" film. This gelatin-coated material was exposed from the back, and processed to remove unexposed gelatin, in such a way that the remaining layer was in relief, much like a carbon print. Exposing the material from the back cut out the old carbon-print step of a second transfer to correct the reversal of the image. Each of the resulting positives—often called "matrices"—was soaked in a dye of the correct subtractive color, and sequentially rolled into contact with a specially prepared receiver sheet, transferring the dye from each matrix over to the receiver. The whole operation had to be done with accurate registration, which required special easels and register pins to make sure everything fit properly. The gelatin in the matrices never moved; it remained where it was. Only the dyes transferred over to form the final image.

A good dye transfer could be the best of all chemical color prints. Its quality came from the dyes used and from the physical appearance of the surface, which looked as though the image had somehow been built up, giving the print a physical presence that modern chromogenic color prints cannot match. I hedge a bit in my praise of the dye transfer process because a bad dye can be awful, but because the process was always touted as being the best, some people think even the bad ones are OK. This is a continual problem with printing processes: like celebrities, they get a reputation, and before too long this reputation can cloud the reality of the process that underlies it. Dye transfer prints were expensive and rare, and could be as bad as anything else. When they did their job well they were, like Marilyn Monroe, better than anything else around.

The Eastman Kodak Company, which made the matrix film for dye transfer, stopped producing it some years ago. I think there are stocks of it out there, cherished by dedicated printers, so it might be that a dye transfer could still be made. It would be a shocker to put a high-grade dye next to a superb digital inkjet print. The computer print, if on a gloss surface, wouldn't have the beautiful physical character of the dye, but it could beat it hands down for color.

In the lower-left corner, under the overmat, we can see the three dye layers, which don't exactly fit each other. The magenta and cyan combine to make a reddish blue and the yellow and cyan together make green; where the three colors overlap we find a pale brown, rendering the tabletop on which the vase rests.

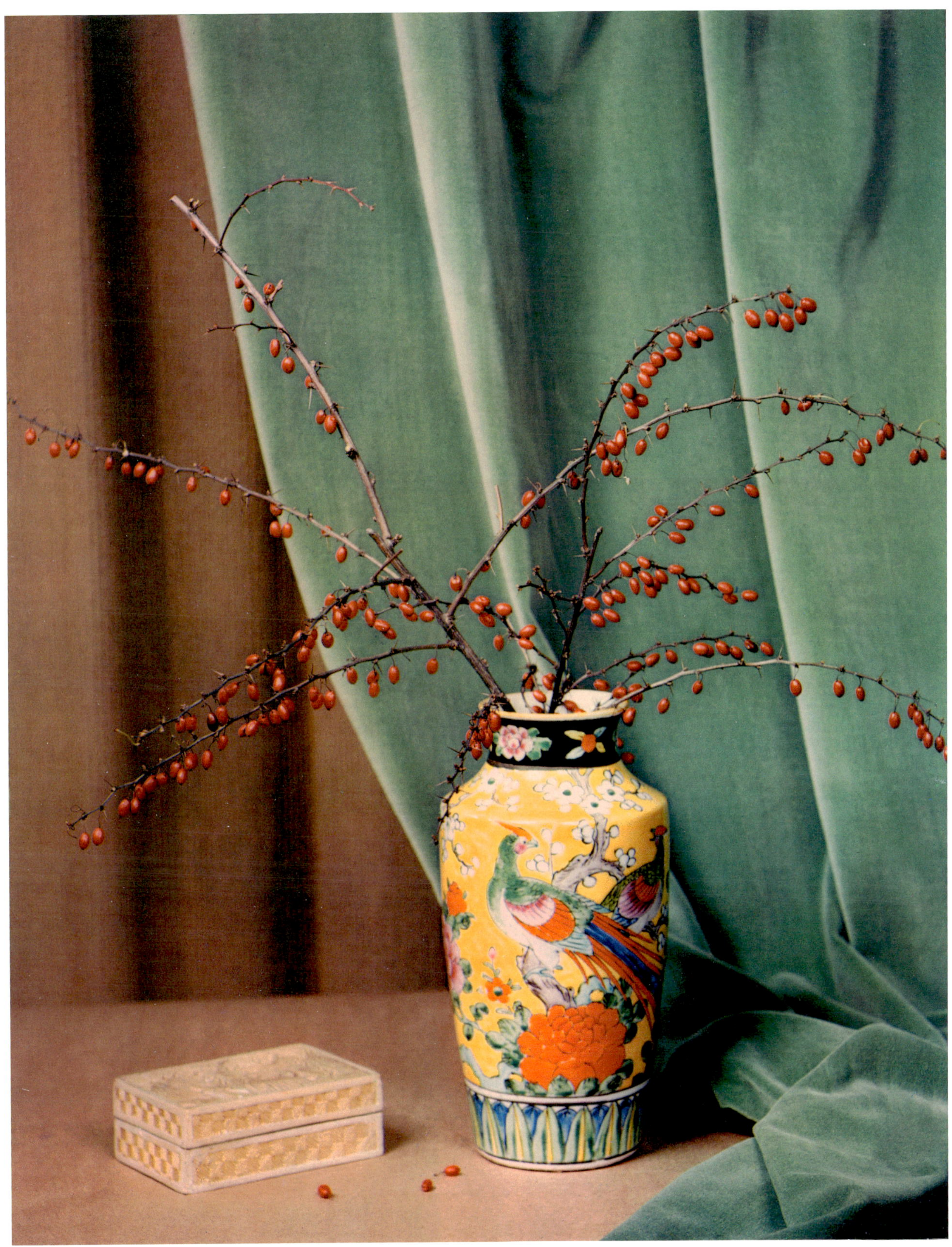

**Dye transfer print.** Adolf Fassbender. *Winter Berries.* 1946. 15¾ x 12⅝ in. (40 x 32 cm). This dye transfer print is not only quite large but also has a beautiful semimatte surface, quite different from the normal gloss used for dyes.

## 9.6 KODACOLOR AND KODACHROME

Color carbon, carbro, and dye transfer were all complicated processes requiring skilled handling and specialized equipment. In the 1930s the Eastman Kodak Company introduced the first widely available color materials that could be handled by the amateur. The processing and printing still needed to be done in a lab, but Eastman had long since built up a huge business of processing and printing film exposed by the public. The new materials were revolutionary in that individual color separations were no longer needed–each single sheet of film held three sensitive layers, each producing one of the primary color records. Like the old individual separations, these emulsion coatings were black and white, but they were converted to dye images of the proper color during processing.

This color revolution started with large film in sheets and movie film for professional use and was followed by 35mm and small-format film for sale in the widespread and lucrative amateur market. These films and papers were miracles of construction. The old black and white films had themselves been complicated enough to require laboratory conditions when they were manufactured — they simply could not be created at home — but the color materials only came about because Kodak, and a small number of other companies, made immense investments to build the factories that could manufacture these terrifically complex materials, and do so in the huge quantities that would make them available at a reasonable cost. The economic reality of single-sheet color materials is that they only come to us because of the advantages of mass production and carefully evolved manufacturing and marketing systems; if we tried to make a single box of 35mm color film on our own, it would cost millions of dollars. We find the same reality in the automotive industry, where the simplest mass-produced car is a miracle of refinement and accumulated experience, only accessible to the common man because of the cooperative economy in which we live. Photography had come a long way from the home-cooking techniques of its origins a hundred years before.

The new materials came in multiple forms: as negatives, to be used for color prints on paper; as transparencies, to make autopositive slide materials; and as coatings on paper to make direct prints from either negatives or transparencies. The suffixes "-color" and "-chrome" designated the differences between negative and positive materials, so we find a whole new set of made-up names to accompany the fabricated Kodak moniker. Kodacolor and Kodachrome were soon joined by Agfacolor and Agfachrome and eventually Fujicolor and Fujichrome. These names are still in use today.

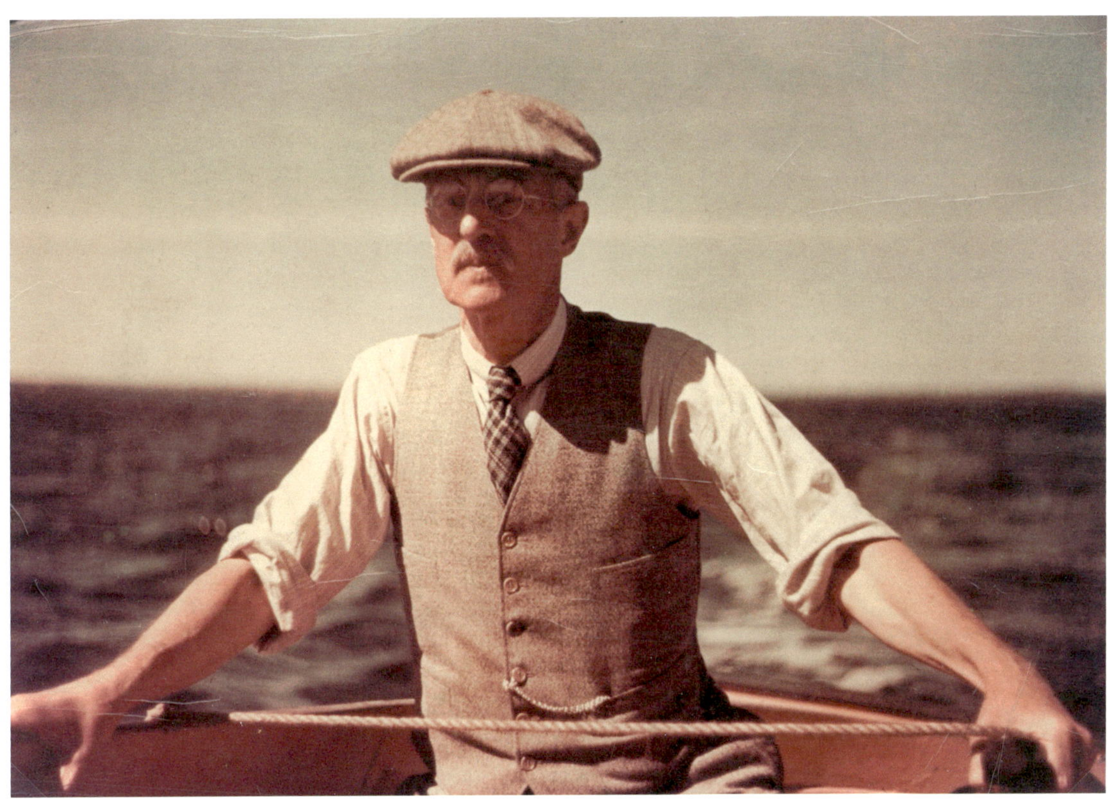

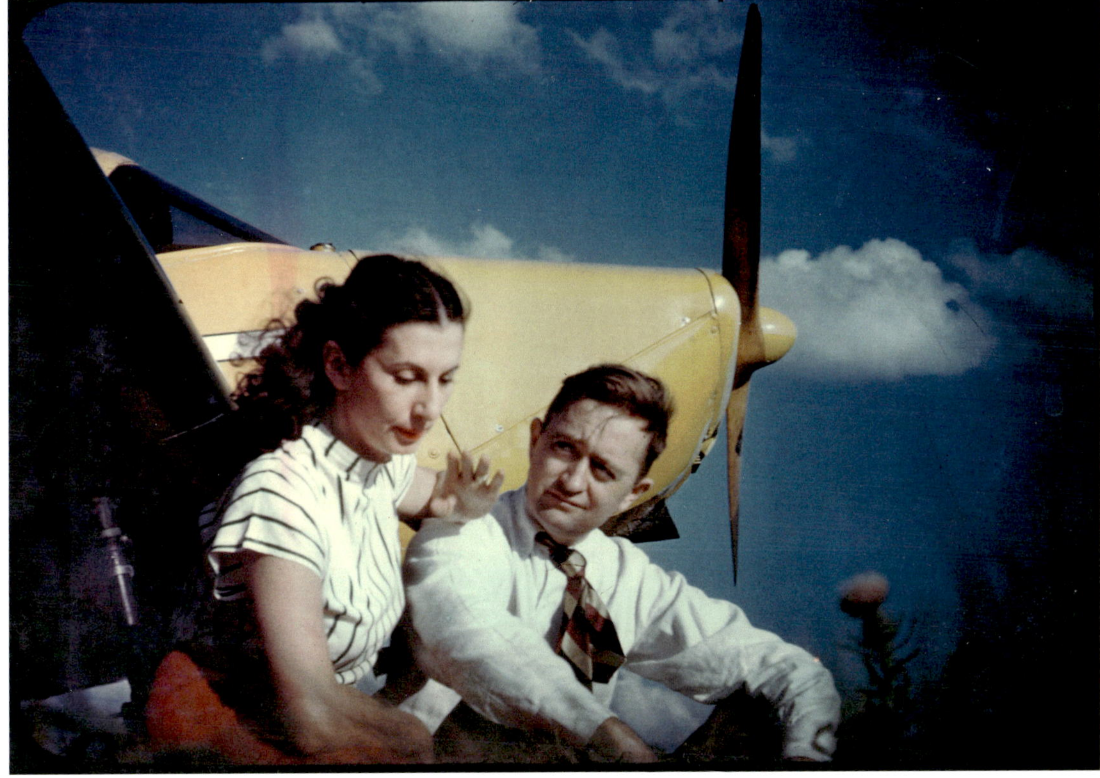

Top: **Kodacolor print.** Photographer unknown. *Edward Wanton Smith.* c. 1939. 4½ x 6⅝ in. (11.4 x 16.8 cm). This print, from 1971, was made from an internegative in turn made from a Kodachrome transparency.
Bottom: **Kodachrome print.** Photographer unknown. *Mariam and James McGlone with their Piper Cub.* 1946. 5½ x 7⅞ in. (14 x 20 cm). This print was made directly from a Kodachrome transparency.

## 9.7 LARGE-FORMAT TRANSPARENCIES

The astonishing single-sheet color processes became widespread and buried the old separation-based color methods. In 1946, Kodak made a new family of materials that could even be processed in a conventional darkroom, using just a few tanks and film-developing racks. The transparency in this new group was called the Ektachrome, and it quickly became the standard for creating original color photographs that were to be reproduced in ink. The one we see here is from the preparatory material for the book *Photographs from the Collection of the Gilman Paper Company*, published in 1985. The original, a daguerreotype, was photographed in the studio with a standard gray scale and a set of color patches alongside it. Transparencies such as this, made strictly as intermediaries for the printing trades, were produced by the thousands, used once, and then packed away in file drawers or old film boxes. They are one of the hidden treasure troves of photography.

The transparency became the standard for reproduction because it has a longer tonal range than a print. If we take any sheet of white paper and put the blackest mark possible on it, the difference in reflectivity between that dark tone and the paper itself can never exceed about 1:50. Within a transparency, though, the black tone can be completely opaque and the white completely clear, so the range of tonalities is unlimited. This extended range gives the color transparency a beautiful look, with saturated colors and brilliant contrast. These materials—which are "autopositive"—also have an extremely fine grain, the result of reversal processing. Transparencies tend to look sharper than paper prints, which have an inherent softness because the white support of the paper inevitably scatters light. The film used to make transparencies is manufactured with a light-absorbent backing—an "antihalation" coating—that eliminates this unwanted effect. On the down side, transparencies often have a color cast to them and are difficult to expose correctly. We say that the "latitude" of a transparency is very limited, which means that the exposure must be exactly right.

In the past, museums made photographic records of their collections with either black and white copy negatives or color transparencies. Today we can make much finer color records with high-end digital scanners, so larger institutions are taking on a huge rephotographing endeavor to create new digital archives. The old transparencies hung around for years in their brown-paper envelopes; we still don't know how well the digital files will last over long periods of time.

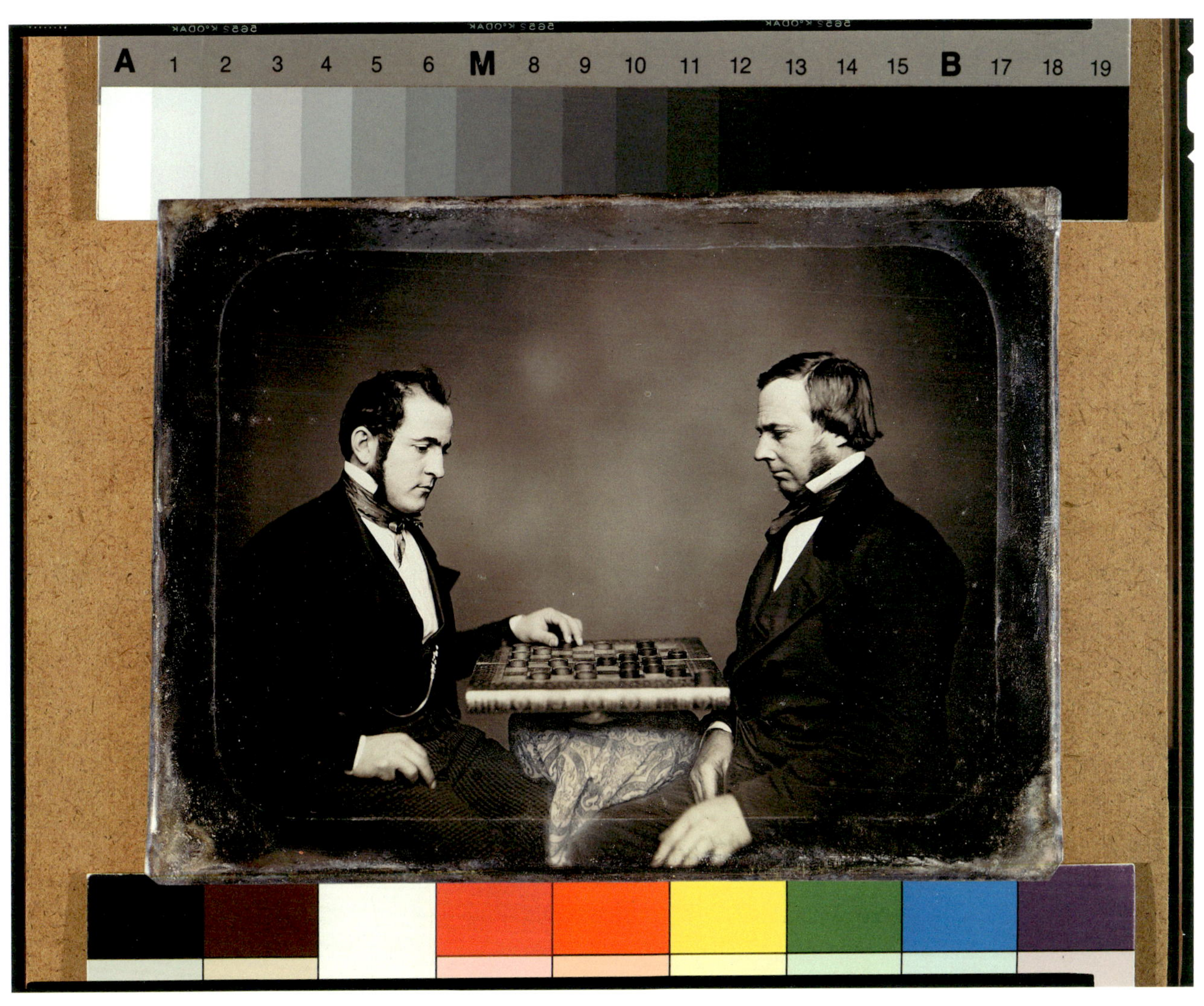


**Large-format transparency.** Possibly Jeremiah Gurney. Two men playing checkers. 1850–52. Daguerreotype
Print: Kodak Ektachrome transparency. Photographer unknown. 1982. 8 x 10 in. (20.3 x 25.4 cm)

## 9.8 CHROMOGENIC OR TYPE-C PRINTING

Only two chemical processing baths were needed to develop a black and white negative or print. The first of these, the developer, chemically reduced the latent image to a visible silver deposit. The second bath, the fixer, removed the unexposed (and consequently undeveloped and unstable) silver salts that remained in the film or paper. Over time, two more baths of convenience were added—one called the "short stop," used between developer and fixer to arrest the developing action, and the other a wash of plain water, used at the end to clean the processing chemicals out of the material. Whether amateur or professional, the black and white darkroom really only needed four trays for making prints and four small tanks, holding basically the same chemicals, for developing film. Color was a different story.

The developing of color materials, whether they ended up positive or negative, demanded extremely accurate temperature controls and a far more complicated sequence of processing steps. First the silver emulsions had to be developed, then the silver deposits to be converted into dyes, then fixing was needed, then some form of stabilization, and then a final wash. If the picture was to be a positive transparency then a bleaching step and a reversal exposure were also needed. This processing originally took place in laboratories—both the professional and the amateur sent out their exposed color film—but in the postwar era processing machines became available that could be set up in schools and large professional darkrooms. Some materials, such as the original Kodacolor and Kodachrome, would always need the outside labs, but other formulations could quite easily be handled automatically in fairly simple installations. The dominant process for making these color prints is commonly called "C printing," which stands for "chromogenic," a term referring to the manner in which the silver images are converted to dyes. C-prints can be absolutely wonderful, and they will continue to exist into the computer age, since they can be exposed with digitally controlled lasers (see plate 12.11).

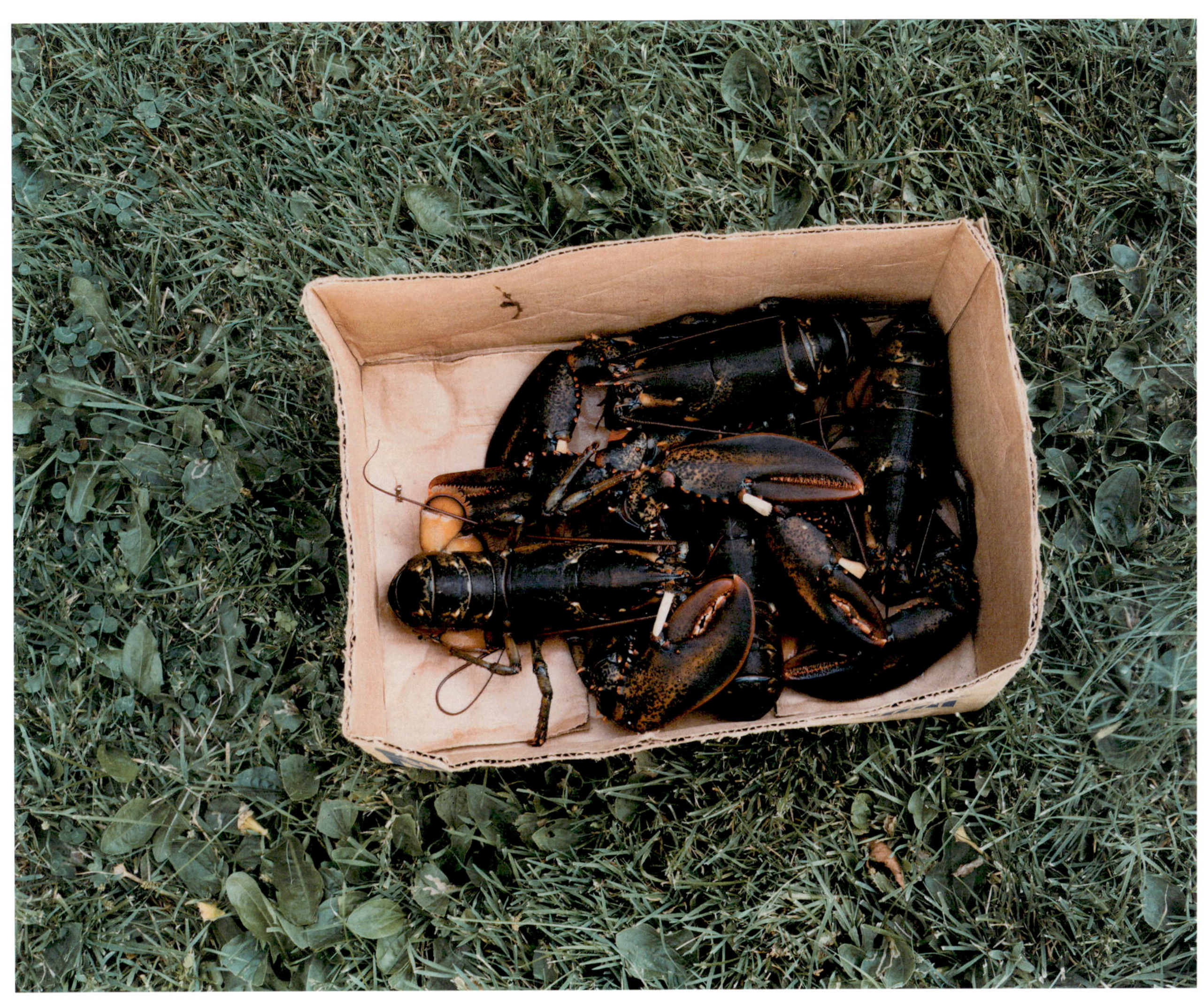

**Chromogenic print.** Stephen Shore. *Castine, Maine.* 1974. 7¾ x 9¾ in. (19.5 x 24.6 cm)

## 9.9 35MM COLOR SLIDES

It is hard to believe just how many photographs there are out there. Many of them exist (or did exist) as 35mm color slides. By the 1950s, small-format cameras had become easy to use, relatively inexpensive, and perfectly suited for the amateur. Their film was sold in rolls that could hold thirty-six exposures, and the practice of sending 35mm film away to labs for processing was long established. None of this had happened by accident, but rather as a direct result of the recognition by manufacturers of photographic materials that there was an immense potential market waiting to be tapped. Photography was built on the foundation of silver, which is what the manufacturers were actually marketing, through the attraction of the value added to the metal by putting it in a light-sensitive form. Today we are witnessing the collapse of that entire industry, since silver is irrelevant in the capture of digital images.

The huge amateur market that consumed 35mm slides has always been a mystery to me. Why did all those people make all those pictures? The impulse must be connected to an effort to retain memories of times gone by. It is somewhat tragic, because as we use technological devices to aid our memories we inevitably reduce our capacity to remember. We see this demonstrated in the mnemonic wonders of oral traditions, which always suffer as writing is introduced to cultures. Color slides are even more mysterious because they are almost never looked at. At least with an album of prints we can take the book off the shelf, easily leaf through it a bit, and then put it away again. The slide requires a projector, a dark room, and almost invariably other people, who have been gathered together to participate in the viewing of someone else's visual history. For me there is no more excruciating event than looking at the family slides.

These little photographic artifacts were only produced for about sixty years. They began to be made when color and the amateur market came together, and they started to fade when digital photography came along, and with it the ability to keep family pictures on the computer. There are literally hundreds of millions of slides getting moldy, being thrown out, and simply being forgotten until a younger generation finds them while cleaning out the old family home. By that time there will be no projectors left, so those too will most likely be discarded. The circumstances of their form will lead to the disappearance—unseen—of a huge portion of photographic history.

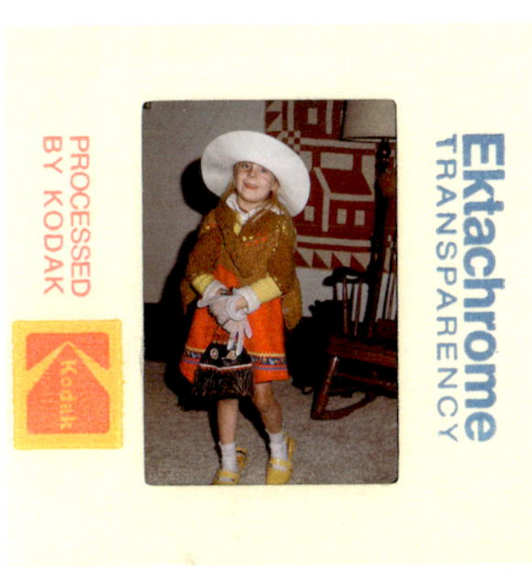


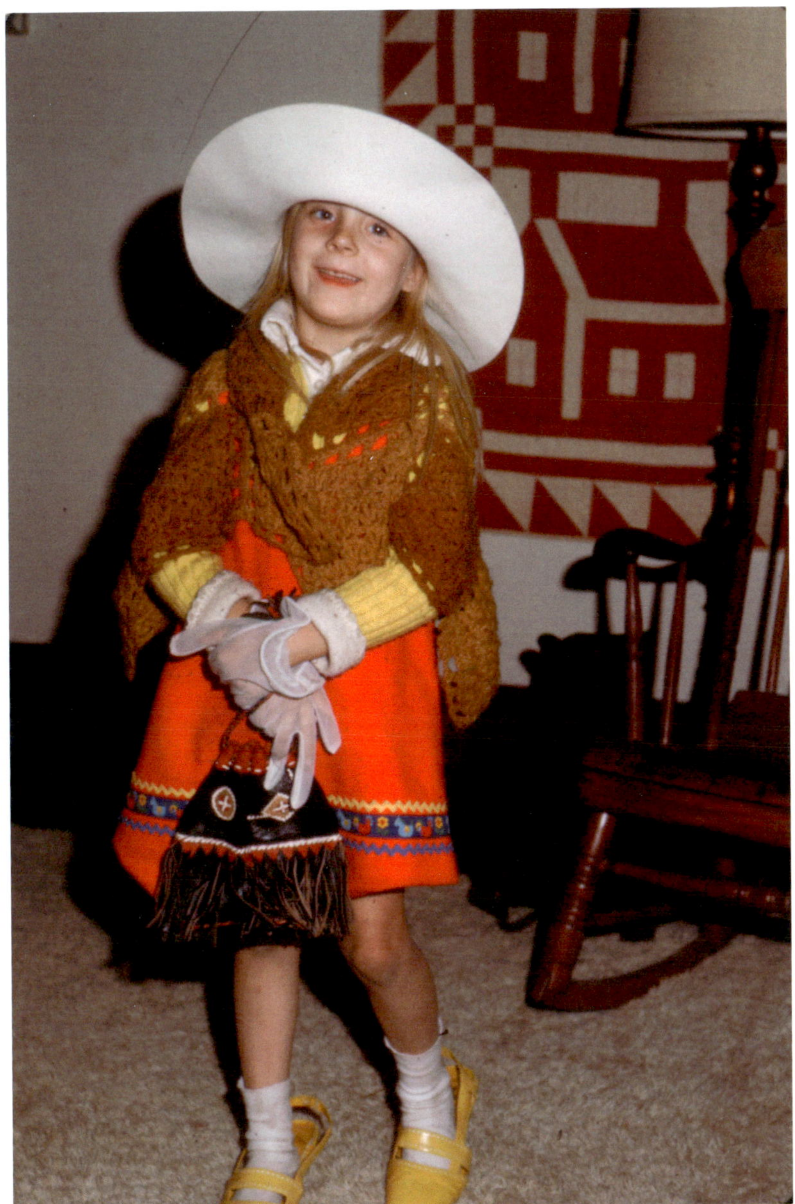

**Color slide.** Beverly Heegaard. Sarah Heegaard playing dress-up. 1973. 2 x 2 in. (5.1 x 5.1 cm)

## 9.10 CIBACHROME

Color photographic prints are most easily made from color negatives. These negatives are immensely complex, since they have to carry the color information for the three primaries in complementary form, and must do so in a way that gives a decent "color balance" to the prints. As all this was being worked out in the mid-twentieth century, the amateur slide market was developing, and a need arose to turn slides into prints. This was not so easy to do—the only practical way was to rephotograph the slide to make a color internegative, then print that.

The answer was to develop a paper that used reversal processing to create a direct positive, so that a slide could be exposed through an enlarger to produce a positive print in a single step. One of the most successful of these "autopositive" processes was the Cibachrome, which ultimately evolved into the Ilfochrome. These prints are identifiable in two ways: they are usually brilliantly shiny and they almost always have black borders. The borders are black because either the frame of the originating slide, the slide carrier in the enlarger, or the blades of the darkroom printing easel have transmitted no light to the edges of the print, leaving those areas an unarticulated black.

Cibachromes were the first single-sheet color material to have a high degree of permanence—which was a bit tough to take because the prints were often terrible. The colors were highly saturated, and complex masking was required in the printing to create decent color balance. The one we see here is successful because it was superbly made and used the somewhat garish colors of the medium to emphasize the picture's content. The orange, red, and green each play their role in the illusion set up by the photographer, and subtleties of color rendition are not necessary for the picture to work well. When Cibachromes are made of scenes drawn from the natural world, outside the studio setting, they almost always fail unless printed by a real master.

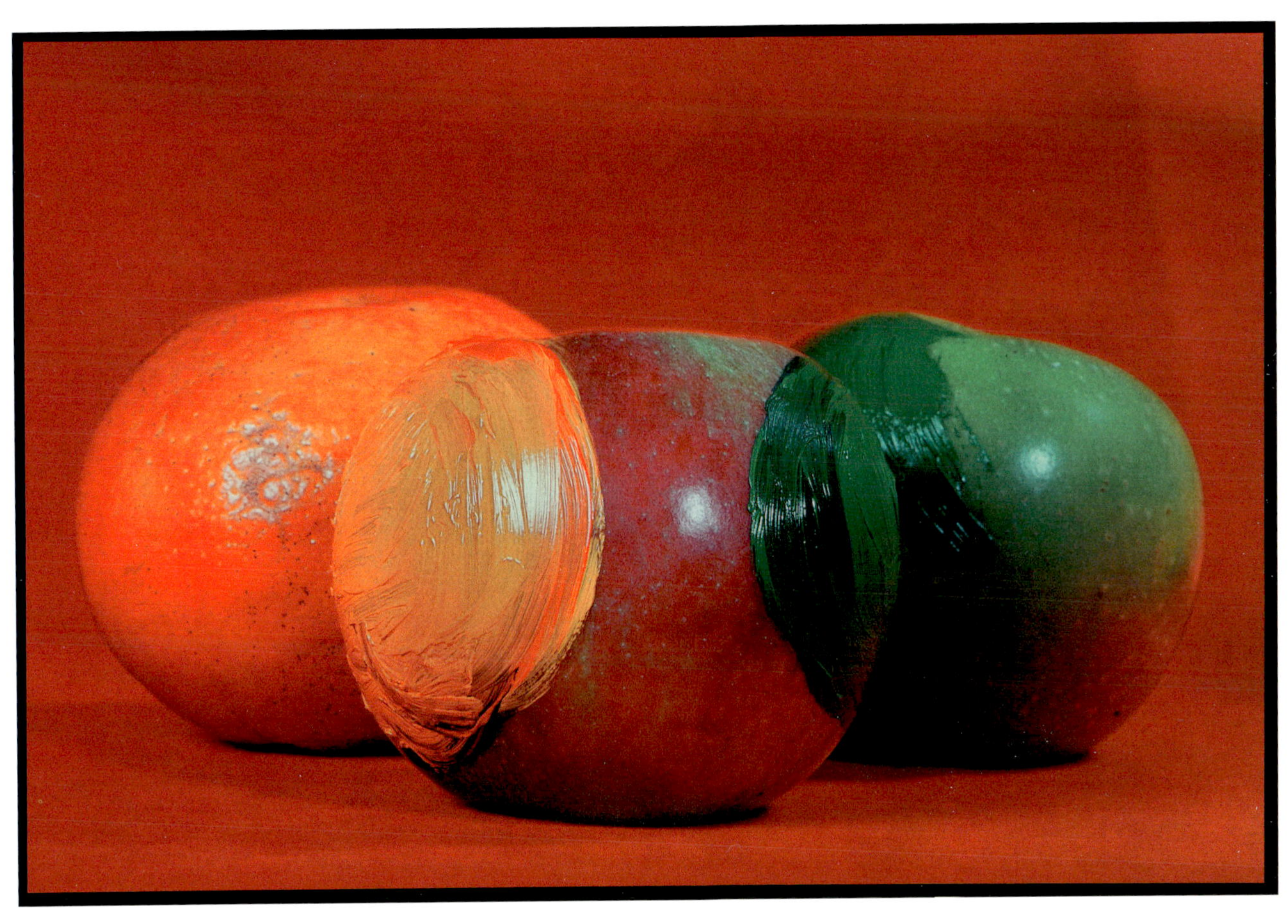

**Cibachrome print.** Allan Chasanoff. *Apples and Orange.* 1983. 9¼ x 13¾ in. (23.5 x 34.9 cm)

## 9.11 POLAROID COLOR

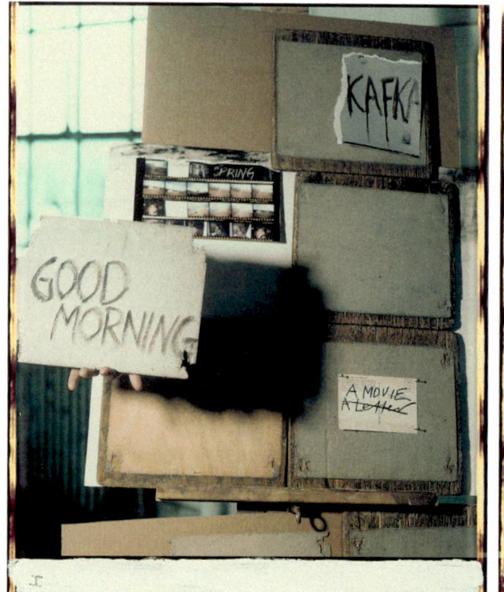


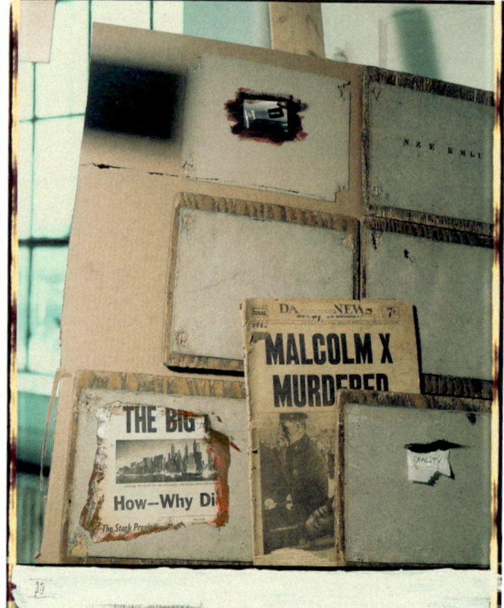


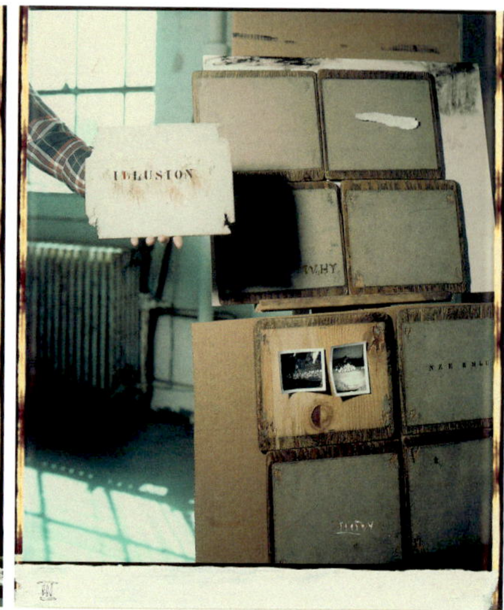


Edwin Land began his work with color by attempting a two-color system, trying to go one better than James Clerk Maxwell, who had proposed three colors as the basis for photographic systems. When Land finally solved the puzzle of instant-developing color materials it was with the more conventional set of three subtractive primaries. Somewhere in there he got a very strange idea—that he could make extremely large-format cameras that could produce superb replicas of famous works of art, making these unique objects available to the masses by existing in multiple copies. Toward this end Land made cameras that could produce Polaroid color photographs six feet high. The whole idea was deeply flawed, because, as anyone who has spent a long time printing knows, replication is never the path to successful reproduction. Instead, any copy made must find its own new form in the materials and context of its new physical statement. Land thought he could match the colors and that would be that, but most pictures affect us with complexities of form that are not simply about values of color and tone. Much of the nature of the originals was simply absent in the Polaroid reproductions. It just goes to show that it doesn't matter how bright you are—and Land was extraordinarily brilliant—you can still get in trouble meddling outside your area of expertise.

Land also made a smaller Polaroid camera that used twenty-by-twenty-four-inch film, and one of the great things the Polaroid Corporation did was to make these machines, along with a technician to run them, available to certain photographers and artists at no cost. Films in other formats were also supplied in exchange for prints made with these materials. A whole generation of photographers had a chance to use these extremely expensive, high-

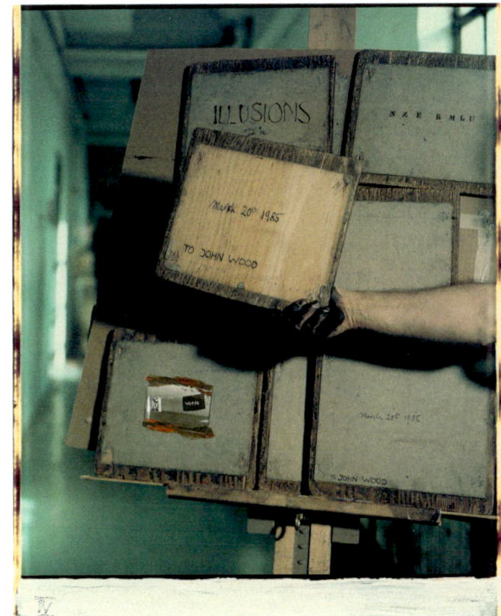

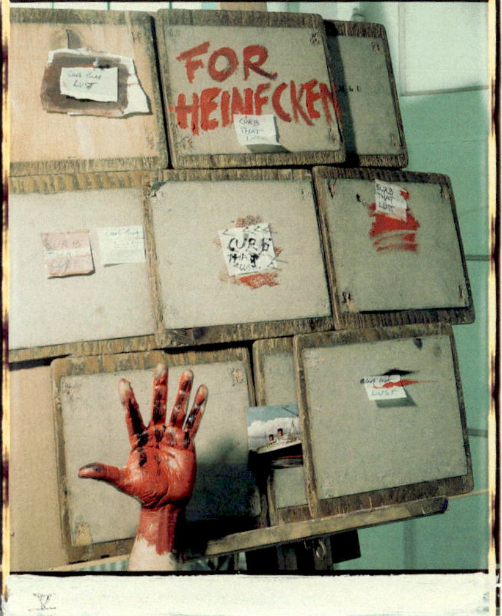

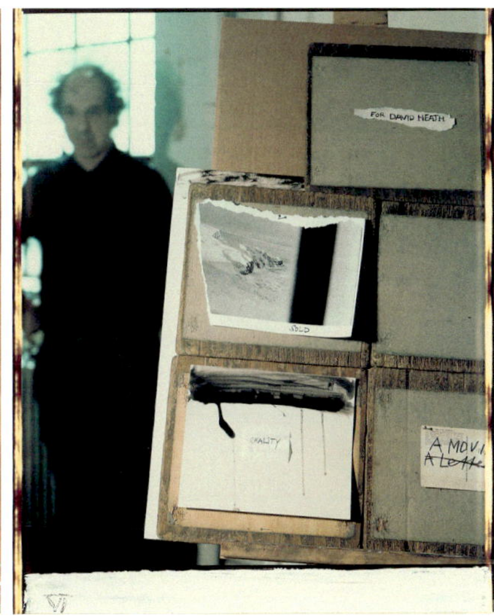


tech color systems without the terrible burden of paying to purchase or rent them.

The twenty-by-twenty-four-inch prints could be absolutely beautiful. The camera was almost always used in a studio setting, eliminating much of the photographic magic that can happen when the things in a picture derive from the world instead of the photographer's mind. One of the great pleasures of this particular set of six images, linked together in a horizontal format, is that Robert Frank has brought the camera to his workshop, away from the antiseptic conditions of the normal photographic studio. The color response of Polaroid color materials to the blue of the sky was quite odd, rendering it with a greenish cast that we see here in the values shown by light coming in from the windows. Large-format Polaroids also often suffered from the presence of a technician, there to make sure things worked out on the pure taking-the-picture level. All we need is someone in charge of lighting things properly to give a repetitive quality to the pictures, but once again in this sequence we find Frank overriding any such concerns as he mixes interior light, from tungsten lamps or a strobe, with the cool blue of the sky.

Despite my quibbles there are terrific twenty-by-twenty-fours out there, made by many photographers who engaged the studio and used it well. Like the daguerreotype, each of these photographs is unique, and every print has been struck by the first-generation light in the camera.

**Twenty-by-twenty-four-inch color Polaroid prints.** Robert Frank. *Boston.* 1985. Six prints, each: 27¾ x 22¼ in. (70.3 x 56.4 cm). The prints also include hand-applied paint and collage.

## 9.12 THE SX-70

The Polaroid processes wound down with a small, beautifully designed camera called the SX-70. Sleek, made of stainless steel with a leather cover, these marvelous devices had reflex viewing and cranked out small square pictures that looked like no others. The cameras were made for the amateur market, and the film for them was designed with a space at the bottom of the print on which the photographer could write notes. This was a clever use of the area needed to hold the processing chemistry that was spread across the image area after exposure. Because Land chose dyes that sharply cut portions out of the color spectrum, Polaroid color materials always had an interesting palette, with intense, saturated primaries. Many SX-70 prints suffered from a yellow cast that obscured these colors, but other Polaroid materials—four by five and eight by ten inches—showed them beautifully.

SX-70 film came in packets of eight sheets, and it was almost irresistible to rapidly expose all eight before even seeing how the first one came out. It took a few minutes for the pictures to fully form, and I always suspected that there was a marketing ploy behind this, to keep the photographer clicking away, and hence spending money, in a way that wouldn't have happened if each exposure could be seen before the next was made. These pictures had a tough plastic cover sheet bonded to the image, and it turned out that you could make marks on them with a fingernail or by squeezing the print when it was still fresh. Many artist-photographers produced interesting work by such physical manipulation of SX-70 prints.

Toward the end of his life Walker Evans was given Polaroid SX-70 cameras and film to work with. I remember him carrying a couple of the cameras in his jacket pockets, with a case of the film in the trunk of whatever car he had managed to enlist to drive him around. Walker would find an interesting subject and rapidly expose a whole pack on it, thrilled with the prospect of seeing the pictures quickly and knowing that he had more than one copy of them. At one point he visited us in Rhode Island (he had conned me into doing the driving) and saw, hanging in our basement, a marvelous old rotten "Dead End" sign that my brother owned. Walker wanted the sign, and my cagey brother offered to trade it for a photograph. Walker said fine, pulled out an SX-70, made five pictures of the sign itself, and offered them to its owner. My poor brother realized he had been had but requested that one Polaroid be signed. Walker agreed, took the selected photograph, and wrote on the front, "for John Benson with grt. pleasure Walker Evans 6/29/86." He died the next year, on April 10, 1975.

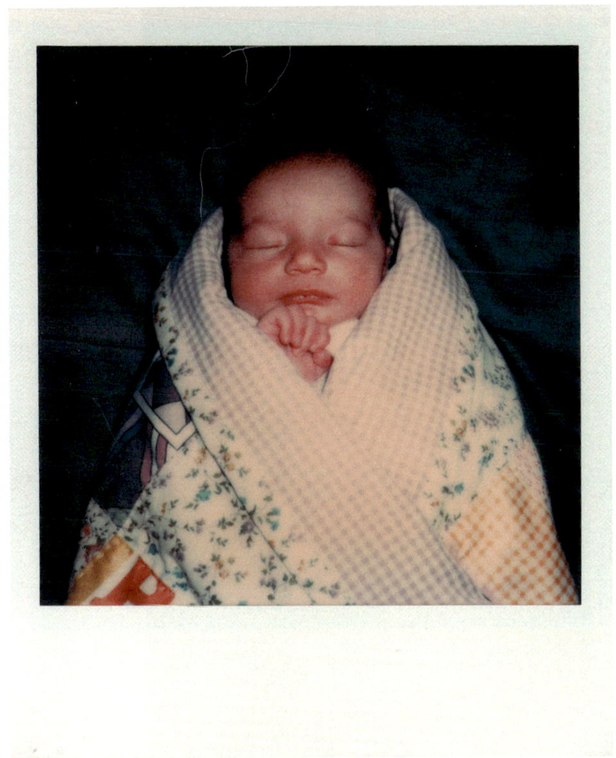

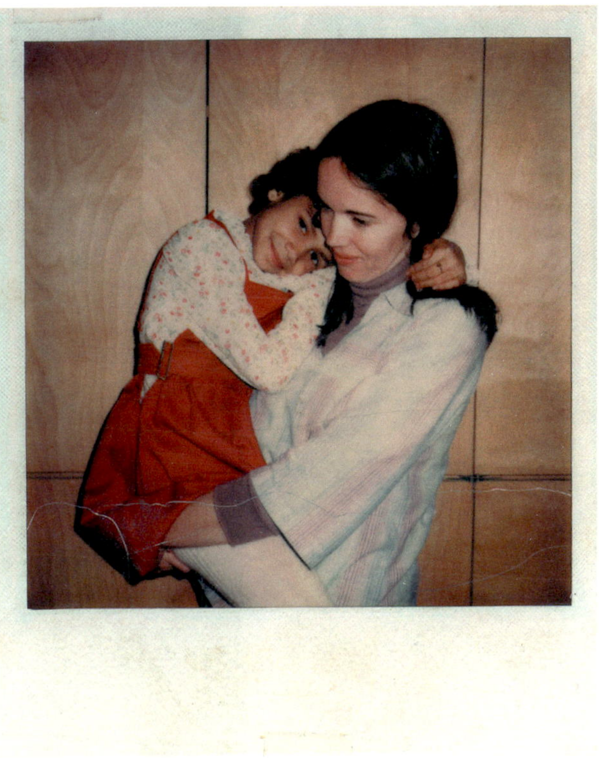

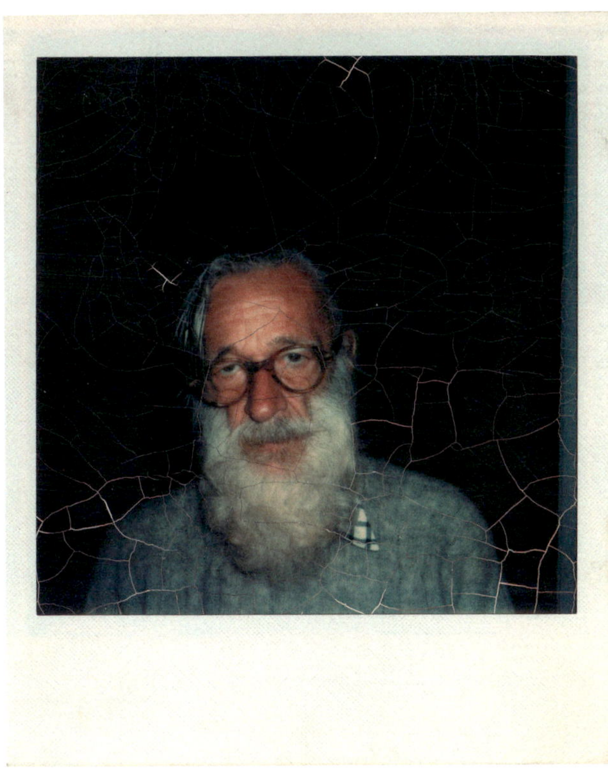

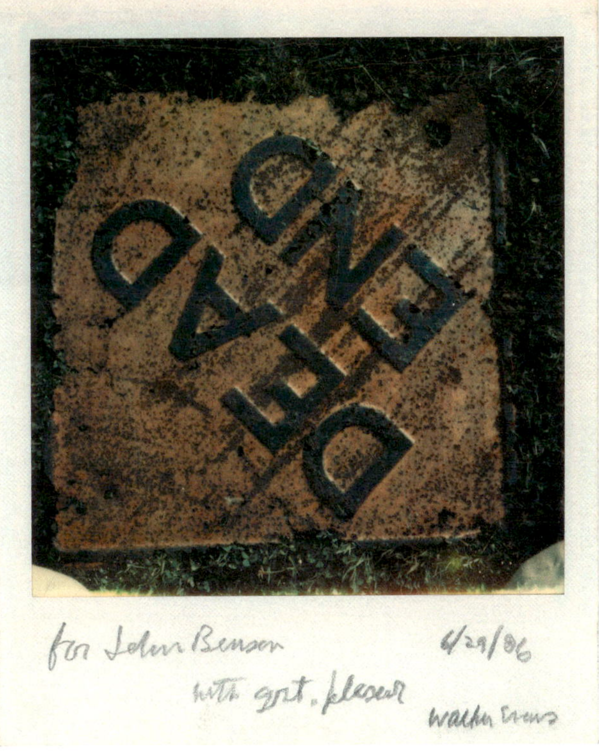


**SX-70 color Polaroid prints.** Top left: Richard Benson. *Abby Sophia Benson.* 1975. Top right: Richard Benson. *Barbara and Sarah Benson.* 1975. Bottom left. John Benson. *Walker Evans.* 1974. Bottom right: Walker Evans. *Dead End.* 1974. Each: 4¼ x 3½ in. (10.8 x 8.9 cm)

# Part 10

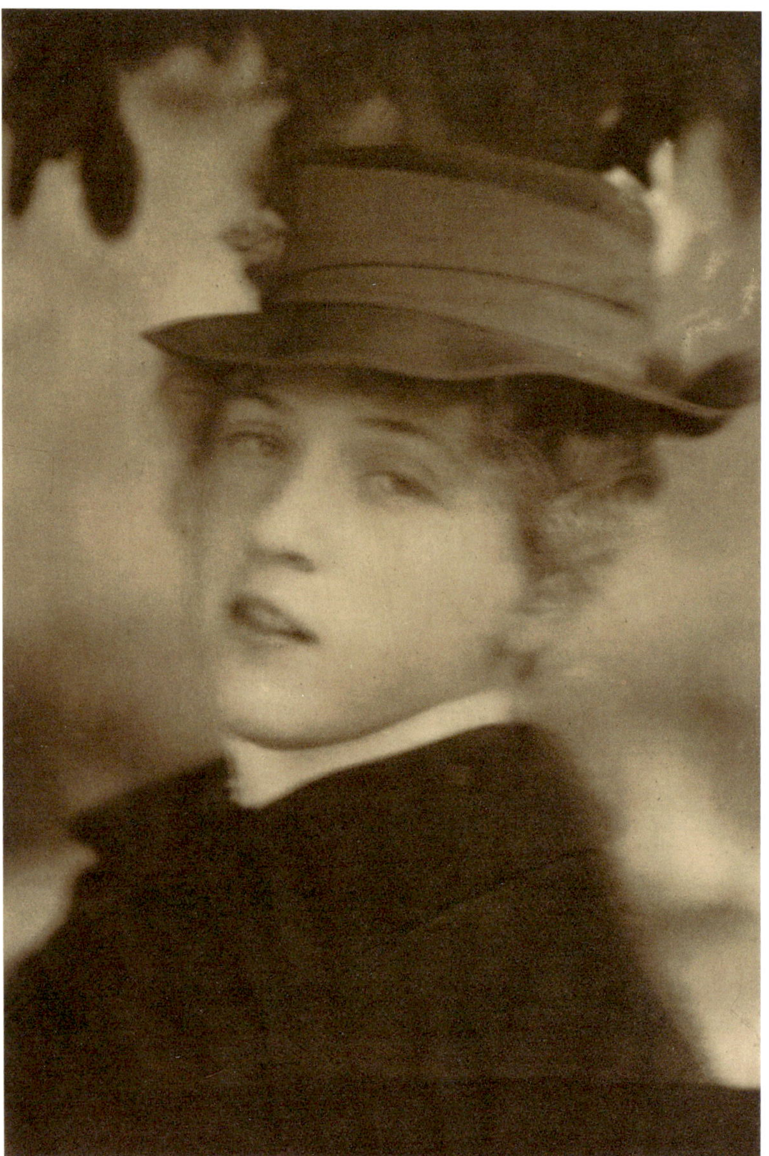

Three of the ink-printing methods—relief, intaglio, and planographic—adapted to the photographic image. Intaglio printing did so first, with the invention of photogravure. Planographic printing was second, in the form of collotype. Relief printing, the oldest of all, was the last to make a workable adaptation, but it ended up with an inexpensive and tremendously successful method in the single-impression halftone. Our examination of photography in ink begins with relief and intaglio because they are the oldest processes.

**Hand photogravure.** Alfred Stieglitz. *Miss R.* 1904. 8⅛ x 5½ in. (20.6 x 14 cm). Plate from *Camera Work* 12, October 1905.

# Photography in ink: relief and intaglio printing

10.1 The question of print quality
*Alterations of meaning in photographic reproductions in ink.*

10.2 Wood-engraved photographs
*Relief-printed photographs cut by hand in wood.*

10.3 Random screen halftones
*Early efforts to develop binary screens for relief printing.*

10.4 Ruled halftone screens
*Halftone prints generated by the use of a ruled glass screen.*

10.5 The letterpress halftone
*The widespread adoption of the mechanical halftone.*

10.6 Magazines
*Cheap ink printing of photographs for mass distribution.*

10.7 Duotone letterpress halftones
*Attempts to improve the quality of the letterpress halftone.*

10.8 Process color in relief printing
*The introduction of inexpensive color printing in ink.*

10.9 Flat-plate photogravure
*Intaglio printing adapted to the photographic image.*

10.10 Manipulated photogravure
*Meddling with the photographic image in photogravure.*

10.11 Art photogravure
*Photogravure as the most beautiful of all photographic ink processes.*

10.12 Rotogravure using mechanical screens
*Replacing the aquatint in rotary photogravure printing.*

10.13 The newspaper rotogravure section
*High-speed rotogravure for the pictorial section of the newspaper.*

## 10.1 THE QUESTION OF PRINT QUALITY

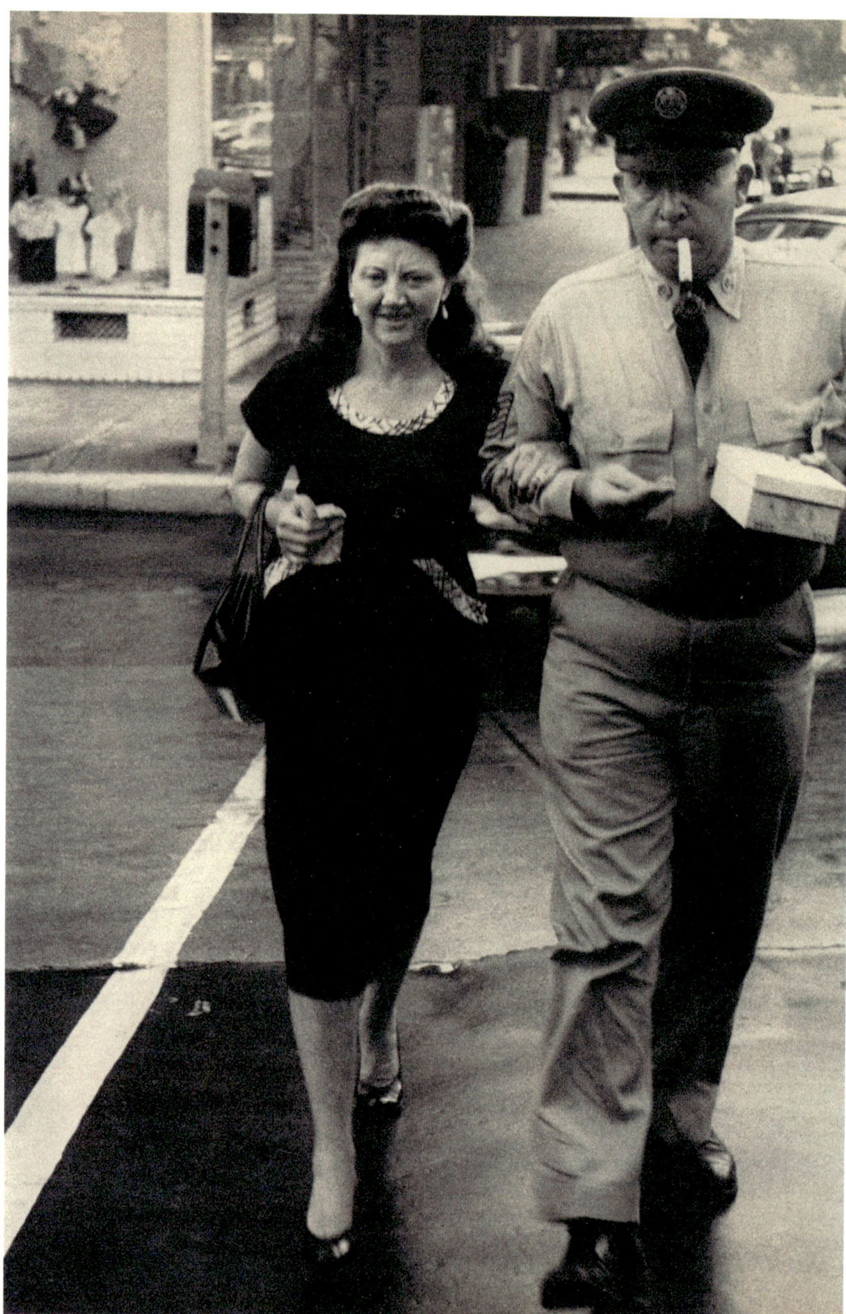

**Rotogravure and photo offset lithography.** Robert Frank. *Savannah, Georgia.* 1955. 6¾ x 4½ in. (17 x 11.5 cm). Left: from the 1959 edition of *The Americans*, printed in rotogravure (Paris: Delpire). Right: from the 1969 edition of that same book, printed in photo offset lithography (New York: Aperture).

When chemical photography is translated into ink, the quality of the reproduction varies tremendously. Even under ideal conditions every printing process would alter the image it reproduces; in the practical world, where publishers' schedules are tight, budgets are limited, and the printer must struggle with his craft, reproductions can often turn out terribly. There has been a steady increase in the quality of ink reproductions of pictures, and today it is possible to make superb books that do justice to the original chemical prints, but this state has been long coming. These two prints, reproduced here quite

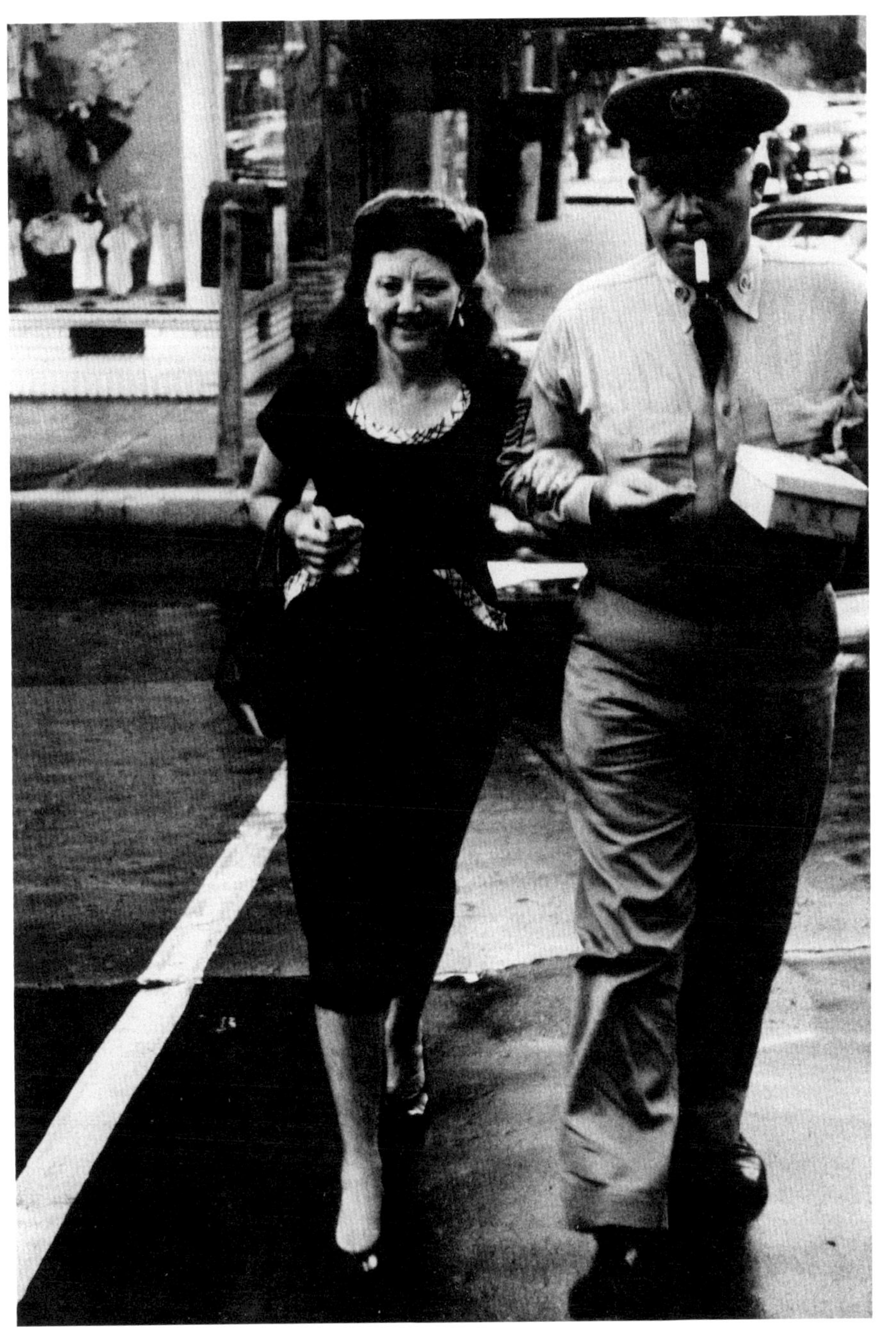

accurately, are from two different editions of Robert Frank's great book *The Americans.* The version on the left is from the first printing of the book plates, done in Europe in 1958, in rotogravure. The one on the right is from the second edition, printed in the United States in 1969, in photo offset lithography. The gravure version (actually published in two editions, with different texts but the same plate pages) is clear and lyrical in its photographic description. The offset version, heavy, plugged up, and rough, was made in the early years of offset, before that technology was working very well. Few copies were made of the gravure edition but many thousands were produced of the offset edition. A complex picture of America is there on the left, but sadly missing in the far more influential print on the right.

## 10.2 WOOD-ENGRAVED PHOTOGRAPHS

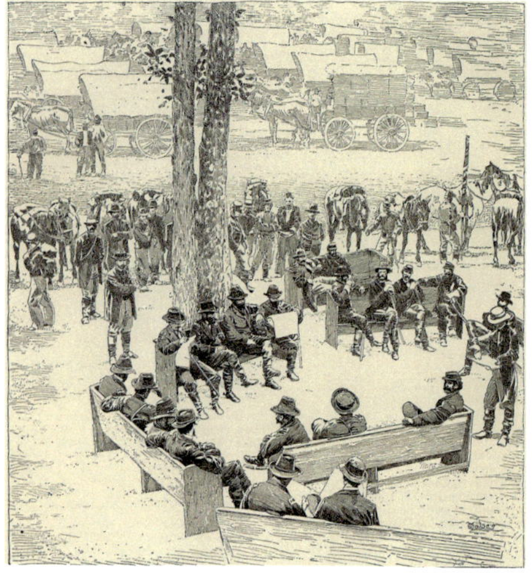

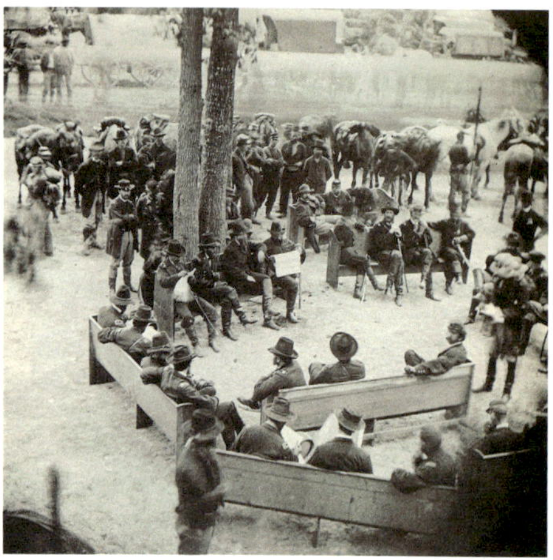

Timothy O'Sullivan. *General Grant with Staff at Bethesda Church.* May 21, 1864. Top: as a wood engraving in *The Century*, c. 1897. Bottom: as a mediocre halftone, printed c. 1966. The wood engraving shows an alternate method of reproducing a photograph. Unlike the plate opposite, this print is chiefly linear, with less attempt made to emulate photographic tone.

The picture on the right originated as a chemical photograph—the photographer is even given a credit line—but the print we see was made from a hand-cut wood engraving. The sequence by which this happened went as follows: (1) the photograph was taken (probably around 1880) using an early dry plate. (2) This negative was printed with a light-sensitive coating that had been applied to an end-grain wooden block. (3) A carver laboriously engraved the block by hand, working with a burin and using the image printed on the wood as a guide. (4) The finished block was locked up with type in a chase. (5) This composite was used to generate a stereotype (a thin metal replica, shaped to fit a cylinder), and (6) this plate, along with a group of others, was mounted on the cylinder of a rotary printing press, to be printed at high speed for use in the magazine *The Century*. I need to list this remarkable series of steps to place the practice of hand-cutting a photograph in its proper context. Photography was mature by this time, and was replacing handwork in the task of gathering data for widespread dissemination by the printing press. The presses themselves were fast, driven by the equally mature steam engine. The odd part of the whole process was that the hand still played an important role in translating the photograph into printable form. It seems that this task of translation should have been easy, but it was actually extremely difficult. The technologies of photography and printing were both well advanced before the emergence of the simple dot-bearing halftone, which ultimately replaced hand engraving.

To this day the task of converting a photograph into ink is fraught with problems—a seemingly simple chore, it almost never turns out correctly. Many of the following pages will be devoted to the various ways in which this translation has been done, and we will address the challenges that have so often led the process astray. The fundamental problem—mentioned earlier but impossible to overemphasize—is that photographs have tonal gradations that ink, when printed by relief or planographic processes, does not. Black ink is always black—it either goes down on the sheet and makes a black mark or it is not there and the paper is white. The solution to this problem has always been to break the picture up into small particles and to vary the size or number of those particles to emulate tone. The wood engraving we see here achieves this through an incredibly refined set of hand-cut lines. When these small marks cover a large percentage of the paper surface the tone appears dark; when they are small or widely separated, that part of the picture looks light. In the next few pages we will concern ourselves with the difficulties faced in carrying out this variation through mechanical means, with no assistance from the mind of such craftsmen as the engraver who made this block.

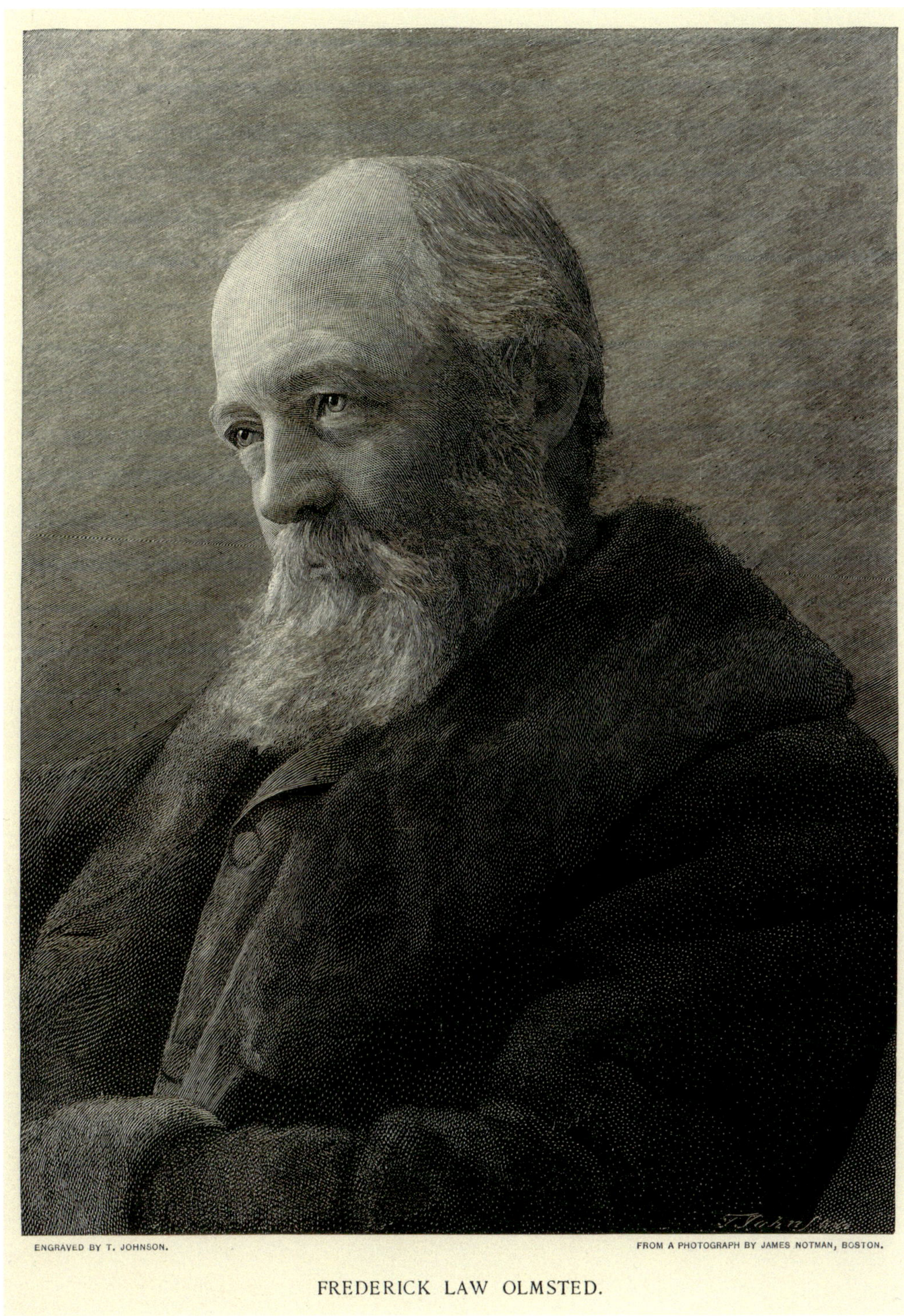


**Wood engraving.** James Notman. *Frederick Law Olmsted.* Print: T. Johnson. c. 1893. 7½ x 5⅜ in. (19 x 13.6 cm). Published in *The Century*, Series 24, issue 46. (May-October, 1893)

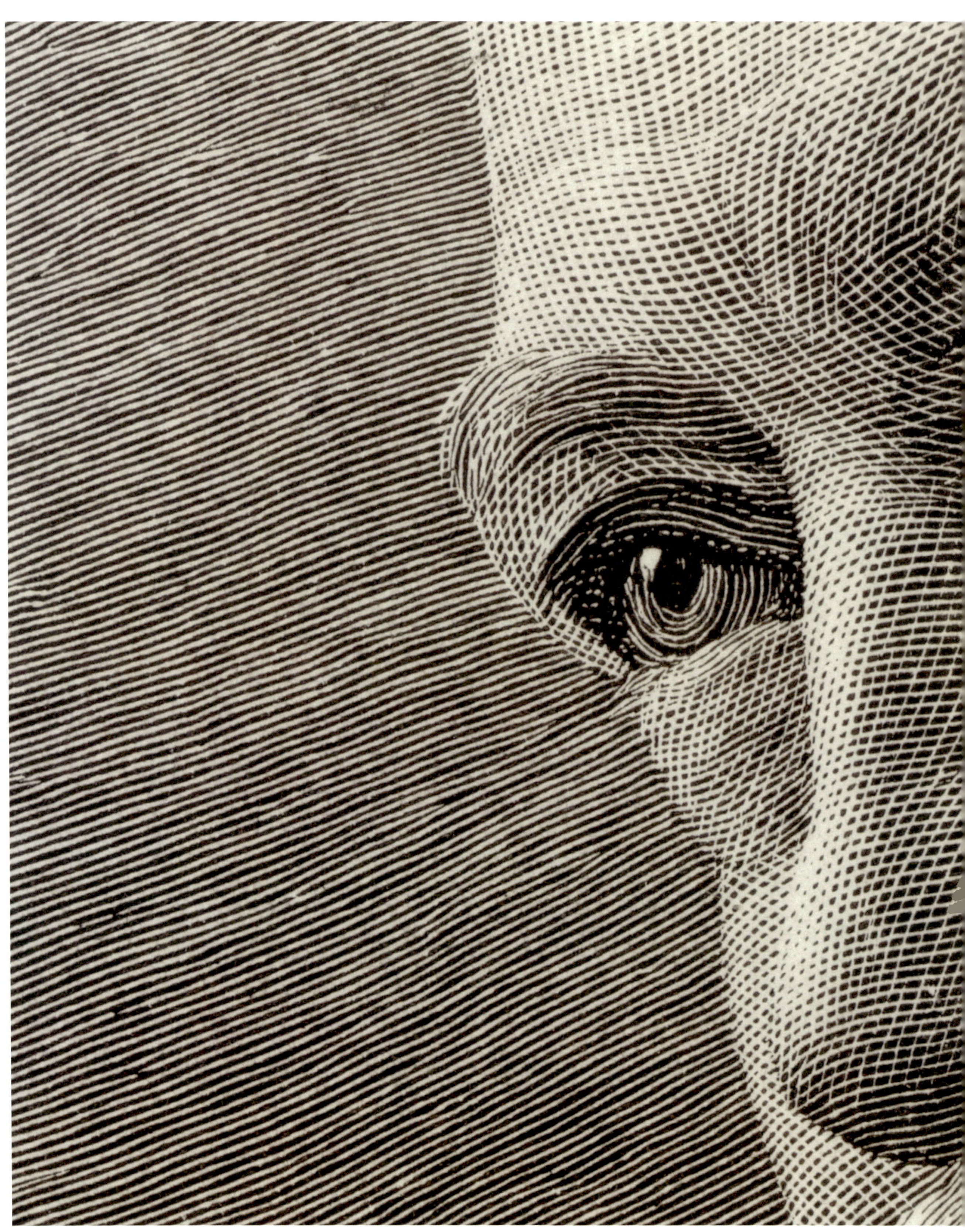

A detail of the previous plate, enlarged eight times from the size of the actual wooden block. This extraordinary network of lines was hand engraved with no tools other than the guide photograph, a handheld burin, and a magnifying glass.

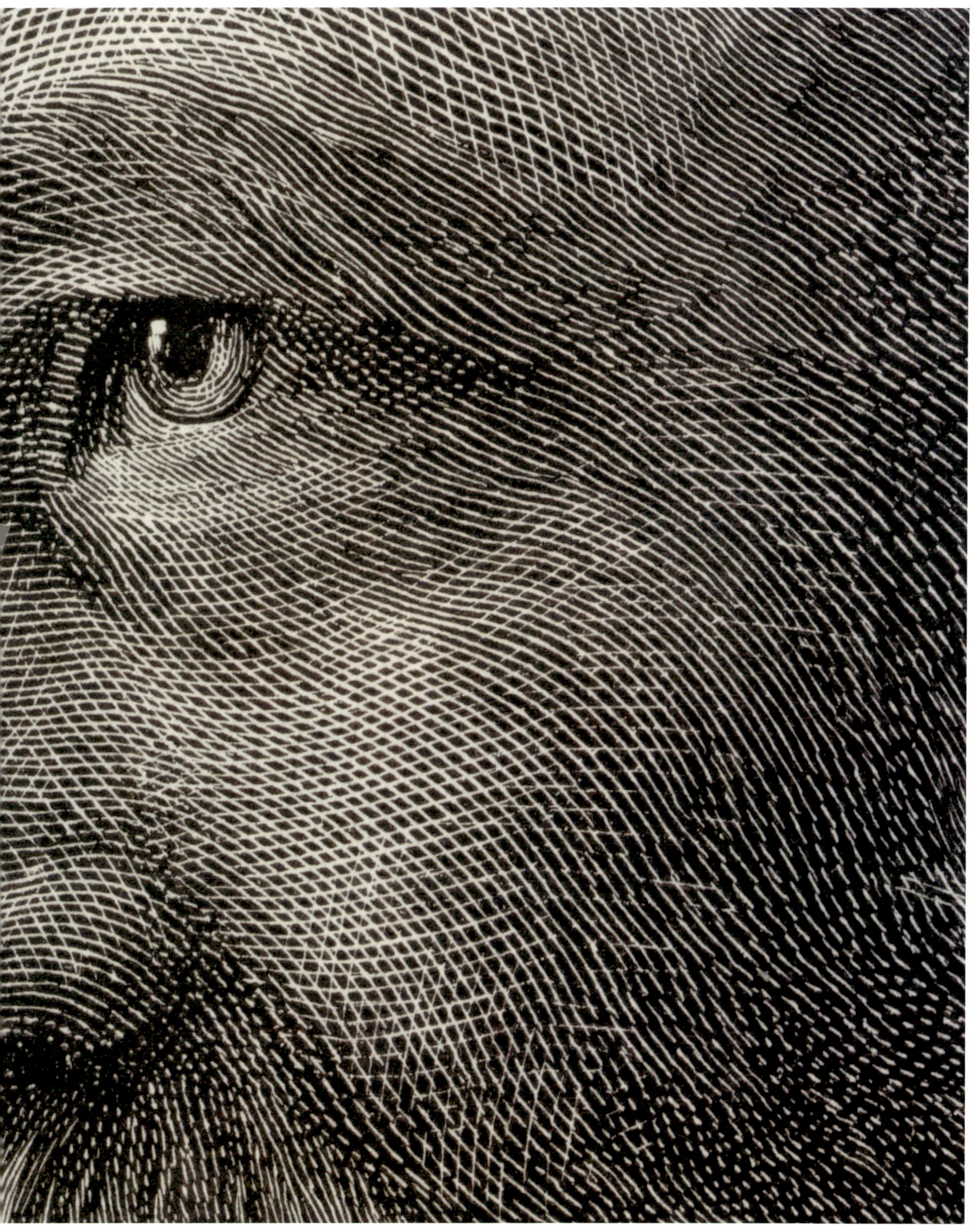

## 10.3 RANDOM SCREEN HALFTONES

The hand-cutting of photographs could only go on for so long before some mechanical method was developed. I need to emphasize here that we are examining relief printing, which in the nineteenth century usually meant letterpress—the metal type used in letterpress printing was creating more pages than all other processes combined. Yet it lagged behind in the mechanical translation of photography into ink. Later on we will examine gravure and collotype (the former an intaglio and the latter a planographic process), which offered translation methods far earlier than did relief printing.

This plate comes from an engineering manual made in the early 1880s. The picture was obviously derived from a photograph—it has the rigid perspective that could only have been drawn by a wide-angle lens. It also has an odd background of trees and sky that would never have been described this way by an artist making an original work; the trees running along the mid-line of the picture are a nearly amorphous blob of middle tones—not the sort of thing one would have created intentionally. To top it all off we have a tiny man standing on the bridge, just to the left of the girders on the right side of the superstructure. From photography's earliest days figures were placed in pictures to demonstrate the scale of the thing being photographed (see plate 5.12).

The print is a true oddity—a reproduction made photomechanically by rephotographing the original photograph through a screen of prepared glass that broke up its tones into a random grain. The principle would be systematized in the halftone, described in Part 10.5, but there the grain would be regular. It is impossible to know just how the screen was made, but it looks as though it was produced from a collotype, a process that we will examine in Part 11. The exciting step we see here is that the screen has done the job of translating tone into a pattern of discrete black and white marks. This was first attempted (as far as we know) by Talbot, the inventor of paper-based photography. It took forty years, from his early trials in the 1840s until the mid-1880s, before this revolutionary idea could be made to work with any dependability.

A detail enlarged four times from the original to show the random grain, which translated the photograph's tones into binary marks that could be printed.

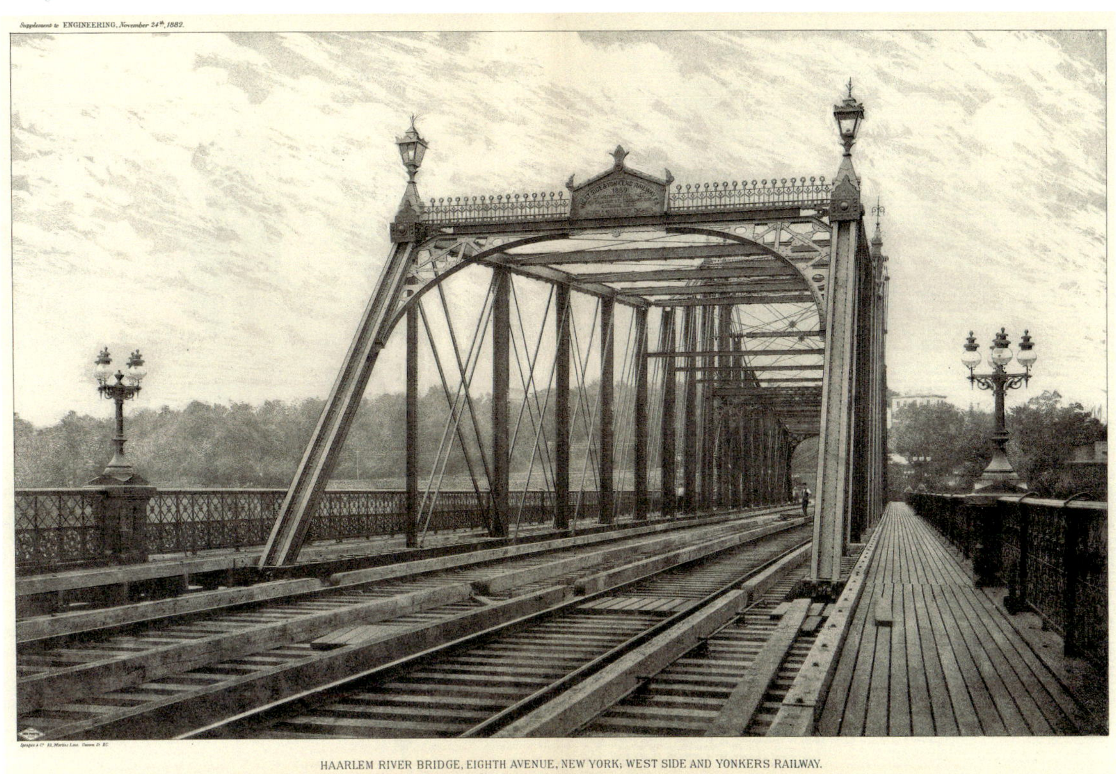


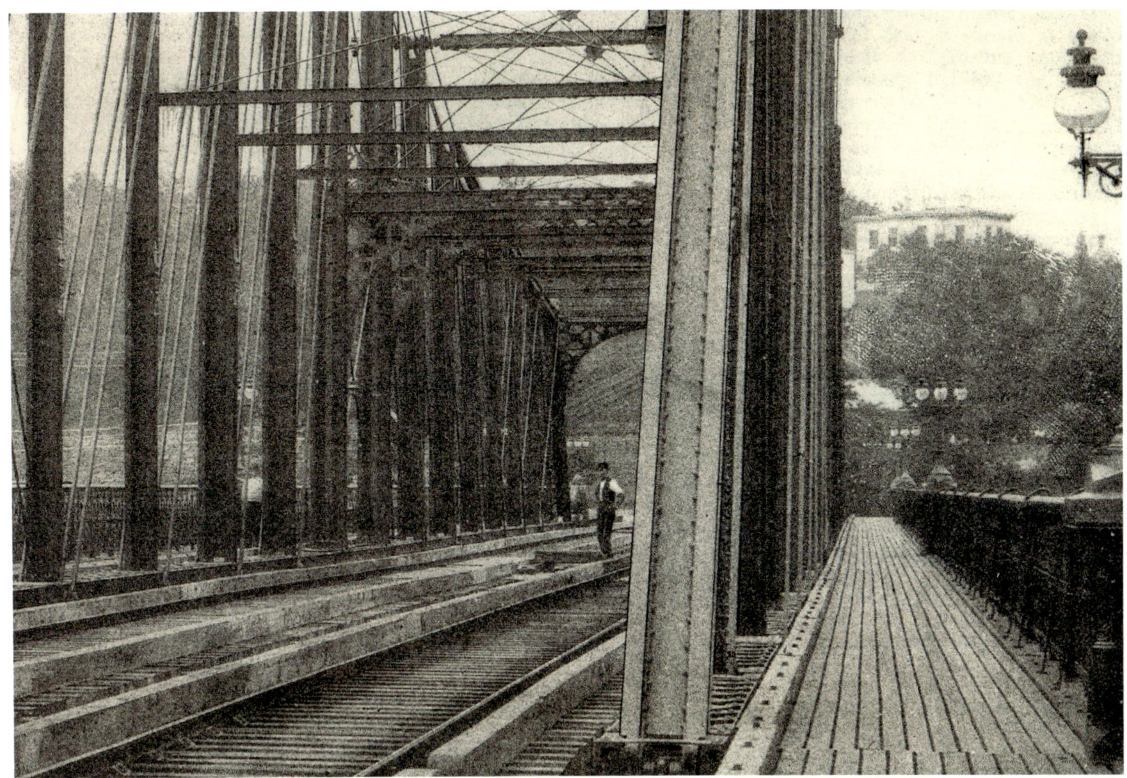

**Random screen halftone.** Top: Sprague & Co. *Haarlem River Bridge, Eighth Avenue, New York; West Side and Yonkers Railway.* 1882. 11¼ x 17 in. (28.6 x 43.2 cm). Bottom: a detail of the print, reproduced at actual size. From a supplement to *Engineering*, November 24, 1882.

## 10.4 Ruled halftone screens

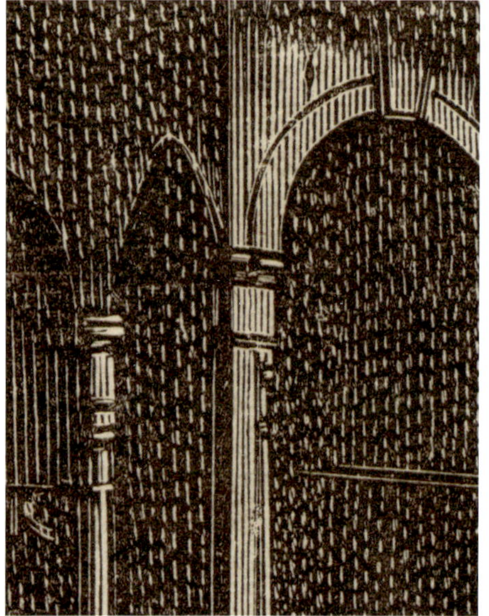

The wood engraving shows only what the engraver chose to reveal—an idealized background of fine marks and a clear linear description of the column and its moldings.

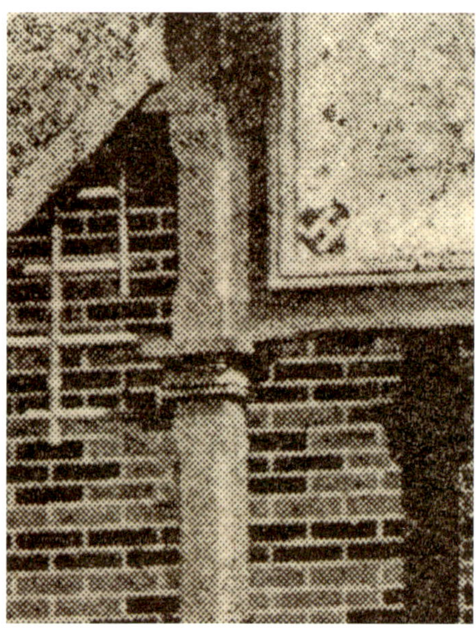

The halftone dumbly renders everything in the photograph—mottled tonalities, random brickwork, and a range of middle grays. Now the column must compete with its surroundings, while in the wood engraving it is isolated for the sake of clarity. Photography by its nature describes all things with equal attention, and the mechanical halftone preserves this characteristic.

This extraordinary sheet comes from a large book celebrating the Universal Exhibition in Paris in 1889. The page doesn't look very impressive until we realize that it shows two photographs, the upper one printed as a wood engraving, the lower as a primitive mechanical halftone. Here we find the old and the new locked up together in a letterpress form. Metal type even shows up on the same sheet—so we have letters made in a lead alloy, hand-generated marks in boxwood, and a chemically etched copper plate tacked onto a wooden support, all working together to generate our sheet.

The lower picture indisputably comes from a photograph, simply because it shows no evidence of the hand. The upper picture must as well because its perspective is photographic. In each case the photographer has stood somewhat to the side of the building, to show its shape, and in both cases he used a fairly wide-angle lens. No doubt this was an old rapid rectilinear lens, a symmetrical design that could be stopped way down to produce excellent wide-angle pictures many years before the invention of the more refined anastigmat lens, in 1898. To top it all off, the pictures, made in Paris, use the standard European format of eighteen by twenty-four centimeters. This was the whole-plate size on that side of the Atlantic in the late nineteenth century, and one of the American tragedies is that we adopted the somewhat turgid eight-by-ten-inch shape instead of this elegant form. The size of the pictures has been slightly changed in the reproductions; the proportions alter a bit throughout the book according to the designer's layout of each page.

The halftone print is nowhere near as good as the wood engraving above it. When I say "good" I simply mean that the new method doesn't have the clarity and tonal range of the old. There is a person on the porch—maybe such distractions were eliminated from the wood engraving—and the background, if muddled, is much more realistic. We could also ask whether the building in the wood engraving had been completed when the book went to press—perhaps it was unfinished, and the photograph provided most of the information needed for the reproduction but the reality wasn't there for the rest. Whatever the case, mechanical reproduction, freed from the judgments of an engraver, contributed to the falsehood that photographs portray some sort of truth about the world from which they derive.

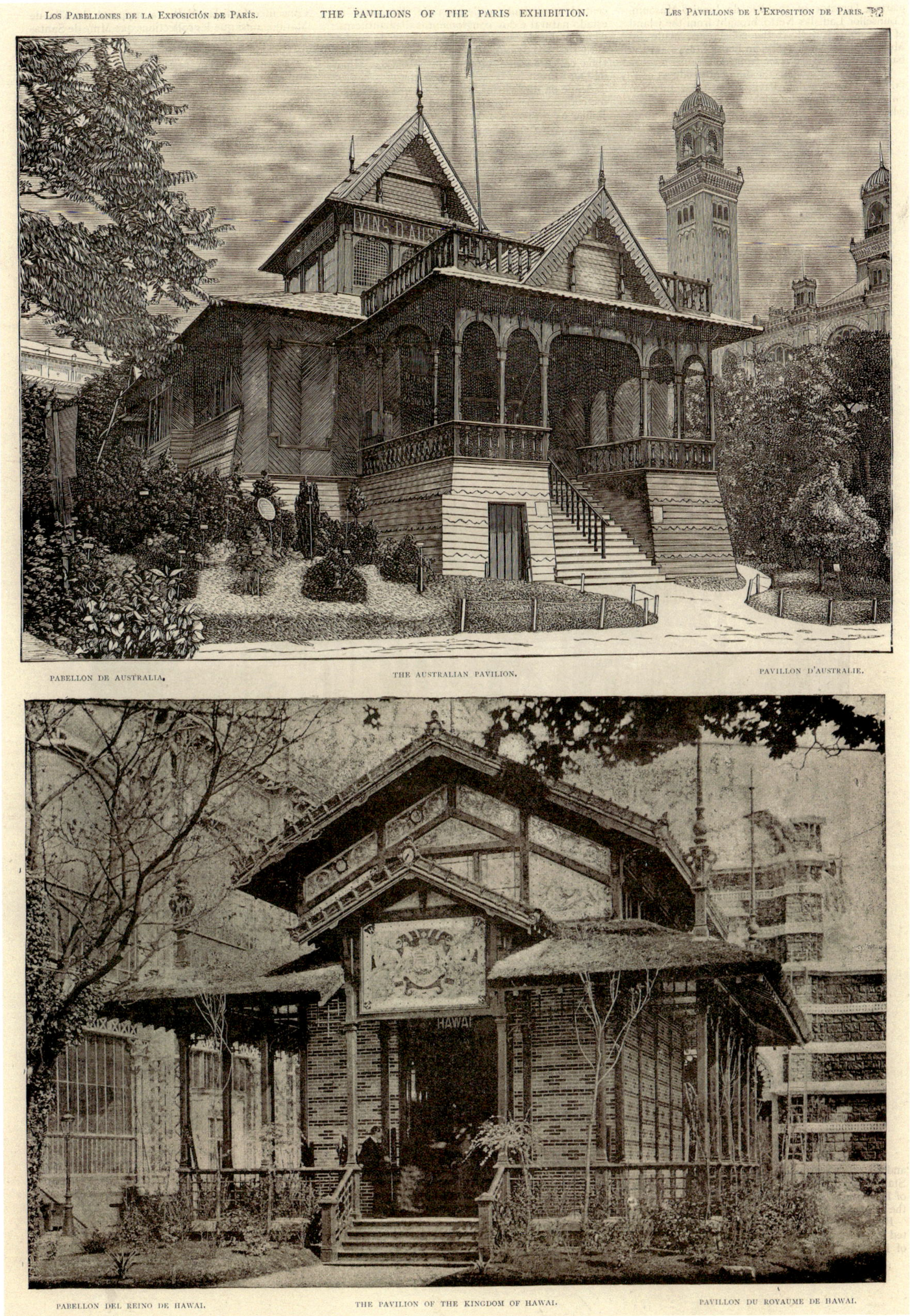

Los Pabellones de la Exposición de París. THE PAVILIONS OF THE PARIS EXHIBITION. Les Pavillons de l'Exposition de Paris.

PABELLON DE AUSTRALIA. THE AUSTRALIAN PAVILION. PAVILLON D'AUSTRALIE.

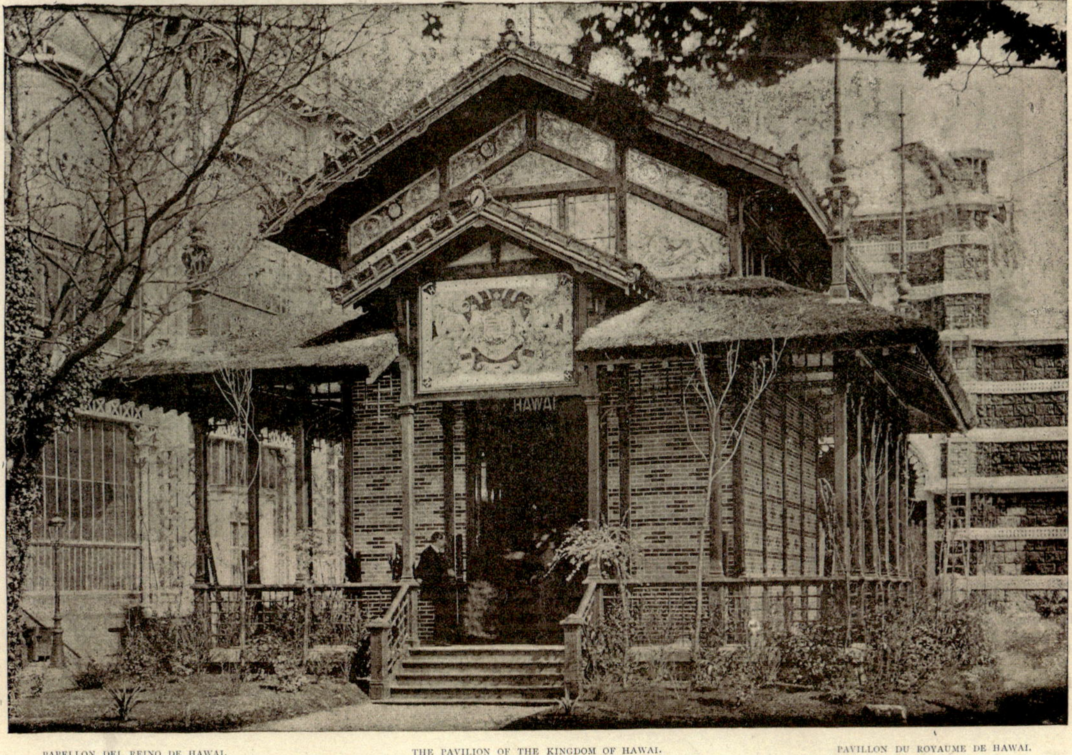


PABELLON DEL REINO DE HAWAI. THE PAVILION OF THE KINGDOM OF HAWAI. PAVILLON DU ROYAUME DE HAWAI.

**Wood engraving and halftone print.** Photographer unknown. *The Pavilions of the Paris Exhibition.* 1889. 15 x 10 in. (38.1 x 25.4 cm). A page from *The Paris Universal Exhibition Album* (Stiassny and Rasetti, 1889).

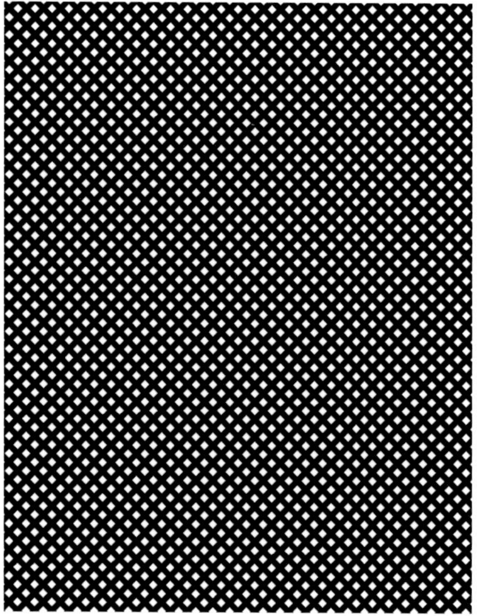

A representation of a section of a glass halftone screen, similar to the one used in 1947 to make the reproductions for The Museum of Modern Art's Cartier-Bresson book. The screen used for that book had approximately 100 clear dots per linear inch, or 10,000 per square inch.

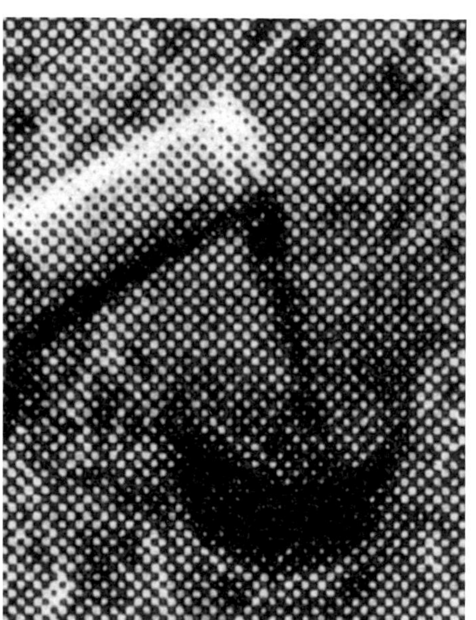

An eight-times enlargement showing the halftone dot pattern. Imperfect inking and squeezed transfer of ink to paper have produced considerable distortion of the halftone dot.

## 10.5 THE LETTERPRESS HALFTONE

The plain one-impression halftone, printed by letterpress, completely dominated mass-produced photographic publications from about 1900 until the refinement of photo offset lithography in the 1960s. The halftone was cheap, easy to make and print, lent itself to the production of stereotypes (which allowed both type and pictures to be printed on rotary presses), and gave a passable level of quality for most uses. A surprising thing about this technique is that it changed so little between its invention and its demise.

The halftone negative was made by photographing the original through a glass screen ruled with a network of tiny apertures. These apertures produced diffuse dots of light that struck the sensitive film or plate. When developed with a high-contrast developer, the dots appeared solid in the negative, but varied in size according to the intensity with which each had been illuminated by the original. The halftone negative thus produced was exposed by contact to a light-sensitive resist coated on a sheet of copper. The resist—usually a fish or animal glue sensitized with bichromate—hardened where exposed to light; the unexposed resist between the dots remained soft, and was washed away, uncovering the copper. Next came an etch (usually ferric chloride), which dissolved these areas of bare copper, the spaces between the dots. As it cut below the surface of the copper it also cut into the sides of the dots, which diminished in size, making the print lighter and lighter as the etching went on. This undercutting could be arrested, through an etching trick with a compound called "dragon's blood" (believe it or not), but the undercutting supplied a practical limit to the ruling of the screen—about 150 dots per linear inch. Smaller highlight dots from a finer screen would be eaten away and not print. No matter how well a letterpress halftone is printed, the image will have a somewhat rough appearance and the resolution will be low when compared to an actual photographic print.

The second major difficulty with the letterpress halftone was that it only printed well on a hard, smooth, clay-coated sheet. The copper plate had to be lightly inked (to avoid filling in the spaces between the dots), then evenly pressed against the paper. Halftones were printed on presses that held the paper on a cylinder, so that the full pressure of the press was applied to the narrow section of the plate that the cylinder contacted. Both paper and copper are hard, so if either one was at all uneven, or if the pressure was not quite right, the transfer would be flawed and the print would suffer. The vast majority of printed letterpress halftones had visible difficulties because of imperfect ink transfer. This problem was never solved, and offset printing, which uses a soft intermediate blanket between plate and paper to sidestep the whole issue, would completely kill letterpress within a couple of decades of its perfection in the years following World War II.

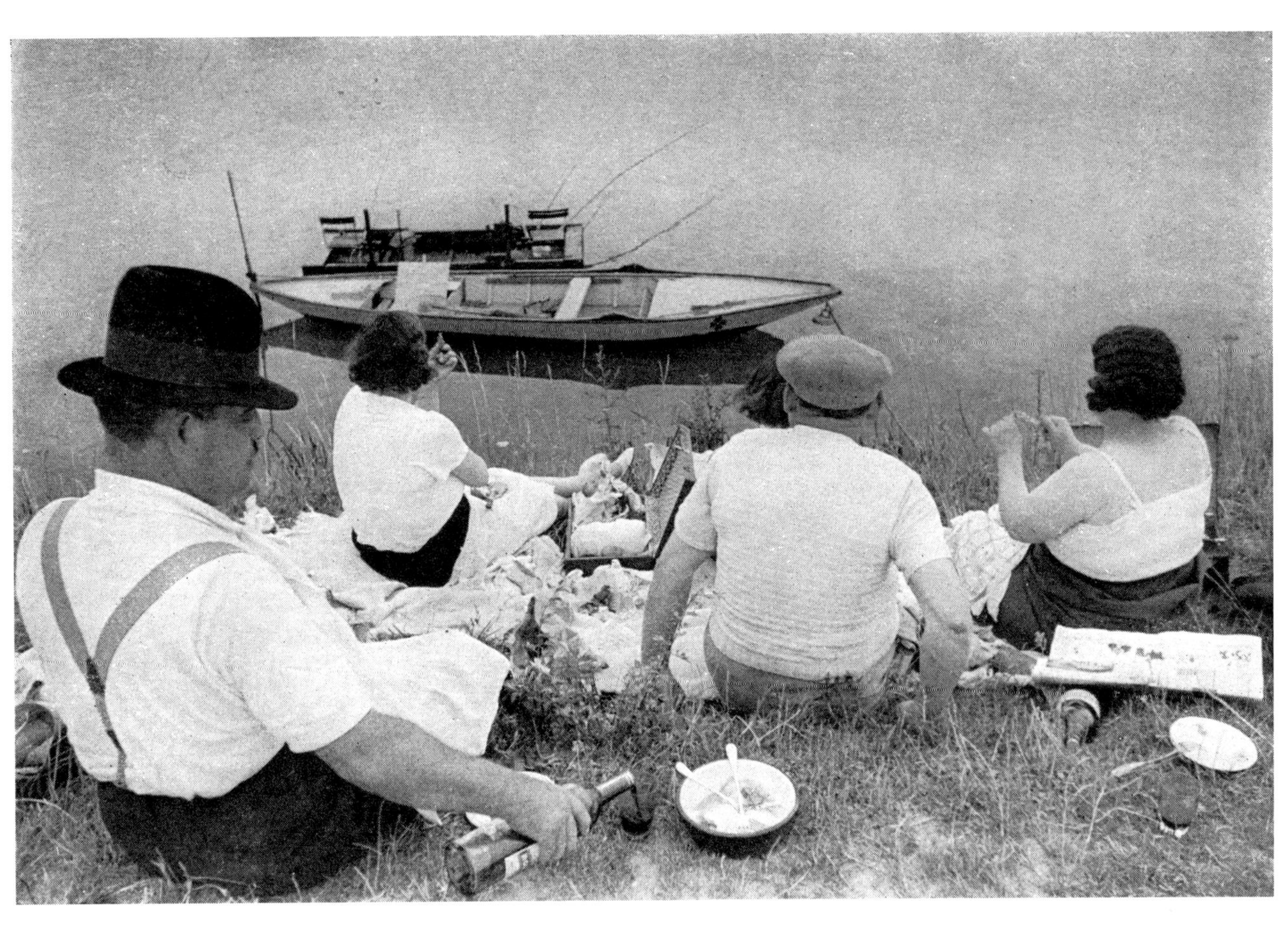

**Halftone print.** Henri Cartier-Bresson. *Sunday on the Banks of the Marne, France.* 1936–38. Print: 1947. 4 x 5⅞ in. (10.2 x 14.9 cm). Letterpress-printed halftone from *Henri Cartier-Bresson* (New York: The Museum of Modern Art)

## 10.6 MAGAZINES

By the turn of the century—that is, of the nineteenth to the twentieth—photographs were everywhere. The medium had been alive for sixty years, the old handmade photographic processes were on the way out, and the dry plate, burrowing its way into society through the efforts of George Eastman, was responsible for millions of photographs. The thing that was missing in all this was the cheap, throwaway, mass-produced photograph. As long as photography was based on chemical processing and individually developed prints, it was destined to be marginal in its social effect.

The cheap and reasonably adequate single-color halftone met this evolutionary challenge. Within the next fifty years an astonishing number of pages were printed holding ink-generated photographs. These turned up in books and newspapers, but a huge portion of them appeared in magazines.

Magazines bridged the gap between the one-day-relevant newspaper and the more expensive, permanent book. They could deal with news and popular subjects and could lie around the house for a while before being thrown away. Most newspapers were local events, printed in enough copies to satisfy the nearby population, and the book tended to be a national item, made in a few thousand or so copies on the gamble that it would reach enough buyers to sell out the edition. The magazines, on the other hand, adjusted the size of their runs to a growing national audience. Rapidly produced—often weekly—their editions routinely went into the hundreds of thousands, and the industrialized world was quickly wrapped in cheap photographs printed as ink halftones.

The halftone block was originally a flat thing—copper tacked onto wood, locked into a chase with metal type. The magazine revolution happened when this simple image-bearing tool became thin and curved and could be mounted on a rotary cylinder. This was achieved through the technique of the stereotype, which was a casting, or electroplated replica, of the halftone block. Stereos were made in a number of ways, but every method ended up with a thin, tough relief plate that rotated in the press instead of moving through it in a reciprocating pattern. Rotation brought speed, and reduced the time spent on each unit printed. Time is money, so this window of efficiency gave rise to millions of photographs that could be looked at, read about, and then casually discarded until the next set arrived at the newsstand or in the mailbox.

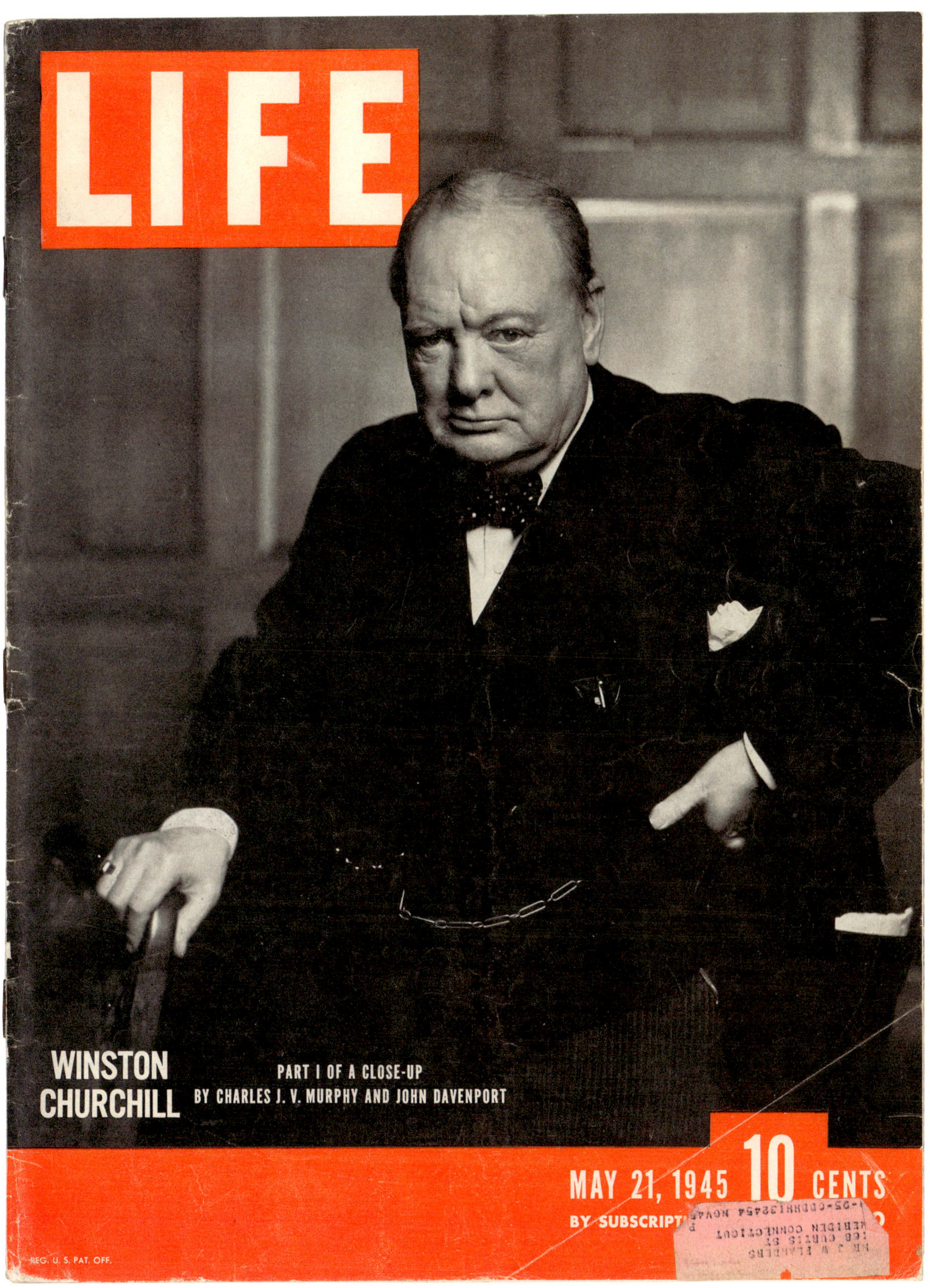


**Halftone print.** Yosuf Karsh. *Winston Churchill.* 1941. Print: 1945. 14 x 10½ in. (35.6 x 26.7 cm). The cover of *Life* magazine, May 21, 1945

## 10.7 DUOTONE LETTERPRESS HALFTONES

The simple halftone aspired to be upper class and to work as a luxurious method for making beautiful photographic reproductions. Its primary limitations were in the dot size—always coarse enough to be visible to the eye—and short tonal scale, imposed by the difficulties of inking and printing a delicate relief plate. A third problem with the halftone was the absence of a single halftone negative accurately rendering the full tonal scale of the photograph. The smooth, even steps of tone in photographic prints became a rough, erratic set of gradations in the simple dot-constructed halftone.

A partial solution was to print a picture in more than one impression, using two different halftone negatives made by photographing the original print twice. The technology wasn't too complicated; it required negative images that were of identical size, which was easy when glass plates were used. When one halftone was printed over another a terrible pattern could form called a "moiré," which was a frequency-interference pattern between the screens if they were not exactly aligned. This problem was avoided by tilting one screen thirty degrees away from the other, a solution that had been discovered by hand engravers many years before when working with overlays of linear designs. It turned out that even without much refinement in the way the halftones were made, a two-impression reproduction, printed first in black and then in gray ink, could look far better than any single one. The second set of dots in gray ink—even though they were pale—added body to the black parts of the picture and made the areas of middle and light values much smoother. This new development—the duotone—appeared in art books and other expensive publications where image quality was the first concern. Duotones first showed up at the start of the twentieth century and became common by the 1930s.

Extremely beautiful photographic reproductions were already being made in the first half of the century by the technique of photogravure (sections 10.9–11), but this intaglio medium was very expensive. The multiple-pass duotone, though more expensive than a halftone, was still far cheaper than gravure, so it had a viable role in photographic ink printing. The presses never really registered the sheets accurately when printing duotones, but the second impression, being gray, could be a bit out of alignment and still improve the reproduction. Perfect registration had to wait for the multicolor offset presses designed to print color for advertising purposes.

This letterpress duotone was printed with two colors: a black and a pale green. The green is nearly invisible when examined with a magnifying glass, but gives a distinct green cast to the print. The register mark, never cut off this proof sheet, shows the two inks and their respective screen patterns.

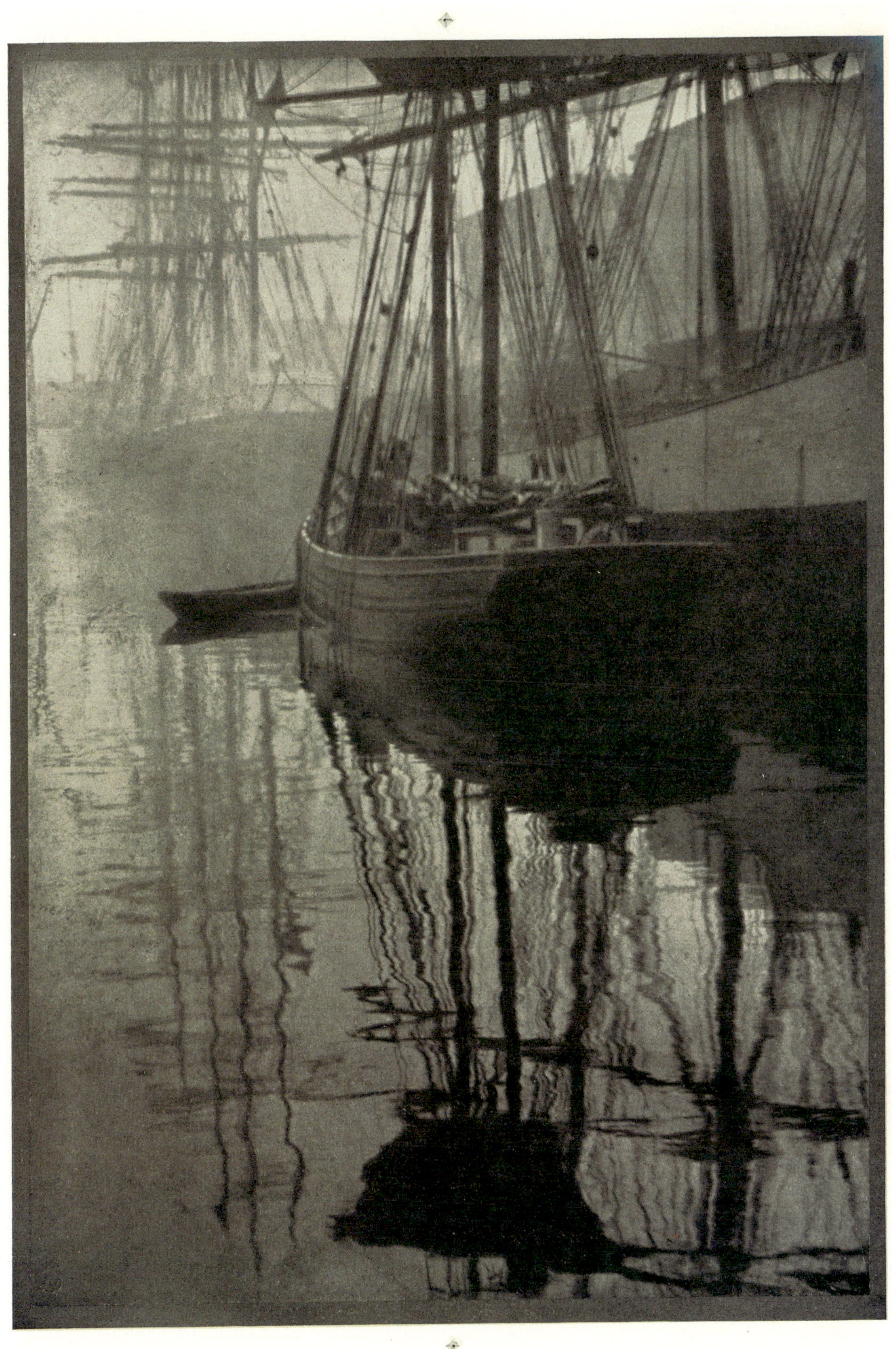

**Halftone duotone print.** Alvin Langdon Coburn. *The Spider's Web.* c. 1905. 10¼ x 7 in. (26 x 17.8 cm). An untrimmed proof sheet for a plate in *Camera Work* 21 (January 1908).

# Photography in ink

## 10.8 PROCESS COLOR IN RELIEF PRINTING

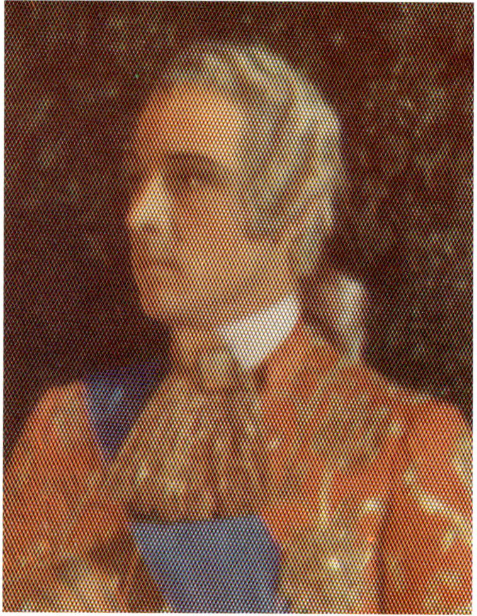

An early color reproduction, using a primitive linear screen instead of the halftone dot. This image was supposedly the first color photograph transmitted by wire, in 1924. Reproduced from *A Half Century of Color*, by Lewis Walton Shipley, published by the Macmillan Company in 1951. Reproduced in approximately actual size.

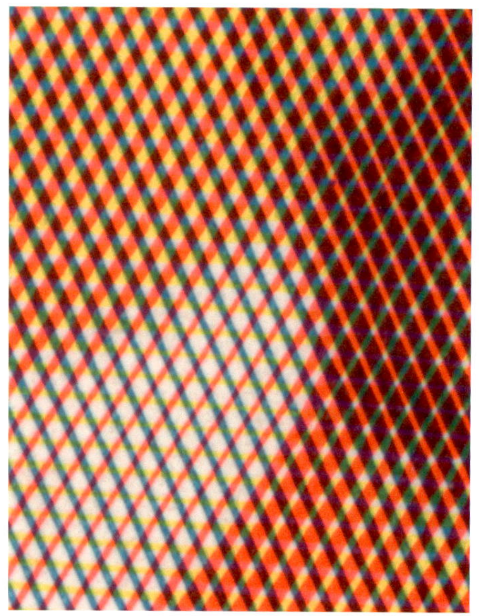

An eight-times enlargement from the print above, showing the screen pattern, which varies in line width to increase or decrease tone. Many different screen structures were experimented with in early color work, all trying to minimize the moiré patterns that result from the superimposition of multiple screens. This particular one resolves the problem by not using a black printer, reducing the number of screens to three.

We should not be naive about the reason for the development of color printing; it was entirely due to the belief that you had a better chance to sell someone something they didn't need if you advertised it in color rather than in drab old black and white. The theoretical basis for color printing was laid out by Maxwell in the mid-1800s, and decades of work in chromolithography had demonstrated the social power of ink images in color. By the 1940s color halftones were making their mark in magazines and books, printed by a method called "process color," which was becoming firmly established. A key element in the spread of color was the construction of multiunit printing presses that could lay down all four process colors—the subtractive primaries of cyan, magenta, and yellow, plus black—in one pass. The history of color photography in ink teaches us much about our society. The color reproductions printed with letterpress were never very good, but color had such commercial power that all printing technologies ultimately became color mediums. From its introduction before World War II, color printing grew so robustly that by the 1970s the printing press manufacturers—by that time making letterpress, offset, and gravure presses—were building more and more presses that printed four colors at once. Today, only sixty years after the widespread introduction of color, the single-unit press is an anachronism and huge, expensive, four- and five-color behemoths are everywhere. They crank out books and magazines and above all marketing catalogs in huge numbers. Today the process is usually photo offset lithography but its roots lie in letterpress, where the simple old copper halftone was refined to print three primaries in register to give the illusion of full color.

Idealized three-color printing, using cyan, magenta, and yellow, never worked properly because it produced an inadequate black, so right at the start a fourth impression, in black ink, was added to the "process" method, which then became known as CMYK printing. It's critical to remember that color photography itself was still being worked out in the 1930s and '40s; only after World War II did chemical color photography become first-rate and widespread. Color in ink was never top-notch until the development of the computer. Designers and publishers of art books tore their hair out trying to make fine color reproductions, and even now, when the technology of printing is completely embedded in the digital stew, pictures often turn out badly. The problems are all wrapped up in the human eye and mind; our eyes record data in three parts of the spectrum and the mind generates the illusion of full color out in the world. The press attempts to do the same, piling illusion on illusion. It is a wonder that it works at all.

**PIONEERS IN** *Color Reality..*

★ Color skeptics are gone. Advertisers recognize the value of color reality as a potent force in telling, with maximum effectiveness, an advertising story. Everything we contact wears its lipstick, its rouge, its painted or printed exterior. The extent to which we respond to color is simply a matter of how skillfully and purposefully color is projected at us.

Study the reproduction of strawberries shown below. Eliminate the color and your reaction as to their edibility is doubtful. Color is the vitalizing note that awakens our appetite and stimulates the desire for possession.

Witness the leading magazines and newspapers. In them we find an ever increasing use of color in the sales messages of successful advertisers.

Now, that important moulder of public opinion, the motion picture industry, is taking to color. Color movies in a not distant tomorrow will supplant today's ordinary movies just as surely as the talkies eliminated the silent pictures.

So it is not a question of whether color shall be used in advertising and printed matter, but how can merchandise best be reproduced in reality with all its sales appeal.

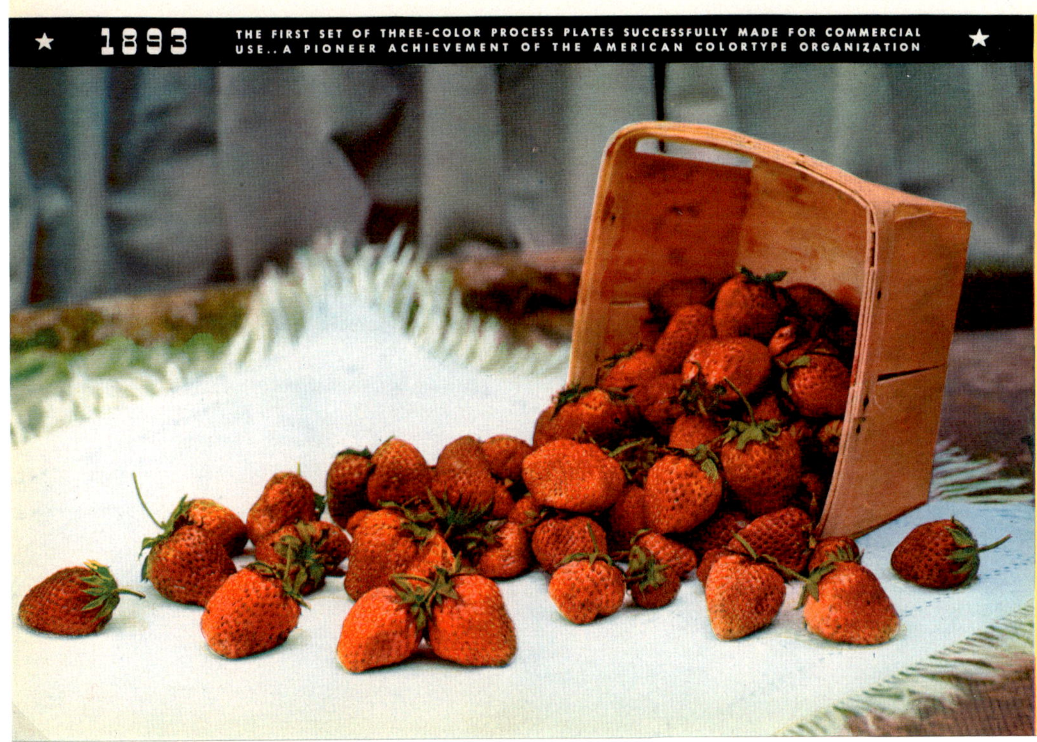


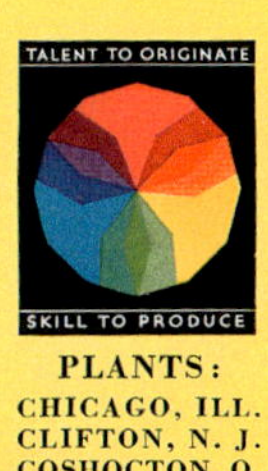


PLANTS:
CHICAGO, ILL.
CLIFTON, N. J.
COSHOCTON, O.

**Process-color halftone print.** Photographer unknown. *Pioneers in Color Reality.* 1936. 13¾ x 11 in. (34.9 x 28 cm). From the trade magazine *Advertising Agency*, September 1936

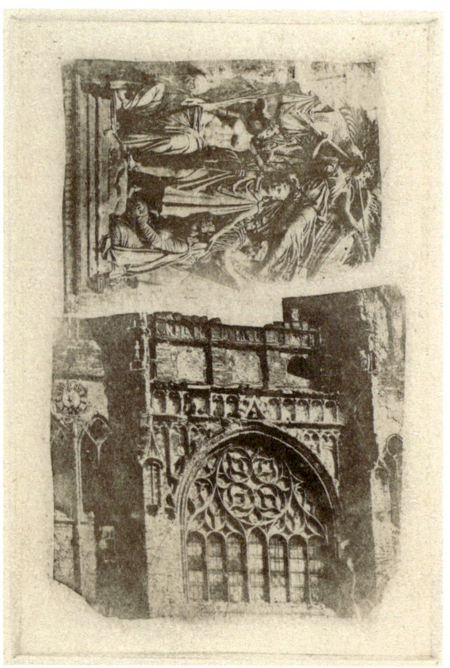

William Henry Fox Talbot. Untitled. c. 1852. 3⅜ x 2⅜ in. (8.6 x 6 cm). Many early attempts were made to print photographs with ink. This small experimental print, which Talbot called a "photoglyptic engraving," was an attempt to make an intaglio reproduction of a pair of calotypes.

## 10.9 FLAT-PLATE PHOTOGRAVURE

We leave relief printing now and move back in time to the adaptation of intaglio printing to the photographic image. The copper plate, dampened paper, etching press, and silky aquatint were all waiting in the wings for the invention of photography. If you believe, as I do, that photography was invented because the printing presses of the world needed more data than the hand could provide, then the early development of photogravure seems an inevitable step. By the 1880s photogravure had reached a state of near perfection, due to final refinements by Karl Klíc. The process combined all the tools of traditional etching and aquatint with the beautiful tonal description of the photographic carbon print. Though the steps in making a gravure are complex and difficult to carry out, we can describe them quite easily, because we have previously described both aquatint and carbon printing.

A copper plate is polished, cleaned, and dusted with acid-resistant grains in exactly the same way as is done for a hand-drawn aquatint. A sheet of carbon tissue carrying a red pigment is sensitized to light in exactly the same way as the tissue for a carbon print. This tissue is then exposed to a film or glass-plate positive (instead of a negative), and the carbon/gelatin image is pressed to the aquatinted copper plate instead of to a sheet of receiver paper. Once the tissue is removed by development in hot water, the plate is dried and then etched, using a heavy solution of ferric chloride in water.

This is where the magic takes place. The crucial ingredient in the resist now transferred over to the aquatinted copper plate is not the pigment but the gelatin. As we remember from earlier on, a carbon print consists of a gelatin layer that varies in thickness according to the values coming from its exposure. Because the gelatin layer now stuck to the aquatint was made from a positive rather than a negative, it is thin in the shadows of the picture and thick in the highlights. When placed in the etching bath the gelatin slowly takes up water and swells, and as it does so the ferric chloride is able to move through it. In the dark areas of the picture, where the gelatin is thin, the iron compound quickly reaches the copper and begins to etch the fine spots left open by the aquatint. The lighter values are etched later, after the necessary time has passed for the gelatin to swell and allow ferric chloride to pass through those areas. After the etch has reached all parts of the picture, it is stopped and the resist and aquatint are removed. The plate now carries a set of ink-bearing pits that have been etched for variable amounts of time in inverse proportion to the thickness of the gelatin layer that had been applied to the surface. This variable depth, when printed, lays down ink of variable thickness to generate tone. Because photogravure depends upon an ink film that varies in thickness to show tonal differences, it uses an ink that is less dense than that for other processes, where the requirement of the ink is to simply be as black as possible.

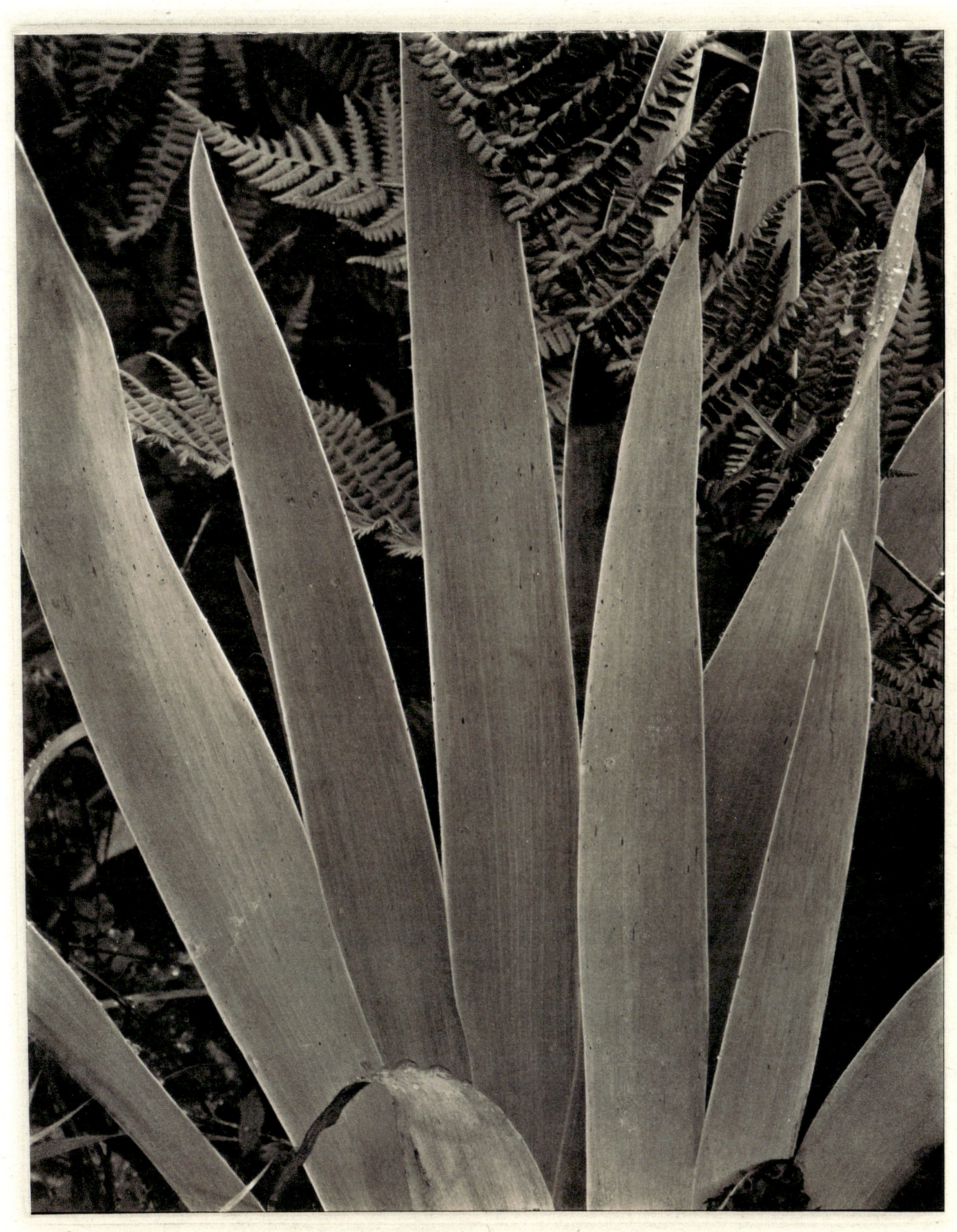

**Hand gravure.** Paul Strand. *Iris.* 1928. Print: Jon Goodman and Richard Benson. 1978. 9⅞ x 7⅞ in. (25 x 20 cm)

## 10.10 MANIPULATED PHOTOGRAVURE

A great advantage of hand engraving and etching was that the artist/printer could work on a plate, proof it, then go back and make alterations to the plate. Early attempts to print photographs in ink often included efforts to retain this capacity to manipulate the image, and the resulting pictures show intrusions of handwork—painted-out skies on halftone blocks, or perhaps evidence of the etching needle at work on photogravures. In either case the desire to meddle in the photographic image was intense and ongoing.

Chemical photography allowed a whole range of manipulations to alter the tonal values of prints and control their color. Global adjustments to the photograph, done through chemical means or through the judicious handling of light in the darkroom, showed no evidence of the hand in the finished print. The complex technologies of ink printing provided new means for altering the photographic image, and we often find heavy-handed alterations made to printing plates. This is not inherently bad but only embarrassing, because the pure photograph has such magical description that any intrusion into it almost always reduces its power. When the intrusion comes in the form of visible work with things like etching needles and paintbrushes, the damage is almost always great—not only does the work show the hand, but the adjustments often interrupt the implied connection between the photographic image and the reality from which it derived. The power that the photograph gets out of its assumed connection to the world from which it was made is almost always stronger than the idea of the artist who tries to alter it.

This pair of pictures shows a classic manipulation carried out in the plate-making process. The top image shows objects photographed against a now vanished background that the printer must have disliked or deemed inadequate. When the gravure was etched, this background was painted out and left blank. Afterwards a fresh aquatint—noticeably more grainy, as we can see in the detail to the left—was applied and a flat tone was etched on it without the use of any photographic image. Thus a bland and obviously ill-fitting background was applied to a superb and complex photographic rendition.

The picture includes another beautiful bit of photographic description. The lower detail on the right reveals the sharp but shallow depth of field of the camera lens, visible in the textured cloth upon which the sculptures rest. The photographer has made the perfect decision of where to place this plane of focus—somewhat toward the foreground, giving objects behind it a slight degree of softness.

A fifteen-times enlargement showing the two different aquatints: one for the sculptures and their supporting surface, the second, much coarser one for the background.

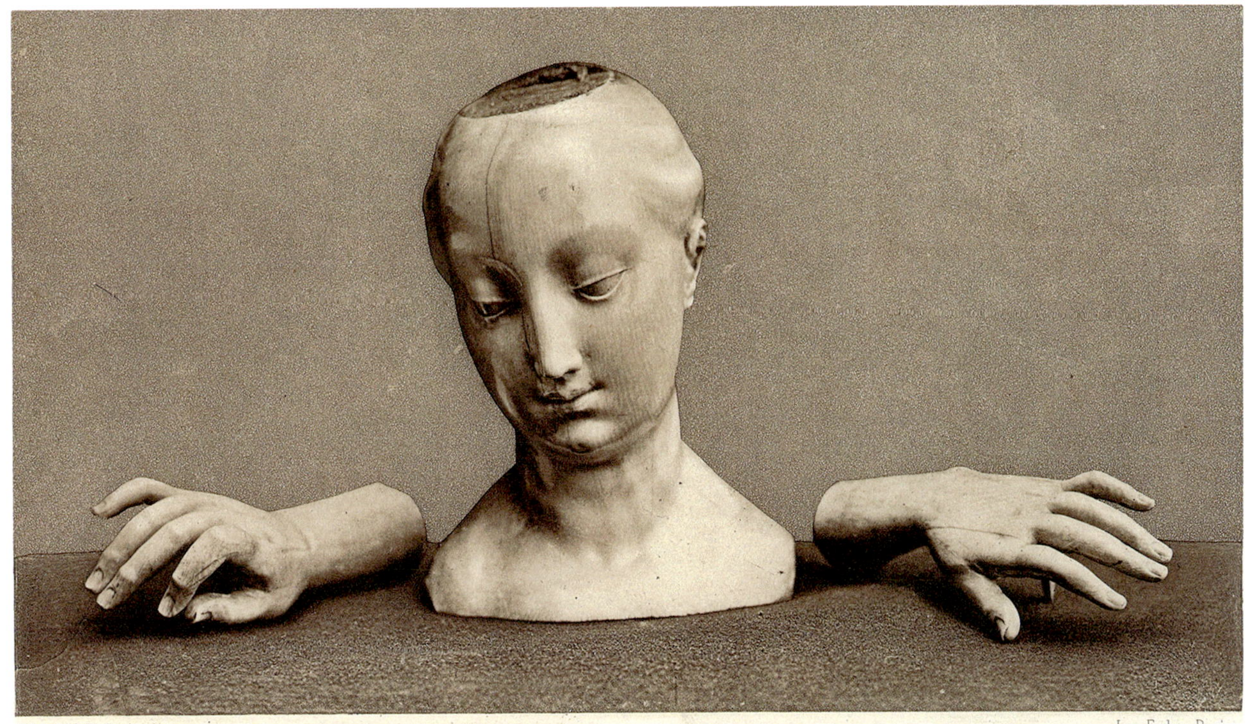


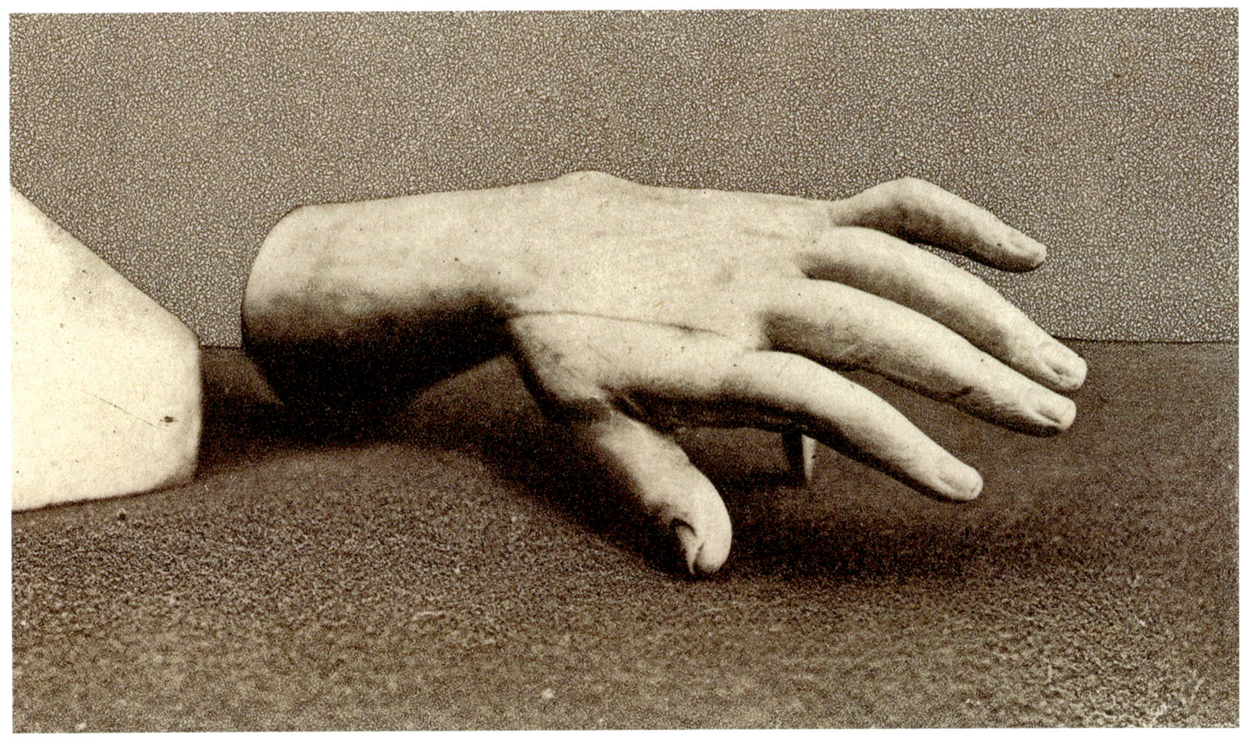

**Manipulated photogravure.** Top: photographer unknown. *Tête et mains* (Head and hands). Print: P. Dujardin. c. 1900. 5¼ x 7⅜ in. (13.3 x 18.7 cm). Bottom: an enlarged detail showing the different texture of the applied background.

## 10.11 ART PHOTOGRAVURE

When an aquatint was well made, it provided printing cells that were virtually invisible to the naked eye. When a gravure resist was properly etched, it not only described a full range of tones but even allowed their internal relationships to be adjusted to make the information from the negative more effective. When both these things happened in a gravure, and the originating photograph had a fine tonal scale, the result could be more beautiful than anything else in photography. Yet the tone and clarity were only part of the reason for this. Much of the glory of photogravure came from its capacity to produce a deep black value on a totally matte surface.

There has long been a war between the glossy surface and the matte. It began at the very start of photography as the brilliant, ultimately glossy daguerreotype battled with the soft, matte-surfaced salted-paper print. When paper won the battle with the decisive tool of the albumen print, it did so with a semigloss surface that could reveal the long range of tones carried by the new glass wet-plate negatives. Later on, when the silver-based developing-out papers came to dominate photography and when chromogenic color papers were made, gloss surfaces won hands down. Even the humble letterpress halftone did its best work on a smooth, nearly polished clay coating applied to wood-pulp-based paper (with disastrous archival effects).

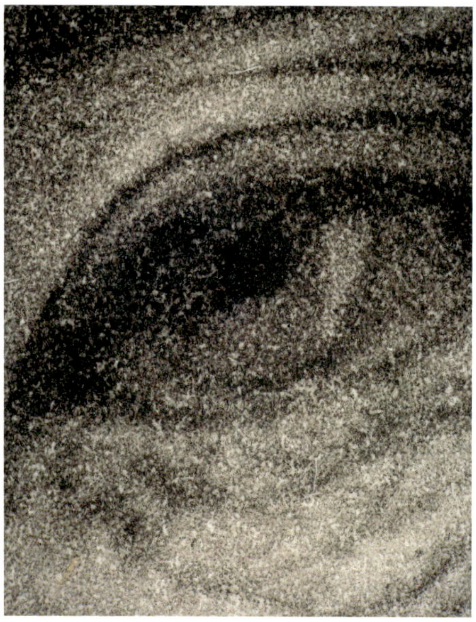

A seven-times enlargement showing the fine grain of the ink-bearing aquatint cells.

I first started as a printer in 1966, and did a project a few years later for the New York publisher Leslie George Katz, who got me hooked on matte surfaces. He would look me intently in the eye and say he wanted a black value in the print to match the black surround in a monarch butterfly's wing. This sort of obsession—which I quickly caught—led us to photogravure, and to attempts to make modern photo offset lithography with the kind of surface that gravure so routinely produces. While nothing can compare with the magical matte surface of hand gravure (well—nothing could until the introduction of inkjet printing), we should be aware that any matte surface fails when compared to a glossy one in a contest of tonal rendition. The gloss always wins, because it can carry a blacker black and show finer detail. The lesson here is to avoid comparing such different things side by side, but instead to come to know them on their own, each in its own context. Matte surfaces are dragged down by adjacent gloss ones, and I learned early on that I should never make a comparative press proof for a book on both kinds of paper, because the gloss would always win.

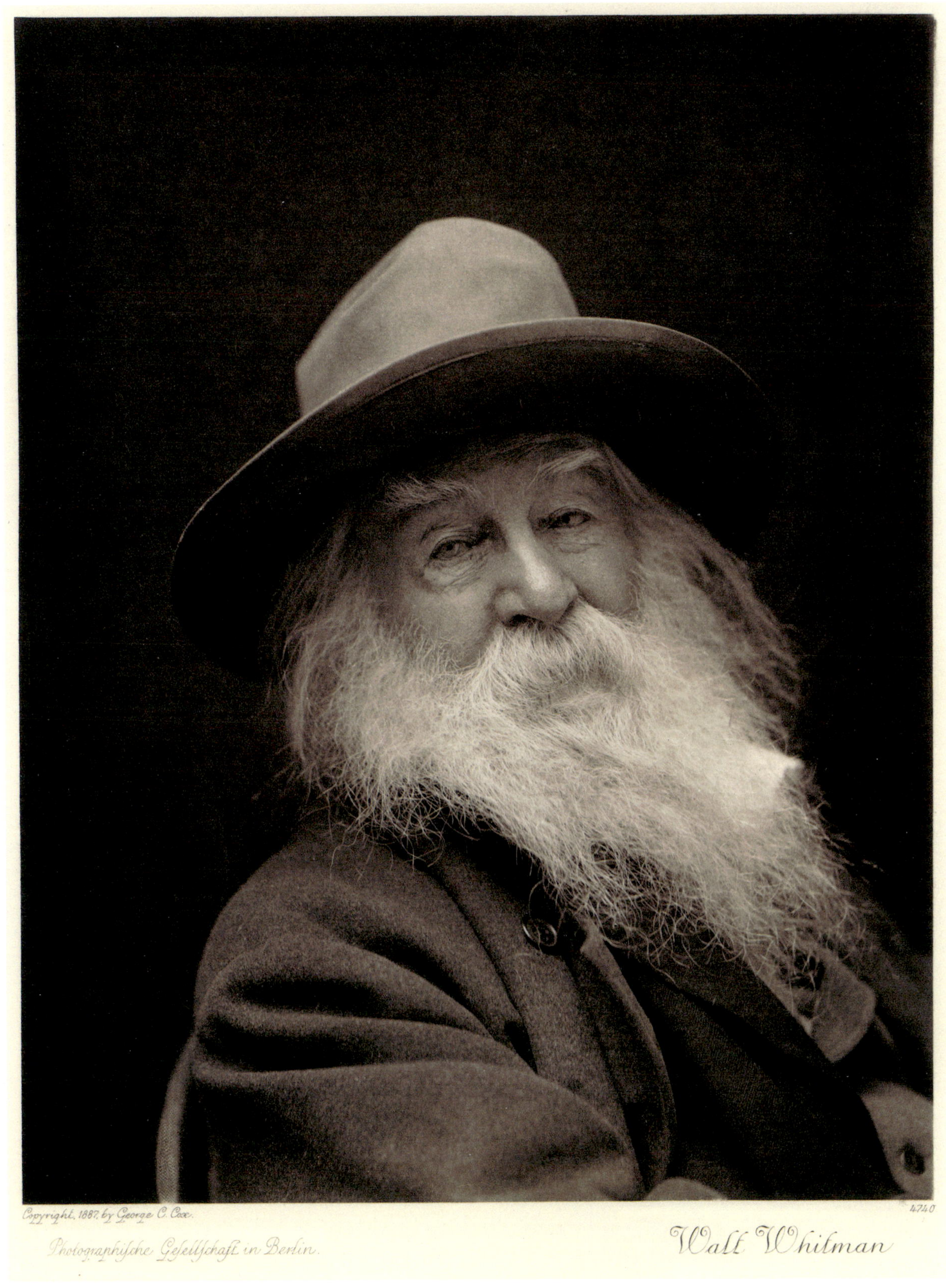


**Hand gravure.** George C. Cox. *Walt Whitman.* c. 1887. Print: Photographische Gesellschaft, Berlin.
10¼ x 7⅝ in. (26 x 19.4 cm)

### 10.12 ROTOGRAVURE USING MECHANICAL SCREENS

Photogravure was a hand process. The aquatint was applied to a flat plate, etched in a sequence of trays, then inked and wiped by hand, and finally run through a press—as often as not driven by a hand-operated wheel. This great process could not enter the long-edition book world until it left the hand behind and became mechanized.

This changeover took place early in the twentieth century. The first thing to go was the aquatint. Finely ruled halftone screens were around by that time, and specialized ones were made for gravure that didn't use dots but instead held a fine screen, a rectilinear grid much like a window screen but in negative form. This screen was exposed to the carbon tissue first and the picture positive was exposed afterwards. Once transferred to the plate, the screen image protected the copper, so that the etching took place only in the screen's tiny "windows." The random cells of the aquatint were thus replaced by square ones, absolutely predictable in form. The next change was to get rid of the flat plate; now the etching was done on thin copper sheets—about .025 inch thick (.06 mm)—that could be wrapped around a cylinder. Later on even this plate disappeared, replaced by chrome-faced cylinders with copper electroplated onto them in which the image was etched. The remaining problem to be solved was the wiping, for which a tool was invented called the "doctor blade." This device, acting like a windshield wiper, ran across the plate surface and removed all the ink from the top but not from the printing cells. The old stiff gravure ink was changed to a more fluid one, and the doctor blade became a very long, thin band of metal that wound steadily across the plate as it wiped, to avoid nicks and grit that could create lines running through the whole print run.

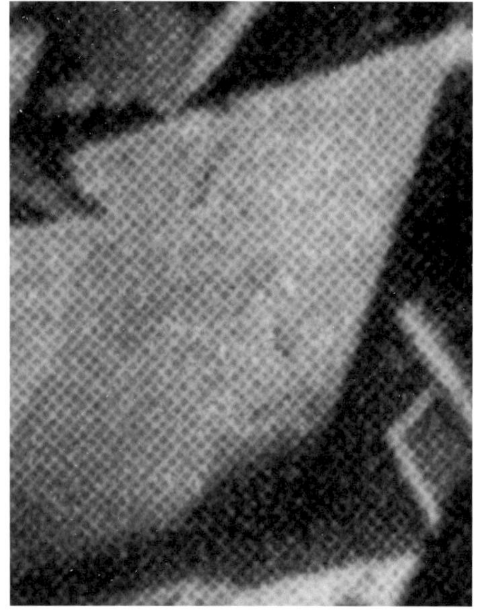

Enlarged eight times, this detail shows the mechanically regular square cells in screen rotogravure. The depth to which each cell is etched varies according to the tone in the original photograph, and the ink is deposited in varying thicknesses to describe those tones.

The old flat-plate photogravure had been called "hand," "grain," or "helio" gravure. The new mechanized form was called "rotogravure," reflecting the purely rotary nature of the presses: not just the plate but the paper were handled by cylinders. This was what made high-speed printing possible. The new gravure retained much of the beauty of the old hand methods. It could use matte inks, and the plates were still made from film positives, so a long tonal range was attainable. The fine printing cells, holding ink of variable thickness, gave a true rendition of tone. This printing became the standard for photographically illustrated books in Europe. The French and Swiss printers reached a high point in bookmaking with Cartier-Bresson's *Decisive Moment* and Frank's *Americans* (there respectively titled *Images à la sauvette* and *Les Américains*), but many other glorious books made in this process are still out there and available inexpensively in used-book stores. The pictures may or may not be great art but the printing is among the very best ever done.

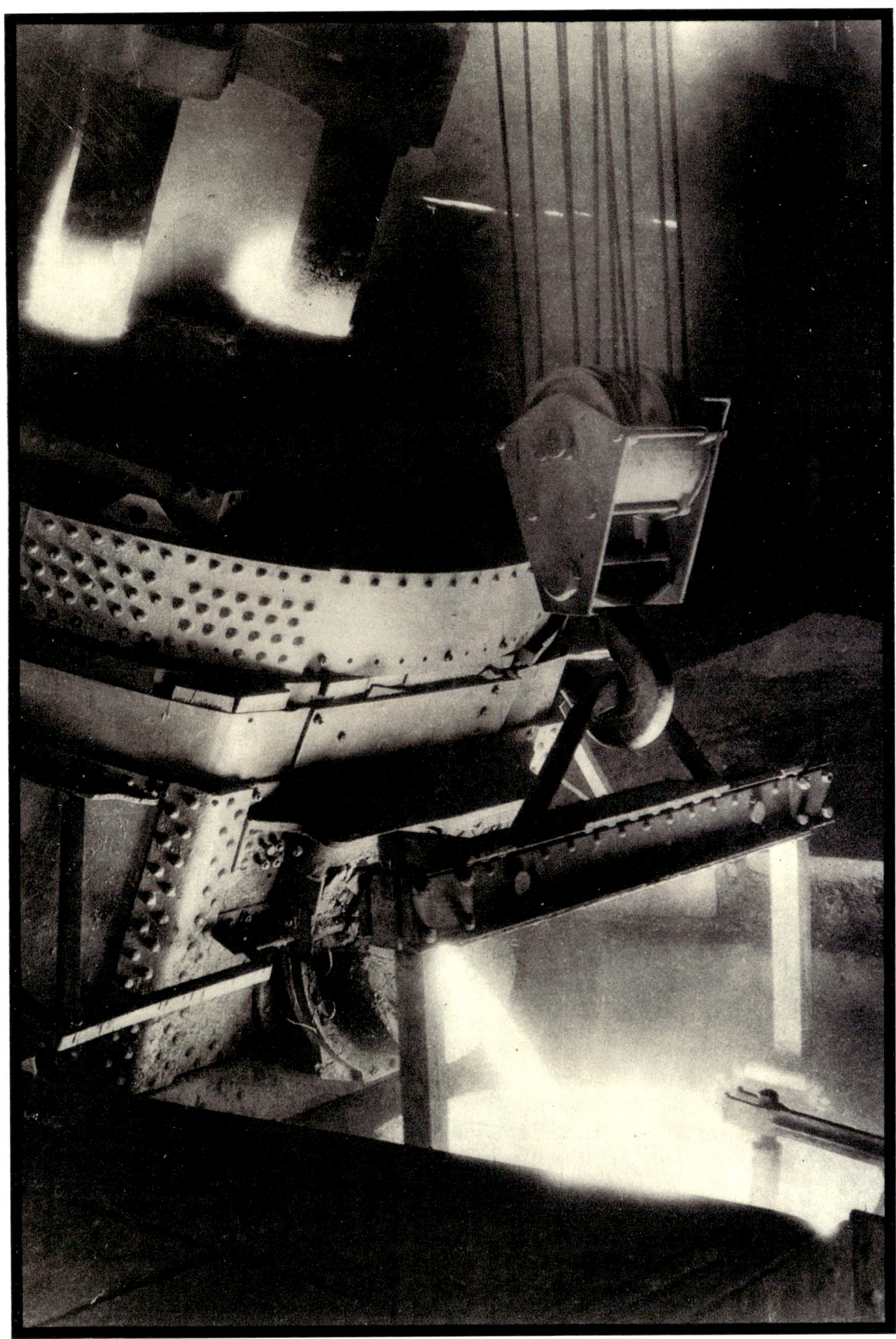

**Rotogravure.** Margaret Bourke-White. *Cradle of Stainless Steel.* c. 1932. 6½ x 4⅜ in. (16.5 x 11.1 cm). From *Fortune* magazine, September 1933, p. 55. *Fortune* was printed in both letterpress and rotogravure, with the more expensive process used for illustrated sections.

## 10.13 THE NEWSPAPER ROTOGRAVURE SECTION

The simple letterpress halftone invaded newspaper work, and by the early twentieth century these throwaway news sheets began to hold rough black and white pictures printed with coarse ruled screens. The images were poor, and as rotogravure became more widespread a new gravure section of the newspaper was created to hold better illustrations than could be printed by the letterpress halftones. Called the "roto" section, this insert was packed with black and white photographs, usually printed in a brown ink to distinguish it from the letterpress section. The example shown here, with a four-color picture, was unusual.

Even on lousy newsprint — rough surfaced and full of acid, so doomed to yellow almost immediately — the gravure illustrations looked great. The pictures were crammed on the page to get as much coverage as possible, and we often find in these sheets a new freedom of design. Letterpress, which printed the other parts of the paper, still drew its data, both letters and pictures, from rectangular parts. The letters, usually set on a Linotype machine, all sat on straight flat strips of metal; the pictures were printed from copper or zinc plates, which were nailed to wooden blocks that themselves were all right angled. Five hundred years after its invention, metal type was still locked up in a chase that could only hold rectangular pieces. These loaded chases were used to make stereos, which could run on cylinder presses, but the old ninety-degree angle dominated the page design. Rotogravure was different: the only requirement for the picture information was that it could be held on film. Photographs still tended to be rectangular, since camera formats were that shape, but when the roto pages were laid out, the designers could tilt pictures, make them round, or arrange things any way they wanted. A new craft developed in the print shops called "stripping," which was the practice of assembling sheets of film into the forms that could expose large single plates like the rotogravure page we see here.

In the period between the wars, photo offset lithography was in its formative years and the printing for it was also done from film, used to expose large, thin plates of zinc or aluminum, so strippers showed up there as well. The craft of stripping was short-lived, because one of the innovations of digital technology has been that the work of assembling printing forms is now all done on the computer. In the early years of the digital age — from about 1990 to 2000 — these new computer-generated forms exposed large sheets of film that then exposed the printing plates. By now — 2008 — even that film has disappeared, and the computer file is used to drive lasers that expose the printing plates directly.

The square printing cells that were so clearly visible in the prior plate are obscured by the paper fibers when printed on rough newspaper stock.

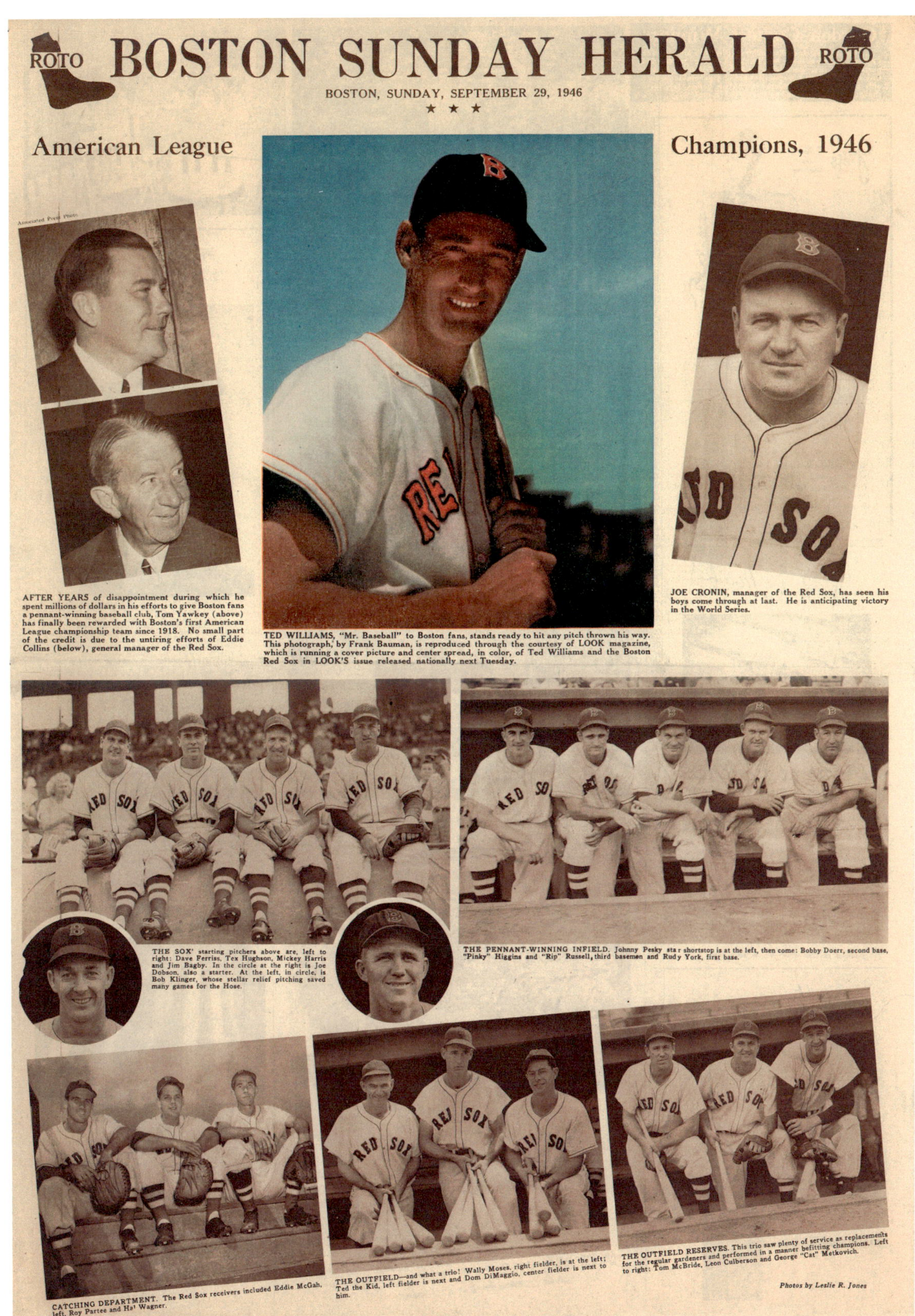

ROTO BOSTON SUNDAY HERALD ROTO

BOSTON, SUNDAY, SEPTEMBER 29, 1946

★ ★ ★

American League Champions, 1946

Associated Press Photo

AFTER YEARS of disappointment during which he spent millions of dollars in his efforts to give Boston fans a pennant-winning baseball club, Tom Yawkey (above) has finally been rewarded with Boston's first American League championship team since 1918. No small part of the credit is due to the untiring efforts of Eddie Collins (below), general manager of the Red Sox.

TED WILLIAMS, "Mr. Baseball" to Boston fans, stands ready to hit any pitch thrown his way. This photograph, by Frank Bauman, is reproduced through the courtesy of LOOK magazine, which is running a cover picture and center spread, in color, of Ted Williams and the Boston Red Sox in LOOK'S issue released nationally next Tuesday.

JOE CRONIN, manager of the Red Sox, has seen his boys come through at last. He is anticipating victory in the World Series.

THE SOX' starting pitchers above are, left to right: Dave Ferriss, Tex Hughson, Mickey Harris and Jim Bagby. In the circle at the right is Joe Dobson, also a starter. At the left, in circle, is Bob Klinger, whose stellar relief pitching saved many games for the Hose.

THE PENNANT-WINNING INFIELD. Johnny Pesky star shortstop is at the left, then come: Bobby Doerr, second base, "Pinky" Higgins and "Rip" Russell, third basemen and Rudy York, first base.

CATCHING DEPARTMENT. The Red Sox receivers included Eddie McGah, left, Roy Partee and Hal Wagner.

THE OUTFIELD—and what a trio! Wally Moses, right fielder, is at the left; Ted the Kid, left fielder is next and Dom DiMaggio, center fielder is next to him.

THE OUTFIELD RESERVES. This trio saw plenty of service as replacements for the regular gardeners and performed in a manner befitting champions. Left to right: Tom McBride, Leon Culberson and George "Cat" Metkovich.

*Photos by Leslie R. Jones*

**Rotogravure.** Leslie R. Jones. *American League Champions, 1946.* 22½ x 15¼ in. (57.2 x 38.7 cm). *Boston Sunday Herald*, September 29, 1946. The designer of this rotogravure sheet is unknown.

# Part 11

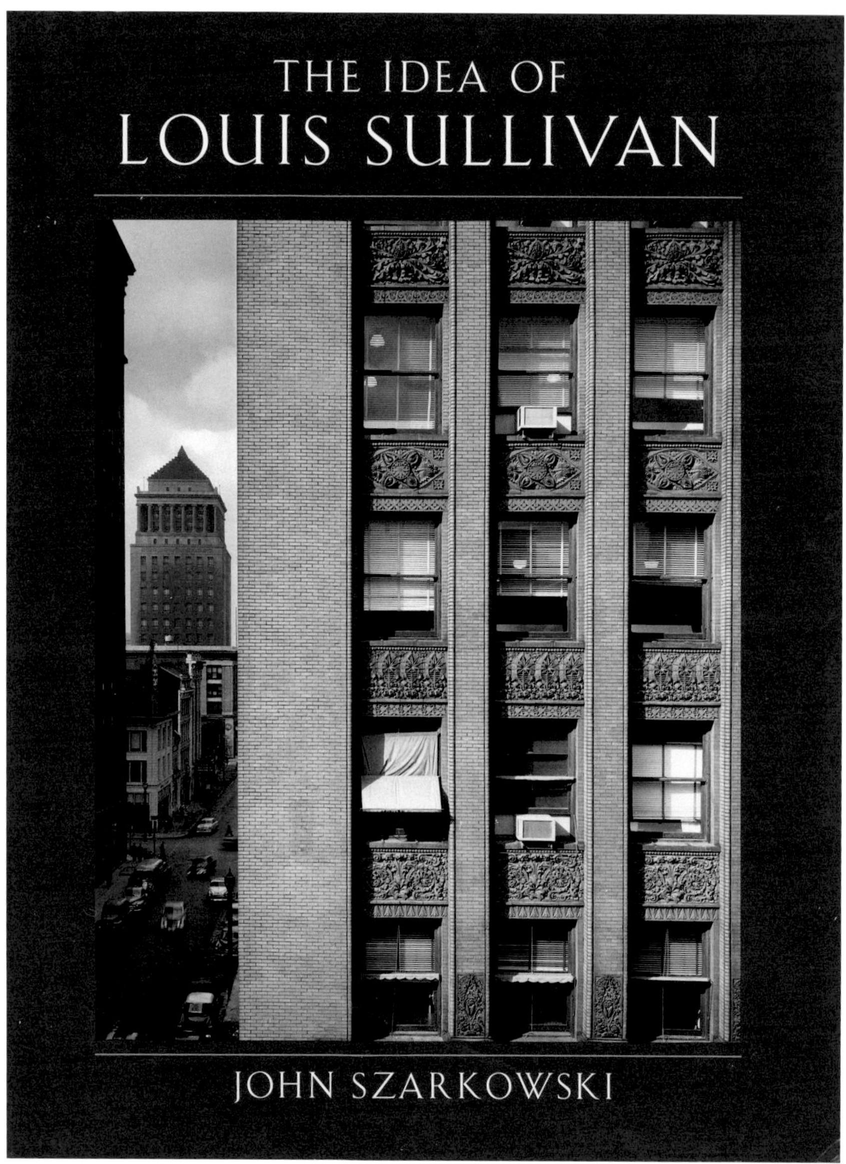


This section deals with two processes: the eccentric collotype, now long dead, and photo offset lithography, which is the dominant printing process in the world today. Offset has reached such a high level that books of photographs made today are far superior to those of a generation ago.

**Photo offset lithography.** John Szarkowski. *Wainwright Building.* c. 1954. Print: 2000. 12½ x 9¼ in. (31.7 x 23.5 cm). Jacket for Szarkowski, *The Idea of Louis Sullivan* (Boston: Bulfinch Press, 1956, reprint ed. 2000). Printed by Cantz, Germany, from separations by Robert Hennessey. Cover design by Jerry Kelly.

# Photography in ink: planographic printing

11.1 Black and white chromolithography
*The old color-printing method applied to the black and white photograph.*

11.2 Collotype
*Planographic printing from gelatin-coated glass plates.*

11.3 Collotype
*Collotype presswork and book concerns.*

11.4 Pochoir
*Color stenciling on top of collotype prints.*

11.5 Collotype quirks
*Double rolling and other collotype oddities.*

11.6 Photo offset lithography
*Early single-color offset printing.*

11.7 The nature of offset printing
*Offset's innovative technology.*

11.8 Offset duotone
*Two-pass printing from halftone screens.*

11.9 Offset tritone
*Complex multipass offset printing for black and white reproductions.*

11.10 Offset duotone and tritone
*Comparing the screen patterns of the duotone and the tritone.*

11.11 Process color in offset
*Four-impression offset printing with the subtractive primaries.*

11.12 Web offset
*High-speed, high-edition offset printing on roll paper.*

11.13 Offset as an art medium
*The atelier that never happened.*

## 11.1 BLACK AND WHITE CHROMOLITHOGRAPHY

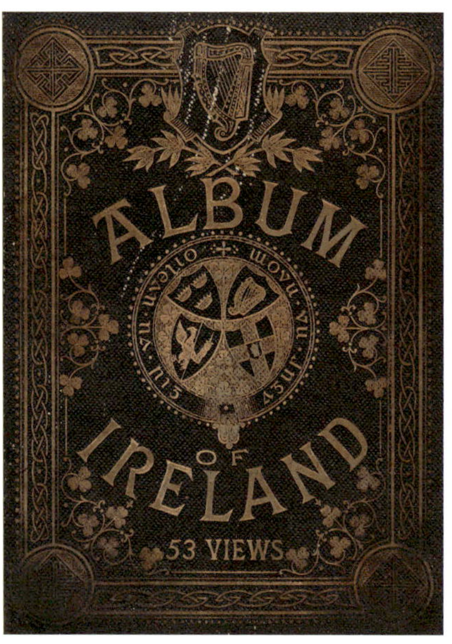


Chromolithographers adapted to the black and white photograph by making hand-drawn translations of it on litho stones, a practice that continued even after photomechanical systems had been developed. These prints were often mounted in small albums and sold to tourists, as part of the immense trade in pictures that fed the need of travelers to bring mementos home. If we tried to evaluate the various ends toward which photography has been applied, we would most likely find that portraiture and tourist photographs have been the biggest categories.

These pictures come from a small album printed in Germany for William Lawrence, an Irish publisher. This firm ran a studio that produced thousands of photographs of Ireland, to be published as original prints and postcards and in small albums such as this one. The publisher faced the old problem of the cost of the original photographic print, which could not be sold in inexpensive versions. By the turn of the century the collotype process was widespread, and postcards and albums were being produced with it, but small and inexpensive chromolithographed albums were still being made as well.

These pictures don't look like any others; they are obviously hand drawn but just as obviously had their origins in photography. The top illustration opposite shows a busy Dublin street full of people and carriages frozen in a moment that only photography could have captured. Unlike the calm and ordered Venice plazas of Canaletto, this one is hectic and arbitrary—the scattering of people derives from everyone rushing somewhere, with no sign of careful arrangement by an artist. The prints have been done with a black and four gray inks, and these grays have been carefully colored to give the purplish cast of the albumen print. The paper they are printed on is white, but another impression in yellow has generated a white rule around the image, emulating the look of a photograph mounted on a support. Even though the pictures are obviously handmade, they still strive to look like photographs. The chemical print, mechanically made by lens and camera, had reached such a level of respectability by the late 1800s that other processes struggled to imitate it.

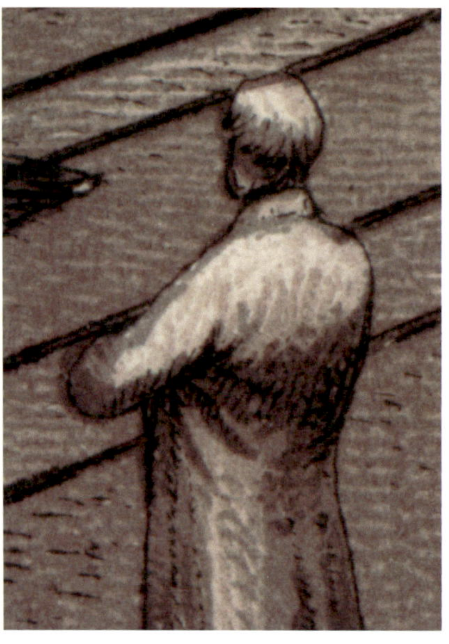

This detail, enlarged six times, shows that four grays and one black ink were used in the reproduction.

The small detail to the left shows that stippling was used in these prints to soften the harsh tonal divisions between the ink colors. Without the stippling, the solid layers of ink would have made crude, posterlike images. Plate 11.9, toward the end of this section, shows the progressive stages of a four-impression reproduction of an albumen print done in photo offset lithography, and that print, younger by a hundred years, is a direct descendant of this earlier hand-drawn set of separations.

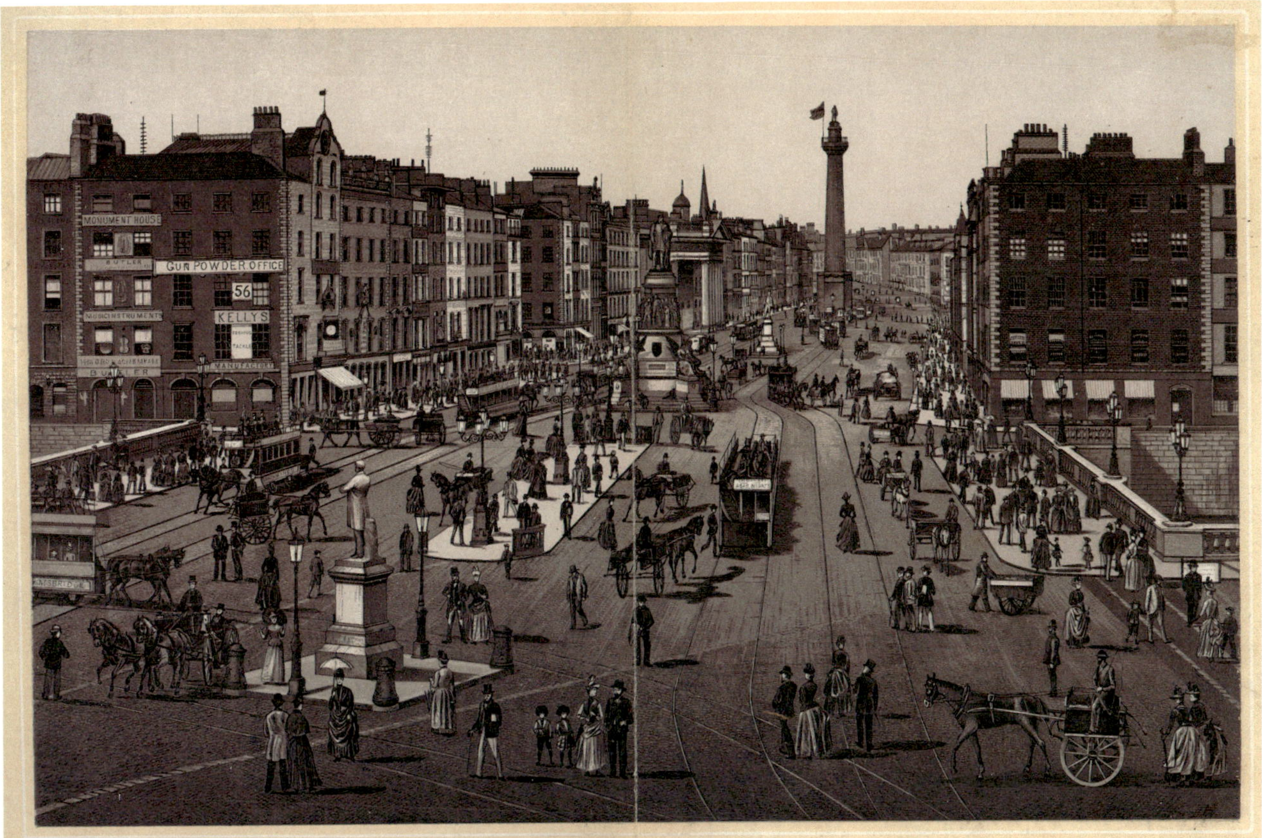

SACKVILLE STREET AND O'CONNELL BRIDGE, DUBLIN.

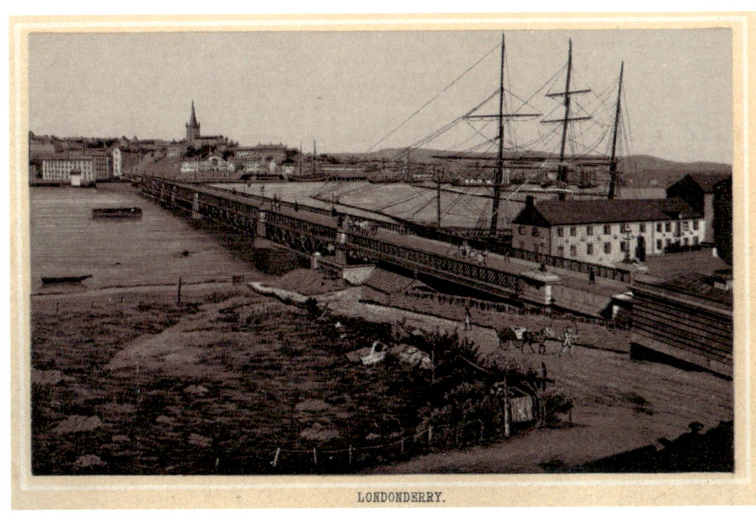

LONDONDERRY.

**Black and white chromolithography.** Studio of William Lawrence. Top: *Sackville Street and O'Connell Bridge, Dublin.* c. 1890. 7 x 10½ in. (17.8 x 26.7 cm). Bottom: *Londonderry.* c. 1890. 3¼ x 5 in. (8.3 x 12.7 cm). From *Album of Ireland: 53 Views* (Dublin: William Lawrence, c. 1896)

## 11.2 COLLOTYPE

Flat-plate photogravure came about as a modification of the older technique of etching. The plates, paper, ink, and presses were in place; all that was required for photogravure was the development of a method to etch photographic information into the printing plate. The next ink-and-photographic process to come along, the collotype, was completely new. Being planographic—printing from a flat surface—it was related to stone lithography. It shared with that process the characteristic of using the incompatibility of oil and water to describe the printing areas, but beyond those two similarities collotype was a brand-new creature, unlike anything before it.

Collotypes were made as early as the 1860s, barely twenty years after photography was invented, and the process was well established in France by the mid-1880s. Commercial collotype died in the 1960s, and when I first started work as a printer, in 1966, at The Meriden Gravure Company in Meriden, Connecticut, it still had three collotype presses running, doing book work. On my first visit to the company I was given a tour of the shop, and my guide, the ancient owner of the plant, let me know that it had long since been accepted that collotype could only be properly practiced by workers of Teutonic extraction. (I'm not kidding about this belief—the three pressmen were named Allendorf, Zande, and Brecklin.) The process was complicated, terribly unpredictable, and erratic at best; but when everything went well, a fine collotype could hold its own against the best of photogravure.

Collotype prints were backward, reversed left to right, unless the copy negatives from which they were made were reversed through a prism. Occasionally photographers would shoot with glass plates put into their cameras backward (that is, with the emulsion facing away from the lens) to produce an original camera negative from which to make the collotype plate. The sharp clarity of the print opposite makes me quite certain that that was done for this picture.

Collotype presses were huge, holding a flat glass printing plate on a massive bed that ran on steel rollers, like a railway truck. The bed moved beneath a set of ink rollers and then under a cylinder big enough to hold the large sheet used for book work. The paper wrapped around this cylinder came into direct contact with the printing plate, and the ink was transferred in a single impression. This arrangement—of the paper directly meeting the plate—was the weak link in collotype, because it was a lithographic process, using a moist plate, and the dampness striking the paper inevitably changed the paper's dimensions. This doomed collotype to be a single-impression process, since the sheets could never dependably be registered for multiple impressions. We find some color collotype, but it is rare, and almost never in perfect register. The old-timers who printed collotype used to say that the way to do a fine limited edition in the process was to print twice as many sheets as needed, spread them out on the floor, and pick out the best ones. There was some truth in this: because collotype plates were dampened manually during the printing, the tone of the impressions varied from sheet to sheet.

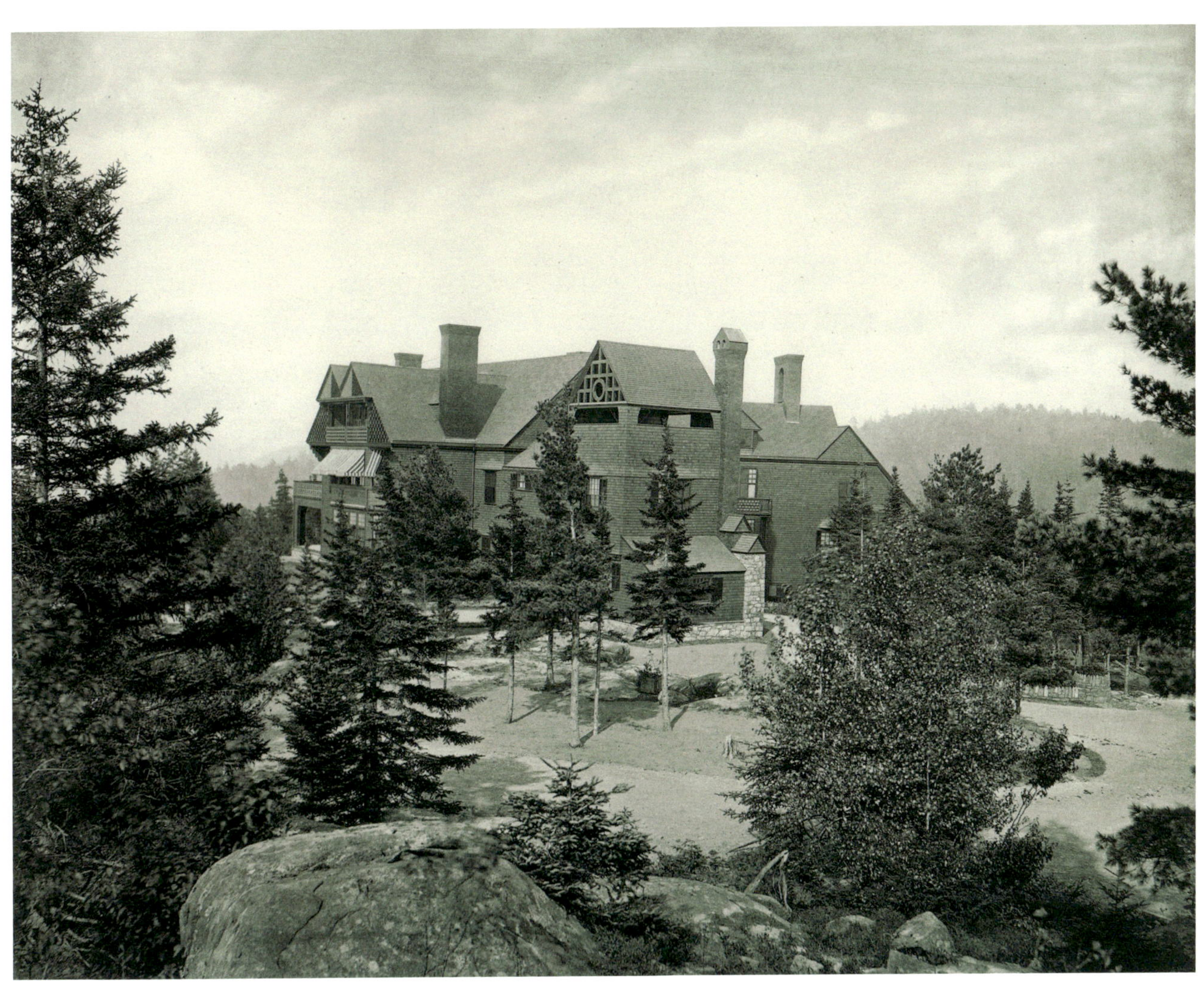

**Collotype.** Photographer unknown. Shingle-style house. c. 1910. 9⅛ x 11¾ in. (23.2 x 29.9 cm)

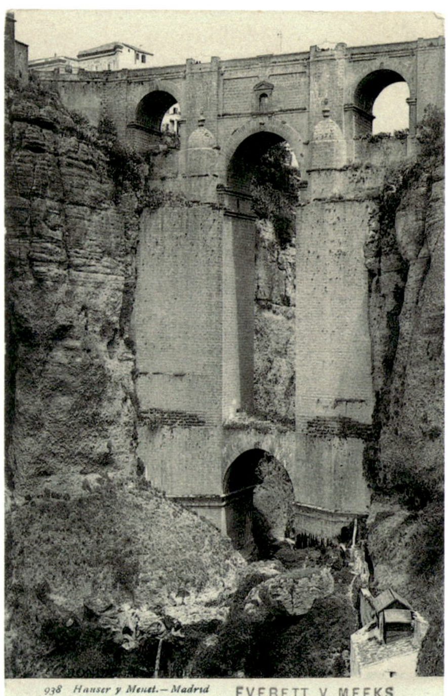


Collotype became the most commonly used printing process for European postcards. This one is an example of a simple, single-impression card, printed in a blackish-green ink. Everett V. Meeks, whose name is stamped on the card, collected postcards and was the dean of Yale's School of Art for thirty-five years.

## 11.3 COLLOTYPE

The printing plate for collotype was prepared by coating a sheet of tempered ground glass with a layer of gelatin containing a bichromate, as a light-sensitizer, along with other ingredients—every collotype shop had its own secret formula. This coating was applied hot, as a liquid. Once poured onto the plate, it was dried by leveling the glass, protecting it from drafts, and applying a gentle heat. Next the plate was exposed with sunlight to a continuous-tone negative (as opposed to the halftone-bearing negative used in letterpress printing), then washed in cold water to remove the bichromate and swell the gelatin. This wash was critical because it produced a reticulated pattern in the gelatin, providing a fine grain that allowed tiny spots of black ink to appear to the eye as varying tones of gray. Where the plate had been heavily exposed the reticulated gelatin would not take up water, and so would accept ink; the less-exposed areas would absorb water, reject the ink, and consequently print lighter. Once processed, the plate could be dried and stored for some time before printing. When it was to be used, the glass plate holding the gelatin image was soaked in water and glycerin, drained, and placed on the bed of the press.

It is an efficiency in book-making to print multiple pages at one time, on a large sheet of paper later folded and cut to make the individual pages of the book. When the book consists of type alone this is easy to do, since slight variations in the printing across the large sheet are usually invisible, and even if they are not, they have no effect upon the content that the printed page is delivering. When illustrations are printed, though, any variation has a strong effect on the picture. The images must all be handled in the same way, and tremendous technical skill is necessary to print eight illustrated pages consistently on a single side of the sheet. We are used to this today, with our multicolor, highly mechanized offset presses, but when collotype was thriving, and twenty-eight-by-forty-inch glass plates were used to print fully illustrated pages, it was something of a miracle that all of the pictures could turn out well. The sheet we see here, printed by The Meriden Gravure Company in 1957, is nearly that size, and shows eleven photographs of sculpture by Donatello. The plate for it was exposed by sunlight to eleven continuous-tone negatives stripped into a single flat, then processed and printed in an edition of about 500 copies. After that many impressions, the plate would have been breaking down, from abrasion to the gelatin surface, so another would be made to print an additional 500 copies. A book such as this, if printed in 2,000 copies, might have taken four complete sets of plates. It is astonishing that cranky old collotype could produce sheets of such beauty.

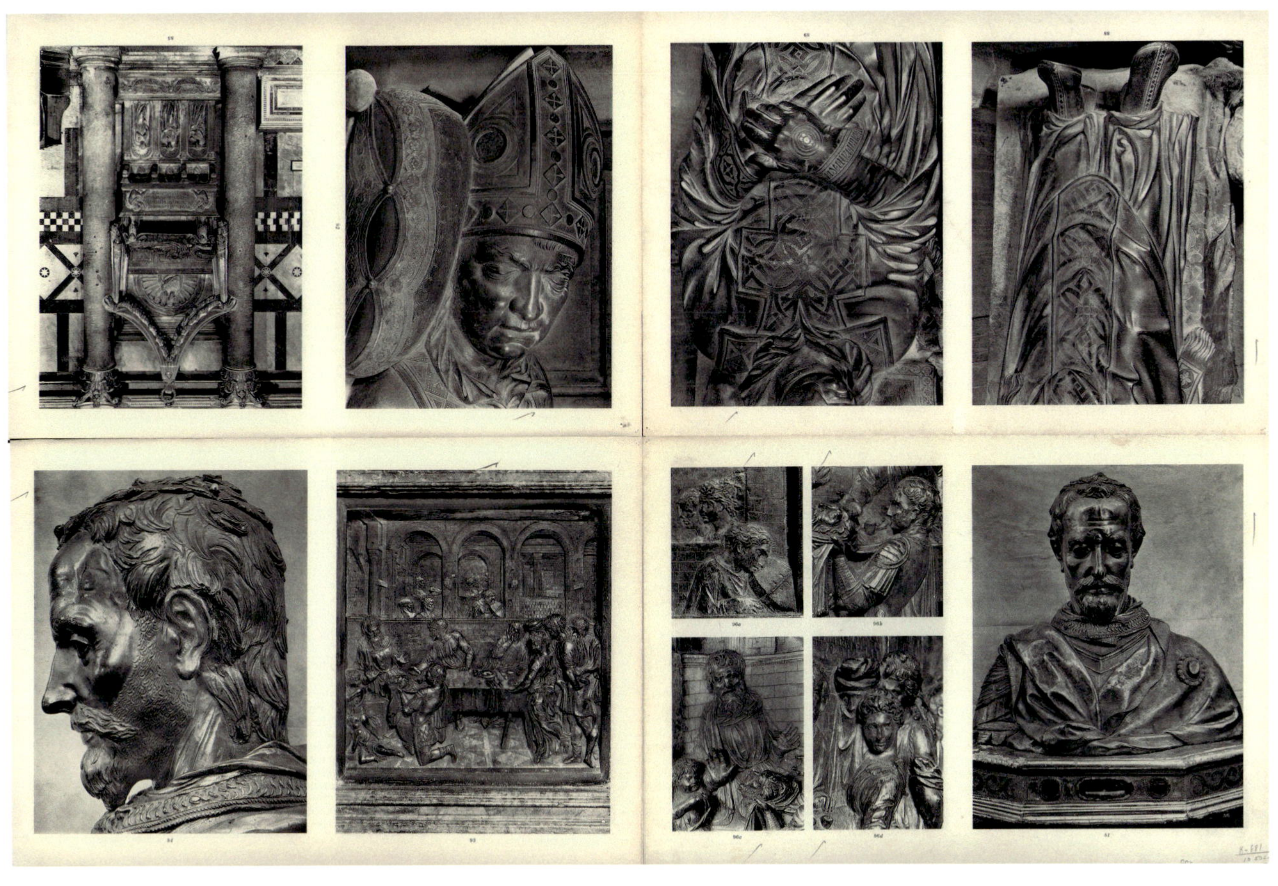

**Collotype.** Press sheet from H. W. Janson, *The Sculptures of Donatello* (Princeton: at the University Press, 1957). 25½ x 37⅜ in. (65 x 95 cm). This was the customer's approval sheet, and it was printed on October 24, 1957.

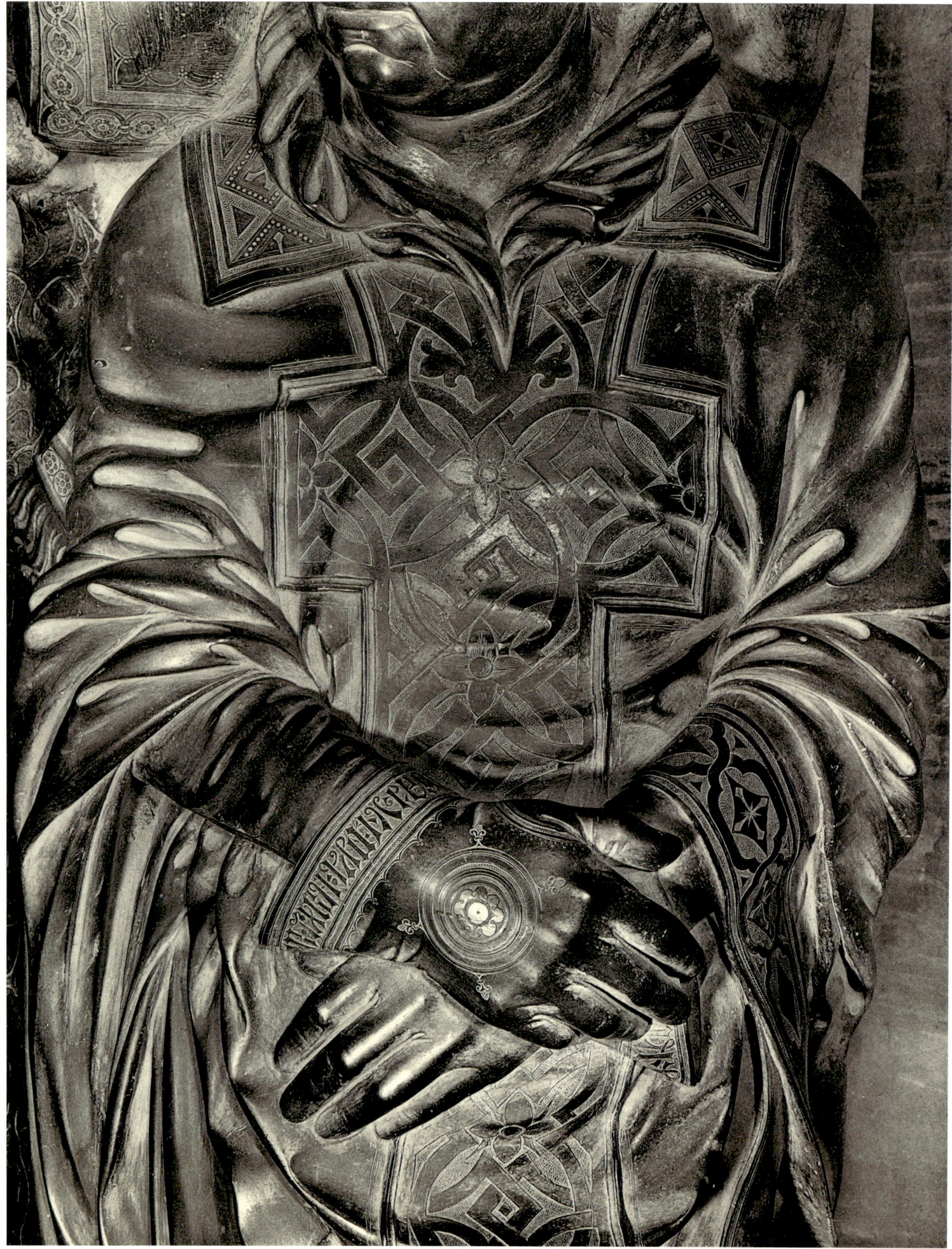

One page from the Donatello sheet, reproduced at 85 percent of the size of the collotype.

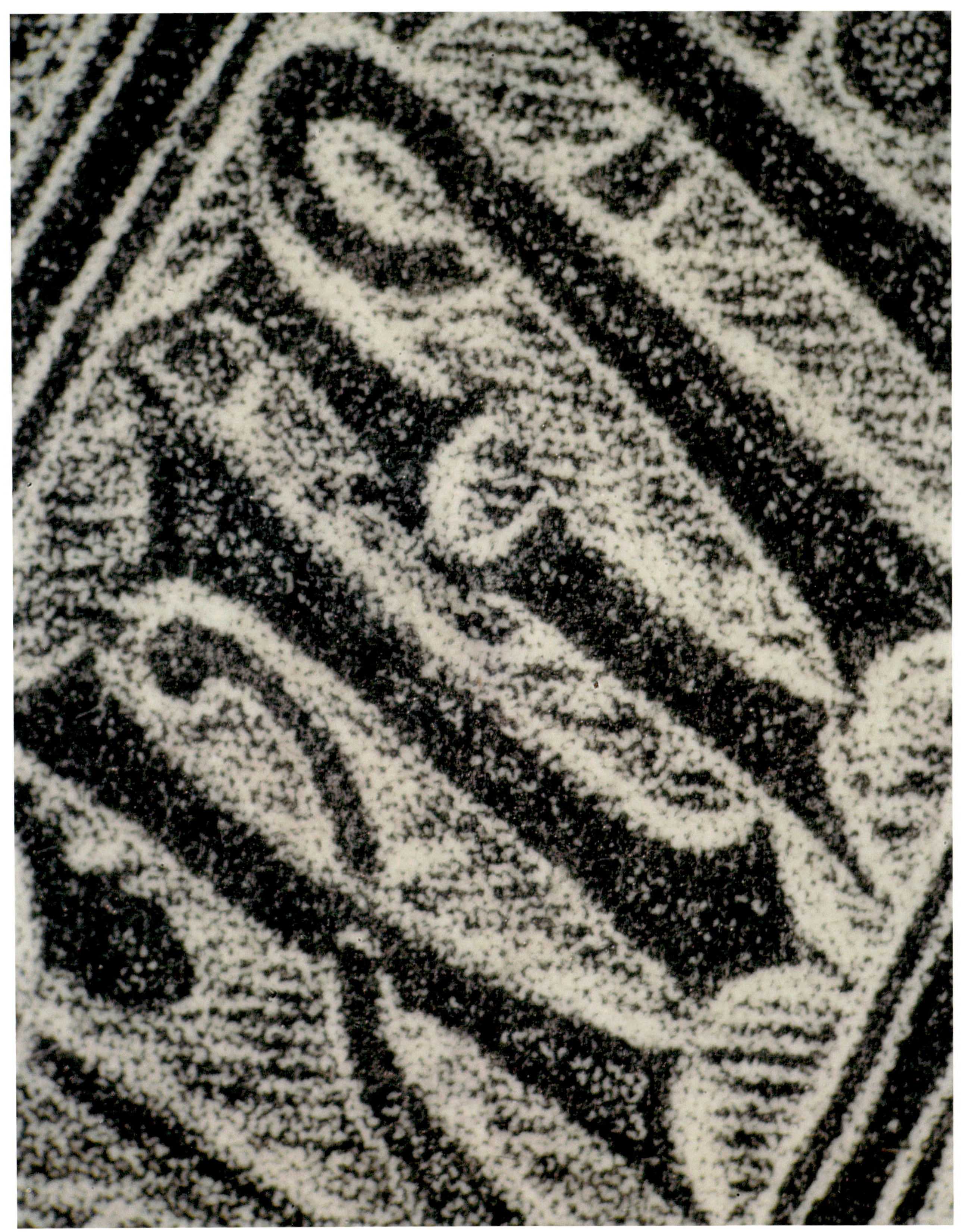

A detail enlarged twenty times from the collotype, showing the random grain of the reticulated gelatin.

## 11.4 POCHOIR

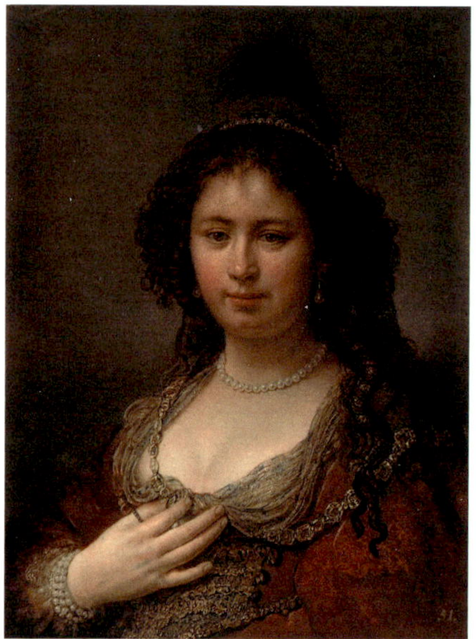

Collotype was used for process-color reproductions but the color impressions seldom registered properly. When correctly done, as in this reproduction of Rembrandt's painting *The Officer's Wife*, process collotype could be great, but pochoir is the more common form in which collotype was used to make color pictures.

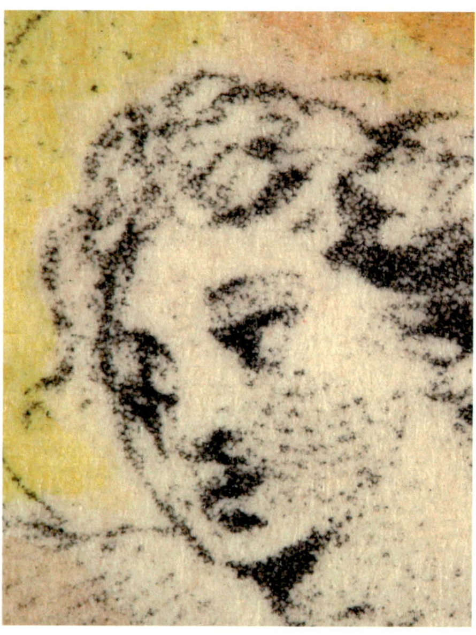

The pale and open black and white impression of the collotype is visible in this enlarged detail.

Collotype was often used to print the black and white skeleton for hand-colored prints. Called "pochoir" prints, these were usually made on good acid-free paper, then colored with stencils. They were most often made for the decorative market but also have a long history of turning up in books. The technical problem in hand-coloring, described in section 9.1, is that the monochromatic framework that holds the applied color must be pale in those areas to be colored. This means, for example, that a pale blue or red tone, which would normally become a light gray in a black and white reproduction, must print as white—the gray would make the applied color "dirty."

Collotype was suited to pochoir for two reasons: its random grain was invisible to the eye, so there was no halftone dot to make the owner think it was a plain old reproduction, and the printing plate was generated from a continuous-tone negative, which could be made with a filter that eliminated most of the dominant color in the original. If the print being reproduced was heavy in the reds, a red filter could be used to make the negative and those areas would be light, allowing the hand coloring to show. The difficulty here was that, if the print had any blues, greens, or cyans in it, they would be rendered dark, making the hand-coloring for those areas worse. This could be somewhat countered by making exposures through two filters—we called it "split filtering"—but even so a good deal of handwork was necessary to get all the colors to disappear.

When process color printing was developed, using the three subtractive primaries, it turned out to need a fourth printer using black ink. The task of eliminating color densities in this black printer was a huge challenge. In the older pochoir a solution had been cobbled up through imaginative filtering, careful developing of the negative, and then skilled handwork to complete the job, but when color was printed from the primaries, and a skeletal black was added, making this black printer right was almost impossible. One of the most amazing benefits of digital technology in the printing trades is that the computer can look at any point in a picture, evaluate the color data present there, and easily eliminate any values that are not neutral gray. By doing this across the entire data field of the picture, the printer can generate a file in which only the neutral values are present—the perfect attenuated-black basis for a color print. This new technology would have been perfect for pochoir but it became available at the very moment that hand-coloring disappeared altogether from printmaking.

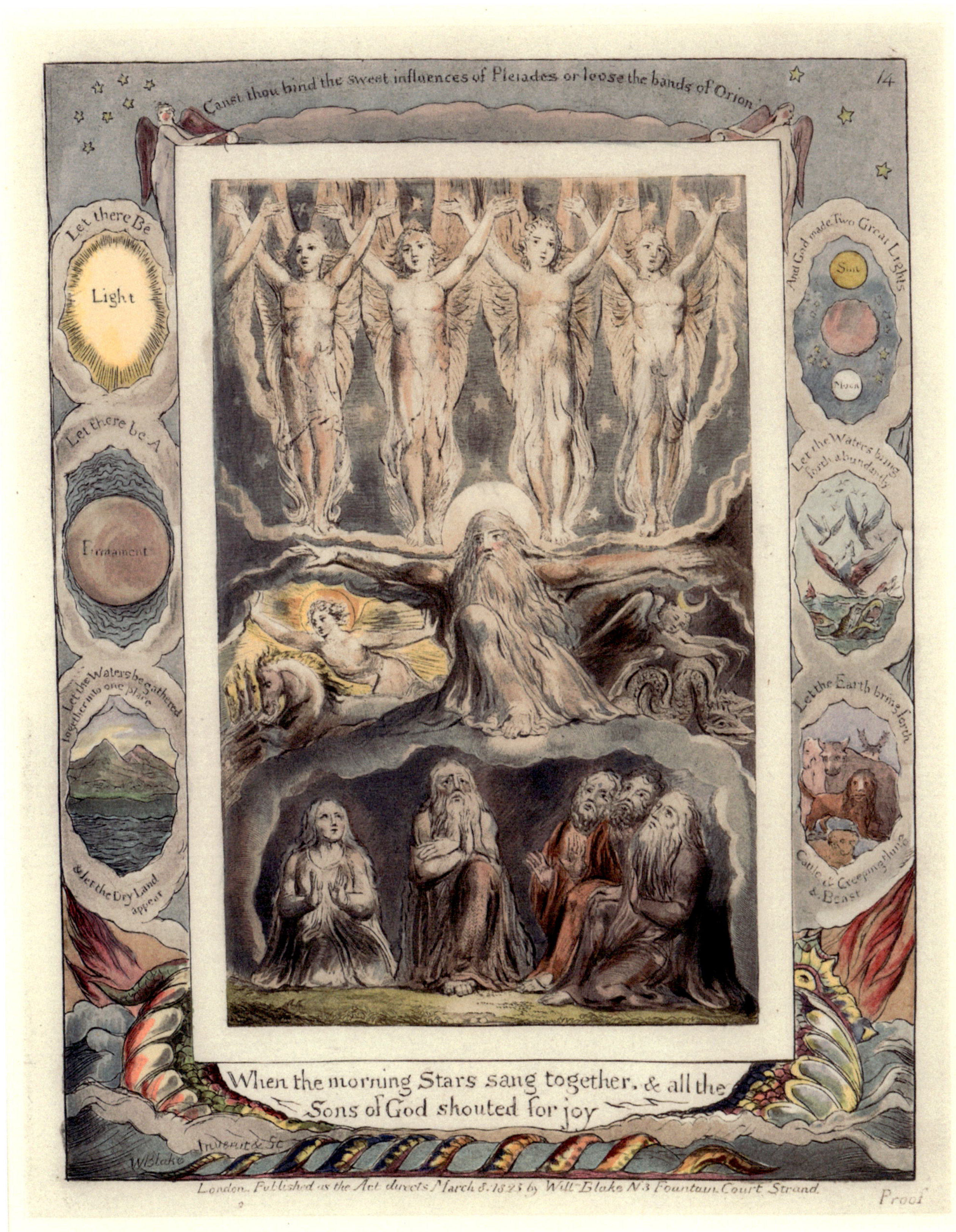


**Pochoir.** William Blake. Proof sheet for *When the Morning Stars Sang Together,* from the Book of Job. 1825. Print: Trianon Press. 1976. 8 x 6⅜ in. (20.3 x 16.2 cm). This print is a hand-colored collotype proof of a Blake engraving that was colored by someone other than Blake himself.

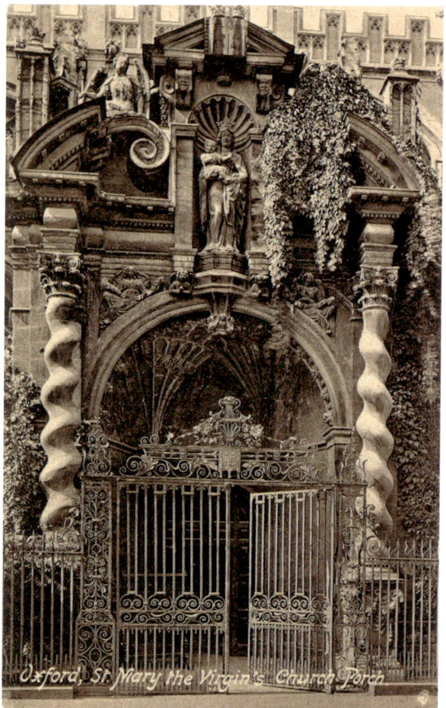


A double-rolled collotype postcard in black and brown ink.

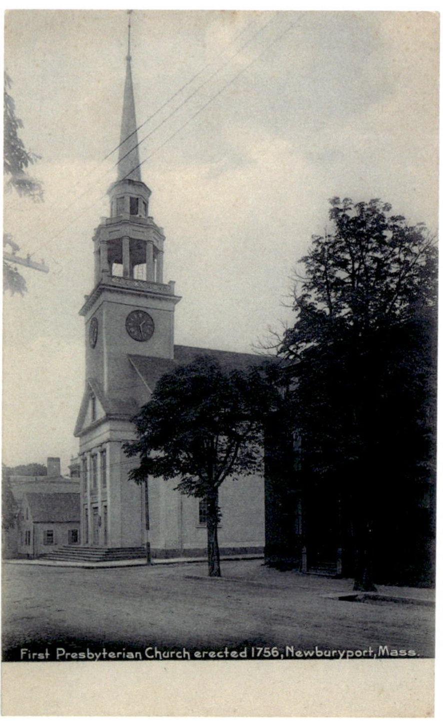


A double-rolled collotype postcard in which the second inking was pale blue.

## 11.5 COLLOTYPE QUIRKS

*Print color.* For some reason the old collotype printers were remarkably casual about the color of ink that they used. In any given publication we can find prints ranging from neutral to brown, green, or blue. The two reproduced here, on the top right, have been taken from a small book titled *U.S. Steel Cruiser Boston*, published by E. H. Hart in 1888. These prints are green and brown but the book has other plates that run the full gamut of collotype colors. When I was a young printer, and working in a shop that still did collotype, the pressmen made quite a fuss about the ink, and even in the 1960s imported it from Europe, where we all assumed it was made by grinding pigment, bats' wings, and frogs' legs into secret formulas guarded through the generations. Perhaps no one paid any attention to color, since getting the prints to turn out decently was such a far greater problem.

*Collotype imitating albumen.* Chemical photography was always expensive because the prints had to be handled individually and their materials were costly. Editions could be printed from negatives, and there was no theoretical limit to their numbers, but the reality of labor and material costs meant that any edition larger than a hundred or so required some sort of ink printing. We saw in section 6.4 how the woodburytype filled this need, but collotype could similarly be made to imitate the chemical photograph and was less expensive. The example below opposite is from a trade magazine that describes the print accurately as a "collotype imitation silver print." The ink has been mixed to have a purplish-red cast, to imitate the old gold-toned albumen print, and the paper is a highly polished clay-coated sheet. I had an old-time photographer tell me that if you went into a large photo studio in Paris early in this century and ordered an edition of fifty or more prints, you were just as likely to receive collotypes as actual chemical prints.

*Double-rolled collotype.* Double-rolling was a technique used to produce richer collotype prints without the need for multiple impressions. The plate was inked with a stiff, dense black ink and then immediately reinked with a soft, colorful one. Once double-inked, the plate was printed in a single impression. The result looked much like the later duotones printed by photo offset, which tend to have a color cast in the light values and a strong, neutral black in the deepest tone. This method was often used for fancy postcards, two of which appear to the left.

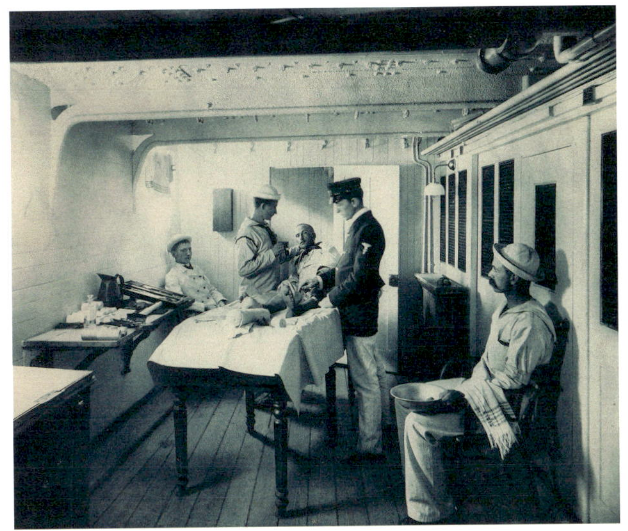

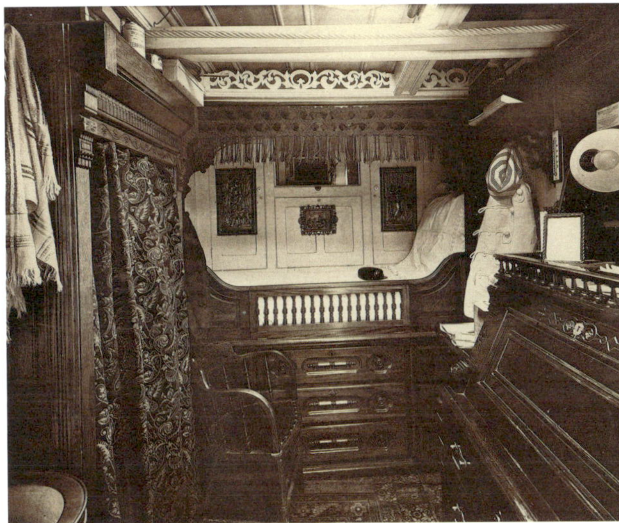

**Collotype.** Two plates from the souvenir book *U.S. Steel Cruiser Boston* (New York: E. H. Hart, 1888). Each: c. 7 x 8¾ in. (17.8 x 22.2 cm)

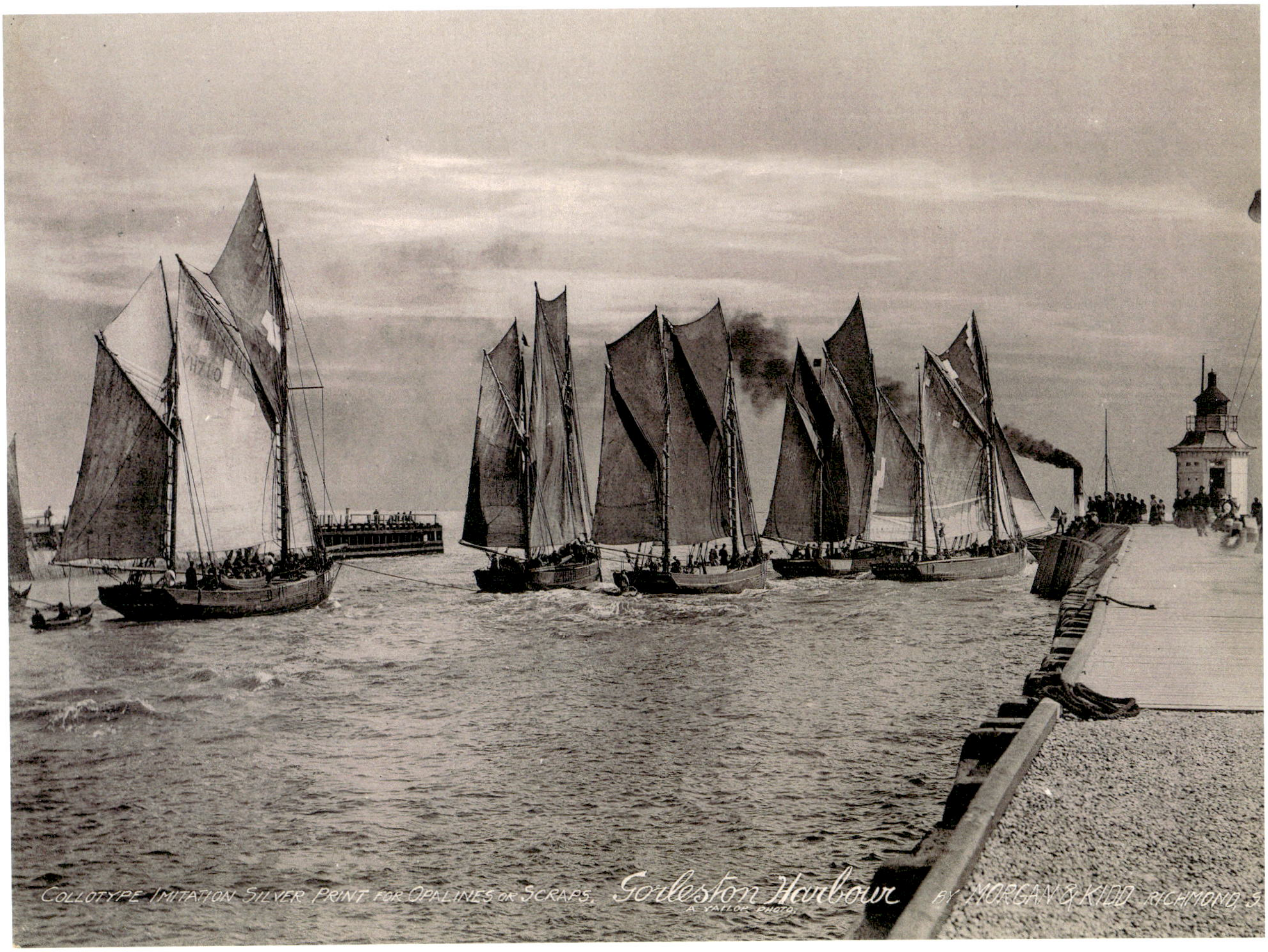

**Collotype.** A. Yallop. *Gorleston Harbour.* c. 1900. 6¾ x 9⅜ in. (17.2 x 23.8 cm). Made as a sample of the process, this collotype was printed in *The Penrose Annual* as an advertisement for the publisher Morgan & Kidd.

## 11.6 PHOTO OFFSET LITHOGRAPHY

Relief printing (as halftone-based letterpress), gravure, and collotype gave the printing trades three terrific systems for reproducing photographs. These processes had their heydays from about 1880 until 1960 — fully eighty years — and they were directly responsible for photography's move out of the darkroom, with its chemical print, and into its modern role as the great visual data-transport system of today. Through the early years of the twentieth century, another process slowly took form that would prove to be the giant of all picture-printing processes. This was photo offset lithography, which, in its final form, brought together lithographic chemistry, lightweight and inexpensive printing plates, and simple, completely photographic data input to the printing press. I will try to be restrained in describing offset (as we casually called it), but it is both my trade and my chief love of all the ink-printing methods, so even while being cautious I will probably say too much about it. More pictures have been printed in offset than by all other methods combined, so a careful examination isn't such a bad idea. Today we are also witnessing the peak of the process's development; it is fully integrated with the computer, and through the next years, as digital printing takes on smaller jobs, the offset behemoth will most likely live on, producing superb printed editions of books, catalogs, and magazines. I think it will be around for quite a while yet.

The process had its origins in chromolithography. As we saw in the large poster shown in plate 2.10, lithography, printing right off the stone surface, could lay down a beautiful solid layer of ink. As soon as light-sensitive metal plates replaced the stones, the halftone, fully refined in letterpress printing, could move into lithography — the old, laborious translation of pictures by hand could be mechanized through the halftone screen. The metal plate and the halftone were vital to the rise of offset, but the central innovation, the one that made it king, was the introduction of the offset blanket. Printers had long known that when a fully inked roller was used to transfer ink to a printing plate, the roller, after the transfer, retained a negative image of the plate, since the ink in the image areas had been removed from it. This observation made clear that a rubber roller could hold an ink image. If a clean roller was passed over an inked litho stone, then rolled again onto a sheet of paper, a positive image could be picked up and transferred to the paper. This practice of transferring, or "offsetting," an image became the core of photo offset lithography: a metal plate was inked, it printed onto a rubber blanket, and that blanket then transferred the image to the paper. The ramifications of this practice were revolutionary.

This picture was drawn by hand, then printed with solid colors and coarse halftone screens. The printer used rough approximations of the subtractive primaries, but there are two blues instead of the usual cyan; one blue has a lot of red in it and the other, lighter one is quite green. Many package labels carried specialized colors, which almost always struck the eye with an intensity that halftone-generated mixes of the primaries could not. This technique, called "spot color," is used to this day in fancy color printing.

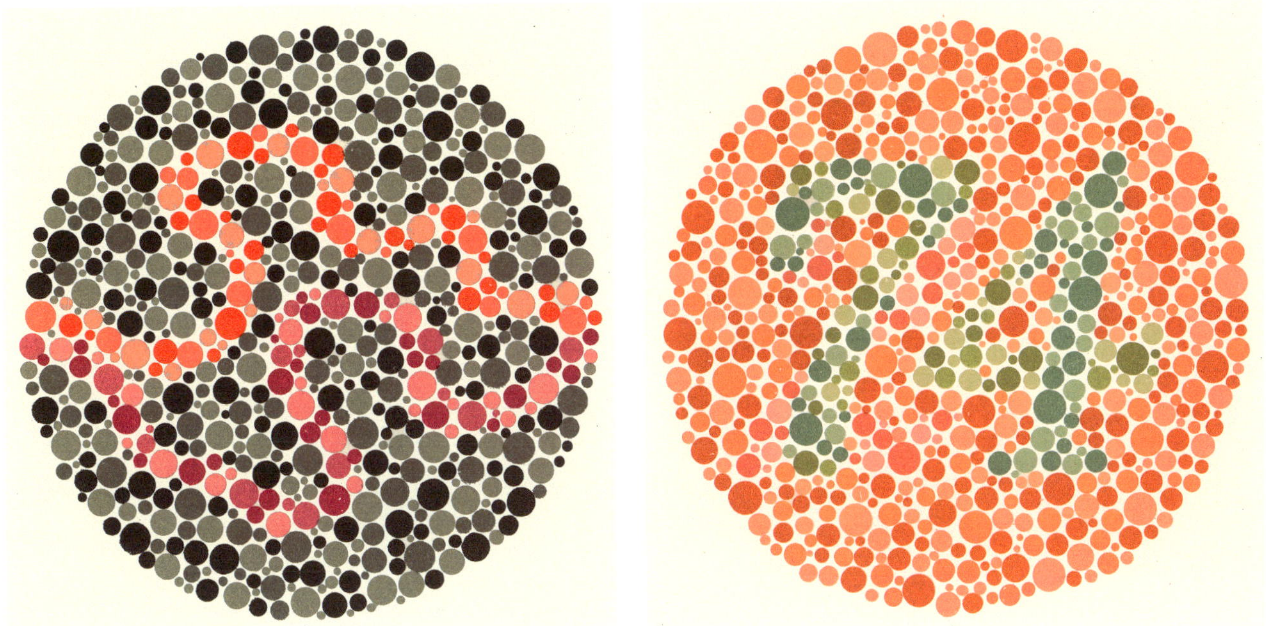

**Photo offset lithography.** Shinobu Ishihara. Two plates from *Ishihara's Tests for Colour-Blindness* (Tokyo: Isshinkai, 1966). Each: 3⅞ x 3⅞ in. (9.9 x 9.9 cm). Developed in the 1930s by Dr. Ishihara in Japan, these beautiful arrays of colored dots, printed by offset, could accurately hold the subtle colors needed to determine slight individual differences in color vision.

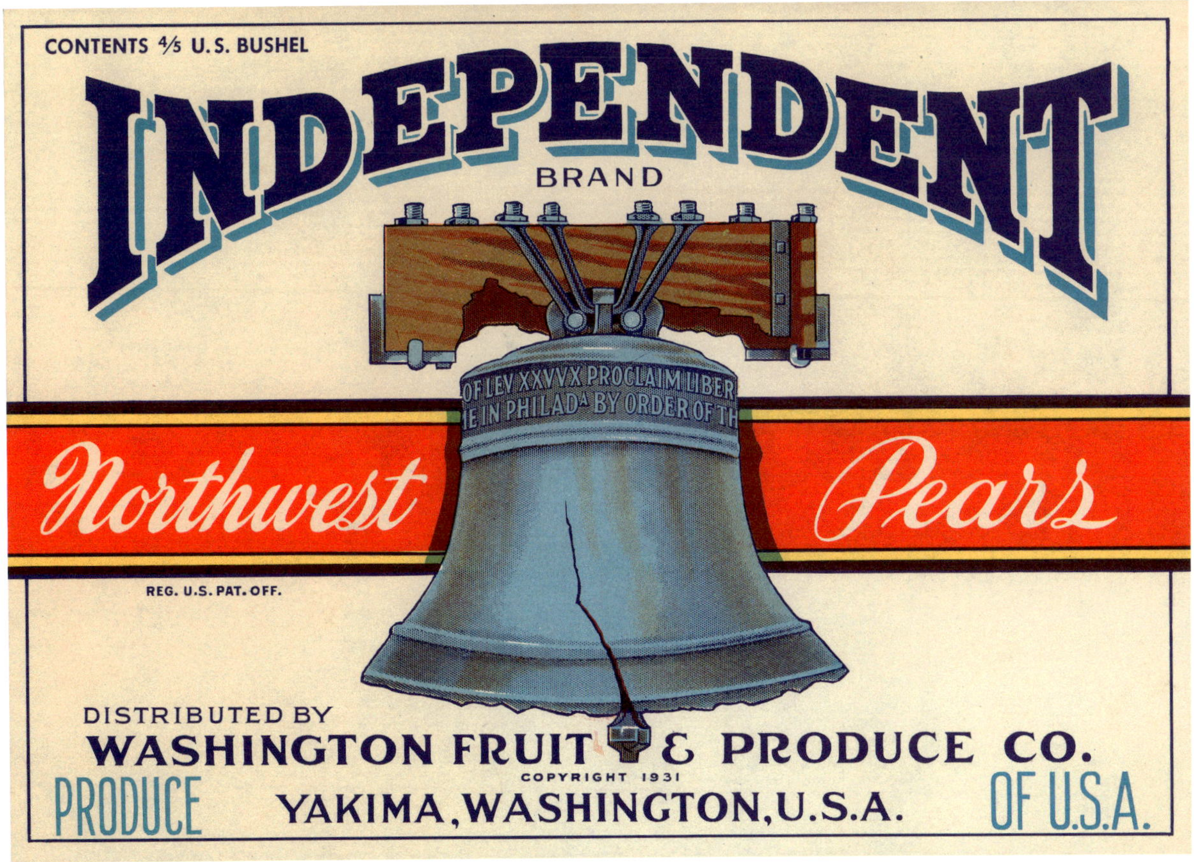

CONTENTS 4/5 U.S. BUSHEL
INDEPENDENT
BRAND
OF LEV XXVVX PROCLAIM LIBER
IE IN PHILADA BY ORDER OF TH
Northwest Pears
REG. U.S. PAT. OFF.
DISTRIBUTED BY
WASHINGTON FRUIT & PRODUCE CO.
COPYRIGHT 1931
PRODUCE YAKIMA, WASHINGTON, U.S.A. OF U.S.A.

**Photo offset lithography.** Artist unknown. Label for fruit box. c. 1950. 7 x 9⅛ in. (17.7 x 25 cm). By the mid-twentieth century, many fruit- and vegetable-box labels were printed by offset. Even on cheap paper, these labels carried brilliant colors and simple but strong designs. They could be produced very inexpensively in short runs, without the need for the costly copper or zinc cuts that would have been required for letterpress printing.

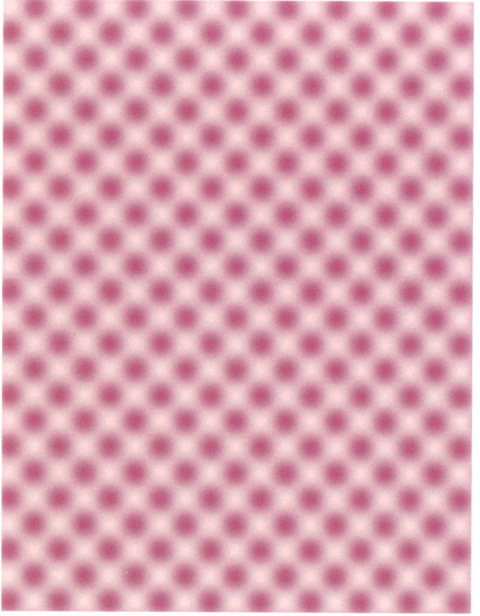

A sixteen-times enlargement of a section of a magenta contact screen, similar to the one used to make the magazine cover illustrated here. These screens, made photographically from the older glass halftone screens, were colored magenta to allow contrast control in the reproduction by filtering the light used in the copy camera.

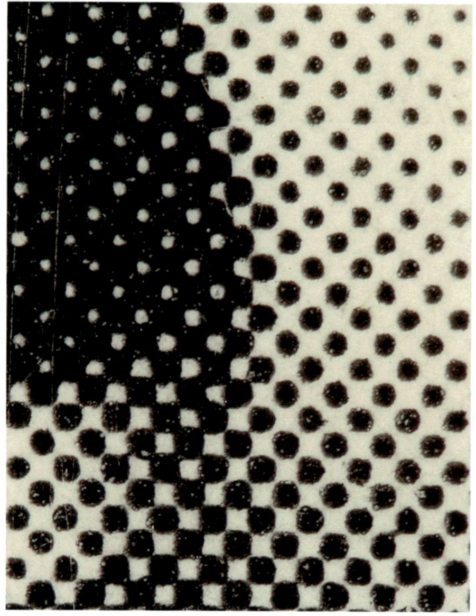

A section of the halftone, enlarged the same amount to show the remarkable sharpness of the offset process. In use the screen is angled at forty-five degrees, which gives the least-apparent dot pattern to normal vision.

## 11.7 THE NATURE OF OFFSET PRINTING

The offset press has ended up with three cylinders, stacked one above the other. On top is the plate cylinder, around which is wrapped a thin aluminum plate holding the image in a polymer coating. Ink and water rollers ride on the plate, providing the ink/water balance necessary for the image to form on it. Beneath the plate cylinder is the blanket cylinder, which is wrapped in a cloth blanket with a thick, smooth rubber face. The ink from the plate transfers to this blanket with each revolution. Beneath the blanket runs the "back" cylinder, a polished steel cylinder with grippers to hold the paper, which bends around the cylinder as it is printed. All three cylinders are connected by a gear train so that they run in perfect synchrony.

The introduction of the rubber blanket between plate and paper has six crucial effects, which we must list:

1. The blanket can "kiss" the paper relatively lightly, transferring ink without distorting the sheet.

2. The soft rubber can conform to, and print beautifully on, a rough-surfaced paper.

3. The blanket acts as a moisture barrier, keeping the water spread on the plate away from the paper, so that it does not swell and change size.

4. The paper—with its fibers and coatings, abrasive over time—never touches the delicate surface of the plate.

5. The image is reversed a second time, so that a right-reading, emulsion-down halftone negative, produced directly in a copy camera, prints correctly.

6. Small alterations to the size of the printed image can be made by changes in the underpacking of plate and blanket.

These mechanical advantages are coupled with a tremendous change in the halftone that was possible as soon as it was printed lithographically. The old relief plates that were used to print halftone-based reproductions could never hold a screen ruling finer than about 150 dots per linear inch, because of technical problems in etching, inking, and transfer. The new lithographic plates, holding images on a plane metal surface with no relief, can easily maintain a cleanly printing screen ruling of 300 dots per linear inch. Such a fine dot is nearly invisible to even the best naked eye, and completely invisible to anyone over forty years old. In offset printing the halftone finally drops out of sight, as ink is laid down in patterns so fine that we fully accept them as tonal.

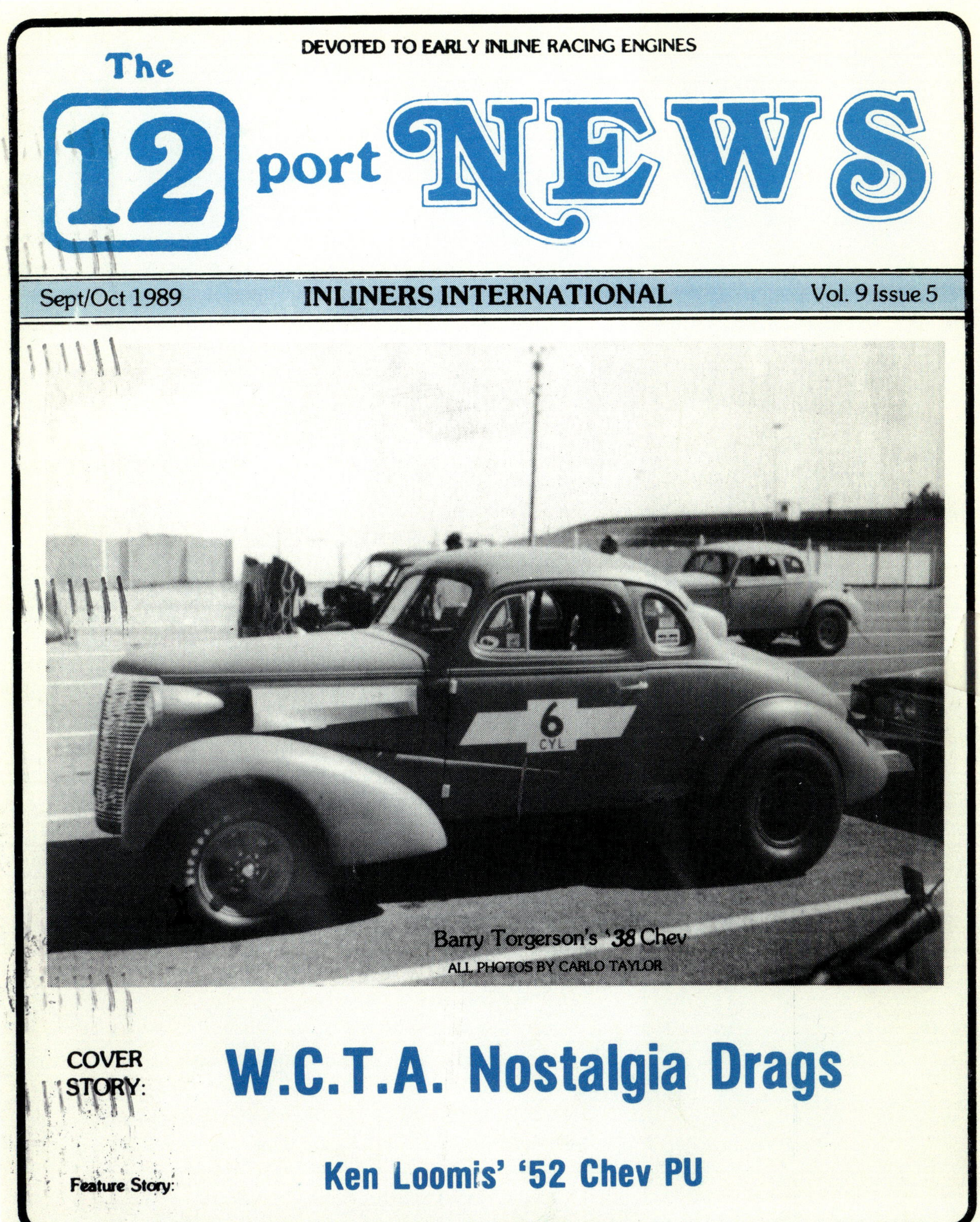


**Photo offset lithography.** Carlo Taylor. *Barry Torgerson's '38 Chev.* 1989. Print: cover for the magazine *The 12 Port News,* published by Inliners International, September/October 1989. 8 x 6¼ in. (20.3 x 15.9 cm). A single-color 100-line-screen black halftone with blue spot-color on coated paper.

## 11.8 OFFSET DUOTONE

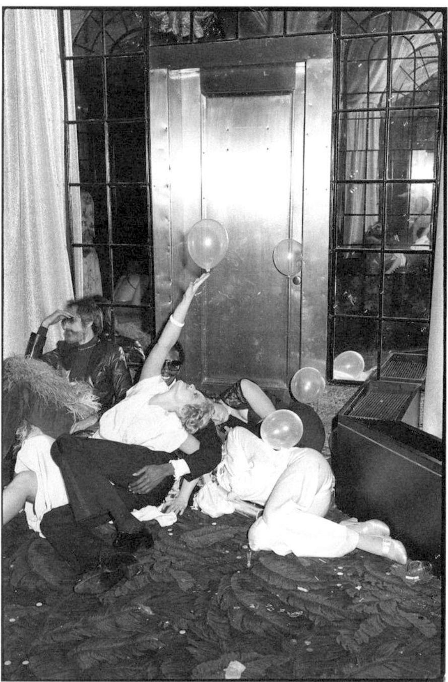

The black impression, shown here by itself, is always printed first, because ink transfers best to an unprinted sheet and a superb transfer is required in order to hold a decent black value.

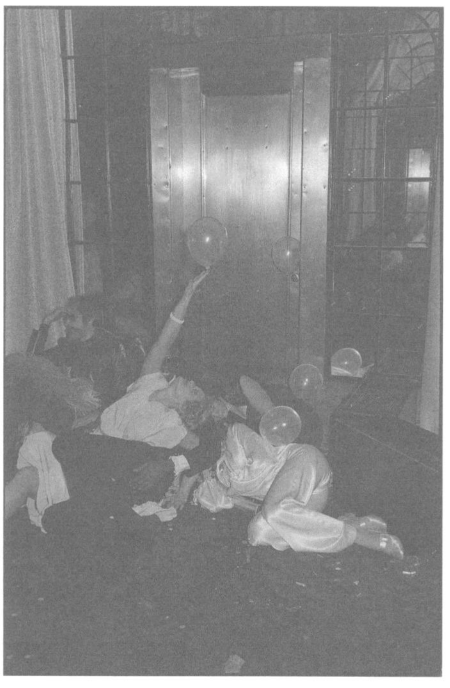

The gray impression is printed on top of the black. Because the gray ink is transparent and lighter in value, it does not obscure the shadow detail rendered by the black printer.

The old relief trick of printing a black and white picture in two impressions was quickly adapted to photo offset lithography. The delicate touch of the blanket, and its effect of keeping water away from the paper, allowed extremely accurate registration: presses were made that could print a black layer on a sheet one day and then perfectly superimpose a gray pass on the next one. This kind of printing—called "dry trap"—also allowed strong matte blacks to be printed on soft paper. Whenever the old letterpress books had included halftones, they had had to be printed on a hard, clay-coated sheet, necessary for a smooth transfer of ink between the metal plate and the paper. Because of the softness of the blanket, offset could print on any surface, giving rise to a new, uncoated sheet—"offset stock"—that had the same appearance as the paper used in beautiful old letterpress books holding type only. Offset presses can handle paper in big twenty-eight-by-forty-inch sheets, often with eight book pages per side, or sixteen pages in all. When folded down, such a sheet produces a "signature" in a book.

Printers were initially sloppy about the tonal structure of their duotones. The early two-impression illustrations, done in the 1960s and '70s, were tonally rich, because of the two layers of ink, but they didn't always replicate the tones of the original very well. Gradually printers unlocked the puzzle of how to expose and develop the halftone negatives so that each color emphasized different parts of the picture scale and, once printed together, did a pretty good job of looking like the original.

In the case we see here the black printer was made contrasty and showed exaggerated detail in the shadow portions of the picture. The gray printer, on the other hand, showed little distinction between tones in the dark areas but had terrific accuracy in the light values. In the print from the two combined, the shadow detail holds, because the gray of the second impression doesn't bury it, and the light values are good, because there is little black ink in those areas, so the smooth gray steps are clear and accurate. This solution was necessary because there was no method for exposing and developing a single halftone negative that could accurately portray all the tonal steps from black to white. The carefully crafted duotone was a solution to this problem.

When properly made, the duotone had a marvelous benefit unavailable in the darkroom: the black printer controlled one end of the tonal scale and the gray printer the other. The ink for each impression could be adjusted on press, so each end of the scale could be independently tuned. This was a tremendous control, allowing reproductions to be accurately pinned down as they were being made on press.

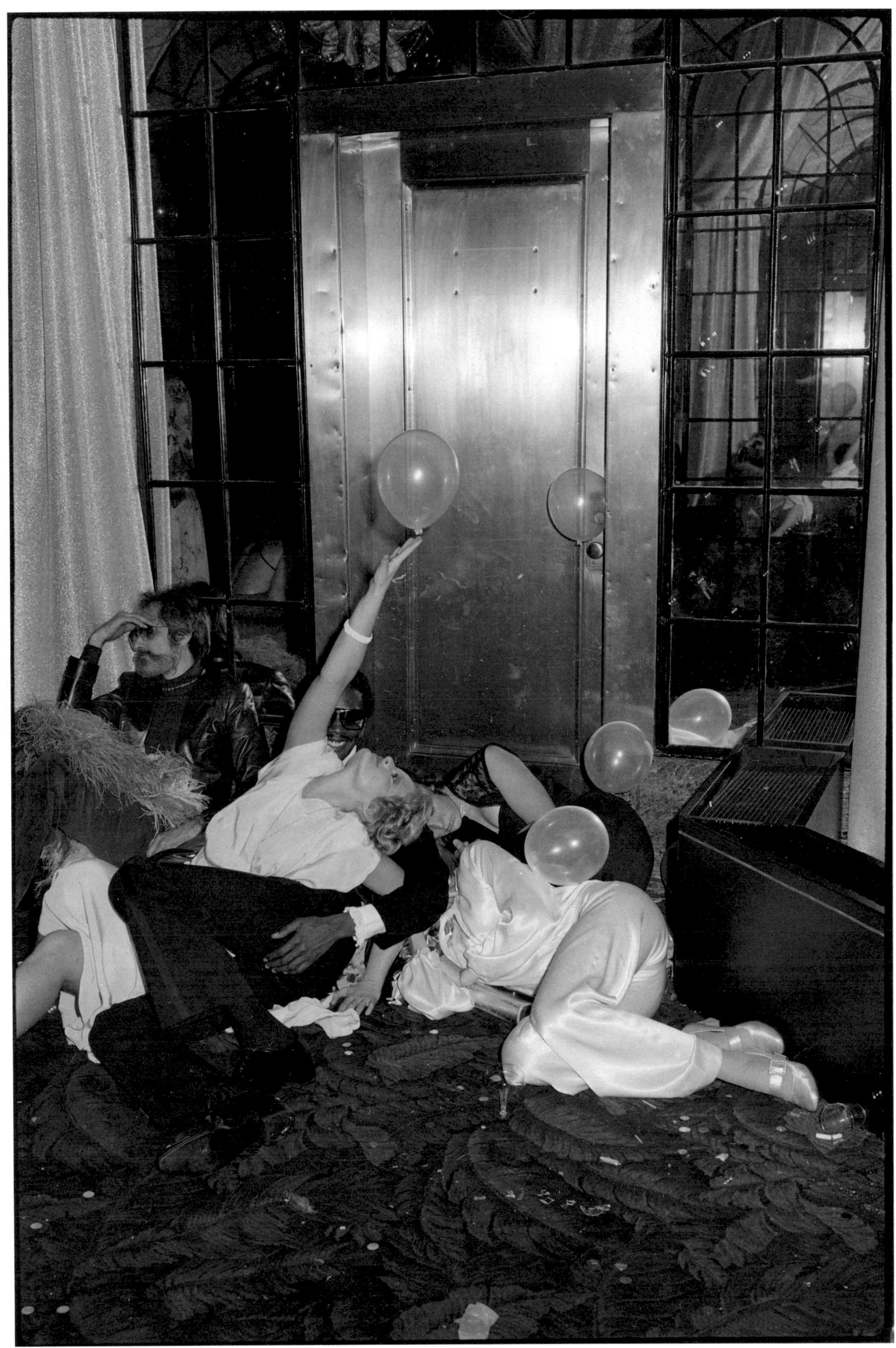

**Photo offset lithography duotone.** Tod Papageorge. *New Year's Eve 1977–1978.* Print: Thomas Palmer. 2007. 13 x 8¾ in. (33.1 x 22.2 cm). The details to the left show the black and gray printers by themselves.

## 11.9 OFFSET TRITONE

The duotone was followed by more complicated printing, in three, four, and even five colors, all to make beautiful reproductions of black and white photographs. These additional colors were particularly needed for the reproduction of photographs from the nineteenth century if the rich variety of their original chemical color was to hold. In the case we see here, a black impression was used to generate the darkest tones in the print, but then, instead of a simple gray, the other inks were warm in color to match the old purple/red of the albumen original. Early black and white photography can also be reproduced with process color (as we do in this book), but the finest reproductions cannot be done that way. The tritone, printing from three halftones in various shades of gray ink, does much the best job.

I make this whole thing sound like a cakewalk but it is actually very difficult to do well. Reproductions never look just like the originals, and all serious ink reproduction of photographs is based on the understanding that the reproduction has to look "right" in its own context—of ink on white paper in a book. This rightness often requires that values in the original be altered in the reproduction. Many early photographs, for example, have turned quite yellow, and if this color is slavishly followed, the reproduction simply looks wrong. Printing requires an understanding of a concept of equivalence: the most accurate replica one can make of anything is seldom a literal copy, but rather a new thing that gives the viewer the impression that it looks like the original.

By the 1980s and '90s, offset presses were appearing with four or more printing units, so that a blank sheet of paper could go in at one end and come out at the other carrying a full-color reproduction. It is important to remember that the huge expense of developing such presses was directed toward better printing of color—by this time black and white constituted only a tiny segment of the offset-printing market. Before the multiunit presses were around, the printer making duotones or tritones faced a terrifying task: the first impression of the reproductions for the whole edition had to be printed and dried, and then the second pass was put down the next day. If the halftones weren't right, then the whole press run, and its expensive paper, had to be discarded. If the book had a large budget, press proofs could be made of the pictures and this dangerous routine could be avoided; the proof, done in only a few copies, could confirm that the halftones were correct, and if they weren't, they could be remade and re-proofed until acceptable. Unfortunately budgets were seldom that fat, and most two- or three-color printing was done with a nerve-racking mixture of terror and faith that the whole thing would turn out right in the end.

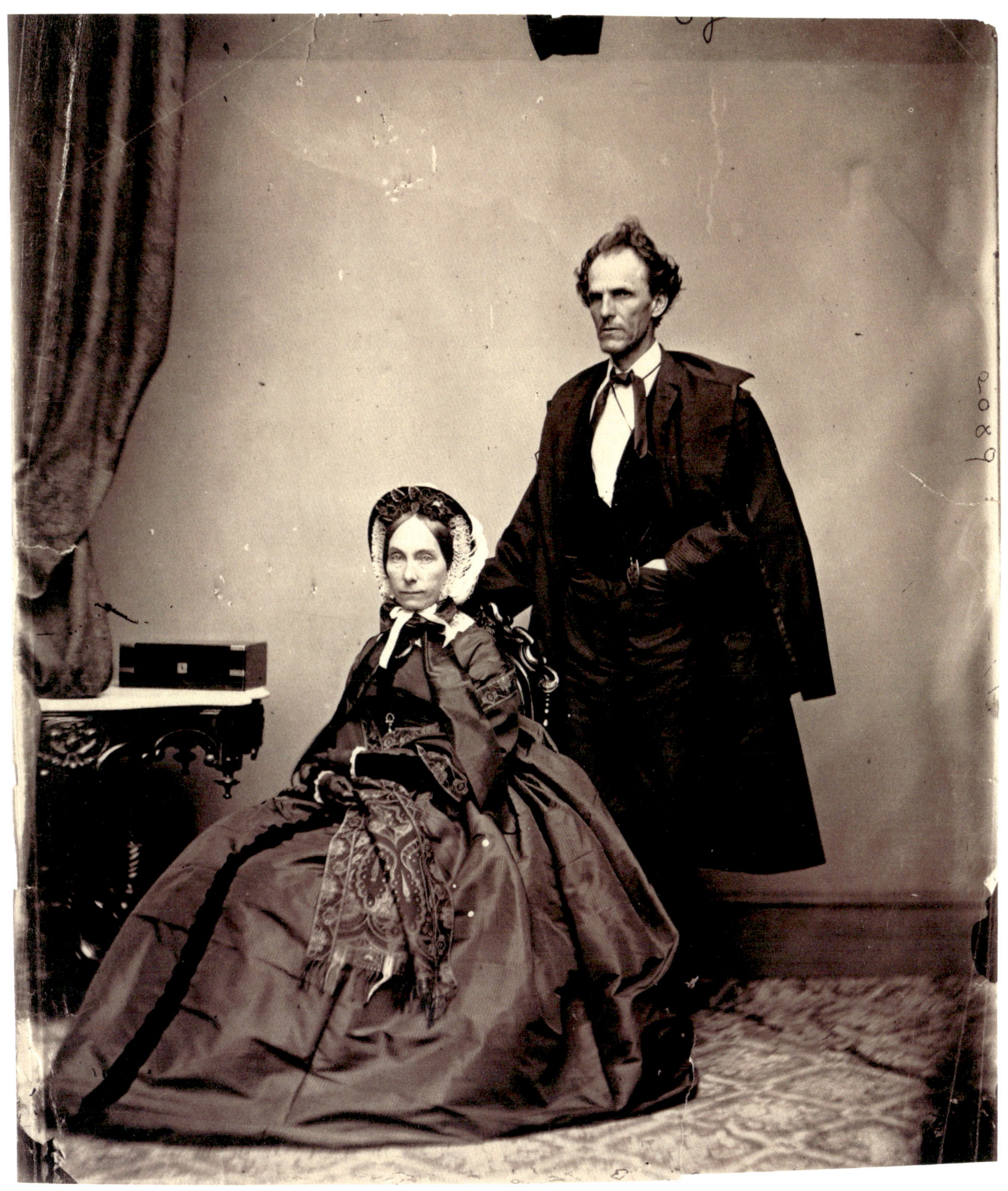

**Photo offset lithography tritone.** Mathew B. Brady Studio. Senator and Mrs. James H. Lane. 1861–66. Print: Richard Benson and Thomas Palmer. 1985. 9 x 7¾ in. (22.8 x 19.7 cm). A multiple-impression proof sheet for *Photographs from the Collection of the Gilman Paper Company* (White Oak Press, 1985)

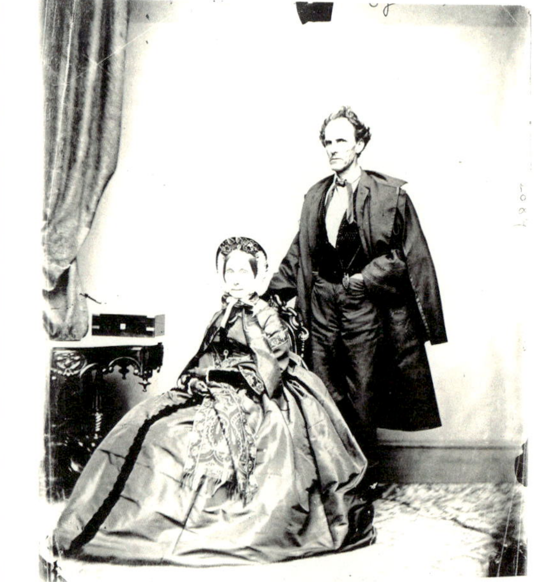

The first impression, from a high-contrast plate, using black ink.

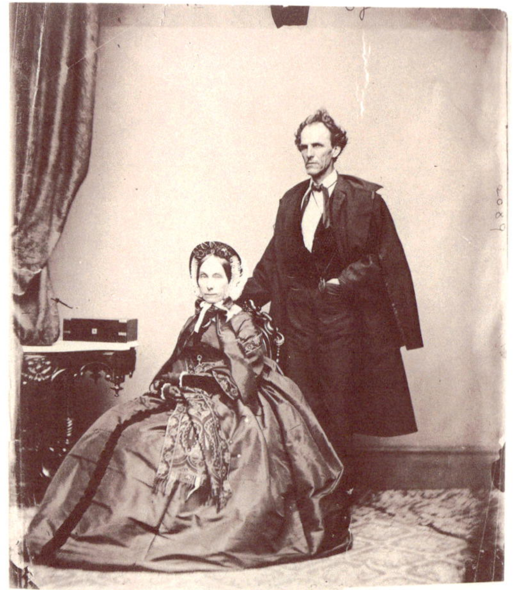

The second impression, from a more "normal" halftone, printed in a reddish-gray ink.

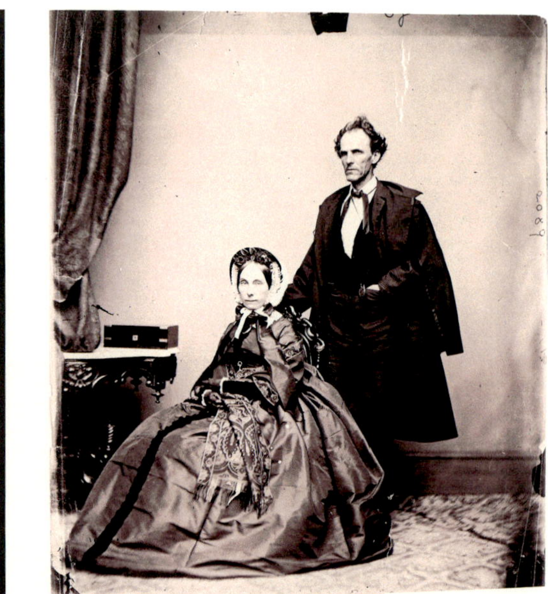

The first and second impressions together.

A breakdown of the stages of the reproduction, with color bars still attached, showing the solid values of the inks used in the printing. This reproduction also uses a fourth plate, which prints an overall varnish but contains no picture data, so I still call it a tritone.

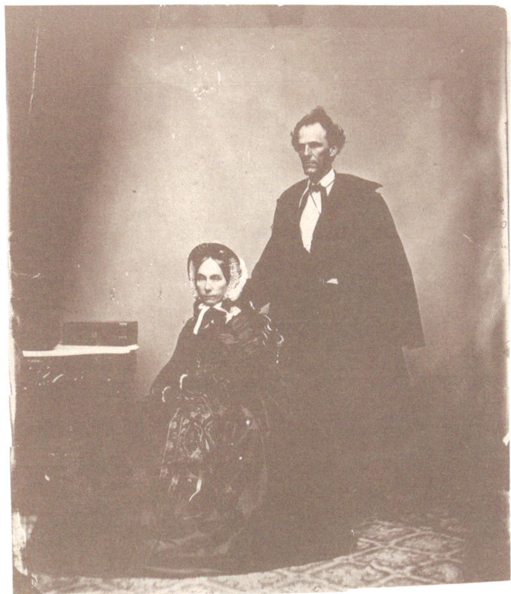

The third impression, carrying no detail in the shadows, and creating a smooth layer of tone in the darker values of the picture.

The final impression, carrying no picture data (except the shape of the picture), printed with a solid of a warm-toned varnish.

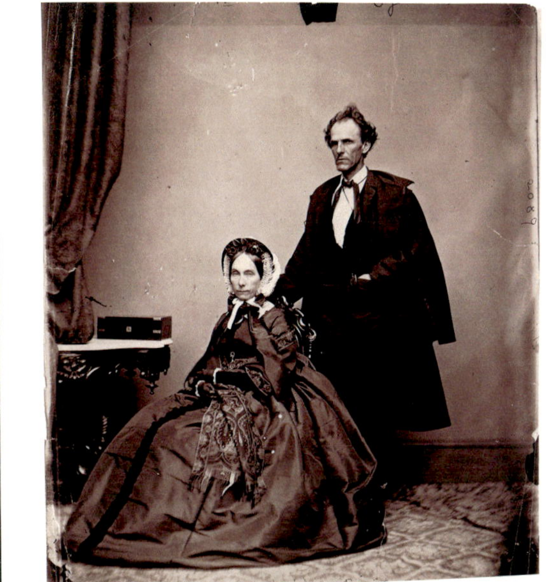

The first, second, and third impressions together.

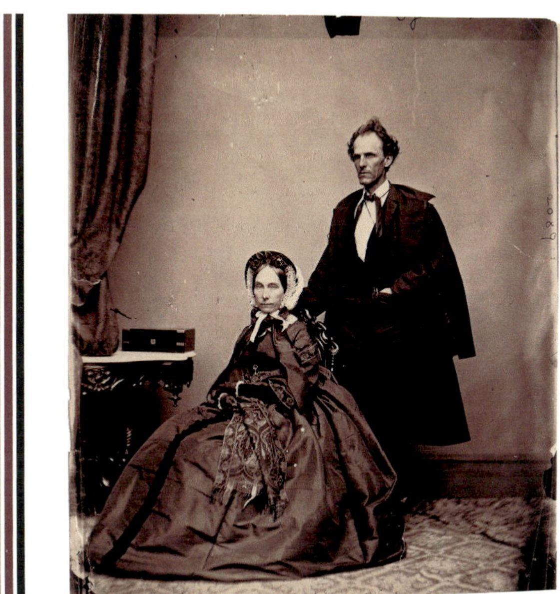

The completed print.

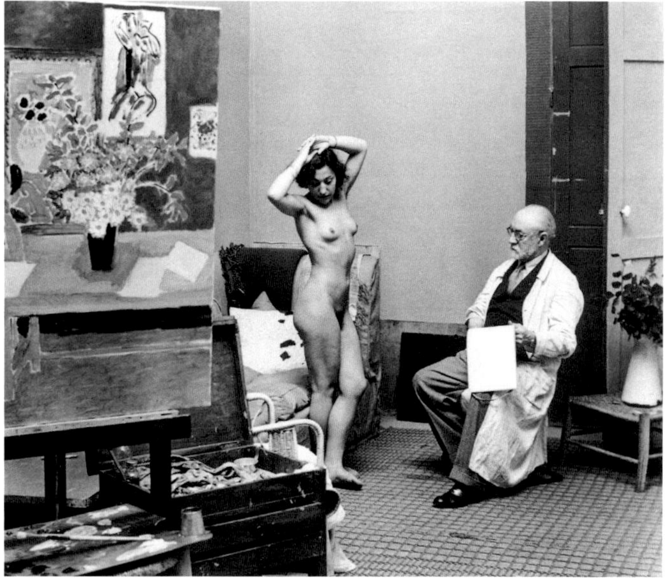

**Photo offset lithography.** Brassaï. *Matisse Drawing Nude Model at Villa d'Alésia.* 1939. Print: 1994. 5½ x 6½ in. (14 x 16.5 cm). From *The Allan Chasanoff Photographic Collection* (Houston: Museum of Fine Arts). A duotone print in black and gray ink.

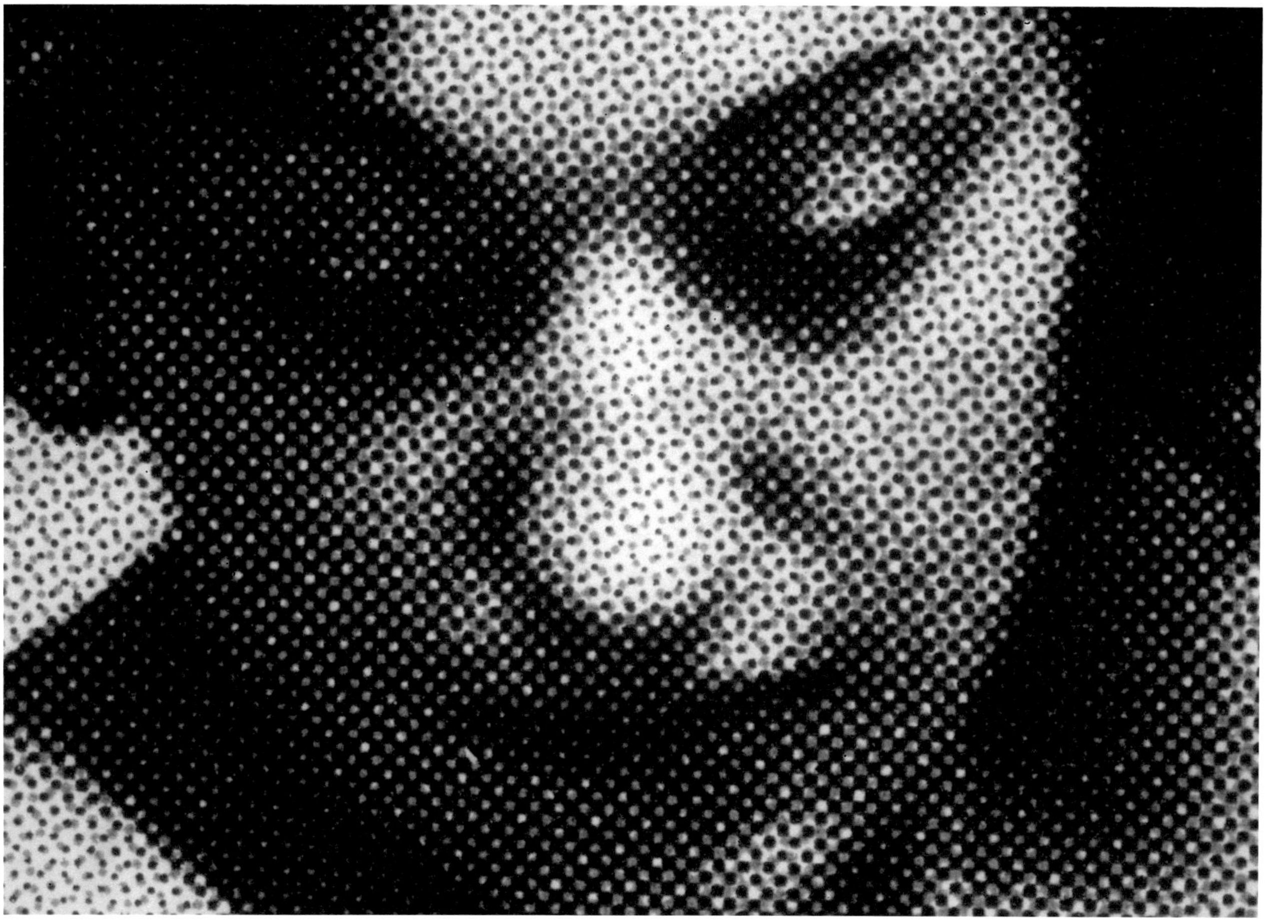

This duotone, which was printed with a 200-line-per-inch screen, is reproduced here enlarged about twenty times from the original. In the dark areas of the picture the gray impression is completely obscured by the black one, but in the highlights the gray dots are obviously larger than the black. This shows that the gray printer carries most of the highlight information and the black the shadow detail. This is the most common form of the duotone.

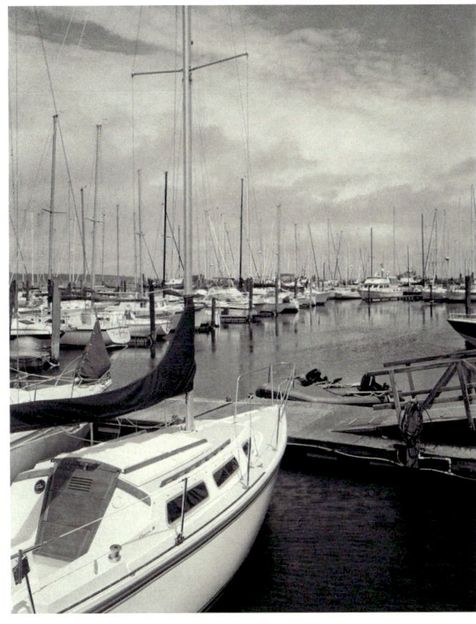

**Photo offset lithography.** Richard Benson. *Bend Boat Basin.* 1985. 9½ x 7½ in. (24.1 x 19 cm). A tritone print in black, dark-gray, and light-gray ink.

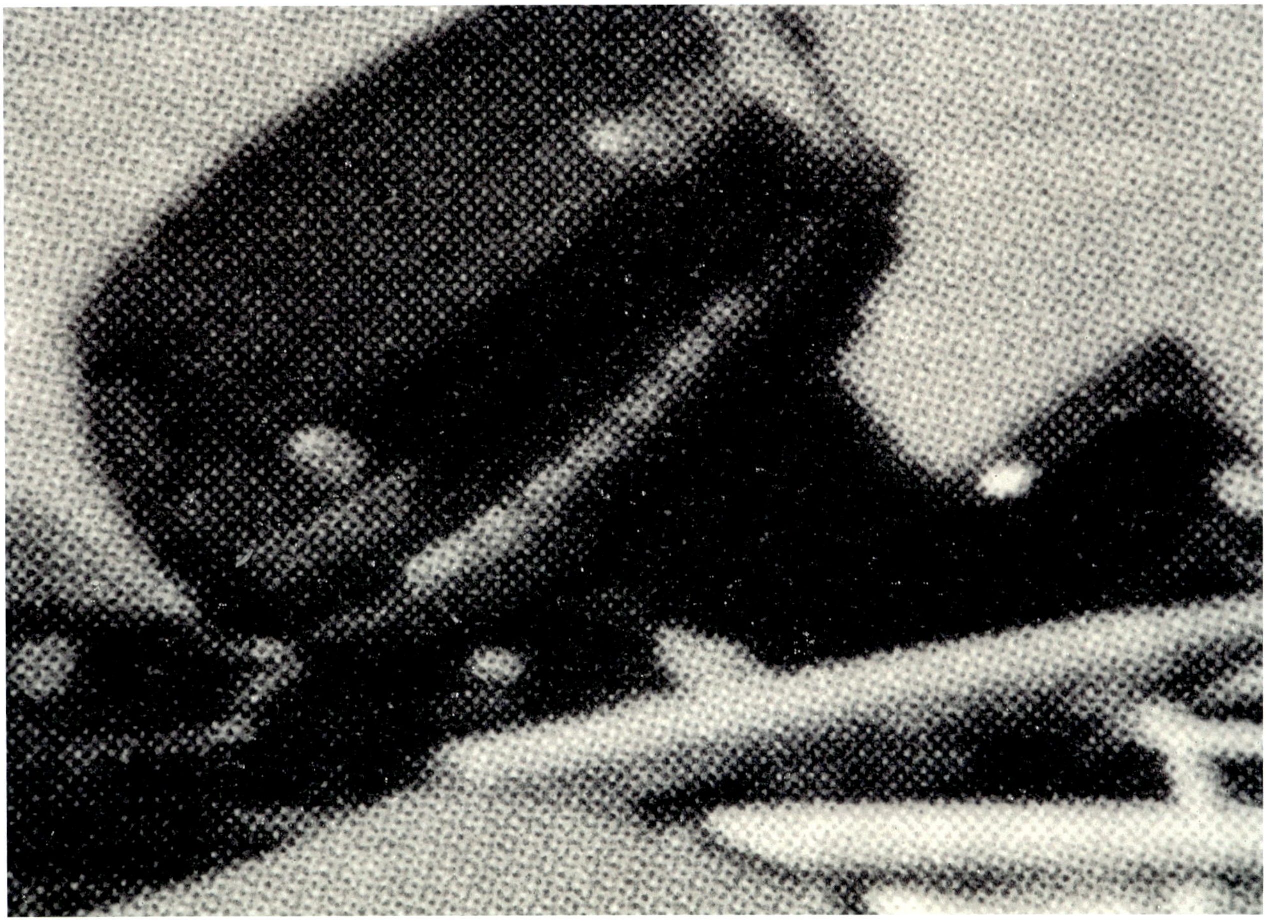

This tritone, printed with a 300-line-per-inch screen, is here enlarged about twenty times from the original. No black-printed dot appears in the lightest values, where only the light gray shows. This light gray becomes a solid for the mid-tones of the picture, where the dark gray carries a large dot and the black a fine one. Thus the black carries shadow detail, the dark gray the mid-tones, and the light gray the highlights.

## 11.11 PROCESS COLOR IN OFFSET

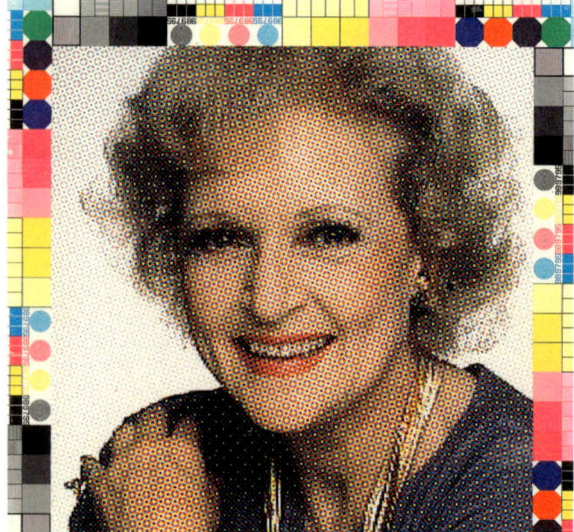

Betty White's test sheet, reduced to the size where our eyes blend the dots and see the picture instead of the halftone pattern.

Color printing was the engine that drove the development of photo offset technology. Printers had long since solved some of the basic problems of color: one was how to angle the halftone screens to avoid moiré patterns; another was to develop filters and inks that fitted each other well enough so that separations made with one filter could be printed with an ink of the complementary color. This particular problem was never fully solved, since no pure inks have ever been developed, but many darkroom tricks, using intricate masking, did a pretty good job of fixing those errors. Color printing also came to depend on the large-format transparency. These color intermediates were photographed to make the reproduction, then were available on press to guide the printing. Not many museums were willing to send their Rembrandt (or Betty White) to a printshop for the purpose of comparison.

Since color was extremely complex, the preliminary or "prepress" work tended to be done in specialized houses—the transparencies were made in the field by professional photographers, and then the separations, masking, and conversion to halftones were done by the specialists. The printing took place at the companies that had the big presses. One drawback to this system was that the division of labor allowed each party involved to blame the others when things didn't work out, as was often the case. In all my glowing descriptions I leave out the fact that the reproductions were almost always poor, whether made in color or black and white. The business of making a replica of anything is to some extent doomed from the start, and when the object being reproduced is a photograph, the job is nearly impossible.

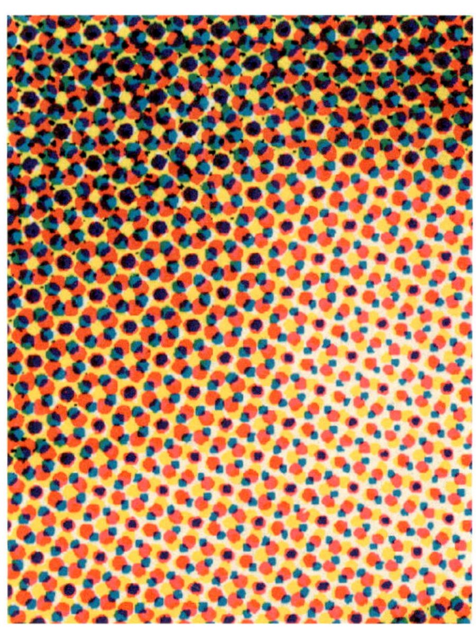

In any multiple-screen print—one that uses more than one dot pattern—some dots are next to each other and some are on top of each other. If the inks are transparent, their respective locations make no difference to the eye of the viewer when seen at a normal viewing distance. This detail shows the basic pattern of four-color process printing using traditional halftone screens.

Despite its complexity, in the end color printing turned out to be easier to do well than black and white. It's hard to pin down the reasons for this. One big one is the development of color proofing systems that could make pretty good prepress replicas of what the halftones would do. These methods used photo polymers in the subtractive primaries; the separation house could make a set for fifty dollars or so to give the customer an idea of what the reproduction would look like. There was never an adequate method for proofing a black and white duotone or tritone. Another reason for the success of color printing was that it could be done badly and still look good. Even if the print was too heavy, or too light, or somewhat out of balance, the colors' interrelationships could still hold and the colors could be enticing even if inaccurate. The fact that the original was seldom seen near the reproduction helped too. But in black and white work, errors in weight and scale could remove whole areas of content, and tonal distortions could murder the picture.

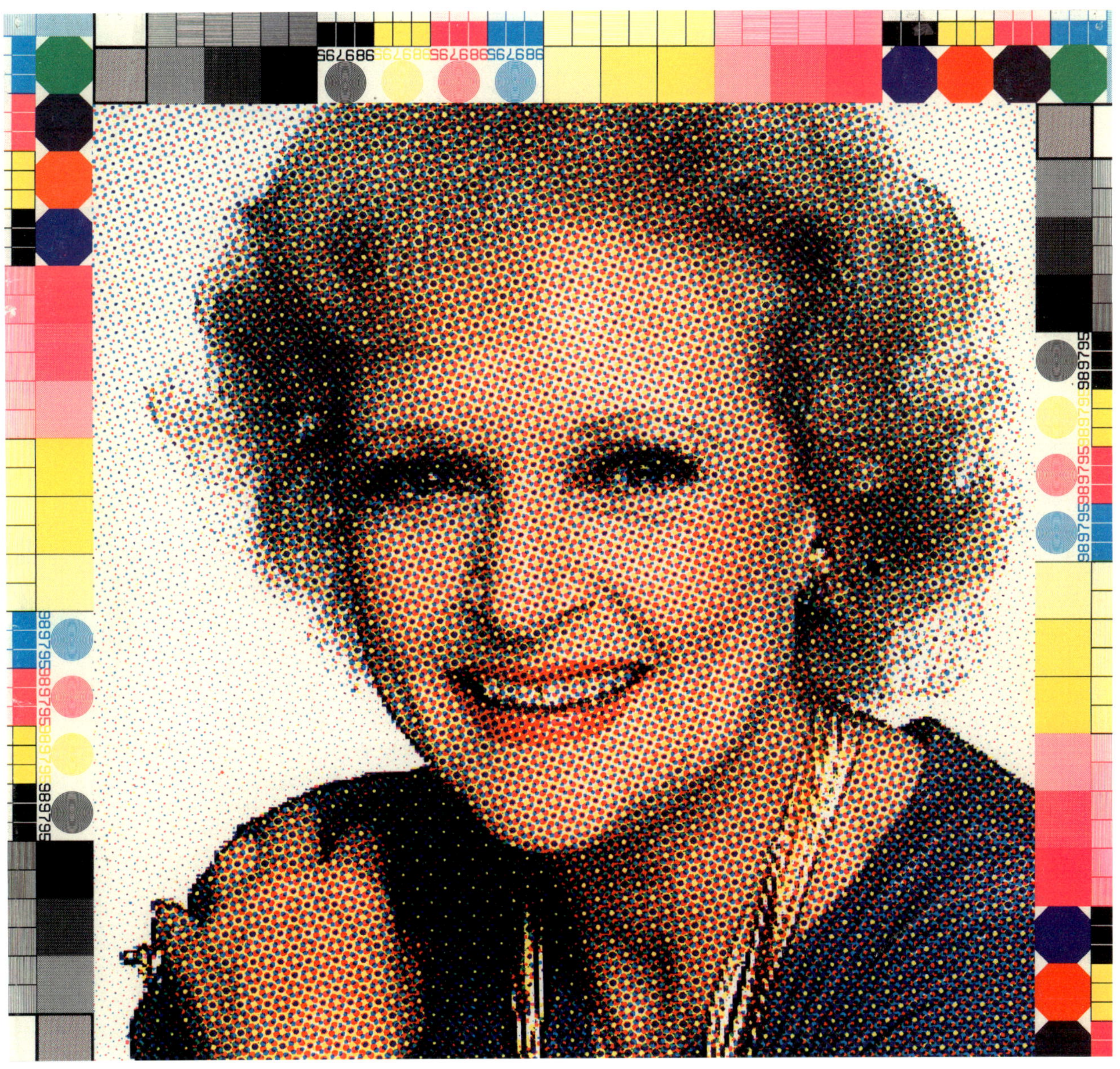


**Process color in photo offset lithography.** Photographer unknown. *Betty White.* c. 1985. Print: c. 1990. 7¾ x 8¼ in. (19.7 x 21 cm). A test sheet designed to calibrate an offset press. The halftone is very coarse, and the small circular patches show if the press is "slurring" the image.

## 11.12 WEB OFFSET

All the offset printing we have looked at so far was done on cut sheets of paper. The printing speeds gradually increased, from about 4,000 impressions an hour in the early presses up to 10,000 or more for the newest ones. If a book is to have 192 pages, and each press sheet holds sixteen pages (eight per side), then twelve sides must be printed. Even with long makeready times such a book can be done in less than a week as long as the edition is no more than a few thousand. When we get to magazines—routinely printed in editions of hundreds of thousands, with a new issue weekly or monthly—the math simply doesn't work out. There has to be a faster way to print.

The answer is web printing. For readers under thirty I must emphasize that this is not the World Wide Web we are talking about, but paper printed on rolls instead of sheets. Web printing was first developed for letterpress newspaper work, where time was a central concern, and it gradually moved over to offset. When a press prints individual sheets, its speed is limited by the need to properly register each sheet moving into it. This cannot be done without stopping the sheet at some point, moving it against register guides, and then accelerating it up to the press speed. But it turns out that there is no speed limit for the actual printing itself; plate, blanket, and paper are quite happy moving ink around at far higher speeds than any sheet-fed press can manage. If the printing is done on a roll of paper, and with a workable, high-speed registration system, there is in principle no limit to how fast a press can print.

That high-speed registration system turned out to be a stroboscopic light, which reads register marks printed on the paper and adjusts the tension of the web to keep things aligned. Web presses are so fast that heat drying is used so the paper can be cut and folded right in the press, which discharges full signatures at the other end. In order to get finished pages the press must print both sides of the roll; this is called "perfecting," and the web press must have eight printing units instead of the four that a sheet-fed press needs for color work. A large web press may be 200 feet long, with the four or five printing units occupying perhaps a third of its length and the feeder, dryer, and folder taking up the rest. Web presses return profits when run continuously, and they even have devices built into them allowing the input rolls of paper to be changed without stopping them. A good web press can print 35,000 to 50,000 impressions per hour, on sixteen magazine pages at a time, with four-color pictures, using halftones of 200 dots per linear inch, printing on both sides of the web. The operators have to wear ear protection, and when things go wrong they do so really quickly, but it is web printing that makes all those magazines, newspapers, and catalogs possible.

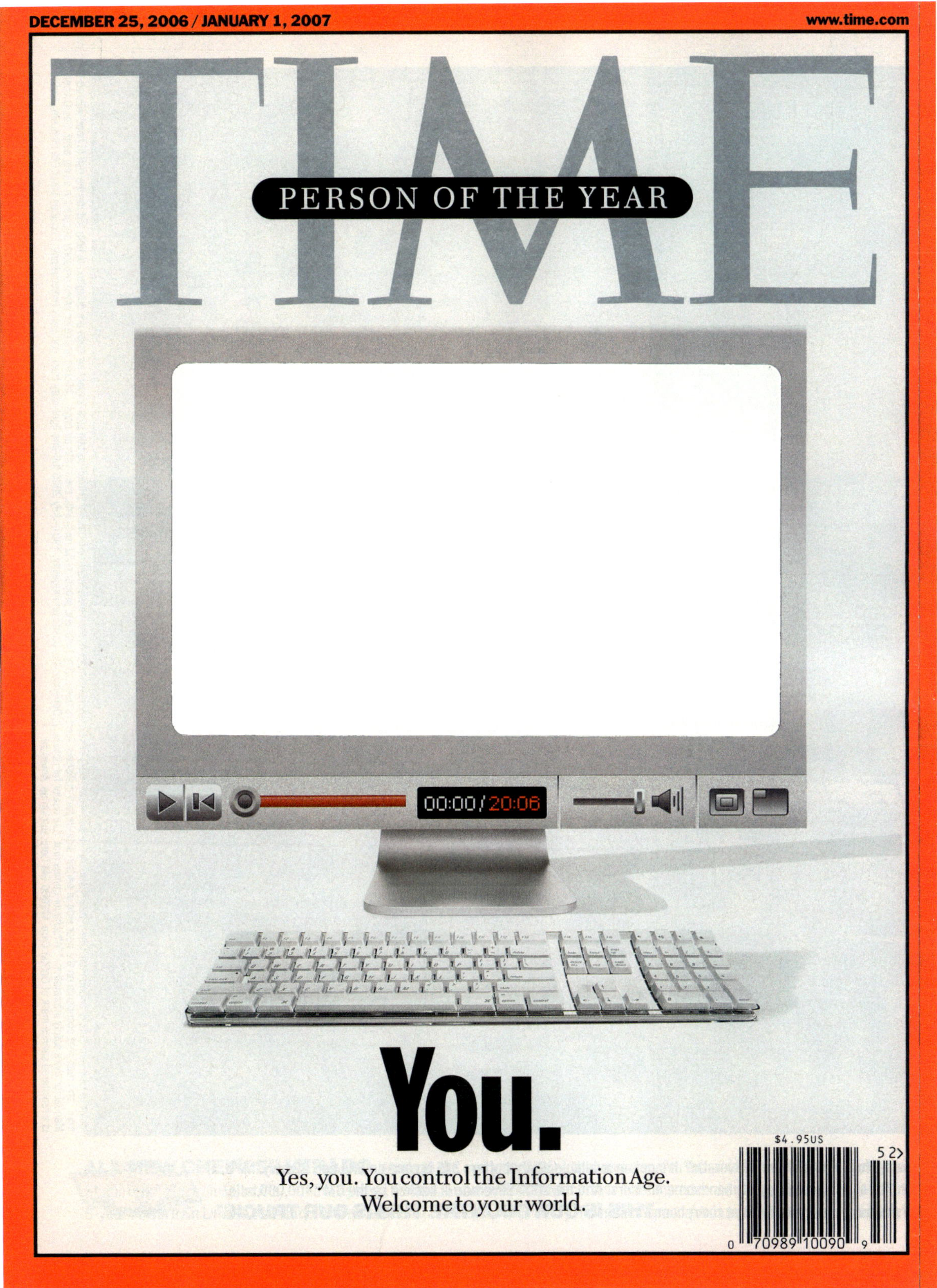


**Web photo offset lithography.** Arthur Hochstein (designer) and Spencer Jones-Glasshouse (photographer). Cover of *Time* magazine, December 25, 2006/January 1, 2007. 10½ x 7¾ in. (26.6 x 19.8 cm). This cover, printed by web offset, has an aluminized plastic mirror stuck on in the monitor area, intended to reflect the reader's face.

## 11.13 OFFSET AS AN ART MEDIUM

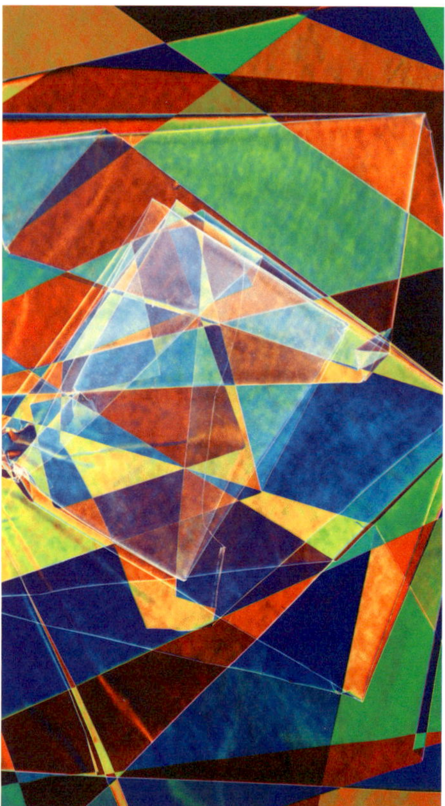

Scott Hyde. *Folded cellophane—Polarized x 3.* 1966. 8½ x 4¾ in. (21.6 x 12 cm)

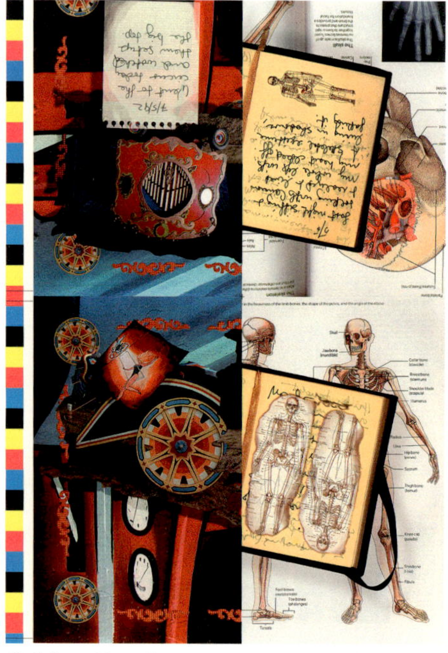

Carl Sesto. Press sheet. 1994. 15¾ x 11¼ in. (40 x 28.6 cm). From *Ordinary Events* (Boston: SMFA Press, 1994). Offset press sheet for a book designed and printed by the artist.

Not too many artists use photo offset lithography as their primary medium. I am one, having done my best work in ink on a single-color offset press (long since junked). Joan Lyons, who made the picture on the right, is another. Syl Labrot—now dead—did remarkable color work in offset, and Lyons, Labrot, Scott Hyde, and Carl Sesto pretty much make up the group I know about. I am sure there are others out there but probably not too many. This is not surprising, because production offset presses are large, expensive, dirty, and dangerous. They had one at Yale in the '70s, in the graduate design department, but it nearly scalped a student once and they had to get rid of it. One has to be extremely careful around sticky ink moving on rotary cylinders at high speed. As if this wasn't bad enough, the artist using this medium also needs to have a copy camera, vacuum frame, arc lamp, and tons of other bits and pieces to have a functioning offset shop.

It is unfortunate that the artist using offset is so rare, because it is a great medium. Ink can be piled up in multiple layers, editions in the few hundreds are easy, and if the inks are chosen carefully, work made this way can be extremely permanent. Small art shops exist for intaglio processes, stone lithography, and fancy letterpress, and some even have offset proof presses on hand, but the pure-offset art shop never really happened. It is even less likely today, because the new digital printing technologies lend themselves beautifully to atelier-scale work. A big inkjet printer, high-end Macintosh computer, and flatbed scanner together cost a fraction of the investment needed for a new offset press.

A tremendous number of older presses are out there in daily use, but ultimately offset will most likely fade away except for large-edition work, done by web printing, and substantial book projects that can justify the initial investment in preparatory work. Maybe fine little two- or four-color presses will then be available cheap, and perhaps a few enterprising souls will grab them and set up private shops, to make art with this great medium even as the digital revolution takes over. A good friend of mine has a printing company with, hidden away among the behemoths, a beautiful little nineteen-by-twenty-five-inch, five-color Heidelberg press. Every time I visit him I make a point of walking by that press to see if they are still using it. When new it must have cost upwards of $500,000, but once obsolete, it won't be worth a nickel. The last time I visited the plant I surreptitiously paced off the length of the machine to see just how much room it took. I could just manage to fit it into my basement workroom.

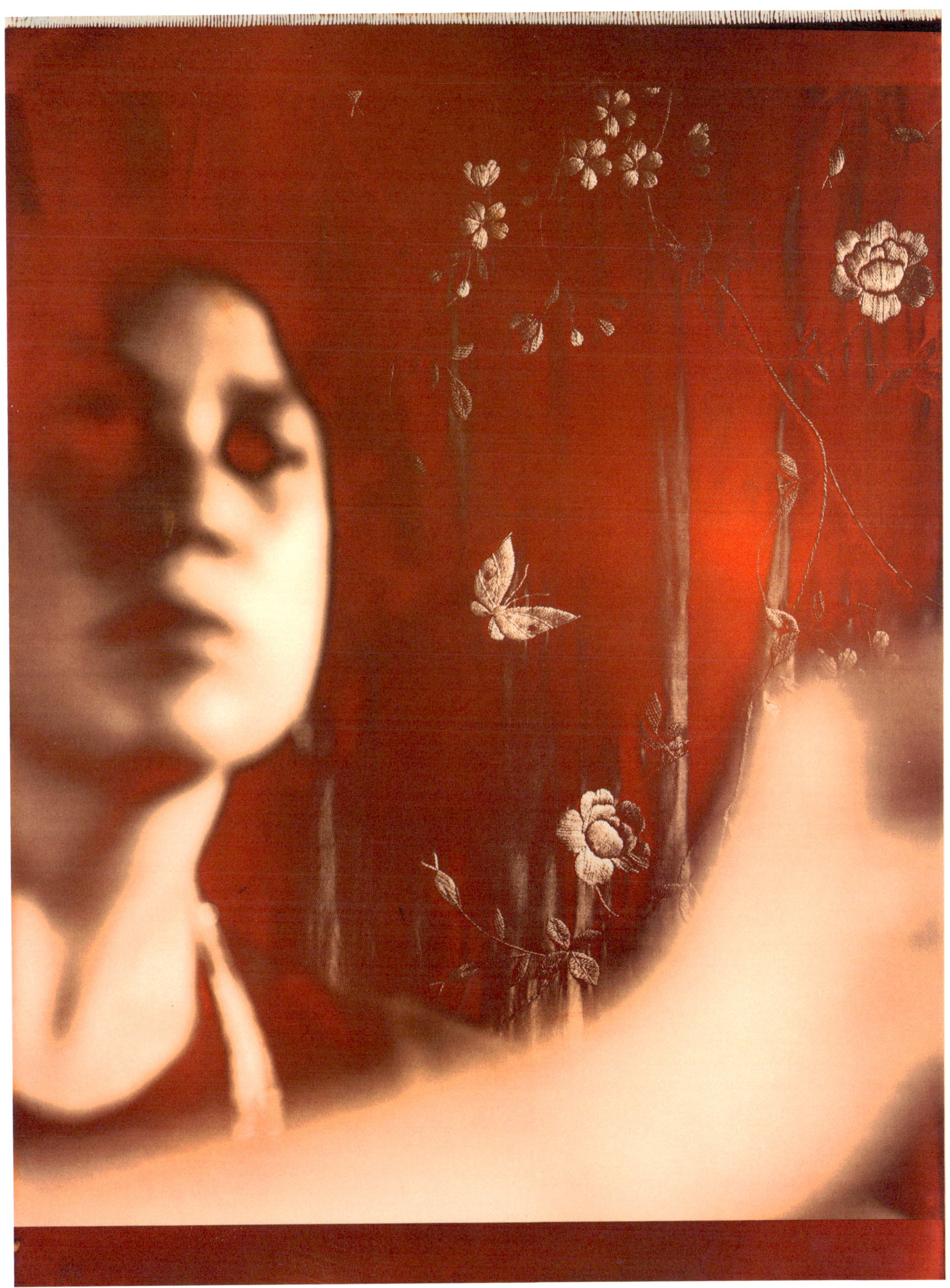

**Photo offset lithography.** Joan Lyons. Untitled, from the portfolio *Presences*. 1980. 22¼ x 16½ in. (56.5 x 41.9 cm). Multipass offset print derived from an original twenty-by-twenty-four-inch Polaroid print.

# Part 12

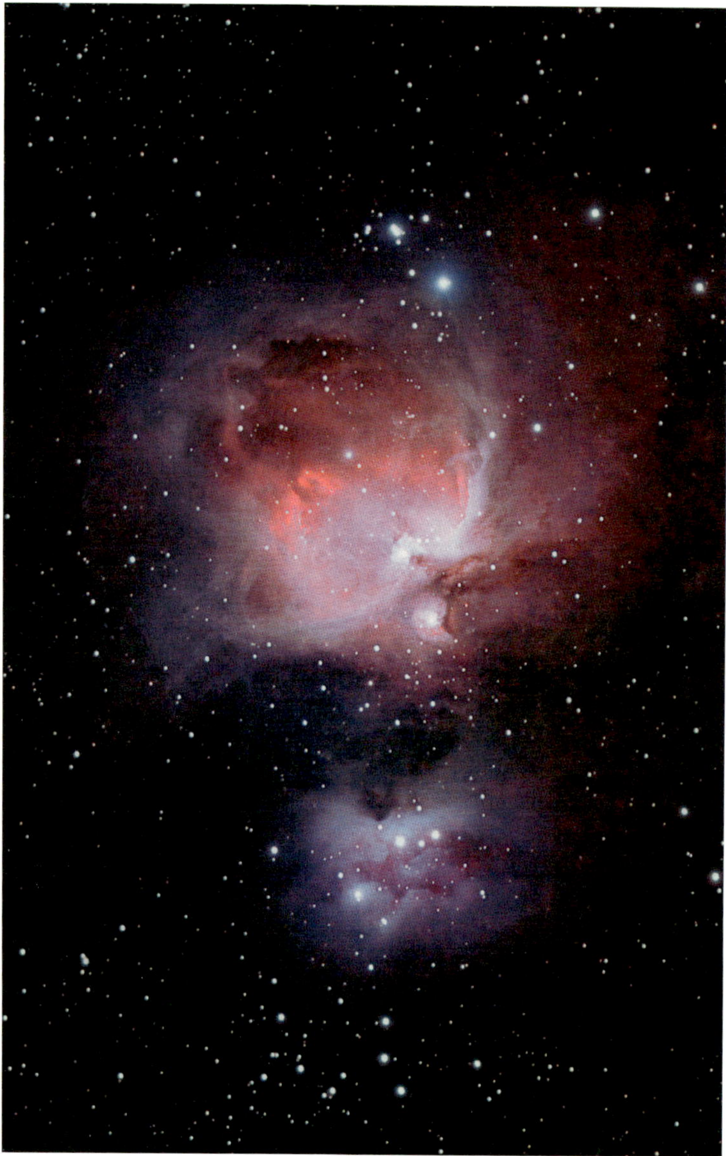

The digital revolution, which first showed its colors in the 1980s, has swept traditional photography away far faster than anyone expected. This book deals with printing, and so ignores the great transformation of cameras from analog to digital devices. But whether used to take pictures or to print them, the old chemical processes are near death and digital media rule the photographic world. Those who don't believe this are almost always over sixty years of age. This section deals—briefly—with some of the new printing systems.

**Photo offset lithography.** Steve Cannistra. *Orion Nebula.* 2004. Taken with a 3½-inch Takahashi refractor and a Canon digital camera, in a 100-minute exposure. Print: 10⅛ x 6½ in. (25.6 x 16.6 cm). Digitally generated web offset reproduction in *Sky and Telescope* magazine, May 2004.

# Digital processes

# Digital processes

## 12.1 THE PIANO ROLL

This is a section of a player piano roll, in which punched holes record the notes for an automated piano to play. The roll does two things: it stores information about the music and it instructs the piano how to play that music. We tend to be muddled about this distinction, perhaps most strikingly in those cocktail-party discussions of the biological code in which we commonly refer to DNA as a blueprint when it is really an active construction tool. The distinction is important, because devices such as this roll are the roots of the digital age, and we can't understand the computer and its power if we aren't clear about what tool does what job. This strip of paper (cut from a far longer roll) acts as a memory device (like our computer's hard drive) but it is also an active tool used in making the music.

The holes in the roll are all round—those that look like long cut-out lines are just a series punched closely together so that they overlap and make a continuously open section. The surface of the paper in any given area is either solid or not, and this division of the sheet into either of two conditions means that the information recorded there is binary. Only two conditions are possible on the paper; there is either a hole or not—nothing exists in between. We have already wrestled with the problem of ink on paper being binary—there is either a black mark, or the white paper, and nothing in between. Much of the technological development in printing has been aimed at getting around the problem of the binary nature of ink—at giving the black bits of pigment the appearance of tone. Here, on the piano roll, we see exactly the opposite going on: the roll has been made to transform the continuous—we say analog—nature of music into a binary code that can store it and then translate it back into sounds. The central activity in the digital age may be the computer's manipulation of numbers, but a huge amount of effort is spent on the task of translation. Information must be translated from some data source in the world into the form in which the computer can handle it, and then, later on, that information must be translated back out, into a new version that may or may not be similar to the form originally imported. The word we use for this translation of information into the computer is "digitized." By this we mean that the smoothly varying information of the world is turned into discrete values that can somehow be stored. In the piano roll those values have a binary form, but we always need to remember that digitization does not necessarily mean something has become binary. We could just as easily turn to a system that used more than two states, such as the method we use to count: for our day-to-day handling of numbers we use ten different ones, and so we say that our counting system is "base ten," whereas the computer does all its work with "base two."

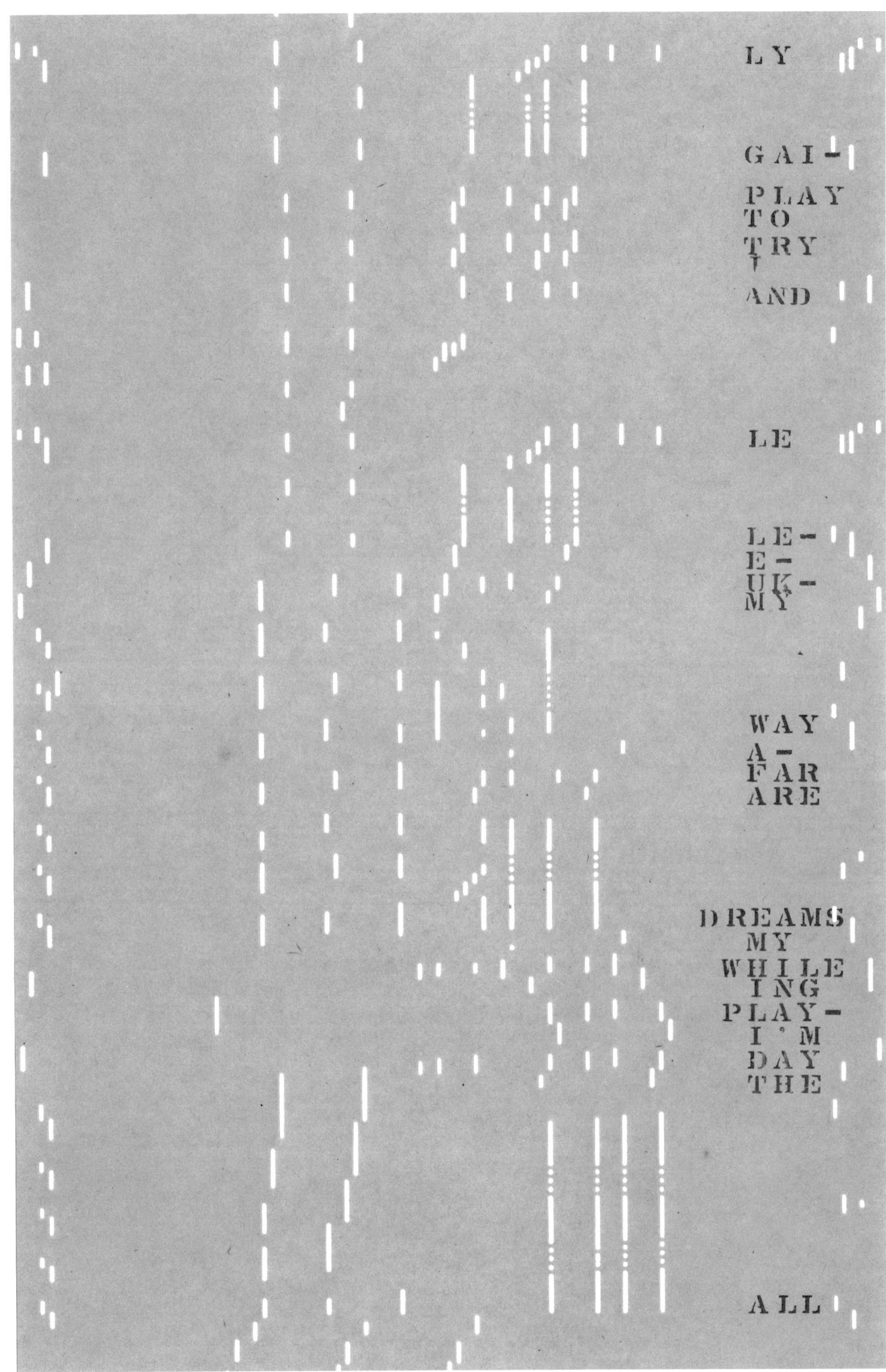


**Punched paper with letterpress text.** Section of a piano roll. c. 1920. 16½ x 10½ in. (41.9 x 26.7 cm). A section of a piano roll holding musical information in the perforated holes and libretto information in printed words to be read by the singer (who appears to be playing the piano). The roll moves downward as it is being played, so time is measured along its length, while bass notes are to the left and treble to the right, so musical tone is described across its width.

## 12.2 IBM PUNCH CARDS

The IBM punch card had its heyday as a data-storage tool from the 1930s to the 1960s. One interesting thing that these cards did, aside from storing data, was translate binary information into electrical signals. Small conductive brushes rested against the card as it was read. If a hole was present, a current flowed; if the paper was solid, it did not. The punched hole was really a switch, and this notion of a switch that was turned either on or off became the basis of the electronic computer. This book is not a history of the computer—and I am certainly not qualified to write such a thing—but we have to understand some of the principles underlying these devices because the computer and its peripherals will shortly be handling every piece of photography and printing that is done. I exaggerate a bit, because there will always be folks who use film and old printing presses, but they—and their work—are already firmly stuck on the banks of the technological river that is sweeping the rest of us away from our solid old analog roots.

If we were to pick the best word to describe the precomputer age of technology, it would have to be "analog." An analog is some physical structure that emulates the form of another. The tones in a black and white photographic negative are a simple analog of the illumination that fell upon that negative during the period of its exposure. The silver deposits change across the negative in continuous variations in density, with one tone smoothly turning into the next. This analog is a simple one because color has been left out; by using black and white film we have chosen to select only a part of the incoming information for our record. That selection, however, is not only smooth and accurate but appears to be continuous and uninterrupted. Until we enlarge it so highly that grains of silver appear, we believe that we are seeing actual tonality in the negative. When such a "continuous tone" negative is digitally scanned into a computer, its information is chopped up into discrete values, each assigned to a particular point on the negative's surface as a numerical record of the tonal density at that point. Because the computer is electronic, this digitization is in binary form, so that it can be handled by switches turned either on or off. The translation is very similar to the one we see on these IBM cards, with one, major exception: the data in the negative is translated into a tremendous number of values, far more than in the relatively crude cards we see here. Like halftone dots on the printed page, digital information must be plentiful, and must shrink below the resolution of our senses, if it is successfully to imitate the analog from which it derives.

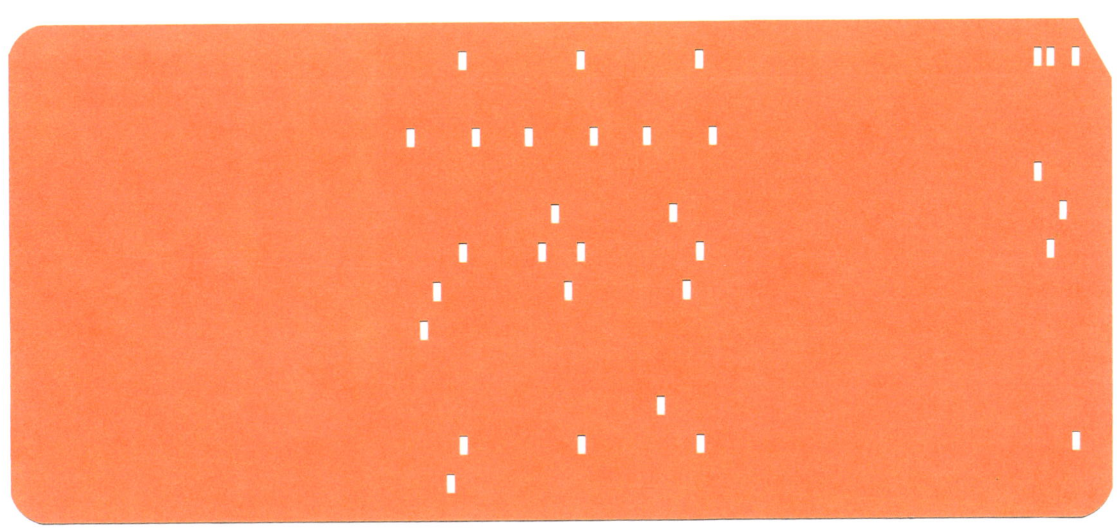

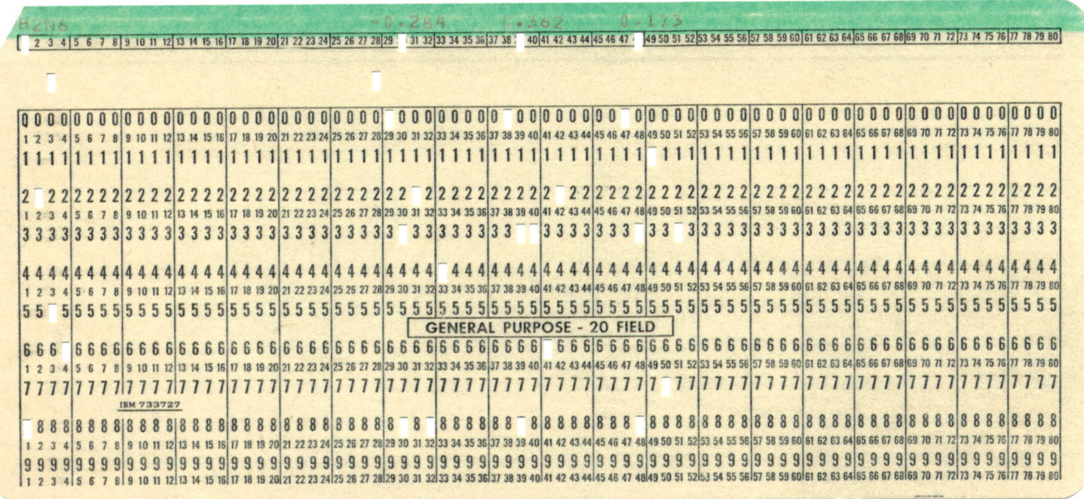



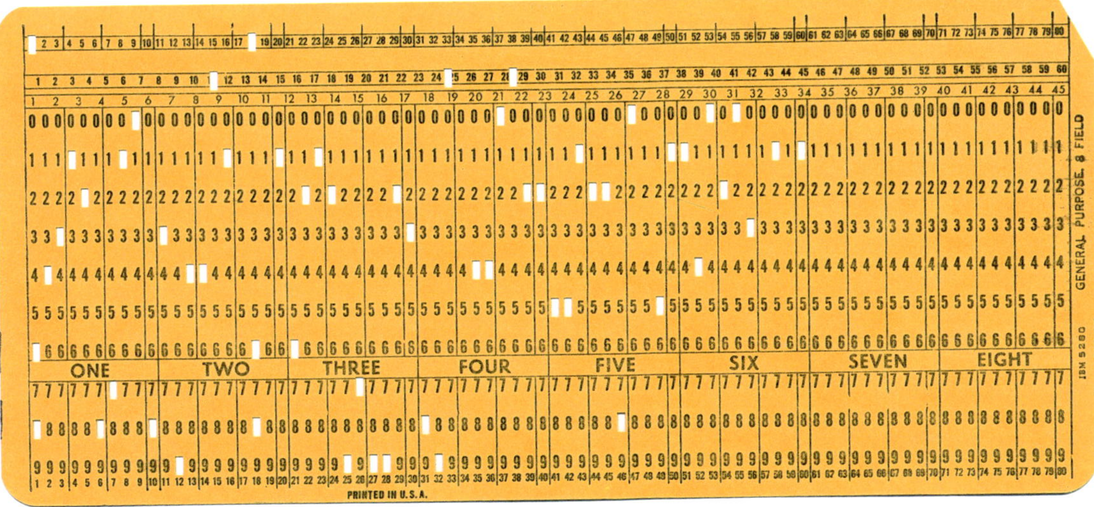



**Punched paper with photo offset text.** IBM punch cards. c. 1956. Each: 3¼ x 7⅜ in. (8.3 x 18.7 cm)

## 12.3 LASER PRINTS

The earliest electronically driven prints — that is to say, those directed by an electrical signal rather than by light — were crude images sent through radio or by telegraph to printers that burned their data onto specialized paper. Electronic printing didn't become really common until the spread of the Xerox machine, invented in the 1920s but not widely used until a couple of decades later. The Xerox made copies by brightly illuminating a document — usually black letters on a white sheet — and using the light reflected from it to create a pattern in a static electric charge on a specially prepared plate. The charge on this plate was used to attract oppositely charged black toner onto a sheet of paper, and that deposit was then set by heat, to make a permanent copy. The sensitive plate was usually cylindrical, and the copy machine thus made could produce readable copies rapidly and cheaply.

The Xerox machine underwent a major transformation when new versions were developed that received the image not from a brightly lit sheet but from a binary-driven laser. The light from the laser would dispel the static charge on the plate in any area it struck, and if the beam was finely focused, and turned off and on rapidly, it could lay down a pattern of dots that could form not just letters but also pictures. The letters were built up out of closely spaced black dots — often as fine as 600 per linear inch (this means 360,000 dots per square inch) — but to create the illusion of tone in reproducing pictures, these dots had to be grouped into larger dots, laid down in patterns that emulated the old printer's halftone.

The new laser-printer halftones were quite crude. When a fine array of dots is used to produce a halftonelike pattern, there is an interlock between resolution and tonal gradation. The easiest way to describe this is to say that a halftone (which the laser could build up out of even finer dots than before) might have a certain number of tonal steps, but a version of that halftone with coarser resolution — say half the resolution — might have as many as four times more tonal steps available to it. This is because the laser can build up halftone dots in a larger number of sizes if it has a larger grid to work in — the fewer the halftone dots per inch, the more dots from the laser are available to build up each one. But a larger grid for each halftone dot means coarser resolution of the halftone. Tonal images printed by laser printers can be highly detailed with limited tonality, or tonally complex with low resolution.

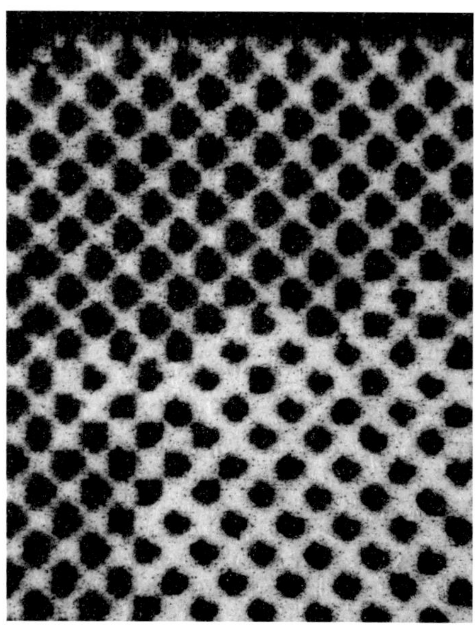

The laser printer has very low resolution and its dots can only be printed as a solid black. In this detail we see the coarse halftone generated by clumping the laser dots together. The halftone pattern thus created is about fifty-six dots per linear inch, seen here enlarged ten times from the print.

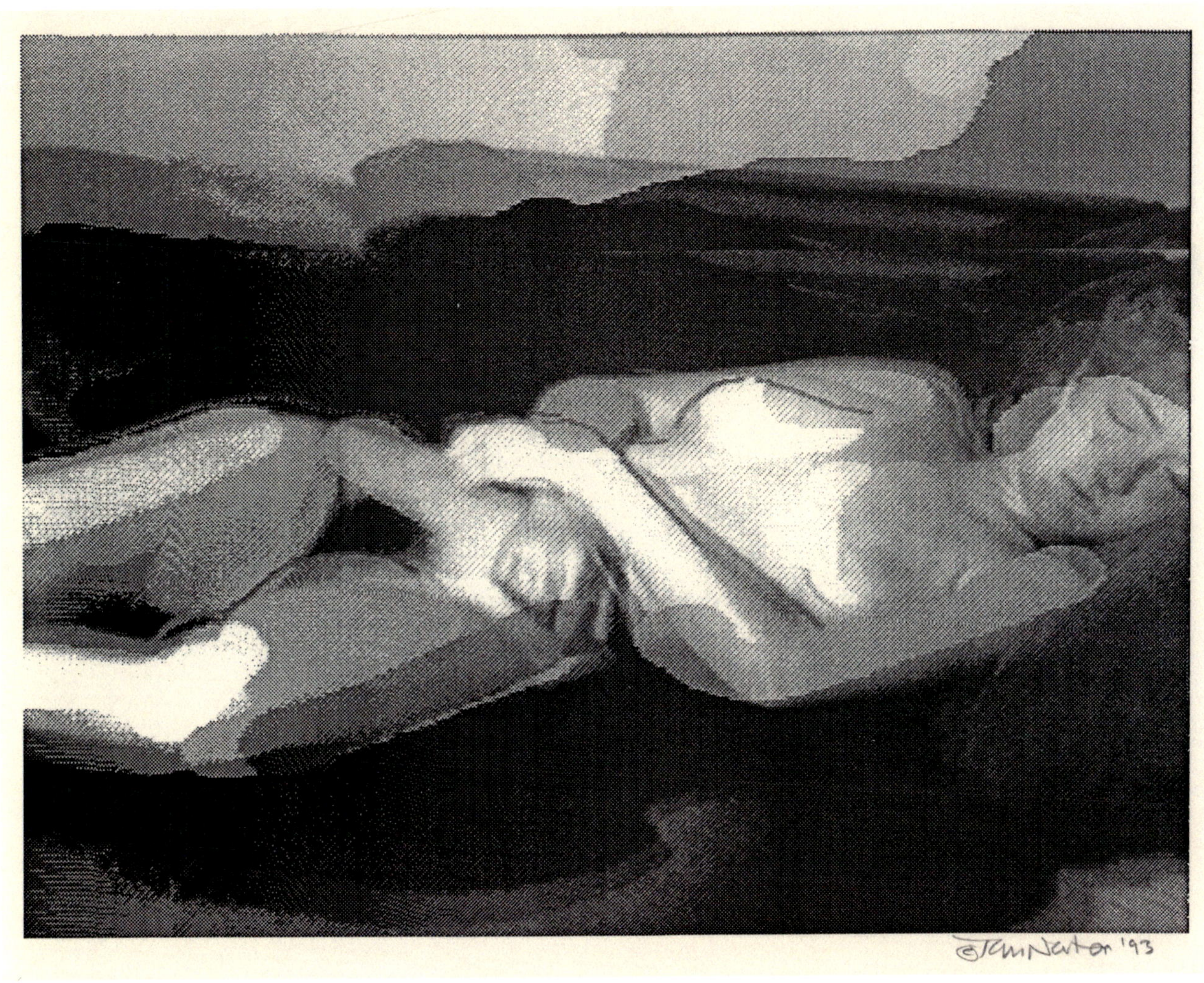


**LaserWriter print.** Tom Norton. Untitled. 1993. 7⅛ x 9⅛ in. (18 x 23.2 cm)

## 12.4 THE CANON COLOR COPIER

In 1987 the Canon company produced a laser copier that made instant images in full color. As in the Xerox machine, the original was laid down on a flat scanning bed and the image was drawn by a laser, but in this case there were four separate drums—one each for cyan, magenta, yellow, and black—that had to have the appropriate static images built on them. Quite early on in the color copier's life, firms were making computer interfaces for them that allowed them not just to copy a preexisting piece of flat art but to print a digital file.

The image quality of these machines is quite high. The toners used are superb and very stable, and the images suffer mainly from an irregularly shiny surface—the toner deposit is often shinier than the paper support, leading to an odd, uneven reflectivity. Today all the small instant-print shops have versions of these color copiers, which are manufactured in a variety of brands and types. A few companies (Xerox, Canon, and Agfa among them) decided to turn the laser-driven color copier into a professional production machine, seeking out a market for high-end printing of books and small publications on demand, to avoid the need to produce large print runs before knowing whether or not a given publication would sell. This potential market is the same one that is pursued by the Indigo printer, which is described in section 13.5. Print-on-demand bookmaking languished for a while, although the technology was already available, but today many small printshops and university copy centers offer such a service. If the binding and page sizes are standardized these small-edition publications can be quite inexpensive.

I haven't seen much original art done with color copiers, but prints made by these devices are everywhere. A good family snapshot might be copied to make a dozen or so for family members, or a unique watercolor might be copied and framed to be sold to tourists in some waterfront shop. The trouble with all this is that these prints are copies and decidedly inferior to the originals. The colors tend to be saturated, and they have often been falsely sharpened, but even so these second-generation prints are commonly mistaken for originals. Anyone collecting old prints should always bring a magnifying glass along to check that prints for sale are not just color copies. The detail on the left shows the fine parallel lines characteristic of the toner deposits from most of these copiers. The resolution on these machines is so fine that they can also emulate the traditional halftone, which gives them a better tonal scale, but with an obvious large halftone dot.

The Canon color copier lays down its toner in a linear pattern, in which the intensity of the lines varies to create changes in tone and color. This detail is enlarged approximately twelve times from the original print.

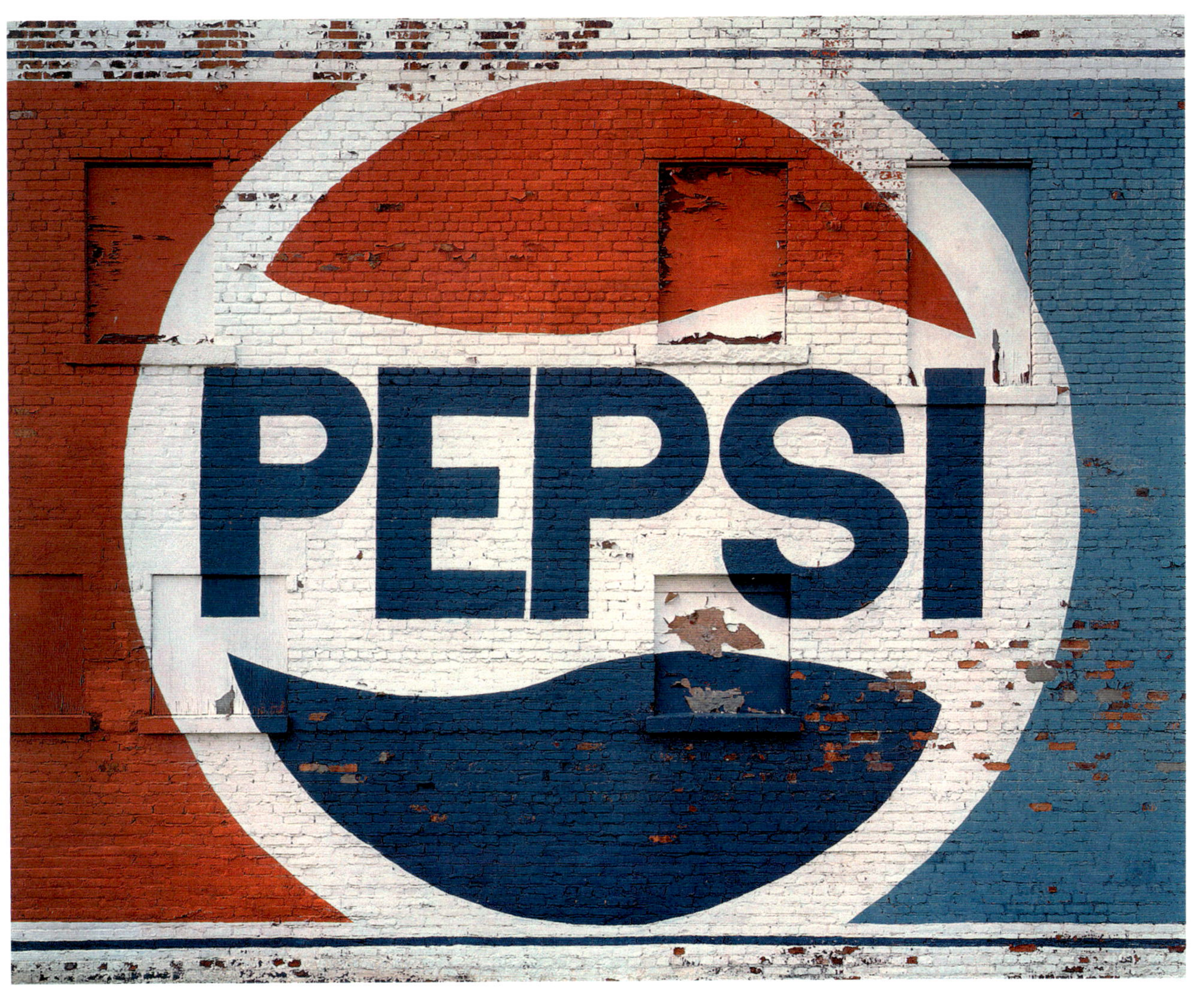


**Canon color copier print.** Richard Benson. *Pepsi Sign.* 1994. 10 x 12⅝ in. (25.4 x 32 cm). This print was made from a digital file produced by scanning an eight-by-ten-inch transparency.

## 12.5 DIGITAL HALFTONES AND STOCHASTIC PRINTING

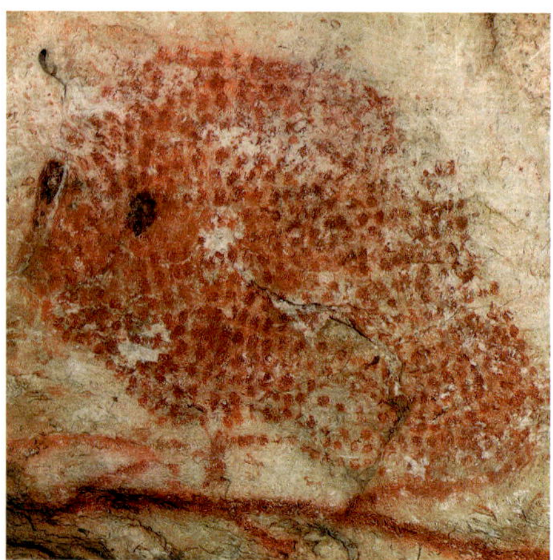

This painting, dating from about 15,000 years ago, is from the cave at Marsoulas in southern France. The image has been built up by blowing dots of red pigment onto the cave wall; this pictorial form, of assembling a picture with random dots, is virtually identical to the stochastic printing used by some digital printers today.

The old printer's halftone dot was an analog creature, not a digital one. It was binary—which is to say that densities in the halftone negative were either completely opaque or completely clear—but the dot itself varied smoothly in size, from a tiny black dot for the highlights of a print to a tiny white dot, in a black field, for a dark tone. These variations in size were an analog of the tones in the picture. When printing went digital the computer developers faced the problem of how to render this dot with the new tools.

The solution was to use an exposure device, called an "imagesetter," with far higher resolution than the halftone dots themselves. When digitally generated film is to be exposed to make a halftone negative for use on an offset printing plate, the exposure device is a fine laser, of the same sort used in a laser printer. If the laser resolution is high enough, it can build up a representation of the halftone dot within a small grid by simply adding more laser dots for each step up in the density required in the final print. If the laser can expose 2,400 dots per linear inch, and a final halftone resolution of 200 dots per linear inch is desired, then the grid within which each dot is built will be 12 laser points per side. Each square in the grid can then fit up to 144 laser dots. A highlight (in a positive piece of film) might be 4 dots clustered together. A mid-tone would be 72 laser dots, set together to emulate a round dot covering half the area of the grid. For a dark shadow tone, nearly black, the grid square would be completely covered with exposed points on the film except for a small group left clear, clustered together, to make a white dot in a black field. By building the image up to emulate the old halftone dot, digital technology can deliver a structure that is virtually identical to the one made by the earlier halftone screens. This makes the offset printers happy.

Stochastic screening was a natural extension of this practice. As the offset presses became better and better, and capable of printing extremely fine dots, some smart character figured out that the tiny laser points didn't need to be clustered to imitate a coarse halftone. In stochastic screening the dots are laid down in the grid in a random pattern, still covering the right percentage of the grid to represent the tone needed in any area, but arrayed as tiny marks in a random pattern. The grain of this pattern can be far finer than in the halftone. Images screened this way have no visible halftone dot when seen by the naked eye, but the resolution of the image is the same as though a coarse dot were still being used. The resolution is determined by the grid size, which remains the same in either case.

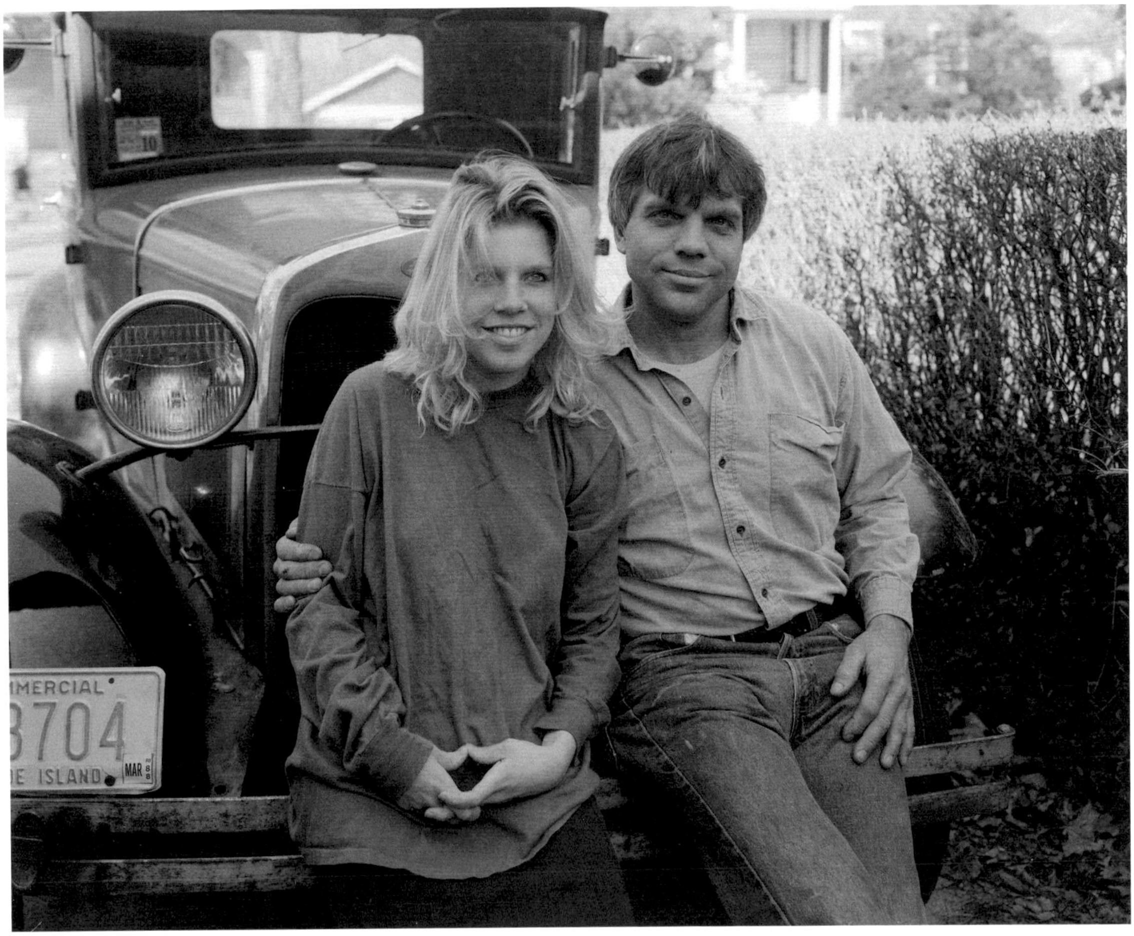

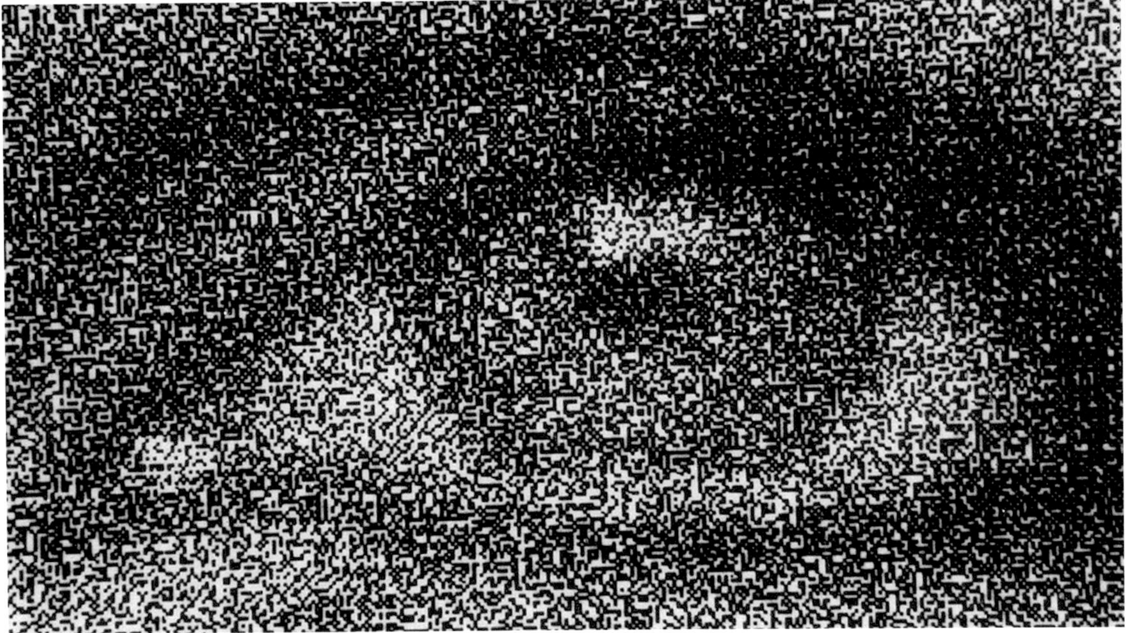

**Stochastic print.** Richard Benson. *Richard and Tanya Donnelly.* 1989. Print: 1994. 11 x 13¾ in. (28 x 35 cm). A gelatin silver print made by loading photographic paper into a film imagesetter designed for producing halftone film.

## 12.6 IRIS PRINTS

The great digital machine that ushered in the computer age of fine printing was the Iris printer. These inkjet printers were developed in the late 1980s as proofing devices for offset presses. They enjoyed limited success in this role because it turned out to be extremely difficult to make their inkjet image closely resemble the ink-printed halftone image that came out of the large offset printing presses. There were other color proofing systems out there, and the Iris never could compete with them. What these machines did do was make magnificent photographic prints on a wide variety of papers. The Iris used a large, rapidly rotating drum to hold the paper and a set of jets to put down a fine spray of ink. These jets were connected to ink tanks by flexible hoses, which allowed them to move slowly along the drum, parallel to its axis, to cover the entire area to be printed. The machine could lay down both fine lines of ink or ink drops of different sizes in a stochastic pattern.

In the beginning, the Iris inks were pretty much just water containing dyes similar to food coloring. The deposits were so delicate that any spot of water that fell on them would create a mark, and sunlight faded the image very badly. These difficulties were finally overcome with the development both of better dyes and of various coatings that absorbed ultraviolet light, and that were sprayed onto the prints to improve their stability. Iris prints began to get a foothold in fine-art printing, and at one point some ambitious marketeer decided to call them "giclée" prints. This deeply stupid name has led many a purchaser to think they have some rarefied creature hanging on their wall when all it is is an inkjet print. "Giclée" has now been applied to prints made with any inkjet printer, so the purchaser of one of these prints can't even be sure of getting an Iris print.

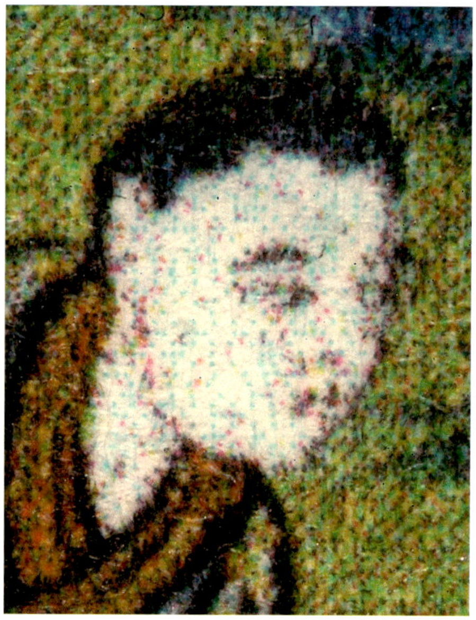

The Iris printer created, for the first time, marvelous photographic prints with highly saturated colors on a truly matte surface. Papers were made with matte surfaces for traditional, chemical color photography, but those papers had always produced inferior colors. The legacy of the Iris, which continues today in all the small- and wide-format inkjet printers, is to produce soft, matte yet intense colors, unlike any that had been seen before. Black and white photographers had the platinum print for matte images but there was no comparable method for color. If an Iris was made on a good rag paper, with the correct sizing, it could produce a tonal scale unmatched even today. Unfortunately a lot of poor pictures were made on fancy paper, complete with deckle edges and sold as high art, but when an Iris print was right, nothing could touch it for out-and-out image quality. There are still a few Iris printers in use, but the superb modern inkjet printers have driven the Iris into obsolescence.

The stochastic dot pattern we see here, enlarged approximately twenty times from the Iris print, appears as cyan, magenta, yellow, and black dots. These tiny points of ink do not vary in value; a dot is either there or not. Because of this go-or-no-go system, any tonal variation must be generated by controlling the number of dots that go down in a given area.

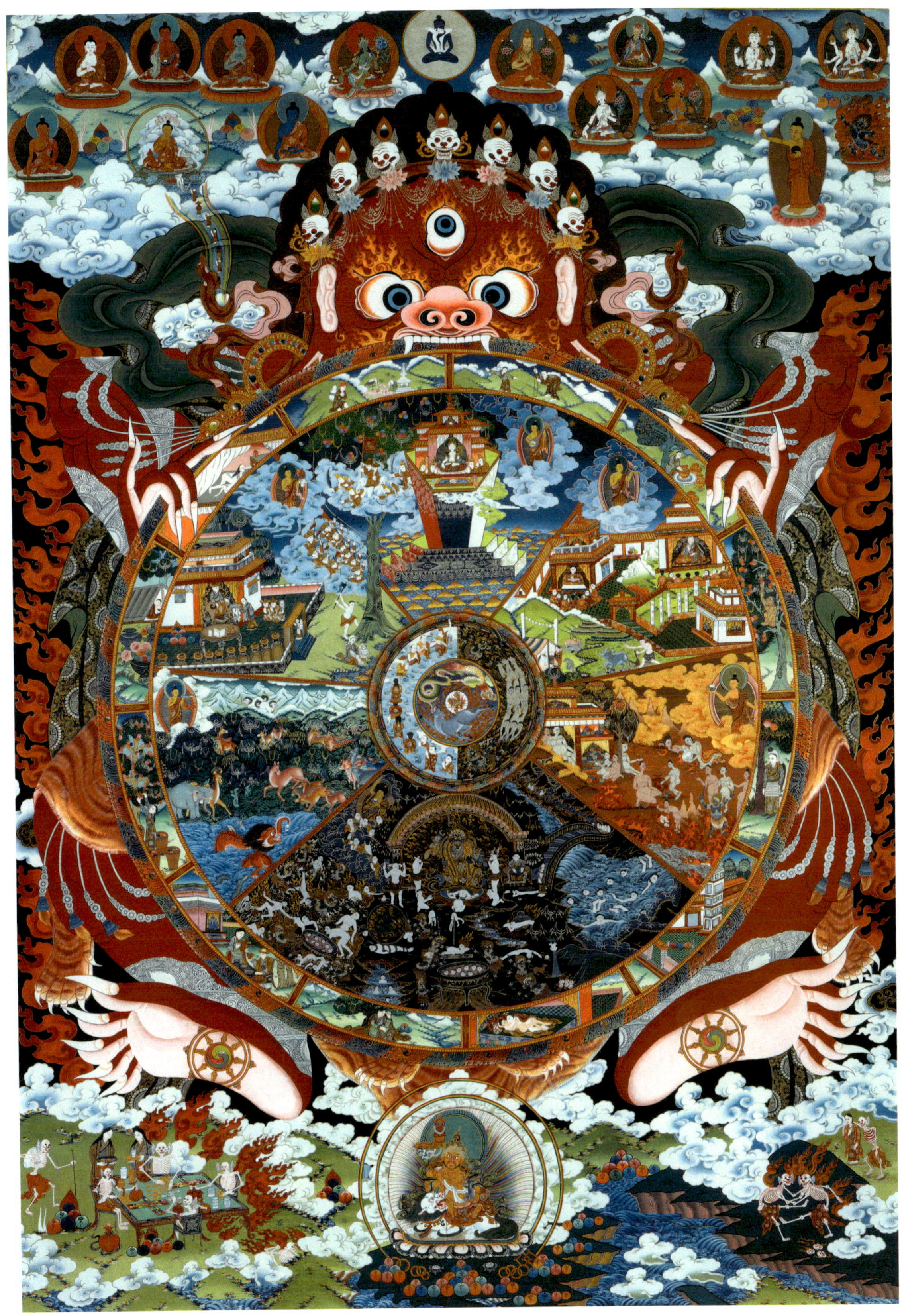

**Iris print.** Workshop of Romio Shrestha. *The Wheel of Deluded Existence.* c. 1995. Tempera on canvas.
Print: Laumont Editions. 1999. 21¼ x 15¾ in. (54 x 40 cm)

This twenty-five-times enlargement from the print shows the soft squares of tone generated from the black dye layer in this black and white print. Unlike a hard halftone or stochastic dot, these patches of dye have variable tonality, deriving from the modulated heat used to transfer the dye.

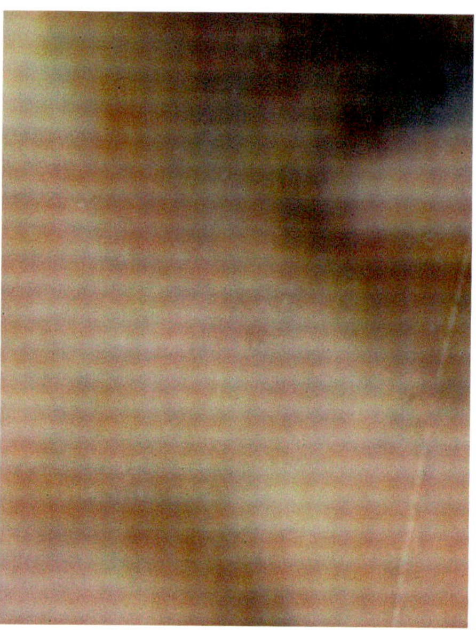

These patches from the color print to the right are also enlarged approximately twenty-five times.

## 12.7 DYE-SUBLIMATION PRINTING

Very early on in the digital upheaval a completely new kind of photographic printer appeared. Called the "dye sublimation" printer, it used tiny heating elements to force a dye onto a receiver sheet. The prints it made were usually eight by ten inches in size, although I remember one model that went up to eleven by seventeen; I don't know of any that went larger than that. The first one I saw was at a small digital workshop up in Camden, Maine, that was funded by the Eastman Kodak Company. The printer, called a Kodak 7000, was an odd-looking device, plain in design, with a pair of handles on the front. It only took me a minute to realize that it had been designed to slip into a rack, like those that held radio equipment in the ham-radio age. I asked the Kodak technician why the machines were designed that way and he said it was so they could fit into the racks of the B-52 bombers for which they were made. These printers were developed so that instant color prints of targets could be generated right on the plane. Like so much other technology that we love, this one came to us from the military.

The dye-sub printer uses a long roll of clear acetate holding solid layers of dye in the three subtractive primaries and black. When a print is made, a special sheet of paper is drawn into the printer and held next to one of the dye layers on its acetate support. Together they are wrapped around a drum. A set of heating elements—200 per linear inch—is lined up across the drum, to be selectively fired by the digital file holding the picture information for that color. As the paper/dye combination moves beneath these heaters, the dye is activated and moves over to the paper receiver. Once a single layer of dye has transferred, the paper is aligned with the section of the acetate sheet holding the next color and the heating operation is repeated, again driven by a file for that color. This is done four times; finally the machine ejects a completed color print. After a single print is made, the length of the acetate support holding the used-up areas is rolled up and a fresh section is ready for the next print.

Dye-sublimation prints look very much like traditional chromogenic prints. They have terrific colors—saturated and smooth—and their surface is usually moderately gloss (although matte paper supports are also made). These printers can also make superb black and white prints, using only the black section of the color band. When examined by magnifying glass the dye appears in soft squares, 40,000 to the square inch. Because the values within each square vary in tone and color, they assemble together smoothly to the unaided eye and look like a high-resolution continuous-tone print. The old halftone screen, in sharply defined solid colors, shows up easily at this same resolution, but the dye sub's soft, particulate structure disappears, just like the stippling in chromolithography that was discussed in sections 3.4 and 3.5.

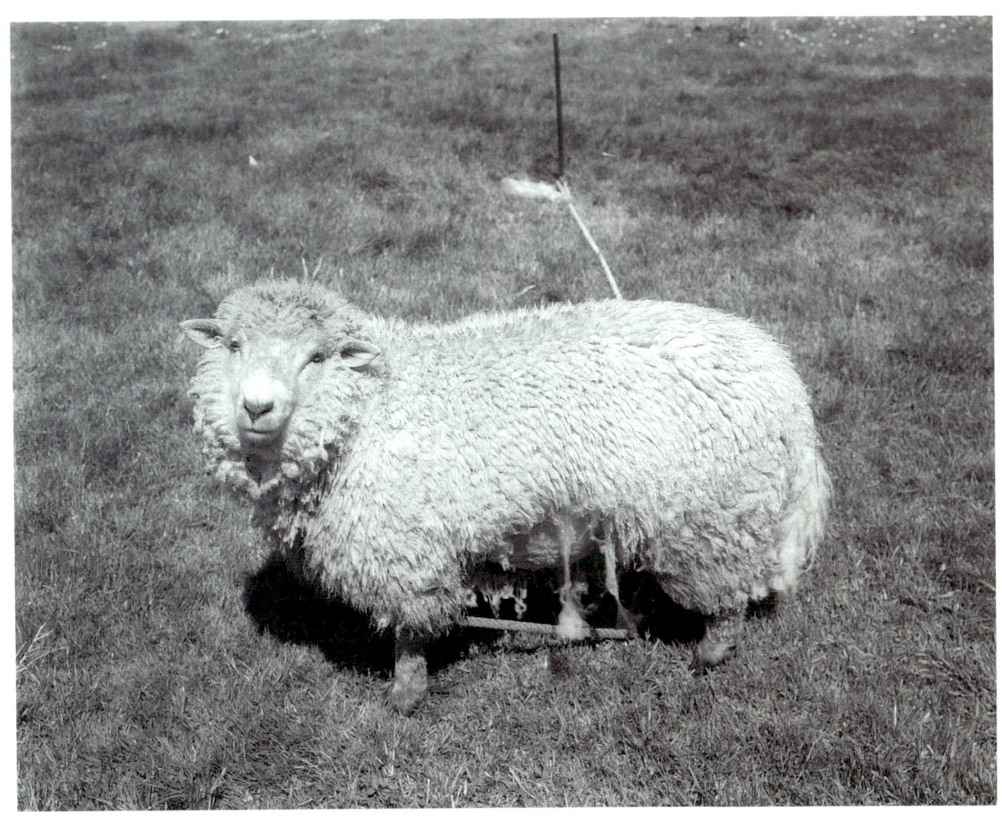

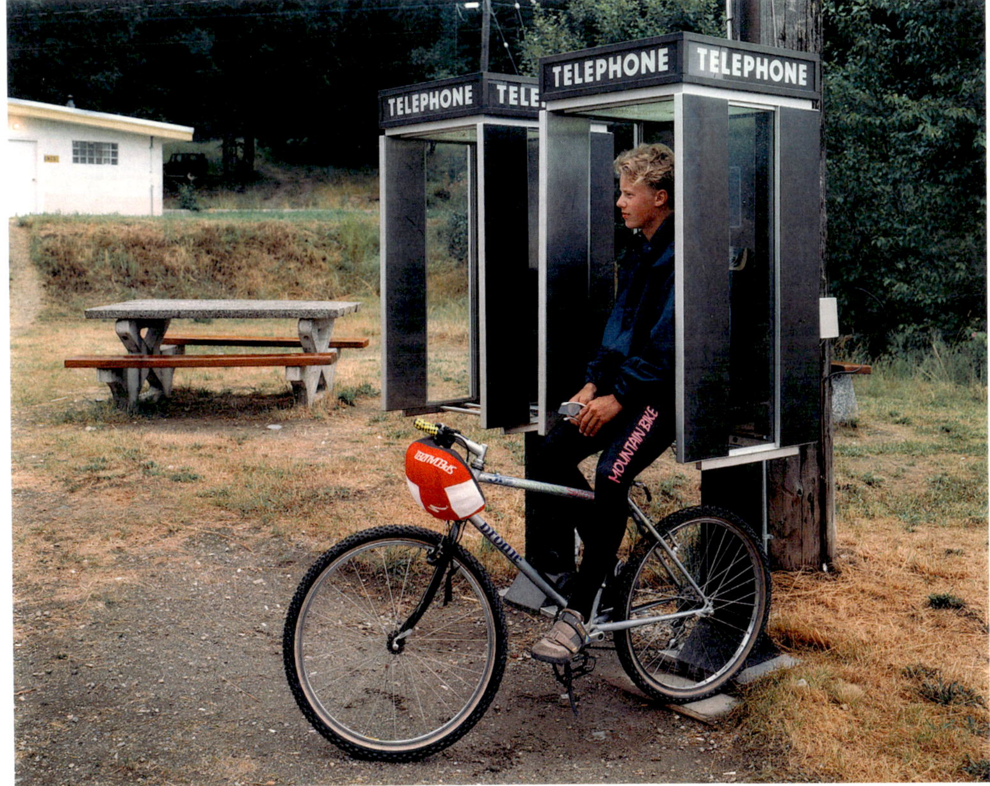


**Dye-sublimation print.** Richard Benson. Top: *Tethered Sheep.* 1995. Bottom: *Boy on Bicycle.* 1995. Prints: 1998. Each: 7½ x 9½ in. (19 x 24.1 cm). A black and white print from the black dye layer only and a four-color print using all four dye layers.

## 12.8 EARLY INKJET PRINTS

Even prior to the Iris printer, crude inkjet printers were used to produce architectural drawings. Called "plotters," these devices used black ink and could turn a computer file into a large drawing to be used in construction projects. The old method of making working copies of drawings was to use a chemical process, such as blueprinting, to reproduce a handmade drawing. The plotter produced a paper version of a drawing that had been made with a computer illustration program, opening the door for the large staffs of draftsmen in architectural firms to become smaller groups of computer operators.

The plotter soon had colored inks, to allow the emulation of drawings with color. (We must always remember the power of color to sell things, whether in a meeting called to sell a wealthy client on an architectural design or on Wal-Mart packaging.) It wasn't long before these machines were used to make prints of photographs, and by the early 1990s a few manufacturers were producing them as wide-format color photographic printers. This particular print is one I made around that time, by scanning an eight-by-ten-inch Ektachrome transparency with an early drum scanner (to make a thirty-megabyte file, which at the time I thought was immense). The print has pretty good color, only a few streaks, and quite a heavy rendition of the shadow areas. The paper I used was designed to dry the ink rapidly and looks like a sheet of plastic.

The early plotters adapted to photographic use had a relatively coarse dot pattern; this detail is enlarged eight times from the print.

The early inkjet printers differed from the Iris printer in that the printing head moved rapidly back and forth across the sheet of paper and after each "pass" the paper advanced a tiny bit so another line of dots could be laid down. The rapidly rotating drum of the Iris, holding a large piece of paper, was eliminated. Since there was no reason to imitate the old halftone, the printers used stochastic screening, and they underwent steady refinement, with new models coming out every year or so. Before long the inkjet printer shook off its architectural roots and became a superb color printing device, laying dots down at a resolution far higher than could be seen by the naked eye. Some of these machines were large, able to print pictures forty-four inches wide by any length, but a whole new type was developed that printed on letter-size or slightly bigger paper. These little machines—desktop printers to accompany the desktop computer—were cheap to buy but expensive to use, because their economic basis was the sale of ink. A printer for letters and family photographs might cost less than $100, but within a very short time the buyer would have spent more than that on ink if a lot of picture printing was done. The machines came with a set of ink cartridges, so the owner became hooked on the new prints well before having to face the $20 cost for each replacement.

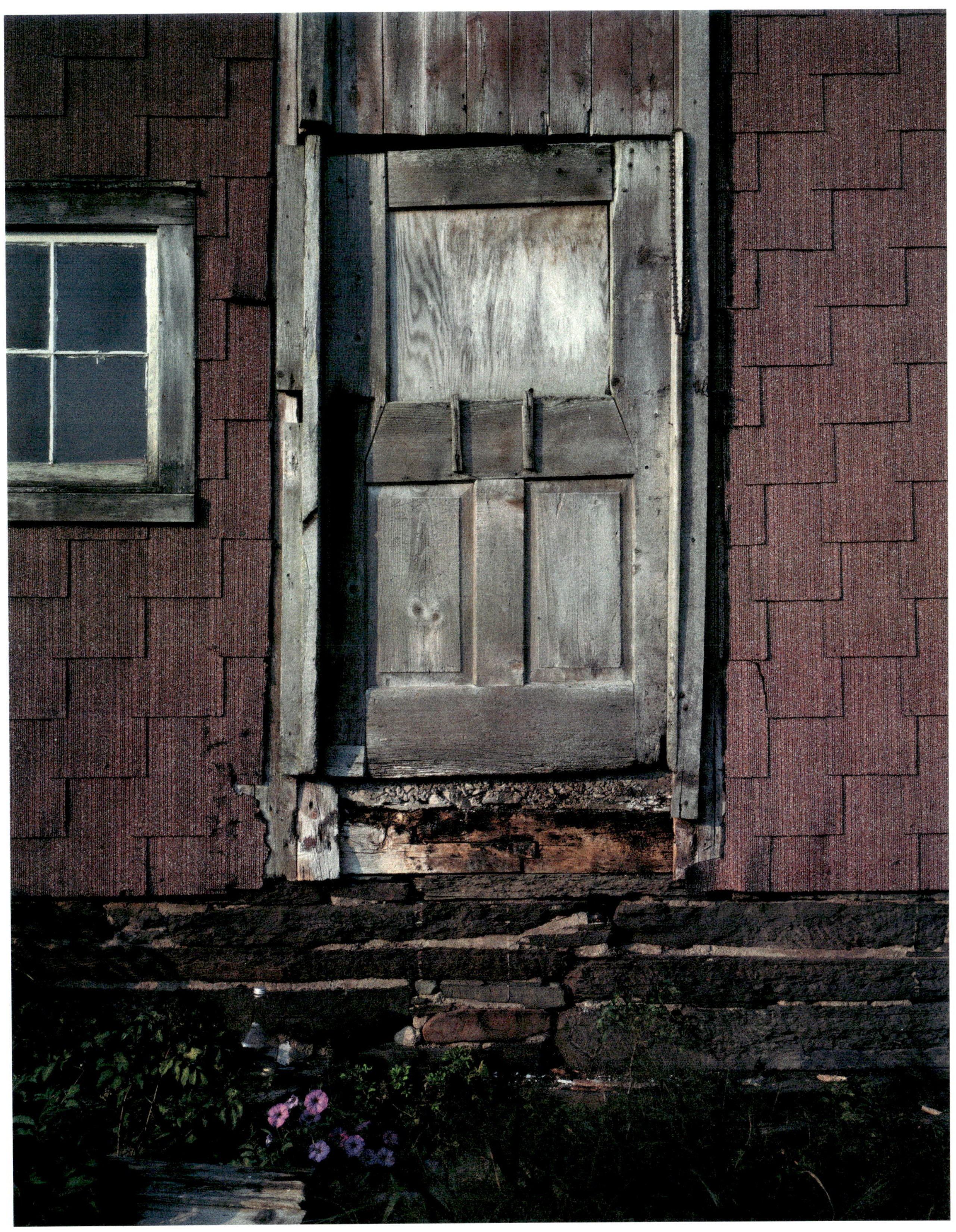

**Hewlett-Packard plotter print.** Richard Benson. *New York State Barn.* 1993. 19⅜ x 15½ in. (49.2 x 39.4 cm)

## 12.9 MODERN INKJET PRINTING

Even though the inks cost a lot, desktop inkjet printers are absolutely wonderful. We need to remember that all the old chemical materials were even more expensive, due to the presence of silver in their coatings. With the new digital printers we become frustrated at the cost of the inks but conveniently forget that we use these machines to make far more prints than we ever made in the darkroom. Had we tried back then to predict what printing device would come out of the computer age, we would never have dreamed up these printers. They are inexpensive, rarely break, print rapidly, and make prints that look as though they have the full tonal and color range of an actual chemical print. This last attribute comes because the technology of the print head has made extraordinary strides. On the best machines these tiny jets, grouped for each color, are able to put down droplets of ink at a resolution of 2,880 per linear inch, which means that a single square inch, if fully covered, could hold over eight million separate deposits. The computers themselves—their memories and processors—have all grown in speed and data-handling capacity to match the ability of the printers to lay down ink. We tend to ignore the miraculous technological path that is traveled every time we click a computer's print button.

As the inkjet printer evolved, the dot structure became finer; this detail has been enlarged approximately twelve times from the print.

Inkjet prints do have some problems. In the beginning, prints made this way tended to fade badly, but by this time (2007) the dyes and pigments used in the best inks are even more permanent than those in the older chemical chromogenic print. There is still a fragility to the prints, partly because they are sensitive to bad chemistry in the air, but also because the ink deposits are physically delicate. The old chemical prints could be manhandled and still remain intact—a pile of silver prints could be shuffled around and perhaps some surface scratching would occur, but the prints would probably still be OK. Do this with a pile of inkjet prints and very soon every one will be ruined. This is such a problem that when I print my own pictures and manage to get a good one, I immediately put it in an overmat, reversing my forty-year-old habit of storing photographs in unprotected piles. You would think that a replacement could be made simply by pressing the print button again, but computers, software, printers, and inks change so rapidly that one never knows if a good print can be made again. Perhaps the most irritating problem with the inkjet prints is that they look very different under different viewing lights. A print that is fine under tungsten light turns quite green under daylight and might shift to red when viewed under fluorescent light. The ink-makers are gradually solving this problem, called "metamerism," but even today a great-looking inkjet print can take on a distressing color cast when viewed under different conditions from those for which it was made.

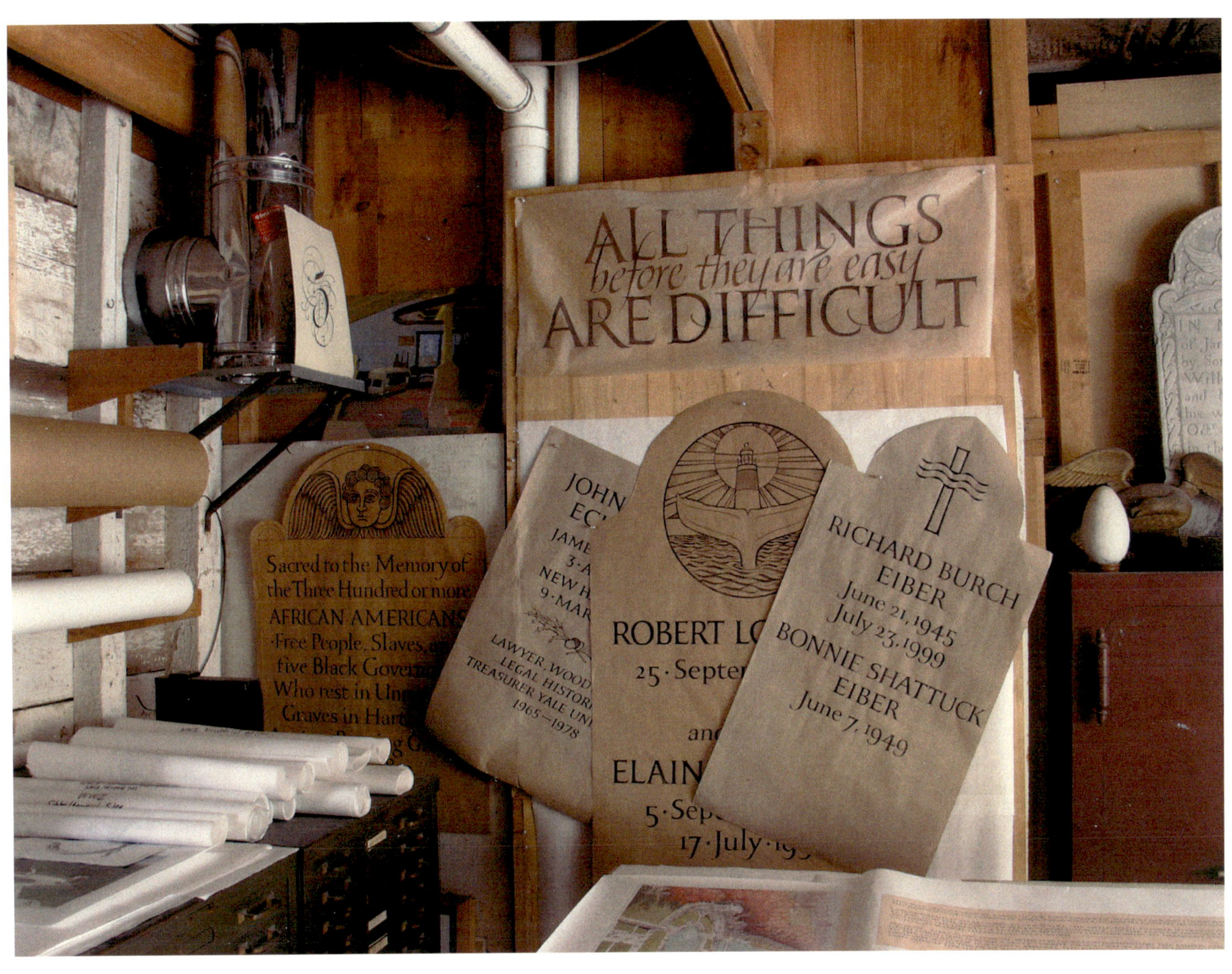


**Inkjet print.** Richard Benson. *All Things Are Difficult Before They Are Easy.* 1998. 7¼ x 9⅝ in. (18.4 x 24.5 cm). This picture was made with an early Olympus digital camera.

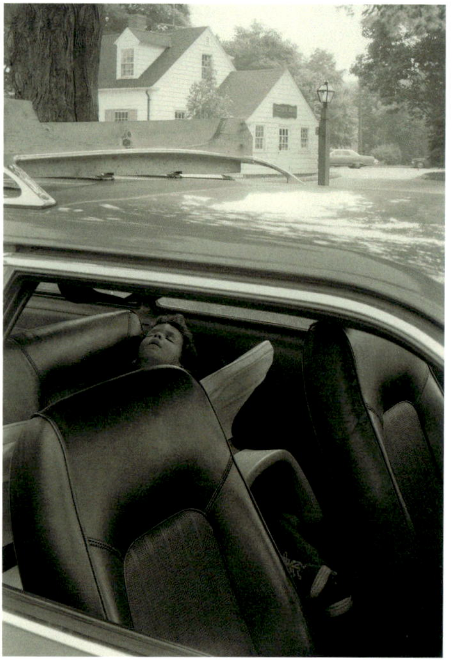

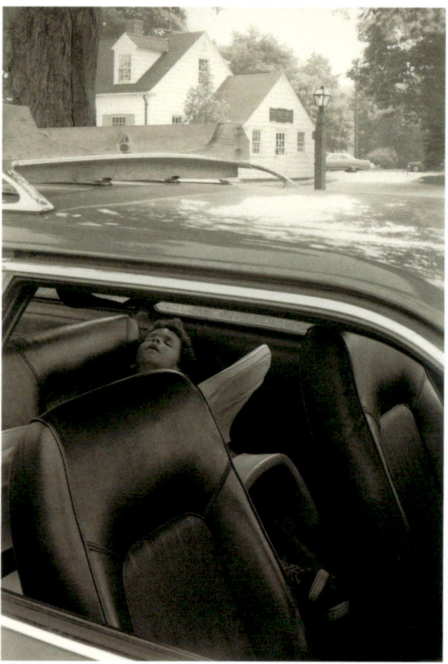

The question of permanence is present in every printing process. Both of these prints—made at the same time, on the same paper, with aftermarket monochromatic inks—started out as neutral gray. One print has turned green and the other brown. These changes might simply reflect the author's sloppy storage, but they could also be due to inferior paper or the presence of volatile chemicals in the air. Whatever the case, some digital prints are surprisingly fugitive in color. Ink manufacturers expend a great deal of research on developing inks that do not fade, but light is corrosive for all pictures.

## 12.10 BLACK AND WHITE INKJET PRINTING

The metamerism problem—of prints shifting color under changing lighting conditions—is particularly bad for black and white inkjet prints. If we make a beautiful black and white print, tuned so the tones are neutral, it is disturbing to walk across the room with it, toward a window, and find the image becoming green. This happens because the bulk of the inks that make up the picture are in the subtractive primary colors. They may be carefully balanced to produce neutral tones when printed in nearly equal amounts at any one spot, but that balance depends upon a specific light source being used to view the print. All inkjet printers have black inks in their ink set, but a print made with just that one ink will be rough and tonally poor. The smooth values in any inkjet print come from building up the image with at least four sets of dots, each in a different ink, and only by using inks in the primary colors can we print both color and black and white pictures with the same ink set. The minute we change viewing lights, such prints can shift in color.

This difficulty can be solved in two ways. One is to use a carefully designed "RIP," which stands for "raster image processor." The file we handle in the computer is not the one that drives the printer. Printers differ from computers in their design, so another translation is needed: a specialized file, which we never see or manipulate, is made to create the final print. The RIP is the device that produces this hidden but essential digital printing file. When used with normal colored inks, a good RIP will make up most of a black and white image out of the black ink (some printers even add an additional gray ink), then supply tone and smoothness by printing weak arrays of colored dots as well. As the percentage of colored ink in a print diminishes, so too does the metamerism problem. The second solution is to give up on making color prints and install a set of monochromatic inks in the printer. Some companies produce these as aftermarket additions, and they can make extraordinary prints that are stable, tonally spectacular, and completely free from color shifts.

These monochromatic ink sets use one or more black inks and various weights of gray. The cartridges or tanks in the printer are replaced with these new ones, and specialized software is installed in the computer to build print tones that match the monitor display. One of the pioneers in the development of these black and white ink sets—Jon Cone—even developed new software that lets the inkjet put down a diffuse dot, producing a print that looks truly tonal, even under the magnifying glass. A fine print made with these inks and that dot structure is as rich in grays as anything silver produced in the long history of chemical photography.

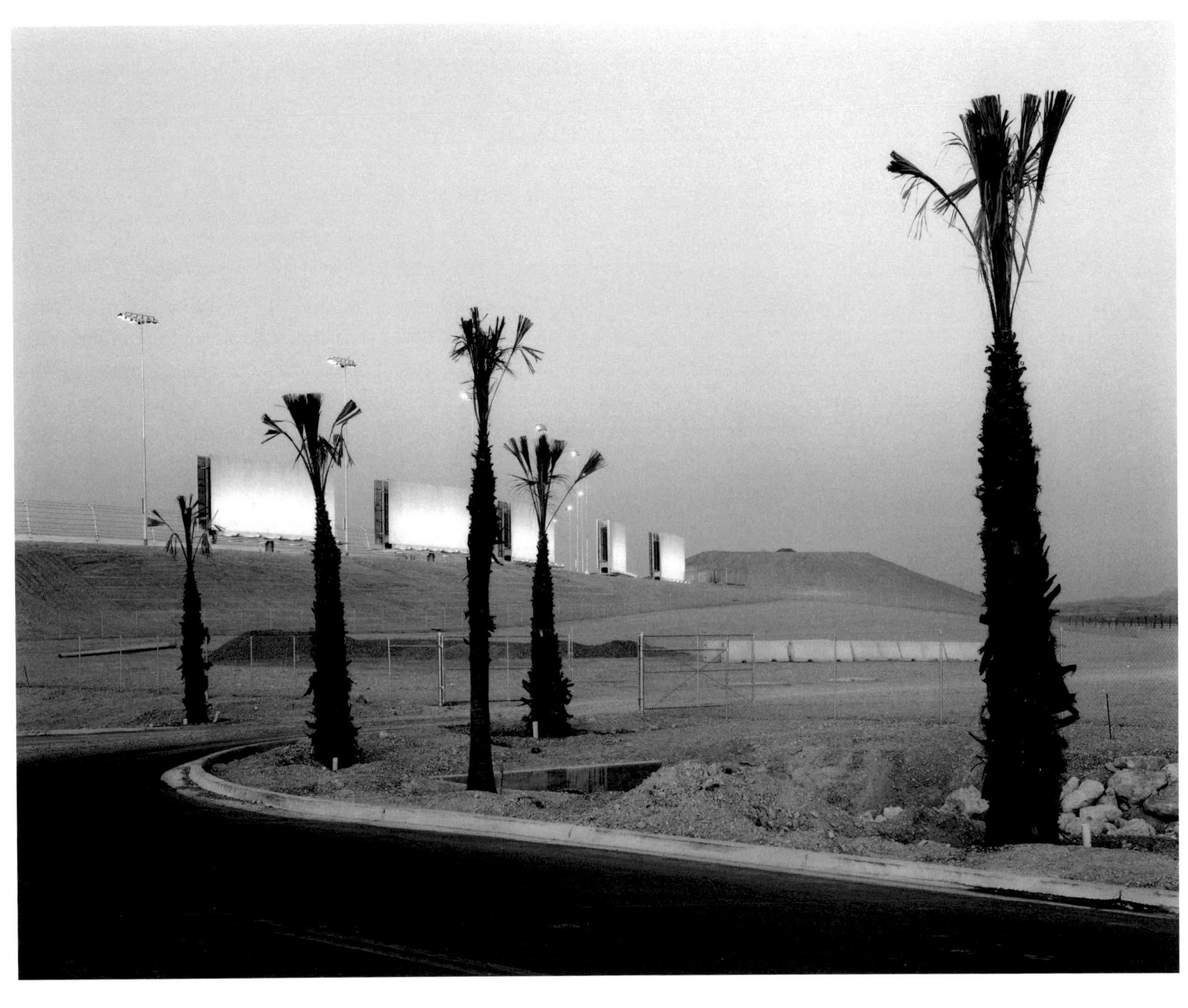

**Inkjet print with monochromatic inks.** Steve Smith. *Las Vegas, Nevada.* 1996. 10¾ x 13½ in. (27.3 x 34.3 cm)

## 12.11 DIGITAL CHROMOGENIC PRINTS

The physical fragility of inkjet prints, and the lack of great gloss and semigloss paper surfaces, has tended to keep them out of the galleries in which photography is classed as high art and sold for substantial sums of money. The dependable old C-print had become the standard for a color photograph that could be sold to a collector or museum, and the computer age grew in influence without really intruding on this old practice. But the computer had long since proved itself a miracle machine for retouching and altering photographs, and for a while in there—roughly 1990 to 2000—the practice arose of scanning an original photograph, doctoring it on the computer, and then generating a new piece of continuous-tone film from it in a device called a film recorder. This machine used tiny lasers to expose the new film, often at a resolution of 10,000 lines per inch, and these new transparencies were to all intents and purposes identical to film exposed in the camera. The really big difference was that the image had been manipulated by the computer in the picture's intermediate electronic stage, straining photography's already dubious connection to the truth even further. The newly output transparencies were ideal for the advertising trade—they built perfectly upon the foundation of deception that underlies much advertising.

Toward the century's end, a new printer came along that eliminated the film recorder by exposing color photographic paper directly with lasers driven by a computer file. This new machine was extremely expensive, costing over a quarter million dollars, but it could output a flawless C-print, indistinguishable from one made chemically in an enlarger. This technology was accompanied by newly developed chromogenic papers that had far greater permanency than the earlier ones. The work flow for these prints then became, exposure of the film in the camera; development; scanning of that film; manipulation of the resulting file in the computer; and then direct output onto conventional chromogenic photographic paper. These new prints slipped easily into the art world, becoming the standard method for producing digitally manipulated color photography with the same respectability as the older, chemical color prints.

We must be very clearheaded about this. There is absolutely nothing wrong with altering or otherwise doctoring a photograph in the computer. Photographs cannot be relied upon to render any sort of truth about the world from which they have been made, and every chemical photographic process that has ever existed involves a degree of handling and manipulating of photographic information to suit the photographer's wishes. If there is any drawback to this new way of exposing the old papers it is that the making of the print is handed over to a laboratory, breaking the ancient practice of the artist physically doing the work of making art.

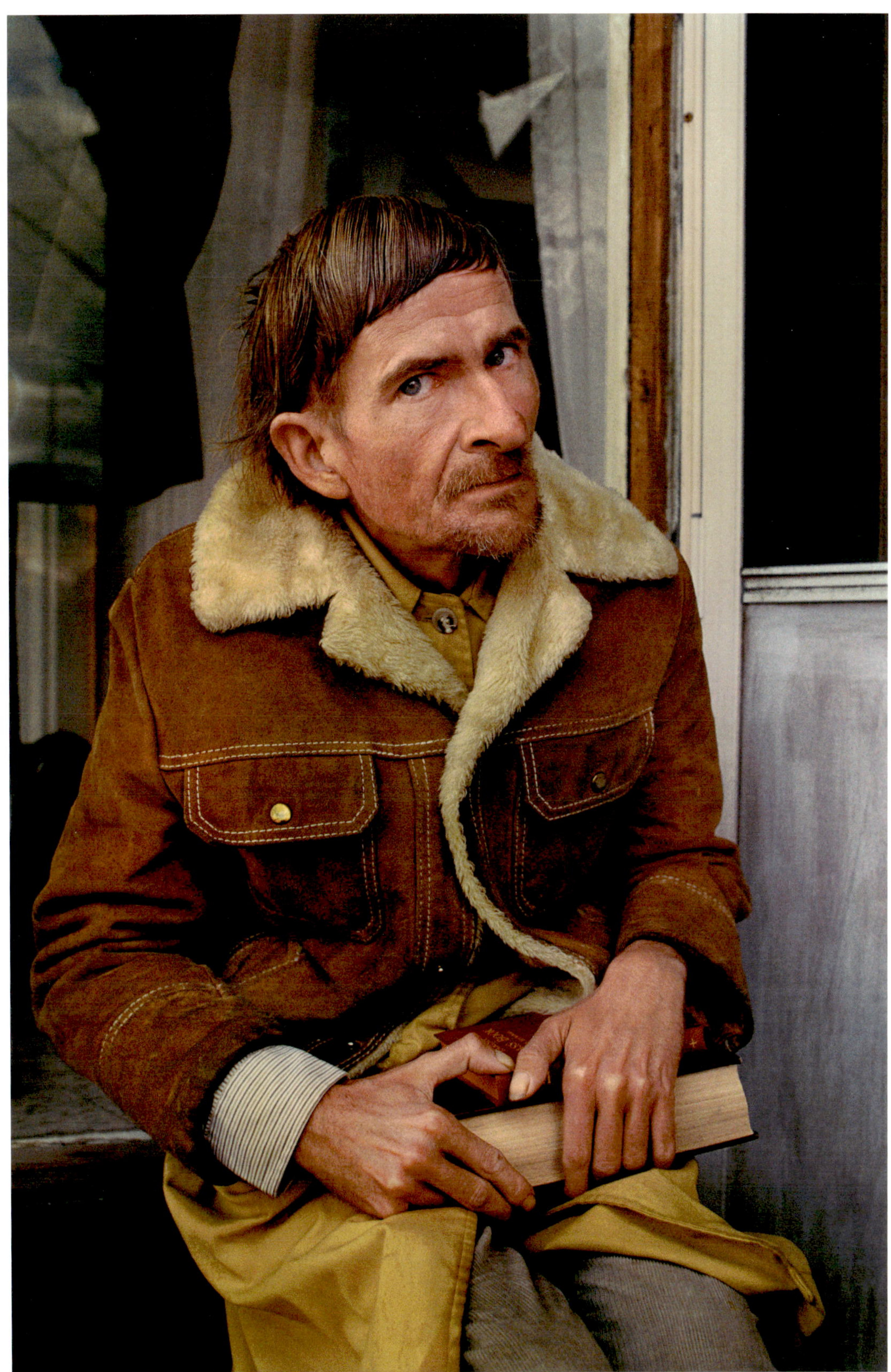

**Digital chromogenic print.** Robert Bergman. Untitled, from A Kind of Rapture 1989. 37 x 24½ in. (94 x 62 cm).

# Part 13

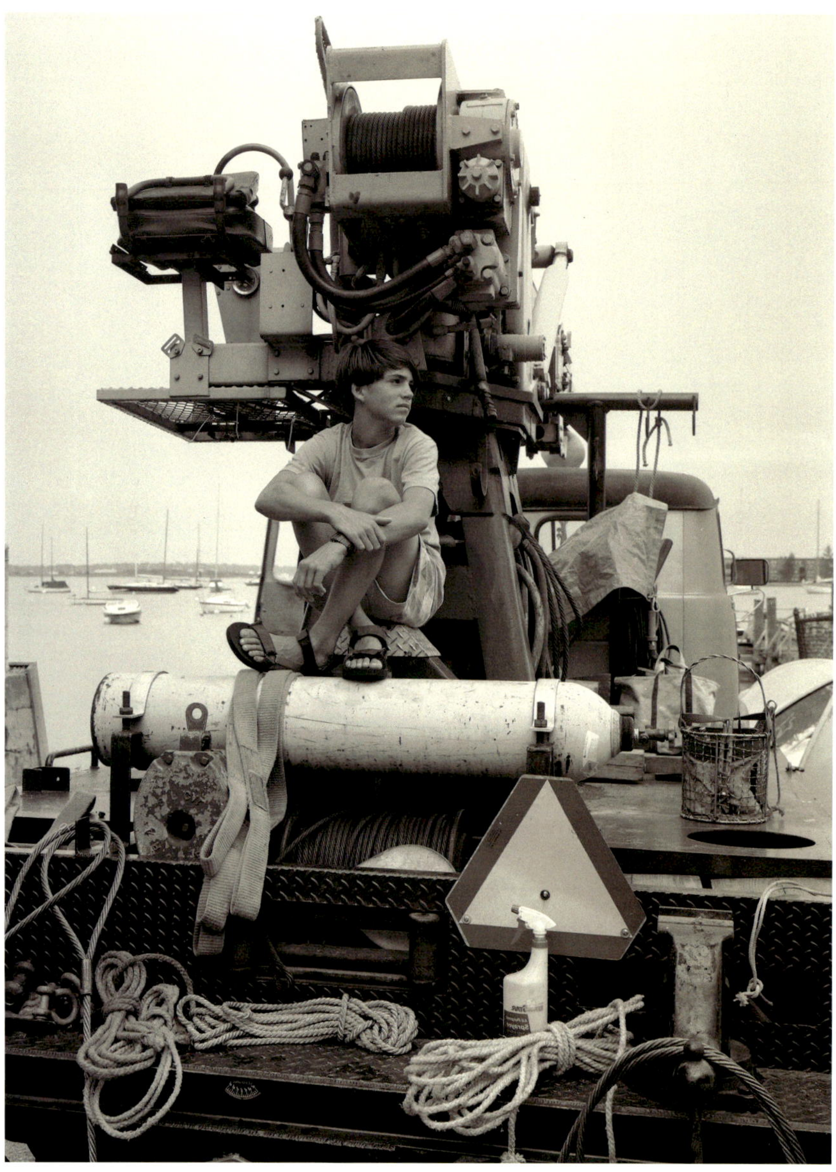

Photography and printing have become inextricably embedded in digital technology. The only chance we have of foreseeing the future is by understanding that human beings and all their actions are likewise intimately tangled with technology of all kinds. Wherever this show is going, the human being no longer travels there alone, but is instead accompanied by a host of rapidly changing technological offspring.

**Pigment print.** Richard Benson. *Daniel Benson on Jon Power's Crane Truck.* 1991. 15¾ x 11½ in. (40 x 29.2 cm). An experimental print made with acrylic paint on aluminum.

# Where do we go from here?

## 13.1 CALIBRATION

This is a test image, used by offset printers to calibrate their scanning, file-tuning, plate-making, and presswork. We must accept the need for such images because virtually all printing done today in ink (and even in photographic labs) is digitally based, and this kind of printing cannot be done properly without careful technical controls. This is the great drawback to the digital revolution in photography and printing—that we must give up the old instinctive, seat-of-the-pants work habits of the traditional darkroom or pressroom and instead be willing to measure and codify visual data to ensure that things turn out the way we envision.

This is a terrible thing. Artists have always placed technique on a lesser level than visceral impulse; when they don't they become craftsmen instead. The line between these two activities is soft and blurry, but the great technical prowess of the finest artists never obscures the fact that their work is valued because their craft carries something far more interesting than the craft itself. A work of art expresses the wisdom of the artist and the craft is the mechanism that brings this wisdom to physical form. This sounds like a bit of a tirade, but I emphasize it because the need to calibrate digital tools and obsessively measure their output is a tremendous obstruction to the artist's work. Photographers have always faced this problem, because of the mechanical nature of their trade, but in black and white photography the best work has always been done with a minimum of technical complexity. The best photographers have always understood how their medium worked, but seldom was great photography done with gray cards and light meters. Exposures were made based upon experience joining feeling, and only when color-reversal materials came along did as basic a tool as the light meter become necessary. I sometimes even go so far as to say that no great black and white photograph was made with a light meter, unless it was being used to hold up the sagging bellows of an old view camera.

This is an extreme point of view, but our test pattern should alert photographers and printers to the great danger lurking in technical controls: that calibration and measurement only have benefits when they connect to established standards, and standards of any sort run absolutely counter to the central tenet of art—that its richest ground is in the field of the unexpected and unpredictable.

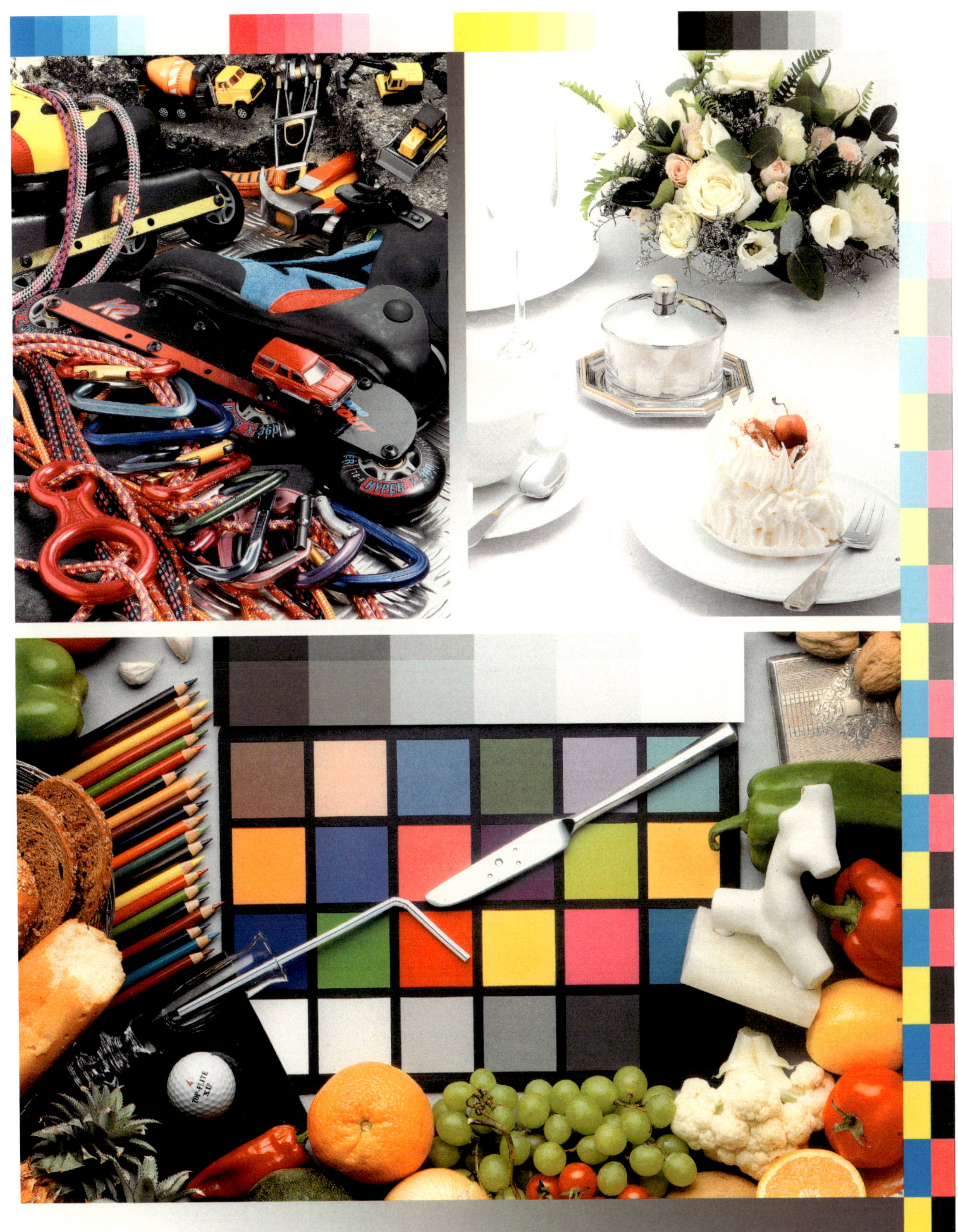

**Prepress polymer proof print.** Calibration page. c. 2001. 10¾ x 8½ in. (27.3 x 21.6 cm). A test image created for calibrating a prepress proofing system to a particular offset press.

## 13.2 COLOR MANAGEMENT

The issues of calibration have a direct impact on any photographer using the computer because the image on the monitor never looks like the print that ends up being made. The biggest reason for this disconnect is that the monitor image is made in additive color and the print in subtractive color. The monitor literally glows while the passive print simply reflects, and each device uses a different dye set to generate the colors. It is possible to build a hood around the monitor and then make a light box around the print, so that they sit side by side and appear somewhat the same, but this ideal is seldom adhered to, and even when followed, it doesn't address the fundamentally different colors that the two systems display.

Another reason why the monitor image and the print don't look alike is that every digital device has its flaws: both the scanner doing the input and the printer doing the output introduce errors in the data handling. Also, the monitor, paper, and inks each have their own set of colors, which differ from one another. Technicians say that each stage has its own "color space," and that there is no hope of making a properly balanced print unless these differences are integrated with each other through some controllable method. What has evolved to do this is a system called "color management," which uses various "profiles" for each machine and ties the profile data from one device to the next, in a chain of information that in theory will make things turn out right.

In a highly controlled laboratory setting these profiles seem to work—sort of. Since the earliest years of their craft, printers have been telling clients that the picture will look right because their methods always work out as planned, but this has never been the case. Color management is based on the premise that all aspects of the process, from scan (or original exposure with a digital camera) to print, can be controlled and that each step along the way will behave as planned. It is possible to use color-management tools to help us make a print, and we can even go to the extreme of buying expensive software to do this, but in the turmoil of technological change (and while trying to follow the instincts of an artist) I have found the system hopeless. If we make photographs and use the new technology to make them, we quickly realize that we are working in an environment similar to that of the automobile in the era of the Model T Ford. We can get great results, but things break down constantly and we have to putter with the machinery. We are a long way away from the time when we can simply turn the key and drive away, secure in the knowledge that we will get where we want to go without unexpected bumps along the way.

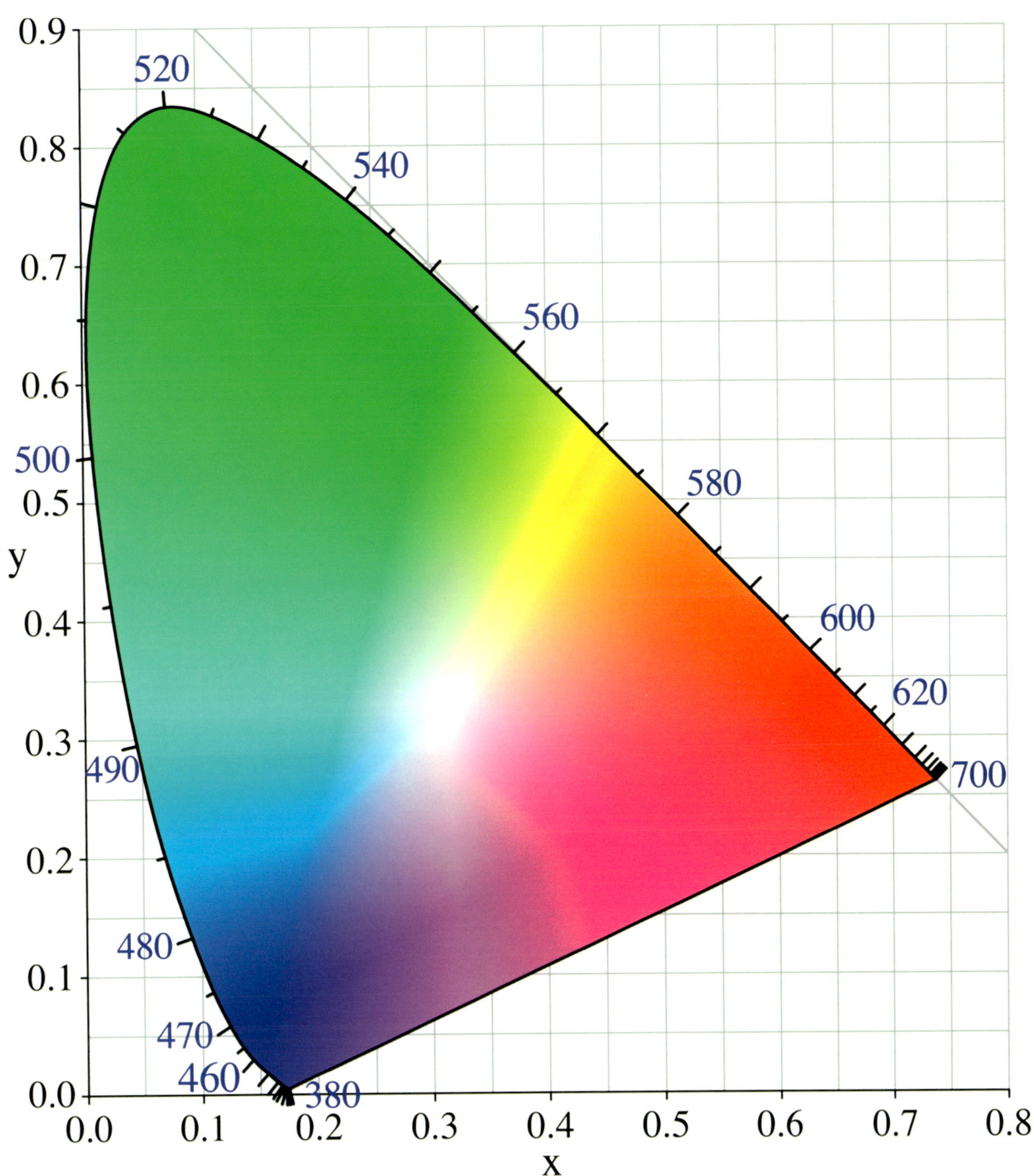


**Web download.** Chromaticity diagram. Downloaded 2006. 1,140 x 1,260 pixels

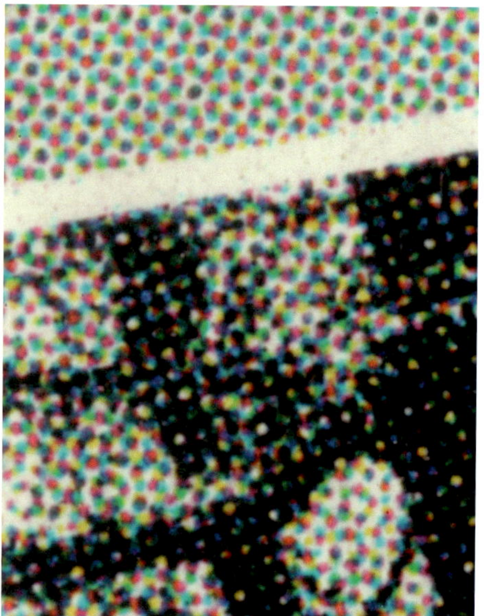

Although printed at high speed on a web press, and using a halftone pattern generated by the computer, the dot pattern shown in this detail has remained the same for the seventy years or so in which process-color printing with halftones has been common.

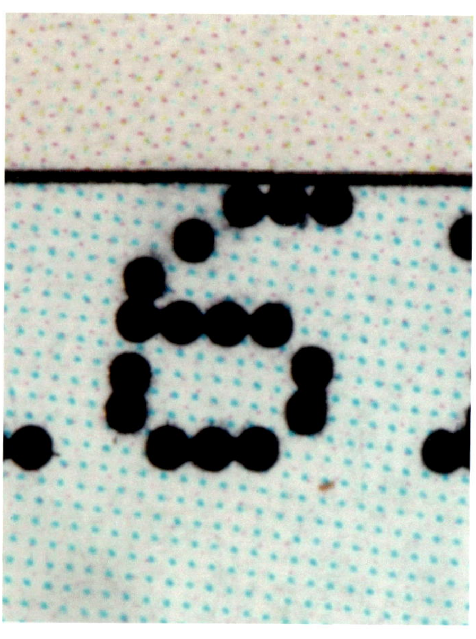

The information customizing the catalog for a specific recipient has been printed on top of the conventional halftone. The coarse dots have been digitally generated, and are printed in poor register, but the numbers they display have changed for every single copy in the thousands of the edition.

## 13.3 DIGITAL EVERYTHING

This is the back cover of a catalog that I received the week I wrote this page. I needed something to show the pervasiveness of the computer, and I could have picked up almost any catalog that arrived in the mail (it's close to Christmas, so there are a lot of them). This particular one is from Light Impressions, a firm that sells archival material for photographic preservation.

The first thing to be said is that I was the second human being to handle this booklet. The first was the postman who put it in my mailbox, and as I took it out, I became the second. People designed it (using computers), presses printed and even bound it (also while controlled by computers), and the U.S. Postal Service delivered it to me, but nowhere in that process did a person touch any part of it. Not only has it remained pure and unsullied by the unpredictable human being but this cheap throwaway catalog, along with thousands of others, is better made than most books ever were. The reproductions are crisp and, when clothing or household goods are being harped, the colors are brilliant. Those of us who cling to the past should be absolutely clear that almost everything about printing is better now than it ever was before, and that this is thanks to today's remarkable digital tools.

I reproduce the back cover because it shows the small pale-yellow and pale-blue rectangles in which code numbers have been printed. Those numbers are unique, and define this catalog as the specific one that was sent to Richard Benson to help him buy stuff. The numbers link to huge databases, generated to place me in a group of likely clients for this company's products. These databases in turn are part of an even larger, nebulous data entity comprising the aggregate of databases from many companies selling many different products. A number of businesses, instead of selling products, instead deal only in sales data, which they market to those who still sell hard goods. We are part of this web, and even though it makes us nervous we happily take advantage of its benefits.

To top it all off, the page we see here has a photograph on it. The history of that picture is as follows: John Sexton made a negative and printed it; the print was scanned, plated, and printed in ink as the cover of his book; that cover was then scanned, plated, and printed on the catalog; I got the catalog, scanned it, tuned it, and sent it to the printer of my own book. Even after all this, the picture looks pretty good. The union of photography, computer, paper, and press is an absolute miracle in its present state.

**Author Profile: John Sexton**

*"I will never forget the first time I saw a print emerge under the dim amber glow of a safelight in a friend's makeshift darkroom more than thirty years ago." That "unforgettable experience" is what began John Sexton's passion for photography and print making.*

*When a student "...I went to see an exhibition by three photographers: Ansel Adams, Edward Weston and Wynn Bullock...I'd never had a photograph in front of me that made your heartbeat skip and made you catch your breath."*

*Today, John's own photographs make your heartbeat skip and your breath catch. He's renowned for his luminous, quiet, black and white photographs of both the natural environment, and of man's technology. Recognized worldwide as a photographer, master print maker, workshop instructor and lecturer, he's also Director of the John Sexton Photography Workshops program, consultant to Kodak, and author of three award-winning books* ***Quiet Light, Listen to the Trees,*** *and* ***Places of Power.***

# a wonderful gift

*for any photographer, artist or lover of fine photography*

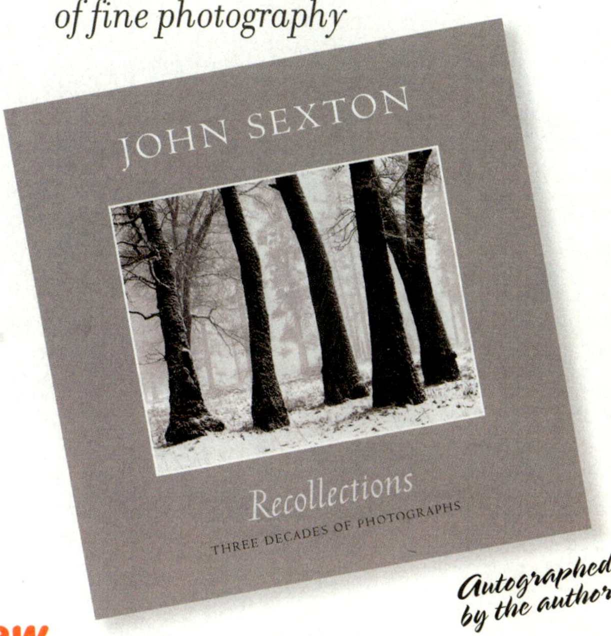


*Autographed by the author!*

LIGHT IMPRESSIONS®
PO Box 787
Brea, CA 92822-0787
800-828-6216

ACCOUNT NUMBER
00641233

HAVE THIS KEY CODE HANDY WHEN ORDERING ⇨ LL6115 YOUR KEY CODE

**new**

## *Recollections: Three Decades of Photographs,* by John Sexton

The purity of a fresh snowfall, enigmatic rock forms, fallen trees touched by a waterfall, are transformed into images of tranquility and wonder when seen through Sexton's eyes. With John supervising every detail, his large-format, black and white images have been magnificently reproduced on luxurious heavyweight paper. None has appeared in a prior Sexton book. In his engaging notes, John relates the adventures and challenges encountered while working in the field and in the darkroom. 140 pages, 12x12 images, hardcover.

**#10665** Sugg. Retail $75.00 **Our price $65.00**

"John Sexton has taken up where Ansel Adams left off, and he has done it with a powerful vision and a strong sense of purpose. His latest book, Recollections, is an essential volume for anyone who loves great photography."
— David Hume Kennerly, *Pulitzer prize winning photography*

**********AUTO** 5-DIGIT 02840
RICHARD BENSON
53 TILDEN AVE
NEWPORT RI 02840-2065

PRSRT STD
US POSTAGE PAID
LIGHT IMPRESSIONS

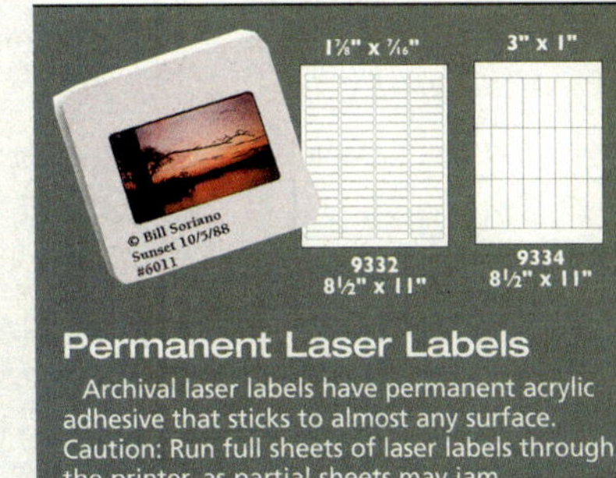


1⅞" x 7/16" — 9332 8½" x 11"
3" x 1" — 9334 8½" x 11"

## Permanent Laser Labels

Archival laser labels have permanent acrylic adhesive that sticks to almost any surface. Caution: Run full sheets of laser labels through the printer, as partial sheets may jam.

**#9332** 1⅞ x 7/16 80/sheet, 20 sheets $13.95
**#9334** 3x1 24/sheet, 20 sheets $13.95

½" x 1¾" — 9624 8½" x 11"

© Leslie Getty
Silver Tray 6/30/88
# 6351

## Inkjet Labels
*With Tear-Proof Covering!*

Premium paper is ink-jet coated for crisp text and brilliant, high-resolution image, and reinforced with a tear-proof polyethylene layer. Ideal for most desktop inkjet printers.

**#9624** ½ x 1¾ 80/sheet, 25 sheets $20.95

© 2006 Light Impressions

**Web offset.** Light Impressions company. Mail-order catalog, back cover. 2006. 10⅛ x 8⅛ in. (25.7 x 19.7 cm)

## 13.4 LONG-EDITION ROTOGRAVURE

This is a spread from *National Geographic*. The publishers of this venerable magazine have long been dedicated to high-quality production, and have sought to maintain this quality as the size of the print run keeps growing. The solution, surprisingly enough, has been to print in gravure, the oldest of the ink-printing systems for photography. We have looked at gravure in its early flat-plate stage, where the inking and wiping were done by hand. In the section on book processes we also saw examples of gravure's rotary version, where screened images were etched to variable depths and printed in longer editions with mechanical inking and printing. Almost all applications of gravure died out as offset became dominant, but one remained: this is magazine work in beautiful color, printed in editions in the many hundreds of thousands.

The cylinders used for this kind of printing no longer carry a plate but print from copper electroplated onto a chrome cylinder. After the print run is completed, the copper is removed, a new layer of the metal is electroplated on, and the information for a new publication is etched into it. This etch is done directly, with a laser, instead of with the old carbon tissue. It might cost $2,000 to make a single cylinder, and a set of sixteen pages might require eight of these, but once they are made, the printing cylinders can print a million copies without wearing out, and do so with absolute consistency. The machines that do this are immense, often printing in multiple units so that all of the signatures are assembled into a complete publication in one operation. The terrific cost of preparatory work becomes practical when it is distributed over a huge edition. A set of cylinders might cost $100,000 for a single edition, but if a million copies are printed, that cost amounts to only a dime a copy. Gravure lives on, making beautiful pages, in the surprising niche of lush, extremely-long-edition color printing.

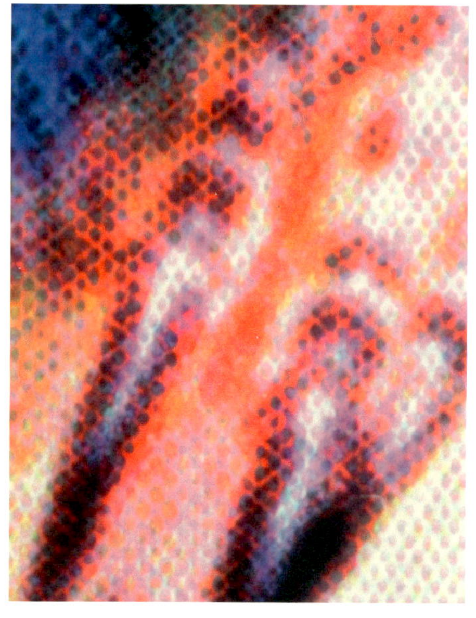

This detail shows the soft gravure printing dots, which vary in strength as well as size. The older, rectilinear dot pattern generated by a gravure screen has given way to circular, laser-etched printing cells.

It is a little like the steam engine. This was the prime mover that drove the industrial revolution, in stationary engines running factories and in locomotives carrying huge loads for pennies a mile. Gradually these old vapor-based machines were driven to obsolescence by the internal combustion engine, burning gasoline in cars and diesel fuel in trains. Most people don't realize that steam still lives, hiding in huge electrical power plants, where it drives the turbines that make 90 percent of all the electricity used in the world. The heat source might come from atomic reactions, and highly advanced turbines might convert the heat to work, but the same old steam powers a large part of our society. Odd hiding places can occur where old technologies live on in new and important roles.

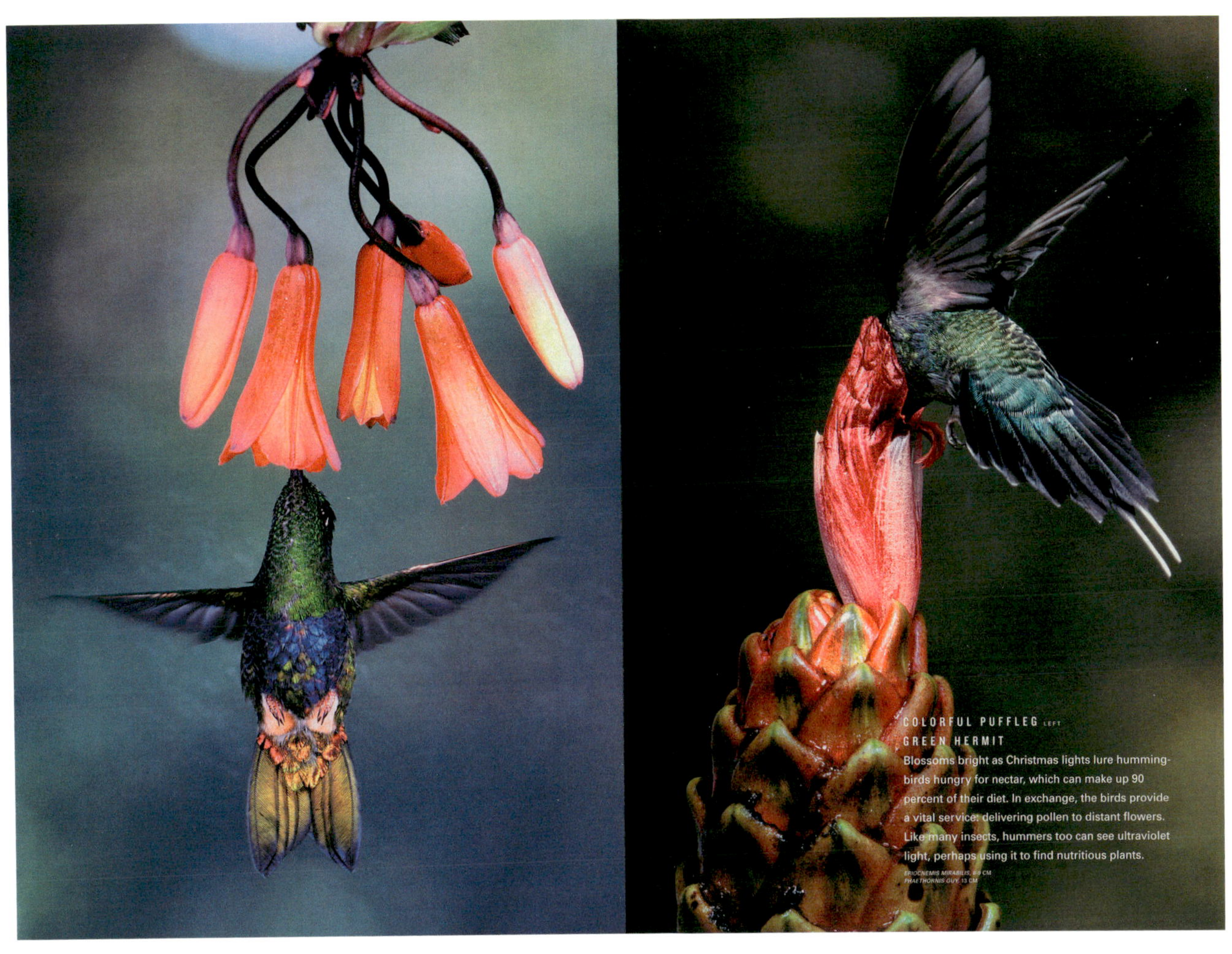


**Web rotogravure.** Luis A. Mazariegos. *Eriocnemis Mirabilis* (left) and *Phaethornis Guy*. c. 2006. Print: 2007. 10 x 13¾ in. (25.4 x 34.9 cm). Double-page spread from *National Geographic*, January 2007.

## 13.5 THE INDIGO PRINTER

The computer has altered all phases of printing but one aspect of the practice has remained stable since books were first printed: the designing, printing, and binding of a book in an edition that can then be marketed. The publisher puts up the money; the paper merchant, printer, and binder all get paid, and sometimes the author even gets compensation too, but all of these funds are handed out at the publisher's risk that the book won't sell. The economics are shocking to many photographers who naively want to have a book of their work published, because the actual making of the book only costs about 15 percent of the retail price (and that's for a really well-made book!). Many publishers regularly lose their shirts on books, and only stay in business because some of the titles they publish hit the big time and make up for the losses. There is an old tale about a publisher who wins the lottery, and instead of retiring decides to keep publishing until the money is all gone.

The stubbornly persistent practice here is that of printing the entire edition at once. This habit can be traced back to preparatory costs and the need for printing presses to be tuned and "made ready" before they can print well. That preliminary work is so expensive that it is only undertaken when a large edition is to be printed. If we print 5,000 sheets on a multicolor offset press, that work might cost about $3,000, or sixty cents a sheet. If we use the same technology to print only five sheets, the run will still cost at least $1,000, because, even though we use much less paper, the prepress work and makeready remain the same. For the small edition the cost per sheet would then be a horrifying $200.

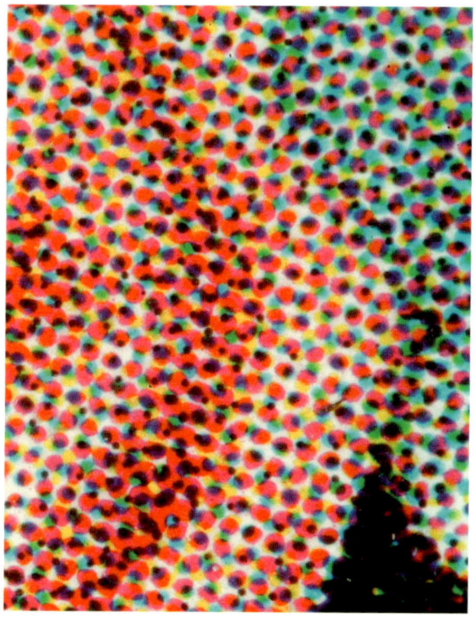

The computer might change this. One specific piece of technology that could do so is the Indigo press, which is now owned and sold (or leased) by Hewlett-Packard. This press is an offset press, still printing on a blanket from an ink-bearing plate, but the plate is electronic and can change its data set with every revolution of the press. That innovation is combined with the equally remarkable one of an ink that completely leaves the plate and blanket with each impression, so no residue remains from sheet to sheet. Rather than having to print the same page repeatedly between make-readies, the press can print the pages of a book sequentially, one after the other. This innovation permits the printing of single copies of a book at a reasonable cost. This technology, like that of the production-level color copiers mentioned in section 12.4, can produce books on demand. Huge inventories, storage warehouses, and publisher's risk could all disappear if this practice became widespread. Even more important, such a development would support the making of books that are only viable for a small audience.

The dot used by the Indigo printer looks identical to the dot used in conventional offset lithography.

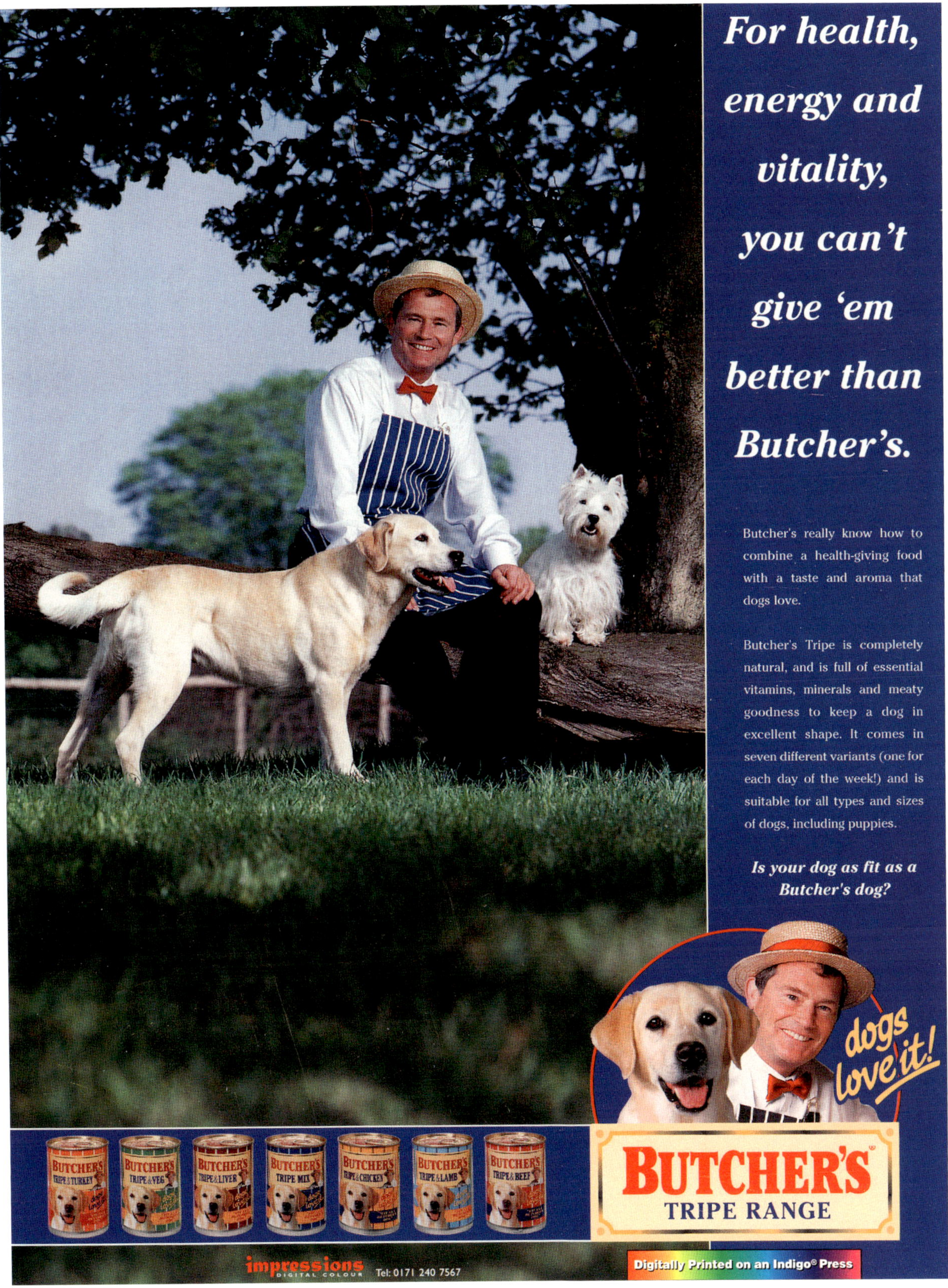


**Indigo print.** Impressions Digital Color. *Butcher's Tripe Range*. 2006. Print: GHP (Gist Herlin Press). 2006. 10⅝ x 8⅛ in. (27 x 20.7 cm). Proof for an advertisement.

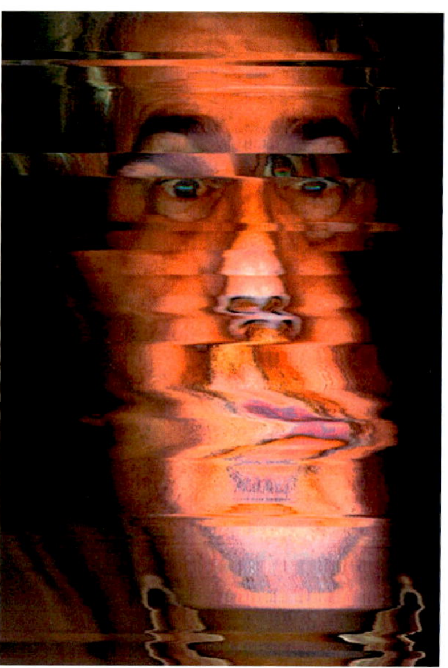

**Digital scan.** Allan Chasanoff. *Self-portrait.* c. 1990. 498 x 347 pixels.

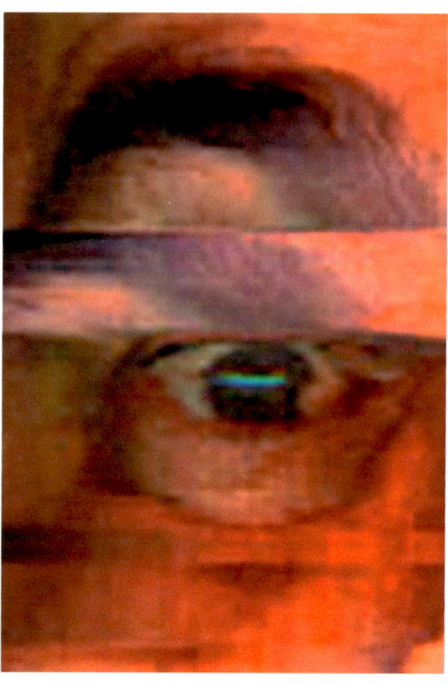

Since the earliest years of photography, light sources have shown up in miniature reflections in the eyes of the subjects of portraits. In this case the light we see is the long one traveling with the scanner bar. Here we see the evidence of a new, lensless imaging system.

## 13.6 SCANNER AS CAMERA

Cameras existed before photography was invented. They used a lens that projected light onto a ground glass, producing a two-dimensional image that could be traced. A pinhole can also project a dim but fairly sharp picture, and natural cameras turn up occasionally using such tiny apertures. The most common one is found in solar eclipses, when every small bit of light coming through the leaves of a tree shows the eroding crescent of the sun. Cameras have used this fundamental structure—of a point projecting a circle of definition onto a flat plane—for the entire history of photography. One of the delights of the computer age is that it has brought us a completely new kind of camera to accompany the old one in our photographic toolbox. We don't call it a camera but a "scanner," and it is a new and very exciting method for gathering visual data.

The scanner began as a rotary device that drew a stream of data from a rotating drum onto which a film transparency had been placed. As the drum rotated, the scanner eye moved slowly parallel to the drum's axis and extracted a spiral thread of tonal information from the transparency. In the first scanners this information was analog, and it controlled an output light that exposed a new piece of film on another drum rotating in sync with the first. By filtering the input light, this system could produce a set of color separations. Between input and output was a set of electronic controls that could tweak the analog flow to control the density of the new film being exposed.

These scanners are still around, but are digital now and very expensive. There is also a new, inexpensive, and common device called the desktop flatbed scanner. Here a series of sensors is strung along a linear bar, which passes along the object to be copied in a direction at right angles to its array of sensors. In so doing the scanner records strings of data taken from an area and builds up a picture. The origins of the principle lay in the Xerox machine, which made copies of printed material by passing a drum beneath it. I remember discovering my grade school's first Xerox—we took great pleasure in scanning unmentionable body parts when no one else was in the office. (Even then this new machine could double as a camera.) The modern desktop scanners are very refined and their sensors can even record quite faraway surfaces. They act as multiple-lens cameras, making pictures with a high degree of depth of field over an extended period of time. Even more exciting, the photographs they make are not taken from a single point: the scanning bar moves and sees its subject from more than one location.

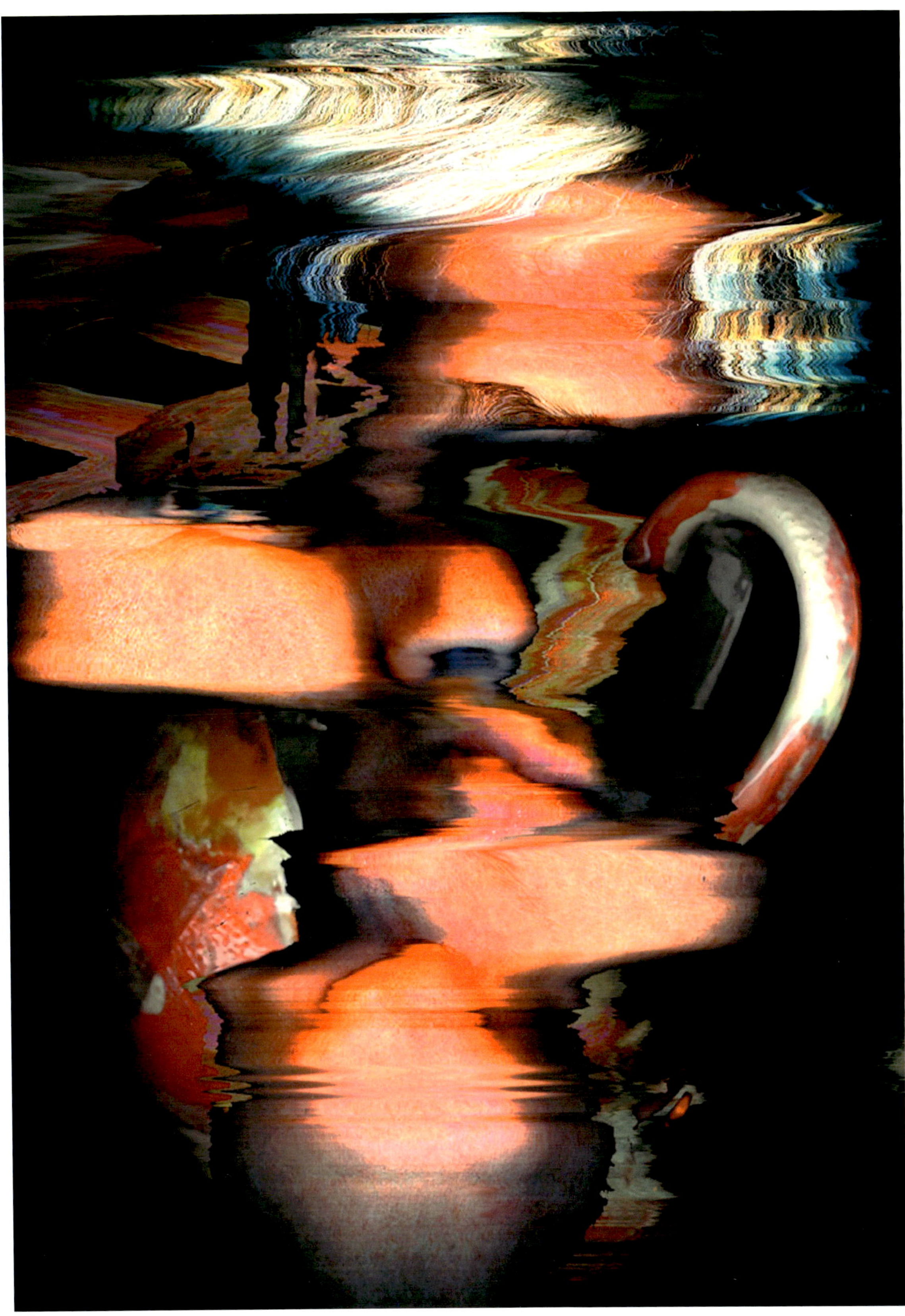

**Digital scan.** Allan Chasanoff. *Self-portrait.* c. 1990. 1013 x 720 pixels.

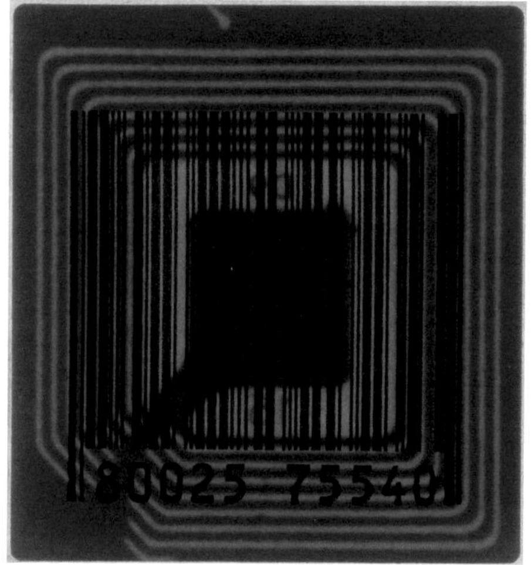

A bar code, shown at top as a reflective print and below illuminated as a transparency. This small inventory device, this one from a bookstore, contains in the dark central area a hidden picture, which, unless it is disabled during checkout, can be read electronically to alert the store that a product is being removed illegally.

## 13.7 PICTURES FOR MACHINES

Throughout the long history of printing, and indeed of all forms of picture-making, images were made for the use of human beings. Something radically new began to take place in commerce in the last part of the twentieth century, in the development of the humble bar code, used to control inventories, sales data, shipment-tracking information, and so on. This simple device was innovative because it became a widespread form of picture designed solely for the use of machines, not people. Machines had been looking at pictures in industry for some time; the registration system for the web press is a good example, in which an electric eye examines a register mark to fit high-speed printing. The bar code, however, moved out into society at large and reduced the activity of the hand even more—data no longer had to be typed into a cash register or written on a slip, because all this was taken care of automatically by the data transferred when a machine read the simple code on the package.

The bar code is read by being scanned. It is interesting that the camera used to access this information is not the old single-lens one of photography but the new one of the scanner. All forms of scanners, from the expensive ones that use a rotating drum to the cheap little ones that fit on our desk, do their work by making a picture that is not for human consumption. When we scan a picture into our computer we never see the data taken in; instead we view an analog surrogate, put up on the computer screen for our convenience. The scan itself is a string of numbers, intelligible only to the computer. It isn't just the hand that is disappearing here but the human being as well.

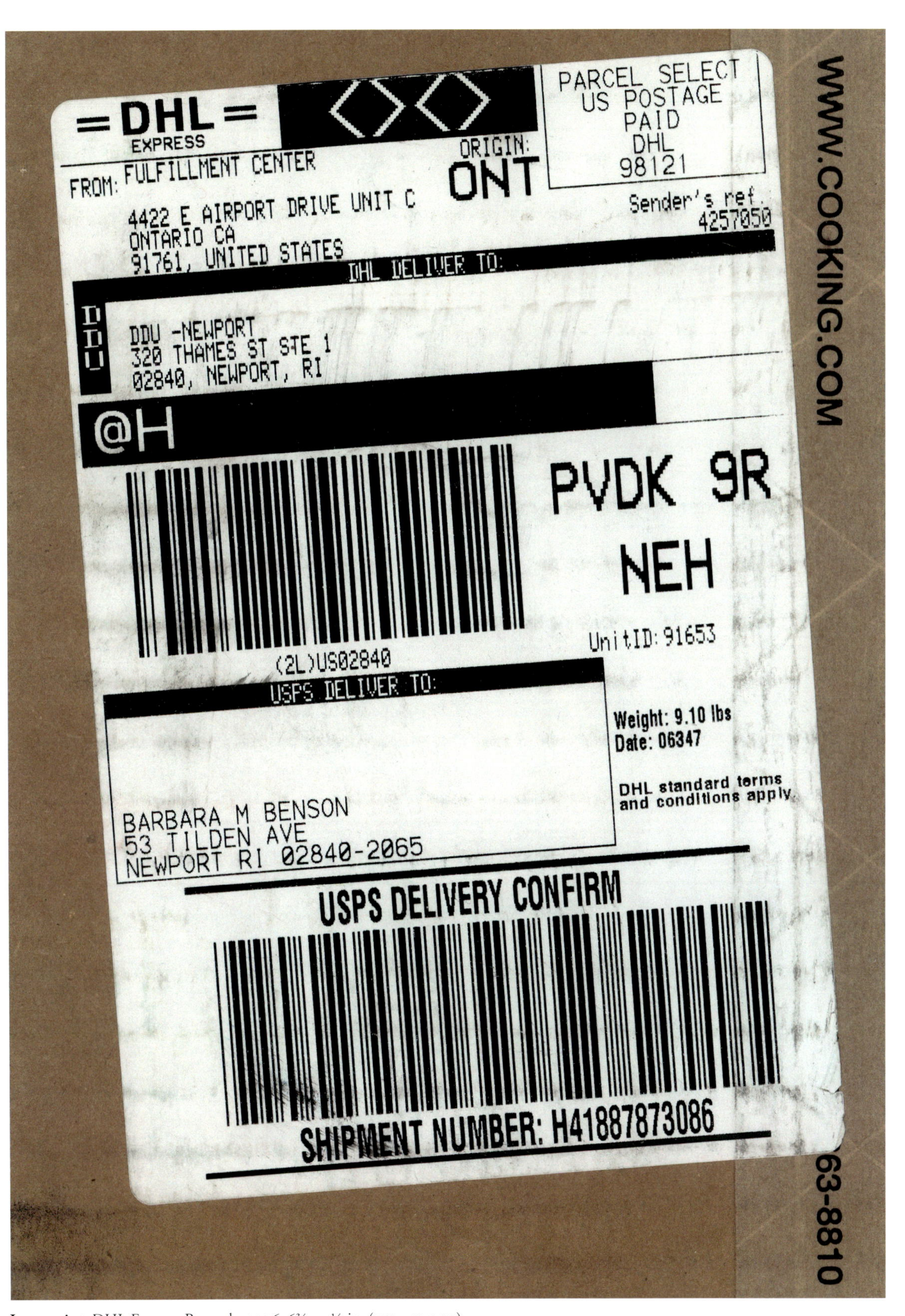


**Laser print.** DHL Express. Bar code. 2006. 6¾ x 4½ in. (17.1 x 11.4 cm)

## 13.8 THE DISAPPEARANCE OF THE HAND

We end with this painting. Made with oil paint on a piece of board, it is physically indistinguishable from paintings made five hundred years before. The artist is certainly modern but his materials and techniques are old; he might have made a photograph of the scene, and used it in the studio as a memory device, but still the picture was made by hand, eye, and mind working together. If we have learned anything in the last few hundred pages it has been that this old way of working is becoming irrelevant. This picture is unique—it hangs on my living room wall—and is seen by almost no one outside my family and friends. The demise of pictures in single copies is one of the first great innovations of printing, which has totally undermined the social role of pictures that exist in only one copy. Photography, even before it linked up with printing, introduced other great changes: the lens replaced the eye as a data-gathering tool and chemical processes replaced the hand in translating that data to print form. Our survey shows the steady adaptation of photography's informational power to the printing presses, and by the end of the last century, the hand had completely disappeared from these unified visual processes. It was still in there messing around until the computer came along, but now we make and distribute multiple copies of pictures that are never touched by the ancient hand/eye/mind activity that made this little painting.

The bar code gives us a warning that the hand is only the first part of the human being to disappear from picture-making. As soon as the power of pictures made for machines is recognized, the whole technological infrastructure we live in will change. As I write this, machines built to understand pictures are still crude; in concentrating on developing the technology to make pictures for people to understand, we haven't quite realized that the technology of picture construction is just the simple, first half of the equation. The second half will be sophisticated devices to access and interpret visual data, and once those become commonplace the human being itself will start to slip out of the big picture and begin to take on a role in the background, planning and directing the show but no longer the central actor on the stage. The devices we make can already go where we are not allowed, through distances in time and space that biology simply can't cope with, and it is just too interesting out there for this practice to do anything but grow. Before too long, technological tools will probably even comprehend what is discovered better than we can.

I think we need to take on this new job and enjoy the technological child that we have been building, and that is so inevitably driving us and our biological relatives into the background. As we do so we need to recognize that some pictures, like the painting we see here, are made for the human being to enjoy, and that they should continue to be made, to exist solely for our individual pleasure.

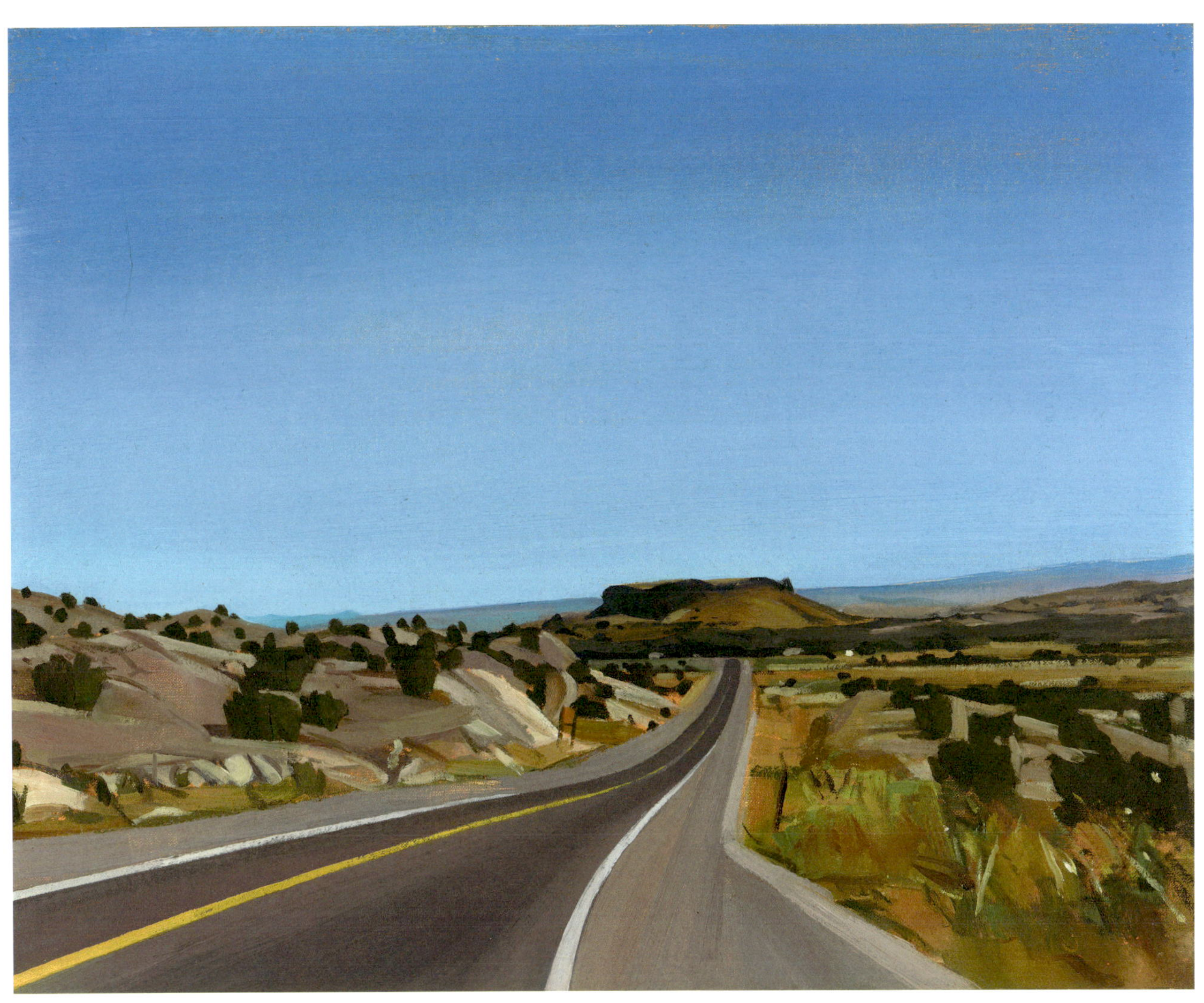

**Oil on panel.** Christopher Benson. *New Mexico Landscape.* 2005. 11 x 14 in. (28 x 35.6 cm)

**acid:** a substance, usually in solution with water, that has a pH lower than 7.0. Acids have a corrosive effect on metals and are commonly used as etches in the printing trades.

**additive color:** *see* primary colors

**albumen** (also albumin): a soluble protein commonly found in egg white.

**albumen print:** a silver photographic printing-out process that was developed to render the long range of tones held in wet-plate glass negatives. The albumen print is a refinement of the earlier salted-paper print, but it differs in using a heavy coating of albumen as a binder for the salt and subsequent silver image. Albumen prints have a long tonal range and strong blacks, and they were almost always toned with gold, producing a purplish image.

**ambrotype:** a lightly exposed wet-plate glass negative that appears as a positive when placed on a black backing.

**analog:** a representation of something that imitates a physical characteristic of the original. The photographic negative is an analog, in silver, of the variable light intensity striking the film during exposure.

**aquatint:** a randomly distributed array of grains of an acid-resistant material, applied to an intaglio printing plate before etching to protect parts of the surface from the etch. The pattern of the grains confines the etching to small cells between them. Those areas not etched act as a wiping guide for the cloth or hand that cleans the inked plate. Ink remains in the cells and is transferred to the paper in the press.

**architectural plotter:** a large-format inkjet printer designed to generate architectural drawings.

**asphaltum:** a hardened asphalt that can be used as an etching resist, whether dissolved in turpentine or in powdered form.

**autochrome:** *see* Lumière Autochrome

**autopositive:** any photographic process that produces a positive image directly from exposure to light. In most photographic processes, light darkens a photosensitive material in such a way that the brightest light produces the darkest areas of the picture, resulting in a negative image that must then be printed to make a positive. Autopositive processes, such as the daguerreotype, tintype, and ambrotype, produce a positive directly with no intermediate negative stage.

**bar code:** a printed pattern of lines, readable by an optical scanner, used to automate product logistics. Bar codes allow manufacturers and retailers to create automated inventories and are used to direct objects during shipping.

**binary:** for printing purposes, "binary" refers to a description of information with only two possibilities: at a given point on a white sheet of paper, for example, black ink is either present or not—there are no intermediate tones. The common halftone, which prints small dots in varying sizes, is a method for generating the appearance of such intermediate tones with only black ink and plain paper. Computers use a binary mathematical system in which 1 and 0 are the only numerals, as these can be efficiently represented by an electronic switch that is either on or off.

**black and white photography:** photography that renders all colors in monochromatic values. Black and white prints have no color information deriving from the scene photographed, but they often have color casts derived from the particular chemical process used to produce them.

**blueprint** (also cyanotype): an iron-based photographic printing process using inexpensive iron compounds and simple development in water. Used predominantly for engineering drawings, the process was also widely used as an amateur photographic printing medium.

**burin** (also graver): a specialized cutting tool, acting more like a gouge than a knife, that is used to engrave lines in metal or wood. Driven by the palm of the hand and guided by the fingers, the burin is held nearly flat to the surface that is to be engraved. Its slanted, usually lozenge-shaped point cuts a groove that varies in depth according to the angle at which the burin is held above the surface.

**burnisher:** a hand tool used to polish mezzotint plates and to do corrective work on etchings, engravings, and even photogravures. Burnishers have highly polished tips made of steel or agate mounted in a wooden handle.

**C-print:** *see* chromogenic process

**calotype** (also talbotype): the first negative-positive photographic process, invented and named by William Henry Fox Talbot. Salted paper is used for both negatives and positives.

**camera:** a light-tight box holding some form of light-sensitive recorder (film or digital sensor), with an image-forming aperture (lens or pinhole) and a means of admitting light for a controllable interval.

**carbon black** (also lampblack): this amorphous form of carbon results from a gas flame burning without sufficient oxygen. Carbon black was the original pigment for carbon printing and gave the process its name.

**carbon print:** a photographic process based on the tendency of a colloid (in this case gelatin) to harden upon exposure to light when previously treated with a bichromate. Carbon prints are made using a sheet of paper called "carbon tissue" that has been coated with gelatin into which pigment has been mixed. After exposure, the gelatin-coated sheet, hardened according to the degree of exposure from the different tonal densities of the negative, is processed to wash away the unhardened gelatin along with the pigment it contains, leaving a print made of the remaining pigmented gelatin. During processing the exposed gelatin must be transferred to a new support. Sometimes this is to be done twice: the transfer to the first support reverses the image, so that it must be transferred from that sheet to a second one to read correctly.

**carbro print:** a variation of the color carbon print, in which the pigment-bearing gelatin is hardened by contact with a bleached silver-based color separation instead of by direct exposure.

**carte de visite:** a small photographic portrait, approximately 2¼ by 3½ inches (6 by 9 cm), that was mounted on a card similar in size to a calling card. These small pictures were very common in the second half of the nineteenth century and were usually made by the albumen process.

**chromogenic process:** a photographic color process that uses three silver images on a single support to create corresponding dye images in the subtractive primary colors. The three superimposed dye images yield a full-color image. Both films and prints are produced using this process. Eastman Kodak's Kodachrome transparencies and Kodacolor prints use the chromogenic process, as do similarly named materials produced by other companies, such as Fujichrome and Fujicolor.

**chromolithography:** color printing using multiple lithographic stones to produce prints with a wide range of colors. The most complex chromolithographs involve many stones, each printed in its own color. Tonal variations are produced by superimposed patterns of stippled dots.

**Cibachrome:** an autopositive photographic color print process, renamed Ilfochrome after Ilford bought Ciba-Geigy.

**CMYK:** color printing using cyan, magenta, yellow, and black, the first three being the subtractive primary colors. ("K" is used to designate black to avoid confusion, since "B" might represent blue.) Ideal subtractive printing would not require black, since the three primaries together should produce it, but practical considerations of press and paper require this fourth ink. CMYK is also used as a file type in the computer, when a four-channel file emulates the colors of the subtractive primaries.

**collodion:** a solution of nitrocellulose in ether.

**collodion wet-plate:** *see* wet-plate process

**colloid:** a general term, not in much favor with chemists today, used to group natural glues and jellies such as fish glue and gelatin.

**collotype:** a lithographic printing process that uses a reticulated gelatin coating on a glass plate as the printing surface. Collotype plates are exposed from continuous-tone negatives without the need for a halftone screen.

**color balance:** color photographs can vary greatly in hue, but when the gray values in such pictures are neutral we say the color balance is correct. Color balance is greatly affected by the hue of the light used to make the picture.

**color carbon print:** a carbon print made by superimposing three carbon prints in register, each in a subtractive primary color, exposed from the appropriate color separation.

**color management:** the practice of controlling color in a wide range of digital processes. Color management is complex and unwieldy, and is based on the premise that color errors in any given stage of a process can be codified and controlled, and that if this is done for all steps in an extended process, then the color rendering can be accurate. The mechanism on which color management is based is the color profile, which handles the specific color rendition of each device and manipulation.

**color mixing:** in traditional mediums such as painting, colors are mixed in a loosely defined manner, and in grade school we were taught that yellow and blue mixed together made green. In modern photography and printing, colors mix in a carefully defined manner. Pure cyan and magenta pigments or dyes, when mixed together, produce blue. Yellow and cyan combine to produce green while yellow and magenta produce red. When light is mixed (as in the computer monitor), blue and green produce cyan, blue and red produce magenta, and red and green produce yellow. Varying amounts of any color produce shades of varying saturation and lightness.

**color profile:** a color table that describes the accuracy and errors of a digital color-handling process. A profile is attached to any file that carries color information and forms a chain of control that runs through the entire process. Cameras, scanners, printers, and computer monitors all have profiles, and these work together (in theory) to allow the proper control of color. *See* color management.

**color saturation:** a measure of the purity of a color—the degree to which it is free of dilution by white or gray. As a pure color becomes lighter it is diluted by white; when it becomes darker it is diluted by gray; and in either case it becomes less saturated. In both subtractive and additive color, saturation is reduced when more than two primaries are mixed. In the subtractive system the third primary produces grayness; in the additive system the third primary produces lightness. In strictest terms, the only fully saturated colors are full-strength examples of a single primary or a combined pair.

**color separation:** the process of photographing an original through filters to produce three black-and-white images, each of which records a portion of the color spectrum. Red, green, and blue filters respectively produce the color records for cyan, magenta, and yellow. These separations, after subsequent adjustment, are printed in register with each other and in the appropriate primary colors, producing subtractive prints that carry a wide range of colors.

**complementary colors:** colors complement each other when they are opposed across the additive and subtractive systems. Thus blue complements yellow, since the increase of one is accompanied by the reduction of the other. The same is true of red and cyan and of green and magenta. *See* primary colors.

**contact paper:** an obsolete type of photographic developing-out paper with a moderate light-sensitivity that made it suitable for printing by contact. These papers used silver chloride as the dominant sensitive chemical, and while much "slower" (less sensitive) than enlarging papers, they were much "faster" than the older printing-out papers such as albumen paper.

**contact print:** a print that has been exposed by placing the negative in direct physical contact with the print material (as opposed to enlargement, when the image passes from negative to print material through a lens system).

**contrast:** a loosely used photographic term referring to the degree of separation between a picture's lightest and darkest tones. A high-contrast print might have bright light values and dark shadows while a lower-contrast image would be grayer at both ends of the tonal scale.

**copper engraving:** an intaglio process using copper plates cut with a burin. Many so-called engravings were made with some amount of etching, marking the copper not with a burin but with an acid or other solvent. Etching was often used to begin a plate that was then cleaned up with a burin.

**cross-hatching:** in linear processes such as engraving, the practice of describing tone by closely spacing black lines on a white ground. Cross-hatched groups of lines often run at right angles to each other, forming a linear grid that appears to the eye as tone when viewed from a sufficient distance.

**cyanotype:** *see* blueprint

**daguerreotype:** one of the first practical photographic processes, publicly announced in 1839 and named for the French artist/inventor Louis Jacques Mandé Daguerre. A light-sensitive coating on a silver-plated copper sheet produced brilliant and sharp images, which, when sealed under glass, have proven to be extremely permanent. Since daguerreotypes are autopositive, each one is unique.

**dauber:** a soft, rounded, cloth-covered tool held in the hand and used to apply color when stenciling.

**developing-out paper** (DOP): the modern class of black and white papers that register a latent image and so need to be developed after exposure to produce a visible image. This term is commonly used to refer to modern gelatin silver papers, which are most often made extremely sensitive so that they can be used in enlargers.

**digital:** in printing and photography this term refers to image data made up of discrete points that are assigned numerical values in order to hold a record of visual information. Digital processes are radically different from the older analog systems, such as film, which record data through continuous material variations.

**digital C-print:** a chromogenic print that has been exposed by lasers driven from a digital file instead of being exposed in a conventional enlarger.

**dry plate:** a gelatin-and-silver-based photographic negative material, invented in the late nineteenth century, that could be factory produced, packaged, and sold at a later date. The dry-plate coating has existed in many variations and has been used on both glass plates and flexible film. When coated on paper, it became the basis of most developing-out papers of the twentieth century.

**drypoint:** work done on an etching plate with a needle, to raise a burr that will catch ink and print without the need of chemical etching. Drypoint is often done as afterwork on etched plates. Work done this way is delicate and cannot withstand long-edition printing.

**duotone:** an ink printing method in which two superimposed halftone images of a single picture are printed with different inks, to render tone more accurately than is possible with a single impression.

**dusting box:** a large box, sometimes suspended in bearings so that it can be turned, used to apply a random aquatint to a printing plate. The material inside is usually powdered asphaltum, which is stirred up in the box and then allowed to settle on the plate surface.

**dye:** a soluble compound or liquid that reflects or absorbs a specific color. Dyes tend to be less stable, or lightfast, than pigments.

**dye sublimation print:** a digital process that transfers dye images to a receiver sheet through the use of heat. Small heating elements, as small as 200 per linear inch, are heated to varying degrees to affect correspondingly small, correspondingly varying amounts of dye. Dye sublimation prints are usually made in color, using the three subtractive primaries and black.

**dye transfer print:** a chemical photographic printing process (as opposed to a digital one) that created a full-color print by the use of three color separations, each controlling a layer of dye.

**emulsion:** a mixture of an insoluble solid or liquid suspended in another liquid. The most common emulsion in photography is the suspension of silver salts in gelatin, used for photographic films and papers.

**end grain:** the grain in a wooden block that has been cut perpendicularly to the growth of the wood. The cells in wood are long and narrow, running parallel to the trunk or branch of a tree. An end-grain surface presents these cells cut across their thin dimension. Because of their density, end-grain blocks can hold extremely fine carving, and when made of a hard wood they can be used in a form with metal type. *See also* side grain.

**engraving:** the process of removing material from a printing surface (usually metal or wood) through the use of a burin. Engraved lines in an intaglio process hold ink, and print; in a relief process they create nonprinting areas.

**enlarger:** a specialized camera used in the darkroom to expose photographic paper from a negative. Consisting of a light source, negative stage, bellows, lens, and stand, the enlarger projects the negative image onto light-sensitive paper, which is subsequently developed to produce the positive image. Because the artificial light of the enlarger is much weaker than the sun, enlargements must be made on highly sensitive developing-out papers. An enlarger allows prints to be made bigger than the negative, although same-size or even reduced-size enlargements are also possible.

**etching:** most commonly, an intaglio printing method in which the ink-bearing cells or lines of an image are formed by chemical action on a printing plate. In plate-making, etching is the removal of metal through chemical action, by an acid or some other solvent. In lithography, etching is the treatment of the printing surface to produce a chemical distinction between printing and nonprinting areas.

**etching needle:** the etcher's primary drafting tool, usually made of steel with a sharp point. The etching needle, which is held like a pen, can draw lines through a resist before etching or can generate actual printing lines when applied with more pressure. *See* drypoint.

**etching press:** a press using two heavy cylinders and a solid steel bed that runs between them. Properly called a "mangle," the press can apply the tremendous pressure needed to squeeze the paper and plate sufficiently to transfer the ink from the plate recesses onto the damp paper of the print. Usually hand driven, these presses are used for printing engravings, etchings, mezzotints, and flat-plate photogravures.

**ferric chloride:** a watery, acidic iron solution that can swell hard gelatin, pass through it, and dissolve copper. Ferric chloride is the etch used in photogravure.

**ferrotype tin:** a high-gloss polished sheet, usually of chromed steel, that can be used to dry photographic paper so that it takes on a high sheen.

**film format:** a loosely used term that refers to both the size and the shape of camera negatives. The 35mm format is also called two-by-three, reflecting its proportions, and the four-by-five- and eight-by-ten-inch formats are the same shape but differ in size. Both the English and the metric systems are used for film formats, so six-by-nine is the same shape as 35mm but is six by nine centimeters in size, on what Americans call 2½-inch roll film.

**fixer:** *see* hypo

**foxing:** a discoloration often appearing on old prints, typically in patterns of rust-colored dots.

**gelatin:** a transparent protein produced from animal tissues, gelatin is the coating used in most photographic emulsions. When wet, it swells in a controllable fashion, allowing the management of the chemical reactions within the emulsion.

**gelatin printing-out paper** (also gelatin POP): a late variant of the albumen print in which gelatin replaced albumen.

**gelatin silver paper:** the modern designation for the common black and white developing-out photographic paper used for much of the twentieth century.

**giclée print:** an ordinary inkjet print, so called to enhance its salability.

**gouge:** a chisel with a concave blade, used for making woodcuts.

**Graflex camera:** an early single-lens reflex camera that used sheet film, generally four by five inches but as large as five by seven inches.

**gravure:** an intaglio process in which a photographic image is etched in a copper support. The image is broken up into ink-bearing cells that vary in depth and consequently hold different amounts of ink, allowing the printed image to carry true tonality. Gravure comes in many forms; the name has become the generic term for a whole family of intaglio photographic printing processes, and the naming of these variations is nearly endless. We find the terms "gravure," "photogravure," "hand gravure," "aquatint gravure," "flat-plate gravure," and "heliogravure" (among others) all used for the same process: hand-wiped gravure prints of photographs made from flat plates. When gravure is mechanized, becoming a rotary process, it is referred to as "gravure," "photogravure," "rotogravure," and just plain "roto" (among others). In Europe the term "gravure" is used to mean an intaglio print, either an engraving or an etching.

**gum bichromate:** a pigment process using gum arabic mixed with pigment to produce a photographic image. Usually applied to rough watercolor paper, this process was a favorite of the Pictorial photographers of the early twentieth century.

**halftone:** a printed image in which the continuous tones of a photograph have been converted into a regular grid of high-contrast dots of variable size. In the past, halftone negatives were produced by photographing an original work through a screen. Modern digital technologies create halftone dots directly, from smaller dots made by computer-run lasers. A halftone negative can be used to create relief, intaglio, or planographic printing plates.

**halftone screen:** originally a glass screen with ruled black lines in a pattern similar to a window screen. When used with the correct high-contrast film and developer, the screen would break continuous tone into dots of varying size. In the 1950s the glass screen was replaced with a film replica, which in turn has now been replaced with screen patterns generated by computer software.

**hand gravure:** *see* gravure

**hypo** (also fixer): the generic term for the solution that fixes, or stabilizes, a chemically printed photograph by removing undeveloped silver compounds from a developed photographic emulsion. The two chemicals used almost exclusively as fixers are sodium thiosulfate and ammonium thiosulfate.

**imagesetter:** an electronic device designed to record digital image files on film. The result—an electronically generated halftone on film stock—could be used to expose photo offset lithographic plates. Imagesetters are now disappearing, since today most printing plates are exposed directly from digital files.

**impression:** the printer's term for a single act of printing. Thus a print in more than one color, and so made from more than one plate, is called a "multiple impression" or "multipass." Also used to designate the quality of ink transfer, so we may have a heavy or light impression, a rough or smooth one.

**Indigo printer:** an offset printing press that uses an electronic plate and polymer inks. By changing the digital file used to expose the plate, each impression can be made to vary from the one before. This means that an Indigo printer can print the pages of a book sequentially, so that a single copy can be produced at a reasonable cost.

**ink:** a marking fluid holding a dye or pigment. Most printing inks use oil as the body fluid, while writing inks often use water.

There is no easily definable difference between ink and paint—both are applied to a surface to change its color—but they vary widely in the specifics of their makeup and their methods of application.

**inkjet print:** a print made by a digitally run machine that distributes small droplets of ink over a surface to create an image. In the overwhelming majority of these machines, a print head holding ink jets moves rapidly across a sheet of paper to apply stochastic patterns of ink in the subtractive primary colors. Early inkjet printers such as the Iris printer used a slow-moving set of jets that applied ink to a rapidly rotating sheet mounted on a cylinder.

**intaglio:** a process using a plate whose low portions carry the ink. The most common intaglio processes are copper and steel engraving, etching, and photogravure.

**internegative:** a copy negative used to make a new positive image.

**Iris print:** *see* inkjet print

**justification:** the practice of spacing letters and words so that columns of type (or hand lettering) are even on both sides. Unjustified columns tend to be even on the left and "ragged" on the right.

**lantern slide:** a 3¼-by-4-inch glass-plate positive made for projection. Lantern slides were most often used for educational purposes; they never enjoyed the broad popularity of 35mm slides in two-by-two-inch mounts, which succeeded them and which in turn have been replaced by modern digital snapshots.

**laser print:** a pattern of toner on paper, fixed by heat. The laser print resembles the Xerox copy but is generated from a digital file instead of an analog light image.

**latent image:** an invisible image produced by changes in light-sensitive silver emulsions. Chemical development makes the latent image visible.

**lens:** a transparent object, typically made of glass, whose polished curved surfaces converge or diverge light. Camera lenses are usually complex, consisting of individual lenses, a mounting barrel, and a diaphragm.

**letterpress:** relief printing from metal type and image-bearing halftone cuts in copper or zinc. Also the actual press used for relief printing.

**linear:** used to describe the response or behavior of some physical process that varies consistently according to the action generating it. Film has a linear response to light in the mid-tones of a properly exposed negative. Many digital processes are not linear, and require complex adjustments to be useful for picture-making purposes.

**Linotype:** a keyboard-driven machine manufactured by the Mergenthaler company to set metal type in rows cast in single lines. Invented in the late nineteenth century, it dominated typesetting for the first half of the twentieth century.

**lithography:** a planographic printing process that uses variations in the chemical nature of a treated stone (or of a coating on metal or plastic) to define which areas of the surface will and will not carry ink. The most common forms of lithography use a water film in the nonprinting areas and an oil-based ink in the printing areas.

**Lumière Autochrome:** one of the earliest color photographic processes, which produced autopositive color transparencies on a glass support.

**makeready:** the preliminary work to prepare a printing press for a production run.

**matrix film:** a specialized film manufactured by the Eastman Kodak company for use in dye transfer printing. The film was exposed, then washed in processing to produce an image in relief. The varying thickness of this matrix held varying amounts of dye.

**metamerism:** some inks' characteristic of appearing to the eye as different colors when viewed under different light sources. Metamerism has been a severe problem in digital printing, and only the newest generations of inkjet inks are free from it. Metamerism usually leads to an image shifting toward red under yellowish light and toward green under cooler light such as daylight.

**mezzotint:** an intaglio process that uses a prepared copper plate roughened with a special tool called a rocker. This textured surface holds ink to print an overall black impression, and is selectively polished to produce lighter tones in chosen areas.

**moiré** (or moiré pattern): an interference pattern that can occur when two or more regular patterns are superimposed. Moirés are a common problem in color printing, but can be minimized by careful adjustments to the angles of the printing screens.

**monotype:** a print made from a plate that itself holds no printing information but carries ink manipulated to create an image. Also a form of machine-made lead type in which individual letters are cast and set according to information transmitted by a keyboard and perforated tape.

**negative:** the photographic record exposed in the camera, so called because it renders light values as dark and vice versa. Negatives have ranged widely in the materials of their support, from paper to glass to flexible film. Today they are disappearing, for they have no place in digital photography.

**neutrality:** a characteristic of tones that have no discernible color cast. On the computer screen, images in the RGB color system are perfectly neutral when the digital counts in the three color channels are identical.

**offset blanket:** in offset lithography, the blanket of rubber-faced cloth that wraps around the press's middle cylinder and perfectly transfers the image from plate to paper.

**offset lithography:** *see* photo offset lithography

**orthochromatic:** lacking sensitivity to red light. Almost all early photographic emulsions were orthochromatic, and modern panchromatic materials (sensitive to all colors) were not common until early in the twentieth century.

**palladium print:** a variant of platinum printing in which the image is formed of metallic palladium instead of platinum.

**panchromatic:** *see* orthochromatic

**pantograph:** a device used to copy two- and three-dimensional structures, usually at a different size. The pantograph is an arrangement of linked parallel bars; the user traces the original with one part of the device, and a stylus or other marking tool moving in tandem with the tracing produces an enlarged or reduced version of the same structure.

**photo offset lithography:** a printing process whose presses use three cylinders: one carrying a thin metal plate, which holds the image; one the blanket, which picks up the ink image from the plate; and one the paper, to which the blanket transfers the ink. Photo offset lithography has been the most common printing process since the 1970s. All modern production offset presses are fully rotary and have two sets of rollers running on the printing plate, one for ink and one for water. They achieve very high speeds—upward of 12,000 revolutions per hour—and are built in serial units so that four, five, or even six or more colors can be printed on a single pass through the press. They are also very versatile: the use of the blanket allows accurate printing on many different surfaces.

**photoglyptic engraving:** a term used for some of the earliest efforts to make photographically derived printing plates. These methods were the precursors to photogravure.

**photograph:** a picture formed by the action of light on a chemical or electronic sensor, and subsequently fixed.

**photogravure:** *see* gravure

**pigment:** an insoluble compound that reflects or absorbs a particu lar color. Pigments are often ground into a fine powder to be used in paint or ink.

**pixel:** the point in a digital image for which the digital values have been recorded. Such images consist of an array of pixels; each one is dimensionless, and the more there are to a given area, the finer the image's resolution.

**planographic print:** a print made by any process that prints from an even surface, using neither relief nor intaglio. In most planographic printing the printing and nonprinting areas are defined by chemical differences; these processes are grouped under the general term "lithography." *See also* monotype.

**plate tone:** smooth and often quite light areas of tone left on an intaglio printing plate through incomplete wiping.

**platinum print:** a photographic print made using the light sensitivity of an iron compound (ferric oxalate) to create an image in metallic platinum. Many platinum prints also incorporate some percentage of palladium.

**pochoir:** hand coloring with stencils.

**Polaroid:** a chemical photographic process, manufactured by Polaroid Corporation in many variations, that produced autopositive prints soon after exposure without the need for darkroom processing.

**positive:** the opposite of negative; widely and loosely used in photographic parlance because the negative was typically the first step in the making of a chemical photograph. The term most often denotes a print but can refer to any tonally reversed image made from a negative.

**potassium bichromate:** a chemical used to sensitize gelatin and other colloids so that they become insoluble when exposed to light.

**prepress:** general term for all the preliminary work done before a job is actually printed. Before the onset of digital tools, prepress for offset printing consisted of making the film for reproductions and type, generating proofs, assembling the film into large flats that fitted the printing plates, and making the plates themselves by exposure through these flats. Today almost all prepress is electronic, carried out on the computer, and only comes to solid form with the making of proofs and the exposure of the plates.

**primary colors:** two different sets of primary colors are in common use. The additive set, used in projected-light devices such as computer monitors and television screens, comprises red, green, and blue. The subtractive set, used in reflective-light processes such as photographic printing and ink printing, consists of cyan, magenta, and yellow. The two systems are complements of each other. Painters historically used a different set of primary colors, considering red, blue, and yellow the primaries because they derived from individual pigments rather than from mixed colors.

**printing:** the production of an image, usually in ink, through the means of some matrix that holds the pictorial information in a reusable form. Prints can exist in single or multiple copies, but in all cases they entail the transfer of information from one physical structure to another.

**printing-out paper** (also POP): any photographic paper that generates a visible image directly from exposure to light, without development.

**printing plate:** for centuries, words were printed by arrays of metal type locked into printing forms. Pictures instead required a plate or block to carry the image. Different processes use a wide variety of materials for the plates.

**process color:** the professional term for full-color printing in ink using the three subtractive primaries—cyan, magenta, and yellow—plus black.

**profile:** *see* color management. Also an alternate name for the silhouette.

**progressives:** trial sheets made by a printer to aid in assessing proofs, usual in color printing and in complex black and white jobs. Four sheets, each printed in one of the four inks of process color that combine to make the corresponding plate, constitute a "set" of "singles." When the set includes additional sheets that show combinations of two or more colors, it is called a "progressive" set.

**proof:** a preliminary test print, made to evaluate content for text or print quality for pictures. In some cases the proof is made on the same press to be used in the production run. More often it is a chemical or other surrogate for ink on paper, to avoid the high cost of makeready and press time.

**red ocher:** a naturally occurring iron oxide used as a pigment.

**registration:** the process of aligning sequentially printed superimposed images to fit each other.

**relief print:** a print made by any ink printing process in which the high parts of the printing surface take ink and transfer it to the print support. The most common relief processes are woodcut, wood engraving, letterpress (from metal type or halftone cuts), and linoleum cut.

**resin-coated (RC) paper:** photographic paper in which the paper base is sealed within a synthetic coating so that it does not get wet during processing. As a result the paper can be developed, washed, and dried rapidly.

**resist:** in etching, the waxy coating applied to a copper plate, through which the artist draws with a needle before the application of the etch. In photogravure, the gelatin carbon print applied to a copper plate, through which ferric chloride is applied as the etch.

**reticulation:** a wormy random pattern created in a gelatin coating by extremes of temperature. It is commonly regarded as a severe fault in improperly developed film. Collotype printing exploits controlled reticulation to produce a printing matrix.

**RGB:** red, green, and blue, the primary colors used in additive processes, such as computer and television displays.

**RIP** (raster image processor): a digital device, either hardware or software, that processes an image to generate the file that drives the printer. RIPs often come with profiles to control the quality of the printing.

**rotogravure:** *see* gravure

**salted paper:** the earliest paper-based photographic material. So named because it was made by coating water containing a soluble salt onto a sheet of paper, which was subsequently coated with silver nitrate to produce a uniform coating of a light-sensitive silver compound.

**saturation:** *see* color saturation

**scanner:** any data-gathering system that employs sequential actions over time. In digital usage the term refers to a device that transfers analog picture information into a set of numerical values. The three most common forms of scanner are hand-held, flatbed, and drum.

**scraper press:** a lithographic press that applies pressure on the paper and printing stone with a stiff leather or plastic blade. The tremendous pressure that a cylinder can apply could easily break a litho stone. The scraper blade avoids this by being stiff enough to print, applying all its pressure on the leading edge, while being flexible enough not to damage the stone.

**selenium toning:** the practice of applying selenium compounds to silver photographic prints to alter their color or enhance their permanence. Unlike sepia toning, selenium is capable of very slight tonal changes, often barely intensifying the blacks.

**sepia toning:** the practice of applying sulfur compounds to a silver photographic print, typically to produce brownish tones.

**serigraph:** a commercial marketing term for the silk screen print.

**sheet-fed press:** the most common printing press, which prints on individual sheets of paper instead of on the continuous rolls used in web presses. Sheet-fed presses range widely in size but are limited in speed by the mechanical demands of handling the individual sheets.

**side grain:** the grain in a wooden block that has been cut in parallel to the growth of the wood. Side-grain blocks can be large and were traditionally favored for woodcuts, while end-grain blocks, smaller but denser and more durable, were preferred for engraving. *See also* end grain.

**signature:** a single printed sheet of paper folded to make the pages of a book.

**silk screen print:** a stencil process employing a finely woven fabric stretched in a frame. The fabric allows ink to pass through areas not covered by the stencil, which can be made by hand or produced photographically. Silk screen printing can produce heavy, opaque layers of color, and fairly fine detail if the fabric is closely woven enough.

**silver halides:** the family of silver compounds, among them silver chloride, silver bromide, and silver iodide, that are highly sensitive to light.

**silver print:** a generic term for all photographic print processes based on the light sensitivity of silver salts. Most commonly, the modern gelatin silver developing-out print.

**spot color:** a particular color, specially mixed as an ink and printed from its own plate to enhance process-color printing.

**steel engraving:** an intaglio process, using plates of soft steel cut either with a burin (often driven by hand with a hammer) or by chemical etching.

**stencil:** a printing process that holds the pictorial information in a pattern of holes through which ink is passed to create a print. Stencils can be simple and coarse, such as those used to stencil shipping cases, or fine and precise, such as those used in silk screen printing.

**stereo:** a term with two distinctly different meanings. In printing, a casting of type and/or halftone images, producing a plate that can be mounted on a cylinder for high-speed printing (also called "stereotype"). In photography, a pair of photographs made with a camera designed with two lenses, to mimic human eyesight. When viewed through a specialized viewer, or by crossing one's eyes, the images merge into an illusion of three-dimensional vision (also "stereograph").

**stippling:** a pattern of closely arrayed dots that emulate tone. In intaglio printing the dots are typically cut by hand; in chromolithography they are made with a fine lithographic crayon.

**stochastic:** in printing, an apparently random pattern of dots used in lieu of the conventional halftone-screen array.

**stripping:** in offset printing, the process of splicing together pieces of film (both for text and image halftones) into large forms for exposure to light-sensitive printing plates. The craft of stripping has disappeared since the introduction of digital prepress.

**subtractive color:** *see* primary colors

**tintype:** an autopositive photographic print on a piece of blackened iron, in effect a less expensive version of the ambrotype.

**transparent colors:** watercolor paints, some oil paints, and most modern printing inks are transparent. "Full color" process printing, using three primary colors (and black), depends on the overlay of transparent inks to produce a wide array of secondary colors.

**trapping:** in printing images in more than one color from more than one plate, the practice of enlarging elements of the image so as to produce a dark line where colors overlap, in order to avoid the more distracting white line that otherwise might result from imperfect registration.

**web press:** a printing press that uses rolls of paper instead of sheets. Web presses can achieve speeds of 50,000 impressions per hour.

**wet-plate process:** a photographic negative process, introduced in 1851, in which light-sensitive silver compounds are held in a collodion coating on a glass support. Sensitive only while damp, this material has superb tonal rendition but demands an accessible darkroom for coating the plate immediately before exposure and developing it immediately afterward.

**wood engraving:** a relief printing process that uses an end-grain wooden block. The carving on a wood engraving is usually done with a burin.

**woodburytype:** a photographic print made with a lead mold generated from a carbon-printed positive. This mold is filled with pigmented gelatin and is pressed onto a paper support to make the print. Relatively inexpensive because it required no silver, the process enjoyed a vogue in the last third of the nineteenth century.

**woodcut:** a relief printing process that uses a side-grain wooden block. The carving is usually done with gouges or chisels.

# INDEX

## ACKNOWLEDGMENTS

I have never understood why spouses are listed last in the acknowledgments. There is little question that all my work stems from the life that Barbara Benson and I have made together, and to her goes the greatest thanks for the years of support and wisdom that she has given me.

The book has grown out of my teaching at The Yale University School of Art, where I have been on the faculty for nearly thirty years. Thanks to Tod Papageorge for his great program at Yale and to the many graduate students who have pushed me to explain things. I only wrote this book because Peter Galassi urged me to, and his continual support for the project has been of the utmost importance. His belief in the book and its accompanying exhibition, and his wise advice, have been central to the entire project.

Many friends have given me pictures, and the benefits of their wisdom, and I can't possibly list them all here. The most important have been John Benson, Doris Bry, Allan Chasanoff, Lee Friedlander, and Tod. Behind the whole project stands John Szarkowski, to whom the book is dedicated; without John none of this would have happened. The origins of my interest in the interaction between photography and printing grew out of knowing Doris, Harold Hugo, Leslie George Katz, and Lincoln Kirstein. These four people started me out as a printer.

David Frankel has been a great editor, cutting all my unnecessary words and reordering my phrases so this mass of trivia made some sort of sense. He bears no responsibility for the errors within, but gets much credit for the parts that do make sense. Marc Sapir made sure the book was produced, and Sarah Meister has seen to a myriad of details. John Gambell has helped with the design and John Robinson and his crew at GHP have been a dream to work with on the physical making of this book. Thanks to all of these essential partners in the project.

Richard Benson

## COPYRIGHTS

© Bachrach Studios: pp. 156, 157
© Estate of Leonard Baskin, courtesy Galerie St. Etienne, New York: p. 6
© Christopher Benson: pp. 49, 313
© John Benson: 209 lower left
© Richard Benson: pp. vi, 139, 161, 181, 209 top, 265, 281, 283, 287, 289, 291, 296
© Robert Bergman: p. 295
Courtesy Boston Herald: p. 239
© Estate of Margaret Bourke-White: p. 237
© The Brassaï Estate/RMN: p. 264
Courtesy Callaway Arts & Entertainment, New York: pp. 284, 285
© Steve Cannistra: p. 272
© Henri Cartier-Bresson/Magnum, courtesy Fondation Henri Cartier-Bresson: pp. 222 below, 223
© Allan Chasanoff: pp. 205, 308, 309
© Jean-Marie Chauvet, Eliette Brunel Deschamps, and Christian Hillaire: pp. 4, 5
© The John Coplans Trust: p. 170
© Walker Evans Archive, The Metropolitan Museum of Art: p. 209 lower right
© Robert Frank: pp. 206, 207, 212, 213
© Lee Friedlander: p. 169
© Frank Gohlke: p. 173
© Beverly Heegaard: p. 203
© Inliners International, Inc.: pp. 256, 257
© 1959 Kanehara Shuppan Co., Ltd. Tokyo: p. 255 above
© Estate of Clarence Kennedy: p. 147
© Joseph Koudelka: p. 167
© Helen Levitt: p. 184
© Light Impressions: p. 303
Courtesy Little, Brown and Company: p. 240
© 2008 Succession H. Matisse, Paris/Artists Rights Society (ARS), New York: p. 177
© Luis A. Mazariegos: pp. 304, 305
© Sam Messer: p. 83
© National Portrait Gallery, London: p. 44 above
© Nicholas Nixon: p. 165
© Tom Norton: pp. 278, 279
© Georgia O'Keeffe Museum/Artists Rights Society (ARS), New York: pp. 141, 210
© John O'Reilly: p. 171
© Tod Papageorge: pp. 258, 259
© 1981 Irving Penn: p. 143
© Stephen Shore: p. 201
© Steven B. Smith: p. 293
© Paul Strand Archive, Aperture Foundation, Inc.: p. 231
Courtesy the Editors of Time Magazine © 2008 Time Inc.: p. 269
© Time Inc.: p. 225
Collection Center for Creative Photography, University of Arizona © 1998 The University of Arizona Foundation: pp. 194, 195
© Washington Fruit and Produce: pp. 254, 255 below
© S. Watanabe Color Print Co. and Kawase Fumiko: pp. 70, 71

## OBJECTS IN PUBLIC COLLECTIONS

Frontispiece. Abelardo Morell. *Book: Pieta by El Greco*. 1993. Gelatin silver print, 17 15/16 x 22 7/16" (45.5 x 57 cm). The Museum of Modern Art, New York. Purchase

P. 44 above. After Sir Anthony Van Dyck. *King Charles I*. c. 1635. Oil on canvas, 49 x 39 1/2 in. (124.5 x 100.3 cm). National Portrait Gallery, London

P. 103 above. William Henry Fox Talbot. *Lace*. 1845. Salted paper print, 6 1/2 x 8 3/4 in. (16.5 x 22.3 cm). The Museum of Modern Art, New York. Gift of Dr. Stefan Stein

P. 103 below. William Henry Fox Talbot. *Loch Katrine*. 1844. Salted paper print from a calotype, 6 7/8 x 8 5/16 in. (17.4 x 21.1 cm). The Museum of Modern Art, New York. The Family of Man Fund

P. 170: John Coplans. *Untitled study for Self Portrait (Upside Down no. 9)*. 1992. Three black-and-white instant prints (Polaroid), each: 3 1/2 x 4 1/2 in. (8.9 x 11.4 cm), overall: 11 7/8 x 5 3/16 in. (30.2 x 13.2 cm). The Museum of Modern Art, New York. Gift of Marsha Plotnitsky

P. 171. John O'Reilly. *Mythic Still Life*. 1985. Collage of black and white instant prints (Polaroid), 3 3/4 x 6 5/8 in. (9.5 x 16.8 cm). The Museum of Modern Art, New York. The Family of Man Fund

P. 177: Henri Matisse. *Red Room (Harmony in Red)*. 1908. Oil on canvas, 70 7/8 in. x 7 ft. 2 5/8 in. (180.5 x 221 cm). State Hermitage Museum, St. Petersburg

P. 184: Helen Levitt. *New York*. 1976. Dye transfer print, printed 1992, 14 x 9 5/16 in. (35.6 x 23.7 cm). The Museum of Modern Art, New York. Gift of Marvin Hoshino

P. 199. Possibly Jeremiah Gurney. Two men playing checkers. 1850–52. Daguerreotype, 5 1/4 x 7 3/16 in. (13.3 x 18.3 cm). The Metropolitan Museum of Art. Gilman Collection, Gift of the Howard Gilman Foundation

P. 201. Stephen Shore. *Castine, Maine*. 1974. Chromogenic color print, 7 11/16 x 9 11/16 in. (19.5 x 24.6 cm). The Museum of Modern Art, New York. Purchase

Pp. 206–7: Robert Frank. *Boston*. 1985. Six color instant prints (Polaroid) with hand-applied paint and collage, each: 27 3/4 x 22 1/4 in. (70.3 x 56.4 cm). The Museum of Modern Art, New York. Acquired through the generosity of the Polaroid Corporation

P. 230. William Henry Fox Talbot. Untitled. c. 1852. Photoglyphic engraving, irreg., 2 5/16 x 3 7/16 in. (5.9 x 8.8 cm). The Museum of Modern Art, New York. Gift of the International Museum of Photography at George Eastman House

Pp. 261–63: Mathew B. Brady Studio. Senator and Mrs. James Henry Lane. 1861–66. Albumen silver print from a glass negative, 8 13/16 x 7 3/4 in. (22.4 x 19.7 cm). The Metropolitan Museum of Art. Gilman Collection, Purchase, Alfred Stieglitz Society Gifts

## COLLECTION OF JOHN BENSON

P. 10, 11. Albrecht Dürer. *The Men's Bath*. c. 1496. Woodcut, 15 1/4 x 11 1/4 in. (38.7 x 28.6 cm)

P. 17: Ludovico Vicentino Arrighi. Leaf from *La Operina*. 1522. Print: Ugo da Carpi. Woodcut, 6 5/8 x 4 5/8 in. (11.8 x 16.8 cm)

P. 45. After Sir Anthony Van Dyck. *King Charles I*. Print: Isaac Beckett, c. 1685. Mezzotint, 13 1/8 x 9 7/8 in. (33.3 x 25 cm)